MOSCOW MEMOIRS

Emma Gerstein

MOSCOW MEMOIRS

Memories of Anna Akhmatova, Osip Mandelstam,
and Literary Russia under Stalin

Translated and Edited by
John Crowfoot

The Overlook Press
Woodstock & New York

First published in the United States in 2004 by
The Overlook Press, Peter Mayer Publishers, Inc.
Woodstock & New York

WOODSTOCK:
One Overlook Drive
Woodstock, NY 12498
www.overlookpress.com
[For individual orders, bulk and special sales, contact our Woodstock office]

NEW YORK:
141 Wooster Street
New York, NY 10012

Originally published in Russian as *Memuary* by Inapress, St. Petersburg, Moscow, 1998.
Published by arrangement with The Harvill Press.

"Lamarck" is reprinted by permission from *The Complete Poetry of Osip Mandelstam*
translated by Burton Raffel and Alla Burago, the State University of New York Press.
© State University of New York. All rights reserved

Selections from "For the Resounding Valour," "Cherry Brandy," "Apartment," and
Verses on the Unknown Soldier are reprinted from *Osip Mandelstam: 50 Poems*, translated
by Bernard Meares. Translation copyright © by Bernard Meares. By kind permission
of Persea Books, Inc. (New York)

Selections from "Under her dark veil she wrung her hands . . .," "MCMXXI,"
"They led you away at dawn . . .," "For seventeen months I've been crying out . . .,"
"Epilogue," "In the Fortieth year" and "To the Londoners" are reprinted from
The Complete Poems of Anna Akhmatova, first published in Great Britain in 1997 by
Canongate Books, 14 High Street, Edinburgh, EH1 1TE

A CIP record for this book is available from the Library of Congress

Printed and bound in Great Britain

1 3 5 7 9 8 6 4 2

ISBN 1-58567-595-4

Contents

TRANSLATOR'S
ACKNOWLEDGEMENTS

My thanks to Larisa Bespalova, who first introduced me to Emma Gerstein, and to Martin Dewhirst, Pavel Nerler, Jennifer Baines and Robert Wells for much-appreciated help of various kinds over several years. Christopher MacLehose and Andrea Belloli at Harvill were very patient and most supportive of this large project. The Akhmatova Apartment-Museum on Fontanka, the Mandelstam Society in Moscow, and Leonid Vidgof provided the majority of the illustrations that so enhance this edition. I owe the greatest debts to Tatyana Litvinov for her encouragement and criticism and to my wife, Tatyana Lipovskaya, for reading and discussing the entire translation. The remaining errors and shortcomings are my own.

John Crowfoot
September 2003

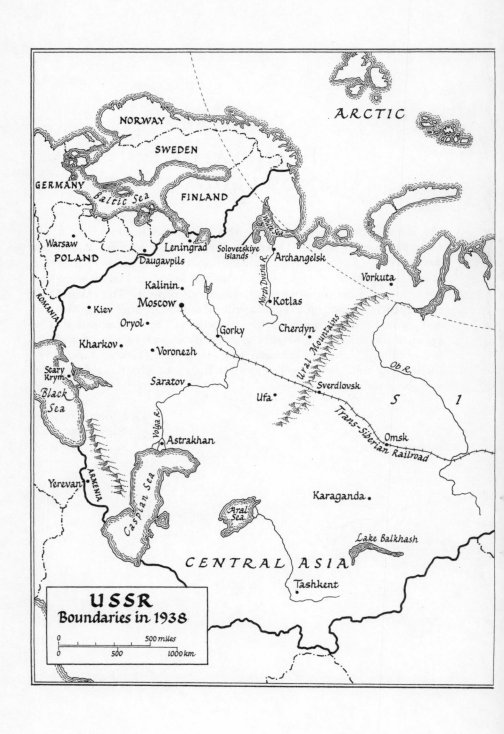

USSR
Boundaries in 1938

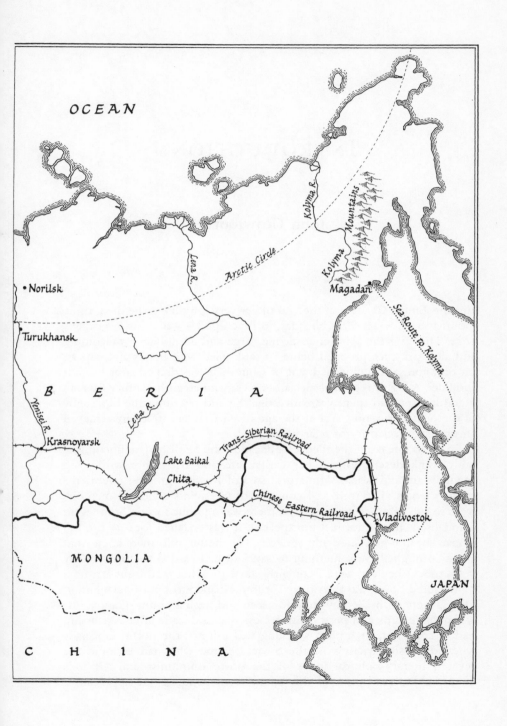

INTRODUCTION

John Crowfoot

Visiting Emma Gerstein at the end of her very long life – she died, three months short of her 99th birthday, in June 2002 – was a curious experience. There sat the spinster academic, large and immobile, a welcoming and alert presence propped behind a desk piled with books and papers; on occasion, a magnificent braid of white hair was draped over her left shoulder. A highly regarded specialist on early nineteenth-century Russian literature, she had spent years investigating and rewriting the biography of the poet Lermontov. Yet at the age of 95 Gerstein suddenly achieved an uncertain celebrity of a far wider kind.

In 1998, breaking the silence of decades, she published an uncomfortably frank description of her earlier life and friendship with Osip Mandelstam and Anna Akhmatova, two of Russia's greatest twentieth-century poets. The tone and contents of Gerstein's collected memoirs were so unlike other accounts that there was a public furore. Some were scandalised. It was not just unexpected, it was uncalled for – as though a spear-bearer had suddenly spoken. The better informed knew that Gerstein might have something to say, and had earned the right to say it. Even so, they too were frequently startled by her forthright attitude: "Unwanted Love" was the title of the longest and most personal memoir. Others were enthralled by an unforeseen and fresh account of apparently familiar events and personalities. Less than a decade after censorship had disappeared, such plain speaking was still not the norm, especially when discussing victims of the Soviet regime who had become the revered literary-political icons of the post-Communist era. "If it is disturbing to read parts of this book," remonstrated one appreciative critic, "then ask yourself how much more disturbing it was to write them!" Many remained sceptical. Why had Gerstein waited so long? The motives for this late exposé were unclear and frequently considered suspect. As to the tone, *unkind* or *mean-spirited* were words used to describe it.

The author of the controversy appeared supremely unruffled. "Well, I think that really is my last TV interview," Gerstein announced during one of my visits, with the self-deprecating humour that lightens her unsettling tale. Satisfaction at her belated freedom to speak, and at the interest being shown in her memories and opinions, was unconcealed. Yet Gerstein was also tickled, it seems, by the incongruous absurdities of a fame she had not sought. Few could have been less concerned with such ephemeral popularity (there was no television in her small, over-heated apartment); few were more aware of the importance and enduring value of the written and printed word.

Emma Gerstein was born, on 25 October 1903, in Dinaburg (Daugavpils in modern Latvia), the second of her surgeon father's four children. After some years the family moved to Moscow, where Grigory Gerstein had found work at one of the city's major hospitals. Emma attended the *gymnasium,* or classic secondary school. At the age of 16 she graduated: following the revolutions of 1917, she notes, the *gymnasium* was called the "United School of Labour".

Grigory Gerstein was appointed head physician at the Semashko hospital. In 1921, the family of six moved into the service apartment where Emma would live for the next forty years. After a while, her father was also retained as medical consultant to the new élite of Soviet Russia. Emma enjoyed a security and prospects not shared by many of her immediate contemporaries. Her father belonged to one of the few professions then accorded unequivocal respect by the Bolshevik regime; though he had not been politically active and never joined the Communist Party, he sympathised with the new order. His sons and daughters seemed assured of a good education and satisfying careers. The eldest child, Vera, the favourite musical daughter, married well; after leaving school, the two boys took up engineering. Only Emma could not settle.

For a brief period after the Revolution, she attended courses at Moscow University, now open to all, but many of the professors she most admired soon emigrated. She thought of moving to Petrograd. Finally, she started a three-year course in Moscow. At first, on the advice of her relatives, she tried the natural sciences: perhaps she would train as a doctor. She quickly abandoned that good intention. Transferring to the university's language and literature department, she graduated in early 1925. Over the next decade there followed a string of unsatisfactory office jobs. One of the few skills Emma acquired was typing. For a time, she was personal secretary to Olga Kameneva, sister of Trotsky and wife of the demoted Party leader Lev Kamenev. Once Kameneva began to dictate a speech she had to deliver to some minor Soviet organisation: "The tumultuous growth of socialist emulation . . ." Neither she nor her helpful secretary could get one word beyond the obligatory, overblown rhetoric of that opening declaration.

Emma's father, aiding her search for work, at times lost patience. "So you don't like the way our society is organised?" Grigory Gerstein demanded of his disconsolate daughter on one occasion. "Then do something about it!" There were few kindred spirits to whom she could turn. Supporters of the old regime were unattractive and often anti-Semitic. There was a prominent revolutionary in the family, her much older cousin Lev Gerstein. He had been sentenced to death by the Bolsheviks in 1922; this verdict was subsequently commuted, and Emma's sister took him food parcels in prison. To Emma such Mensheviks and Socialist Revolutionaries were a tedious lot and restricted in their outlook. Not a member of any class defeated by the Great October Socialist Revolution of 1917, she felt isolated and out of place. "With my naturally luxuriant head of hair, mournful face and sharp tongue I only provoked irritation," she remarks, recalling the first job she lost.

Her parents and brothers each later faced their own moment of traumatic disillusion with the new regime. For the time being, sister and brothers unkindly recalled that Emma had always been something of a misfit (as children they had teased her for her ugly nose): "O, she's no good at anything, she'll never get anywhere." In the late reflection "Of Memoirs and More Besides", which ends this volume, Gerstein recalls how as a child she conceived a passion for writing that was mocked and dismissed by sister and cousins alike: ". . . scraps of paper with my scribblings could be found, scattered in every corner of the apartment." Whatever the sources of her persistent oddity, a succession of increasingly modest jobs drove her to despair. Emma attempted to poison herself. She was caught in time: her friend Lena happened to phone, and Emma admitted what she'd done. After consulting the family, an alarmed Grigory Gerstein sent his daughter to a sanatorium to recover.

There, at Uzkoye, in October 1928, she met Osip and Nadezhda Mandelstam. Which is where this book begins. The encounter changed the whole course of her existence. As Gerstein freely confesses: "Acquaintance with Mandelstam was . . . my 'initiation' into another life where everything was judged by different standards." She felt instantly

drawn to the unusual couple. Soon they were friends, and for the next
ten years Emma would be one of their immediate circle.

Mandelstam is regarded today as the twentieth century's "literary martyr"
par excellence. Descriptions of his life are, inevitably, distorted by the
knowledge of his tragic end, and this has only added to the legend. A
promising young poet when his first book was published in 1913,
Mandelstam's outcast status in Soviet literature "was defined as early as
1923",[1] says the classic account. The poet then had fifteen years still to
live, yet his fate, it is often implied, was foreordained. Gerstein's opening memoir "Near the Poet" tells a different story.

Recalling their years of close acquaintance, and episodes petty and significant, Emma Gerstein modifies perceptions of the poet's circumstances and
complex personality, restoring a valuable sense of the ambivalence and uncertainties of the period. Shortly before meeting Emma, Mandelstam and his
wife, Nadezhda, had come to Moscow from Detskoye (formerly Tsarskoye)
Selo, near Leningrad. Soon the couple had reason to be dissatisfied.
Translation as one important source of income was about to vanish, thanks
to the dispute with Gornfeld.[2] Over the next few years, the Mandelstams
lived in a dozen different locations around the city, including Emma's own
room. Still, in 1928 volumes of Mandelstam's verse and prose had just
appeared, and after a while his situation and mood took a turn for the
better. In 1930 he again began to write poetry and to get some of his new
work published. Far from being a faded and irrelevant voice, he was winning
new admirers and confirming his old renown. Allocated one of the rooms
for writers at Herzen House, in 1933 the Mandelstams received an entire
apartment. On two occasions the poet gave well-attended recitals in the
Soviet capital. It was therefore not simply frustration that led him to compose
and recite the Stalin epigram, the seditious poem for which he was arrested
and exiled in May 1934. Uncertain and precarious, the revival in his fortunes
also made its contribution to that display of bravado.

Mandelstam's act of defiance cast a long shadow over the poet's last
years and the life of his closest acquaintances. The dramatic account of
Gerstein's own involvement conveys the agitation and excitement that
surrounded the poem from the outset:

One morning, unexpectedly, Nadya came to see me; in fact, she
rushed in. Her words were brief and urgent: "Osya has composed
a very outspoken poem. It can't be written down. No-one, apart

---

[1] Nadezhda Mandelstam, *Hope against Hope* (London, 1999), "Theory and Practice".
[2] See Appendix 1.1, "The Gornfeld Affair".

from me, knows about it. We need someone else to memorise it.
You're the one. After we die, you'll make it public. Osya will recite
it to you; then you'll learn it by heart with me. For the time being
no-one must know of this.

Gerstein's irreverent, affectionate portrait of the poet during the preceding six years prepares the reader for a significantly different interpretation
of that subversive work and its consequences. Mandelstam's "fussy, highly
strung character" contrasted, in her words, with a direct gaze and an unexpectedly "firm, warm handshake"; trying later to catch his contradictory
nature in a single phrase, she suggested that Mandelstam had "a cruel
mind but a kind heart". This little accorded with the canonical account.
For what she describes, above all, in her recollection of the Stalin epigram
is not a resolute and solemn opponent of tyranny but, first and foremost,
a poet exhilarated by a successful composition – with the fateful consequence (for himself and for others) that, despite his own warnings, he
could not resist sharing his new work with more and more listeners.
      Gerstein affirmed Mandelstam's gift of prophetic utterance, in this
and in his later works. He could foresee what others did not. She would
not accept the subsequent tale of martyrdom – that the poet was now
doomed, death merely postponed for a further four years. A more alarming picture emerges from her first memoir. By the late 1930s, when the
Mandelstams returned to Moscow from exile, the situation was increasingly dangerous for all. Yet only the personalities of Mandelstam and
Nadezhda, Gerstein suggests, would ensure that the circumstances proved
fatal: "Nadya could not withstand Mandelstam's elemental craving to
live and work freely and openly; her own gambling instinct constantly
incited Osip to keep trying to do so." It is a disturbing and controver-
sial suggestion. In the last analysis, however, it only deepens the sense
of a human and individual tragedy.

Not until forty years later did Gerstein finally begin to write her memoirs.
On a visit to the banished Mandelstams in 1936, she was confronted by
the couple. She was reluctant to petition the Party's Central Committee
or the Writers' Union on their behalf. "You'll write memoirs after I'm
dead", Osip taunted, "but you don't care about the living poet?" Gerstein
was furious. Mandelstam hastily changed the subject. At the time, as she
tells her readers, the idea of writing about him would not have entered
her head: it was loyal friendship that bound her to the Mandelstams,
not literary ambition or curiosity.
      Outliving almost all her generation, Emma Gerstein put the unhoped-
for freedom of her last years to good use. The first memoir was published

when she was 83: "Longevity", Gerstein was fond of repeating, "is the only salvation." Exceptional firmness of purpose and enduring clarity of mind go some way to explain the qualities of her work. A strong incentive was also needed before she would tackle such reminiscences again. A first attempt was halted in the late 1950s by none other than Akhmatova, aghast at Gerstein's candid portrait of Mandelstam. In the interim, his widow Nadezhda's two volumes of memoirs *Hope against Hope* (1965) and *Hope Abandoned* (1970) became key underground texts for the whole of the Soviet bloc and indeed "shaped an epoch" (that much Emma would concede). Until there was good reason to respond and, preferably, new evidence to support any criticism, it was not worth challenging what Nadezhda had written. An opportunity in 1977 to read literary specialist Sergei Rudakov's letters from exile in Voronezh seems to have changed matters.

Here was private, informal and wholly contemporary testimony by one who saw himself as a friend, rival and amanuensis to the banished poet. It revealed a picture in many ways not dissimilar to that Emma had begun to draw of Osip and Nadezhda. This was further proof that the widow's epoch-making account had misrepresented the actions, motives and character of others. In her second memoir, "Mandelstam in Voronezh", Gerstein prefaces extensive excerpts from the letters Rudakov wrote to his wife in Leningrad with her own recollections. For these also concerned Emma's later life and continuing friendship with both Nadezhda and Akhmatova. In the frustrating and inconclusive post-war attempts to discover what had happened to part of Mandelstam's poetic legacy, Emma was often their hapless intermediary.

"I write detective stories," Gerstein once explained, defining her particular genre of literary research. In her introduction to "Mandelstam in Voronezh", she offers an investigation dedicated as much to deciphering the character and motivation of the main actors as to establishing chronology and fact. Nadezhda's extraordinary accusation ("the theft of our archives had been part of a deliberate plan") is revealed as groundless. What motive could she have had for this and the other examples of "irresponsible gossip" in her books? In a late memoir entitled "Nadezhda", Emma would subject her behaviour to a pitiless cross-examination. Here Gerstein focused on Rudakov's wretched widow. Under threat of poverty or sheer terror, Lina Rudakova sold and destroyed manuscripts which had been entrusted to her husband; she then deviously concealed the fact from all, including Emma. Gerstein could not condone or excuse such acts (the prolonged deception was the worst part of it), but the attempt to understand this minor figure, caught up in a much larger tragedy, is wholly characteristic of the author's approach. It also, incidentally, sets the behaviour of contemporaries in perspective.

The late 1940s and early 1950s were terrible years in Gerstein's life. The mounting anti-Semitism of that period is mentioned only briefly here. Elsewhere she has described losing her job at the publishers Literary Heritage and avoiding the then criminal charge of unemployment with a phoney yearly certificate from the director Zilberstein. Then he grew too nervous even to support that weak deception. Such was the grim and deepening despondency of those years. Standards of behaviour established by terror since the 1930s, and again reinforced after the war, are graphically stated in a 1954 letter written by the poet Tsvetayeva's daughter. Writing from exile in the Far North to Dina Kanel (whose own story intertwined with that of the Gersteins), Ariadne Efron mused:

> I consider our friendship, your relationship with your husband Adolf and his treatment of your deceased sister's children . . . entirely natural. It seems entirely natural to me that . . . poor, old, chronically sick Aunt Lilya scrapes together a parcel for me – though it is now fifteen years since she started helping first Mama and my brother, and now me! Yet by the standards of recent times, it would have been entirely normal for Adolf to remarry in 1940, for Lyalya's children to be put in a home and for Aunt Lilya to have disowned me fifteen years ago . . .

In her quiet, undemonstrative and sometimes diffident way, Emma did not desert any of her adoptive "family" and friends. But as she herself noted, they did not provide her with work: she still had to earn a living.

Work and money would be a constant struggle and uncertainty, however modest Gerstein's requirements. By the late 1930s, however, she had at last found her vocation as a literary researcher. It was a late start, and in that era of enforced subterfuge and cryptic allusion, curious parallels and contrasts may be noted, in passing, between Mandelstam and the Lermontov she so assiduously brought to life. Both awkward characters with friends and enemies at court, they were exiled for rebellious verse (and for duelling: "at ten paces our words have no sound"). Both died early, in confused and disputed circumstances. Emma herself commented: "All my work was animated by a sense of inner resistance." Whatever the motives, her rigorous and painstaking literary investigations undoubtedly did much for the style and contents of the distinctive memoirs she eventually wrote.

And there Gerstein's account might have ended. It could not provide younger readers with the draught of vicarious heroism they imbibed while reading Nadezhda Mandelstam's memoirs. They were works by different authors, written for different purposes and, as important, under different conditions. More restrained and thoughtful, Gerstein's two early memoirs had a muted reception in the late 1980s when they were first published abroad as a *New Look at Mandelstam*. They appeared as an émigré volume in France, and only the second section, "Mandelstam in Voronezh", was soon republished in the Soviet Union. Still, Gerstein had already achieved a great deal. She had cleared the reputation of Sergei Rudakov, killed fighting the Germans, and offered a vivid alternative portrait of Osip Mandelstam, who died on his way to Kolyma. At last, there was a response to Nadezhda's famous and widely admired books by someone who had known the poet and his widow at the time described, and had known them well. In offering a new look at Mandelstam (and Rudakov), Emma also sketched the tale of her own life. But as yet these were the bare outlines. Much was left unexplained. She had not begun to describe her lifelong attachment to Anna Akhmatova nor her involvement with another who shared, and survived, many of the ordeals of Mandelstam and Rudakov.

That revelation needed further prompting. It came in the late 1980s, so Gerstein says, when she grew increasingly irritated by the "dreadful" publications and TV appearances of Lev Gumilyov. As something of a substitute for his mother, Akhmatova (she had died in 1966), Gumilyov became a hero of Gorbachev's *perestroika*. Writing regularly for the press and speaking on television, he not only broadcast his views, as a historian, about the Huns and Khazars; he also talked about his famous parents. Emma again began to write. Throughout the 1990s this task, crowned by the publication of these memoirs, gave her (in her own words) a renewed interest in life.

If by the mid-1930s she was less absorbed by the Mandelstams, not the least reason was her concern for another, who would spend 13 years in prison. In her third, longest and most personal memoir, "Unwanted Love", Gerstein for the first time describes her odd and profound relations with Akhmatova's son Lev (or Lyova). These were baffling to onlookers but indubitably sincere: "You love him?!" an amazed Nadezhda whispered to Emma, inconsolably apprehensive when Lyova was expelled from Leningrad University. After their first affair, precipitated by his summons to secret-police headquarters, theirs became a strong but irregular attachment. (One inattentive response to these memoirs labelled Gerstein an "embittered old maid". This is laughably far from the mark. In 1940, as she describes, Emma gave a spirited public defence of the single woman's right to her own life, work and accommodation.) The pre-war liaison with Lyova would lead the faithful Emma to aid and assist mother and son for the next twenty years.

The rest of her book is devoted to those who survived, displaying many forms of endurance and courage. The one person to emerge from the memoirs undiminished both as an artist and as a human being is Anna Akhmatova. Her tragic figure towers over the others – not only metaphorically, since she (like her son, Lyova) was little short of six feet tall. Akhmatova's story had been told before, but never quite from this viewpoint or proximity. Through close contact with both mother and son, Gerstein came to appreciate the deep-rooted tragedy of their entangled lives, something always partly veiled from others. As one who knew and understood Mandelstam *and* Akhmatova, Gerstein's memoirs also restore a wider balance and perspective. At times, the Mandelstams suggested that Akhmatova's position was the easier: as a woman she was shielded by her husband; as a poet her work was more readily understood. Yet ambiguous as Mandelstam's status might be, until Stalin's famous 1934 order to "isolate but preserve" him, he intermittently enjoyed opportunities to publish and recite his works that were wholly denied Akhmatova, an outstanding poet whose former husband Nikolai Gumilyov, the father of her only child, had been shot as an anti-Bolshevik conspirator in 1921. For some years their son, Lyova, was kept out of harm's way, "running round the cabbage patches" of provincial Bezhetsk. Then the young man went to Leningrad to live with Akhmatova and her current husband, the art historian Nikolai Punin. By the end of the 1930s, both men had been arrested and released, while Lyova was detained again, for a time threatened with execution, and then sent to the camps. In 1938 Akhmatova was put under constant surveillance. Mandelstam died that December; Akhmatova's ordeals would continue into a yet bleaker period.

Three soon-reversed changes of fortune were the only respite Akhmatova earned in all those years: as a poet in 1940 and during the war; as both writer and mother in 1945. Lyova's return from the camps and then the front was soon succeeded by a further and painfully prolonged term of imprisonment that ultimately drove mother and son apart. Gerstein understood the distress that her son's situation caused Akhmatova, even when jealous maternal feeling kept her at a distance. One incident says much of these involved relations. After Lyova's first arrest, Emma took an apparently incoherent and raving Akhmatova by taxi to seek the help of a fellow-writer: at that moment, the poet admitted long after, she was not just bewailing her loved ones but composing a poem. Lyova's first arrest and subsequent imprisonment, the whispered conversations in the prison queues – these would stir Akhmatova secretly to conceive the poems that make up her *Requiem*, a tribute to those who suffered then as she did: it is, one commentator has suggested, a work of "an immediacy that both transcends and falls short of poetry".

In 1949 Lyova was again arrested and imprisoned a second time for the previous offence. With a great many other such "repeaters" he was sent back to the Gulag: they had already proven they could survive there. One aim, doubtless, was to break the will of his now sick mother. The cynicism of the post-war years, more chilling than the horrors of the '30s, would lead Akhmatova to produce a different kind of verse.

How does a poet address a tyrant? Gerstein touches the most sensitive of issues for her two heroes, and their admirers, when she confronts the poems they addressed to the Leader. Akhmatova's post-war cycle "In Praise of Peace" (and Stalin) was a calculated though agonising gesture: "Legend speaks of a wise man who saved each of us from a terrible death." These poems, published in 1950, did not improve matters. They did prevent them, perhaps, from getting any worse. Her son remained in prison where his tormentors demanded a confession that Akhmatova was an English spy; meanwhile her own arrest was again demanded by the secret police chief Abakumov.[3] Gerstein evokes the enduring humiliation to which Akhmatova then subjected herself by committing this public act of dishonesty. In the late 1950s, giving copies of the new volume of her poetry to friends, Akhmatova would paste over the compromising texts with other poems she had written.

Certain poems by Mandelstam (and Pasternak) in the 1930s were a more complex matter. They reveal a genuine fascination with the Stalin phenomenon and an attempt, through verse, to grasp the realities he represented. Not content to leave matters at the level of discomfort with the very existence of these "aberrant" compositions, Gerstein probed further. After the Stalin epigram, Mandelstam felt a periodic urge to restore contact with the Revolution and, even, with the Leader. "Everywhere", on his return from exile, Gerstein records, "Osip gave inspired readings of his 'Ode' to Stalin." Yet if that was a transparent attempt to find favour with the authorities, the Leader's image would surface in more perplexing forms in some of his other poems of 1937.

---

[3] In June Abakumov informed Stalin that "reports from agents and information obtained under interrogation . . . testified that the poetess was an active enemy of the Soviet regime". Stalin responded: "Continue investigation and surveillance" (*Novaya gazeta*, 20–26 March 2000).

Gerstein the friend recounts what she saw. Little more movingly illustrates her "tender attachment" to Akhmatova than her vigil beside the sleeping poet in October 1935 when, following the arrest of husband and son, Akhmatova aged overnight. Gerstein the scholar continued, to the end, to follow new leads. Provoked once more into writing, this time by a Petersburg academic (she was now 91), Emma tried in "Anna Akhmatova and Lev Gumilyov" to unravel the puzzle of a third poet's apparent influence over Stalin in the mid-1930s. Two of the Leader's inexplicable acts of clemency towards Mandelstam and Akhmatova are linked to the name of Boris Pasternak. For a brief period, Gerstein suggests, the suicide of Stalin's wife's bound the dictator to a man he regarded as a "cloud dweller". The new lead had appeared only in 1990, when one of Pasternak's private letters to Stalin had finally been published.[4]

Emma's reflections on these mysterious ties were in part, perhaps, provoked by her own biography. The suicide of Nadezhda Alliluyeva in 1932[5] and the failed attempt at a medical cover-up affected her own future. By a strange quirk of fate, she owed her late chance to take up literary research to the pity others felt for her stricken father (the story is told in Chapter 5 of "Unwanted Love"). She was offered a post at the Literary Museum, and though, as usual, the job did not last long, it brought the 33-year-old Emma the contacts and experience she needed to begin a lifetime's work.

Gerstein had now told the story of her life. The voice and attitude were distinctive. In memoirs of Mandelstam by Akhmatova, Kuzin, Shtempel and Nadezhda herself, it was an epic portrait that emerged. In Gerstein's dissenting recollections the features that came to the fore all undermined that monumental and heroic image: it was, in fact, Mandelstam at his best and worst. "There are also my own memoirs," Emma noted stoically in 1995 – "but people do not like to consult them since they never quite follow the established path." What were her motives and intentions?

As Emma in great old age considered a photograph of three elderly women – herself, Nadezhda and Akhmatova, gathered to mark the latter's birthday – she observed, half-seriously: "Just look at us. I'm the one normal person there, with those two Witches and *grandes dames*." It took some effort for Emma to free herself and her contemporaries from the spell of those formidable women. After so many years, it would hardly be surprising if some resentment surfaced, towards one and quite possibly both of them. In her attempts to disentangle fact from legend,

---

[4] Included here as Appendix 1.4, "A Letter to Stalin".
[5] See Appendix 1.2, "Alliluyeva's Suicide".

Gerstein several times noted how her own words and recollections had been bent to serve another purpose.

"The strangest things happen", she commented dryly, "when memoirists use the words of others to record their reminiscences." The memoirist in question was, of course, Nadezhda Mandelstam, and a facile explanation for this entire volume could be found in the animosity that separated Emma from the poet's widow throughout the last twelve years of Nadezhda's life (she died in 1980). To the end Emma would regard Nadezhda and all her works with an irritation that often surfaces in these memoirs. "I'm accused of defaming the dead," she remarked to me. "And what, then, was Nadya herself doing?"

Gerstein might well be harsh and even, on occasion, pitiless in her descriptions and judgements. She was "not afraid to contradict Akhmatova or 'spoil' Mandelstam's biography", noted the critic Andrei Nemzer, neither did she "fear to present herself in a less flattering light and subject her own life to painful analysis". It is not a long-delayed settling of scores that provides the key to the undiminished passion and conviction of her memoirs. Spurred by the love and admiration she had felt for Osip and Nadezhda Mandelstam, and for Akhmatova and her son, Lev Gumilyov, Gerstein's memoirs recall the tests faced by her strong and taciturn loyalties. The conflicting thoughts and emotions roused by such memories were, however, also subjected to the painstaking appraisal of a scholar. A long-suppressed need for confession, the researcher's insistent cross-questioning of the evidence and a chronicler's awareness of posterity – the constant interplay of these rival demands gives the book its momentum, style and distinctive tone. As Nemzer put it: "A highly qualified literary historian and a woman of rare sobriety of thought, Gerstein deliberately oversteps the bounds of the memoir genre."

Nevertheless, this book did grow, in a sense, out of Emma Gerstein's long acquaintance with Nadezhda Mandelstam. There is a glimpse of what their friendship once meant in two letters from the poet's widow. Writing to Nikolai Khardjiev in early 1940, Nadezhda noted that only Emma among her few women friends was continuing to write to her in Kalinin. In April of that year she urged her faithful correspondent to get on a train and visit her. Given their later irreconcilable hostility, Nadezhda's closing words now have a sad and ironic ring. Concluding that they were not likely to meet soon, she leavened her reproaches with mock formality: "Therefore, Emma Grigoryevna, we can only trust to heaven where, after death, we shall choose some well-appointed little cloud for our posthumous aerial voyages."

The affection that bound Akhmatova and Gerstein did not cool.

Appreciating her unstinting support and attempts to reconcile Lyova and his mother, Akhmatova, from the first, had also taken a serious interest in Gerstein's early literary studies. In a diary entry for 6 December 1939, Lydia Chukovskaya mentions how she called on the poet to find her and the literary critic Lydia Ginzburg engaged in a discussion about "someone called Emma" and her suggestions of a court conspiracy against Lermontov.[6] In the late 1950s a now "wealthy" Akhmatova gave Gerstein a typewriter to supplement her minimal earnings. In 1964 *The Destiny of Lermontov*, Gerstein's collected studies of the poet's biography, brought her fame beyond narrow academic circles and among the admiring reviews was one by Akhmatova. In her 62nd year, thanks to the support of Kornei Chukovsky, Anna Akhmatova and Irakly Andronikov, Emma was at last admitted to the Writers' Union. A year later she finally moved into a small self-contained apartment of her own.

Gerstein was not an aquiescent member of the literary establishment. In 1967 she signed a collective letter in defence of Solzhenitsyn,[7] but neither that act nor her belated, and modest, degree of recognition and basic comfort would, perhaps, impress Nadezhda Mandelstam. Only in 1964 was Nadezhda again permitted to live permanently in Moscow. By then she had dashed off her impassioned first volume of memoirs, known in English as *Hope against Hope*. From the mid-1960s it circulated widely as an underground publication. Close friends had seen it earlier, and Emma Gerstein was certainly acknowledged to be a "close friend" in that volume. By the time *Hope Abandoned* appeared in 1970, Emma had been demoted to mere friendship (compare biographical notes to both volumes), and anyone reading the sarcastic reference in that text to "our Lermontov scholar" would realise she was a former friend, at that. Wisely, Emma left the portrait of Nadezhda to the very last of her memoirs. For that remarkable woman displayed a capacity not merely to influence and impress an enraptured younger generation or her foreign devotees (see Clarence Brown's shrewd sketch in the preface to *Hope against Hope*) but also to assert her will over such strong personalities as Akhmatova. Nadezhda successfully interposed herself and her interpretation of the past between later readers and those of her own circle and generation. By then Emma had known Nadezhda for over thirty years. How should she react to the actions and statements of someone who, for so many,

---

[6] "She's no great writer," a critical Chukovskaya commented of Emma to Akhmatova (29 October 1942) when they were in Tashkent together during the war. "She's a faithful friend," replied the poet, "and that's far more important."
[7] Among her 80 fellow Union members supporting Solzhenitsyn were Tatyana Litvinova and Alexander Gladkov, a quotation from whose diary ends this Introduction.

would become a cherished icon, revered over the next two decades as an oracle, archetypal Bohemian and symbol of unbowed opposition?

Slights and an offhand negligence, Gerstein reflected, had formed part of their relationship from the very beginning. Early on, Emma felt that Nadezhda was "a creature of a different kind". Their "very lively" relations compensated for the rough treatment often meted out by the forgetfully self-centred Mandelstams. Indeed, Gerstein felt bound to admit, "those wounds and sarcastic remarks, and certain of the disappointments, bound me even more closely to the two of them". To her all the Khazin family felt like relatives, and if the youngest child appeared, at first sight, to be the oddest of them all, then by common consent Nadya was, at the same time, the most attractive. "She was over-rich," Gerstein suggests, "like a strong blue cheese." In a discontinued earlier draft of her memoirs, the very opening of that frankly titled "List of Grievances" recounts a favourite Khazin family story of a birthday party for the seven-year-old Nadya. When the table was laid, the parents went into the nursery to summon the girl and her guests, only to find Nadya playing alone. "Where are your friends?" "They've gone home." "But why?!" "I hinted they should go." "How did you hint to them?" "I said: 'Get out, I'm fed up with the lot of you.'"

The last and the shortest of Gerstein's memoirs, "Nadezhda" (first published in 1998) caused the greatest uproar. For all its new-found openness, post-Soviet Russia was still a prurient society. Direct mention of the younger Nadezhda's bisexuality by a woman who had belonged to her circle and was now herself in her nineties infringed more than one strong taboo. These inclinations had long been admitted, Gerstein's critics fumed, in conversation and in certain published references. This and her other revelations and hypotheses make uncomfortable, even at times unpleasant, reading; yet there was, as always, good reason for such an explicit statement. For instance, the tale of the "Young Lady of Samatikha" (as she is nonchalantly called in *Hope against Hope*), and of her part in Mandelstam's last arrest, required such a preface. Nadezhda herself warned that what she had written in her memoirs was "the truth, nothing but the truth – but not the whole truth". The third and final mention of the incident in this book at last reveals the anxieties that Mandelstam's wife confided to Emma at the time.

Elsewhere Gerstein's punctilious approach can make for more pedestrian prose. In one innocent context, she cautions the reader that, in the "total absence of documentary evidence", she is relying exclusively on what she remembers; at other moments she scrupulously offers the source and confirmation for statements about events she herself did not witness. Yet once accustomed to the style and manner of Gerstein's recollections, re-reading Nadezhda Mandelstam's first book can be a surprising experience. When the Soviet Union still represented a powerful political and moral threat, *Hope against Hope* was a source of inspiration and determination to many inside and outside the USSR. Open the book at "Theory and Practice", the chapter that describes the role of informers, and the reader is plunged into a stream of statements, allegations and judgements, in a style of presentation that runs counter to Emma's demand for proof or silence. (Nadezhda may sometimes have been right. This could not justify the libelling of others, Emma asserted, among them the unfortunate David Brodsky with whom Nadezhda opens her book.) As important for the historical accuracy and conviction of the text, Nadezhda's fast-paced narration also shows scant concern for chronology. Hindsight repeatedly takes over, making for a better fable but constantly anticipating and antedating the full and bitter understanding that came only with time.

In her unforgiving portrait "Nadezhda", Gerstein permitted herself to be as outspoken as Mandelstam's widow. Emotional blackmail, guilt over an unconsummated suicide pact, risky games with the feelings of others: it is an uncompromising indictment, only slightly softened here by an epilogue drawn from a later article. *Moscow Memoirs* thereby issues a much-needed caution to readers. Of course, these memoirs do not replace the testimony of Nadezhda Mandelstam, but that is of concern only to those who, consciously or not, demand a single, incontrovertible authority. Emma's own recollections of the poet's wife enhance appreciation and understanding of her partisan and assertive texts by showing more fully the character of their inimitable author.[8] Solitary and self-sufficient, Gerstein wanted to know only as much about her friends and acquaintances as they would tell her. Her depiction of an earlier Nadezhda throws into clearer relief the prickly character whose tiny kitchen, now she was established back in Moscow, was regularly filled by a succession of visitors, ready to absorb her vivid tales and trenchant lessons – for a decade and more, after all, Nadezhda had earned her living as a teacher.

Once Nadezhda committed her outspoken reminiscences to print, it was inevitable, perhaps, that the two should fall out. The last straw, however, was an opaquely motivated dispute in 1968 involving Nikolai

---

[8] Nadezhda came to prefer a different image of herself when young: hence the folded corners of a 1920s photograph (see p. 413) that altered her pose.

Khardjiev. The controversy over the accuracy and fairness of Nadezhda Mandelstam's books is easy to grasp, especially after reading *Moscow Memoirs*. The intense feeling generated by the long-promised Soviet collection of Mandelstam's poetry, finally published in 1973, is matched, for outsiders, by its initial obscurity. Gerstein offers little to explain the latter conflict, and today it demands greater context.

For a brief but memorable period in the late 1950s, various kinds of poetry became immensely popular and officially tolerated in the Soviet Union: football stadiums were filled for poetry readings; the young gathered around the statue of Mayakovsky, recently erected in Moscow, to recite their own works. Neither mass enthusiasm nor official tolerance would last. It did reflect a widespread, often deeply felt appreciation of a need for such free and direct expression, once the grip of terror and censorship had eased. In its own way, Nadezhda Mandelstam's first book of memoirs was unofficially the high-water mark of that period, the short-lived political Thaw following Stalin's death. This only made the foot-dragging over Mandelstam's rehabilitation as an artist the more frustrating: no longer banned, he and Akhmatova remained officially undesirable. Only gradually were individual poems by Mandelstam published here and there during the 1960s, and usually in journals on the periphery – Alma-Ata, Tbilisi, Tashkent, Voronezh – as though the poems were themselves still in exile. In the USA, meanwhile, a full but often inaccurate collection of his works began to appear. Fifteen years after an official commission was set up to publish the poet's works in his own country, a censored and incomplete volume of his poems was finally issued there in what was, by Soviet standards, a very modest print-run.[9] Since the 1934 charges had still not been withdrawn (the ban remained until 1987), much written after the Stalin epigram was, like that seditious poem, inevitably excluded. Yet Nadezhda's irritation and concern became particularly focused on the editor of the book.

Nikolai Khardjiev had been an obvious choice. Apart from his formidable qualifications, he had also heard many of the unpublished poems of the 1930s as they were written, from Nadezhda herself. Now his approach began to alarm her. At one point she claimed that he had appropriated some of the texts without permission. "Fortunately, I seized the archive back from him and it's already in the West," Nadezhda later

---

[9] Publication of a volume of Akhmatova's works for which Gerstein prepared the prose section was held up from 1967 until 1976 because the editor of the poetry there, Lydia Chukovskaya, signed letters defending the dissident authors Sinyavsky and Daniel and supported Solzhenitsyn.

wrote, "otherwise it would have been destroyed." That there were likely to be serious textological problems in dealing with Mandelstam's poetic legacy was hardly surprising. For example, Emma recalled a version of the Stalin epigram that was dramatically confirmed when the KGB released Mandelstam's autograph of the poem over half a century later, in 1987. She had quietly taught that poem to others and always disputed the version of this (and other Mandelstam poems) reproduced in the US edition. Khardjiev was a man "of whims and caprices", as Emma makes clear in her memoirs, but if he now worked slowly, his labours on the 1973 volume were painstaking and meticulous: Akhmatova had valued his judgement and opinions for good reason. Whatever the rights and wrongs of the dispute, it was one in which Gerstein felt both personally and professionally involved, and she took Khardjiev's side. Coming after *Hope against Hope*, the quarrel permanently separated her from Nadezhda.

Emma did not respond publicly for twenty years. Indeed, since the key text of these memoirs, "Near the Poet", and the book itself were published in Russia only in 1998, the delay in response lasted nearer three decades. "I had my reasons," Gerstein replied curtly when asked about her silence. She was stirred to react, in fact, when important new evidence appeared or when private and unchecked recollections and surmise threatened, through publication, to acquire the status of undisputed evidence.

Following Nadezhda's example, Gerstein published certain texts abroad. Apart from a number of literary studies referring to the early nineteenth century, there were only two short contemporary comments on the reasons for Lyova Gumilyov's long detention in the Gulag. She made an exception in order to protect Akhmatova from her son's as yet muted claims that his mother had abandoned him in the camps. There were also good reasons not to write. Ever since Nadezhda's two volumes of memoirs had begun to circulate there had been a steady hum of indignation among those who considered themselves, their relatives, acquaintances or friends to have been misrepresented or libelled by the poet's widow. Yet faced by a regime that still suppressed many of Mandelstam's later poems and certain works by Akhmatova, and that banned publication of Pasternak's *Doctor Zhivago*, elementary solidarity required that any criticism be subdued. A clash with Nadezhda would not only be unpleasant, it would be counter-productive. Certain things, moreover, could begin to be discussed only in a free atmosphere.

As important, perhaps, was the urge to get on with what was left of life. An era of severe disappointments and tribulations lay behind.

There were other more positive tasks: throughout the 1970s Gerstein helped to edit and publish Akhmatova's original studies of Pushkin; in 1986 a new and expanded edition of her own *Destiny of Lermontov* appeared. In the end, perhaps, there also remained on Emma's part some pedantic respect for priority and the order of publication. Nadezhda's and Akhmatova's memoirs, though long published abroad, became generally available in Russia only in the late 1980s and early 1990s – until they were to hand, much of the polemical and critical thrust of Emma's own work would remain incomprehensible to a wider readership.

A literary scholar of Gerstein's experience would most certainly have left behind a record of her views on the gaps and inconsistencies in the available documentary evidence. At one point she astonished me with a proposal to go on to the Internet to correct the garbled publication of an interview she had given. Instead she decided to make comprehensive notes and place them in her archive. "What a gift that would have been to world anti-Semitism," she joked, "two old Jewish ladies quarrelling for all to see." Scholarly concerns determined her own priorities: first came the condensed and deceptively simple "Near the Poet", which stripped away the accretions of myth and legend; the revelations of Rudakov's testimony and of her own recollections in "Mandelstam in Voronezh" then offered detailed confirmation of Nadezhda's method and persuasive distortions. The opportunity to write and speak freely thereafter, it seems, did indeed sustain Gerstein through her last decade. For years there had been talk that Akhmatova had neglected her imprisoned son. The chance systematically to refute Panchenko's open repetition of that complaint within months of its publication was a bracing and extraordinary change of tempo. For so long Emma had been an intelligent but necessarily taciturn observer, a participant whose actions were known to few.

Perhaps words from Akhmatova's 1965 review of *Destiny of Lermontov* are now equally applicable to Gerstein's memoirs and could as well be used of the portraits she paints here – of Akhmatova herself and of Mandelstam – as of Lermontov. The poet (wrote Akhmatova) "has long been a stylised figure . . . Emma Gerstein sets aside this stylisation and, quite freely and simply, describes a living person: one who argues, thinks and suffers and, at the same time, in her hands, does not cease to be a great poet".

Never once moving from Moscow, Emma Gerstein had lived to see the Soviet regime come and go. When hand and eye were already failing, a formidable memory and command of her material continued to guide her pen. Now she was writing for younger generations, sometimes 70 years her junior.

Even those in their 50s and 60s, she asserted, did not really understand the Soviet 1930s: her youngest Russian readers, meanwhile, sometimes had as vague an idea as many Western contemporaries about the system that for seven decades had held millions in thrall. Emma saw not only her memoirs in print but also the republication of all her academic and occasional journalistic pieces. When I explained that delays to the English translation of *Moscow Memoirs* were partly due to the demands of a book about the war in Chechnya, Gerstein permitted herself a sigh of frustration: an intensely lived knowledge of Lermontov and *his* campaigns in the Caucasus fuelled her just audible complaint: "But what's new about that?"[10]

In 1999, the year after her memoirs appeared, Emma confessed that, at long last, "the laws of nature are beginning to affect me". Praised for her publication, she noted, with the melancholy misgivings of a literary scholar, that books are forgotten: "in an altered world, occupied with very different things", would she still find a reader? This could well be the fate of her volume, she worried. Somehow, that seems unlikely.

Though Emma Gerstein's volume of memoirs was compiled from different works, composed over a period of twenty years, remarkably little has been omitted in translation. The structure of this edition from these six memoirs was proposed by Ms Gerstein herself. The only subsequent changes were a shortening of "Mandelstam in Voronezh" and its separation into an epistolary diary and a commentary (the latter forms Appendix 2), and a similar shifting of Lev Gumilyov's Gulag correspondence to the end of the book (Appendix 3).

In translating and editing Emma Gerstein's memoirs, the text has been prepared for the general reader. Footnotes explain the numerous references and allusions that concern literary matters, historical events, personalities and obscure aspects of life in a vanished civilisation (the translator is, if anything, a historian not a literary specialist). The translator's "Five Notes" in Appendix 1 throw extra light on key incidents, unfamiliar realities and one intriguing piece of correspondence. A map and short list of biographical notes complete the apparatus. Those who want more can exploit the detailed index and the other books cited here.

---

[10] "How appalling it is, this war in the Caucasus, from which officers always return sick and aged by ten years, and filled with revulsion by the slaughter," wrote Sophia Karamzina in an 1837 letter that Gerstein quotes in *The Destiny of Lermontov*. "It is especially lamentable since the war is without purpose or results."

(Victor Terras' compendious 1991 *History of Russian Literature* proved especially informative and valuable.)

There remains one insuperable weakness in the English edition. Emma Gerstein's memories and shrewd comments indisputably have a value of their own, but it is her unique link with two of the greatest Russian poets of the twentieth century that gives them particular interest. Accordingly, versions of eleven poems by Mandelstam and ten by Akhmatova have been included here. Disappointing for English readers, these offerings are quite inadequate to any who know the originals. ("Must you include these 'translations' of Mandelstam and Akhmatova?" asked a dismayed acquaintance, equally at home in Russian and English literature.) It would have been easier, indeed, simply to let the persevering track down English translations of the poetry for themselves. Prose may survive the transition to another language, poetry rarely does. As Mandelstam himself declared in his *Conversation about Dante*, if a text is capable of paraphrase, then that, to his mind, was "surely a sign of non-poetry".

No claims are made for the versions in this book, least of all those I attempted myself. As deployed here their purpose is frankly functional. A stanza or, in some cases, an entire poem (the Stalin epigram, for instance) was added in translation to make fuller sense of Gerstein's comments: her original readers naturally had access to these works or had long known them by heart. Sometimes, she made play of details and implications not preserved or emphasised in existing translations; elsewhere she insisted on variant readings: both necessitated new versions. It was then a short step to a free-standing and lightly annotated selection of those poems by Mandelstam and Akhmatova that were mentioned in the text, in particularly striking or poignant circumstances. Even in a travestied form, they give some impression of the themes and variety of the two poets and retain a faint echo of their distinctive voices.

Yet supposing an adequate poetic equivalent existed in English, it would still not restore another vital dimension: the intense admiration and respect with which their native readers rewarded and sustained the authors. First acquaintance with many of their works was a semi-clandestine activity. Long after Stalin's death, the uncensored poetry of Akhmatova and Mandelstam was among the literature immediately confiscated when dissidents were pursued from the 1960s to the 1980s. Nor were the officially tolerated works often easy to come by.

A scene from that more recent past offers a fitting conclusion to this introduction. It took place not long before Emma Gerstein began to write her memoirs. In early 1974 a second printing of the long-awaited

Leningrad edition of Mandelstam's poetry suddenly came on sale. A
Moscow writer made the following entry in his diary:

> 15 January. This morning they sold Mandelstam at the Bookstall.
> After the previous disappointments a list was drawn up of over 200
> people. Lev put me down as #65. At 9.30 a.m. and even earlier
> there was a crowd waiting outside . . . The temperature was 19
> below zero. We went off, once in a while, to warm up in some
> neighbouring financial institution. Sometimes, as always happens
> in queues, amazing rumours began (they wouldn't bring any, they'd
> only have 50 copies, only people who brought their Writers' Union
> card would get one). At about 11 the books arrived. The shop's
> director announced that 200 copies would be put on sale. People
> lined up.

A member of the Union, queuing up outside the Writers' Bookstall
in the centre of Moscow, the diarist was lucky. He'd left his card at home
but was able to buy a copy for 1 rouble 45 kopecks ("They say it's
already selling on the black market for 50–80 roubles"). Pleased with
his good fortune, he forgot to mention an odd coincidence: 15 January
1974 would have been Osip Mandelstam's 83rd birthday.

October 2003
Geldeston

I

NEAR THE POET
[1986]

At the Sanatorium

The day I arrived I could not help noticing one couple. A young woman of intelligent and rather refined appearance entered the dining-room. Her husband followed. A dry, haughty face with a long lower lip and an elegant beak of a nose; greying hair that receded far from his high forehead. "Probably an art professor from GAKhN," I said to myself.[1]

Once seated, they carefully considered the menu: could he eat liver? She had a quiet, pleasant voice. The liver proved tough and the "professor" quite toothless. Irritably, he began to say something to the waitress; a row seemed likely. His wife did nothing. Her slanting pale blue eyes cast a brief glance of veiled curiosity at the other diners. This calm silence and her prominent, bare, broad-templed brow imparted an obscure gravity to the whole scene. Chastened, the waitress brought a different dish.

As the guests left the dining-room, they began to plan a programme of evening entertainments. The "professor" was approached: would he not recite something? Turning to a round-shouldered man in an airplane pilot's uniform, he acidly demanded: "Supposing I now asked you to fly; how would you respond?" All were dumbfounded. Exasperated, he began to explain. Poetry was not a form of recreation, and it was just as much work for him to write, or even read, verse as for his colleague to fly a plane. The holiday mood was spoiled. With a disdainful growl, the "professor" (or poet, as I now knew) added something about "parlour games". His wife meanwhile held everyone in the same pensive and direct gaze.

---

[1] The State Academy of Art Studies.

It was 29 October 1928 at the sanatorium of the Scholars' Aid Commission, not far from Moscow. Out of season, few academics were at Uzkoye, but their family members and other professions were represented. My father, a Moscow surgeon, had sent me for ten days' convalescence: I had suffered a severe emotional shock and arrived in a depressed state. I was 25 years old.

Next morning, the couple passed me in the corridor. He held her elbow and walked with a slightly mincing gait; her step was firm, though she was noticeably bow-legged. A snatch of conversation reached me: "Really, I should challenge him to a duel!" said Mandelstam, his upper lip twitching faintly (by now I knew the poet's name). I felt sure that he wanted to fight yesterday's pilot. I was mistaken. The prickly rejoinder had nothing to do with anyone at our sanatorium, as soon became clear: it referred to his dispute with Gornfeld over the translation of *Till Eulenspiegel*.[2]

It takes little time to become friendly at sanatoria and rest homes. By Nadezhda's birthday on 31 October, we had become acquainted. Mandelstam's wife proved a convivial and entertaining companion.

She was now 29. "A year to the next zero," she joked.

We first met in the library, which was also the sitting-room. On the walls were radio sockets, but there was no loudspeaker; we listened through earphones.

This was Mandelstam's favourite pastime. Had a tuft of hair not poked above the headstrap, he would have resembled a woman in a bonnet. He could not have cared less. Sitting cross-legged on the couch, he listened most intently to the music. Occasionally, he beamed and bounced up and down, but for the most part his face and even his pose expressed deep attention and respect.

I do not remember Mandelstam ever naming a performer, but he always noted the day's programme: "It's Chopin today," or "I'm off to listen to Mozart."

Not once did I hear him complain about the deadening timbre of that mechanical device. He adored the radio. Of this there would be further proof when the Mandelstams were staying on the Kropotkin Embankment in Moscow, at the Hostel for Visiting Scholars. Divans stood against all four walls of the square sitting-room. A guest seated herself, opened a book and put on earphones. For a while, Mandelstam restrained himself. At last he dashed, muttering, out of the room, and through the closed door we heard his rapid steps and outraged cries

---

[2] An account of this literary row is provided in Appendix 1.1, p. 424.

in the corridor: "Either one reads, or one listens to music!" The woman was totally bemused. She had not been disturbing anyone, had she?

"A ball is a complex ritual," I exclaimed. Walking in the park at Uzkoye, a chance companion had begun talking of Society life before the Revolution. Mandelstam noted the remark. My views on the social and aesthetic meaning of that festive rite probably struck him as more entertaining than genteel reminiscences of balls at the Moscow Assembly Rooms. Thereafter, the Mandelstams often singled me out to accompany them on their walks.

It was a casual aside: "We are such unsettled people, all three of us," said Mandelstam. I took this as recognition of the inner anxiety that then consumed me.

Nadezhda discerned in me a resemblance to her elder sister. Anya always ate alone, was withdrawn and reticent, and came and went at the bidding of her intuition, which seldom misled her. Before the Revolution, she studied early French literature at the faculty of historical philology. Now she survived on whatever work came her way and lived in the dark back room her uncle had given her in a large communal apartment in Leningrad. I would like her sister, Nadezhda believed. When Anya later came on visits to Moscow I indeed took a strong liking to her and she responded in kind. At Uzkoye, though, she was described as an emotionally disturbed woman, unable to cope with life. Hardly the most pleasing comparison. Nadezhda was actually paying me a special compliment, or so she thought. Contemptuous of "primitive" people, she preferred those who deviated from the norm and guessed at (or imagined) such aberrations in others. Her sympathetic attention had a beneficial effect. She had no inhibitions whatsoever, and as we talked I gradually overcame my innate reserve.

Sometimes Nadezhda would not join our walks in the park, preferring chess and billiards, games Mandelstam did not play. Then the two of us strolled alone.

Not a trace remained of the reserved, forbidding figure I had encountered that first day in the dining-room. Mandelstam had a humorous turn of mind and took a lively interest in the petty dramas of life at the sanatorium. Of these there was no shortage, since restrictions of monastic severity were in force. Grown men and women posted a lookout by the doors so the director would not catch them executing the daring steps of the Charleston or dancing the foxtrot. Both were prohibited. It was not a crime to sing French songs. Once I was so carried away that, accompanied on the piano, I sang my favourite "Je cherche auprès Titine" (the melody served as the leitmotif for Charlie Chaplin's *Modern Times* [1936]). A French translator joined in and then performed several more Parisian ditties herself. The administration had no grounds for complaint: the rules did not cover such an unheard-of occurrence. Still, it would be less disturbing if the "patients" all sang "That noble sea, blessed Baikal" or (in Ukrainian) "The wide Dniepr wails and moans." I kept Mandelstam informed of every such event. I was in an open ward, and I saw and heard more than the Mandelstams, who had a room to themselves. His animated cross-questioning recalled the aunt who never left home but each day learned the latest news of Combray's inhabitants from her elderly maid (cf. Proust, *Du côté de chez Swann*, 1913). My comparison was eagerly accepted, and for several days I was Françoise and he was Tante Léonie.

Nadezhda fell ill. All day Mandelstam was in a state of agitation, seeking help and advice. But as soon as the doctor had made his diagnosis, prescribed treatment and confined her to bed, my afternoon walks with Mandelstam resumed.

On our return, I would tell Nadezhda of her husband's despotic ways. He could not imagine my taking any path but the one he indicated. "He treats me like a chauffeur," I complained. "'Right, left, straight on,' he tells me. I'm left with no choice but mute obedience." Soon "chauffeur" was also part of our humorous ritual.

Our conversations were not always so light-hearted. I was seeking consolation and, probably, was rather frank. I think so, because one such earnest dialogue ended with an appeal: "I am unfortunate, aren't I?" Mandelstam looked at me most attentively and gravely. "Yes, you are unfortunate," he said: "but do you know? Sometimes unfortunate people are very happy."

For the rest of my life, I would be convinced time and again of the truth of this aphorism. Acquaintance with Mandelstam was thus my "initiation" into a different life where everything was judged by other standards.

To begin with, though, our conversations took a somewhat Freudian turn and revolved around the theme of eroticism – "the first thing that comes to mind, when you wake up each morning", as Mandelstam put it.

We were discussing the sources of his perception of life. Nothing, he said, so depends on eroticism as poetry. "What about music?" I interrupted. "Surely music is also linked with eroticism? Why poetry specifically?" "Because I happen to have a certain experience in such matters," Mandelstam replied peevishly. He halted abruptly, struck by a sudden conjecture:

"You have read my poetry?"

"No."

He became appallingly angry. I began to make excuses:

"But I know – well, people told me – that there is a wonderful poet who lives in Tsarskoye Selo."[3]

"We haven't lived there in years!"

"Everyone is entranced by your new poems –"

"What new poems?"

"But you have just published a book, haven't you?" I said in confusion.

"There's no new verse in it! I have not written poetry now for many years. I am writing . . . I have written . . . prose . . ." Mandelstam shouted angrily.

Panting with irritation, he abandoned me. Alone on the empty path in the deepening twilight, I watched his receding figure with its shuffling, odd splay-footed gait. He almost ran, ignoring the footpaths, stumbling and sinking into the muddy earth, until he came up against the tumble-down fence and leaned his head on the rail. Behind me shone the lights of the sanatorium. How could I return alone? What would I tell Nadezhda? I sat on a bench, abashed and perplexed. Meanwhile, Mandelstam approached with a slow calm step. He also sat down and, eyes sparkling through their long lashes, began to quiz me: "Well, and how did you imagine this Mandelstam? A sober character, with a big beard, perhaps? Who lives in a palace . . .?" He was especially amused by the invention of the beard: no-one at that time wore beards apart from old-fashioned professors.

Reconciled, we returned home. That evening, Nadezhda nevertheless enquired: "Whatever were you and Mandelstam talking about?" I gave the best account I could. "He's just flirting with you," she snapped. I'm not sure. I remembered how he told me, with some disappointment, "I toss you a ball, but you don't catch it."

For some reason, Mandelstam constantly recalled Larisa Reisner during our walks. He remembered an episode, from before his marriage, when he called to accompany Reisner to a masked ball. "Larisa Mikhailovna is stroking a toad," he heard the maid announce. She meant to say her mistress was "ironing her jabot" [one mispronounced letter separates the

---

[3] Small town outside Petersburg which grew up around the imperial summer palace.

two statements in Russian]. In the 1960s and '70s, I read this anecdote several times in memoirs about Mandelstam, though the details varied.

Responding to some of my stories, Mandelstam once drawled: "Larisa Reisner was also *heavy* artillery!" From Nadezhda's tales I knew that he had in mind Reisner's affair with Nikolai Gumilyov.

Reisner's tactlessness, Mandelstam said, was "inspired". Now married to Fyodor Raskolnikov, she attended a diplomatic reception. A French lieutenant arrived. He was so good-looking that a stunned Reisner got up and walked towards him. And there they stood, embarrassed, face to face, two handsome creatures. "But she had a most unattractive walk," I remarked. "Not at all," Mandelstam replied in astonishment. "She danced along . . ." (he gazed thoughtfully and solemnly into the distance, as always when seeking the right word, then added) ". . . like a wave on the sea."

We walked out to the main road to buy cigarettes at a co-operative shop. I had never been in the countryside at that time of year. I was acutely aware not just of the dark ponds and paths of the autumnal park and the mysteriously gleaming windows of the former Trubetskoi mansion but also of the wild, bare trees, the low grey horizon and the occasional small house at the roadside. I wanted Mandelstam to share my mood. But, no, he hated it all: slush, despondency, miserable buildings and the nondescript faces of those we passed. "I am a city-dweller," he declared.

One of the women on my ward was young but so debilitated that she always returned to bed after breakfast. In the sitting-room one day she asked Mandelstam: "Do tell me about Gumilyov." I thought: He'll get angry and treat the request as cheap curiosity. But nothing of the kind: he described a meeting with Gumilyov during a journey, perhaps even at a railway station. I had loved Gumilyov's poetry since I was 15 and revered his memory. For some reason, though, I do not recall a single word of Mandelstam's story. All I remember is the loving, respectful tone in which he spoke of a friend and fellow-poet, and his concluding words: "That was the last time we met."

It would soon be 7 November, the eleventh anniversary of the October Revolution. I was glad to be here and not in Moscow. Everyone in the city would join the demonstration and give me disapproving looks for staying at home. Yet which column could I have marched in? (Although there would be trouble at the labour exchange, I had left my job.) And it was impossible to visit anyone that day: the trams did not run, and the streets were crammed with singing marchers who tossed their comrades up in the air each time the procession could not move forward and came to a halt. No, it was not for me.

The gala evening was modestly celebrated at Uzkoye. As I recall, there were no visiting performers. Instead we were all invited to the main hall, and a radio was set up there. We listened to a broadcast of the celebrations, probably from the Bolshoi Theatre – official speeches followed by a special concert. The effect on Mandelstam is hard to describe: "Charity performances, recitations, plump sopranos from the 1890s," (he was almost shouting) "the same arias, over and over again . . ." A young architect turned in amazement to the rest of the audience: "I can't understand why Mandelstam, of all people, should be so upset. *He* isn't responsible for the concert programme!"

The next day when we came to lunch, we saw an additional, lavishly laid table. Many important comrades had gathered there to relax over the holiday. It was strange to see Nadezhda's reserved, elegant brother Yevgeny Khazin in such company. His hazel eyes, also slanting, had a cold brilliance, and his manners were impeccable: how he peeled a pear with his long-fingered, delicate hands! So many new guests had arrived that there was no room for him at our table. We had more fun and chattered away. After the meal, Mandelstam said I had no reason to be so diffident: "You're good at defending your views . . . and keep those you're talking to at a respectful distance." It was a purely Mandelstamian approach to the problem of conduct.

Osip Mandelstam, 1920s

We know what profound meaning Mandelstam attached to the concept of "inner conviction" and how often he was hurt by the failure of a chance acquaintance to keep his distance. In the author's aside in *Egyptian Stamp* (1928) he exclaimed with good reason, "Lord, let me not be like Parnok!" The Parnok, whom "women and hotel doormen held in contempt" and who was among those "disliked by the mob". Such incompatibility was highly typical of Mandelstam.

His impulsive character did not always disclose his best qualities. Frequently the worst traits came to the fore, not so much individual failings as those of family and background. Given his impressionable nature and intense excitability, this took dramatic forms and often led to the false belief that he was a vulgar figure. Such an attitude encouraged others to be overfamiliar in their dealings with him. Yet he knew that his intellect and poetic genius were unique of their kind and entitled him to a respectful deference. The discrepancy was a source of constant distress for Mandelstam. I only recognised this later when, for five or six years, I saw the Mandelstams regularly in Moscow.

I returned home immediately after the Revolution Day holidays. The Mandelstams stayed on at Uzkoye. I came back to visit them and brought him a Russian translation of Proust's *À l'ombre des jeunes filles en fleur* (1920). I found Mandelstam on a couch in the sitting-room, wearing earphones.

I cannot understand why, but I suddenly felt a terrible sadness. I sensed something alien about him, as if he were setting off down obscure, fanciful and exotic paths. This momentary sense of loss and despair was a fleeting premonition and just as promptly forgotten.

And there we were, strolling and chatting in the park with Nadezhda. A damp snow had fallen, and she was dressed for wintry weather with a certain athletic elegance she alone possessed. Later I learned that the flat-topped leather cap, with its smooth fur lining and earflaps, and the brownish jumper had been bought from a quite ordinary co-operative shop. Today it is inconceivable how ugly the objects on sale there usually were, but Nadezhda could always spot something usable on the shelf. She shared her brother's sharp eye and good taste: he wore knitted gloves as if they were calfskin and cut a dashing figure in his waterproof.

When we came back and entered the room, Mandelstam was lying on the bed and gazing into the air. Next to him lay the Proust. Mandelstam muttered to himself, then isolated words could be heard, finally he quoted a complete phrase. "Only a Frenchman could say that!" he exclaimed in disgust. It was a naturalistic description of the awakening of sexual feeling in the novel's young hero.

We again went out for a walk, but this time only Mandelstam and myself. He continued thinking about Proust, "the pathos of memory" he termed it. The book prompted a wave of recollections about his own childhood. He was no longer speaking to me, but addressed the ponds. Frank and painful admissions. Complaints about his difficult childhood and incompetent upbringing: they continued taking him to the women's bathing place for too long; he found it very unsettling to be caned by his governess.

He drew me towards the ponds, one stretching darkly after the other.

On their banks, his pliant voice loudly declaimed entire sentences, with unexpected metaphors and meanings that I could not penetrate. It was an irrepressible improvisation, directed not at me but towards the farther of the ponds, and I vaguely recalled how Pushkin wandered above the same small lakes, singing his verse and frightening the ducks.

I last visited the Mandelstams at Uzkoye on the day they were leaving. We sat with their suitcase in the taxi. The engine throbbed and, as if keeping time, Mandelstam also shuddered with irritation. We could not leave. We were waiting for a woman who was also returning home after treatment. The same person, in fact, who had asked about Gumilyov. Mandelstam lost his self-control. He cursed and kept crying, "The meter, the meter!" Of course, the woman soon appeared, but Mandelstam's dissatisfaction did not pass. When we dropped her outside her apartment building, she invited the Mandelstams to call on her. As soon as we set off he remarked caustically: "She supposes we are now acquainted." I was exultant. Our acquaintance, it seemed, was firmly established.

In Moscow, Mandelstam made me a present of his books. *Egyptian Stamp* carried an "old-fashioned" dedication, as he himself described it, dated "20 November 1928". A few years later, however, Nadezhda took back his *Poems* (1928). They were short of a copy to submit for a possible new edition at Khudlit, the publishers. I objected but when Nadya contemptuously remarked, "What do you need it for?" I took offence and surrendered the book. She probably tore out and destroyed the inscription. Mandelstam had concluded with the words, "Thanks for the Proust".

In Moscow

Mandelstam distinguished his author's copies of *Poems* (the 1928 republication of *Stone*, *Tristia* and subsequent verse) by the colour of the binding. "Vanilla, strawberry and pistachio ice-cream," he would joyfully declare. I was given a "strawberry" cover, which resembled that of *On Poetry*. This collection of his essays, published the same year, had not yet sold out, and I bought a copy in a book shop.[4] It left a staggering impression. Mandelstam's dismissal of the nineteenth century in the title essay – back to the orderly and rational eighteenth century, he proposed, or forward into an unknown, irrational future – filled me with apoca-

---

[4] "[M]ade up of articles written between 1910 and 1923 and united by a common idea," commented Mandelstam in the preface. See Osip Mandelstam, *The Collected Critical Prose and Letters*, ed. Jane Gary Harris (London, 1991).

lyptic horror. Though my learning proved deficient, everything about
the way he wrote and reflected in the remaining articles was close to my
perception of life. I appealed to an old school and university friend to
share my rapture. "Poor fellow," she could not help remarking, when I
read extracts to her. "Who is he writing for?"

Lena's practical attitude was well founded. On the eve of Stalin's Five-
Year Plans, articles written and published at the beginning of the NEP[5]
were treated as inane absurdities. Mandelstam was losing his readers.

Nor did he have a home of his own.

From the day I first visited the Mandelstams in Nadya's brother's
room on Strastnoi Boulevard until 1933, when they were allotted an
apartment in the writers' building on Nashchokin Street, I would go all
over the city (and beyond) to see them, wherever they were renting a
room or staying with friends and family:[6]

> on 1st, 2nd or 3rd Brest Street (I do not remember which
> now) between the Garden Ring and Belorussky Station;

> at a new flat-roofed house on the corner of Spiridonevsky
> and Malaya Bronnaya streets;

> with Mandelstam's brother Alexander, in his room on
> Starosadsky Street;

> on Pokrovka Street;

> at the Kropotkin Embankment, the Hostel for Visiting Scholars;

> in Caesar Ryss's room in Apartment 20, at 10 Bolshaya
> Polyanka Street;

> at Herzen House on Tverskoi Boulevard: a narrow room with
> one window, later a large room with two or three windows,
> both in the right wing;

> again at the Bolshevo rest home and a second time at Uzkoye;

---

[5] The New Economic Policy, introduced by the Bolsheviks in 1921 at the end of
the Civil War, permitted petty capitalism and the market to exist again. The
acronym NEP came to define a brief, ambiguous but vivid interval brought to
an end by forced industrialisation and the collectivisation of agriculture after 1928.
[6] See Appendix 1.3: "Living Space", p. 425.

two or three times at 6/8 Shchipok Street where they lived
with me;

and yet again with Nadya's brother Yevgeny Khazin, at
6 Strastnoi Boulevard.

No matter where they were, I do not recall Mandelstam at a writing table.

No, there were exceptions. For instance, when Alexander Mandelstam
brought round his article. Then working in the book trade, he had to
contribute to a specialist publication, but he was no writer or, to be
more exact, found it hard to concentrate. Mandelstam sat down at the
table beside his brother and helped him patiently and lovingly.

In the large sunlit room on Tverskoi Boulevard, I occasionally found
Mandelstam sitting at a small kitchen table with a vast colourfully illustrated volume of Pallas or Lamarck open in front of him. Such a large
book could not be read lying down.

During the very first winter of our acquaintance, Nadezhda and
Mandelstam lived with me at Shchipok Street next to the Semashko
Hospital. My father was head physician there until 1929. After that date,
those not members of the Party could no longer hold administrative
posts (he would head the surgical department until the late 1930s). In
the '20s, it was still the rule that only medical personnel could live in
the hospital grounds. As a result, when everyone else's living space was
constantly being reduced, we were very grandly accommodated: our
large, detached one-storey house had a glassed-in veranda, its own garden
fenced off from the hospital grounds, and even stables in the courtyard.
At the same time, Father's position trapped his children, since his living
quarters could not be exchanged for other accommodation.

Our family consisted of six adults, each with different occupations and
interests, all a little cranky in their own way and forced by circumstance
to live together. Each had a separate room. One of my brothers married
a cousin who lacked the usual Gerstein quirks but was richly endowed
with oddities of her own. They had recently had a son. Dropping by to
see me, the Mandelstams heard my little nephew say his first very difficult word. Thereafter they often recalled how he jumped up and down
on my couch with radiant eyes and triumphantly announced "Eego-
lo-chka" [little needle]. Somehow Mandelstam found it a particularly
moving experience.

For us, home was a focus of passions, tears and stubbornness, and we
concealed the scars left by the hurt we inflicted on one another. This
was especially evident in the tension that surrounded our mealtimes. But

Nadezhda was able to win the attention of every member of the family despite the frenzied competition of my cousin (sister-in-law).

Nadezhda and my father discussed their impressions of other countries: as a child she had visited Switzerland several times with her parents.

She and my elder sister, her contemporary, compared "facets", as Nadezhda referred to the individual configurations of eyebrows, nose and forehead. They both had foreheads of the Italian Renaissance type. My sister had graduated from Professor Goldenweiser's piano class at the Conservatory, and this gave Nadezhda a reason to describe games of chess she had played with him at some rest home.

She and my mother talked about Sofia Andreyevna Tolstoy: "It was no easy matter being the wife of Lev Tolstoy," remarked Nadezhda.

In the kitchen, our housekeeper cast morose glances in her direction as Nadezhda cheerfully baked shortbread.

Very soon, Nadezhda had nicknamed us "Habsburgs". We came, it seemed, of ancient stock, and this made us weary and refined people, just like the later offspring of the Austrian Imperial dynasty. I was discovered, a few days later, to have "Ehrenburg eyes", the same grey and clever gaze. "She has to make a character of everyone she meets," commented my ironic friend Lena. "That's the essence of such worldly sociability." With Mandelstam, however, similar conceits evidently had different roots. I had an Egyptian profile, he said. I was astonished, and he also expressed surprise: "But don't you remember? The Pharaoh in his chariot . . . his bodyguard beside him . . . or a column of soldiers in profile . . . Well, you're like that spear-carrying warrior." I don't know if I really bore any outward resemblance to an ancient Egyptian. To tell the truth, I had a poor recollection of what the Pharaoh's chariot looked like – as if it mattered – but Mandelstam had correctly guessed one thing: it was a family trait to act as a "bodyguard". We all offered a supporting shoulder to anyone we looked up to or supposed to be less fortunate than ourselves. As life tried and tested me I ceased to lean on others and began to offer them such support.

Restlessness

I often went to Nadezhda's brother Yevgeny to see her and Osip. At the time, the watchword of Mandelstam's life was "the rejection of literature". He did not want to be a writer. He did not consider himself a writer. He hated the writing desk. He was careless with books he didn't need, bending back the covers, tearing out the pages, and using the paper and card for any purpose that came to mind.

"Trampling Moscow under foot", they named it in their private language: for calling Mandelstam the Poet a has-been, for considering his prose to be "not realist" and his essays to be incomprehensible, and because it was there that the Gornfeld dispute deprived Mandelstam of the translation work that had just started coming his way.

"We'll set up shop," Mandelstam's imagination took flight. "Nadenka will be on the till . . . Anya [Nadezhda's older sister] will serve behind the counter."

"And what about you, Osip Emilievich, what will you do?"

"There's always a man in such places. Surely you've noticed? In the back room. Sometimes he stands in the doorway, once in a while he goes over to the cashier and speaks to her . . . That's who I'll be."

But soon the eloquent tirades resumed, and he was again running out to the telephone in the corridor to cajole, complain or demand a reply. He would return and consult us, then run back to the phone and finally, exhausted, throw himself down on the divan, with his arms around "Nadenka". At times he would devise games. The two of them drove me to distraction with one of these pastimes, "Emma needs a compress". They started wrapping towels round me, I fended them off, they roared with laughter, and I also began to laugh though I was not that amused.

The complaints, accusations and declarations were dictated to Nadya.

Again he would dream up new patrons and live in anticipation of the appointed hour.

Falling on the divan as if tumbling into water.

Once he threw himself down . . . and went straight to sleep.

Head resting on a folded arm, he lay on his side, knees bent, and all his limbs acquired a peculiar lightness. As though the slender but strong hand, the now more delicate lines of his face and even his strangely proportioned body had all submitted to a mysterious harmony. It was quite unlike a reclining figure: he seemed to float in blissful repose and be listening.

Decades later when anyone mentioned Osip Mandelstam in my presence, I always wanted to exclaim: "How beautifully he slept!" But I kept quiet, for fear of appearing ridiculous.

This experience is comparable only to the shock I felt at the spectacle of the dead Mayakovsky. He lay on a table, straight and light, with a face bathed by death, and – despite the arresting sight of his heavy, iron-heeled boots – he appeared to be flying.

One time Mandelstam and I went to the Khazins [Yevgeny and his wife] on Strastnoi Boulevard. Tsvetayeva's *Tsar-Maiden* and Gumilyov's *Pearl* were laid out on a little table with other volumes of poetry.

"Just like the dentist's," Mandelstam growled quietly and sat down cross-legged on the broad divan. In the conversation that followed, I asked his opinion of Akhmatova's poetry. Gazing into the distance he spoke not of the love themes in her lyrics but of her descriptions of nature. He compared her poems to the depictions of landscape in the Russian classics, but neither in Turgenev nor in Chekhov could he find a parallel. Muttering names, he ran through a list of writers until he reached the one definition that stood comparison: "Aksakov's steppe".

Muttering was one of his ways of talking (in all I counted four). It was a barely restrained emotional reaction: he "thought aloud", moving his lips, almost groping for the words – yes? no? perhaps . . . ? No, this is it: and a thought took shape as a brilliant aphorism (No. 1), which sometimes developed into an impassioned improvisation with devastating logical deductions (No. 2). There were never any mechanical, run-of-the-mill phrases with Mandelstam.

When he dictated his article on literary translation to me, however, it was neither mutter nor improvisation but a loud rhythmic declamation (No. 3). He tested each phrase aloud, pronouncing the words triumphantly and admiring their disposition.[7] "Torrents of Hackwork" was published in *Izvestiya* on 7 April 1929 and was one of the phases in his battle with Gornfeld, which had grown into a major literary row.[8]

He dictated the article to me in a room they were renting somewhere near the Belorussky Station. It is a hard business, always living with someone else's worn and tasteless furnishings. At times, Nadya grew tired of it. Once she lay down on the bed and covered herself from head to foot with the blanket. Mandelstam grew cross: "Nadenka, this is a pose . . . It's 1910-ish . . . You're the Chamber Theatre,[9] Nadenka!" She leaped up.

Returning from the city one day, Nadya merrily described the usual shouting match on the tram. They were pushing their way towards the exit, themselves shoved and poked, giving virtuoso abuse in response. The opposition had the last word: "Toothless old man." About to descend, Mandelstam poked his head back round the carriage door and exultantly declared: "There'll be teeth next time!" With that triumphal cry, they got off the tram.

---

[7] Gerstein later describes a fourth quite different "social" style of speaking; see "At Herzen House", p. 31.
[8] In July 1929, Mandelstam's "On Translations" appeared in *On Literary Guard* magazine (Appendix 1.1; see p. 424).
[9] Founded in 1914 by Alexander Tairov, the Chamber Theatre "declared war on philistinism".

We went to the cinema to see *A Descendant of Genghiz Khan* [1928]. Mandelstam had a note of admission, but it was no easy matter to speak to the manager. I stood a little way off, listening to Mandelstam shout and the disapproving cries of the queue: I saw their astonished looks. Mandelstam almost trembled with exasperation and was yelling indignantly. How overjoyed I was when we finally got inside. But Pudovkin's famous film did not please him at all. The lyricism of the Mongolian landscape which formed the backdrop to the action enraptured me, but Mandelstam shrugged, "It's an engraving . . ." Discontented, he explained that the cinema demanded movement not still-life scenes. Why borrow subjects from another art form? It was just a blown-up engraving.

Sometimes we went to the Satire Theatre. It was in the Arcade on Tverskaya Street where *Moscow Komsomol* had its offices (at one period in Mandelstam's life he worked for the newspaper).We never saw anything interesting at this theatrical revue. The actresses were typical of the time: they might be attractive and have good figures, but their smiles were cold and their eyes empty. Only one sketch sticks in my memory. It depicted tenants at a meeting of the house-management committee. The actors wore realistic and appropriate costumes, but their increasingly heated discussion was conducted not in words but in mooing, miaows and barks. A gentleman with a small pointed beard, wearing a collar and tie, was particularly fine: this relict of the old regime barked malevolently with the varied intonation of an accomplished troublemaker.

As we returned after the show, I complained of a despondency and boredom not just on the stage but among the audience as well. How wretchedly everyone was dressed, and how little their faces revealed. Mandelstam was incensed. Excitedly, he began to assure me that audiences had been no different before the Revolution. Amateur performances, charity fundraising evenings, social dramas at the theatre – everywhere, he recalled, there was a philistine audience far worse than today's. "I miss none of it, not one thing," he exclaimed passionately.

Mandelstam recognised only the present. For him the day before did not exist. And there was no way back. His comments about our present existence, the much-vaunted "Soviet reality", could be summed up in a very few words: "They led us here and abandoned us."

As well as the *Moscow Komsomol* offices there was also a canteen in the Arcade. You stood in line and fetched your own food, and I was astonished by the speed and efficiency with which Nadya chose from among those unappetising little bowls. Nor was Mandelstam at all dismayed by the cheap plates and cutlery and the not particularly clean surroundings. The Mandelstams were undemanding. He was wearing a coat of inexpensive

grey striped material that went very well with his shaven (matt) face, dark
eyes and the elegant carriage of his head. One of the *Komsomol* staff made
him angry. Mandelstam, hands shaking with rage, began to push the plates
about the cheap table before running out of the canteen, his eyes flashing. "He's changed a great deal," the editor told me later. "He's become
so quarrelsome." But I had enjoyed Mandelstam's furious eyes and the
sharp words he hurled at his companion. He was already growing disillu-
sioned with his *Komsomol* colleagues. He rang one of them at home, in
a hurry to share a new idea for the newspaper, but his acquaintance had
the day off work and postponed their conversation to the following morning. This bureaucratic indifference in one so young astounded Mandelstam,
and he ceased to expect a lively response from his new friends.

The Russian Association of Proletarian Writers, RAPP, was preparing
to hold a conference. Mandelstam avidly followed the preliminary sparring in the literary press. We attended the gathering. In a large and not
very full hall, Mandelstam went up to one after another of the writers
sitting in the front rows of the audience. Then he walked up the broad
passage to the rostrum and handed a note to the organisers: he wanted
to address the conference. They did not call him. He returned home
downcast.

The RAPP magazine *On Literary Guard*, attacked Mandelstam for his
prose, especially "The Chimera of the Revolution", a chapter[10] in *Noise
of Time*, and for his poetry ("The Century", 1922). Leopold Averbakh
was eloquent, assured and fearsome. Mandelstam began to waver:
"Perhaps they're right after all, I am a class enemy? A bourgeois poet,
do you think? Outmoded?" And it was impossible to tell whether his
twitching upper lip signalled irony or alarm. The curving, susceptible line
that joined nose and mouth was a Mandelstam family trait shared by all
three brothers and evidently inherited from their mother. In Osip's case,
this mild tic was accompanied by an inimitable vibration of his voice.

It was August 1929 when Lena invited me to spend ten days at
Podsolnechnoe. Today the Artists' Union has a retreat there, on the
shores of Lake Senezh. Then it was a rest home open to all, and there
was nothing to remind one of painting or of Blok (although his
Shakhmatovo estate was nearby).

At mealtimes, the toiling masses kicked up a tremendous fuss. The
food was inadequate, they said, and they walked around half dressed.
Their dissipated manners alarmed me. But in such a large company there
are always one or two with whom you can talk and go on walks. Apart

---

[10] Also given the alternative title "Sergei Ivan'ich".

from Lena, I passed the time with another pleasant woman, and we were all befriended by a man still in the Komsomol though he was 27 or 28 by then. He spoke of his own edgy condition and that of his comrades as if it were some kind of achievement. One had trembling hands. Another couldn't sleep if light penetrated the smallest crack. A third could not bear sudden noises. All this was due to the Civil War and, perhaps, work in intelligence or simply in the Cheka.[11] Incidentally, no matter how many I met, these young men all loved to reminisce about their first wives, who had also belonged to the Komsomol and then, for some reason, had

Cover of Noise of Time, *1925*

left them. The deserted husbands pined. They probably missed not their departed companion but the extravagant emotions of the first years of revolution. In 1925, at one of the idiotic offices where I worked, I listened to the tales of a former political officer in the border guards. He had served somewhere on the USSR's southern frontier. The Red Guards, he told me, simply could not get used to peacetime conditions. Towards evening, one of them would become frenzied, point a revolver at his temple and shout: "Say the word, and I'll end it!" And this, moreover, for no apparent reason.

Chatting with my new Komsomol acquaintance at Podsolnechnoe I mentioned the publication of Sverdlov's letters from exile in the periodical *Press and Revolution*. Writing to relatives from Siberia, Sverdlov complained about Djugashvili, with whom he lived, and described him as petty-bourgeois and anti-Semitic. Djugashvili was none other than Stalin. My acquaintance was disturbed: how could he have missed such a thing? It was very important. Evidently, like any remotely independent-minded Komsomol at the time, he was anti-Stalin.

---

[11] The Extraordinary Commission for the Combat of Counter-revolution, Sabotage and Speculation; first title of the Soviet security service or secret police, 1918–22.

We got talking about *Egyptian Stamp*. Earlier he had read and even enjoyed *The Noise of Time* (now incorporated in the new volume), but *Egyptian Stamp* was totally incomprehensible. I disagreed and tried to explain the meaning of Mandelstam's prose, but it proved no easy task. Obviously, I didn't understand the book myself.[12] Back in Moscow, I admitted as much to Mandelstam. His explanation was most good-natured: "My thoughts leap implicit links."

A while before, I had shown him an essay of mine that no-one would publish. Mandelstam found it terribly dull. "They wrote like that in the 1890s," he said: "you've even made it quite lively, but we must write differently today." The 1890s again! They were a bogey for Mandelstam, the epitome of all that was cheap and tasteless, whether in literature, the arts or everyday life.

Returning from Podsolnechnoe, I found the Mandelstams had moved once more, to the grey corner building on Spiridonevsky Street. They were renting a room in a small self-contained apartment inhabited by an engineer, his wife and their seven-year-old son.

Early autumn, Indian summer: it was the best time of year in Moscow. The city echoed and hummed as its lush greenery gained a yellow tinge. On the flat roof of the newly built apartment block, Mandelstam breathed it all in.

Towards evening, Kirsanov called unexpectedly. Mandelstam also took him up on the roof. When they came down, he was in a lively mood and content that they had talked about poetry. Long after the poet had left, Mandelstam went on chanting a stanza Kirsanov had written. It began: "Robin Hood came to see us . . ." (unfortunately I don't remember the rest). And as he repeated it, over and over, he walked, almost dancing, round the room.

On another occasion, it was not a verse, a line or even a word that enthralled Mandelstam but the letter D in one particular context.

I was sick and lying in bed, reading the just-published *Twelve Chairs*. Mandelstam came to visit. He was delighted to see Ilf and Petrov's novel and quoted from the book without looking. "Galkin, Palkin, Malkin, Chalkin and Zalkind!": he knew the members of the Moscow tavern band by heart. The first four names were a rapid gabble, but he empha-sised the last letter of "Zalkin-D!" as though setting down a heavy log.

---

[12] In 1926, several chapters of *Noise of Time* were reprinted in Paris in the émigré newspaper *Dni*; *Egyptian Stamp* was published in the Leningrad monthly *Zvezda* (May 1928) and, four months later, as a separate book.

His voice at that moment was resonant and melodious, with extraordinary overtones in the lower registers. Repeating the surnames again and again, he found different ways to stress "Zalkin-D!" and could not stop laughing.[13]

Mandelstam laughed not like a child but like a tiny infant. His toothless mouth opened and closed while tears streamed from his tightly closed eyes. He dried his beautiful curling eyelashes and shook his head.

Sometimes he spoke with great passion about politics. The struggle within the Party against the "Right Deviation"[14] prompted a series of reflections that ended with a simple and commonplace observation: now they were all lying low, waiting to see who came out on top. Another time, his unexpected formulations and rigorous arguments led him to predict a new world war. Squatting on the corner of the divan, he raised his index finger: "Buy sugar!" he concluded grandly.

It was just a game, of course, but it left a strange impression on me. In our family, it was considered contemptible to hoard supplies.

That day, Mandelstam was very short. This happened once in a while. He was, in fact, of a classic medium height but sometimes he appeared taller and at others, below average. It depended on his posture, and that was dependent on his inward state.

In Armenia, Nadya later told us, in full view of everyone else, an enormous goitre-like tumour began to swell up on Mandelstam's neck. In a few hours, it had shrunk away. We have a name for such miracles today – we talk about "allergies" – but then we had never heard anything of the kind.

All this is evidence of Mandelstam's extreme nervous sensitivity. He was in a state of constant inner activity. Hence the conflicting descriptions of his outward appearance, which was difficult to capture in a static portrait.

Besides, Mandelstam was strangely proportioned. The disparity between his upper and lower torso was striking. A very straight and handsome back, broad shoulders and a head of elegant form and regular oval shape were planted on a wide and heavy pelvis. This was obvious from the incorrect disposition of his feet: heels together, toes turned out. The result was a gait that was partly a shuffle and in part defies all definition. Perhaps the famous backwards tilt of Mandelstam's

---

[13] The final letter of the last surname identified the one Jewish member of the band.
[14] Moderate force in late 1920s headed by leading Bolshevik Nikolai Bukharin. Mandelstam first obtained his personal support in 1922 when Yevgeny Mandelstam, his youngest brother, was arrested.

head, which seemed to express emphatic pride, was linked to this physical defect. As if that mannerism kept his entire body in balance as he
walked.

Return to Poetry

Some of Mandelstam's new poems found their way into print;
more circulated privately and were never published in his life-
time. As a guide to this crucial but at times bewildering
distinction, the poems then published are always indicated as
such in the main text; for others consult the footnotes. [tr.]

On Starosadsky Street, in the room of his absent brother, Mandelstam
and Nadezhda gave me a bleak reception. "We're poor," a hurt
Mandelstam announced. "You'll find it dull here." Vividly Nadya began
describing how one visitor after another came bearing gifts of money or
food. Even Klyuev had turned up, his outstretched hand awkwardly prof-
fering a little sandwich speared on a stick: "It's all I have."

After the "Armenia" cycle of poems appeared [*Novy mir*, March 1931],
Mandelstam's name as a poet gained new resonance: their present lack
of money would otherwise have hardly evoked such sympathy in Moscow.
Even my acquaintances reflected the quickening public interest, especially when the latest poems – among them "Batyushkov", "Lamarck" and
"Park of Culture" – continued to appear in *Novy mir* [June 1932]. My
friend Lena's husband, the artist Alexander Osmyorkin, had smiled scep-
tically on hearing of my new friends. "Oh, 'Till Friday'?" he teased,
repeating Mandelstam's nickname (he made a practice of asking for
money on those terms), and told other then current anecdotes about
the poet. Now he began to speak of him with respect. He greatly admired
his new poem "For the Resounding Valour" (written in March 1931),
but commented that the last line was "a bit heavy-handed":

> For the resounding valour of ages to come,
> For the high-sounding name of the great human race,
> I've cut myself off from honour and joy
> At my ancestors' feast, from my cup and my place.
>
> The wolf-hound century leaps at my throat
> But it isn't wolf's blood that flows through my veins,
> You'd do better to shove me, like a cap, up the sleeve
> Of the hot fur coat of Siberia's plains

Where I needn't see cowards or glutinous muck
Or bloody bones ground within wheels,
So the primeval splendour of the blue Arctic fox
Will gleam for me all the night long.

Lead me off in the night where the Yenisei flows,
where the pine trees reach up to the stars,
Because it's not wolf's blood that flows through my veins
And none but an equal shall kill me.

Mandelstam himself did not like the last line. Reading the poem to me, he said he could not get it right and was even inclined to cut it altogether.[15]

Strange as it seems, Mandelstam's return to poetry also had an effect on my life. His poems reverberated, that was the reason. Hitherto I knew only from Nadya how "Osya" read his poems, rhythmically waving his arms. Now his voice accompanied the trivial and important moments of our life, adding new colour and depth to our daily experiences.

The way the poems "Midnight in Moscow" [*Literaturnaya gazeta*, 28 November 1932] and "Still far from patriarch or sage . . ." transformed reality into poetry left a particularly strong impression. For we watched it happening. The walking stick with a white knob appeared because Mandelstam began feeling giddy and short of breath when he went out. Then there were the time-filling activities of an unemployed man who aimlessly wandered the streets or ran errands, for instance, to pick up the washing from the Chinese laundry. The constant hunt for cheap cigarettes so as not to run short in the evening; cadging a smoke from passers-by. And the Moscow summer nights in an unfamiliar rented room into which, like a talisman, they carried their possessions: a handsome but ancient rug bought in better times from a second-hand shop; the crudely decorated kitchen wall-clock that appeared from somewhere else. Through the open windows came the noise of the city – not just as it fell asleep but as it woke, with the nocturnal testing of tramlines. Two preliminary hammer blows on the rail, an echoing sound that reached every house. Often they then made adjustments, tightening bolts and tapping. This is all reproduced exactly in "Midnight in Moscow":

---

[15] Mandelstam's penultimate version of the last line was "And my mouth has been twisted by lies." First published in the Soviet Union in 1965. (Translation: Bernard Meares, 1977).

> You'd say: some way off in the workshop
> Two clowns, Bim and Bom, have settled in.
> And tiny hammers and combs go to work,
> Now a mouth organ plays
> Now a child's toy piano:
> Do-re-mi-fa
> and Sol-fa-mi-re-do.

The only poems I didn't like were those that struck me as rhetorical: "Grand Piano" [*Novy mir*, June 1932] or "Canzone".

I was at Starosadsky Street when Boris Lapin dashed in to see Mandelstam. He had just looped the loop in a plane – such excursions over Moscow were then on offer. With astonishing precision, Lapin described the shifting perception of sky, land and aeroplane, and demonstrated how the earth shot towards him. Mandelstam thereupon recited "Canzone" to him. Yet no matter how energetically he read, for me the poem again failed to make the expected impression. Mandelstam kept trying to draw me into conversation, but I declined, not knowing what to say. "Don't pretend you're stupid," he commented with vexation.

The Mandelstams' post-Yerevan period was marked not only by new poems but by a new friendship ("I was forced awake by friendship, like a shot").[16] Before I ever saw Boris Kuzin, Nadya had talked endlessly to me about the marvellous man they met in Armenia. A zoologist, he studied insects and went on expeditions to Central Asia. At that time, such people were a rarity and themselves regarded as exotic creatures. He was a follower not of Darwin but of Lamarck, and in 1929 defended his point of view in public debate at the Communist Academy. He kept his head shaved and wore a starched collar; he had long arms like a monkey, Nadya said, and a purely Muscovite pronunciation acquired from his nurse, not from literature.

Soon I met him at the Mandelstams' and could add several further touches to this portrait. A lightly pockmarked face. He was proud of the pure-bred form of his head; it was that of a thinking man. A friend was similarly well endowed; together they went to hear Bach at the Conservatory and always sat in the same seats in the ninth row of the stalls. Another friend (or the same person?), whom we had not seen, brought him jazz records from abroad – his favourite musical genre

---

[16] From the poem "To the German Language", published with a dedication to Kuzin in *Literaturnaya gazeta*, 28 November 1932.

after Bach. He loved the poetry of Mandelstam, Gumilyov, Kuzmin
and Bunin. Kuzin knew foreign languages and constantly re-read
Goethe in the original. Moving among professors, he would tell us
stories about the daily life of Moscow's academics. He himself had a
job at the University Zoological Museum. He lived with his mother
in the Zamoskvoreche district on Bolshaya Yakimanka Street. In 1930
he was 27.

Mandelstam had his own way of discussing things with Kuzin. I was
with them once when, drinking wine, they considered nineteenth-century
composers. No-one was left unscathed. "And Glinka? Is he alright?"
Kuzin was testing Mandelstam's taste. "Mm, he's alright," Mandelstam
nodded his head in reply. It was a dialogue of those who understood
each other very well.

Once, though, Kuzin told Mandelstam that he was dissatisfied with
"Today we can remove the transfer" and "Still far from patriarch or
sage". In the first poem Mandelstam was in open polemic with the White
Guards; in the second, he lauded "the ostrich-fan armature as they start
building the Lenin apartment blocks". Evidently, the discussion became
quite heated. I found Mandelstam on his own, murmuring in distress:
"What was that all about? A commission from the other side? I have not
the slightest desire to accept it," and he lay down on the bed, staring
fixedly up at the ceiling.

Kuzin also criticised Mandelstam's use of Russian. In one poem,
Mandelstam had employed the wrong preposition; in another, Kuzin
doubted whether a word was appropriately used. Mandelstam dismissed
these comments. Evidently, "Today we can remove the transfer" was
written when the Mandelstams were living in the room of Caesar Ryss,
opposite the clock at the beginning of Bolshaya Polyanka Street. I was
glad that they also were now living in Zamoskvoreche, but Mandelstam
did not share my enchantment with the small side streets straight out
of plays by Ostrovsky.

Nadya's brother Yevgeny, Kuzin and I made up the Mandelstams'
regular family circle. Old friends also dropped by. The most frequent
visitors were Yakhontov, who came with one or both wives, and Morgulis
(who came without). Now and again other writers would call, the famous
and the young. Among the latter was the translator Bogayevsky. Once
he brought news that an acquaintance had been exiled. He commented:
"Only discreet people now remain in Moscow."

One heady spring day Nadya called and rang up Morgulis: "I can't help
it, I must make an assignation with someone." Her playful tone affected
me instantly, like champagne. As a result of this fool's play, Morgulis

came to Shchipok Street and left with Nadya for their tryst "beneath the clock". He was an inimitably jolly character, and they executed a dazzling duet. Morgulis had a long Jewish nose and slightly bulging eyes that changed colour but remained inscrutable. He chattered away, his head bobbing and bowing, and recounted the unbelievable things going on in "literary circles".[17] He made himself indispensable to all kinds of people. "It's more than adaptation," Mandelstam once remarked. "It's a kind of mimesis."

Boris Kuzin, early 1930s

Nadya gaily recounted that Morgulis stole books, but the Mandelstams were not afraid of him. "From you, never!" he had assured them.

That summer of 1931, Morgulis not only found himself a job but took Nadya with him. The work at the newspaper *For Communist Enlightenment* actually suited her very well. A year before, in search of earnings, she had got in contact with some publishing concern. I went with her several times and saw the women hanging on her every word. They commissioned an article on children's literature, and she wrote a scathing critical analysis of Kornei Chukovsky's books. His verse was derivative, she declared, and cited the literary sources from which, in her opinion, he had borrowed the rhythms, rhyme and intonation of his poem "Crocodile". The article was read aloud to a rapturous and respectful audience but not published. Now Nadya felt very sure of herself at the newspaper: "I have as much authority as an old-time senator."

Mandelstam composed many humorous "morgulets" about Morgulis and Nadya at *Communist Enlightenment*. I remember the first two he wrote, only one of which has been published:

---

[17] Alexander Morgulis (1898–1938), translator and author. First became closely acquainted with the Mandelstams in 1925–7 in Leningrad; after 1932, board member of Writers' Union. He was arrested in 1936 and died in prison.

> I cannot rid my mind of
> Old Man Morgulis's eyes:
> With horror there I read
> *For Communist Enlightenment.*
>
> No, the eyes of Old Morgulis
> Do not suit his appointment.
> They'll drive him out, they'll fire him
> from *Communist Enlightenment.*

When Nadya went into hospital, Yakhontov often visited Mandelstam. This was on Pokrovka Street, among the "plush" and dusty furnishings of a wretched rented room. The same room from which Nadya evicted an intrusive journalist, calmly warning, "The leg's broken, don't sit there!" or "Be careful, the ceiling drips here," etc. Her handling of such situations was brilliant.

Calling one time, I found Yakhontov in top hat and tails.[18] The spectacle was not in the least bizarre: his pose fitted the room like a scene on a carefully arranged set. He and Mandelstam were reciting some of the poet's comic verse. It described the dramatic dilemma now confronting the owner of the apartment. Hearing that a full-length fur coat could be had in Siberia at a very reasonable price, she let the room to raise some money and off she went. Her mother and son stayed behind in Moscow. The Mandelstams could not pay, however. The only way to ease his conscience was to assert superiority over the hapless philistines by composing and chanting derisory verse.

To heighten the effect, Yakhontov, on his way back from the toilet, had filched the neighbours' kettle as he passed through the shared kitchen. Now it stood on the chair next to his top hat.

Mandelstam began in epic style: "So yearned Karanovich for Siberian furs / She took a bad lodger at Pokrovka Street."

Yakhontov joined in: "'Granny, there'll be no fur coat!' / the grandson, panting, ran in: / 'That Mandelstam couldn't give a damn.'"

There followed a rapid scene change, just as in Yakhontov's own stage performances. Without a pause, both speakers began a second poem on the same theme, and together recited:

> Call me, Granny (He he he!)
> And I shall come to see you now:

---

[18] Vladimir Yakhontov (1899–1945), founder of the "One-Man Theatre", friend and admirer of Mandelstam since 1927.

    Should I dress for dinner, or
    Appear in a long fur-coat?

Yakhontov's powerful and resounding voice rang with a calm force. Mandelstam quavered in a thin, deliberately insolent and bleating tenor. Their "He he he!" was particularly vile.

  Yakhontov read out a letter from Lilya Popova, his first wife and permanent director, who was in Central Asia. She set down her ideas about future productions for Yakhontov's "One-Man Theatre". Mandelstam praised the letter. There was an awkward moment, however, when Yakhontov recited his new work, an adaptation of the second chapter of *Yevgeny Onegin*. Mandelstam did not approve. I cannot remember his exact words, unfortunately, but he superbly defined the poem's light touch, conversational verse and buoyant airiness. Yakhontov's dramatic rendition, in his view, suited Nekrasov's poems, but was inappropriate to *Onegin*. Yakhontov's eyes cast daggers. Soon we left together, since we were going in the same direction.

  It was then that Yakhontov declared that he could not work with Mandelstam's prose; it was too densely written.

Gradually, our house in the hospital grounds changed character. People started living in the basement. Then we lost the large drawing-room; it was turned into a dormitory for the nurses. Every nook and cranny in the other wings became crowded with people. The main hospital building housed an entire village, relations of our caretakers and orderlies. The manager got them all residence permits and found them jobs.

  With less living space, I had to move into a different room in our apartment. Once settled, I invited the Mandelstams to a modest "house-warming". We were just sitting down to eat when he disappeared. Where could Mandelstam have gone? He was not making a telephone call; he was not in the kitchen or anywhere else. Finally, I had the sense to check my father's study.

  Papa stood in the middle of the room gazing down with a certain perplexity (he was a tall man) as he listened to Mandelstam. The latter had come to a halt. Gesturing with both hands as though raising a heavy object from the floor, he was fervently making a point to my father:

  ". . . he can't think up anything by himself . . ."
  ". . . the lack of inventiveness personified . . ."
  ". . . a kind of parasite . . ."
  ". . . a task-master of the kind who forced the Hebrews to work in Egypt . . ."

  Do I need add that he was talking about Stalin?

Highly satisfied, Mandelstam returned to my room.

"Your father has a child's perception of things," he told me. "His ideas about everything are clear but primitive."

When all my guests had left, Papa came in to see me: "That Mandelstam of yours is a downright infant. He was talking such out-rageous nonsense, infantile chatter . . ."

The Mandelstams still had nowhere to live. For a week or so, I let them use my room and slept with my mother. In his militant despair, Mandelstam quickly reduced the room to uninhabitable chaos. The little white window drape? Pulled off one nail and hung back crooked. The clean counterpane? Trampled all over in filthy boots.

He went to pieces with a will, and for him the very process was an active demonstration. Mandelstam grew unrecognisable: grey stubble on his flabby cheeks, deep wrinkles beneath his eyes, a crumpled collar . . . At which point he began to resemble a character from my earliest child-hood in Dvinsk.[19] An extremely agitated man ran about the city in a bowler hat and suit, white underwear showing through his torn trousers. Once he rushed into a shop, provoking laughter, indignation and pity. People gave him some coins, and he turned to leave, spitting out curses and threats. Struck by the beauty and tender rosy cheeks of my nine-year-old sister, he halted, stroked her face with his filthy rough hand and said, with indescribable tenderness, "a lebenke" ("precious little life", Yiddish). Then he hurtled out, once again yelling and cursing. I would long have forgot-ten the episode had not Charlie Chaplin and Osip Mandelstam made me remember unlucky "Alebenke", as we children referred to him.

Once, greatly upset, Mandelstam described an incident that had just occurred. He had been to see Khalatov, head of the State Publishing House. For a long time he sat waiting in the secretary's office. Other writers walked past into the director's study, but the secretary would not admit Mandelstam. When Katayev arrived and was immediately received, his patience ran out. "I am a Russian poet," Mandelstam proudly shouted and left the office, slamming the door.

Mandelstam was forever dashing out to the telephone. If someone caught him making a call in the corridor, when he ended the conversation and replaced the receiver he would grandly retire to their room with his head held high. Wounded pride lay behind such behaviour, said Mama. She sensed a great poet who lacked recognition. When Papa finished reading

---

[19]Known as Dinaburg in the pre-1914 Jewish Pale of Settlement; today Daugavpils in Latvia.

Mandelstam's poetry, he conceded that he was gifted but said that his verse was totally outmoded. Antiquity had its beauty, of course, but it was hardly what today's young people needed. Mandelstam could not instil cheerfulness and determination, Father concluded.

Mama liked to read Blok, and I had his epic poem *Retribution* in the Alkonost edition. She was drawn by the description of a family tragedy and found parallels with my sister's experiences. The relevant chapter was marked throughout by Mother's pencil. Mandelstam picked up this volume, drenched with tears and sighs, and began to write rapidly in the margins. Then with a proud gesture he handed it to me: "There, now you can sell it. Any second-hand bookseller would give . . . 50 roubles!"

The book disappeared during the war, and I cannot precisely recall Mandelstam's acid remarks, which he signed and dated. Let me just give the gist, as I remember it.

In the preface, Blok listed various events that together made up the "integral musical thrust" of the epoch: "Andrei Yushchinsky was murdered in Kiev, and again there was reference to the use made by Jews of Christian blood."[20] This offensively "objective" phrase outraged Mandelstam. He underlined it and added a marginal note, referring to the following sentence on the next page: "Finally, that autumn Stolypin was killed in Kiev, and this signified that the country was no longer being run by the gentry and official class but wholly under the control of the police department." Mandelstam then provided his own commentary on both phrases, beginning with a parodied repetition: "And again there was reference . . ." The same words prefaced his comment to several lines of verse in the poem itself. The polemic was powerful and politically astute, and I lament the book's loss to this day.

That same autumn of 1931, a son was born to Mandelstam's brother Alexander. Soon Mandelstam was affectionately calling the child his heir. It was a difficult birth, and the mother was in labour for 72 hours. All that time, Mandelstam either sat with his two brothers in the hospital waiting-room, or the three of them went outside and wandered together round the building.

He dashed into our apartment in a thoroughly dishevelled state. The new mother needed to be examined by a specialist. Mandelstam asked me to ring Father at the hospital, but it was impossible; he was operating. Finally, Father came home. I warned Mandelstam that he must wait while

---

[20] The charge of ritual murder against the Jew Mendel Beilis was examined and dismissed at a famous trial of 1911.

Papa recovered and had something to eat: then I would ask him to call a colleague "among the Kremlin hospital consultants", since Father also worked there. Mandelstam walked rapidly and impatiently up and down the corridor, lying in wait for Papa. Finally, he could stand it no longer and grabbed the telephone. "I am calling from Professor Gerstein's apartment," he began. Having established his credentials, Mandelstam reached agreement with the consultant and took him to see his sister-in-law.

At Herzen House

The Mandelstams were given one of the rooms for writers at Herzen House, on Tverskoi Boulevard. Small and elongated, the room was on the low ground floor of the right wing. Where the kitchen was I do not remember; I suspect there was none.

It's laughable to suppose that the Mandelstams could furnish it themselves. All they possessed were two spring mattresses and a tiny kitchen table donated by a new acquaintance, a middle-aged lady with a "troubled soul" (quipped Nadya) who had been enthralled by Mandelstam's monologues.

I went with him to visit her and there observed yet another of Mandelstam's ways of speaking. This was not the agitated utterance when, stirred by some fleeting emotion, Mandelstam could not rest until he had converted the feeling into a brilliant verbal improvisation (the next day, it is true, stung by some fresh comment, he might begin to prove just the opposite of yesterday's assertion, and with the same irresistible conviction). I don't believe such words could have been memorised and

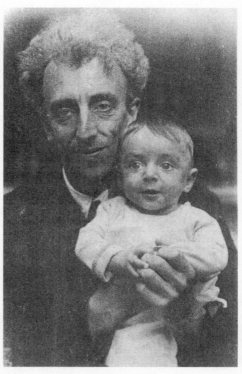

Alexander Mandelstam with his son Sasha

repeated. They were a stream of thoughts transformed, before his listener, into speech. When invited out, his manner was different. With a definite goal in mind, Mandelstam suited his talk of music and literature to his audience: he wanted to entertain, make a pleasant impression . . . and enjoy a proper meal.

As we got ready to visit his benefactor, Mandelstam was calm and composed. For artistic effect, however, he discarded his stiff collar and tie. This was to heighten the contrast, I thought, between his utter poverty and the incomparable elegance of his words. During the meal, he took melodic flight in response to a question about Chopin from our hostess. She did not get another word in: on these occasions, Mandelstam performed without the participation of others. They were dazzling monologues.

He asked me to accompany him because he could not stand being alone at that time and always preferred to go anywhere with someone else.

Nadya was at *Communist Enlightenment,* and he didn't know what to do with himself in the mornings. Once he came to *Krestyanskaya gazeta,* where I then worked, and bashfully, like some supplicant, pulled the door ajar and beckoned me with his finger. I went into the corridor, and he began pleading with me to stop work and go out for a walk. He was afraid to go by himself, and he could not stay in their room; he had not the nerve to disturb Nadya, though her office was even closer to Herzen House than mine.

On days when we began work later, I would often first call on Mandelstam. Sometimes we went out into the small square in front of Herzen House; sometimes we sat on a bench on Tverskoi Boulevard.

Pasternak's wife and small son were then living in the other, better wing of Herzen House. It was famously a period of domestic upset for Pasternak, who was separating from Yevgenia in order to marry Zinaida Neigaus. Several times I saw him leave the writers' dining-room in fretful preoccupation, a set of covered dishes in both hands: he was taking lunch to his abandoned family. If he met friends, he would put the little saucepans down on a bench and give long, almost tearful accounts of his family affairs. Sometimes he picked not friends but mere acquaintances. Then his plaints and confidences gained a wide circulation. This chapter in Pasternak's biography found reflection in *Second Birth* [1932], his latest volume of poetry.

We sat with Mandelstam on Tverskoi Boulevard and discussed the new book. Mandelstam did the talking, of course, yet it was not a monologue. Rather, a dialogue with a taciturn companion. He needed only light prompting for the conversation to flow: as he spoke, tossing out incomplete phrases, you sat there, a mere onlooker, as the thoughts took shape.

"To read Pasternak", Mandelstam had written long before, "is to free one's voice." He enjoyed repeating Selvinsky's witticism (the "renowned" pun, he said) about "parsnip froth and almond cliché".[21] He devoted much thought to Pasternak at this time and in passing would let drop various remarks – "Pasternak is unimaginable outside Moscow", "Pasternak can only write in his study, sitting at the table" – whereas Mandelstam himself did not write at all but, so to speak, was carving in stone (an allusion to *Stone,* his own first collection).

This time, he talked about *Second Birth.* He rejected today's Pasternak, the new verse was ornamental and overburdened . . . Mandelstam's words were a rough draft, not memorable until the one essential definition burst forth: "Soviet baroque".

I do not remember many visitors in the narrow room on Tverskoi Boulevard. Of his writer-neighbours only Klychkov, who lived in the opposite wing, came to see Mandelstam. Once when I was there, Shengeli called. Mandelstam had given him his *Fourth Prose* to read. It was "one of the gloomiest confessions yet published", said Shengeli and recalled Jean-Jacques Rousseau.

Soon a large room with two or three windows became free on the same corridor. The Mandelstams moved, and their old room passed to the poet Ruderman. He was married with a child, and his wife was indignant that the Mandelstams had been given the larger room. "Ruderman is a young and active poet," she yelled in the corridor: "Mandelstam's an old man who's stopped writing. And even if he does write something once in a while, all the same he's outdated, a poet from the past." Mandelstam was then 40, and his "Armenia" cycle and several new poems had just been published in *Novy mir.*

Though the new room was next to the old and the windows faced the same way it seemed cheerful and sunny. Perhaps the bright wallpaper and lack of trees directly in front of the windows played their part. It also felt as if the life of the Mandelstams had entered a more peaceful period. This can be seen in his verse of the time, such as "Moscow Park of Culture and Recreation" [*Novy mir,* June 1932]. Reading Lamarck and Pallas also had a soothing effect on Mandelstam.

I remember typing up two poems for him. "Impressionism" arose from a visit to a museum. Of the other ("Alas, the candle is melted")

---

[21] "Pasternakipi i mandelshtampy". In Russian *pasternak* means "parsnip", and the German *mandel* (Russian *mindal*), "almond".

he said with a smile that the last two lines were about my friend Lena. He nicknamed her "the Hellene" because of her cheerful and broad-minded conversations on erotic and romantic themes: "And they let scoundrels into the bedchamber, seeing a value in this."

People on their way to Herzen House dropped in to see him more often. Nadya always returned from work in a cheerful mood, with new anecdotes, and pushed the little table over to the divan so that she could sit and enjoy her meal with her feet up.

In the morning, Ivan Aksyonov often called by. Evidently he was learned in many disciplines. Finding Mandelstam reading Pallas, for instance, he talked with him for a long while on geographical subjects. After he had gone, Mandelstam could always think better. His forehead was clearer and seemed to increase in size, becoming a "dome of comprehension", while his movements grew calm and fluent.

By this time, the magazine *On Literary Guard* had been closed down. RAPP was disbanded, and this nourished hopes of a literary revival. Discussing the news with Mandelstam, Aksyonov declared that Averbakh was a gifted commentator and compared him with Pisarev. Mandelstam did not object.

On one of my visits, I found Mandelstam on his own, sitting on a chair in the middle of the room, with a small volume in his hands. He was flipping through the pages.

"Now this is Blok's most brilliant poem!" he cried and read:

> How hard to walk among people
> And affect to be still alive
> And tell those who've not yet lived
> Of the tragic play of passions.

It was strange to hear the familiar lines recited with Mandelstam's brisk delivery and moving intonation. In fact, he left his stamp on everything. Once, at our apartment on Shchipok Street, as though the wind caught him up and set him down at the grand piano, he played a Mozart or Clementi sonatina, known to me since childhood, with exactly the same nervous, upward-flying intonation. How he attained this effect in music I do not understand, since the beat was not broken for a single bar. Evidently, it was all a matter of phrasing.

To Mandelstam it did not matter who had written a poem, himself or another. If the verse was real poetry, he took pride in it. He never felt envy.

Herzen House, the right wing

When Mandelstam himself wrote a new poem, he thought the world had been reborn. He would read it to friends or acquaintances, whomever he met first. On a still spring-like June evening, I went with Yevgeny Khazin to see the Mandelstams. He came out of the building and, standing under the porch among the green shoots in the courtyard, read us "Like a reveller with a magic cane" ["Batyushkov", *Novy mir*, June 1932]. The words flowed like a melody, from forte to piano, with rising and falling intonations. The last verse was like a barcarole from the second line on: "You are of the city, and friend to its dwellers."

I would always hear Mandelstam's voice in certain lines that I memorised from his poems. How he accentuated the fencing strokes in the last but one verse of "Lamarck"!

> And Nature stepped back from us
> As though [*parry*]
> She had [*parry*]
>   No use for us: [*thrust!*]
> And drove the elongated brain
> As a rapier into dark sheaths.
>
> (*Novy mir*, June 1932)[22]

---

[22] For the full text, see "Five Poems by Osip Mandelstam", p. 90.

At the end of the 1940s, I met an old friend after many years apart. We had a good talk, but something was missing. It was like revisiting child-hood places – we are amazed that everything's so small: where are those heights and depths we met at every turn? But then a poem by Mandelstam was mentioned. Reminding each other of the words, we recited it aloud with one voice. How everything regained its radiance! We ourselves gained significance, as though an experienced director had given us the best positions on stage. It was then that I understood that in the past we had met to the sound of verse. It had accompanied us as though we were strolling through a garden where clear water bubbled in the foun-tains or as if we were in the forest talking about our own important affairs, only half aware of the singing stream and the calling of the birds.

Mandelstam was no longer alive when I realised this.

The poet himself had no time for idylls. For him, no difference existed between the mundane and the poetic. There were no elevated and base objects. All was fed into the same process of creative transformation. Hence his unexpected assessments of those around him, and his im-passioned interventions in the events of daily life. And here everything hurt and disappointed him. Mandelstam would complain about the "land-scape"; he meant the people whom he had to meet, and the stifling air.

Once, hoping to find peace and laughter in the cheerful room on Tverskoi Boulevard, I was met by commotion and disarray. Over the divan dangled an enormous piece of wallpaper, torn from the ceiling halfway down the wall.

"It's frightful," the Mandelstams greeted me. "There are bed bugs here!"

I offered the usual practical advice on how to get rid of the horrible insects. Mandelstam would not hear a word of it. He wanted to throw every object out of the room; they might live in chaos but without the bed bugs. It seems to me that he had a natural inclination to destruc-tiveness, and to a disordered form of comfort.

On another occasion, he was much taken by the idea of shaving "Nadenka's" head.

"But Osip Emilievich, it won't look nice," I intervened.

"I like a prickly aesthetic," he replied dismissively.

The more poems he wrote, the more he was irritated by the writers constantly crossing the courtyard. Standing by the open window of their room, hands in his pockets, he would yell after one of them: "There goes that scoundrel X!" It was only then, looking at him from behind, that I noticed how his ears protruded and how much, at such moments, he resembled a "nasty little boy".

Literaturnaya gazeta organised an evening of his poetry, and it was held in Herzen House itself. I stayed at home with Nadya. In the end, we grew tired of waiting for him. I went to reconnoitre and found I was late; people were already leaving. Down the staircase came Kornely Zelinsky, saying something to his lady friend about estrangement from contemporary life, a narrow field of vision and Mandelstam's feeble intonation.[23] I did not listen more closely, but the impression was of something sickly and staggeringly unlike the rich timbre, harmony and urgent passion of Mandelstam's poetry.[24]

The next year, he had a major evening recital at the Polytechnic Museum. Again Nadya was absent. Mandelstam did not permit her to attend his public readings. At his wish I accompanied him in the car. In the dressing-room he was immediately surrounded, and I went to take my seat in one of the first rows next to my inseparable friend Lena. The old Moscow intelligentsia had emerged from its haunts to attend the recital. Lena and I gazed at the crumpled faces of these long-suffering and underfed people, their eyes aglow with melancholy intelligence. I particularly recall the pale face of the artist Lev Bruni, listening intently to the reading (he was hard of hearing).

Mandelstam's voice was rather weak for such a large auditorium; microphones were not used then. Nevertheless the poet upstaged Boris Eichenbaum, despite the latter's acute and bold opening words, and his experience as a lecturer and articulate public speaker. "He is an academic, when all's said," I whispered to Lena.

How strange it was for me to watch Mandelstam, in his everyday jacket, pale under the merciless overhead illumination, and listen as he read my favourite lines, spreading his arms and reciting in his usual style: "So the convict sings his rough lament, / As the thin streak of dawn rises over the prison."[25]

It should have been Yevgeny Khazin sitting next to me, not Lena. But his wife had come, treating it as a great social occasion. She took little interest in Mandelstam's verse. Nadya would give very funny accounts of her complaints: writers and artists didn't gather at her flat,

---

[23] A leading "Constructivist" writer who had, in 1930, denounced his earlier views in an article in *On Literary Guard* magazine.

[24] In a letter to Eichenbaum, Khardjiev gives a different account of this recital in November 1932: "He is a poet of genius, of valour, a heroic man. A grey-bearded patriarch, Mandelstam presided as shaman for two and a half hours. He recited every poem he had written in the past two years in chronological order!"

[25] "My eyelashes sting, and a tear has welled up in my heart" (March 1931). Published posthumously in New York, 1961; Alma-Ata, 1965; Leningrad, 1973.

like they did at "Sonya's", she lamented. (Sonya had married the Constructivist poet Nikolai Aduyev and then the celebrated playwright Vsevolod Vishnevsky.) "You can have Osya," offered Nadya. Her sister-in-law candidly retorted: "He's not famous." Now, however, posters advertising the Mandelstam evening had appeared, and many well-known people intended to go. Yevgeny's wife also went. During the interval, a feather boa draped across her arm, she stood conversing energetically with Tatlin. Meanwhile, Yevgeny hovered between them and myself, looking so discomfited and helpless that my heart winced for pity.

In which year did I go with Mandelstam to visit the "kind elephants"? (It was Nadya's nickname.) I can't remember whether we set out from Tverskoi Boulevard or Nashchokin Street.

The "kind elephants" promised to treat Mandelstam to a recording of Bach's *St Matthew Passion*. He could not afford to miss such an evening, since "religious" music was not performed at the Conservatory. Nadya was sick, so I went with him, overjoyed at the chance to hear this inaccessible work.

During dinner Mandelstam delivered his expected orations. The meal did not pass without an awkward incident. Giving me some butter, he managed to tip almost all the contents of the butter dish on to my plate. Under the alarmed and attentive gaze of our hostess, I had to put it back (my plate was quite clean). The man of the house was, I think, an educated economist; she was in charge of the Moscow Regional Library, a very large plump woman with big hands and feet. There were several other guests around the table: a young girl, someone who worked on the radio (it was he who had brought the gramophone and records), and skinny Sergei Bondi, the renowned Pushkin specialist.

The foreign recording had been made by renowned singers and a famous orchestra. It was such an experience for Mandelstam that he hardly noticed the words of explanation with which the comrade from the radio prefaced each new record. When it was finished and Mandelstam, after the usual courtesies, was preparing to take his leave, there was a suggestion to run through the entire programme once more. Mandelstam tried to make his excuses. I supported him, but nothing helped . . . we had to stay. He listened for a while but it was more than he could bear. Moreover, our "master of ceremonies" became more relaxed and voluble. Mandelstam interrupted. At first he tried to explain calmly to those present what poor taste was. But after the other guests' uncomprehending responses Mandelstam grew more and more heated; he started shouting, and ended with a shrill and penetrating exclamation: "We are now engaged in masturbation!" He fled the room in despair. I followed. Our kind host pushed past me and led Mandelstam into his study, as if to say: Let me calm him down myself. This was so successful that a short while after, Mandelstam walked steadily into the hall and immediately began to put on his coat. Next, the girl came out of the room with the bag I had forgotten – a battered object, which had long lost its strap; bewildered, she passed it to me, holding it a little disdainfully by the sides.

We returned on foot. Mandelstam said that rows were a quite neces-sary phenomenon, repeating the ideas contained in *Egyptian Stamp* and other comments to be found in his prose.

We walked down the middle of the road, along the quiet, small streets of the Tverskaya–Yamskaya district. They were wider and straighter than the usual Moscow back streets. If only we could live somewhere like this in the provinces, Mandelstam said wistfully. He complained about Moscow and the pace of life on its streets, which did not accommodate man's inner world. He talked of office workers who squeezed and pushed each other every day in the trams. "I could not live like that," he said with horror. He was in a melancholy state of mind.

Once in the daytime, the door opened and Victor Shklovsky walked in. Without a word, he sat down by the window and said abruptly: "I'm just back from the White Sea Canal. More horrific than the war."

After a pause, he related what talents the Russian nation possessed. What master craftsmen the peasant prisoners were turning into there. As I recall, Shklovsky had gone to see a relation who was working on the canal as a prisoner.[26]

Then they began talking about Kleist, whom Mandelstam had praised in his poem "To the German Language". Shklovsky and Mandelstam walked diagonally back and forth across the room, towards each other, as they argued. Each developed his thoughts with such a quantity of "implicit links" that it was hard to make anything of their elliptical comments. I felt superfluous. But I remained, remembering that Mandelstam had once said: "You never distract me."

Nadya and I confided to each other that we did not like certain poems by Mandelstam: "Canzone", "Grand Piano", "Lamarck" – "No, you mustn't say that about 'Lamarck'," Nadya interrupted. "Tynyanov explained to me that it's superb: it foretells how a human being ceases to be human. A movement in reverse. Tynyanov called it a work of genius."

---

[26] Along with other writers, Shklovsky (1893–1984) contributed to the 1935 *White Sea Canal* volume in praise of such forced labour.

Nadya's recently widowed mother, Vera Yakovlevna, came up from Kiev and stayed with her son. Yevgeny lived nearby and she spent most of the time with the Mandelstams, so as not to hinder his wife Lena's work. As usual, the mother did not spare her daughter-in-law.

"Today she collapsed into an armchair," Vera Yakovlevna would mock her, "and started boasting: the State needs us, we are indispensable . . ." She was referring to the task of designing the decorations for Moscow during the public holidays. The artists Sonya Vishnevetskaya and Yelena Fradkina, working as a team, had been awarded the job. Yevgeny Khazin's former and present wives thus became important figures.

Once in a while, his wife visited the Mandelstams on Tverskoi Boulevard. She was there when Klyuev called. Nadya invited him to sit at the table, but he meekly settled on the low window-sill: "I'll sup my *shchi* here." Yevgeny's wife, with her long, made-up face, dressed with practical elegance, even gaped slightly. With curiosity she observed this beggarly wanderer lift the spoon to his mouth in slow and serious concentration.[27]

Though Nadya did say that when arguing, Klyuev would sometimes "forget himself and begin to talk like a junior university lecturer".

It was then that the Cossack poet Pavel Vasilyev, who had come to the capital from Siberia, began to attract attention in Moscow. This handsome 22-year-old was a tall, curly-haired blond, and of exceptional physical elegance, with sensitive flaring nostrils. Mandelstam took a strong liking to him. Vasilyev reciprocated, often dropping in, reading his verse and chatting enthusiastically with Nadya. Over a period of two to three years, he was gradually transformed from a novice into a fashionable poet who had access to the "high society" then taking shape in Moscow's literary and artistic circles. He was a rowdy character. Reviewers and commentators criticised him, and privately it was said that he was under the influence of Mandelstam. This led to Mandelstam's impromptu couplet: "The cat neighed, the stallion meowed, / And a Cossack copied a Jew."

I was passing Herzen House on the tram. I got off, wanting to see them, but after a glance through the low window had second thoughts. Nadya was lying on the bed, her blue eyes gazing attentively at someone and listening to what he said. At her feet stood Mandelstam. Before them was Zvenigorodsky. He was reading his verse. Mandelstam and Nadya

---

[27] For Klyuev's fate, see Vitaly Shentalinsky, "The Arrested Word", *The KGB's Literary Archives* (London, 1995; published in the US as *Arrested Voices* [New York, 1996]).

had suddenly taken him up, declaring that he was Russia's second Tyutchev. This quite turned the old man's head. The last of his kind in Russia, he was now living the difficult life of a member of the intelligentsia, poorly adapted to contemporary existence.

Once Yakhontov called with both Lilya Popova and Dinochka Butman. His two wives were wearing identical light-coloured, curly goatskin coats. Everyone admired the coats. But in reality Nadya was captivated by Lilya alone. She was the only one of her kind, Nadya said. Describing her shyness, Nadya remembered how she would not go anywhere in Detskoye Selo[28] and didn't know what to say: she would enter and, without a word of greeting, stand mutely in the middle of the room. The daughter of a locomotive stoker, Lilya lived with her parents in Kislovodsk. She proved to have the powers of a medium, and a hypnotist began to perform with her at the local circus. Yakhontov saw her, fell in love and brought her back to Moscow. From Nadya's description one would fall for Lilya without setting eyes on her. One day Klychkov visited the Mandelstams and, fixing me with a passionate eye, quietly asked Nadya: "Is that Lilya?" He was utterly crestfallen when he learned his mistake. Such were Nadya's talents.

They did not have a telephone on Tverskoi Boulevard, and so Mandelstam asked me to go and call Yakhontov from a pay phone; for some reason he had not visited for a while. Yakhontov could not come. He was in heavy demand during the holiday weekend, like all actors who did stage turns. They each picked up several performances for the same evening and rushed hectically from one venue to another. Yakhontov's explanation did not satisfy Mandelstam. He began to run him down. Yakhontov was an "ageless youth": "He's already 30, but he acts as though everything still lies ahead." At that age, someone who lived exclusively on their own hopes was deficient, said Mandelstam angrily. One must live in the present.

It was impossible to guess his response to the most commonplace remark. On another ocassion, he reacted quite differently to Yakhontov. The actor had the habit, someone said, of picking up women in the street. Leaving home, he would already be equipped with a variety of love notes and then select a suitable text for today's chosen target. It was abnormal, they said indignantly. Mandelstam commented thoughtfully: "Here we call it schizophrenia. But somewhere like Paris, that's how any man behaves. All of Maupassant is based on such behaviour. Everyone reads him here, but no-one is surprised."

---

[28] New Soviet name of Tsarskoye Selo until mid-1930s.

Adelina Adalis began dropping by frequently. Ilya Ehrenburg visited from Paris and came to see Mandelstam together with Svyatopolk-Mirsky. Adalis took part in the sharp debate that followed. Ehrenburg admired the progressive politics of the Soviet Union and was enthralled by the "building of socialism". We did not like Ehrenburg for praising at a distance what we ourselves had to endure. Mandelstam explained how hard it was for him to work here, but Ehrenburg would not hear a word of it.

When he and Mirsky left, everyone joined in a lively discussion of what he had been saying. "What can you expect?" Adalis exclaimed: "He's a man and 40 years old; that's all there is to it."

Nadya assured me, however, that Ehrenburg "understood everything" and had shown her a lithograph depicting Hell, so far as I recall, in something of the spirit of Pushkin's "Faust": "So this is the exile of earth's children? What order and silence!" Ehrenburg compared this immutable eternity with our socialist paradise.

"It's impossible to live without wine of some kind," exclaimed Mandelstam, sitting by the window. The monotonous daily routine was intolerable for him. Perhaps he should go away somewhere? Ring up another city? Stir up a public row?

He was sitting cross-legged on the divan and, capriciously and childishly, presented his demands to a kind uncle. It was again Shklovsky, who had just called by. "I must have . . . and I need . . ." demanded Mandelstam, not altering his pose but bouncing higher and higher. Shklovsky listened with a smile. Mandelstam, carried away, was devising ever new paths to salvation: "We must go the Central Committee and tell them . . .", "request a study trip . . . to be provided with . . . accommodated", "persuade the State Publishers to give a large advance . . ."

"You must talk to Gypsies in their own language," Shklovsky replied, with the same little smile carved on his face.

In their wing of Herzen House, on the ground floor, lived a little-known writer with whom the Mandelstams apparently had no dealings. Yet when he died, Nadezhda became fervently involved in organising his funeral. She insisted that the coffin lie in Herzen House for people to say their farewells; she went to the management committee and demanded that they hold a civic service, and she shouted that a refusal would violate the statutes of the writers' committee. I couldn't see what she was getting out of it. Did she want to protect the widow? Perhaps there was something about this writer that I did not know? Or was it

simply that Nadya's gift for public activity had been aroused and she
was expressing her justifiable indignation?

There was a family with whom the Mandelstams were acquainted: the
lawyer O, his wife and their little daughter. Leaving home one day, they
saw a queue outside the Registry Office, located in the building where
they lived. As we know, marriages, divorces, births and deaths are all
recorded there. Remembering only the last of these categories, the little
girl naively enquired: "Are they waiting for coffins?" The child's remark
struck them as apocalyptic. Nadya repeated after the parents, "It's very
likely it'll come to that." Then we did not know that millions of our
fellow-citizens would be buried without coffins, and as yet it had never
entered my head, at least, that Mandelstam would be among them.

On the ground floor, next to the Mandelstams, lived the poet Amir
Sargidjan[29] and his wife. They were all on friendly terms, and as neighbours would visit each other. Then Sargidjan borrowed 75 roubles from
Osip and did not return them. This infuriated Mandelstam; of course,
he had now run out of money. Standing by the window, as usual, and
restlessly examining the passers-by, he saw Sargidjan's wife coming home
with a basket of food and two bottles of wine. "Look at that!" he shouted
so all the courtyard could hear: "A young poet won't pay back a debt
to his older comrade but invites others to come round and drink wine
with him!" Words were exchanged, and a quarrel began. This ended
with the woman's demand that her husband give Mandelstam a beat-
ing. He did just that and struck Nadya as well.

The Mandelstams insisted that the matter be brought before a
comrades' court. Nadya marched up and down in front of Herzen
House, showing off her bruises and announcing to every acquaintance,
with shining, merry eyes: "I was beaten by Sargidjan; Sargidjan beat up
Mandelstam . . ." When the hearing was held in Herzen House, the
little room was packed to overflowing. Alexei Tolstoy[30] chaired the
meeting.

I did not go since I was at work, but that evening Yevgeny Khazin
dropped by and told me everything. Always reserved, even he shouted,
stamped his foot, and leaped up and down on his chair in outrage at
the decision of the court. Not only did it not decide in Mandelstam's

---

[29] Amir Sargidjan was the literary pseudonym of Sergei Borodin (1902–1974),
who wrote historical novels and began publishing under his own name in 1941.
[30] Alexei Tolstoy (1883–1945), writer, emigrated after the Revolution, returned
in 1923 and became a leading "fellow-traveller".

favour, but Sargidjan escaped without any rebuke. This was a misfortune for Mandelstam because it became an obsession: he himself described it in precisely those terms.

Gravely chanting, he dictated to me one of his many formal statements about the event, expressed with his characteristic brevity and use of metaphor. A thought from that text stuck in my mind: a minor act of baseness, Mandelstam asserted, differed in no respect from a major act of baseness.

In April 1933 the Mandelstams left for Stary Krym. For yet another year, however, Mandelstam would be tormented by this dispute, which in his mind grew in significance. His hatred became focused on the figure of Alexei Tolstoy.

Three to four months later, they returned to Moscow. Something had changed. I sensed it the very first time we met. But I left immediately for a month in a rest home. When I returned that autumn, the feeling of change seized me still more firmly.

Mandelstam had grown an elegantly clipped little beard in which white hairs now showed. His shoulders had broadened, he had put on weight, and had it not been for his constant nervous mobility, he would have seemed altogether sturdier. On Nadya's face I began to note signs of age. In October she would be 34 and one could already sense a woman who had reached her mid-30s.

Her brother started to exhibit a kind of rigidity. It seemed to me as though his emotions had been replaced by reflexes. His mother, a doctor by training, had already remarked the previous winter that Yevgeny's "veins were calcifying". Speaking of him, Mandelstam commented that 40 was a critical threshold for a man. If one cleared that hurdle successfully, then one could live thereafter without any thought for one's age. Yevgeny and I parted for a while, but two months later we made things up. "We can't quarrel," he explained: "we're relatives." Something had gone from our relations, but something new had been added.

My contemporary, the 30-year-old Boris Kuzin, had also changed. Where now were the fervour, the gleaming eyes and the resounding laugh with which he had returned in 1930 from an expedition to Central Asia? He became more gloomy and neurotic with each passing year. Occasionally, he called to see me. But he never stayed after 10 p.m., repeating the same words each time he left: "I must get back to Mama. She'll be worrying. And I must read before I sleep." He was finishing the second part of *Faust*. (As I have said, he read Goethe in the original.) I couldn't make head or tail of this behaviour until Nadya revealed what had been going on. He was regularly summoned by the GPU.[31] His investigator demanded that Kuzin become one of their "undercover employees" – i.e. an informer. He was threatened with arrest and assured that a "non-informer" was himself a counter-revolutionary. "Just think what will happen to Mama if you are arrested." "Mama will die." "What a cruel young man you are." According to Nadya, the GPU's demands on Kuzin related only to university affairs. In 1933, Kuzin was indeed arrested but not held for long.

The Mandelstams invited him to go on vacation with them to Stary Krym. The

Yevgeny Khazin, 1960s

widow of the writer Alexander Grin was living there. She appeared in Moscow soon after her husband's death and came to the capital frequently thereafter on business connected to his literary affairs. The Mandelstams became friendly with Nina Grin, and she often visited them. The following year she blossomed into an attractive 40-year-old widow. As she strolled beneath a decorative parasol, she vaguely recalled the beauties painted by Kustodiyev. She also came up to Moscow during the winter months.

Kuzin returned from Stary Krym earlier than the Mandelstams. They had gone on to Koktebel, where they collected pebbles on the shore and talked with Andrei Bely, then also, as it happened, staying at the Writers' Home there.

Soon after returning to Moscow, the Mandelstams moved to another apartment. This change coincided with a new period in Mandelstam's life. At Nashchokin Street, he was swept up by a burst of poetic activity and a profound crisis that affected every part of his existence.

---

[31] Soviet secret police, 1922–34 (after 1923 more correctly called OGPU).

Apartment 26, 5 Nashchokin Street

The move to a self-contained apartment was not unexpected. It had been prepared little by little, and was actively discussed, throughout the previous winter. The apartment block was one of the first residential co-operatives, and each candidate was considered by the writers themselves. At the very mention of the name they groaned: "Oh no, not Mandelstam!" I was indignant that such a major poet was not given an apartment and said so whenever I visited the Osmyorkins. But their acquaintance the poet and writer Konstantin Bolshakov objected: "Be reasonable. Mandelstam has no right to an apartment in the Writers' Co-operative Building – he's not even a member of the Poets' Union."

The energy of the Mandelstams overcame all obstacles. His name was added to the list of the co-operative's members. Who paid for him and whether, in fact, any contribution was made on his behalf I do not know – until the very last day there was a feeling of some uncertainty. According to the laws of the time, a tenant could not be evicted if his bed already stood on the disputed territory. Nadya was well aware of this. As soon as the date was named on which the residents were to move in, she took up her post the night before at the main entrance, a mattress beside her. The moment the door was open the following morning, she raced up to the fourth floor – there was no lift in the building – and was the first to rush, clutching her mattress, into the apartment. (I do not recall if any friends helped her.) A lock was put on the door; the occupation was complete.

We thought the little flat enchanting. A small hallway and, opposite the entrance, a door leading into the tiny kitchen. To the right – indescribable luxury! – a bathroom and beside it the toilet. Next along the right-hand wall was the entrance to a long narrow room that led directly into a second room of equal length but much wider. Both doors, moreover, were in the near corner so the first room hardly felt like a connecting passage.

There was no gas ring as yet. The kitchen was therefore used as a third living-room and set aside for guests. Food was prepared in the hall-way on a small paraffin stove, and when the gas ring finally appeared, it was set up there as well.

The apartment was remarkably furnished: there was almost nothing there. In the largest room, to the right of the door, unpainted boards stretched the entire breadth of the wall, forming shelves for books from Mandelstam's library. God alone knows where they'd been stored until then. Apart from the Italian poets, I remember an unbound volume of

Batyushkov (his *Études*, I think), Pyotr Kireyevsky's collection of folk songs, Khomyakov's *Verse* and *Tarantas* by Sollogub with illustrations by Prince Grigory Gagarin. Other than books, each room had chairs and its own divan – i.e. a spring mattress under some covering – and in the big room there was also a simple table on which the telephone stood. It was this spareness that was so charming.

Of course, you could hear everything in other parts of the building. Mandelstam took the large room, which backed on to the neighbouring apartment on the next staircase. The moaning of a Hawaiian guitar could constantly be heard; Kirsanov lived there. The walls were insulated with felt, and, as a result, the very well-heated apartment was full of clothes-moths. Everyone tried to catch them, clapping their hands in the air.

These details were echoed in Mandelstam's "Apartment", a poem of that time.[32] It concluded:

> Not Hippocrene's spring but one faster,
> An ancient current of fear,
> Will burst through the jerry-built plaster
> Of the vicious home I have here.

Earlier unremarked traits of the Mandelstams were revealed in this new home. Above all else, hospitality. They shared what they had, cosily, cheerfully, simply and with a certain artistic style. Wishing to recompense their acquaintances for an existence hitherto spent in strange apartments, the Mandelstams took pleasure in putting up old friends. Their first invitation was to Akhmatova. But she could get away only in midwinter. I had still never seen her.

For a while, Vladimir Pyast, back from internal exile, slept at the flat. At first, Mandelstam found his presence agreeable and interesting. Then he began, with some surprise, to mention a tiresome habit their guest had. Pyast did not go to bed until 3 a.m. His hosts also stayed up, but soon noted that he was not at all inclined to converse. They decided to leave him alone after midnight, but found that Pyast neither wrote nor read but still would not go to sleep. "What *is* he doing in there?" Nadya laughed: "Probably saying his prayers." Mandelstam denied this: "It's some kind of vigil." Judging by his description, Pyast sat in a semiconscious state, neither sleeping nor waking, and did not have the strength to change his position, get undressed, lie down or fall asleep. After all he had suffered, Pyast was afflicted by extreme nervous exhaus-

---

[32] Written November 1933; not published in Russia until 1987. (Translation: Meares).

tion. I came to understand it later, after the Yezhov purges, wartime bombing, hunger, disappointments and many other misfortunes. In the post-war years, I would often catch myself thinking: I'm like Pyast.

Incidentally, I experienced a similar stirring of associations in the 1960s when I received a small flat in a residential co-operative. I could not stop cooking and cleaning and took a joyous pleasure in every petty domestic activity. "I'm Galina von Meck," I kept saying to myself. This was also a legacy of Nadya's stories. After Mandelstam's death, she lived for a while with von Meck who, on her release from the camps, had settled in Maly Yaroslavets.[33] When she visited Moscow, Nadya would describe how slowly and thoroughly Galina tidied her room, spending two hours cleaning her chamber pot. This syndrome could be observed in many former camp inmates.

A young man Mandelstam had known at the *Moscow Komsomol* daily, now for some reason homeless and penniless, used to stay the night at the flat. Let's call him X.

One evening I found the Mandelstams in a state of fussed anxiety. They were running in alarm from the room to the bathroom, washing and shaking out various items. "D'you know what? X has brought lice into the house. What can we do?" Late that evening the doorbell rang. Even Nadya, who was never embarrassed, was thrown into confusion. Mandelstam opened the door and, not permitting X into the apartment, said simply and directly: "Look here, X. You're lousy. You must go to the bath-house, wash yourself and disinfect all your clothes. Come back after that. Today, regrettably, we cannot let you stay." I could see from X's face that he was horror-stricken, but he did not seem offended. Mandelstam possessed an extraordinary quality: at important moments he could be both decisive and direct (it was very hard to deny a homeless person a bed for the night). Given his fussy and highly strung character, this quality was always unexpected, as was his firm, warm handshake and the way he would look his companion straight in the eye.

Of their old visitors, Dligach continued to call. A poet who had worked with Mandelstam at *Moscow Komsomol*, he came accompanied by Dinochka Butman. A character actress, almost a midget but with the large head of a beautiful woman, she had by then parted from Yakhontov. She did not want to marry Dligach, however. Standing next to him in front of a mirror she would say, "I was Yakhontov's wife; could Dligach take his place?"

---

[33] Beyond the 105-kilometre limit around Moscow established for such former offenders.

Lilya Popova remained director and most important member of Yakhontov's theatre. She was now married to the theatre's musical director (his name was Tsvetayev, I think). Unfortunately, he was imprisoned in a labour camp. Lilya had an unshakeable faith in the "rehabilitative" purpose of that institution and after visiting her husband would say what a wonderful psychologist and educationalist the camp director was. Her husband was guilty, she believed. He had kept a diary in which he confided ideas similar to those of Nietzsche, Spengler – "and all that sort of thing", Lilya disdainfully concluded, as she related this sad story to Nadya and myself. She was entirely on the side of the Moscow investigator who had regularly called Tsvetayev in and taught him how to think straight.

Every day for some three to four weeks, the poet Vladimir Narbut came to see the Mandelstams, accompanied by his wife Serafima (Sima), with whom Nadya was on close terms. Sima was considered a "vamp", and indeed there was something predatory in her features. An elongated oval face, a pure-bred aquiline nose with delicate nostrils, heavy eyelids, and her graceful, high-arched feet all contributed to the impression of harmony.

Sima brought her unstitched fur coat to Nashchokin Street and was trying to restore the light, perfume-drenched garment herself: she didn't have the money for a furrier. It was already below zero during the daytime, and, she said, she caught the pitying glances of the other passengers when she entered the tram in her light autumn overcoat.

At this time Narbut was not earning anything. The Mandelstams shared what they had. Nadya and Sima cooked gruel and porridge and made pancakes of some kind; on the days when Mandelstam received his food allowance, they prepared meat dishes. With Sima's assistance, these meals were served most elegantly.

Lilya Popova, 1928

Narbut was tall with a limp and kept one hand in a glove, a legacy of the Civil War. He wore an excellent English suit and had the proud appearance of an eccentric landowner. To myself I called him the Prince.

Naturally, these very old friends of the Mandelstams were swathed in Nadya's tales. She had her own version of the story, familiar to literary Moscow, of Sima's first marriage to Yury Olesha: she had fled, like Nastasya Filippovna,[34] from Olesha to Narbut and then back to Olesha; Olesha then married her sister. In short, it was the tale of the Sisters Suok who will be familiar to readers of Olesha's *Three Fat Men*, memoirs concerning Bagritsky (who married the third sister) and the story later written by Valentin Katayev. Sometimes the Mandelstams would refer mysteriously to Narbut's renewed jealousy or Olesha's latest escapade, and as Mandelstam talked his tone would acquire an indescribable solemnity.

Narbut's political biography was full of dramatic incidents. I knew only what Nadya had told me, however, and that gives me no right to say anything publicly on the subject.[35] Two years earlier, I had seen Narbut at certain meetings which he attended as director of the "Land and Factory" publishers. He had himself organised the publishing house but now had lost all such posts. I remember Nadya describing how "yesterday" Narbut spoke all evening about the rapid industrial development of Japan, and one could feel that he was simply itching, as Nadya put it, to be actively involved in serious politics again. From my other acquaintances, one-time graduates of the Bryusov literary institute now working for various publications, I heard much less approving accounts. In their words, Narbut had very much gone down in the world; he surrounded himself with dubious characters who hung around with him at the radio, where he was doing disgraceful hack-work. This was not at all apparent at the Mandelstams'.

I very much wanted to invite the Narbuts home but our whole set-up was unsuitable for receiving guests, especially since Sima was such a good housewife. Even Vladimir on his own I would not have invited to a "student" tea-party. He was the Prince, not a Khazin or Kuzin; they were easier to cope with.

Preparations were under way for the first Congress of Writers, and polemical articles appeared in the press about poetry and prose at the

---

[34] Beauty loved by Dostoyevsky's *Idiot* who left him for a rich merchant.
[35] Among the former Acmeists, only Narbut (1888–1938) joined the Bolsheviks and held high government and Party posts before being expelled from the latter in 1928. Arrested in 1936, he died in prison.

"new stage" in the country's development. Despite their apparent
independence and indifference, Mandelstam and Narbut closely
followed this campaign. Once Narbut came by and announced very
gravely to Mandelstam: "We have decided to publish a magazine. It
will be called . . ." "What?" "Simeon Yakovlevich." All Narbut's irony
about the current debates on poetry found expression in the name
and patronymic of Nadson.[36] Mandelstam was more concerned about
prose. Detesting "descriptive" literature, he once muttered, bitterly
and sourly: "Soon people will attend a meeting of the house management committee, attack one another and then go straight home and
write about it."

The future balance of literary forces could be discerned in the press
discussions leading up to the Congress. Mandelstam began to realise that
no place had been prepared for him in this new Table of Ranks.[37]

At that moment Bonch-Bruyevich energetically started to collect writers'
manuscripts. He paid well, and everyone needed money. Writers made
for the Literary Museum. The rouble equivalent of the materials offered
was assessed mechanically in terms of each writer's "specific gravity".
Mandelstam's manuscripts were valued at 500 roubles. Offended, he
entered into correspondence with Bonch-Bruyevich and received the
most delicately formulated clarification that, according to general opinion, Mandelstam was a poet of secondary importance. The specialists
had not advanced very much beyond Ruderman's wife, who, as I
mentioned, accused Mandelstam of being behind the times. I myself
once met with unexpected failure at my new workplace, the Central
Bureau of the Department for Research Workers. No sooner had I begun
working there than Mandelstam exclaimed: "Emma will get us trips to
sanatoria and rest homes." Dutifully I raised the suggestion with the
senior lecturer in agricultural sciences who was the volunteer head of
the social-services section. "Mandelstam?" he reacted. "There's no poet
of that name. Once long ago there was such a poet . . ."

In 1931, Mandelstam wrote: "Time you knew: I'm also a contemporary. Just try to tear me from this age . . ." ("Midnight in Moscow",
published November 1932). Now he continued to hear himself scepti-
cally described as "detached from the spirit of the age". Returning from

---

[36] The position occupied by Nadson (1862–1887) in the 1880s showed that
Russian poetry was indeed in poor shape, "not because his poetry lacked content
but because it totally lacked style and a distinctive form or manner" (Terras).
[37] System devised by Peter the Great to formalise precedence of rank and title
in every branch of government service. A famous 1935 film, based on Alexei
Tolstoy's novel *Peter the Great*, would implicitly identify Stalin and Peter.

a walk in an infinitely melancholy state, he told us what had just happened. He had bumped into some writer who began a lively conversation and carelessly repeated that Mandelstam was being ranked among the "neo-classicists". "There's a stick in my hand!" Mandelstam had yelled angrily. After such outbursts he was always miserable.

He submitted the manuscript of "Conversation about Dante" to the State Publishing House. It was returned without a single critical comment, but had numerous question marks in the margins. If I am not mistaken, these were added by A.K. Djivelegov.

The new and innovative opera by Shostakovich, *Lady Macbeth of Mtsensk*, was staged at the Nemirovich-Danchenko & Stanislavky Musical Theatre. I was at one of the first performances. In approximately the fifth or sixth row on the other side of the aisle sat Mandelstam. He was alone. I went up to him in the interval. Mandelstam was so agitated that he appealed in a state of high excitement to someone sitting in front of him: "This is Wagnerism!" They became engrossed in an intense discussion.

The Sargidjan affair continued to obsess him. Once Mandelstam was lying on the bed, with Klychkov sitting beside him. With irresistible eloquence and passion, he yet again described what had happened a year before. Klychkov listened attentively and then remarked: "Of course, he was wrong. He should have given back the money first, then hit you." Mandelstam did not immediately understand what Klychkov was saying; his negligent tone was so at odds with the devastating sense of his reply. In an instant, though, he shuddered and screamed: "Nadenka, we're throwing him out!" At that moment I was on my way to the kiosk for some cigarettes. The tall, long-haired "wood-sprite" Klychkov caught me up by the door on to the staircase and fled, groaning and laughing. I did not take long and returned apprehensively, expecting to meet a storm of indignation. In the first room Nadya was sitting calmly, gazing absent-mindedly into the distance with her enigmatic, modest-yet-sly blue eyes. I glanced into Mandelstam's room, and what do you suppose? He was still lying there, while on his bed sat Klychkov, and they were hugging and kissing one another. They had made their peace.

Sometimes Mandelstam would put on his good suit (acquired, I think, from the hard-currency shop using the coupons from Nadya's inheritance), have his beard trimmed at the barber shop and feel himself a true "Petersburger". Citing Claudel in conversation with me, he grew cross: "You don't know Claudel? Don't you understand French?"

On the same landing was a writer with a young Polish maid who lived in. Ascending the stairs at the same time, Mandelstam noted once again her well-bred beauty. Then he lay down on the bed, musing and raising his index finger triumphantly: "It's not what it seems!" he repeated. Mandelstam suspected that she was no housemaid and that there was some secret romantic or political story involved.

On the ground floor, opposite Klychkov, lived the satirical writer Victor Ardov, with his young wife, an actress at the Moscow Arts Theatre, and her little son from her first marriage, Alyosha Batalov. Nina Olshevskaya was one of the first post-Revolutionary graduates of Stanislavsky's school, which he describes in *An Actor Prepares*. Her beauty had a varied ancestry: Polish aristocrats, Russians and Tatars. Gleaming dark hair, dark high-coloured cheeks and eyes that were, in Khardjiev's words, "like coals" all prompted him to call her the "Gypsy". Nina Olshevskaya and her close friends Nora (Veronica) Polonskaya and Sveta Pilyavskaya formed a galaxy of irresistible women. They gathered in Ardov's new apartment where, it seemed, there was as yet no furniture apart from the divan and the three-leaved mirror in the corner of the bedroom. Ardov got to know the Mandelstams, and the two families were on neighbourly but not very close terms.

Sometimes, when bringing home an acquaintance he had met out walking, Mandelstam rang the Ardovs' doorbell. If Nina opened the door, he would comment: "A pretty girl lives here," bow politely, say "Goodbye," and with a smile take his guest up to the fourth floor. (Nina Olshevskaya recalled this in the 1980s when we would meet to record her reminiscences of Akhmatova.)

That was the domestic background to the dramatic events of this critical year in Mandelstam's life.

Conflicts, Great and Small

Nadya brought back a new catchword from the Crimea, "returnees". She had acquired it from Andrei Bely. He told of the joys of meeting those who had returned from banishment and exile. There were many such people of his acquaintance: not only did he belong to the most elevated ranks of the Russian intelligentsia, but he was also linked with the Anthroposophists, who were banned and dispersed in the 1920s. Andrei Bely, as everyone knew, was an active member of the society.

Alluding to the Copernican vision of the world as he thought aloud, Mandelstam linked his own new attainments with Koktebel. Much that

he said, it seemed to me, was now redolent of his conversations with
Bely. And it was then that I heard an echo of Spengler's philosophy in
his words although I well remembered his irritated mutter ("German
professor!") when reading *The Decline of the West*.

I do not recall Mandelstam then talking about political matters. Yet he
said what he thought of the gaping wounds of our time in "A cold
spring. Famished, timid Crimea".[38] The poem would later become known
with distortions that destroyed its artistic value. This is evident from the
very first line as incorrectly published in the US edition of his collected
works:[39] "A cold spring. Hungry Stary Krym".

To some, the poem seemed flat, especially beside the explosion of
colour, sound and scent in "Ariosto", which he also wrote then in the
Crimea. This was not Mandelstam's type of poem at all, asserted Yevgeny
Khazin, and could just as easily have been written by Khodasevich. But
Osmyorkin was at once enraptured by the precision with which the poet
had caught the inimitable features of the Crimean landscape: "that same
sour and biting smoke", because stoves were fed with cakes of pressed
dung, "the Easter foolery of the decorated almond" and the "felted
land", from the soft carpet of fallen tamarisk leaves which covered the
ground. (The American edition made a complete muddle here: "grey-
ish" instead of "sour smoke", and not "the felted earth" but the nonsensical "in felt overshoes".)

There were those who disapproved of Mandelstam's poem "The
Apartment" ("The apartment's as quiet as paper,/ Empty, without any
schemes") and accused the poet of trying to emulate Nekrasov.
"Mandelstam is degenerating," was the reaction of Boris Glubokovsky,
a friend of the Osmyorkins who proved a snob. Eight years in the Solovki
labour camp had not made him change his attitude to art and poetry.

The response of the few other listeners to whom I could read this
poem was interesting. My friend Lena's mother, a dentist and a progressive member of the intelligentsia who did a great many kind deeds as a
member of the polyclinic's trade-union committee, suddenly burst into
tears and said: "That's exactly what our life is like." An artist of my
acquaintance, also actively involved in the Creative Workers' Union, took
a more down-to-earth view: "The bastard. They give him an apartment

---

[38] Written after they had seen for themselves some of the brutal consequences
of collectivisation. Not published in Russia until 1987. For the full text, see
"Five Poems by Osip Mandelstam", p. 92.
[39] The first attempt to gather and publish (in Russian) all of Mandelstam's works
was the four-volume collection (eds G.P. Struve and B.A. Filippov) that appeared
in the US between 1967 and 1971.

to which he's not entitled – and that's how he thanks them!" Osmyorkin alone sensitively grasped the image of withdrawn isolation and hopelessness that the verse embodied.

"Emma, he's a predator!" Nadya greeted me in despair. "He doesn't want my mother to move in with us. That was the only reason I ever grabbed this flat!"

With some affectation, she recounted a dream in which Mama pleaded, collapsing into her arms, "Save me!" Very harsh words were said about Mandelstam, illustrating his egotism and capacity for making those around him do as he wanted. She understood that he was not being wilful; the artist was forced to behave this way because he must defend his talent. But today she did not repeat her favourite remark: "If Osya is not unruly he will not write verse." No, she complained bitterly about him, asserting that all poets were predatory, and she did not want to put up with it.

Nadya's desire to take in her mother was understandable. Vera Yakovlevna had become a widow in 1930 and was living alone in Kiev. The older children could not accommodate her. Anya had neither a room of her own nor regular earnings, while Yevgeny shared one room with his wife. Things were further complicated because Mandelstam was supposed to invite his father to stay. The old man was living the whole time in Leningrad with his younger son Yevgeny. As soon as Mandelstam became settled – i.e. acquired a flat and was awarded a personal pension (not very large, it's true), a food allowance and a privileged book subscription – the idea arose of its own accord.

The internal feud, concealed from other eyes, continued for some time. Mandelstam's father came to Moscow and was very well received by Nadya but, for some reason, was unhappy. He did not want to go out to buy paraffin and privately complained to me in his strange German-Jewish accent: "I'm onvell" (I remember the expression since it became a favourite phrase of Lena and myself). After living for quite a while at Nashchokin Street, Emil Mandelstam returned to his younger son, and soon his place was taken by Vera Yakovlevna, though not yet for good.

It was then that Nadya thought up the plan of moving her mother into one room with Mandelstam's father. We were so stupid that we did not realise how insulting the proposal was. And when Vera Yakovlevna refused outright (he would smoke, or snore – some unfamiliar old man, not on your life!), Nadya turned it all into a joke: "Mama's too ladylike." Zhenya and I would repeat this like idiots and laugh.

Victory in the end went to Vera Yakovlevna. She shifted all her belongings from Kiev to Moscow. When the large bedstead with its nickel-plated

knobs was set up in the half-empty room of the Mandelstams' apartment, their artistic habitation lost its charm. But that did not happen
straightaway.

Vera Yakovlevna grew to be part of the Nashchokin Street set-up, and
soon all the guests were following Nadya's example and referring to her
as a "lovely old lady". In fact, she was not at all attractive. She had a
harsh, squeaky voice, and her manner was overfamiliar. Only her short-
ness and elderly plumpness allowed one, with considerable latitude, to
proclaim her "a darling". She was, however, a clever woman and valiantly
endured the astounding disorganisation of her children.

Twenty-five-year-old Marusya Petrovykh became one of the Mandelstams'
circle without my noticing. I knew that Akhmatova had helped to acquaint
them, but when and how I had only a vague idea since I was absent from
Moscow for a long while that autumn.

To begin with, I paid not the slightest attention to Marusya. From
time to time, a new girl or young woman would turn up at the
Mandelstams'; they would be keen on her and then she'd vanish, leaving no trace in their recollections or conversation. Marusya struck me
as a trivial creature. A scarf like a Young Pioneer's neckerchief; a fantasy
of the new dress she'd make and wear to the premiere of *Twelfth Night*
at the Arts Theatre's second stage; and excited accounts of her Caucasian
adventures during which someone at the hotel had deliberately separated
her from her husband (Petya was an agronomist, if I remember rightly).
She chattered about parties at home when the chairs were pushed to
one side and the young danced a foxtrot while the outraged neighbours
banged on the walls . . . I tried mocking her childish tone and empty-
headed tales, but to no effect. The Mandelstams took her seriously. He
considered her a good and professional translator of poetry. Both firmly
invited her to visit them, and she evidently was happy to accept.

Yet another novelty were Nadya's new stories about Akhmatova and her
son, sitting side by side like "two doves". Where had she seen such a
thing? In Leningrad? In Moscow? Lyova Gumilyov had indeed passed
through the capital on his way to join an archaeological expedition in
the Crimea. But Akhmatova? Had she also visited? I never found out.

Nadya already knew all about Lyova. He was absorbed by early Russian
history, knew the subject like a scholar, and his range of interests evidently
derived from Khomyakov. He took no interest whatsoever in girls; he
adored his mother.

Lyova went on archaeological and other expeditions only as a seasonal
occupation. As the son of Gumilyov, he could not find any permanent

work nor could he go to university. Thus he was without official social status, almost like those formally "deprived of rights".[40] The Mandelstams had the idea of pressing, with my support, for him to be accepted as a member of our trade union (using his contract work on these expeditions as the pretext). Of course, I agreed. The Central Bureau of the Department of Research Workers, where I was then employed, was attached to the central committee for the Educational Workers' Union and thus, in turn, under the overall control of the Central Council of Trade Unions.

Sometime in October, an absent-minded and independent young man with a rucksack on his back called at the Bureau. Addressing me formally as Emma Grigoryevna, he introduced himself: "Lev Gumilyov." In appearance he was little different from all the other provincial research workers who then gathered constantly at the Bureau. He provided certain essential bits of information about himself. As he was leaving, he asked with childish levity: "D'you like a sweetie?" and tossed a boiled sweet on to the desk. Two days later he left Moscow, and I visited the Mandelstams. Nadya was quick to pass on his dismissive comment: "The usual office floozie." Such was the executed Gumilyov's son in the role of a petitioner.

Nevertheless, I took up his case with great zeal. To begin with, my superiors were well disposed ("Such people require a special approach"), but when the matter finally came before the highest authority, the Presidium of the Central Council, the times had already changed, and there would be no more talk of any "special approach". I was to witness this in regard to other cases as well.

Lyova, meanwhile, remained in the same insecure position as before.

One morning I was visiting the Mandelstams. The doorbell rang. Lyova came in, radiant with joy, having seen in the Old New Year (13 January) at Marusya Petrovykh's. It seemed he was again in Moscow and staying with the Mandelstams at their invitation.

"Where's my darling boy?" exclaimed Mandelstam if he did not find Lyova at home. He hardly let him out of his sight; they were always running off somewhere together. Once they came back from a pawnshop where they had stood in line all day. Excitedly they described their triumphant verbal sparring, as they waited in the queue. Lyova had seized the most aggressive girl by the hand. "Be my wife!" he suggested. This tickled Mandelstam.

---

[40] Representatives of the pre-Revolutionary order, from government officials to priests and businessmen, were officially deprived of a range of civil rights until 1936.

He took Lyova with him to the State Publishing House, where, at the end of the working day, he read "Conversation about Dante" to some of the assembled editors and authors. "Was it interesting?" I asked Lyova. "Very." "Did it go off well?" "Superbly." "Did they discuss it?" "No." "But why?" "Not one of them understood a word. And I didn't understand a thing either." "So what was the good in all that?" "It was interesting, nevertheless."

On another occasion they came home excited and keyed up. They had just visited Klyuev. Mandelstam quoted his poems and showed how proudly Klyuev read them. Wide shirt-sleeves billowing like balloons, it had seemed as if Klyuev was moving under sail.

This visit hardly displayed the caution with regard to Lyova that the Mandelstams had loudly proclaimed at his first appearance. Even less cautious was the involvement of Lyova in Mandelstam's feud with Alexei Tolstoy. Lyova was supposed to stalk him and give Mandelstam advance warning that he was on his way. Then Mandelstam was supposed to rise up before the "Count" and slap his face. As part of this operation, the two friends, young and old, would sit for hours in some canteen or bar at the Nikitskie Gates [on the Boulevard Ring] not far from Tolstoy's house. This was not the district's only attraction. Close by was Granatny Street, where Marusya Petrovykh lived. She did not go out to work, and, without doubt, they would call by during the day.

Jealousy and rivalry were sacred attributes of passion in Mandelstam's understanding.

"How interesting! Just the same happened with Kolya," he exclaimed. His head began to whirl with memories stirred by Lyova of Nikolai Gumilyov in the hungry Petrograd winter when both poets were in pursuit of Olga Arbenina.

Andrei Bely died. Upset, Nadya told us what had driven him to the stroke that ended his life. His book of memoirs, *Between Two Revolutions*, had just appeared, with a preface by Lev Kamenev in which all of Bely's literary activities were termed a "tragi-farce" acted out "on the sidelines of history". Bely bought up all the copies of the book he could find and tore out the preface. He continued visiting the book shops until he suffered the fatal stroke. The Mandelstams were at the funeral. Nadya noted that only one schoolteacher boldly brought her students there to say farewell to a literary genius. Other teachers, evidently, could not rise to the occasion: some were ignorant and simply did not know who Bely was; others knew, but did not dare involve schoolchildren in this event. I also did not attend, although Bely's death was a great shock. I had been brought up on the poetry of Blok and Bely since I was 15. His "Symphonies" were a revelation while I loved *Silver Dove* even more than *Petersburg*. But that was long ago now. Life had changed drastically since then, and I was so overwhelmed with my "duties" that I could not ask for time off work to attend an unofficial ceremony. Besides, I always found open expressions of emotion difficult and avoided any kind of demonstration. I was deeply moved, however, by Mandelstam's verse on the death of Bely.

He sent these poems to Bely's widow, but she did not like them. What could be the reason? Had she really read anything better during those days of bereavement? I did not note any signs of hurt or irritation, but I could see that Mandelstam was sincerely and deeply disappointed.

Never expecting to hear my comments on his verse, he now wanted to know exactly what I had found so appealing in both his poems. I tried, in general terms, to define how I felt about them. I said something to the effect that they represented the continuity between epochs and that, having acutely denoted the primacy of Bely's philosophical and poetic thought at the turn of the century, Mandelstam had expressed this in terms of our contemporary outlook, of which he himself was the spokesman. "You are the most intelligent woman in Moscow," responded Mandelstam with satisfaction. Probably K.N. Bugayeva, Bely's widow, did not approve of the verse he had sent her because she could not grasp its meaning.

Soon after, Nadya gave me a present. It was a draft of one of the poems that the poet himself had rejected. Unfortunately, it has not survived. My friend Lena, to whom I gave it for safekeeping, destroyed it.

The draft was a scrap of paper, about one-sixteenth of a normal sheet, on which Mandelstam had written in a tiny script. He had corrected the text several times, then rewritten two lines above a text that was entirely deleted, before crossing out everything thoroughly from beginning to end. The lines were probably intended for the middle stanzas of the poem that begins "Two or three accidental phrases pursue me" ("10 January 1934"). Deleted several times, the text was difficult to decipher, but the abundance of complex words that I recall is very characteristic of Mandelstam's philosophical lyrics. It is impossible, therefore, to agree that this was the draft of another work on Bely's death, "Where Did They Bring Him from? Who? The One Who Died" (though Nadezhda Mandelstam incorrectly asserts as much in *Hope Abandoned*). That lost poem, which parodied the senseless colloquial speech of curious philistines, would not have demanded the difficult quest for expression so evident in the rejected draft. Nadya gave me the text as an

interesting specimen of handwriting, not at all for the purpose of preserving the contents. The Mandelstams appointed me sole custodian of a
quite different and earlier text.

One morning, unexpectedly, Nadya came to see me; in fact, she rushed
in. Her words were brief and urgent: "Osya has composed a very outspoken poem. It can't be written down. No one, apart from me, knows
about it. We need someone else to memorise it. You're the one. After
we die, you'll make it public. Osya will recite it to you; then you'll learn
it by heart with me. For the time being no-one must know of this.
Especially Lyova." Nadya was very wound up. Without more ado, we
went to Nashchokin Street. Nadya left me alone with Mandelstam in
the large room. He read aloud:

> We live without sensing the country beneath us,
> At ten paces, our words have no sound
> And when there's the will to half open our mouths
> The Kremlin crag-dweller bars the way.
> Fat fingers as oily as maggots,
> Words sure as forty-pound weights,
> With his leather-clad gleaming calves
> And his large laughing cockroach eyes.
>
> And around him a rabble of thin-necked bosses,
> He toys with the service of such semi-humans.
> They whistle, they meow and they whine:
> He alone merely jabs with his finger and barks,
> Hurling one decree and another like horseshoes –
> In the eye, in the face, the brow or the groin.
> Not one shooting but swells his gang's pleasure,
> And the broad breast of the Ossetian.

Today the Stalin epigram is well known. But having read the closing
couplet, Mandelstam exclaimed: "No, no! That's a bad ending. There's
something of Tsvetayeva about it. I'll leave it out. It will do well enough
without it . . ."

Then he read the whole poem again, closing with enormous fervour:
"'Hurling one decree and another like horseshoes – / In the eye, in the
face, the brow or the groin!' The Komsomol will sing that on the streets!"
(he was swept up by his own exultant mood) "in the Bolshoi Theatre
. . . at congresses . . . from every tier and balcony . . ." And he marched
around the room.

Searing me with a direct fiery gaze, he halted: "Watch out. Not a word. If they find out, I could be SHOT!"

Tossing back his head with especial pride, he again marched back and forth across the room, rising on tiptoe each time he changed direction.

Then Nadya and I withdrew, and she began to recite the poem to me, line by line. Straightaway she told me an alternative version of the fifth line: "Even the dogs in his courtyard are plump."

It was all deeply buried and concealed, I thought. Before Mandelstam was sentenced I told no-one else about the poem and naturally did not recite it to a soul. When the Mandelstams once began talking about the epigram in my presence, however, Nadya placidly commented that Nina Grin preferred the other version. "Stunned" is not the word. So I was not the only one in on this secret? Neither had I known there were different versions of the text.

Akhmatova

"He was stifled by his own unpublished verse" (Akhmatova).

That was how the time passed, before the storm broke, during Mandelstam's last year of life in Moscow. Into this explosive atmosphere flowed a new current. In February 1934, Akhmatova came to visit.

In honour of her arrival, Mandelstam prepared a long, humorous address:

". . . If your head begins to spin, fall back on the working class";

"You will speak and we shall listen – listen and understand, listen and understand . . ."

Akhmatova was given the kitchen (minus gas ring), and the tiny cell was christened the "shrine". Similar titles were assigned to the other rooms, but I do not recall them now.

Mandelstam and Akhmatova would talk alone. Only once, when I had to glance for some reason into the "shrine", did I catch them together. With childish enjoyment they were reading aloud in Italian from the *Divine Comedy*. To be precise, they were not reading but somehow acting out different parts, and Akhmatova was self-conscious about her involuntary bursts of rapture. It was strange to see her wearing glasses. She was standing, a book in her hand, before the seated Mandelstam. "Well, you go on," they prompted one another. "Now it's your turn."

Once they came home, merry and animated, after being invited out together. Mandelstam had committed several gaffes in the space of an evening. He had greeted the wrong person with the wrong words, used inappropriate expressions as they made their farewells and, above all, was openly bored by the new version of *Oedipus in Colonus*. Shervinsky had translated jointly with Nilender and the latter, it seems, was reading it that evening. Domestic jokes and puns contributed to Mandelstam's humorous quatrain:

> Acquainted for many years
> Shervinsky invited us home:
> To hear Oedipus fall in step
> And march beside Nilender.

Akhmatova was friendly with Shervinsky, but poets and artistic figures of this type were anathema to Mandelstam. Since I heard many enthralled comments about Shervinsky from his pupils, in particular my friend Lena, from actors studying at the Theatrical Arts Institute who gave public recitals, and from other translators, I asked Mandelstam's opinion. "A young man from Prechistenka",[41] he answered indifferently, referring to the younger generation of the families that formed Moscow's academic élite, "and he's not changed at all."

Towards the end of February, Akhmatova began getting ready to return home to Leningrad. Lyova went to the station to see her off. As soon as the hall door closed behind them, Mandelstam tossed himself on the divan and exclaimed: "Nadenka, how good that she's gone! That was too much electricity for one home."

A kind of bleakness settled on the Mandelstam flat after Akhmatova's departure. There surfaced a hint of irritation towards her. It was easy for Akhmatova, suggested Nadya with a touch of ill will, to maintain a majestic indifference when she was shielded by Punin. No matter how tangled her domestic situation, living in that household did provide a minimum of security. Mandelstam, on the contrary, had to wage a daily war of survival.

He claimed that Akhmatova was already an unofficially recognised classic. Once we talked about her poetry, and among his approving words there was nevertheless a passing comment on the "mannered style" of her early verse. Though he did add: "Everyone wrote like that then." After the usual muttering, Mandelstam declared, disapprovingly,

---

[41] District along street of the same name in central Moscow.

At Nashchokin Street, 1934 (l. to r.): Alexander Mandelstam, Maria Petrovykh, Emil Mandelstam (father), Nadezhda, Osip Mandelstam and Akhmatova

"Auto-eroticism". On another occasion Nadya sharply criticised the tasteless endings of several poems in *Rosary* [1914] and *White Flock* [1917]: "How could she write, 'Even he that caressed then forgot,' or 'He gave a calm and awful smile'?"

Lyova made me a gift of the photograph taken for his identity document. On the back he began an acrostic:

> Enamel, diamonds and gilt
> Might adorn the Egyptians:
> My damsel's graceful figure . . .

He could get no further. Walking about the room, he bombastically and repeatedly chanted the lines. Mandelstam grabbed the pen from him, quickly altered "graceful figure" to read "figure might enhance . . ." and added energetically:

> A yard of Cheviot or tricot.

In March, Lyova returned to Leningrad, but a month later he was back in Moscow. The Mandelstams, however, would not let him stay. As when Akhmatova was with them, he slept at the Ardovs'. There he found actresses, Victor Ardov's racy anecdotes and an uproarious atmosphere in which Nadya eagerly played her part. Mandelstam, meanwhile, relapsed into a most unsettled state. No sooner had Lyova climbed the stairs from the Ardov flat than Mandelstam would greet him with the words: "Let's do something naughty." And they made a trunk call to Akhmatova in Leningrad.

Mandelstam's manic condition did not subside. Where he was rushing off to, whom he saw and whom he talked to, I did not then know. Subsequently, it was clear that he was still seeking an opportunity to slap Alexei Tolstoy and was reading his Stalin poem to almost anyone who would listen.

By now he was again missing Akhmatova. He demanded over the telephone that she come back to Moscow. Once, after such a conversation, he turned to me, beside himself with irritation: "When it comes down to it, we are Acmeists, members of the same party. Her party comrade is in trouble, she's duty-bound to come!"

Akhmatova arrived on 13 May. They spent one whole day together. Late that evening, GPU men appeared with a warrant for Mandelstam's arrest. The search of the apartment continued all night. Osip was taken away.

Mandelstam's Arrest and Exile

On the morning of 14 May, I came to Nashchokin Street. With tears in her eyes and her hair down (it was then still black), Akhmatova opened the door. She had a very bad migraine, something, she said, that never happened to her. I learned everything.

The translator David Brodsky, they told me, had paid his first ever visit to the Mandelstams that evening. To the dismay of his hosts and the tired Akhmatova, he stayed late and was still there when the GPU men arrived. His visit struck them as suspicious: had Brodsky been sent to observe their reaction to a late-night ring at the door? (These suspicions were quite groundless, apparently, and found no confirmation later.)

Nadya told me privately that one of those conducting the search went to the house management committee and returned with a document recording Lev Gumilyov's temporary registration with the Mandelstams. Showing it to Mandelstam he demanded threateningly: "What's this then?"

She and Akhmatova told me how they searched the apartment and examined any manuscripts . . . For ten days, we tormented ourselves with hypotheses. Why had they picked up Mandelstam? For striking Alexei Tolstoy? Or for his poems? I could not be frank with Akhmatova; I thought she did not know about the Stalin epigram.

I called at Nashchokin Street as often as I could, in my free time before and after work. The stairs were kept under surveillance. The doors of the other apartments were always ajar: a maid was chatting to someone or a couple were flirting.

Soon the other residents began to say of the Mandelstams: "People used to gather there." There could be no worse accusation. If "people gathered", that meant there was a "group" or "conspirators". "Who 'gathered'?" Nadya demanded sourly. "Emma? Boris Sergeyevich [Kuzin]?" She considered that Aduyev was behind these rumours.

Some ten days later, Nadya was summoned by telephone to the Lubyanka. The investigation had been completed. Mandelstam was banished for three years to Cherdyn. If she wanted, she could accompany him. We sat at Nashchokin Street and waited for Nadya to return. She came back shocked and harrowed. It was hard for her to give any coherent account.

"It was for his poems. 'Stalin', 'The Apartment' and the Crimean verse ['A Cold Spring']. Mandelstam, concealing nothing, frankly recited all three. Then he wrote them down."

"What? With the last two lines? But he'd left them out!" was my reaction.

"He recited and wrote them out in full. A written version of the Stalin poem was already lying on their table."[42]

Osip himself had told her. She had seen him. With heartbreaking tenderness, she said: "How he clung to me: 'Nadenka, the things they did to me!'" According to Nadya, the interrogator had a written version of the variant known only to Marusya Petrovykh and taken down by her alone.[43]

Mandelstam was cross-examined about the Stalin epigram. "Who's this 'We'? On whose behalf are you speaking?" They wanted to identify and convict a counter-revolutionary group. "We reported back to higher authority," the investigator told Nadya. Stalin was not named, but it was clear that his words were quoted: "Isolate, but preserve," that was their instruction. This saved us all from being arrested and charged.

---

[42] He recited "For the Resounding Valour" and "The Apartment" before being confronted with written copies of the Stalin epigram and the Crimean verse. See Shentalinsky, "Mandelstam Street", in *KGB's Literary Archive*.

[43] The interrogator quoted alternative third and fourth lines: "All we hear is the Kremlin crag-dweller, / The murderer and peasant slayer"; see Shentalinsky, *ibid*.

Nadya's first despairing words to me were: "Emma, Osya named you."
She watched me with anticipation and fear. Mandelstam said he had
never written down or circulated the poem about Stalin, and it was
known only to members of his family: his wife, brother [Alexander],
brother-in-law and Emma Gerstein.

Nadya's account was confused: "They pretended that they were shooting his 'fellow-conspirators' in the next room." According to Nadya,
Osip shouted: "How dare you shoot Emma Gerstein? She is a thoroughly Soviet person." In 1936 in Voronezh he told me a different story. It
was the investigator, supposedly, who shouted at him: "How dare you
slander Emma Gerstein, who is beyond doubt a Soviet person?" What
actually happened during the interrogation I do not know, of course,
but at that time I fully accepted the version Nadya passed on to me as
the truth.

"Congratulations!" said Akhmatova when we found ourselves alone
together in the smaller room. "Now you also are on their files." I was
shocked by her sensible remark. Had I been able, at that moment, to
cast my gaze forward, perhaps I might have taken more notice of her
words: for the next twenty years, the only words I would hear from
every official, personnel department, editorial office, credentials commission and the Writers' Union were "Your application is refused". But that
day I was hardly capable of such thoughts.

Nadya continued: Mandelstam could not hold out for long and soon
named those who were not just "family members" but everyone to whom
he had read his poem, among them Marusya Petrovykh. "Ah! the theatre-
lover," responded the investigator, and Nadya found this suspicious. She
had accused Marusya, even before Mandelstam's arrest, of having left a
typed version of his "New Poems" that Nadya had given her, on the
window-sill. "And why does she come round here, 'wringing her hands'?"
Nadya now said with irritation.

She expressed her suspicions as though they originated with
Mandelstam. Yet after Akhmatova had visited him in Voronezh and heard
at first hand his account of the investigation, suspicions about Marusya
Petrovykh were removed once and for all. Until her death Akhmatova
would meet Marusya, and their friendship throughout the ensuing 30
years remained unclouded.

Akhmatova and I were sitting next to Nadya on the divan in the large
room while friends came and went, fussed around, collecting money and
other essentials for the coming journey. The door opened, but the moment
Sima Narbut set foot in the room, Nadya exclaimed: "Sima, forgive me,
I can only see close friends and family now." And there sat I.

Nadya was in a semi-delirious state. She mentioned Shengeli and Narbut and expressed certain suspicions (Osip had also read his poem to them, it turned out). But why suspect them when, as I now know, 14 people had heard the poem, and where is the guarantee that there were not still others? The artist Tyshler, for instance, claimed that Mandelstam had recited the poem to him in the presence of several other people.

Only later in Voronezh did I learn the identity of some of the others to whom Mandelstam had read the epigram (Akhmatova, Pasternak, Kuzin). And twenty years would pass before I learned, only from Akhmatova herself, that Lev Gumilyov also knew of the Stalin poem then (something against which the Mandelstams had specifically warned me).

. . . It was time to go. Nadya stuffed the money people had collected and brought to her into her old battered handbag, tossed some things into a bag and left. I watched her with awed admiration. Akhmatova, Alexander Mandelstam and Yevgeny Khazin left together. They asked me to stay behind with her mother, Vera Yakovlevna.

Zhenya came back late, emotionally drained. He told us how Akhmatova left for Leningrad, from the other station, and how they waited for Nadya and Osip . . . The details of his account I do not now remember; they have been overshadowed by the description of this event in Akhmatova's *Leaves from a Diary*.

That unforgettable day has been described twice. By Akhmatova and by Nadezhda. There also exist unpublished versions of Akhmatova's memoirs about Mandelstam. In the better-known published account, Akhmatova, listing the "beautiful and elegantly dressed" women who visited Nadezhda when Mandelstam was under arrest, continues: "Meanwhile Nadya and I sat in our crumpled knitted jackets, yellow-faced and wooden. With us were Emma Gerstein and Nadya's brother."

In a different variant of *Leaves from a Diary*, dated 28 July 1957, Akhmatova describes Nadezhda's arrival in Leningrad after Mandelstam's second arrest in 1938. "She had the most terrible eyes. 'I shall only calm down', she said, 'when I learn that he's died.'" Some paragraphs further on, Akhmatova concludes: "At the beginning of 1939 I received a short letter from a friend in Moscow: 'Our friend Lena has had a child and our friend Nadya has been widowed,' she wrote."

In several of the copies[44] she gave to people Akhmatova indicated the identity of those mentioned. The "Moscow friend" was Emma Gerstein,

---

[44] These were illegal typewritten copies. The text was not published in the USSR until 1989.

while "our friend Lena" was Yelena Osmyorkina. I should add that Lilya, the Osmyorkins' daughter, was born on 30 January 1939, while "our friend Nadya" – i.e. Nadezhda – asked me to come to Nikolai Khardjiev's apartment on the day I returned home from Leningrad, in order to tell me that Mandelstam had died. I shall have more to say about that terrible day.

In *Hope against Hope*, Nadezhda writes the following about my visit to Nashchokin Street on 14 May 1934:

> My brother Yevgeny was still asleep when we rang to tell him the news. On the phone, of course, we used none of the taboo words like "arrested", "picked up" or "taken away" . . . We had worked out a code of our own and we understood each other perfectly without having to give anyone's names. Both he and Emma Gerstein quickly came over to the apartment. All four of us then left, one after the other at short intervals, each with a large shopping basket or simply with a wad of manuscripts in his pockets.

I do not know which of us carried Mandelstam's manuscripts from the apartment. Where would we take them? Akhmatova did not live in Moscow, and Yevgeny and I could also expect to be searched since we belonged to Mandelstam's immediate domestic circle.

I remember this differently. And I remember well, because I remained in possession of "material evidence": for the next 27 years, whenever I spring-cleaned my room, a schoolchild's briefcase with a dangling, half-torn-off handle regularly caught my eye, until I threw it away on moving to a new apartment. It belonged to Nadya. We had stuffed it full of the Khazins' family documents in order to burn them in the little stove in my room. These were papers compiled to collect money from a New York insurance company on the death of Nadya's father in 1930. It so happened that the hard-currency stores had just opened,[45] and the Khazins could legally receive coupons in return for this money from the United States. Nevertheless, they were concerned that the papers might be used as additional evidence of the Khazins' bourgeois origins (and goodness knows what else) if there was another search. Incidentally, I did not read these documents. I carried them out of the Mandelstam flat, which was under surveillance, and spent the whole night feeding them into the stove. The paper was so thick, however, that it was not completely consumed. Certain pages had to be pulled out and burned

---

[45] It was a criminal offence for private citizens in the USSR to hold foreign currency.

over a candle. This is the "exploit with a candle" so inaccurately described by Nadezhda Mandelstam in *Hope Abandoned*:

> The end of the last poem . . . ["Where have they brought him from?"] is missing. After our apartment was searched I gave the page with this poem to Emma Gerstein. It had lain on the floor, unnoticed by the men conducting the search. When we were on our way to Cherdyn, she took fright and burnt it. For some reason I am repelled by the fact that instead of throwing it into the stove, she held it in the flame of a candle.

In *Hope against Hope*, she refers to the "wads of manuscripts" that Akhmatova, herself, Yevgeny Khazin and I carried out of the arrested poet's apartment. In her later book there is only one page "unnoticed by the men conducting the search", which she then, for some reason, entrusted to me although, Nadezhda Mandelstam claims, it was the only existing autograph of an unpublished poem on the death of Andrei Bely.

As I have said earlier, she was mistaken.

Once the Mandelstams had left for Cherdyn, I recovered a little and gave thought to my own position.

To be on the safe side, I handed the letters that I cherished, and verse by certain poets, to a cousin who was very fond of me. However, she would not risk accepting an autograph text of Mandelstam, who had just been sent into exile, and I had no right to insist since she had nothing to do with that side of my life. My oldest friend, Lena, suggested I give it to her mother. "We always take her everything we wish to keep from prying eyes," she said. "Shura [her artist husband] even keeps 'pornography' there" – i.e. what our zealous critics termed pornography at that time.

Several days later, however, Lena came to tell me that her mother had handed back the Mandelstam text; she was already safeguarding the papers of her friend's son, a youth who had been exiled for belonging to a Zionist or Menshevik group (I don't recall which).

"All right then, give it to me. I'll think of something," I said.

"But I put it down the toilet," answered Lena.

I was shattered.

"You couldn't read it anyway," Lena said in self-justification.

At that moment, the Mandelstams unexpectedly returned from Cherdyn. Distressed, I told Nadya of this sad episode and Lena's response.

"Those are just the kind of drafts that textual critics examine," Nadya commented sadly.

In Moscow, the Mandelstams were supposed to be given a new place of exile. Apparently, they were offered a choice and preferred Voronezh to the other permitted towns.

In Nadya's stories about their journey to Cherdyn there was a truck that frightened Mandelstam: the driver had the face of an executioner (in my imagination I now see a cap pulled down over the eyes and a hard mouth, or a sickly smile and reddish beard – I have seen both types). Mandelstam was convinced they were taking him to be shot. He did not want to get into the truck. "Couldn't they have found a driver with a more human face?" asked Nadya indignantly. She boldly sent telegrams to Moscow, addressed to the Central Committee, the GPU and Stalin himself: "A poet has been driven mad . . . That is a major offence against the State: a poet has been sent into exile in a state of madness . . ." Nadya screamed along the telegraph wires. When Mandelstam was assigned to Voronezh in place of Cherdyn, we discussed who had helped achieve this. Was it Akhmatova who had petitioned Yenukidze? Was it Bukharin who had written to Stalin that "poets are always right, history is on their side"? Or was it Pasternak, whom, as we now all know, Stalin telephoned about Mandelstam? I said, half seriously, half joking: "It was you, Nadya. You gave even Stalin a fright." I had great admiration for her.

Mandelstam was offended to be placed among political exiles in Cherdyn: Mensheviks, Socialist Revolutionaries, members of the Bund . . . Feuds broke out between the former members of the different parties. A line in his Voronezh poem "Stanzas" is devoted to them: "I did not see the end of the slandering goats' squabble." (I heard the line from Nadya as well.)

The Mandelstams remained in Moscow for two or three days. Osip was in a numbed, motionless state, and his eyes were glassy. His eyelids were inflamed and would never recover; his eyelashes fell out. One arm was bandaged, but not in plaster. His shoulder was broken after he jumped from a window on the first floor of the Cherdyn hospital.

While Nadya ran off to register their documents at the relevant GPU department, I stayed behind with him. Osip lay on the bed, a fixed stare on his face. I found it unnerving to be left alone with him. It seems that we went out for a walk. I was helping him put on his tie. He yelled crossly: "Careful . . . my arm."

They were seen off at the station by Alexander Mandelstam, Yevgeny Khazin and myself. On the way there, we called in at the GPU on

Kuznetsky Most to collect yet more documents. We were openly being followed. From there we took the tram. Nadya and her brother sat with the luggage on the front platform of the second carriage, while Mandelstam, his brother and myself stood on the back platform.

Unconsciously, I watched Mandelstam sizing up the road with a critical eye. Before I realised what he was up to, he leaped with his bandaged arm from the moving tram. He managed the jump magnificently and calmly walked across the dusty, cobbled station square, dodging between the carts and automobiles, and avoiding the people bustling about and dragging their sacks towards the station. None of us had the nerve to jump after Mandelstam, and we did not know what to do. Only on the rail platform did we sigh with relief when he walked up, silent and thoughtful. Saying farewell, he embraced me and I tried not to catch his wounded arm. In the carriage next to the window sat a hefty, rosy-cheeked blond in a cap with a light blue band.[46] He did not take his eyes off us.

Nadya often came up to Moscow and sometimes stayed for three or four weeks at a time. This was necessary in order to keep hold of the flat, maintain old ties, look for literary translation work and, to tell the truth, have a break from Mandelstam.

In the early period, it was very difficult to be with him. He still had not recovered from the shock of being at the Lubyanka and then in Cherdyn. He could not be left alone. During one of Nadya's first trips away, her mother went to take her place but categorically refused to repeat the experience. Vera Yakovlevna described to me in detail Mandelstam's condition and behaviour in Voronezh. Two episodes have remained in my memory.

They were walking in the city together. It was hot and dusty. Mandelstam was suffering a paroxysm of bilious irritation. He demanded that Vera Yakovlevna walk faster. He shouted at her and cursed, but she could not go on: her shoe had chafed her foot. "Hey, grandpa," a passer-by reproached him. "What are you howling at your old woman for?"

"He thought I was Osip's wife, not his mother-in-law," concluded a horrified Vera Yakovlevna.

In the room Mandelstam stood for a long while at the window and did not say a word. Suddenly, he shouted: "A swallow . . . a swallow." "Osip Emilievich, what's the matter?" "But don't you see the swallow flying there."

---

[46] A blue-cap or GPU officer.

"I looked out of the window," continued Vera Yakovlevna. "There was no swallow; in fact there were no birds at all. He's mad, I tell you, those were hallucinations."

Poor Vera Yakovlevna. With her sober doctor's approach, she could not know that the swallow is a constantly recurring motif in Mandelstam's poetry, a major image in its symbolic system. In that mean Voronezh room, Mandelstam was summoning or lamenting his muse: "Teach me, frail swallow that has forgotten how to fly" [*Verses on the Unknown Soldier*, 1937].

A letter arrived from Nadya in Voronezh.

Whatever "taboo words" did she avoid there!? Although the letter was sent through the post, it was written in the style of a Party directive. In short, one-syllable phrases the following was brought to my attention. Nadya must come up to Moscow on business concerning the apartment. Someone must take her place with Osya. Mama is sick, no-one else can come to Voronezh, "So you will have to go," wrote Nadya.

A bare order, not a single word of human sympathy. Total indifference to my own circumstances. Not even indifference but disdain: she knew very well I was concerned about someone who was also under surveillance and much dearer to me than Mandelstam. I had forgiven Mandelstam his behaviour under interrogation. I had forgotten about certain hurtful and difficult moments in our relations. Naturally, when tragic days struck and Nadya was so in need of friendly support, I disregarded all else. But this only encouraged new demands: "So you will have to go." What about my job? How was I supposed to exist thereafter?

I shared my worries with Dinochka Butman. She volunteered to go to Voronezh instead of me. For an entire month she was there, sharing one room with Mandelstam. I do not remember how she managed. Later, Nadya could not find one kind word to say about this tiny woman.

Nadezhda Mandelstam, Voronezh

Whenever Nadya came on a visit to Moscow, I would call to see her –
so did all their old friends – and she went to see anyone she pleased.
Even now the sight of mandarin oranges recalls how we ran out to get
them from the buffet at the Kropotkin metro station during our evenings
together. Through her I got to know Khardjiev. Until Mandelstam's
arrest, he had rarely visited them (more often when Akhmatova came to
stay). Now he would visit Nadya each time she came from Voronezh.
He became one of those ready to give the Mandelstams all the material
support he could muster. I knew nothing of this. Once, however, when
he was extremely vexed with them (and they knew very well how to
reduce their closest friends and family to such a state), he burst out: "If
only you knew what I sold in order to send them money – a first edition
of Konevskoy!"[47]

Each time, Nadya brought Mandelstam's new poems to Moscow and
recited them, taking pleasure in every line, repeating those that she liked
particularly: "the tent-like feasts of sparks", for example, or "The boyish
ocean rises from the freshwater stream, tossing cupfuls of water at the
clouds." She read in a rapid staccato, but did not possess the poet's
musical ear. Once Klychkov begged: "Don't imitate Mandelstam, just
read it out – I can't understand otherwise." No matter how much
Klychkov loved Mandelstam, he gave an unfriendly sniff when Nadya
brought the poem, "What street is this? It's Mandelstam's Street".[48] It
seemed immodest to him. He considered that Mandelstam was exaggerating his own importance.

To begin with, Yevgeny and I did not like the Voronezh poems and
did not understand them. Only the Kama poems did I love straightaway,
especially "The day was five-headed". I adored this poem and recited it
to all my friends ("The dry-ration Russian folk tale. The wooden spoon
– Hey-halloo! / Where are you, you three fine lads, from the iron-gated
GPU?")[49] But we regarded this as his Urals cycle. Zhenya said: "They
gave him all of Russia." The first purely Voronezh poems, on the contrary,
struck us as overdone or rhetorical and strained. It was "Goldfinch"
[December 1936] that changed our minds: "I'll throw back my head,
My goldfinch – Let's look together at the world." I immediately sensed
a new classic.

Nadya told of Mandelstam's work in the theatre and on radio, and
of what pleasure he gained from touring musicians. This is evident in
his playful and masterly "Violinist". On the other hand, Nadya was

---

[47] Ivan Konevskoy (1877–1901), an exponent of early Russian symbolism.
[48] For the full text see "Five Poems by Osip Mandelstam", p. 93.
[49] Not published in Russia until 1987.

crudely derisive of those who came to Voronezh; she avoided meeting
them. She derived particular pleasure from accusing writers of cowardice.
Her eyes even gleamed as she did so. Once she arrived in Moscow in
an almost exultant state: Ehrenburg had spent three days in Voronezh,
and given a recital there, but did not visit them.

She was displeased with Akhmatova for her poem "Voronezh": "She
came to visit an exiled poet and what did she write about? A monument
to Peter? . . . The battle of Kulikovo Field?!" Probably this explains why
Akhmatova added a new concluding stanza to her poem in the 1950s.
I am convinced it was not there in 1936. What could have prevented
Akhmatova reading it to Nadya at that time? For reasons of censorship,
Akhmatova was not able to include "Voronezh" in her 1940 collection
From Six Books, but her closest audience would have known such tragic
concluding lines:

> While in the disgraced poet's room
> Fear and his Muse take turns on duty
> And night advances
> That knows no dawn.

In *The Flight of Time* (1965), the poem is dated 1936, but textual
analysis also indicates a later origin for the final verse. Would she really
have written of unending night looming towards a living poet? Clearly
this was written in retrospect. Such a bitter and ironic intonation appeared
in the poems of Akhmatova's later period, when sharp-witted colloqui-
alisms, verging on banter ("Fear and his Muse . . . "), began to enrich
her conversation as well. The sharp breaks in rhythm are also stylistic
evidence of the "late" Akhmatova.

In my view, this spoiled the poem. The desire to speak frankly
about the fate of Mandelstam did not clarify but confused the text.
I did not see the manuscripts of Akhmatova's poems, and in particular that of "Voronezh". Therefore, all I have just said must remain a
hypothesis.

Soon after the events of summer 1934, I was dismissed from my job
with 24 hours' notice and given an appalling reference. I made do as
best I could until 1936, when I finally found work at the Literary
Museum. This was not a permanent post, however, but contract work.
As soon as I received my first pay, I went to Voronezh. The exhausting
journey took 36 hours, if not longer. I remembered Akhmatova's recent
visit to the Mandelstams. Yevgeny and I saw her off from Moscow. He

did not immediately think to order her some bedding from the conductress. When I realised what had happened, there were no more mattresses or linen to be had. Unhappily I told Akhmatova, who was sitting straight-backed on the hard carriage seat. She replied with queenly negligence: "No matter."

Nadya met me at the station. When we reached their room, Mandelstam asked straightaway: "For long?" "Yes," I answered cheerfully. "For the entire May Day holidays." "For three days?! Might just as well not have come!" A pause. "I thought you would stay for a month, at least three weeks . . ." "But I do have a job, Osip Emilievich." "Not a permanent job."

They were then living in quite a good room, recently rented in one of the city's best apartment blocks. It had been built for engineers and technical personnel, a new three-storey brick building. The flat had all modern conveniences, but the bath-tub was covered with a sheet: the inhabitants were not allowed to use it.

The other tenant was a young man. His main occupation was billiards. They nicknamed him "The Actor". The Mandelstams suspected that he had been put there to keep a watch on them. (And I had so thoroughly concealed in Moscow that I was going to Voronezh.) On the second day of the holiday, he returned home totally drunk. Nadya bustled around him and, after pulling off his boots, finally got him to bed. "There's something down-to-earth and unladylike about her," Khardjiev once remarked approvingly, when speaking of Nadya.

The streets of the city were crammed with people out celebrating. There was not a single educated face in sight.

The following day, Mandelstam felt unwell. I went with him to see the doctor on duty at the regional Party committee polyclinic. It was in the bright, semi-basement premises of another new building.

The doctor listened coldly and attentively to what he had to say. His upper lip trembling, Mandelstam described at length and in pseudo-scientific terms the nature of his affliction. The word "aorta" played a great role in this monologue ("The aortas swell up with blood", *Unknown Soldier*).

At the Mandelstams', I also became acquainted with Sergei Rudakov. His wife Lina Finkelstein had come from Leningrad to visit him during the holiday.

Mandelstam was in a very unsettled state. He was impatient to go somewhere . . . anywhere . . . Later, reading the poem that ends "When the burden of evenings lay down on hard beds . . ." I would always remember that day in Voronezh. How well that's expressed! The personification of exile.

Suddenly, two youths, about 20 or 22 years old, flew into the room. The father of one was director of the co-operative – i.e. in plain terms a grocery store. He had an official car. The boys were going out to admire the banners, red flags and illuminations, and they invited Mandelstam to come with them. He was very eager. He consulted Nadya, but the answer was clear from the outset: he would go.

He came back from his outing in a state of joyful excitement. The boys (there were now four of them) pulled out a bottle of wine. They asked Mandelstam to read something and leaped up in rapture when, with unrestrained fervour, he recited "Cherry brandy":[50] "Let me tell you in all frankness: / It's mere raving – cherry brandy! – angel mine."

The third day of my stay in Voronezh. Tomorrow morning I would leave. Mandelstam began talking to me very firmly. Since I did not wish to stay longer, I was obliged to do what Nadya would have done in Moscow had I taken her place. I must go to the Central Committee and tell them: Mandelstam was wasting away in Voronezh, he was not being given any work, he was dying of hunger. The last presented difficulties: during the holidays Mandelstam had enjoyed both chicken and condensed milk.[51] So I could not rely on my own emotions here. But that was not the problem. How could I go to the Central Committee and make demands if I was incapable of dealing with the head of our department? I resisted stubbornly. This had no effect. Finally, I told him what I should have said to begun with: "Whoever is going to let me in to see the Central Committee?"

"Don't worry," Mandelstam replied grandly. "If you simply say that you have come from the poet Mandelstam, they will immediately want to listen to you."

"Perhaps, but not where they issue passes [into the building]."

"Very well," Mandelstam conceded graciously, "then go and see Stavsky."

He began to instruct me how I should talk to the general secretary of the Union of Soviet Writers. It was a quite hopeless undertaking, because I would not gain admittance to see Stavsky, and even had I got into the *Novy mir* offices, where he was chief editor, I would have blenched at his first hostile reply: his reactions certainly would have been unfriendly. I rejected this plan too.

"Perhaps you're just afraid?" asked Mandelstam provocatively.

"It can't be excluded," I replied calmly, but already with restrained fury.

"Aha!" Osip shouted boastfully, looking round at Nadya.

---

[50] For the full text see "Five Poems by Osip Mandelstam", p. 89.
[51] At the time neither cheap nor easily obtained under the Soviet system of rationing and shortages.

She was standing a little way off, in a beret and short leather coat, manuscripts of worker-correspondents and novice writers in her hands (the editors of the local Kommuna publishers gave her them to read). Nadya was listening closely to our conversation.

"Aha," Osip cried, looking straight at Nadya. "You'll write memoirs after I'm dead, but you don't care about the living poet?"

I could feel myself growing pale with rage. Today, forty years later, I am writing memoirs, but at the time I had no idea of doing such a thing. Close personal ties then bound me to the Mandelstams, not my historical and literary interests.

As the blood drained from my face, something like fear was reflected in Osip's eyes.

"Nadenka, let's leave it," he said. "I know Emma's face. She is now inexorable."

Nadya hurled the folder of manuscripts aside and they spilled out, fanning across the floor.

"It's a crime against the State to keep you here!" she cried. "I can't be bothered with such nonsense . . ."

She shook her fists in the air and her coat flew open.

"Nadenka, that's enough," said Osip imperiously. "I need to talk to Emma."

We remained alone together. As usual, after his outburst Mandelstam became calm and affectionate. He sat next to me: "I'm fond of you . . . naturally our conversation was emotional."

All this meant was that Nadya was desperate to go to Moscow and needed a replacement. Now he could not stay behind with just anyone – he must have a close acquaintance. (Rudakov was a man, after all, which was not the same, and during this period their relations were somewhat strained.) He had no desire to consider the political implications or my position. It was then that I finally brought up his behaviour under interrogation. I had never once permitted myself to do so when I met Nadya in Moscow. Faced by the Mandelstams' ever-mounting demands, however, I decided at last to speak out. Confidence in a friend has to be mutual, when all is said and done. Mandelstam began explaining to me: "You yourself understand that I could not name anyone else. Not Akhmatova surely, nor Pasternak? Kuzin was out of the question, as you well know . . ." (He was alluding to Kuzin's recent arrest and the watch now being kept on him.) "As to Lyova, well . . ." he said meaningfully, playing on my special feeling for Lev Gumilyov.

It's quite sad to learn that you have been selected in advance as a sacrifice to save others. I did not say so, but Mandelstam sensed the awkwardness. To smooth things over, he cited the investigator who had called me

"a thoroughly Soviet person".
This was neither here nor there.
As I already knew, very soon
nothing survived of Mandelstam's original intentions,
unquestionably approved by
Nadya. Both Pasternak and
Akhmatova ended up on the list
of people to whom he had read
the Stalin poem.

He began telling me how
scared he had been at the
Lubyanka. I recall only one
episode that Osip confided to
me with astonishing frankness:
"I was being taken somewhere
in the inner lift. Several people
were standing around. I fell to
the floor. I was thrashing about
when suddenly, above me, I
heard a voice: "Mandelstam,

Mandelstam, Voronezh

Mandelstam, aren't you asham-
ed of yourself?" I raised my head. It was Pavlenko."

What could I say to that?

In the end, we decided that I would track down Lilya Popova in
Moscow and give her a note from Mandelstam.

The train was due to leave early in the morning. The Rudakovs knocked
softly at the door; Lina was also returning home to Leningrad. We set
off for the station. The Mandelstams did not see me off or say goodbye; they did not wake or get up.

This gave me every right, I thought, not to carry out Mandelstam's
commissions. He did not dare post the letter to Lilya, however, and I
could not refuse to pass on a message from an exile.

Popova lived in what was then considered the distant outskirts of
Moscow, beyond the Savyolovsky railway station. Much earlier I had heard,
from Nadya herself, how Lilya and Tsvetayev were living in a room big
enough to hold their grand piano but nothing else. All day long she
would lie thinking on top of the piano as she prepared her next production. She remained director and literary adviser of Yakhontov's theatre.

The picture that met my eyes was quite different. A neighbour let me
in. She told me that Lilya had gone to see her husband in the camps.

He had already been imprisoned for some time. The woman was evidently very kind-hearted and helped Lilya. She told how the two of them put together parcels for Tsvetayev. She then carried them to various small towns where she posted them. And what wonderful mittens she had knitted for Lilya to take to him. She touched on the other concerns that beset a woman with a husband in the camps.

We immediately felt we could trust one another. Still, given the circumstances, I could not bring myself to leave her the letter that the exiled Mandelstam had sent for the absent Lilya. Returning home, I burned the note. Before doing so, I glanced at its contents. In his elegant, flowing hand, Mandelstam had written: ". . . Lilya, if you are capable of the unexpected, you will come . . ."

Mandelstam's term of exile ended in May 1937. They returned to Moscow and I visited frequently. Once again I would remain on my own with Mandelstam.

Several people immediately came to see him at Nashchokin Street. Once the bell rang, I opened the door, and there stood my former schoolfriend Ilya Feinberg. He was now a professional writer and the author of *1914*, a documentary account of the imperialist war. His greatest interest, though, was Pushkin, and after the Great Patriotic War [1941–5] he became a leading Soviet Pushkin specialist. He found Mandelstam lying in bed. Nevertheless he joyfully greeted the "returnee" and started to talk to him about Tynyanov's *Pushkin*. Mandelstam had read the first parts of this novel in Voronezh and enchanted Feinberg with his inimitable opinions of Tynyanov's unfinished work. Nadezhda, fearing that Mandelstam would become overexcited, took his pulse; Ilya and I withdrew to the other room and went on talking about our former schoolmates.

During one of those first days, Mandelstam stood looking out of the window next to the divan. He had intended to go to bed, but instead began talking about Moscow. The city disturbed him. There was something here he did not recognise. He did not speak of departed and now dead friends. No-one then did. For everyone these losses sank to the depths of their soul and a mysterious radiance mounted from within and permeated all their deeds, words and laughter . . . Anything but tears! Such was the character of those years.

Mandelstam began to speak of the people he had seen in Moscow. It was a brilliant improvisation. I recall: ". . . and enigmatic Khardjiev with his large head . . ."

Calm again, Mandelstam pensively began: ". . . And the people have changed . . . They are all somehow" – he moved his lips, searching for a definition – "They are all somehow, somehow . . . DESECRATED."

There was an infinite sadness to his words; he spoke from the depths
of his heart.

Akhmatova arrived. She stayed with Sofia Tolstaya-Yesenina in one of
the back streets near Prechistenka or Ostozhenka.

I walked her home from the Mandelstams'. We reached the flat and
remained alone in the room set aside for Akhmatova. She lay down on
the divan and then herself suggested (for the first time since we had become
acquainted) that she write out some of her poems for me: "Well, which
would you like?" I asked for "The Muse", "If the moonlight terror over-
flows" and "I hid my heart from you". Tearing the centre page from a
notebook, she wrote each poem in pencil on a separate side of the sheet,
adding: "Copied 10 June 1937, Moscow". "And on the fourth side", she
proposed, "I shall write . . . this for you." It was "The Incantation" ("By
the untravelled path, / Through the unmown meadow, / Across the
cordon of night"). I did not know the poem. She dated it "15 April 1936"
and explained: "The 50th birthday of Gumilyov."

When I returned to the Mandelstams they asked one question after
another. I showed them Akhmatova's autographs. "Couldn't you ask for
new poems?" said Nadya with contempt. "Everyone knows those."
Mandelstam objected: "No, 'The Incantation' is new." "Yes, but . . ."
and Nadya said something disparaging. Mandelstam would not agree.
That's it, I've now remembered how to define his intonation on such
occasions: he spoke with respect, solemnly confirming his words with a
gentle nodding of the head.

He was in his pyjamas on the divan; Nadya was on her way out. The
two of us remained behind.

He was radiantly happy and read *Verses on the Unknown Soldier*
from beginning to end. Then he asked me to write it down from his
dictation: "No need to punctuate: everything will find its rightful
place."

He sat in his favourite pose, cross-legged on the divan, and dictated.
The second section began: "Cold, feeble folk shall murder, freeze and
starve." The entire order of the sections was quite different from that
accepted today. The lines about Leipzig and Waterloo were completely
absent. Evidently, Mandelstam considered that they overburdened the poem.

When he reached the line "Ash-tree clarity, sycamore vision", he interrupted himself: "Mm, how fine that is!"

> Ash-tree clarity sycamore vision
> Slightly blushing rush back to their home

> As if casting spells with fits of fainting
> On both heavens with their fading fire

"What flight, what movement . . ."

Still sitting cross-legged, he bounced on the spring mattress and repeated, screwing up his eyes in pleasure, "an ash-tree clarity, sycamore vision". It was a bravura ending, theatrical and firm, and he looked me straight in the eye:[52]

> And squashing the worn-out year of my birth
> In my fist with the crowd and the herd
> I whisper through bloodless lips:
> "I was born on the night of the second and the third
> Of January in the eighteen ninety-first
> Untrustworthy year, and the centuries
> Surround me with fire."

He knew how to bring the recital of his poems to an effective climax.

Then he asked me to read the entire text aloud. "You read well," he said, "and I'd like to remember the way you make it sound.

"This will be the final version," he decided. And signing it "O.M. May 1937" he handed the text to me.

Alas. The authorised version of *Verses on the Unknown Soldier* was lost during the war, and with it went my copy of Blok's *Retribution* with Mandelstam's marginal notes and *On Poetry*, the collection of his articles. They were all borrowed by Sergei Rudakov, but in August 1943 he was arrested. There was no-one to ask where they'd gone.

And another similar evening.

Mandelstam once again lay on the divan, but his gaze was empty and motionless. I sat opposite, and we barely conversed. Finally, he announced: "You know what? Someone sent me a new Italian book about architecture. But, of course, Italy is Fascist . . ." Restlessly, he turned something over in his mind.

"Really, I ought to go to the GPU and report this. Why are you looking at me like that?"

His eyes were quite glassy, just as on his return from Cherdyn.

"But wouldn't you go to the GPU if, for instance, you learned of a political plot against our country? Or a military secret of the Fascists

---

[52] One of Mandelstam's longest poems, begun in Voronezh in spring 1937. (Translation: Meares).

which threatened our State? Of course, you'd go. Yes, yes . . . You could go right now . . .

"Yes! You're the one who should go to the GPU. You will say: 'They are sending literature from Fascist Italy to the poet Mandelstam. He does not know who is foisting these books on him. It is an act of provocation. Measures must be taken to shield a Soviet poet from . . .'"

And so on and so forth. I listened to him with embarrassment. Fortunately, at this moment Nadya returned. Rushing to catch the last tram, I left without a word to her about this conversation.

I felt very disturbed. Mandelstam appointed me to preserve the secret of his anti-Stalin poem, and now he was sending me to report to the GPU. But that was not the worst: it was painful looking at someone who had been so severely traumatised.

The next morning I woke with a heavy heart. What was that horror the evening before? I had hardly opened my eyes before the phone rang. Either Nadya or Zhenya, which I do not remember, urgently summoned me to the Mandelstams'. I decided that Osip had gone to the GPU and that something terrible had happened. Yet when I rushed into the flat on Nashchokin Street, I was greeted by an incomprehensible scene.

Mandelstam was sitting on a chair in a suit, wearing a tie and boots, and Nadya was not around. With a negligent smile he turned to me and said ingratiatingly: "Do you know, it seems that I do not have the right to live in Moscow. We knew nothing of this. In Voronezh when I was given back my passport they did not say a word about any 'minuses' [towns where he was prohibited to reside]. This morning, a policeman came by and demanded that I leave Moscow within 24 hours.

"Nadya has gone into town . . . to kick up a fuss, and to collect money . . . Meanwhile you and I shall do the following. We'll go out on to the staircase, and I shall have a fit. You start screaming. Then run out into the street, stand outside our entrance, and gather a crowd: 'It's a disgrace! They're throwing a poet out of his flat! A sick poet is being banished from Moscow!' Meanwhile I shall be there in the entrance, thrashing about. By that time Nadya will come back . . .

"Well, let's go."

I froze on the spot.

"I can't do it," I muttered.

He tried insistently to change my mind.

"But why ever not?" Osip began to grow cross. "Simulation is the most well-tried form of political struggle. Now, do come along . . ."

"No."

"You stupid woman!" Osip yelled and began to drag me by the hand. "Let's go! I'll show everyone what real political faking means. I'll show them!"

At this moment Nadya raced in. Her entire appearance expressed a single threatening query.

"Nadenka, she won't do it."

Nadya cast a disapproving look at me.

The subsequent conversation was rapid, sharp, indescribable and immediately forgotten. I left. What happened further that day, I do not know.

Within the space of 24 hours, Mandelstam had demanded that I report to the GPU and join in his "political struggle" with that same organisation. I wanted no further part of this game. It had become too evident that the Mandelstams needed me not as a friend, a companion or an admirer of his work but as a servant with no life or personality of her own.

Soon I learned that they had decided on a course of action that few at that frightful time had the nerve to risk. It was based on Mandelstam's profound belief in the power of his talent, the strong-willed obstinacy of his wife and their passionate desire to remain in Moscow.

Probably it would have been more sensible to get Mandelstam away, somewhere beyond the 105-kilometre zone [surrounding the capital], or to Stary Krym where Nina Grin continued to live. Whether he would have met or escaped the same fate there, we cannot say. It was madness, however, for anyone to hang around Moscow and Leningrad in 1937 without the right to reside in either city, and to hover persistently before the eyes of blood-crazed officials or mortally frightened writers and editors. For the sick Mandelstam it was triply insane. Yet Nadya could not withstand Mandelstam's elemental craving to live and work freely and openly and Nadya's gambling instinct constantly incited Osip to keep trying.

Everywhere Osip gave inspired readings of his "Ode" to Stalin, hoping it would find favour with "higher authority". But the poem only made a good impression, it seems, on Lilya Popova. She tried persuading Mandelstam to write a penitent letter to Stalin, and herself threatened to send such a letter to the Leader, if the poet would not. "And you know, she's capable of it, she's that kind of person," Yevgeny would say to me, in horrified anxiety. Rightly he feared that it would invite catastrophe to mention the author of the shocking epigram while the convulsion of arrests and executions continued.

Mandelstam's triumphal Bolshevik poem was not at all to the taste of the current leaders of literary fashion, but he did not realise it. "What is he up to? They've no use for him whatsoever," lamented my friend. "And his surname won't impress them much either." In strictest confidentiality, he revealed that at *Novy mir* they had suggested to a famous Soviet writer that he change his Jewish surname for a Russian pseudonym.

Still, it was very hard to resist Mandelstam's impassioned determination. This was also apparent in casual domestic episodes. Mandelstam forced Yevgeny's mother-in-law, he told me, to interrupt her singing lessons ("she deserted her little singers!") in order to ask some barely acquainted tenants on the next floor if Mandelstam might use their telephone. He was thrown into such despair on discovering that the Khazins' phone was out of order that strict Melita Abramovna was obliged to betray all her principles. Returning to their room, however, she murmured: "The man's insane."

My friend Lena described how the Mandelstams came to lunch and the anxiety they brought with them. But their hosts quickly adapted. Mandelstam held interesting conversations about literature, and Osmyorkin was proud to support a persecuted poet. He made several pencil portraits. One of these sketches as they sat at table I liked very much; it wonderfully caught the likeness of Mandelstam.

Sometimes the Mandelstams appeared to forget their woes and consciously resolved to enjoy themselves. Once they came to visit me with Natalya Shtempel, who had arrived from Voronezh, and the four of us drank wine together. They came to see me only during the day. I could not allow them to spend the night illegally in my father's apartment.

Nadya said that the Shklovskys' maid had been so well drilled that as soon as the Mandelstams appeared, she immediately fed them, even if their hosts were not at home. At first they also frequently spent the night there, but Vasilisa peeked from behind the curtain and saw (or perhaps she imagined) that someone outside was watching them. Then the Mandelstams began to sleep at Maria's Grove [a district] in north Moscow, supposedly in the room of Shklovsky's older sister-in-law, who was formally registered there, but in fact at Nikolai Khardjiev's. The windows of her ground-floor room looked out on to the street, and it filled the Mandelstams with dread. They moved into Khardjiev's nine square metres of living space, and he surrendered the divan, sleeping instead on the camp bed.

I was walking along a deserted Alexandrovsky Street on my way to see Khardjiev. It was already dark, the pavements were covered in slush, and I kept to the middle of the road. Coming towards me I saw Mandelstam, in a short black fur coat, stamping through the mud with his head held high; next to him trudged a downcast Nadya. I called out and nodded to them, but Nadya gave a vague stare and Osip murmured, without turning his head and barely moving his lips: "We don't know you, we don't know you."

That's a bit much, I thought to myself. Another one of Nadya's tricks.

When I reached Khardjiev, however, all was made clear. He opened the door with a sombre expression. "They brought some nark with them," he announced. The Mandelstams had called without warning. Soon they noticed a shadow outside the low window, which looked out on the inner courtyard. Someone insolently looked through the glass into the room. Khardjiev quickly threw open the window, and a man moved away unhurriedly and concealed himself round the corner. The Mandelstams sat for a while, could stand it no longer and left.

I told Khardjiev how I had met them. We understood the reason for their strange behaviour: they had wanted to protect me from observation.

That was the last time I saw Mandelstam.

And that is the way I remember him now. Head held high, a short black dog jacket pulled up around his ears, a matt face and a tenacious, sideways gaze in the semi-darkness of the street lights.

Where were they going that evening? I don't know. On several occasions they again spent the night at Maria's Grove and it was from Khardjiev's room that, encouraged and satisfied, they set out in spring 1938 for the sanatorium at Samatikha. Mandelstam did not return. As we know, he was arrested there on 3 May and taken to Butyrki prison. In September, they sent him to the transit camp near Vladivostok. It is impossible to describe that period.

In January 1939, I returned from Leningrad to Moscow. Little time had passed, yet how drastically everything had changed. In Leningrad it was as though I had spent three weeks in a burned-out ruin. During the autumn of 1938, Akhmatova separated from Punin. He had a new companion. Lyova had been arrested, and his terrible case was still dragging on. Akhmatova moved into a different room in Punin's apartment. I lodged in Osmyorkin's studio at the Academy of Arts, but not many of his friends now remained in Leningrad. These misfortunes cast a shadow over those once-cheerful quarters.

I had gone to Leningrad to give a lecture on the "Circle of Sixteen" at Pushkin House. The study of Lermontov changed the course of my life. To begin with, it was indirectly linked with the Mandelstams. In January 1936, Boris Eichenbaum stayed in Moscow at their apartment on Nashchokin Street. With him was Morgulis. He introduced me to

Eichenbaum and everything started from there. The invitation to Pushkin
House was, in fact, a great achievement. It came against a background
of universal grief, but there was no contradiction in that. All my work
was animated by a sense of inner resistance.

In Leningrad I visited Akhmatova in her new and unfamiliar room.
The bottom drawer in the cupboard would not close: the rusks she was
collecting for Lyova got in the way. On the floor lay a bag for provi-
sions. I would go and buy tinned food to take to him in prison, and
ran errands for Akhmatova. It was cold at Osmyorkin's studio.

Tension induced by success and heartache, the Leningrad climate and
the constant rushing about made me ill, and I left the city with a high
temperature. I found myself in a carriage with workers from the Kharkov
tractor plant, returning home from an excursion. They all sang Revolutionary
songs. Mine was the top bunk and I had to jump to get on it. My head
was spinning, and I could not clamber up. I asked someone to change
places. Not one of those cheerful lads would agree. All night as everyone
snored I stood out in the passage. Someone took pity and said I could sit
by his feet on the lower bunk. Feeling thoroughly humiliated, I accepted.

In Moscow, my one desire was to get to bed as quickly as possible.
As I opened the door into our apartment, the telephone rang in the
corridor. "It's probably for you," Mama said. "Nikolai Ivanovich
[Khardjiev] has been ringing for the last three days. He's already rung
again today."

Yes, it was Khardjiev.

"Come here without delay."

"I'm thoroughly unwell. I've only just got home."

"You must come."

"I can't."

"Emma, you must come. It's essential."

I went.

On the divan lay Nadya.

The parcel had been returned. Mandelstam was dead.

We sat the whole day together. Nadya sometimes stood up, sat down
on the bed and said something. She talked about Fadeyev. He had broken
into tears on learning of Mandelstam's death: "A great poet has died."
Nadya gave a bitter smile: "They didn't protect him, and now they're
exaggerating. Osya wasn't a great poet."

Khardjiev went out to find me a taxi. The poet Petnikov stayed behind
with Nadya. He lived in the south and had arrived in Moscow that day,
intending to stay with Khardjiev. But he found Nadya there with her
devastating news.

Once home, I collapsed. I was in bed for three weeks. What was happening to them, I wondered?

I sent two reports of Mandelstam's death to Leningrad. Picturesquely describing my return by train to the Rudakovs, I added, as an aside: "Nadya is now a widow." Sergei guessed immediately and told his wife: "Mandelstam is dead." She simply could not believe I might insert such terrible news in that cheerful letter.

To Akhmatova I wrote: "My friend Lena has had a daughter and friend Nadya has become a widow."

Nadya left to stay with Galina von Meck in Maly Yaroslavets.

In the early spring, I went to the Great Hall of the Conservatory, hoping to attend a concert by a foreign musician who was touring the Soviet Union. It was sold out. I stood by the entrance in the hope of buying a spare ticket. In that festively excited crowd, I unexpectedly caught sight of Nadya. She was standing in a beret and short leather coat, barely recalling her former self. She had not lost weight. But it was as if she had dried up and then hardened in that state. The skin stretched tight across her face. She spoke in monosyllabic, ungrammatical phrases. The foreign virtuoso did not interest her. She wanted to listen to the music "that Osya loved": his favourite pieces were announced on the poster. I went home so as not to compete for a ticket with Nadya. I sensed that if she stood there alone, people would not pass her by. The dry brilliance of her eyes was unbearable.

Written late 1970s–early 1980s. First published in *Novoye o Mandelshtame* (Paris, 1986).

Five Poems by Osip Mandelstam

Osip Mandelstam, 1913
(Yelisaveta Kruglikova)

Tennis

Among rough garish dachas
A hurdy-gurdy roams.
A ball soars on its own,
Magic bait.

Brute force subdued,
Clad in alpine snow,
What Olympian duels
With that quick-limbed girl?

Lyre strings ring too feeble.
A gold racket's stronger cords,
Were braced and cast to the world
By the youthful Englishman:

Weaving the ritual of the game,
So lightly armed
As if some warrior Greek,
Enamoured of his foe!

May. Thunder cloud in tufts.
Withered grass and leaves.
Engines and horns all round –
The lilac's petrol-scented.

The cheerful sportsman swallows
Spring water from the ladle;
Again the war resumes,
With a flashing naked elbow.

1913

Published in Stone, *1913. [tr.]*

Cherry Brandy

"ma voix aigre et fausse . . ."
(Verlaine)

I'll tell you bluntly one last time:
It's only maddening cherry brandy, Angel mine.

Where the Greeks saw just their raped Beauty's fame,
Through black holes at me there gaped Nought but shame.

But the Greeks hauled Helen home in their ships.
Here a smudge of salty foam Flecks my lips.

What rubs my lips and leaves no trace? – Vacancy.
What thrusts a V-sign in my face? – Vagrancy.

Quickly, wholly, or slowly as a snail, All the same,
Mary, Angel, drink your cocktail, Down your wine.

I'll tell you bluntly one last time:
It's only maddening cherry brandy, Angel mine.

2 March 1931

*Published New York, 1961; Tbilisi, 1967.Written during an informal
celebration at the Zoological Museum with Boris Kuzin and his colleagues.
Nadezhda said that "cherry brandy" meant "nonsense" in a long-standing
Mandelstam quip. [tr.]*

Lamarck

An old man, once, as shy as a boy,
A timid, clumsy patriarch . . .
Duelling for Nature's honour?
Fiery Lamarck, of course!

If everything living is only a brief mark
For a day time takes back,
I'll sit on the last step
Of Lamarck's mobile ladder.

I'll lower myself to snails and molluscs and crabs,
I'll rustle by lizards and snakes,
I'll go down those firm gangways, over wide ravines,
And shrink, and vanish like Proteus.

I'll wear a horny robe,
I'll say no to warm blood,
I'll be over-grown with suckers and I'll sting
Deep in the ocean's foam, like a tendril.

We passed the ranks of insects
With ripe liqueur-glass eyes.[1]
He said: "Nature is all ruptures,
Nothing can see – you're seeing for the last time."

He said: "Enough harmony –
You loved Mozart in vain:
A spider's deafness is setting in, and here
The trapdoor is stronger than we are."

And Nature stepped back away from us –
As if we were superfluous,
And the longitudinal brain she inserted
In the dark sheath was like a sword.

And she forgot the drawbridge,
It came down too late
For those with green graves,
Red breathing, and supple laughter . . .

May 1932

Published in Novy mir, *Moscow, June 1932. [tr.]*

"The Mandelstams' biologist friend Boris Kuzin, a neo-Lamarckian himself and opposed to Darwinian notions, was indignant about this poem. Mandelstam had interfered in matters that were not his concern or speciality," comments Mandelstam specialist Pavel Nerler.

"The literary specialist Yury Tynyanov, on the contrary, considered the poem to be a brilliant exposition: it was a prophecy, he believed, of how man ceased to be human. As Nadezhda Mandelstam recalled Tynyanov's argument: 'this was neither a rejection or ignoring of real life but the terrible degradation of living beings that had forgotten Mozart and rejected everything – mind, sight and hearing – in this kingdom of spider-like deafness. It was all horrifying, like the biological process running in reverse.'

"The poem also then caught the attention of many Russian émigrés; Nikolai Otsup interpreted it as 'a striving away from culture into proto-history'. An official Soviet reviewer, on the contrary, identified himself with the spider-like deafness 'That's us' and concluded:

'Do we need to be especially vigilant to recognise the usual hostile assertion, opposed to our reality, about Huns and destroyers of the subtlety of human emotions?'" (*Literaturnaya gazeta*, 23 April 1933).

Crimea

The spring is cold. Crimea, shy and hungry,
As under Wrangel, just as guilty,
Bundles on the ground, patches on tatters,
The vapour, just as sour and biting.
The hazy distance, just as handsome,
The trees, their buds beginning to swell,
Stand like strangers, and only pity
The Easter folly of almond blossom.
Nature does not recognise its own features.
And the terrible shades of Ukraine and Kuban –
On the felted land starving peasants
Stand at the gate, but do not touch the latch.

May 1933

Published Moscow, 1987. The poet knew the Crimea and the secluded resort of Koktebel before the Revolution. During the Civil War (1918–21) he found himself trapped there, as it was contested by Red and White forces, the latter led in their final retreat from Russia by General Wrangel. In late spring 1933 he and Nadezhda witnessed the consequences of collectivisation there. Some three million starved to death; many more had already been deported. In 1934 Mandelstam confirmed and counter-signed the text copied out by his interrogator at the Lubyanka.[tr.]

Mandelstam Street

What street is this?
It's Mandelstam's Street.
What the devil kind of name is that?
No matter which way you say it
It always comes out crooked not straight.

But little was straight about him,
His morals were not lily-white
And therefore this street
Or, rather, this pit
Bears the name of
That same Mandelstam.

April 1935

Published Tbilisi, 1967. This alludes to the second of the five addresses at which the Mandelstams lived in Voronezh: No. 4, 2nd Lineinaya Street, near the rail station. The ominous "pit" apparently refers to the location of the small, one-storey wooden house at the foot of a sloping narrow alley. [tr.]

MANDELSTAM IN VORONEZH
[1986]

I. The Missing Manuscripts

The only published references to this ill-fated history are in Nadezhda Mandelstam's *Hope against Hope* and her casual remarks in *Hope Abandoned*. These statements stand in need of serious correction. Frivolous and offhand, they confuse the sequence of events and thereby distort what happened. When Akhmatova, Nadezhda and Khardjiev were negotiating with Rudakov's widow, I often acted as go-between and after she died in 1977 I was given access to her archive. I thus feel duty-bound to make public all I know of the affair.

1

I became acquainted with the Rudakovs in 1936 in Voronezh. I had gone to visit the Mandelstams during the May holidays, and Sergei Rudakov and his wife, Lina, called to see them every day. The holiday over, Lina and I left in the same rail carriage: I went back to Moscow, she travelled on to Leningrad. That summer, Rudakov was allowed to return home from exile. Subsequently, whenever I visited Leningrad, or the two of them were passing through Moscow, we would meet.

I knew then that Rudakov, while in Voronezh, had worked on the commentary Mandelstam was composing to his published works. As I was aware, the poet also saw him as the future editor of his collected verse and so entrusted Rudakov with preliminary drafts and final hand-written versions of his poems. And after Akhmatova met Rudakov there through the Mandelstams in February 1936 and discovered that he was a passionate admirer of Nikolai Gumilyov, as well as a textual critic and poetry specialist, she handed him part of her Gumilyov archive to work on. Until the very outbreak of war, she often saw the Rudakovs in Leningrad. On 28 May 1940 she gave him her collection *From Six Books*, with the dedication "For Sergei Borisovich Rudakov, a keepsake. A. Akhmatova". Exactly when she handed him her Gumilyov archive I did not know. In 1974, Natalya Shtempel, the Mandelstams' Voronezh friend, told me she received a greetings telegram from Leningrad in 1937 signed: "Akhmatova, Mandelstam, Rudakov". Before the war, she recalled, she had several such telegrams in her keeping, sent from Leningrad during Mandelstam's last brief trips to the city. Both poets, in other words, had kept in touch with Rudakov.

The war caught Nadezhda in Kalinin. She and her mother moved there in 1939, after exchanging the Moscow apartment for a small house, jokingly referred to in her letters as the "palazzo". On trips to Moscow, she always saw Khardjiev and myself, several times staying the night at my apartment, and she corresponded with us both. When the invading Germans approached Kalinin, she and her mother were evacuated and transported to distant Kazakhstan. There she worked on a collective farm. With great difficulty Akhmatova managed to get them transferred to Tashkent. Nadya's brother Yevgeny had already been evacuated there. Staying in Moscow throughout the war, I began corresponding with them all.

In one letter, I informed them that a wounded and shellshocked Rudakov had appeared in Moscow. Nadezhda responded on 29 July 1942: "Warmest greetings to Sergei Borisovich. Hug him for me. I'm so glad he's alive. News reached us that this young and gifted literary specialist had perished and we'd mourned his loss. Most likely he'll take offence at being called 'young', but may he forgive us. I also imagine he was a brave and resolute warrior. Is he an officer or a private?" Nadezhda then turned to Mandelstam's manuscripts: "I took my belongings when we left Kalinin but had very little there. And in Leningrad all is lost, probably, and those are things I shall never see again." On 19 September she again mentioned Rudakov: "Give greetings to Sergei Borisovich. It would be so good to see him. Tell him my last letter from Natasha [Shtempel] was in February. I don't know how she is, and miss her very much." By March 1943 she was asking: "How is Sergei Borisovich? If he's in Moscow, give him my greetings." This was in a note added to a letter from Akhmatova. In turn, Akhmatova enquired about our common friends: "Where are Sergei Borisovich and the Osmyorkins?" That summer Nadezhda cautiously asked Khardjiev: "What have you heard about Sergei Borisovich? He hasn't gone back to the front, has he?" (Evidently, a justified concern for Rudakov could be detected in my letters.)

In May 1944, Nadezhda received my devastating news. Rudakov had been killed at the front. On 17 May, she wrote to me: "You realise what Sergei Borisovich's death means to me. It is one of the most terrible losses of these years. For God's sake, stop hiding everything from me. It's very wrong of you."

From Tashkent, Akhmatova and Nadya sent a telegram of condolences to Rudakov's widow in Sverdlovsk: "Lina Samuilovna, We shall never forget dear Sergei Borisovich. Nadezhda Mandelstam, Anna Akhmatova." It reached her on 7 May. Writing from Sverdlovsk on 3 June 1944, Lina told me that she had also received a letter from Nadezhda. Stunned by her loss, Lina described her feelings:

> More than anyone else, I'd like to talk with you about him. I'd also like to recite his poems to Akhmatova – "Annushka", as Seryozha called her. The dreadful thing is, I want to describe my anguish and torment to him. Sometimes I catch myself wildly imagining that I'll write to him as soon as I get home. And about the poems. I want to read them to Akhmatova. But I think that reading "Marina" to Annushka would be just a little awkward somehow. (Seryozha always said, half in jest, that Annushka was a little hurt that he was working on O[sip] E[milievich] and Nik[olai] Step[anovich] Gumilyov], but not her). And immediately comes the thought that I must write and ask him, whether to read her those poems.

Lina returned to Leningrad in autumn 1944. Who was dead or alive? Who was still at the same address, and who had been bombed out? Fortunately, she soon saw Akhmatova at a concert at the Philharmonic. During the interval, she went up to her and whispered, "Everything is safe and sound." Akhmatova told me this in spring of 1946, when, after a two-year interval, she again visited Moscow. But I already knew that the archive had survived. As soon as Lina was back, she wrote to me: "Everything is in order." This was not wholly unexpected. Before Rudakov's arrest in August 1943 – he was convicted of abusing his position to aid a friend (and died while serving in a punitive battalion) – he had received an official reply from the house management committee concerning the condition of his Leningrad room. When his sister Alla was being evacuated from the city, stated the reply, she had sealed the room and given the keys to the committee. All the furniture was either burned or sold, there remained only books and manuscripts. It was unclear whether the autograph manuscripts of Gumilyov and Mandelstam were among them. Now Lina confirmed that they were unscathed. Sergei Rudakov, however, was no longer there to celebrate the fact.

Akhmatova and Lina met at the Philharmonic in 1944. And they certainly saw one another again. This is confirmed by Akhmatova's hand-written copy of her poem, "In Memory of a Friend" which she gave to Lina with the dedication "For S.B.R. [Sergei Borisovich Rudakov]", dated 8 November 1945. (The poem was printed in 1946, without any dedication, in issue 1–2 of *Leningrad* magazine.) I am not aware in detail of what they then decided about the Gumilyov archive; all I know is that it remained, by mutual agreement, with Rudakov's widow.

In all of Stalin's reign, these years marked the peak of Akhmatova's public recognition. She was published continually by Leningrad and by Moscow literary magazines, and a new book of her poems was already being bound at the printers. Akhmatova was chosen to sit on the board of the Leningrad branch of the Writers' Union, and she attended offi-cial celebrations and sessions of the Union's poetry section. At home, where she lived with her son Lyova, who (after the camps) had come back from the war, there was no stopping the flood of new acquain-tances.

In these circumstances Lina felt inhibited and did not rush to see Akhmatova. On 2 March 1946, Lina wrote to me: ". . . I need you to be there. I have not visited A.A. Once my lecture's done I shall go immediately" (she was then preparing to speak at the pedagogical insti-tute about her work). 26 May 1946: "I have not visited Annushka." (Between ourselves we often called Akhmatova that, not in imitation of Rudakov's private language but to avoid the curiosity of the censors.) 19 July 1946: "Thank you for the information about A.A. I heard her read those poems on the radio. I'll go to see her in the nearest future."

But less than a month had passed when the decree concerning *Zvezda* and *Leningrad* magazines struck like a bombshell. Akhmatova's position changed drastically.

After the war, the house where she lived on Fontanka was handed over to the Arctic Institute. This enabled the secret police to keep a close eye on Akhmatova's visitors: all who approached the entrance booth into the grounds of the former Sheremetyev Palace had to show their passport. I do not know whether Lina visited Akhmatova during this tense period (for my part, I think it would have been unwise), but a year later, on 2 August 1947, she wrote: "I haven't seen Annushka, but I think that in the nearest future I shall pluck up the courage to go and visit her."

Only at the end of 1947 did I manage to get away to Leningrad, so constrained had I been by my own difficulties and uncertainties. For the first time I saw Akhmatova in her proud condition of disgrace. Until then, I had only sent her letters and greetings when someone else was going to Leningrad.

I stayed with Lina. In our free time we talked often and a great deal about Sergei, and also of the manuscripts she had cherished (or so we thought) as sacred relics. She did not show me Gumilyov's letters to Akhmatova or his other autograph texts and I felt no right to a glimpse of them. We did examine the Mandelstam autographs, however, and I held and sorted through the texts. Incidentally, Lina did not show me all of them. The suitcase with the manuscripts lay under her mother's bed, she told me, and she didn't want to open it in her presence. Her mother was a stranger, she complained; she didn't understand Lina's loyalty to her husband's memory, and begged her to sell off his library and archive. Privately, her mother wished her to remarry, but Lina repeated: "No better man than Seryozha existed on this earth, or ever shall."

When I visited Leningrad again, a year later, I found them in very straitened circumstances. Lina's subject, "psychotechniques", on which she intended to write her dissertation, had been abolished. She was forced to leave the research institute and take a poorly paid job at the local library, working from noon to 8.30 p.m. each day. Her mother received a tiny pension for her deceased husband (a doctor in Kiev). Their relations, on the other hand, were warmer: now they clung to one another.

These were the years from 1946 to 1949, it must be remembered, a shaky bridge between the calamities of wartime and a new wave of repression: second arrest and exile for many, reprisals against those captured by the Germans, and now unemployment for Jews as well. For unimportant figures like ourselves, such misfortunes seemed to mark an irresistible slide towards the abyss. So I felt a vague, not even conscious, sense of surprise when Lina told me that by lucky chance they were selling a karakul coat on instalments at some dressmakers' shop and she was buying it.

I recall two other episodes that have a bearing on the subject.

The first time I saw Akhmatova after the *Zvezda* decree, during my 1947 trip to Leningrad, we met only in some public place or when visiting her friends. She could invite no-one to Fontanka since Punin's eight-year-old granddaughter Anya Kaminskaya had scarlet fever and the apartment was quarantined. For this reason, Akhmatova told me, Lyova had even moved out for a while because he was now registered as a postgraduate student and attending the Oriental Studies institute. On most occasions, he and his mother came together when we met. Returning once to Rudakov's widow, with whom I was staying, Akhmatova accompanied me part of the way, and Lyova walked with us. As we approached Kolokolnaya Street, where Lina lived, he turned back abruptly and said: "I shall go no further. They should not see that I know this address" – i.e. the place where Gumilyov's manuscripts were being kept. Possibly this was merely a pretext; perhaps Lyova was in a hurry to go somewhere else. That is not the point. We were all convinced that the precious papers remained quite secure in Lina's hands. When I reached the apartment, I told her what had happened.

A year later, in autumn 1948, I again stayed with Lina in Leningrad. We all found ourselves in yet worse circumstances: Lyova had been excluded from his doctoral studies, Lina was working at the local library, I was trying unsuccessfully to get a job at Pushkin House in Leningrad, while Akhmatova was down to her last money, the advance she received in 1946 for the unpublished collection of her verse. My final evening I spent with Akhmatova and Lyova at the house on Fontanka. As Lyova escorted me to the train, we called at Kolokolnaya Street to pick up my case. We sat there for a while. When Lyova went out for a minute, Lina asked, apprehensive and suspicious: "Why did he come here? He didn't want to let on that we're acquainted before!" I thought then that she was frightened of Lyova. Living in Leningrad, she knew better than I that storm clouds were gathering over his head. Now I surmise that she had begun selling off the Gumilyov manuscripts (hence the new fur coat?) and imagined that Lyova knew.

I would not go to Leningrad again until 1955. Lina, however, usually spent her vacation near Moscow and would then visit the city. It was spring 1949 when we met and she astounded me with unexpected news. There had been a regrettable mistake: she did not have the Gumilyov archive, and had never had it. She explained this misunderstanding. The trunk containing the manuscripts stood in the corridor of their communal apartment, and the neighbour's children, in all probability, had used Gumilyov's manuscripts to make crackers. On returning from wartime evacuation, she had not sorted through Seryozha's surviving archive and had taken quite another envelope to be that containing the Gumilyov papers. Lina asked me to tell Akhmatova. It was a difficult mission, but my relations with Lina permitted me neither to refuse her request nor doubt the truth of her extraordinary revelation. And so I passed on this nonsense to Akhmatova! Today I have irrefutable proof that what Lina told me then was quite untrue. But I obtained the evidence only in 1973. In the 1940s and '50s things looked quite different.

Akhmatova received my information with considerable disbelief. She could not resist the suspicion that Lina had been selling Gumilyov's letters and manuscripts. "It's pure gold, don't you understand," she told me. She often recalled Lyova in this context. If he learned of the archive's disappearance, she worried, he might do something rash, and in his position, anything was risky. At other times, on the contrary, she would say with dreamy menace: "I'll turn Lyova loose on her, and he'll deal with her as he knows how," or yet more drastically, in their own private slang, "He'll make mincemeat of her."

I defended Lina. She probably did not feel strong enough, I suggested, to touch the dead Sergei's precious papers. I repeated her idiocies: "It was easy for her to make a mistake. She took another envelope for Gumilyov's letters to you." Akhmatova spoke quietly and sternly, fixing me with a steady glare: "She couldn't make a mistake! There were folders there!" She almost began to shout: "Folders!" and, choking with rage, incoherently: "Zoya . . . carried them . . . on a sledge." (It has not proved possible to identify which Zoya of her acquaintance Akhmatova had in mind.)

At one of my subsequent rare meetings with Lina, she cautiously asked: "Do you mean Akhmatova didn't believe me?" As gently as I could, I explained that it was indeed a very odd situation. For three years she had assured us that the Gumilyov archive was with her, safe and undamaged; now in the fourth year, this proved to have been a mistake. How could it have happened? Lina merely shrugged her shoulders.

Outwardly, our relations remained the same. I could not believe that she had deceived me or imagine that she could dishonour Sergei's memory in such a crude manner. Occasionally we exchanged letters. On 17 November 1951, for instance, she wrote: "When I was sick I re-read Sergei's letters, from Voronezh and the war years. How much I'd like to read some of them with you, especially the Voronezh letters. How much of objective interest and importance there is there." And 13 August 1952: "How's Annushka?" Then our correspondence ceased altogether. Meanwhile, vague rumours had began to reach Akhmatova: Gumilyov drafts from among those given to Rudakov were occasionally turning up in private hands or even at Pushkin House. This reassured her a little. Someone who had paid large sums for them, she believed, would not readily let go of the papers, and they would not disappear abroad, the thing she feared most of all. From November 1949 onwards, Lyova was again under arrest, and this banished all Akhmatova's other concerns.

A new incident forced me to think again.

At the end of September 1954, I received a postcard from Lina in Leningrad. She informed me – as she had not done for some while now – that she would be passing through Moscow shortly and asked me to stay home that day. At the appointed hour she appeared, and after we had greeted one another the following dialogue took place.

"You have no idea what's happened to me since we wrote?"

"How could I?"

"I was arrested."

"When?"

"In March 1953."

"After Stalin's death?!"

"Yes, two days after."

She had been picked up in connection with the "Jewish plot", she said, and held until the accused doctors had been cleared and rehabilitated.[1] She described various details of her imprisonment, and these did not prompt me to doubt their authenticity. She talked of the investigation ("they did not get as far as torture") and of how astonished she was when they called her out for interrogation and told her that she could go.

I was surprised that her Moscow acquaintance A.D.A. had not let me know at the time. But there then followed a statement that numbed all emotions. This was why Lina had come to see me: at the MGB[2] they had confiscated all the Mandelstam manuscripts, she declared. She began to describe in vivid and emotional detail how they had taken nothing during the search of her room apart from those manuscripts!

I was so appalled that she reproached me: "My arrest has made no impression on you. All you care about is the disappearance of the manuscripts." "But Lina, that was a year and a half ago. Here you are, alive and unharmed, while the Mandelstam manuscripts have gone." Recovering, I said, thinking aloud: "You know, you could still go to the MGB and officially request those papers. They sometimes return things." (Remember, this conversation was taking place in September 1954.) There followed an outburst that I could not withstand: "I wouldn't go there for anything! I'd like you to try. I don't want to draw attention to myself. With our dreadful neighbours. With my situation at work. Don't say a word to me about it. I walk five kilometres to avoid going near that building, I cannot bear to think –" and so on and so forth.

I enquired how Nadya had taken the news. Another surprise! Lina, it turned out, had still not informed her. Was she again hiding behind my back? Did she want me to perform that mission as well? Nothing of the kind. When we went to sleep – she lay down on the camp bed next to my bed, head to head – I spoke firmly into the darkness: "We must tell Nadya immediately." I heard something inconceivable in response, but

---

[1] The alleged "killers in white coats" were all Jewish medics.

[2] Post-war title of the State Security ministry.

forgot exactly what she said. Almost five years later, Akhmatova reminded me of her words: "Don't you remember how she told you, 'Don't poke your nose into other people's business'?!" I remembered; that indeed had been her final reply. I was then totally bemused: why had she come to see me? Evidently, she had not expected me to greet her "confession" with the sober proposal that she make a formal application to the MGB.

My conversation with Akhmatova took place in 1959, more than two years after Mandelstam had been officially rehabilitated. A collection of his verse was due to be published, and Nadezhda decided to make one last attempt to learn from Rudakov's widow what had become of the manuscripts. Until then, obviously, she had done nothing to contact Lina. In the 1950s, at least, when I advised Nadezhda herself to apply to the MGB, requesting release of the manuscripts confiscated from Lina Rudakova, she replied with indescribable venom: "Do you really imagine I gave Rudakov anything of value? They were nothing but copies . . . I've got them all . . . there might be a few drafts, perhaps . . ." I said not a word. If we had reached the stage of outright falsehood, there was no more point in discussion with Mandelstam's widow than with the widow of Rudakov.

The latter's mendacity was finally exposed when Akhmatova invited her to call. In Nadezhda's presence, Akhmatova began talking to her very politely and even presented her with the 1958 edition of her poems. The dedication dates the conversation precisely: "Lina Rudakova, with Akhmatova's greetings, 2 January 1959, Leningrad". As far as I recall, Akhmatova wanted simply to find out who had bought Gumilyov's letters and manuscripts and, perhaps, to buy them back, and to get more detailed information about the Mandelstam manuscripts. However, Lina had probably forgotten what she told me in 1954 and declared that her mother had tossed Mandelstam's manuscripts into the stove in a panic as soon as they had taken Lina away. For me this was the last straw. I was forced to agree with Akhmatova and Nadezhda that it was impossible to believe a word when there were such discrepancies. I could not, however, share their doubt that Lina had been arrested. (Running ahead, I may add that I later saw a certificate from the Regional MGB in her private archive, stating that she had been held in the remand prison from 10 March 1953 and was released on 15 April that year.)

We can now summarise the first part of the long history of the manuscripts entrusted to Sergei Rudakov.

For comparison, in *Hope against Hope* Nadezhda writes:

> The manuscripts remained with the widow and she did not
> give them back. In 1953 she met Akhmatova at a concert

and told her everything was safe; half a year later she informed Emma Gerstein that at the last moment she had been arrested and everything was confiscated.

Then the story changed, she was arrested and "mama had burned everything". What really happened could not be established. All we know is that she sold off some of the Gumilyov manuscripts through intermediaries, not making the sale herself.

Akhmatova was beside herself but there was nothing we could do. Once, on the pretext of publishing an article by her husband, we invited Rudakov's widow to visit Akhmatova but it was impossible to get any sense out of her.

Two different events have been conflated here. The indeterminate word "everything" is used to link the Gumilyov and Mandelstam manuscripts. It was 1949 when Lina told Akhmatova, with my help, that the Gumilyov manuscripts were missing; only in 1954 did she tell me of the "confiscation" of Mandelstam's manuscripts. It remains unclear why Nadezhda did not take back the Mandelstam manuscripts from Rudakov's widow after 1949, having learned of such a serious loss. It may be said that she was then living and working in the provinces and could not easily get in touch with Lina. That is true. But from 1946 onwards, she paid long visits to Moscow every summer and regularly travelled to Leningrad to see Akhmatova.

For a number of reasons, I saw Nadezhda in 1951 only in Moscow. She asked me for all the details of this history, and I described it exactly as I have done here, even including Akhmatova's exclamation about Zoya and the sledge. Nadezhda used the latter detail as she saw fit: in both her books, she states that Akhmatova took her Gumilyov archive to Rudakov on a sledge. This is utterly absurd. Anna Akhmatova was afraid of crossing the street and always attracted the attention of passers-by; and this was at a time when she was writing the poems that made up *Requiem* and *From Six Books*. Can one imagine Akhmatova dragging a sledge through Leningrad in the late 1930s, loaded with Gumilyov's letters and manuscripts? The strangest things happen when memoirists use the words of others to write their reminiscences. Nadezhda's own carelessness, on the other hand, for which there was no justification, is concealed in her narrative. To leave Mandelstam's manuscripts for an indefinite period with a woman whose reputation was already in doubt was unforgivable negligence. Instead of describing this, Nadezhda moves the Philharmonic encounter between Akhmatova and Rudakov's widow eight years forward. By implication,

Akhmatova took no interest in the letters and manuscripts of Gumilyov for a long period and remembered these precious relics only when she met Lina by chance at a concert.

What does it mean to say, "The manuscripts remained with the widow and she did not give them back"? To whom should she have returned them? No-one asked her for them! It is impossible seriously to refer this to a conversation 15 years after the death of Sergei Rudakov. The date, 2 January 1959, is shamefully concealed in Nadezhda's memoirs by the careless word "then" ("then the story changed"). This "then" came after Mandelstam's rehabilitation and the contract with the Poets' Library to publish his verse.

The saga was still far from finished. In her memoirs Nadezhda treats the next instalment with unexpected panache and an inappropriate levity: "Khardjiev did best out of it. He worked his way into her favours and she gave him Rudakov's letters and permission to copy all he needed. Khardjiev is a great flatterer, after all, a Circe; handsome and, when he wishes, a charming person."

It was not at all difficult, in fact, to make contact with Lina Rudakova. Before the war, she lived with Sergei in communal apartment No. 6, 11 Kolokolnaya Street, and would continue to live at the same address after the war and until her death on 19 December 1977. Naturally, Rudakov's widow could not show their entire correspondence to a stranger. Descriptions of his daily meetings with Mandelstam were there mixed with personal, private and household matters. Only she could separate the two, and she did so selectively, giving Khardjiev far from all the letters. Her selection was not successful. She particularly chose those texts in which Rudakov made rather strange claims against the poet, but she failed to notice the authorised copy of a quite unknown poem by Mandelstam and another of his poems with unknown variants.[3] When I read the letters in their entirety after Lina's death, I realised that by then she had a poor memory of what her own archive contained. In particular, she had forgotten Mandelstam's letters to Rudakov. As we shall see later, these throw light on the poet's attitude to his younger friend and differ markedly from Nadezhda's depiction of their relations.

Khardjiev "worked his way" into Lina's favours very simply. Remembering that there was a great deal of value concerning Mandelstam in the Voronezh correspondence, and lamenting the loss of the original poems, I recommended to Khardjiev that he take a look at these letters. For that purpose I went to Leningrad to see Lina in 1958 or 1959. She

---

[3] "Your slender shoulders shall redden with the lash": see "Nadezhda", p. 401.

met me with a guarded and gloomy air, and I was saddened to see the empty bookshelves: Rudakov's wonderful library had already been sold off. I urged her to show the editor of the Poets' Library volume as much of the surviving materials as she could. Rudakov's name would certainly be mentioned in the edition, I explained. The prospect stirred her interest ("Oh, in that case," she burst out) and led her to welcome Khardjiev. When he returned from Leningrad, however, and showed Akhmatova and Nadezhda excerpts from the letters, they were horrified, and Khardjiev himself was shaken, by Rudakov's tone and claims.

But here begins the second part of the Rudakov saga, which for many years entirely changed attitudes towards him.

2

In Akhmatova's unpublished memoirs we read:

> In Voronezh, Sergei Rudakov attached himself to Mandelstam and, regrettably, proved not at all the fine fellow we thought him. Evidently, he was suffering from a type of megalomania if he believed that he and not Osip was writing the poems. Rudakov was killed in the war, and I shall not go into the details of his behaviour in Voronezh. However, all that is connected with him should be treated with great caution.

These apprehensive lines are written in the plural – "we thought". In the hint of Rudakov's improper behaviour in Voronezh, a second voice is most distinctly audible. Akhmatova spent only six days in that city, and in all the succeeding years, as we have seen, her relations with Rudakov remained friendly. His letters from Voronezh? There he does indeed attribute himself a far too active role in Mandelstam's poetic work, which resumed before his very eyes, but nothing specific about "his behaviour" can be gleaned from what he wrote to Lina. In the rough draft of a separate note entitled "Rudakov", Akhmatova's hint is deciphered: her passionate rebuke concludes "meanwhile, Nadya divided all the food into three equal portions."

The claim that Rudakov sponged off the Mandelstams is graphically embroidered in *Hope against Hope*. "I could see that he frequently hindered M., and often I wanted to show him the door," writes Nadezhda. "M. did not allow me. 'What will he eat?' he would ask, and all continued as before." It is rather strange to hear the exile Mandelstam described as a well-off philanthropist. Perhaps he used to share his last scrap of stale bread with Rudakov? But no. Asserting that Rudakov "ate and drank" with them, Nadezhda declares: "For us this was a relatively comfortable period, with translation, theatre and radio work, and it cost us nothing to keep the poor boy." It was quite difficult for any Soviet family to "keep" a 26-year-old man, let alone an exiled poet with an unemployed wife, living in a strange town, and privately renting accommodation (i.e. paying three times the usual rate). This in itself makes one doubt the memoirist's veracity. However, we have more specific information. The details of Rudakov's domestic relations with

Nadezhda, early 1960s

Mandelstam, and the material conditions in which all three lived, are not neglected in his letters, which I later read from beginning to end. As I can testify, he made his contribution towards household expenses and shared responsibility for buying food and performing other domestic chores.

There are many further absurdities in the sketch of Rudakov that Nadezhda includes in her memoirs (see Chapter 57, "Archive and Voice", *Hope against Hope*). The entire tone of her description gives a wrong impression of Mandelstam's close companion, but before discussing that we must correct the factual errors. Nadezhda writes:

> Sergei Rudakov, the son of a general, was banished from Leningrad when members of the gentry were expelled from the city. His father and elder brothers were executed at the beginning of the Revolution. He was brought up by his sisters, and led the usual Soviet childhood of a Young Pioneer: he did well at school, even graduating from a higher-education institute, and was about to embark on a quite decent career when exile blighted his hopes. Like many children without parents then, he very much wanted to keep in step with the

times. He even had a distinctive literary theory: one must write only what would be published. He himself wrote refined and, for that time, fashionable verse that was not without the influence of Marina Tsvetayeva; he chose Voronezh in order to get closer to M.

Beyond the first sentence, the entire passage is riddled with mistakes and inaccuracies.

His father and older brother, the Rudakovs' fourth son, were not shot in the first years of the Revolution but in the early 1920s – i.e. at the beginning of NEP [the New Economic Policy]. During the First World War, General Rudakov served under Field Marshal Brusilov. In the Civil War, apparently, he fought with the White Army under Kolchak, but in 1920, like Brusilov, he decided to join the Red Army. According to those who knew the Rudakovs well, it was unhappy chance that father and son were executed. The incident occurred in Novonikolaevsk in either 1921 or 1922. A commission arrived and demanded that General Rudakov publicly confess and renounce his mistaken past. He refused, saying that he had served Russia faithfully all his life. In that case, said the commission, you face execution. They then asked the same of Igor, his son, who was still a military cadet in 1914 but had ended the war as a decorated St George cavalier. "My reply is the same as Papa's," he said. Both were shot.

As concerns Rudakov's three elder brothers, the oldest committed suicide in 1913 because he could not marry the woman he loved (she was Jewish), while the other two died fighting during the First World War. For some reason, Nadezhda says these young officers were "also generals". All I know is that when Sergei was sent to the front in 1941, his superiors wished him the good fortune of rising to his father's rank.

Rudakov's mother, Lyubov Sergeyevna (née Maximova), died in 1932 when Sergei was 23 years old. He always lived with her and her three younger daughters. His three older sisters were married and had families of their own; the younger three indeed surrounded Sergei with love and admiration, the only surviving brother of five and the youngest member of the family.

I do not know the grounds for Nadezhda's strange observation concerning the political attitudes of those orphaned in childhood. It is certainly debatable and, in any case, can have no relevance to Sergei. When he lost his mother, he was already an adult and, furthermore, married with a small daughter of his own. And Seryozha was at least twelve when his father died. I do not know how he studied at school, but am certain that his was not the childhood "of a Young Pioneer".

As an organisation the Young Pioneers came into existence only in 1922. By then Seryozha was 13 and his childhood was over; behind lay something oppressive, denoted in letters to Lina by the single word "Ufa".[4] Soon mother and children moved from the Volga region back to Petrograd;[5] at that time this was still possible, in spite of her husband's execution. To begin with, they lived with her sister and only later organised a separate household. Sergei's acquaintances of the time recall a most gloomy apartment crammed with portraits of Tsarist officers, his father and four elder brothers and the naval officers also among Rudakov's relations. You could not contemplate inviting schoolfriends into such a home. Not at all, in fact, the "usual Soviet childhood of a Young Pioneer".

Contrary to Nadezhda's assertion, Rudakov did not complete his studies. In 1928, he was accepted by the literary department of the Higher State Courses at the Art History Institute in Leningrad. He did not graduate, though, since the courses and the institute itself were both closed in 1930. This was a great blow for learning and the arts. The most outstanding figures in contemporary literary studies lectured and taught at the Institute: Tynyanov, Shklovsky, Eichenbaum, Tomashevsky and Engelgardt. Most of the students were transferred to other higher-education institutions, but Rudakov was left stranded because of his social origins. Tynyanov, it is true, had noticed the student at his seminar and invited him to help prepare an edition of the works of Kuchelbecker.[6] To earn his keep, however, Rudakov was forced to work part-time as a draughtsman. Soon he, his first wife and their child had to go south and stay with his mother-in-law in Kerch: his wife, another former student at the Institute and the daughter of a Jewish doctor, was not accepted by the family, and Rudakov's jealous mother and sisters gave her no help in raising their child. In Kerch, where Sergei earned a living from architectural drawing, he grew despondent and would travel back to Leningrad – to visit his sisters, work in the Public [today National] Library, go round all the second-hand book shops, talk to his friends about literature and, most important of all, see Tynyanov. He also saw his wife's friend Lina Finkelstein. They became intimate, and soon he left his first family and married Lina. They set up home, living separately from the Rudakovs.

He now had another attentive audience for his literary ideas, besides his adoring sisters. Lina was enthused by his loud declamation of his

---

[4] Capital of the Bashkir republic.

[5] The name given to St Petersburg in 1914 and retained until 1924.

[6] Vilgelm Kuchelbecker (1797–1849), poet and critic, lycée contemporary and friend of Pushkin; active in 1825 Decembrist uprising; imprisoned and exiled to Siberia.

favourite poets, and she admired the verse he wrote. She studied piano with the noted Maria Yudina and herself taught music to the daughters of Tynyanov, Kazansky and other academics. Yet she did not become a professional musician. Instead, she entered the university and by then, it seems, had already graduated.

Sergei, meanwhile, had no prospects of a literary career. He was acquainted with Gukovsky, who had just made an inspired rediscovery of eighteenth-century Russian literature, and he knew Tynyanov's secretary Stepanov and other representatives of the "Leningrad School", as they were called by hostile literary specialists in Moscow. His only hope, however, remained Tynyanov. Sergei longed to participate in the publications of the Poets' Library series: there he could have prepared texts and analysed poetry without fear of being labelled a "formalist". Just as unattainable for him was Pushkin House. No-one would offer Rudakov a researcher's job without a diploma and, with his unrealised gifts and evident potential as a competitor, no-one would give him a contract to work on the Poets' Library publications. The edition of Kuchelbecker's verse appeared in the small-format series only years later. By then back from Voronezh, Rudakov found an acknowledgement of the help Tynyanov had received from S.B. Rudakov . . . on page 284. It was the historic and terrible year of 1937. Rudakov had returned from exile, but he remained of gentry status and Tynyanov could do no more for him. In an earlier handwritten reference supporting Rudakov's efforts to return to Leningrad, Tynyanov gave a fuller account of his work:

> Sergei Rudakov is a talented literary specialist and textual critic. Under my direction, he helped prepare the collected works of Kuchelbecker for publication in the Poets' Library series. In assembling the printed texts and comparing them with manuscript versions, he exhibited not only exceptional thoroughness, ability and professionalism as a textual critic but also a genuine scholar's feeling for his material. These qualities lead me to believe that if S.B. Rudakov continues his work on the publication of the Russian classics he will undoubtedly become a valued researcher into Russian literary history.

The recommendation is dated 5 December 1935. Lina sent a copy to Voronezh and, of course, Rudakov did not fail to show it to the Mandelstams.

What did Nadezhda care for Tynyanov's opinion? Later, in *Hope Abandoned*, she would list him among those who "did not want to

think": "Shklovsky, Tynyanov, Eichenbaum, Gukovsky, the élite of literary studies in the 1920s – what could one talk about with them? They
merely rephrased what they had written in their books and did not react
to the spoken word." From her memoirs we learn that the names of
these scholars nevertheless impressed her. Tynyanov's opinion of
Rudakov, it is true, she assigns to another.

Apparently, Tynyanov's pupil was not Rudakov but another Voronezh
exile, Kaletsky. The substitution becomes apparent when Nadezhda
describes Rudakov's "vices": "He was, for instance, far too arrogant and
offensive towards another of our visitors, Kaletsky, who also came from
Leningrad and was a student of our acquaintances, Eichenbaum,
Tynyanov and others . . ." In fact, Kaletsky was a Muscovite and had
graduated from the Moscow Theatre Institute at which the Leningraders
Tynyanov and Eichenbaum never taught. Kaletsky moved to Leningrad
only after his time in Voronezh. A scene intended to demonstrate his
"inner strength" merely illustrates the author's inability to reproduce
human dialogue and the language of a particular era and milieu:

> The modest, retiring youth Kaletsky sometimes said things
> that others then did not have the courage to say aloud. Once
> with horror he told M.: "All the official bodies we know are
> useless and could not withstand the mildest test — Soviet
> bureaucratism is dead and decaying. But what if the army is
> in just the same condition? What if war suddenly breaks out!"
> Remembering what he had learnt at school, Rudakov
> declared: "I have faith in the Party." Kaletsky was embar-
> rassed and blushed. "I have faith in the People," he said
> quietly.

The scene is bogus from beginning to end. No-one ever talked that way
at home among the intelligentsia. I cannot speak for Kaletsky because I
did not know him, but at least three of those present would have begun
to argue immediately in a competitive display of eloquence and erudition. Incidentally, the bureaucracy was not stagnating at all; on the
contrary, it was going from strength to strength. Why should Kaletsky
have been worried about the condition of the Red Army if it was led
by such brilliant commanders as Blucher, Tukhachevsky, Yakir and
Primakov? No-one then doubted the war-readiness and fighting capacity of the strictly disciplined Red Army (as Mandelstam wrote in May
1935, "And I'd like to protect and preserve / this crazy calm in its long
army coat"). The contrast between Party and People is a complete
anachronism. Replaced for 15 years by "Class" or the "Masses", the term

'People'[7] had only just been rehabilitated. In everyday conversation the word was not yet current. Mandelstam was impulsive and detected the slightest insincerity; his wife was sharp-spoken and intolerant: could they have listened in silence to two wooden fools spouting such cheap claptrap?

By then Kaletsky was 29, a senior lecturer at the Voronezh teacher-training institute and a schoolteacher. He was actively involved with the local literary magazine *Podyom*, which published many of his articles and reviews. I do not know the circumstances under which he was banished to Voronezh, where he spent about two years. In a letter to Lina (14 April 1935), Rudakov mentioned meeting him at Mandelstam's and indicates that Kaletsky had already been there for a year and a half. The Mandelstams arrived in Voronezh in late June 1934 and, consequently, knew Kaletsky for many months before Rudakov appeared.

During the first part of his time in Voronezh, Mandelstam did not write poetry. He began again in April 1935, in other words when he spent almost the entire month alone with Rudakov. Of their contact, which coincided with (or prompted) the rebirth of Mandelstam as a poet, his widow writes (in *Hope against Hope*):

> Rudakov appeared when I was away, hanging about in Moscow and trying to have us transferred somewhere else. In my absence he spent almost a month with M. As we returned from the rail station, M. told me he had a new friend: not Boris Sergeyevich [Kuzin] but Sergei Borisovich, who intended to write a book about poetry and was altogether a fine lad. After his illness M. probably had little faith in his own capacity and lacked a friendly listener for the poems that had again appeared. But he was never able to work in a complete vacuum; I don't think anyone can.

Yet why the complete vacuum? Kaletsky, a language specialist and a well-disposed regular visitor, was there. For all his inner strength, however, his visits did not provide a creative stimulus. It was Rudakov with his "crazy talk", his "resounding nonsense" and his excessive self-regard who stimulated Mandelstam to start writing poetry again.

To Rudakov's many sins is further added an "original literary theory", supposedly his own invention, that "one must write only what will be

---

[7] The Russian term *narod* ("people", "nation") has much of the resonance of *Volk* in German.

published". It is hard to find much originality here. Akhmatova once told me of a young but already well-known literary specialist who was privately reproached for an article containing harsh and offensive remarks about the Acmeists: "I am a professional and have to be published," came the confident retort. He indeed published a great deal. Rudakov did not see one line in print. Before the battle in which he was killed, he left instructions for his wife with a fellow-soldier in the event of his death: she was to publish everything he had written. Lina never managed to get any of his works into print. Only in 1979 was I able to publish Rudakov's "The Rhythm and Style of the *Bronze Horseman*", a study which Tomashevsky had rated very highly as far back as 1941.

It is also odd to hear the poems Rudakov wrote, "not without the influence of Marina Tsvetayeva", being described as "the refined verse then in fashion". In the 1930s, refined verse was considered fatally outmoded. People imitated Mayakovsky, or covertly alluded to Yesenin, and more subtle poetry-lovers admired the "intimate" and "incomprehensible" Pasternak; the activists of the Komsomol were enthused by Bagritsky, Tikhonov, Aseyev, Selvinsky and Lugovskoi; still others wrote the names Bezymensky, Svetlov and Utkin on their banners. No-one knew Tsvetayeva. Her books were not sold in second-hand shops and were most certainly not reissued. What she published abroad as an émigrée did not reach the Soviet reader, and her poems were not quoted in our periodicals. Rudakov indeed loved Tsvetayeva and even had a handwritten copy of the "Poem of the End", but in this he was swimming against the current, part of an educated minority, one of a handful of connoisseurs of Russian poetry.

Another of Nadezhda Mandelstam's taunts cannot pass without comment, since it is highly anachronistic. In her fictional portrait she makes Rudakov express himself in the old, worn clichés used by the losers of the pre-Revolutionary years:

> Rudakov's other tiring characteristic was his constant moaning. In Russia, he considered, the environment "always devoured talented individuals" . . . M. could not stand such conversations: "Why don't you write now?" An argument would always flare up and Rudakov, after complaining about his conditions – his room, money, mood – would lose his temper, and leave, slamming the door. An hour or two later he returned as though nothing had happened.

Listing the "conditions" that prevented Rudakov doing the work he loved, Nadezhda omitted the most important of all: banishment from his native town. For this meant separation from his adored wife, obligatory visits to the NKVD,[8] getting a new [internal] passport every three months, unsuccessful attempts to find permanent work, and the commission to paint a brown boot for a cobbler's sign . . . This and similar jobs he would obtain, with humiliation and much bother, from another Leningrader who had found work with a co-operative. "In Voronezh Rudakov did not even try to get a job," Nadezhda claims. "He still hoped that his wife would get him released with the help of one of the leading generals who later perished in 1937." I know nothing of any "generals", but among writers the Rudakovs placed their hopes not so much on Tynyanov as on Babel. He was friendly with Lina's parents, and Rudakov saw him in Moscow on his way to Voronezh. In 1935, Babel regarded the mass exile from Leningrad as a temporary phenomenon; he assured Rudakov that his stay in Voronezh would last no more than two months.

Despite the hopes raised by Babel, Rudakov found a job at a design bureau. This was not without the help of Mandelstam, who was acquainted with a major Voronezh architect. In June 1935, however, Rudakov had already been sacked and could only take comfort from the same bureau's promises of contract work. He was forced to live on any temporary earnings that came his way, and on money sent by his wife. This deeply demoralised Rudakov.

One final correction. This refers to wartime. Earlier I quoted Nadezhda's letters from Tashkent: they show that she only received news about Rudakov from me. But her habit of writing memoirs from the words of others leads her to offer her own description of his life in Moscow[9] and of the circumstances under which Rudakov, invalided out, was then sent back to the front and died. In this slipshod tale all the facts are distorted: "After he was wounded Rudakov became a military commander in Moscow. One of his relatives came to see him and said, as a convinced Tolstoyan, that he could not fight. On his own authority, Rudakov released him from service but his deed was exposed: he was sent off to a punitive battalion and was killed immediately." Rudakov was not a military commander. He taught at the army training college. The "Tolstoyan" was no relative but an acquaintance, the husband of one of Lina's friends from her piano studies with Maria Yudina. Rudakov was billeted at the district military registration office. To aid the "Tolstoyan", he abused his access to the office forms and

---

[8] People's Commissariat for Internal Affairs, the Soviet security force or secret police (1934–43).
[9] See Appendix 2, "Mandelstam and Rudakov", p. 443.

stamp to postpone the man's military service. The latter had expected complete exemption, but was then called up unexpectedly. Rudakov took such a risky step, I should add, out of kindness, not out of respect for the man's principles. "X couldn't fight," he explained to me. "He was simply afraid, poor thing."

Rudakov was arrested, spent three months in Butyrki prison and was then condemned to ten years in the camps. The "Tolstoyan", as I remember, was given an eight-year sentence, which he spent restoring bombed buildings in Moscow and working on the Volga–Don canal; he survived for a good many years after his release. Rudakov himself asked to be sent back to the front from the camps and, as he expected, was assigned to a punitive battalion. In the very first engagement, on 15 January 1944, he was killed and "atoned with his blood for the crime". What a tragic family. All five brothers were shot and died before their time, while two sisters starved to death in the Leningrad Blockade.

Having depicted Rudakov as a sponger, time-server and careerist in *Hope against Hope*, Nadezhda was still not satisfied. Another anti-portrait of Rudakov, the most overstated caricature, can be found in her uninhibited second volume, *Hope Abandoned*:

> The sons of executed fathers convinced themselves and others of the delight and good sense of working to order. They demanded not just time-serving but an unconditional shift of allegiance to the victor . . . Such a one was the unfortunate Rudakov, the son of a general, who persuaded Mandelstam passionately that the time had come to use the language of the contemporary world. During the war he was very upset that he was a plain lieutenant and not a general, like his father and brothers, who had also died. This was his only grudge since he refused to think about anything . . .

It is hard to say which is more outrageous in these few lines: the personnel-questionnaire approach to people ("children of executed fathers") or her primitive interpretation of Rudakov's frustrated exclamation in Moscow. He was irritated that everyone congratulated him on his promotion to lieutenant. "I should have been a Rokossovsky!" he explained to me. Naturally, he was not referring to formal rank but to the talents of a military leader that he suspected in himself. I might note that he was a very brave soldier.

The most unpleasant aspect of Nadezhda Mandelstam's irresponsible gossip is her open settling of private scores by playing on the political preferences and aversions of her uninformed readers. They cry with one voice: How magnificently she has reflected the epoch in her books! Defamation, slander and demagogy indeed shaped that epoch. Nadezhda not only depicted the time in which she lived but also embodied its defects.

Why did Nadezhda need to destroy Rudakov? She herself said the reason lay in his letters to his wife from Voronezh. And she drew her own conclusions from these texts.

> As we read the letters we realised that the theft of the archives was no accident. It had been thought up by Rudakov, and his widow merely carried out his intentions. What we took to be a purely mercantile interest, to get a good price for the original poems, turned out to be the result of Rudakov's own febrile ideas. It is hard to say what would have happened if I had died. Possibly, Rudakov would have seen justice done and claimed the poems as his own. However, he would have had a hard time of it, since the majority of the poems were circulating in hand-written versions.[10]

We can only assume that Rudakov ordered his wife to "steal the archives" from the next world. For had this been the plan while he was still alive, Lina could easily have claimed, on returning from evacuation, that everything had been burned by those who remained trapped in Leningrad. No-one would have been the wiser. It is sheer fantasy to imagine that Rudakov intended to steal the Mandelstam archive. Unfortunately, Akhmatova also believed this nonsense. In her note "Rudakov" (which she herself never published), she writes brilliant but, alas, unjust lines about Rudakov's "theft": "The very idea that one could steal something from the impoverished, exiled and homeless Mandelstam! What a radiant and noble thought, how cautiously and elegantly it was executed and with what care for [Rudakov's] descendants and his own, evidently posthumous, glory."

Rudakov had many shortcomings. These are revealed in his letters and were subsequently augmented by the behaviour of his widow. But there are no grounds for accusing him of stealing the Mandelstam manuscripts. Unfortunately, Nadezhda and Akhmatova's combined efforts to crush Rudakov, once and for all, were crowned with success.

---

[10] E.G.: This sharply contradicts Nadezhda Mandelstam's insistent statements elsewhere that for between 15 and 18 years Mandelstam's poems were preserved in her memory alone.

They forgot, however, that
there was yet another participant in this drama. He also has
the right to be heard, and his
voice is of decisive importance.
Osip Mandelstam left sufficient
written testimony of his confidence in Rudakov and friendly
feeling towards him. He was
aware of the latter's grudges
and even his claims to "co-
authorship", but adopted an
extremely indulgent attitude to
these pretensions. With his
characteristic capacity for harsh
criticism, he managed to tell
Rudakov all he thought of his
poems. In psychological terms,
the encounter between the two
is a very interesting page in
Mandelstam's biography.

Sergei Rudakov, 1930s

3

In autumn 1973, the daughter of Lina Rudakova's Moscow friend,
A.D.A., rang me up: Lina was very ill, she informed me, and in a state
of great anxiety. Why, she was asking, had her instructions not been
carried out? The speaker was entrusted to pass on a package containing
manuscripts to me: "Gumilyov papers, you know, the ones that she has
been guarding all her life," the voice on the telephone casually explained.
Well! All comment is superfluous, as they say.

After much toing and froing – we could not agree a time or place –
I received a small despatch case containing nine letters from Gumilyov
(one to his mother), several not very important letters addressed to him,
manuscripts of his translations published by the World Literature publishers and notes for lectures on poetic theory. To these were attached several
unimportant materials from Luknitsky's collection. What part of the
original contents of the archive I had been given was impossible for me
to establish. Gumilyov's letters to Akhmatova preserve traces of her work:
in her own hand she had added dates, notes and numeration. Once again
I was obliged to act as a go-between and handed this small collection

to its rightful owner, Lev Gumilyov. He passed it to Pushkin House.

I saw Lina several times thereafter, and tried as best I could to ensure that Rudakov's historical and literary works about Katenin and about the *Bronze Horseman* were published. We also talked about the archives, but never reached any firm conclusion.

She confessed that it had been a mistake to deceive me in 1954 when she had laid blame for the disappearance of the Mandelstam autographs on the MGB. She did not have the nerve, supposedly, to admit that they had been burned. With sincere conviction she told me that "All had been returned to her!" with the exception of Mandelstam's poem about Kerensky and newspaper cuttings showing photographs of Russian writers with Marinetti (taken in 1913 when the Italian Futurist visited Petersburg). She was forced to sign a statement that she surrendered these papers voluntarily and this evidently traumatised her. On returning home, she and her mother began to burn the Mandelstam archive. Concerning the Gumilyov archive, she firmly declared that she had nothing more and had never possessed any more. Once again I believed her. But in a further conversation, already old and weak, she let slip how hard it had been, during one of the dreadful periods in our history, to burn the thick pages of the accounts book in which Luknitsky had written out information for Gumilyov's "Life and Work". A typed version of this chronicle has survived apparently, but the original might well have borne comments in Akhmatova's own hand. It was now clear how right Akhmatova was: Rudakov had been given substantial amounts of archival material.

Certain details concerning the Mandelstam archive left me deeply perplexed. Rudakov's letters lead one to conclude that under Mandelstam's dictation he filled at least 20 notebooks, providing a key to his poetry. Yet Lina assured me several times, very agitated and convincing, that she had burned only one notebook (the most valuable of all!). A poem in Mandelstam's hand was inserted between each page, with one or two phrases of commentary entered in the notebook by Rudakov. This was merely an index, it seems to me, to the other notebooks. Lina assured me she had never had anything more. "As far as the commentary to Mandelstam is concerned," she wrote to me on 31 July 1971, "it did not exist as such. There was a notebook with brief notes to the poems."

Now it is impossible to clarify anything: there is no-one left to ask. All we can do is thoroughly study Rudakov's letters to determine what he and Mandelstam did and in what order. In the second part of this section [and Appendix 2] I attempt such a reconstruction.

There remains one other, quite infinitesimal lead. I am no longer physically able to pursue such investigations as require travel, so let me share this idea with other researchers. Rudakov's letters reveal that he often sent a copy of Mandelstam's verse and his own ideas about the work they were doing in Voronezh to a friend in Leningrad. He is no longer alive. They say he had no family. Those who knew him are also dead. But there is an address that might offer a lead, if such a miracle were possible, to some of Mandelstam's papers. And it will take a miracle since Rudakov sent this address to his wife in Sverdlovsk during the first weeks of the war. The town to which his comrade had moved was subsequently occupied by the Germans, and Rudakov's Leningrad friend was Jewish. No-one now knows what happened to him, so what hope can there be for their correspondence? And still . . . On 18 August 1941, Grigory Leokumovich was living at apartment No. 1, 135 Morskaya Street in Rostov-on-Don. Perhaps someone will find something.

I very much regret that Lina did not allow me to examine Rudakov's letters thoroughly during our last meetings; instead she read excerpts aloud, confusing dates and immediately hiding away the letter she had been reading from. (Today Rudakov's archive is divided between the National Library in Petersburg and Pushkin House.) I was not keen to spend long with her, I must admit. Had I overcome this feeling, and had she not been so secretive, I could have asked her, point-blank, several questions about the notebooks Rudakov mentions. It was not to be.

One of the last times we met, Lina told me to go and see Rudakov's daughter from his first marriage. She and Masha had become friendly only in 1951. It is typical that until the 1970s I had no idea of her existence; I think the Mandelstams never knew anything about her. Now Lina warned me: after her death Masha would receive her entire archive. And that was what happened. For one whole month, Masha and I did nothing but read her father's letters.

II. Selections
from Rudakov's Letters[11]

1 TWENTY DAYS,
30 MARCH–20 APRIL 1935

In Rudakov's first letters we see the landscape that would play such a role in Mandelstam's new poetry, we meet the poet in the room praised in his verse ("I live on the majestic outskirts") and, through the eyes of Rudakov, we see Mandelstam at work.

MARCH

30: Here I am in Voronezh.

31: It's an extraordinary city in a topographical sense. The centre is as flat as a table. Revolution Avenue is a smaller Nevsky Prospect, an arrow not a street (and both the old and new houses are good of their kind). But turn off the Avenue and immediately it's Moscow or Kiev, steep drops and literally ravines. In the gaps between houses on these side streets you can see the horizon a hundred kilometres away and a small river below the town.

APRIL

2: If I had not come home at ten past one last night (the lights go out

---

[11] For convenience, these excerpts are set in diary form. Selected by E.G. from Rudakov's frequent letters to his wife in Leningrad, they have been further abridged here. E.G.'s comments are italicised. Unless otherwise indicated, the notes are hers.

at 1.30 a.m.) I would have written a wonderful letter yesterday. But it's even better like this. I'll tell you everything when I'm home again, when I come back: the sight of the steppes, the railway and the now exceptionally swollen River Vorona; the quickly advancing evening that lingers long in the twilight. Then night falls.

A rissole and cocoa in a café. Afterwards sitting on an improvised divan in a crooked room; a primus unusually easy to light; and walking around the uneven floor. Stepping out into the pitch-black night to go home through the rear balcony door of the little house, which stands on the outskirts of the rail-workers' quarter . . .

Lina, have you guessed? That was Mandelstam.

Meanwhile life goes on. I look for jobs at various organisations. Don't imagine that Mandelstam prevents me (we went together).

Write down just a few of Vaginov's pieces for the two of us (!), whatever Irina will give you.[12] Send one or two of his publications. . . . Mandelstam is also very keen to see the Tynyanov in the "Contemporary", you can't find it here [T.'s novel, "Pushkin", just published in the *Literary Contemporary* periodical].

I feel amazing. The silence has ended. I can speak and think. And I'm incapable of thinking in silence.

Winter ended yesterday and the asphalt on the Avenue is dry. Voronezh recalls an ocean. The alleys and back streets are drowning in mud. But already there are no streams.

4: This is the first time in my life (not counting Kostya Vaginov with whom there was also a little of the kind) when I truly feel that I'm with a friend (a male friend). You'll see him when you come. What's important now is how we get on: we eat together, read Shcherbina and Sumarokov, and his quite exceptional new poems (pre-Voronezh). About my ideas of him, and my conception of Konevskoy and Gumilyov, we hold disputes in which, Kitty, I feel my tremendous strength and rightness (if that was the case next time with Tynyanov!).

It's not a good idea to get too deeply in argument in view of his nervous condition and because he's not obliged to accept re-education in his 26th year of literary activity – it's unthinkable even. I simply watch how he thinks, how he talks of others, passes judgement. It's a new higher level.

My poems are a separate matter; in essence they are the summation of a historical conception. My power lies in an awareness of this, and that means a great deal, enough to make living worthwhile. But I'm

---

[12] Rudakov's sister Irina was married to the poet Konstantin Vaginov's brother Alexei. She and her husband both died during the Leningrad Blockade.

always true to myself and will be among those who last. At moments he so reminds me of Kostya [Vaginov] that I fear for him. His health is very bad. But the poems, the poems, Lina – they will be with us (he has nothing written down here, he will write them out or dictate them) – are amazing, octaves.

These aren't conversations at the Evropeiskaya [hotel].[13] This is life as equals, steady and with all its own qualities – money, galoshes, rooms and everything human.

Above all, and despite everything, he is the brilliant poet who wrote "Solominka" and "Venetian Life". And this isn't on the stage or in the dressing room. Only one thing is important here: in a certain sense, no individual can be genuine 24 hours a day and such proximity allows one to see those genuine minutes that others would not have sufficient desire to capture.

Apart from anything else, I see in him a profoundly unhappy person. His habits and manners can all be explained [by that].

I make him shave and polish his boots outside (and I'm the messy one!).

He's 43, and looks older, more worn, but when he's calm it's the same Mandelstam who was drawn with an upstanding tuft of hair on the cover of *Apollon* (no beard, because he's shaving!).

6: I have a room, that's to say, the half room shared with an actor – I wrote about both. My things are already there and today I shall sleep at home for the first time. The past night I slept at Mandelstam's. I've already unpacked my mackintosh, it's hot spring weather here. Now the only worries are work and money: I have a room and it's miraculously cheap.

Yesterday we went to a concert by the violinist Barinova (Mandelstam got us in for free). She has the most extraordinary Tsvetayeva-like temperament, a youthful 22 years of age and an untheatrical vivacity. (When I said so, Mandelstam was surprised: how could I have spotted a genuine resemblance to Tsvetayeva when I had never seen her? But the rhythms of her verse?!) And see what I achieved. After a year or more Mandelstam wrote his first four lines of poetry. About her, Barinova, after the things I said –

> Play on until the aorta bursts
> A cat's head in your mouth

---

[13] When Mandelstam gave several recitals in Leningrad in late 1933, he stayed at the hotel and was visited there by local writers. Among them was Rudakov, who recited his own verse, which was harshly criticised by the poet.

Three devils there were, you're fourth,
A wondrous last devil in her prime.

That was meant to be the last of six verses. When we got home the
beginning appeared

After long-fingered Paganini
All fiddlers run
In a gypsy crowd

Long-coated would be better than long-fingered, I said.

I'm writing this at Mandelstam's. The balcony door is open and opposite stand the railway signals. It's an unpainted work by Raphael,
Mandelstam says, the background is already prepared.

The house stands on a hill. There's a view of the lower town and the
improbably swollen but already shallower Vorona. From time to time a
train passes. I'm writing on a volume of Sumarokov. Mandelstam is translating [de Maupassant's] "Ivette" which makes him surly with dislike.

7: M. is my salvation; he has any number of worries and keeps me occupied. He's feeling terribly unwell and imagines he has every kind of sickness
including, it seems, gynaecological disorders. He's just like a child. I'll tell
you more when we meet. It would be impossible to forget. Today I took
M. to the consultant. The latter didn't tell him anything in particular and
the infant calmed down. Yesterday evening I spent with T.A. and co. and,
probably, he got nervous being left on his own. He derides "Ivette" and
then praises it, and translates terribly fast and smoothly but he soon tires.

I'm so happy I took volume VIII of the Sumarokov. The Eclogues
are blissfully soothing . . . Shepherds in love and always the same pattern
. . . It annoys Mandelstam but I'm entranced.

8: I read Vaginov to M. and he was terribly against him, apart from the
last poem (about wind, snow and the dying nightingale) to which he
took a great liking: "Now that is a truly posthumous poem."

Lina, it's even frightening and awful, the vastness of my thoughts and
the scale of my plans. At first M. was outraged: "What is this, a pocket
history of Russian literature?" But at that point my strength started to
become evident, as did (strange as it sounds) his helpless conservatism.
I fought back with [quotations from] his own verse! . . .

9: My life here now has a set pattern. While I wait for my documents
to be processed and, consequently, for any talk of a job, we live a "care-

free" existence. I get to M. by midday (it's three good tram stops from my building and the third, moreover, is beyond the railway line and out of town). There I have my second cup of tea since breakfast. He translates, I read (yesterday it was Yazykov which he brought, with Batyushkov, from Moscow). We go out on the balcony without coats. The tree growing next to the balcony lowers its boughs and they bear enormous buds, from which the green, still-unfolded leaves protrude. There are no leaves or grass anywhere yet.

Then we go out. We walk to Petrovsky Square (it's on my way home) where an idiotic Peter [the Great] stands with an outstretched arm. In his other hand he holds an anchor and by the pedestal lies yet another anchor. Peter the Anchor, M. calls him. The garden is small, behind it a slope leading down to the river, and the area beyond can be seen. Before Peter stands a fountain that doesn't work. From there M. goes on various bits of business or accompanies me to the post office to collect my letters (if the post was late the previous afternoon, I call in the morning before I go to M.). We pay visits to friends, go to the shops, and to the telephone exchange (his calls to Moscow). We eat in the middle of the afternoon, sometimes together, sometimes separately since he goes to a dining-room for special dietary needs.

10: M. picked up the "Contemporary" and started having a go at Stepanov. And it was actually rubbish: moreover, M. was twice feebly denounced there. He was in a terribly bad mood. The Tynyanov made him furious with revulsion. I can see a little of what he means. The language draws on outdated strata (1920s to 1930s). And the scenes with Pushkin's girlfriends are a bit overdone. Overall, though, it gave me pleasure: M. is implacable . . .

Translating "Ivette" he utterly lost his temper and uttered an immortal phrase: "Who are these Frenchmen? What can you discuss with them? A cat who's been dosed with too much valerian. Only their Mérimée is worth something."

Later that evening we had a monumental discussion about my poems. Worse than in the Evropeiskaya hotel. What's the problem? I don't understand. He talks of me with the same lack of understanding that the worst readers in the world display towards him. The only really true thing he said, was that 90 per cent of my pieces are about poetry and lie within a narrow literary world of associations . . .

15: M. spent the whole day in anticipation of a phone call (to Moscow between 4 and 6). The line was too busy and he was not allowed to make his call. He was in such a nervous state he almost went crazy. To his joy, he was able to jump the queue that evening and get through. The ladies' arrival [Akhmatova and Nadezhda] from Moscow has been delayed again, now until the 18th.

At home we together fried a six-egg omelette, drank sweet tea with a buttered roll and – alas! – it was 11.30 p.m. But we were now in a wonderful mood for conversation. We began with Komarovsky and ended with me. I lost my temper and began to use him (M.'s poems) to demonstrate my arguments: the evolution of poetry since Nadson (from nothing to Gumilyov and Mandelstam). He is thinking more clearly but alas, not without naive remarks: "Just tell me, in two words, the general meaning," he says. But you'd need to write a volume to express those two words.

17: M. is alarmed: a move to a new apartment and quarrels with the owner but NY is still not here (she'll come on the 20th). I reason with him but he's going out of his mind. I'm now writing from his room. It's a pity you won't see it, the new room won't be the same.

M. now wants to write an article about Formalism. And here I am, a flawed pupil of Tynyanov, Eichenbaum and co., or a supporter of their cause, or the creator of new approaches – even after all our conversations it's still not clear to him.

18: . . . And "Ivette" is already finished.

Being near M. gives me so much that I cannot now describe it all. It's like living alongside Virgil or at least Pushkin . . . No end of ideas about this. What's important is something elusive, not the literary trifles themselves. Although they're present as well (and must be remembered for anecdotes and biographical details).

There was an evening in memory of Mayakovsky (with Yakhontov). The acoustics were appalling and Yakhontov could not be heard. He was giving far too many performances and M. also got his address wrong and did not manage to talk to him. Today we went to the Summer Theatre to hear Gauk play Brahms and Wagner but left early (the matinee performance was packed with children who made it impossible to listen).

20: 5, 6, 7 and now 8 p.m. – M. has been furiously at work. I've never seen anything like it. It's a rare sight.

The result is definite: either there'll be nothing (apart from poetry) or else my book about M. Or an article now in the local magazine. At a distance it's unsurpassed and cannot be described. I stand before a working mechanism (perhaps an organism, it's the same thing) of poetry. I can see the same as inside myself, but this is in the hands of a genius, who will come to mean more than we can understand now. He is no longer a human being but a Michelangelo. He sees and understands nothing. He walks up and down, and mutters: "A black fern by green night . . ." To get four lines he pronounces four hundred. I mean that quite literally.

He sees nothing. Does not remember his own poems. Repeats himself and selecting among the repetitions, writes something new.

A magnificent life lies ahead. And work of a kind that the

2 Lineinaya Street, Voronezh

world has not seen. I'm studying a heavenly construction, the secret of which is concealed from mere mortals: I'm studying the living Mandelstam.

21: Today he moved into the centre of town. I said goodbye to the room with its balcony and incomparable view across the river, beyond the railway track. You know, these twenty days are such an epoch that they cannot be separated from the landscape.

2 THE "SECOND BOOK", MAY–NOVEMBER 1935

On 26 December 1935, Rudakov wrote to his wife from the hospital in Voronezh:

> During the daytime I again slipped into the empty ward and there worked on the [New Year's?] poster and wrote about O. Not very much so far, 18 small pages. At times I thought something wasn't going right but when I read yesterday's

work and imagined what I'd say if someone gave me such
notes about Gumilyov I decided it was essential . . .

*That day he returned to the idea (mentioned on 2 November) of compil-
ing a "Second Book" that would gather and organise biographical incident
and detail from events in their shared life in Voronezh:*

In no particular order I jotted down hieroglyphic facts on a
large sheet of paper: about 30 such episodes. Then I began
to group them on separate sheets of paper. The principle:
vices. Dante's *Inferno*, so to speak . . . This is the considered
structure of the Second Book – i.e. that which it might now
become in contrast to the First Book,[14] which was created,
for the most part, without any plan."

*It is not known whether Rudakov ever compiled the proposed volume but
his letters offer a rich if unprocessed source on which he would have drawn
for the "Second Book".*

MAY

8: Nadine left today. At the station she went wild and upset poor O. so
much that he said, in a trembling voice: "Nadenka, don't be angry,
you're going away, aren't you?" And he lost his walking stick which, it's
true, we later found in the buffet. I feel terribly sorry for him. He became
very quiet and made some cocoa for himself and for me. He dirtied his
hands on the saucepan, wiped them on his forehead and walked around
all evening with a zebra stripe.

9: There's a hitch with O.'s passport and he has been running between
the Voronezh and Moscow telephones all day. He suffers from this [offi-
cial] stupidity, drops cigarette ends on himself, catches fire, is scared and
puts them out, pours tea past the cup and is almost in tears. I calm him
down as far as I'm able: for an hour I told him things that had happened
during the construction of this building and that, and he was back to
normal and clear-headed again. He went off to the telephone exchange
and I went home . . .

10: . . . the passport is sorted out. Nadine is in Moscow and he is gradually calming down. Again a wonderful period has begun.

---

[14] See Appendix 2, "Mandelstam and Rudakov", p. 429, for Gerstein's account
of this lost commentary to the poet's works. [tr.]

12: O. keeps worrying about his affairs and there are only rare moments when he brightens up. Playing chess with Kaletsky gives me great pleasure. I'm reading Konevskoy and am literally crushed by his extraordinary verse. M. and I read him together. M. is getting quieter. I slept from 1 to 3 p.m. at M's. Then we read Vaginov . . .

21: It's a pity that I'm not writing down all I see and hear but letters will preserve a great deal. He again read his poems in memory of Bely. He was very close to him in recent times. He stood, he says, in the honour guard [at his funeral] and before that "the Pilnyaks stood there, vertical corpses above a living corpse". In the confusion the lid of Bely's coffin fell on Mandelstam's back.

Our conversations about Vaginov are endless.

22: Last night I had the pleasure of seeing Voronezh after 3 a.m., a sleepy and enormous Voronezh, expanded by the night and retreating through the air to the Mandelstamian Fields of the Central Black Earth Region. I'd gone to bed and was asleep. I heard a knock at the outer door. The landlady's voice and a reply from outside: is Rudakov, S.B. here? Can you imagine my joy? It turned out to be Osyuk who had not managed to phone Nadine and, taking fright, ran off to see me (on the way he dropped off at the telegraph office but he did not send a telegram: he only dirtied his 3000-rouble suit on the newly painted barrier). I took him to the telegraph office, sent Nadine an urgent telegram and sat with him until dawn. When it was light I took him to a visiting Muscovite (a very kindly acquaintance of his) and went off to work.

JUNE

1: We looked through the books he had been brought from Moscow, among them two volumes of Khlebnikov and Shklovsky's *Hamburg Reckoning*.

7: These are the kind of notes I find pinned to the Mandelstams' door:

> 6 June: "I'm at the doctor's. My sinuses are playing up. Wait for me."

> 7 June: "I'm either at the clinic next to First of May Gardens or the polyclinic on Engels Street, with the laryngologist. Come and find me. I urgently need to show them my X-rays."

8: Recently we talked about lost works. Today I said: "Then there's Gumilyov's 'Dragon'. We know 6 chapters but there were 12." He: "That's his good fortune, it's a bad poem." In my company he has not praised a single line of Gumilyov, apart from "With the Gypsies" (provisionally).

11: An episode. Kaletsky was playing chess with me. O. was getting worked up because local literary people were not paying him any attention. "If Yesenin or Vasilyev were in my position they would have an influence on society. What am I? A Katenin, a Kuchlya . . . Bonch-Bruyevich offered 500 roubles for my archive and when I kicked up a fuss he wrote me an honest letter: 'I and my colleagues consider you a second-rate poet; don't take offence or be angry with us, others give us their archives free of charge . . .' I am not Khlebnikov (Kaletsky says) I'm a Kuchelbecker, a comic figure now and perhaps for ever."

27: O. knows that I'm writing verse (at home). He saw Zabolotsky's "Autumn" in the notebook you sent me. He asked me to read it and I gave a wonderful recital. He and N. sighed and became animated. It ended with his voluble insults: "He addresses readers as if they're idiots . . . It's all fundamentally unhealthy. And the poetry isn't Zabolotsky, it's something of yours." I said it was from *Izvestiya*. N. remembered seeing it . . . "Well, in that case it's like you, and what was said more concerns you . . ."

JULY

5: My present day went as follows. I gave money to my landlady and then to M. (housekeeping for four days or so) and we organised a dinner at their place. Nadine cooked the food I had bought (a vegetable soup, fried eggs, and pancakes with strawberry jam – as a finale M. ran out for 300g of ice cream). Then rain. Chess with Nadine. If she doesn't take back her moves I don't lose: I don't take back my moves though it's hard for me (habit). The Chamber theatre is here on tour. O. knows them and we decided to see *Sirocco*. We arrived late and were seated in the orchestra pit (very cheerful and a good view). The actors admire Osip. Yesterday the actress Natalya Efron visited them; tomorrow several of the performers will come.

9: M. is engrossed by radio work (Goethe, which they've asked him to submit again; it was three weeks' work by Nadine, with O. dancing around). He is getting ready to go to the collective farm for the newspaper. This invigorates and entertains him. No poems. He's preoccupied. I got the

Sumarokov when he wasn't home and showed it to Nadine. She was thrilled! Then O. came, and so was he. They both read some of it.

11: A long day. Most of it, passport business. A queue at the police station, several hours and a passport (three-monthly). Visits to the post office and the Mandelstams during intervals in the waiting.

22: Now about M. It's 1 a.m. and the moon is already half full. At five past noon they departed for ten days, perhaps more, to Kalach station. God, what an emptiness immediately – i.e. the absence of the insistent background of those hundred and more days. We parted most tenderly . . . We promised to write. Understood and said how we'd grown accustomed to one another. It will be very difficult to part from them altogether. The last few days O. has been absorbed with my literary legalisation. He implores me to write verse, at least a light article about Kuchelbecker and reviews. It's all slightly playful but sincere and heartfelt, even if it is a brief impulse. N. is behaving quite wonderfully (understanding and accepting my role for O.)

31: At 9 a.m. I was woken by the Mandelstams. I'm writing you the first and most important [news]. They are in a good spirits. O. is cheerful. They lived at the Peasant Club. O. enchanted the Party leaders, had a horse and a car and travelled 60–100 versts around the district with the Party officials to see things at first hand. Nadine says he charmed them but does not say how, since she wasn't there. It was because he did not have his loving wife beside him, who would have said "Shut up, you clown," when he got carried away, she says. O. says to me: "For two and a half hours I felt as though I was Ryabinin (secretary of the Party regional committee) when he inspects the region. They thought a failing writer who'd suffered setbacks had come to them . . . but I . . . but I . . . I issued them with up to 12 important directives, and countless minor instructions . . ." When I ask exactly what they were, he gives a crafty laugh: he could not repeat them, he says, it was an inspiration. In essence, he showed off in front of them and truly enchanted them with his personal charm, which radiates superbly from him given the appropriate atmosphere.

August

6: O. is a madman, a manic character. You remember the saga of his illness, the same thing now with his collective farm trip. He can only talk and think about that.

14: A letter from Nadine today. Osya is engrossed in a new wave of observations. They'll be back by the 20th.

SEPTEMBER

During the earlier part of the month Lina was in Voronezh. Rudakov's correspondence with his wife resumed on 25 September.

26: The Osiks[15] have a new anxiety . . . although their finances are getting better he has also agreed to do a programme of Gulliver among the giants (Zabolotsky did the scenes "among the Lilliputians"!)

28: Things are going badly for me with the Osiks. Nadka has started to squabble. She simply won't accept that I do not want to eat with them. She's taken offence. Oska reacts to the most petty matters. He only behaves sensibly during clear-headed moments (as before).

They don't have any money for tomorrow. In two days, though, he'll be paid by the radio. I offered them money for a day: "Really! No money, no returned favours!" Earlier when I offered to bring in some water, she pretended that she hadn't even heard my words, and so on. Oska urges me to lunch [with them] and it's all such a tangle of domestic unpleasantness, that I can't describe it.

OCTOBER

2: All day (from 2 p.m.) with M. Again biographical conversations with N., deciphering of dedications etc. If you disregard her foolishness about money and housekeeping then everything could be fine all the while . . .

5: O. went a little crazy during the day. Their room is being decorated, and it's dirty though tolerable. N. is going to Moscow and I'm afraid to stay with O. We'll both go off our heads or, to be more precise, he'll drive me crazy.

7: O. has been given some ephemeral post at the theatre. He is youth-

---

15 After a month together, Rudakov often referred to Mandelstam by the initials M. or O. Following Lina's visit in September 1935, this at times became a less respectful Oska or Osik; from then on, Nadezhda, a familiar "Nadine" from the start, was almost invariably Nadka. Sometimes the couple was jointly referred to as the Osiks.

ful and merry. Where are the despair and madness? They remain only in tiny doses.

9: Today I went to change my passport. Quite a lot of red tape but I am calm now and endure all the different stages quietly and peacefully. I dream of a more or less tolerable job, with 200 roubles a month so that it would be easier for you . . . and so I also didn't have to share things with O.

11: Here they continue their *Steel* making.[16] A (new) hold-up: N. worries about the political message of the programme and is scaring Osya that it will be an ideological failure. That's rubbish but he is partly affected. The real reason why there's a certain cooling towards the *Tempering* is that he now has a 400-rouble salary at the theatre and was immediately gripped by a laziness about work.

16: N. called in the morning and together we went to their room. Played chess (I won, 15½ to 4½). Towards evening they were working on an abridged version of the play *Platon Krechet* for the radio. That same evening the premiere of Goldoni's *Servant of Two Masters*. We did not sit together but wherever there were empty seats. At the end Osya, amazed and pale, came up to us: "Something extraordinary happened to me: I forgot who I am, it's a split personality . . ." N. made a joke of it: "A servant of two masters" (i.e. radio and theatre).

26: Part one of *How the Steel Was Tempered* was made from a montage of excerpts. Since they did not satisfy Osya artistically, he retold a great deal in his own free style, adorning the poor author with his manner and, so to speak, endowing him with his own beauty. I did part two: it was an honest compilation of quotations.

Today he read part one to the radio people. They took fright there: "How can we declare a book approved by the government as stylistically unsuitable?!" The broadcast has been cancelled. The money will be paid only for the first chapter. It's likely (though not yet certain) that they will not be given any more work at the radio. O. is proud: "Again I could not accept an alien system, I offered myself and they do not understand me" (i.e. I'm a genius) . . . One of the staff in the deputy director's office began to console him: "It's not your role." He began to shout: "I do not have, and never have had, my role . . ." (I'm young,

---

[16] Radio version of Nikolai Ostrovsky's Soviet novel *How the Steel Was Tempered* (1934).

in other words, most promising and limitlessly talented). It's all clown-
ing about . . .

N. again intends to sell the apartment. It never stops.

NOVEMBER

3: O. is worried about money and this meant that I had to ring Yevgeny
[Khazin] and Shklovsky (!) once again. But a telegram came that 500
roubles for the Maupassant were being sent and they calmed down. He
is now no longer really ill . . . But O. still wants to be sick in order to
live on benefits. It's all pointless messing about and exhaustion. I'm fed
up with it and I hope it will soon end.

8: Nothing special today. O.'s health was a little worse, perhaps fatigue
after he went outside for the first time and excessive mobility. In the
evening capricious and went to bed so we didn't do any work.

He says that his period of official work has ended. He doesn't want
to work for either the theatre or the radio any more. On the street,
meanwhile, the loudspeaker yells *Krechet* though not in his adaptation.

9: . . . Again I'm eating with the Osiks but only once a day, the rest of
the time at home.

10: Now there's been a row, as if that was needed. Today I quarrelled
with Oska.

For a long time (before you came and while you were here) his biography and work etc. have been all-important. One objective observation
from my side. Our work proceeds one teaspoon every five days and so
on. My mood is affected by Tynyanov's silence and all the Leningrad
past with Gukovsky, Pushkin House etc. And here I have no literary
employment because of him – *Podyom*, radio and so on are all closed
[to me] . . . The row began when I said: "If I had a finished and
published work, then you would also have a different attitude to my
present plans, not to mention the attitude of Tynyanov and literary
specialists as a whole towards me." He was outraged that I was accusing him of kowtowing before literature, HIM – the dethroner of literary reputations! . . . I shouldn't have started but once begun (i.e. having
immodestly drawn attention to myself) there was no need to soften the
blows . . .

N. intervened. If he had been deprived of Dante, as I had been
deprived of all literature, then he would not have written his

"Conversation" and without Gumilyov, Akhmatova, Georgy Ivanov and co., perhaps he wouldn't have existed at all. He went completely off his head at that. He began shouting that everything authentic and genuine always finds an opening and so on and so forth. I don't have the temperament to repeat it all; the "all" did not amount to much anyway. The important thing is that for him I am now moving into the ranks of those who "do not understand" him.

12: Peace with O. We are reading Shevchenko, all three of us at the same time. O. and I rhythm and intonation, and N. the pronunciation and translation. A miraculous racket.[17]

14: Today an unexpected Leningrad. Kaletsky came for his things. A job at the library of the Academy of Sciences and other such matters (Oksman, Pushkin House, a recommendation from Eichenbaum, etc.) His appearance sets us back. It stirs envy and something else as well. But he still complains that 350 [roubles a month] are in material and psychological terms too little for him . . .

19: Concerning the situation with the Osiks. There are no consequences of the quarrel in a direct sense but a certain falsity can be felt. To put it crudely: N. clearly sees the necessity of my presence (at the least so that there was some "company") and she then tried to smooth everything over. And that was all with one eye on her own convenience. She's going to Moscow, after all, and O. would go broody if alone. So she understands that she must keep me happy. All her behaviour has that aim. Sweetness and light. O. is more stupid and simpler since he (unceremoniously) blurted out: if only you'd waited a month with that work, but you're taken up with it all the day.

I most respectfully said that it is very harmful for me to take on too much, time is passing, but this was totally essential and it was a rare chance, perhaps, to get some regular earnings.

20: Went to the cinema with the Mandelstams. *Hostile Paths.*[18] In parts extremely convincing – i.e. in the portraits and natural acting, but as a whole false and objectionable. When the lights went on and all stood, the impressionable O. addressed his astonishment to the entire auditorium: "Nadyusha, how could that be the end? It's a bad film, is it? How

---

[17] Taras Shevchenko, classic nineteenth-century Ukrainian writer. Nadezhda had been educated in Kiev. [tr.]
[18] 1935 film directed by Olga Preobrazhenskaya. [tr.]

could that be?" The audience began giggling at the despair in his voice. But he was upset and ruffled like a sparrow.

Yesterday the psychiatrist gave his findings: exhaustion of the nervous system. O. is already frankly saying that the aim of these medical "investigations" is to draw attention and make his presence known, not to get treatment.

Today I saw Kaletsky off. O God, when shall I leave?

23: N. is making up to me, that's because she's about to go. O. is in an absent-minded and depressed state. All the time she calls him, "My child, my fool." (All the time: "Fool, do you want some tea?" etc.) Or this moment. O. is sitting cross-legged on the bed and N.: "I've seen them banish children and old men but it's the first time I've seen them exile a monkey." And O. smiles with an idiotic appearance. N. is "concerned" about my condition and my health. I eat with them in the daytime but at home in the morning and evening. I'm giving a little money (i.e. a moderate amount). Now N. whines: "Don't leave O. while I'm away."

3 THE PLEKHANOV HOSPITAL, 25 NOVEMBER–11 JANUARY 1936

27: [from the hospital]: The Red Cross doctor already came on the 24th but decided (as did I) that I only had a sore throat. I was lying down for one and a half days at M.'s. They were extraordinarily attentive. When I discovered my skin was turning red on the 25th a panic began. I was taken to hospital. I left Mandelstam a note authorising him to collect my letters . . . N. will not go to Moscow for the time being since Mandelstam is afraid of falling ill and cannot remain alone.

[No date] Mandelstam to Rudakov

Dear Sergei Borisovich,
Without you I don't want to do a thing: our life has changed entirely. Trosha called.[19] Greetings from us all.
You are the finest fellow in the world,

O. Mandelstam

[A note was added by Nadezhda]:

---

[19] Rudakov's room-mate Trosha was a worker and Komsomol member.

Everything is going well, so I'm thinking of writing to Lina Samuilovna and then in 2–3 days' time phoning her. You'll also be able to write to her in a couple of days' time. Let us know, through the doctors, how you are feeling, and what we can send you to eat (caviar? wine? butter? biscuits?) and whatever else you'd like.

I shall also write to your sisters in a couple of days' time.[20] Keep cheerful and get well.

N. Mand[elstam]

10 December 1935, Nadezhda Mandelstam to Rudakov

My dear Sergei Borisovich,
The second day running Osya has not been able, as he wanted, to write you a long letter. We got your letter today (Osya isn't home) and I decided to start writing a little to you "on his behalf", and exonerate my old man (although, of course, he's a wretch). There's feverish activity at the theatre now, that's why: they're about to stage two new productions and Osya's lending a hand (you there, lend a hand!). He sits in on rehearsals, writes the programmes and so on. It's bizarre but he evidently likes being part of the theatre.[21] Today Wolf [theatre director] grabbed him and asked why he was getting so thin. He really does look very bad, very weak etc. But his Stakhanovite temperament does not permit him to go to the sanatorium and he continues cavorting about. Yesterday: 11–3 rehearsal, 4–6 writing the programme, 6–8 discussing programme text at the theatre, 8–11 "The Aristocrats" (he watched the show so as to do a radio adaptation), 11–12 at the baths! Now they're rehearsing; after eating semolina he went to see Yelozo [editor with local paper and magazine]. Because of all his distractions I've put off going to Moscow. I find it very irritating but I don't want to abandon him now when even strangers notice how shabby he's looking. I feel terrible that we haven't brought you anything (food-wise). I know how bad things are at the hospital. But we're in a

---

[20] Sergei's sisters Alla and Lyudmila, also banished from their native city, settled in Saratov for two years. Apparently they returned to Leningrad at the same time as their brother.
[21] From October 1935 to August 1936, M. was a consultant at the Bolshoi theatre in Voronezh.

deep hole now: until the 14th we have nothing but the theatre work, got in a muddle and so on. By the 14th we'll again be in working order.

I was very glad to get your letter and hear of Lina Samuilovna's trip. I'm very sure about it, almost certain.[22] Yes, and your letter arrived together with a very pleasant one from Alla Borisovna. Now Trosha is going to send her a reply, at his own expense, with news of your condition. Have you written to her yourself? . . .

Oska talks about you a lot, and misses you. You'll be offended but (referring to your illness) he called you a poor boy. I heard it myself.

As far as work goes, don't get downhearted: Osya will keep on working and I'll bring you masses [of material] back from Moscow.

But I hope you'll have a dig in the trunk yourself and pick everything you need there.

Trosha is a very kind good person. He has a simply wonderful attitude to you. He's now going to save us and send my letter to your sister (I don't have enough to buy a stamp!)
Best wishes

N. Mandelstam

Osya has come back. He was just sitting at the Kommuna library, with the theatre reports but it's no good him writing now. It'll just be nonsense, he's very tired.

17 December 1935, Mandelstam to Rudakov

Dear Sergei Borisovich,
    What can I say for myself? I'm extremely tired. My mood is stable and positive. I'm on good terms with the Theatre. I'm doing something there (not just paperwork).
    I'm thinking of going to a sanatorium for a month. The theatre dealt with the money side as though I was a long-serving employee. I'll go, I think, around the 20th. The neurological clinic in Tambov does not appeal: I've chosen the ordinary sana-

---

[22] In December Lina went to Moscow, hoping to secure Sergei's earlier return from exile. Hence the suggestion that he himself would soon be able to sort through the Mandelstams' trunk at Nashchokin Street.

torium in Lipetsk. All I need is a room to myself. I've begun a serious discussion with the Writers' Union (partly through the branch here, starting with Voronin). Told them what I thought. They are replying. This is very important and cheering, that's good. Tomorrow I'll be issued a 3-year passport. I got a note from Eichenbaum who stayed at our apartment in Moscow.

Nadya is going to take all the Voronezh poems to Moscow.

It was a good concert. The cellist Tsomyk. He was playing a Stradivarius. Tell the doctors to fit you up with earphones. It's good for convalescents. I'll see what I can do about it at the Radio Committee.

If you don't have any plans for a vacation, wouldn't you like to join me at the sanatorium? You could arrange that. And you must get back your strength. (Write to L. Samuilovna) [phrase added between the lines, E.G.]. We could do two weeks' work there.

Agreed?

Warm greetings

Yours

O.M.

4 NINETEEN THIRTY-SIX

JANUARY

1: One of the orderlies came into the ward, calling the nurse to the telephone. She wasn't there so they say to me: "Someone's asking about you, go to the phone yourself." "May I speak to Bogomolov? This is the writer Mandelstam, I'd like to enquire about the health of Sergei Rudakov." "Hello, Osip Emilievich." He came back because his condition had "drastically worsened." He's concerned about me. It's all quite human . . . And then sounds a note in his recognisable voice (all the rest was in an anxious tone): "Bother, I'd counted on you already being home."

8: O. telephoned. His poems have been accepted by *Krasnaya nov*. I said that Pasternak's poems were in *Pravda*[23] and that one ought to be cautious and exercise foresight in publishing. And at once there was not

---

[23] Two poems by Pasternak in praise of Stalin were published on 1 January 1936 in *Izvestiya*. See "Akhmatova and Lev Gumilyov", p. 346. [tr.]

the hint of artificiality in our conversation . . . again he is living and working (he's talking about poetry, after all, his own verse). But maybe it's only the telephone.

10: I'm being discharged tomorrow.

11: A telegram from O. (delayed in Tambov, "missing you, write"). Went to see him. He wasn't in. Nobody was there. To the hairdresser's. On the way met Trosha. He was almost offended. Waited while I had my hair cut. Told me that the Panovs have taken over Oska's room. He's complained about them to the prosecutor and they have replied with slanders. O. is staying with Peskov, who works for *Podyom*. Where can I find him?

12: . . . O. himself is in a tragic state. Very weak, can hardly walk. And his nerves are bad. He stays with various writers. I tracked down Peskov today. He's fresher than the others. Very young. He was doing some carpentry in the yard. We had a quick talk about O. To be more exact, I listened to him. O. stayed two nights with him, one with Wolf (the theatre director) and one with Sergeyenko (the writer). To begin with O. was in good heart and they drank a little. O. read vast quantities of poetry. The next few days he began to get worked up, N. was not coming.

13: Lina, it's not because I consider myself especially sinful but because I know how I differ from the mass of people (a difference that does not always please everyone) that I again see my triumphal forgiveness in the next world. Yes, that is the most important. The logic is as follows: he who can give much, shall also be permitted to do much. As in Pushkin's "Mozart and Salieri": "Genius and evil deeds are things incompatible." All of this is a generalised reaction to my new (first-second) meeting with O. Maybe he is a madman one hundred times over. Only a weak person cannot endure him. Those who can are worth talking to. He's done quite enough to infuriate me: but what use would I be to anyone if I just became sour because of that? I've seen him twice, for 15 minutes during the daytime at *Kommuna* and all evening at the Marants' apartment. A pity I did not write about the first meeting.

Here it is now. I enter the Writers' Union room. An unshaven, highly energetic O. is shouting into the telephone that the police are obstructing the prosecutor's decision to eject the Panovs and restore the room. He gives me a deep nod and a smile. We go out into the corridor. He is excited and wound up, and has been thrown off balance by my sickness and the fear of infection, the trip to Tambov and the room business. We decide to meet at 6–7 p.m. at the Marants'. The impression is that his mental state is completely unsettled, his eyes are glittering.

With the Marants. To be exact, the apartment they're now sharing with O. He is almost normal. See what's happened: a penitent Panov rushed into the Union, deferentially promised "won't do it again", and tomorrow the reinstatement. God, how wonderfully M. speaks. That's language and thought for you. Although his general condition is of nervous disturbance. Now his tale.

Osip Mandelstam, mid-1930s

He fled to Tambov, so frightened was he of scarlet fever. He was crazy there. Made friends with a tractor driver who said to him: "Leave here, they (patients) don't like you and want to beat you up." The reasons were as follows. O. was looking for a peaceful corner and shifting from one ward to another (infuriating the staff). He found an empty ward and lay down. Eight patients started banging on the door. He leaped out and began shouting, calling them all bastards etc.; the head doctor was called; five ran away, three remained, one of the three was offended by the insults cast at O. but he said, "I called them bastards, and I was right." Then the fellow, according to O.'s tale, organised a Red Partisan attack. O. in his underclothes fled to the doctor's office and there he cursed everyone . . . In the end they gave him back his money (!) and discharged him, "due to a drastic worsening of his condition". He was bowled over by Tambov. Wonderful town houses. One car in the whole place. Couldn't find any shops (needed to buy a button). Voronezh a metropolis by comparison.

We drank tea. We were overjoyed by our meeting. All the same, I don't know anyone else like him. If only he'd write more poems. Evidently the devil would make sure they were good.

Practical matters. While I was ill they summoned me to the NKVD. I talked to some older man for almost two hours in sympathetic terms about Kuchlya, Yury Nikolayevich [Tynyanov] and my lack of desire to study Koltsov and Nikitin in Voronezh. [Rudakov told me that they tried to convince him that he had made the wrong choice in studying Mandelstam, E.G.] I couldn't make out whether this was their initiative or they were instructed by Moscow to make my acquaintance. He said he didn't know anything yet about my appeal. He seemed to want me to return quickly. I gave a very interesting description of Kuchlya and working with manuscripts. He asked about life in Leningrad. Left in a wonderful mood.

15: As we went with O. in a horse-cab to the station to meet NY I thought of you. Snow, a light wind, warm. Of course, we shall ride like that around Leningrad and the islands. O. recalled Blok's lines: "The Yelagin bridge, the snort of a house, and the voice of the beloved . . . "

21: O. feels very bad. Today he even suggested that I wrote to Pasternak about his hopeless medical condition. I'm not in favour of just raising a fuss but he scared me that he might die. It's all very well (i.e. my objections) but he really is weak and poorly. Don't know what the evening will be like. They are at the doctor and I'm waiting in their room.

22: All the past days have passed in the constant turmoil of his concerns about his illness. Now things have brightened up. They both praised to the sky my silhouette profiles extravagantly and even timidly murmured about a "re-examination" of my landscapes. It's all the more interesting because I find I can draw him. Do you know Kruglikova's album of writers' portraits? The Mandelstams say that mine was better. I'm doing my O. just right.

23: *This day Rudakov received an official refusal to re-examine his case from the USSR prosecutor-general's office.*

24: The Osiks got so worked up that they were sure Akhmatova was already setting out . . . But let's see what comes of this. O.'s main interest: "But will she bring some money?" While I'm concerned about the Gumilyov manuscripts – it's all rather mercantile. In the language of my fellow-lodgers this is termed "to think clearly" (which fits somewhere between "deceive", "steal", "trick", "get a cushy berth" etc.) They consider that all people "think clearly". The Mandelstams' affairs are all of this kind.

28: Today the Osiks provoked a row with me about the silhouette profiles. At first sight they liked them very much. Today according to O. there is "no dialogue of lines" and, in N.'s view, "the skull is not moulded and there's no centre (!?)" As a result we quarrelled in a polite way. For the first time, perhaps, it had an effect because he is accustomed that I "conceal my work and thoughts" and he "most properly does not disturb me". That's his position! In other words, while using up vast quantities of my energy, he has fenced himself off from responsibility for all else in our relations with a most polite formula . . . I don't want to see them tomorrow . . . Even less to read them poems. I already know the reaction, so why get irritated for nothing.

Could you not find out, through Papa's acquaintance, more detail about the history of the refusal [to reopen my case]? It's most important.

What you wrote about the negative influence of Oska's friendship seems unreal to me. Furthermore the local [Writers'] Union has expressed a desire to meet me and, in particular, concerning my work with Mandelstam. They've known about it for a long time but spoke openly now. I talked to Kretova (deputy editor of *Podyom*) and she asked me to ring Z. [not identified] . . . Write and tell me what you think of this. I'm afraid you'll be dissatisfied.

5 AKHMATOVA ARRIVES

FEBRUARY

1: Relations with O. are now steadier and that's all down to my restraint and forbearance. It's almost impossible to work sitting in their room and their "manias" distract me. Today they were madly waiting for Annushka but she got held up in Moscow. I start to leave and they dissuade me. It's good that my fellow-lodgers are hardly at home in the evenings. The room is warm. But outside there's been a frost of minus 30 degrees for two days now . . .

2: Went to M. They're cheerful, although also excitable. I eat with them and since N. had already begun to eat the fried eggs two were set aside for me on which O. wrote: "The personal property of SBR, 2.II.36 Voronezh."

An unusual day because I did not work, but passed the time lying down, cracking jokes and playing the fool with O. We read Pasternak, discussed a future Voronezh and all in tones of hilarity. We imagined (this grew gradually from our phrases) that we would become servants of a "cult" (alas, it's almost impossible to convey) – the important thing was that this was against a background of the voluble Yelozo, the Union, Pasternak, Kaletsky, the "landlords", Vdovin etc. We forced N. to make us *gogol-mogol* [a dessert], since the "congregation" would supply us with more eggs. This was all a serious pretence, with genuinely serious digressions.

O. formerly used to praise Pasternak. He says he read him once in 1924 and all the other acclaim was simply by inertia. Now he was disenchanted.

Talked about Zabolotsky, Khodasevich and Tsvetayeva and he (and I) very much want to re-read them. To be more exact, I'd read to him. If you can, bring them with you.

O. wrote "Shengeli" on the "Nord" cigarette packet [Shengeli published *Nord* in 1927] and we remember that "Glider" was both the name of a cigarette and of another collection of verse by Shengeli. We started testing out names for cigarettes: Tristia sounded good but not Stone, The Egyptian Stamp was excellent. My Sister Life, cigarette papers.

And then he signed the photograph: "This photograph was taken in Voronezh by Wolf, in December 1935. S.B. Rudakov made a copy and it would appear to belong to him, evidently it is his property, O. Mandelstam 2.II.36". We decided to write out all the diagnoses of the last two months (there were a great deal) on the other copy of that photograph.

We began to add up their earnings over 18 months. In Voronezh 7200 roubles, in Moscow 14,700 and taking into account "presents" from relatives and acquaintances the total was up to 25,000. In round figures that gave 1,400 a month but N. insisted that it was 700.

5: The main event of the day is Akhmatova's arrival. It was all very much like the preceding days: the Osiks were just waiting for the trip to be cancelled and accompanied these surmises with a variety of offensive declarations about the mean nature of friends etc. All of this – i.e. the prehistory – is very funny material for inclusion in the [second] book.

. . . A most important event: permission and funds have come from Moscow through Litfond for Oska to go south for treatment (Crimea, Caucasus etc.). For the time being this is uncertain and may be delayed because of Akhmatova.

The arrival was as follows. We left O. at home. It was fatiguing for him to walk and, most important, he was "seriously" ill, judging by the telegram sent to Akhmatova, and could not be revived. N. and I went to the station. Platform, crowds.

Akhmatova in an ancient coat and herself old. A nightmarish appearance. I found a horse-cab for them. O. was half crazy from emotion.

When she took off her hat she was transformed. It's as you said at the Pushkin meeting, when she is animated, her face is wonderful and has no age. Magnificent hair. But I'm not yet used to her and the minutes of drabness are simply awful, almost hideous.

A. began to change her clothes and O. and I went to the shop. As soon as we were out of the door he began to sigh and groan that she was the one who needed treatment, not him. I'm sure he'll run off to Stoichev [head of local Writers' Union] about this tomorrow. He's obsessed with medical treatment.

There's a Dobrolyubov festival at the moment. To let A. rest, O. and I went to the musical college for a Dobrolyubov evening and sure enough O. grabbed Stoichev and began whispering: "She's come all this way, I don't want it to be just for me. Wouldn't you like to organise some meetings for her? Help her to settle in here, she doesn't have anywhere to live or any comfort . . . " Stoichev barely managed to free himself.

What's quite amazing is N.'s behaviour. All her foolery has gone, none of her arrogance and, on the contrary, she's ingratiating herself with Annushka.

6: At the Mandelstams'. O. is still crazy. For him Akhmatova's arrival is of public importance. He's already concerned whether it will have any effect on the future [for him here].

There is now no shade of strain. With Akhmatova I am looking at scraps of my textual criticism. She has something of the standing of Oksman.[24] She didn't expect to see what she found, it seems. Lina, I don't like it when people are aware of someone's majesty and tremble (as Yesenin did when he first saw Blok). However, when we were talking and she, recalling O's poetry reading at the Guild, mentioned "Kolya", I shivered. How extraordinarily beautiful she is! Can you imagine walking arm in arm with Gumilyov? All you can imagine I then experienced when I took her to the Marants.

7: In the morning I went to fetch Akhmatova from the Marants. Things are gradually calming down with the Osiks. They have applied for treatment in Sochi. They are full of life.

O.'s nobility now begins. He told A. about my poems and they began to organise a recital. N. took a lively interest; she has not heard them. After lunch we all sat down. I was a little uncertain of my voice, afraid that I would be nervous and read badly. To concentrate I chose a partner – i.e. N., clear, intelligent and affectionate eyes . . . I couldn't

---

[24] Julian Oksman, literary specialist and deputy head of Pushkin House in early 1930s; later sent to the Gulag.

tell you everything but it all turned out well, without the shadow of a doubt on my side that I had triumphed.

That evening they read Dante, talked and joked a great deal. Together they are very merry. My poems, it seems, deeply moved N. Disappointment: A. is already preparing to go home.

8: A disturbed day. Everyone is upset. Wonderful that A. and I are very much in agreement in our views of O. She's a tremendously wise person; together we prepared lunch together, cooking a *shchi*, which turned out deliciously. The minus is that much time and effort goes on O., his plans and politics. On the other hand, you feel sorry for him, he's also down-hearted, in anticipation of her departure.

9: Today O. (in addition) read poems from 1930 and the ladies flattered him, asking for more, and were lavish in their praise. Evidently A. will leave on 11th.

With O. we discuss A.'s poetic silence:

He: "She's a carnivorous seagull: when there are historic events you will hear Akhmatova's voice and the events are only the peak, the crest of a wave – war, revolution. Steady and deep-flowing periods in life do not stir her to poetry and this finds expression as a fear of repeating herself, as an excessive exhaustion during the pause."

He told her that Pasternak was harmful. Formerly he created more completely than others the kind of thing that they started doing *en masse*, and tastelessly. That applied to almost all who have written over 15 years: it's also O.'s "Slate Ode" and A.'s fear. Perhaps that was too sharp: there is also friendship and respect for Pasternak.

Now the most important of all. I am sitting on the divan with Akhmatova and wondering how to formulate the question of working on Gumilyov. The Mandelstams have still not talked of this with her. We sat there in silence . . . She turned to me and said: "When you are in Leningrad I shall show you everything," and so on. Telepathy.

10: Talked a great deal about work with Akhmatova. Her trust is unlimited, all that is needed is time in Leningrad and then everything I have thought of will be done. We understand each other in an instant, as though I had been in the Guild of Poets with them . . . even down to trifles: in some context she mentions Komarovsky, I begin to talk about him and we each recite aloud to one another, or rather together, word for word from "Francesca".

She: "Yes, it's something to know Komarovsky. Do you know, Kolya used to say: 'It was I who taught Vasya how to write: at first his verse was a limping beast . . .' And he was right, of course."

Perhaps I should have gone to see her long ago but without the direct conditions under which we met now, perhaps what was needed would not have happened.

Lina, what I've learned about O. and everything to do with him means a great deal but the calm, eternal brilliance of Akhmatova has given me all I could imagine.

11: Akhmatova left today.

I committed a theft. I took *Anno Domini* from Tolmachev's sister, handed it to A. and she wrote me a dedication. The book will stay with me and no devil will take it away again. In pencil:

"For Sergei Rudakov, a keepsake of my days in Voronezh, Akhmatova, 11 February 1936, at the station."

N. gloomily recalls her visit while O. and I sit in different corners of the room, for some reason angry with one another (jealousy?!). By evening they stirred themselves and began to talk. Confirmation had come from the Litfond in a telegram: "A trip to Stary Krym has been reserved."

17: O. is creating indescribable hell – offence at A.'s departure, uncertainty about their vacation, diseases real and imagined, lack of money.

19: O. has winkled some money out the theatre and it's peaceful once more.

6 THE "SECOND BOOK" (CONT'D): AN ENDLESS QUEST, FEBRUARY–JULY 1936

21: Snow keeps falling, but dry and soft. It's not cold. The Mandelstams went to a concert (the bass Steshenko from Chicago).

27: Now a mass of unseemly particulars with O.'s landlords. Shouts, screams, turning out the lights, again shouts, and their craziness in response.

MARCH

10: Called at the [Writers'] Union. They held a preliminary discussion with me. Their attitude to Mandelstam is incorrigibly negative, even dismissive (despite what he said about them). Hence their scepticism about my work but simultaneously they show an interest.

14: Yesterday M. moved to a new room in a good apartment block for engineers.

16: What's happening with the Union? This is what.

There was a citywide symposium for those working in the arts with a report by Plotkin on formalism (he came down from Leningrad specially to deliver it). This, as you probably know, was a reaction to the article in *Pravda*. I also went. Such barbaric stupidity that it's senseless for me to push myself forward anywhere with my work.

. . . I couldn't sit with O. The new room is very well appointed but has had a coarsening effect on them, they're bad-tempered. Perhaps because it's harder for them to complain about their domestic conditions. O.'s like a crazy person, only talking to himself while N. is a silly woman from some caricature and no-one you can talk with.

27: Today O. took fright at some registration formalities. Then I walked him to the theatre. On the way back:

> O (flattered and satisfied): Has your anxiety passed?
> Me: You were the anxious one. And if I had been feeling anxious the feeling could not have passed since nothing has happened to me.
> O: Really? (Pause) You're attitude to me is so down to earth. I envy you: you've managed to protect yourself and get by. You do not value those around you.
> Me: Do you?
> O: I take a moral not a mundane attitude. You have lost nothing but I am a broken man.

What's the good of pointing out his "immorality"?

APRIL

7: This evening went to Beethoven's 4th Symphony with M.

13: O. put on another performance today. We were coming back from the theatre together when he went pale while crossing the avenue and clutched his heart. I barely succeed in dragging him to Kommuna. "I'm dying, I'm dying," he cries. We put him on a chair but he leaps up, drinks water and yells: "Nadenka, I need Nadenka." We take a horse-cab. He's better at home; I run for the doctor at the polyclinic. He gives him a camphor injection and a doctor's letter. As soon as the doctor is out of the door M. feels better and the speculation and holy foolery begin. (Letters to his brother, Pasternak, telephone calls etc. . . .).

MAY

A long interval followed since Lina soon came to Voronezh.

11: It's still early (8 p.m.). I promised to call on M. in the evening . . . N. mysteriously gave me a letter to send to Zhenya, her brother, adding, "Read it." Here it is:

Zhenyusha,

After his fit Osya is recovering very poorly. He's very weak. Worst of all, Gerke's suggestion (cerebral sclerosis) is finding confirmation: additional symptoms have appeared. He can still be cured, if he responds to treatment.

But soon it will be late.

Let Anya know [i.e. Akhmatova, E.G.]. She must arrange treatment (at Matsesta [Black Sea resort]). We cannot put it off. We need a dacha this summer and, if June and July pass favourably, then Matsesta in August. We need a lot of money. For the dacha and a course of baths. What will happen?

He looks extremely well but that means nothing.

Evidently I shall raise a stink. I'll wait a few days more for Pasternak and Anya. Let them get a move on. If they let me down again, I shall go into action. Osya is not dying. That, of course, may disappoint everyone. But he could drag on, a condemned man, for another 2 to 3 years. He might die without warning and that, in our circumstances, would perhaps be for the best. I won't ask the Union for money. The dacha is not treatment but just something like recreation. Simply to slow things down a little . . . But they'll say they've already done everything or perhaps they won't give a thing. To hell with them.

Nadya

Write. N.

My comment. The [remark about M.'s] good appearance is for me, so that I don't think that appearance (and I'm the only one to see him)

is decisive in this case. That was why I was instructed to read the letter
. . . As concerns money: I picked up some at the theatre, N. rang up
the Union yesterday and Kretova sent 50 roubles (with a note of receipt
which Nadezhda signed: "For Mandelstam from the medical fund of
Kommuna"). O. is cheerful, spouts well-meaning nonsense and is imagining the things he might do (go to a lunatic asylum, or to the dacha,
or write to Maya Rolland,[25] asking her to send him gramophone
records).

12: Here I am sitting with them. Peace and well-being are conditional-
ly restored. Their reaction to Shura [M.'s younger brother Alexander]
is even worse than to Akhmatova or Emma. He was not even regarded
as their loudspeaker but as a postman. They were brusque with him. He
brought 800 roubles for the reprinting of O.'s translation of Vazha
Pshavela (a Georgian poet, translation of 1921).[26] That mad couple are
furiously spending the money so as to howl with hunger more quickly.

27: O. is playing the invalid since he wants to gain the [medical] commission's approval. These events are presented in a letter to Boris Pasternak.
Here it is:

Boris Leonidovich,

Yesterday the collegium of the 2nd polyclinic met. O. was
recognised as disabled and incapable of work and was sent before
the disability commission.
This commission should have been of a medical and curative
nature. Instead it was a mockery: they did not give me an answer
to a single question of a medical nature, so as to avoid accepting
any obligations. O. is effectively without medical aid. Official medicine is merely protecting itself. Private doctors do not want such
a patient. Professor Gauthier was here and he treated O., despite
his social position, but now he has left.
The commission wrote the following note:
"Polyclinic No. 1 of the Voronezh theatre local trade union
committee. Mandelstam, O.E., aged 45, is suffering from
cardiologopathy, arterial sclerosis, the after-effects of a reactive
condition, and schizoid pyschopathy. He should be sent to the

---

[25] Maria Kudashova, wife of the French writer Romain Rolland, and an acquaintance of M.'s from Koktebel in 1915–16.
[26] Volume of Pshavela's longer poetic works, re-published in Moscow 1935.

specialist commission to determine how far he has lost his capacity to work. Signed: Azorova, Shatoilo and Zemgel. 27 May 1936."

In a week's time O. will be confirmed an invalid. This is an honorary title. He can die quietly, as the disabled are supposed to do. He will receive a disability allowance of 8 roubles 65 kopecks. He can sell cigarettes, that's one of their privileges. The Writers' Union still recommends M. to earn the money for his own treatment. He has been refused the right to leave the Region. The doctors say nothing because there is no medical institution of the necessary type in the Voronezh Region . . .

I am not asking you to go to Prosecutor Leikevitov . . . Everyone goes to him and leaves empty-handed . . . I prefer a simple statement: no-one has done what they could for O. Without self-deceptions such as a visit to the prosecutor. I hope that my request will be respected.

Nadezhda M.

Only in Moscow could I get a proper diagnosis. I have been refused permission to go to Moscow for medical consultation.

It is not known whether Pasternak received this brazen and demanding letter. After reading or listening to something similar, Yevgeny Khazin sent the following letter to Mandelstam's youngest brother Yevgeny who lived in Leningrad:

Yevgeny Emilievich,

It's quite essential to go to Voronezh. The illness has turned into outrageous delusion. Instead of getting treatment, crazy notes are being sent in all directions. O. is in an extremely overexcited state. In the latest medical report sent here have been added to his heart diseases "remnant syndromes of a reactive condition and schizoid psychopathy". If things carry on like this, the result will either be heart failure or the madhouse.

The worst of all is that Nadya is thoroughly infected with this delusion. I am afraid that she herself is now the driving force. In other words, two people on the verge of insanity are being left entirely to themselves (while O. is truly seriously ill).

It is quite essential that local doctors be consulted and the nature and extent of the sickness be diagnosed. Then it will be clear what needs to be done.

I think that he is now in need of a sanatorium, even that in Voronezh. The most ordinary type of hospital would now be a salvation, if only we can snatch O. from this state of domestic delusion.

It would be good if you travelled via Moscow.

Yevgeny Khazin

Running ahead, we may note that on 17 June Yevgeny Mandelstam arrived in Voronezh. Evidently he had seen Akhmatova in Moscow and brought with him news and, in all probability, money as well.

31: I called on the Mandelstams. The woman from the radio was there again (Gauk's former wife, also from Leningrad). She was running on about her own affairs.

For some reason the Mandelstams were tense and dissatisfied. They'd been to the Party regional committee, it turned out. O. had been taken ill there and they brought him back in a car (though it was only a short walk away). He explained: "Nadyusha was showing how ill I can be." Afterwards "I felt weak, my pulse rate increased and I didn't even feel faint. Sergei Borisovich, again I am getting caught up in these flaps." N.: "I'm not to blame if you have the soul of a maenad and come back to life at the thought of any fuss" (this was for the benefit of the lady, so as to explain the vigour of his urge to run off somewhere again. It did not look good, after a "car" he should be lying down.)

What did they need? Everything. And now there were groans about the dacha (they could have gone away with the 1,500 roubles they had recently squandered), and new money.

Then the lady naively said: "What? You have such a room, such living conditions and you want a dacha as well?"

He: It's good for the health to lie on the grass and go for walks along the footpaths.

Lady: And there what else will you want? Then what will you ask the Little Gold Fish for?[27]

Everyone (N., O., and myself) very amused by her lively grasp of the essence of such "fuss". A stir in the room. Smiles (slightly embarrassed in the case of N. and O.).

He: As you have guessed, this is a forced substitute for activity and literary work.

Me: The vital persistence of the spirit!

He: Yes, yes.

---

[27] In Pushkin's folk tale, the magic fish grants wishes. [tr.]

JUNE

10: After a succession of uncertainties and groans they decided to go to a dacha not far from Voronezh. First they were going to Pavlovsk, then to Zadonsk. Yelozo gave N. a newspaper mission for a month and after that they'd just stay on there, living off the theatre and subsidies from Moscow (from friends and quite frequent, up to 500–600 roubles a month). Before their departure they also bought books. They were to go with their landlady and her daughter.

16: They say the eclipse will be quite noticeable in Voronezh. The morning of the 20ᵗʰ the Mandelstams are leaving for Zadonsk. He will no longer be on the theatre's books after 1 August.

17: O.'s youngest brother Yevgeny came here for a single day. All very business-like.

18: O. went to see a new professor (I've forgotten his name). He said: "You've the heart of a 75-year-old man but you'll live for a while yet." He rejected the detailed accounts of his predecessors, paradoxical, and O. cheered up.

At 9 p.m. we listened to the broadcast about the death of Gorky. The end of an epoch. The Union was intending to ring up Moscow about O.'s health. An hour before the news about Gorky [his death], O. rang up Stoichev: "During these days of anxiety for Gorky I request that you do not raise my condition."

At home: "And what a terrible way to die, just before the eclipse. Gorky in his coffin, and there's an eclipse." Then he grabs me by the arm and pulls me to the window: "Look there, a tramp. Gorky has died and a tramp walks past. You don't see them nowadays . . . "

20: Today at exactly the same time as yesterday's eclipse O. left on a bus for Zadonsk.

. . . They'd wanted to watch the eclipse together but I deliberately declined since I was sure they would either oversleep or stop watching halfway through. I watched alone from the slope above the river. I felt hungry, bought half a bottle of milk from a passing milkmaid and drank it all with enormous pleasure. The Mandelstams left noisily and with a lot of junk, amid wails and alarms. Where does this dying man keep such reserves of vivacity?

To all other freedoms has been added yet one more, freedom from Mandelstam and from the Mandelstams. The city is free, so to speak.

This is deliverance from the hypocrisy of the last weeks of our relations. It's sad, and joyous and something of a relief.

28: Received a letter from the Mandelstams, which speaks of two (!) telegrams sent poste restante. They are flourishing and invite me join them on holiday.

JULY

1: I'm packing my things, handed in *Onegin* and got 100 roubles, and will go for a day to say farewell to the Mandelstams. Then my ticket's ordered and I'm coming home.

My *Onegin* is authentic if reduced in price. A compilation of literature about him, prepared by me. Perhaps this is the transition from stagnation in Voronezh to Pushkin House?

8: Here I am in Zadonsk. Our farewell was more than touching. For the future this meeting in Zadonsk was very positive. Somehow it will be better at a distance. I can pick up the papers I need in Moscow. That, and the general tone of our meeting, leave a better, not a worse, feeling. Let that be my farewell from Voronezh, a friendly farewell.

7 EPILOGUE

[Autumn 1936] Osip Mandelstam in Zadonsk to Sergei Rudakov in Leningrad

Dear Sergei Borisovich,

Thanks for your note. I'm not sick now but in very low spirits.

I don't know what to do with myself. NY is much worse: she's very weak and has changed a great deal. We cannot live in the city: one, we've nothing to do there and, two, we can't afford a city room. Perhaps we'll move to Sosnovka.[28] Write and tell us what you're doing as often as you can. Send us books.

I want to read the Spanish poets. If you can, get hold of 1) a dictionary and grammar book, 2) an anthology and 3) the best

---

[28] The Mandelstams did not move to the suburb of Sosnovka but rented another room in Voronezh. In May 1937 the poet's three-year term of exile ended, and they returned to Moscow.

authors, lyric and epic. We are plagued by petty concerns. We are both in need of shoes and Nadya needs a winter coat. I doubt we'll cope with that problem. It makes it difficult to move around.

Write to us poste restante. Where and how we're going to live, we don't know. Do write.

Yours
O. Mandelstam

Compiled late 1970s–early 1980s. First published in *Novoye o Mandelshtame* (Paris, 1986), then in *Podyom*, 6–10 (Voronezh, 1988).

II

Unwanted Love
[1993]

After a lengthy silence he replied: "Your taste is appalling!" I had recalled, in passing, one of his nasty remarks, and the memory sent him into a profound reverie. He had made the comment long ago. This belated penitence – for what else could his reply mean? – appeased me: it was not so much an admission of my bad taste as of his appalling character. We must return to a much earlier period.

The war was in its final twelve months. He had returned, having left Moscow in 1941 to join the home guard. Sent to a military hospital, he was then evacuated to Central Asia. Then he was home again. His room was freezing cold; there was no firewood and no way of making tea. I gave him shelter: after Father's death, space could be found for my old friend at our apartment, which was habitable and at least partially heated.

Each day, he went all the way across Moscow and gazed round his empty room; he took one (and only one) book off the shelf and read it as he moved about on various bits of business or when standing in queues. In the evening he read the same book and would not let me see what it was. Once he came into my room, however, opened one of these precious volumes and read aloud: "I must not only punish but punish with impunity. A wrong is unredressed when retribution overtakes its redresser. It is equally unredressed when the avenger fails to make himself felt as such to him who has done the wrong." It was a virtuoso reading, from beginning to end, of Edgar Allan Poe's novella *The Cask of Amontillado*, in Konstantin Balmont's pre-Revolutionary translation. The hero meets his enemy, dressed as a jester, at the Carnival: "He had on a tight-fitting parti-striped dress" and a "conical cap and

bells" on his head. The avenger entices the jester down into the cellar
and treacherously walls him up in a niche saturated with nitre. The devil-
ish procedure is accompanied by the sadistically methodical explanation
of each step that brings the enemy nearer his death. The reproaches,
pleas, pathetic laughter and groans of the victim are accompanied by the
tinkling of the bells on his cap.

My entire room, it seemed, was now filled with the sound. Subtly
aware of each word's shades of meaning, my companion repeated "and
his little bells rang". Then he threw me a fiery glance and declared, "I
hate him . . . ferociously." There followed the endless tale of the feud
between Shklovsky and Khardjiev. The older and younger man had been
at daggers drawn for 15 years and, in the most varied circumstances,
always found new cause to revive their dispute – it would be embar-
rassing to mention some of the pretexts they employed. "Well, you understand . . ." said Khardjiev, and I did. As Mandelstam had commented
long before, I was endowed "with a terrifying capacity to understand".
The poet, as is well known, rejected such an accommodating attitude.

Despite the comforting warmth of the stove, there were days when
we grew estranged. One such evening, casting a cold glance at me,
Khardjiev uttered the words that so offended: "You've become like your
aunt, the one I've never seen." I should have thrown him out but he
went himself, quietly pulling the door to as he left. Alone, I opened the
writing-table drawer. It was empty. When had he removed his manuscript?
It had lain there, with my blessing, ever since the publishers had returned
it. Well-informed editors passed the manuscript round, reading it avidly,
but declined to publish it. Too good? Probably. Before the war, there
were still writers who would not begin exploring a historical theme until
they had researched it for themselves, examining unstudied materials and
developing their own understanding of the subject. Only then did they
set themselves purely literary goals and begin to write. My friend's books
of this kind were a diversion from the main work of his life. But in such
"ephemeral" works he always chose an original, if not necessarily brilliant, hero and immersed himself in the events of other epochs and countries. In this case, I think, the book dealt with the feats of some scholarly
adventurer, perhaps a spy, in the Middle East. Khardjiev had published
several such biographical works, but this, for some reason, was not
accepted. Publishing houses have any number of reasons for rejecting a
good book! A manuscript in which so much skill, ingenuity, determination and talent have been invested then lies in a drawer at home and,
like surplus ballast, distorts the entire course of the author's life. Strange
tastes and appalling characters blossom in a poisoned atmosphere.

The war did not permit us to dwell long on personal relations. I grew resigned to my friend's absences and, if I'm to be frank, found it restful without his caprices. Unexpectedly, I heard his voice over the telephone. As if nothing had happened in December 1944, he rang up and told me excitedly: "I've just seen Lyova."

From that day on, almost imperceptibly, Nikolai Khardjiev again established himself as part of my household. We were used to one another. Momentous events in the world at large – we were marching on Berlin! – and the highly original domestic arrangements within the apartment together created that special sense of comfort we commonly call "friendship". Sometimes I was on night-duty at the Literary Museum. Once, coming home, I found a note on the table:

Emma,

I've finished the book but somehow it reminds me of nothing so much as a corpse. I feel awful. I can't sleep. Headache, confusion and so on. Someone called out to me, during the night, "How do you do, Your Solitude?"

Oh Emma. Yesterday I lost the green stone from my cufflinks in your room, between the bed and the wardrobe. I was terribly put out.

To reassure myself that I exist in time, I showed some persistence and breathed life back into the clock. Since yesterday morning it has been muttering away to itself. All else when we meet.

Find the green stone (when next you sweep).

That was the kind of message I would find in my room during the last weeks of the war.

We spent much time together. Once early in 1945 the postman brought a letter. Khardjiev groaned and exclaimed, "Lyova doesn't love me!" The letter was from Lev Gumilyov, but not addressed to him.

A writer who reached the front after a period of banishment wrote that an angel in the guise of Lyova Gumilyov flashed past his eyes during an attack. Yet throughout the war Lyova was first a prisoner in the camps at Norilsk and then a free worker at the Norilsk combine. No-one was allowed to leave there before the war ended. Only in September 1944, I had received a letter from him, sent with the last autumn ship to leave Turukhansk.[1]

---

[1] Labour camps and settlements above the Arctic Circle could send mail and receive supplies only during the months when the northern sea route remained open.

Dear Emma,

I was very glad to get your letter.

It's nice to know an old friend has not forgotten me, despite our lengthy separation. It was also good to learn that you have met with success as a researcher. Undoubtedly, there is no more noble activity in the world; the most onerous of all my privations is being cut off from the world of scholarly studies. Today I envy everyone living west of the Volga. I'm fed up with Siberia. My life is something out of Jack London – skis, tents, boats, snow, water, mosquitoes etc. You ask about friends and a sweetheart. There are two men with me, ordinary workers, and over the past year I have only seen three females: a hare caught in a trap, a roe deer that came into our tent by accident and a squirrel that someone killed with a stick.

Nor are there any books, indeed there's nothing worthwhile here. Mama is apparently in good health and has returned, as I've learned from Nadezhda Yakovlevna's [Mandelstam] telegram, to Leningrad. She herself does not write or send me telegrams. That's sad. Through all my difficult years I never gave up research or literary activities, but now it seems it was all pointless. Now as then there is nothing else in my tedious life.

It's hard writing letters. How much easier it would be just to talk, kissing your fingers as I did so.

Sincerely yours,
L.

The letter, as the text shows, was a reply. I wrote to him in May 1944 when Akhmatova had arrived in Moscow from Tashkent.

She had brought me some of Mandelstam's manuscripts ("Nadya sent you these") and showed me Lyova's latest photographs. Wearing a close-fitting striped "sailor's" shirt, he had close-cropped hair and his hand-some grey eyes were gloomy. I wanted to let him know that I was alive and unharmed, despite the bombing of Moscow and the adversities of wartime existence behind the front lines. But Akhmatova did not give me her son's address.

I then was guilty of an unworthy deed. She briefly left my room. Immediately, I opened the handbag in which she kept her private letters (she always carried them with her) and copied down the address or, to be more exact, the box number. Akhmatova had twice recited this lengthy figure in a confused and rapid gabble.

No reply came, so I forgot about my letter.

The triangle[2] tucked in the side of my door, astounded me. The letter itself was like a voice from the next world. That was in September yet in December, apparently, Lyova turned up in Moscow. I couldn't make any sense of this. Khardjiev called to see me, however, and all was made clear. His authentic account did not prevent me listening, the following day at the Literary Museum, to sensational tales of Akhmatova's son's passage through Moscow on his way to the front. He was going as a volunteer, supposedly, but had only accomplished this by slashing his wrists. It was hard to imagine someone dragging himself in a "cattle" wagon from Siberia to Moscow with bleeding wrists, but, strange to relate, the stories were not so far from the truth. After the war, Lyova himself told me the details. He was indeed eager to get to the front and several times applied to be sent there, without success. Finally, he went to see the military commandant and, holding a razor to his wrist, threatened: "I am now going to slash my veins and smear your mug with my blood. Then the devils will grill you in a frying pan" (the officer was terrified of the Last Judgement). "So they let me go."

Today yet another description of this event circulates among the Akhmatova memorabilia. Employing already worn clichés of military and prison literature, it cannot be regarded as genuine testimony. Zoya Tomashevskaya, daughter of the well-known literary specialists Boris Tomashevsky and Irina Medvedeva, writes [*Oktyabr*, June 1989]:

> I shall never forget how, during the winter of 1943, Khardjiev rushed round to us one night on Gogol Boulevard and demanded warm things for Lev Gumilyov, who was being moved from the camps to the front. A folded note, tossed from the window of a railway prison wagon, miraculously reached Khardjiev.
>
> Warm clothing was needed, but Khardjiev never owned anything of the kind. He had no possessions whatsoever and did not even wear a fur hat in winter. Now he hastily tried to collect some things and find that "prisoners'" wagon standing in a siding . . . and he found it!

This story should be compared with Khardjiev's own recollections of this event. They were published in 1989[3] as a commentary to a letter he received from Lev Gumilyov, then already serving in the army. "Give

---

[2] Distinctive folding letter form for officially censored mail, used during the war years.

[3] "Akhmatova in Letters to Khardjiev, 1930s to 1960s", *Voprosy literatury*, 6 (1989).

my warmest greetings to Irina Nikolayevna [Medvedeva]," wrote Lyova. "Thanks to you and to her, I arrived comparatively well fed." Evidently those travelling to the front on a military train were not short of warm clothing and footwear; they needed money to stock up on food to augment their meagre official rations. This became clear the moment the two men met at the railway station. Gumilyov's first phrase is not reproduced in Khardjiev's note but I remember it well since he came to me directly from the station and immediately repeated it to me: "Nikolai Ivanovich, money!" Lyova exclaimed. Only a close acquaintance could be addressed in this way; Nikolai Khardjiev was an intimate of Akhmatova and Punin's household. Naturally, he did not find Lyova thanks to a letter thrown, on the off-chance, from a train. Only those convicted and on their way to the camps threw letters out of train windows. Lyova was permitted to make calls from a public telephone at the station in Moscow and managed to reach Shklovsky and Victor Ardov. They at once came to the train. Lyova asked Shklovsky to let Khardjiev know he had arrived in Moscow.

Khardjiev received a note from Shklovsky at the writers' canteen and immediately went to the Kievsky Station. He was joined by Irina Medvedeva, a friend of Akhmatova's, who happened to be eating at the same table. Khardjiev recalls:

> It was winter 1944. With considerable difficulty we managed to reach Platform 5. Sentries were guarding the entrance to the platform. I explained why we had come to a restricted area, and they sympathetically permitted us to walk past the closed, windowless wagons. The sentry repeatedly called out "Gumilyov"; at each wagon came the reply, "Not here." Finally, a soldier leaped from a distant wagon and we joyfully recognised Lev Gumilyov. One might have thought he was going not to the front but to a symposium. Listening to someone so fervent about his studies, I felt sure that he would return alive and unharmed from the war.

In this last assertion, Khardjiev's early impressions have been displaced by later memories. Both he and Medvedeva, on the contrary, came away from seeing Lyova with the gloomiest feelings. He was travelling, they thought, in a train for those serving in punitive battalions, and they expected the very worst would befall him.

Khardjiev had 60 roubles in his pocket and immediately gave them all to Lyova. Medvedeva was quick to grasp the situation. She vanished and sold the next ten days' worth of bread-ration cards for the entire

Tomashevsky family to the first buyer she could find. Passing the money to Lyova, she kissed and blessed him.

From then on, I was in a constant state of anxiety. I decided to talk to everyone who had seen Lyova that day. My unannounced visit to the Tomashevskys' apartment on Gogol Boulevard struck them as most peculiar. When I met Ardov in the metro, on the contrary, he hoodwinked me with his calm, offhand manner into believing that Lyova was going to Iran to work as a translator. I was yet more astonished by Irina Medvedeva's attitude. "Poprishchin, Poprishchin," she repeated. Lyova's account of the discovery he had made reminded her of Gogol's madman. Lyova equated its significance to Marx's theory. He was in a hurry, apparently, to describe his theory of *passionarnost'*,[4] which he later elaborated so fully. However, it was an ironic expression that earned Medvedeva's most thorough disapproval: "Let's move away from the God-bearers,"[5] Lyova remarked, leading her and Khardjiev to a quiet place on the platform. Medvedeva was shocked. Did she really imagine she could teach Lyova to love the Russian people?! Two months passed. Khardjiev was visiting when the postman brought me a letter from the front. The stamp on the triangular note was dated 5 February 1945 and carried the return address Field Post Box 32547-B. Lyova wrote:

Dear Emma,

You can hardly imagine how disappointed I was to leave Moscow without seeing you.

Only the hope that the war will end soon and that I shall come back "cheerful and alive by a familiar road" can be of moderate consolation.

I do not live badly now. The greatcoat suits me, and we have a real abundance of food, sometimes they even hand out vodka; and travel in West Europe is much easier than in Northern Asia. Most pleasant of all is the variety of impressions. Mama is not writing to me, and that's sad. Write, I shall be happy to get a letter from you.

I kiss your hands.

L. Gumilyov

---

[4] After reading Vladimir Vernadsky's *Chemical Composition of the Earth's Biosphere* (1965), Gumilyov found a scientific explanation, as he thought, for the problem of ethnogenesis described in his theory (see note 7, p. 166).
[5] Romantic strains of radical and messianic thought in pre-Revolutionary Russia saw the "People" as God-bearers.

Of course I wrote immediately, but the reply from Lyova was already marked April. Days of good fortune never lasted long in his life. As usual, he had experienced unpleasantness of some kind in the army; what exactly happened, I was never to learn. However, the hint in the April letter was clear:

12 April 1945

Dear, kind Emma,

I only received your letter today. The reason is that, after many an adventure, I have changed addresses; but the lads are forwarding my mail. Your letter roused me for several hours from a state of misanthropy. I've grown unaccustomed to good treatment and do not expect it, so I was moved and upset. But do write. My address is Field Post Box 28807-G.

So far, my war has been successful: I was part of an offensive, captured a city, drank ethyl alcohol, ate chickens and geese, and took a particular liking to the jam. The Germans, attempting to catch me, several times shot at me from a cannon, but they missed. I liked fighting; it is much more dull behind the frontlines.

Mama is not writing to me. I imagine that I am once again the victim of psychological games. I'm not surprised since "the salvation of the drowning lies in their own hands".[6]

I learned that lesson in good time. I have not written to Nikolai Ivanovich [Khardjiev] because I lost his address. Please pass on my greetings.

I have one other request to make of you. Shklovsky saw me at the station and suggested that I send him the manuscript of my tragedy, with a view to publication. I sent it but have lost that address also. I will be most grateful if you find out what has become of my manuscript and write back to me. I am sending you my verse, which in part describes my mood and the circumstances in which I find myself.

Please forgive this muddled letter, the sausage-makers [the Germans] do not make it easy to concentrate.

I kiss your little hands,

L.

---

[6] Quotation from Ilya Ilf and Yevgeny Petrov, *The Twelve Chairs* (Moscow, 1928).

Soon the war ended, and Lyova would return home unharmed. The four months left before demobilisation he spent near Berlin. We kept up our correspondence. I criticised his verse, something I now regret. He was no poet, of course, but in those moving days of victory when Lyova could look forward to being a free man, I should have kept quiet. Shklovsky also responded with something like disappointment or regret to Lyova's tragedy (apparently it was written in verse) and did not begin looking for a publisher.

Lyova's grudge against his mother is most evident and insistent in the letters quoted here. I do not know exactly why he received no letters from Akhmatova during this period. Most probably it was the result of misunderstanding, and of the whims of the censors and the postal system.

Perhaps Lyova's own exaggerated caution played some part. Letters began to arrive after the war had been won. The following hypothesis occurs to me. So long as the battle for Berlin continued, Akhmatova's silence was a kind of charm: she believed there were superstitious omens in every word she wrote. When the danger had passed, Lyova was deluged by his mother's postcards.

Still in Berlin, he wrote to me: "I have received a most laconic postcard from Mama. I am as angry with her as one can be with one's mother; and I shall be reconciled to her no sooner, probably, than half an hour after we meet again" (21 June 1945); "I have received three such very laconic postcards from Mama that I became even angrier. Well, when we meet we shall make our peace" (12 July 1945); "I am no longer angry with Mama and shall not try your patience" (14 September 1945).

The laconicism of Akhmatova's letters would irritate Lyova in the 1950s, when he was once again in the camps. In fact, Akhmatova had probably stopped corresponding with relatives and friends ever since Nikolai Gumilyov's execution and her own unofficial condemnation as a disgraced poet in 1925. This lasted for many years and was only interrupted during the war. Constant surveillance made itself felt in crude ways.

Akhmatova was especially traumatised by the opening and inspection of her correspondence. She found it so oppressive that she began to write letters almost in telegraphic style. Someone persuaded her that censors in the camps read postcards more quickly than sealed letters. Therefore, she would write Lyova two, three or even four postcards at a time. He found this hurtful and irritating, especially because, in his view, Akhmatova wrote dryly. But, aware of strange and hostile eyes, she could not express her feelings. I have leaped forward, however, to a different era. With the onset of victory in May 1945, I repeat, Lyova was deluged with postcards from Akhmatova. After many adventures he returned to Leningrad, where a separate room, next to his mother's, awaited him at Fontanka.

Their relations, occasionally disrupted by the inevitable domestic squabble, remained affectionate and harmonious until his last arrest in 1949. The renewed separation continued for seven years and gave birth to a great many misunderstandings. Unhappily, these culminated in a final row that led to the complete breakdown in their relations that clouded the last five years of Akhmatova's life.

We are now halfway through that journey. Before passing to the many years of my acquaintance with Akhmatova, we must return to an earlier period that I have already described. Even the most gifted writers of our "'60s generation", for all their achievements and admirable qualities, cannot imagine the daily life of people in the '30s. To them it all blurs to form a single murky current, "The Soviet way of life", which supposedly remained unaltered throughout seven decades.

During those long years, my relations with Lyova naturally passed through various phases. There were long periods of complete alienation, even hostility, but I consider the best epitaph to be the dedication he wrote when presenting me a copy of his famous *Ethnogenesis and the Biosphere of the Earth*:[7] "For dear Emma, a keepsake from Lyova, 2 February 1991. L. Gumilyov." Set against the last interviews he gave on television and in magazines, these simple human words strike me as a moment of clarity in an overcast mind. They take me back not to the 1950s (when, for the sake of the past, I refused to abandon Lyova during his long imprisonment) but to the 1930s, of which later generations know so little. And with a vivid, new-minted clarity, my memory conjures up the intonations and gestures of those whom I once held dear:

> "You will speak, and we shall listen and understand, listen and understand . . ." (Mandelstam's greeting to Akhmatova when she came to stay with them at Nashchokin Street).

> "Where's my favourite boy?" (Mandelstam, on not finding Lyova at home; he was then also staying at Nashchokin Street).

> "Lyova, don't slouch . . . Never talk like that again . . ." (Akhmatova)

---

[7] Gumilyov's presentation of his theory of *passionarnost'*, published in 1979. "From 1930 to the present, the author has gathered material and written about the deeds of the Huns, Turks, Khazars and Mongols," he wrote in the early 1990s. "His labours led to the Steppe Trilogy, which was published in seven books and 150 articles."

"When Gumilyov was shot, Lyova was nine years old; his fellow pupils voted not to give him any textbooks." These were then distributed by the schools where even the youngest classes were supposedly self-governing (from Akhmatova's own verbal accounts).

"Such people demand special treatment" (my union superiors about Lyova when, at the request of the Mandelstams, I was seeking their help for him). And still they turned him down.

"He's with us" (GPU[8] telephone call to Akhmatova in 1933, when Lyova was picked up during a raid on the Orientalist Eberman's apartment. From Akhmatova's own account.)

"You are a Sadducee" (Lyova sparring with Nadya who praised the LEF[9] and asserted that we were unconscious Marxists).

"When you die, Mama, I won't bury you like that" (Lyova on hearing of Eduard Bagritsky's funeral).

"*Yok* . . ." (With relish Lyova introduced Turkic words [in this case, "No"] in conversations with the biologists Kuzin and Leonov about their work in Central Asia).

"In the entire Soviet Union there are only two people who understand Khlebnikov: Nikolai Ivanovich and Lyova" (Akhmatova).

"The lion [*lev*, in Russian] pursued Maria in the wilderness . . . Joseph was long-suffering . . ." (from Mandelstam's "Sonnet" about Maria Petrovykh, whom both he and Lyova were pursuing).

"How interesting it is! Kolya and I had just the same experience" (Mandelstam remembering his amorous rivalry with

---

[8] The Soviet secret police; from 1934 known as the NKVD.
[9] The "Left Front in Art", a 1920s avant-garde grouping and journal of the same name, brought together "Futurist writers, Formalist critics and Constructivist artists".

Nikolai Gumilyov for the affections of Olga Hildebrandt-
Arbenina. Compare his poem "Because I Could Not Keep
Your Love . . ." and Gumilyov's "Olga": "Elga, Elga! rang
across the fields").

"Is she some kind of siren?" (Akhmatova on Maria Petrovykh).

"Ha ha ha, he he he . . ." (the general mood of the
Mandelstams' apartment).

"My damsel's figure might enhance a metre of tricot or
cheviot" (Mandelstam correcting and continuing the acrostic that Lyova addressed to me).

"Lyova, you're costing me a lot" (he lacked three kopecks
for a mug of beer and had asked me for the money).

"And that's for you" (something about the combination of
Lyova's impoverished clothes and his merry, intelligent look
prompted the beer-seller to give Lyova a full mug before his
turn).

"Carefree laughter . . ." (Akhmatova in a throaty and constrained
voice, on hearing me chatter with Lyova in the next room).

"What a relief she's gone, Nadenka. Too much electricity in
one apartment" (Mandelstam after Akhmatova's departure
from Moscow).

Chapter 1

Returning home from the Mandelstams' on one occasion, I waited at
the Kropotkin Gates for the No. 18 tram. Nadya had sent Lyova to buy
paraffin, and he stood next to me at the stop, holding the can and talking of philosophical matters with a simple and genuine interest. It
reminded me of the "boys" Mandelstam describes in the "Tenishev
College" chapter of his *Noise of Time*: "Little ascetics, they were monks
in their own childish monastery, where there was more inner life, harmony
and order in their notebooks, instruments, glass retorts and German
booklets than you find in adult lives." By this time there were hardly
any inspired youths in Moscow. We encountered only little bureaucrats

and vigilant members of the Komsomol: at best they were honest and pleasant but hopelessly limited girls and boys. I was convinced of Lyova's intelligence and noble interests, irrespective of his famous parents. He was a successor to the great Russian thinkers, I felt, and not heir to the gifts of his father and mother.

From that day onwards, Lyova began visiting me at home. The Mandelstams were amazed and Akhmatova apprehensive.

One Saturday evening in March 1934, Lyova came to see me. Negligently dangling a small letter by one corner, he proffered it to me as if I were a tram inspector checking tickets. It was a summons from the GPU that Akhmatova had forwarded in a panic from Leningrad, probably with some recent visitor. They invited Gumilyov to come in for a talk.

"Could you see me off at the station?" he requested. "No-one has ever met me or seen me off in my life."

That morning he had been to the Lubyanka, he claimed, shown them the summons and demanded that the GPU send him back to Leningrad: he had no money for the fare. They threw him out. I had no doubt that his tale was true. Many was the time I had witnessed his provocative behaviour on the tram or in public places.

This news perturbed me. I was staggered by the spectacle of his existence, which offered him no refuge on this earth. "Who is the fairest of them all?" the fairy-tale queen demands, and the mirror always replies, "In this land, beyond all doubt, you . . . but . . ." So whenever I asked in like fashion, "Who is the unhappiest person in the world?" I would tell myself, "You are, but . . ." and remember the nobility with which Lyova bore the miseries of a life in which he was buried alive . . . He left me the next morning. For many years, I could not forget the words "My papa," torn from him like a heartfelt sigh.

That evening, I went to the Mandelstams' to fetch Lyova and accompany him, as promised, to the rail station. They were infuriated. Nadya managed to whisper something revoltingly vulgar in my ear, and when we left Mandelstam followed us with a disapproving gaze.

We took the tram to the dirty, crowded station. Lyova talked of his sense of renewal: "I feel I'm about to take to the sky." Had he said goodbye to Marusya Petrovykh? I asked. He could not see the necessity. I insisted that he call her from the station. In the telephone booth he stood facing the apparatus. I looked at the slender neck above the fur collar, and the bowed head in a peaked cap, and I loved him.

The cheap overnight train was at the far end of the station. We said our tender farewells on the platform. From a window in the mail wagon, three-quarters boarded-up, a strange man looked down at us. A black, hard, tenacious gaze.

For some while, there was no news at all from Leningrad. Not knowing what was happening, I wrote to Lyova at Fontanka but the Mandelstams rang up Akhmatova and learned that he was well and had gone to visit his grandmother in Bezhetsk.[10] Aware that I had written, Nadya began to imagine the scene: my letter lay at Fontanka, and Punin and Akhmatova each passed comment on it.

Only three weeks later did my neighbour bring me a postcard that supposedly had been lying at the hospital office all that time. Lyova wrote: ". . . the weather's bad, I'm out of sorts . . . If you want, I can come back quickly . . . my friend has gone to Siberia for five years on a business trip." Later I learned that the GPU had summoned Lyova only to return his documents. A friend picked up during the same raid, however, had been sentenced to five years' imprisonment.

Lev Gumilyov, 1934

It was April. Snow and rain fell together, and the mud outside was impassable. I had a sore throat, and my arms were in bandages (a nervous eczema). "Where's that man who kept bandaging your arms?" my little nephew would recall unexpectedly, several years later. By that time, the man was beyond reach. It was hard to imagine that he was alive somewhere. And what was his life like? Now he was a prisoner in Norilsk: "that man" was Lyova. For the present, though, it was still April 1934. Without warning, and at an awkward moment somehow, he turned up in Moscow. He brought a poem that he had written in the train when he had last left. It began: "The gift of words, unfathomable to the mind / Was promised to me by nature."

The Mandelstams were displeased by Lyova's arrival. Osip composed a spiteful epigram about Lyova and myself which Lyova then recited to me. It referred to the handsome 18-year-old hero of Kuzmin's novella,[11] loved by all the women and especially by the men: the charming adventurer took

---

[10] In late 1917, Nikolai Gumilyov's mother Anna moved from the family's plundered country estate at Slepnyovo to an apartment in Bezhetsk, a nearby small town.
[11] Mikhail Kuzmin's 1907 *Adventures of Aimé Leboeuf*, set in eighteenth-century France, followed his novella *Wings* (1907), the first openly homosexual work of fiction in Russian.

full advantage of this. "Aimé Leboeuf loved older women . . ." began Mandelstam's epigram, and continued something like "Yet did those old ladies love him . . .?" I have no recollection of the rest. For my part I revealed to Lyova that Nadya said he was a degenerate. This courteous exchange did not prevent us ending our evening amiably and peaceably running down the Mandelstams.

I gave Mandelstam not the slightest indication that I knew of his nasty epigram. However, he presented me with a similar offering himself. This was a cutting from the *Ogonyok* weekly about the lion cub Kinuli ["foundling"], which had been tamed by Vera Chaplina, the famous wild-animal trainer. Mandelstam underlined certain phrases to indicate a new storyline. I have lost the first page, but the second is before me and sufficient to show what Mandelstam was getting at:

Seizing him by the scruff of his neck I dragged him into my room

the lion cub began to lick me

the former enemy selflessly spent the nights

in carrying out the experiment

I took in the lion cub not simply for amusement. I wanted to
     test my twelve years of experience

it turned out that affection can achieve a great deal

I shall continue my work

Meanwhile, my relations with Lyova, wonderful at a moment of peril (that passed safely, thank goodness), now relapsed gradually into a banal affair, and that did not appeal to me. We parted as if acting out Akhmatova's 1911 poem, "I Clasped My Hands beneath the Black Veil . . ." with its emphatically indifferent closing lines: "And with a calm, awful smile / said 'Don't catch a chill.'"[12]

Despite our separation, I had to invite Lyova to visit once more since he still had certain manuscripts from the Gosizdat [State Publishing House] consultancy. I was reading them to earn some money and shared the work with him. Lyova appeared but announced that someone in a bar had stolen the works of these amateur poets from his pocket. Instead he had brought me his own new poem, which could not fail to succeed. It was no recompense for the loss of the manuscripts, however, which

---

[12] See "Eight Poems by Anna Akhmatova", p. 318.

promised major difficulties for me at Gosizdat. I reacted coldly to his poem. He left, nervously disappointed.

During a conversation several days later, Nadya mentioned that Osya had been most complimentary about the third and fourth lines of this poem: "Ah! how bitter the cup of sorrow, / Do not love me, wife". I had barely managed to claim it as "my" poem when Nadya sharply interrupted: "Don't be so silly! It's all just for Marusya!" Both hurt and touched, she was jealously protective of the four-way amorous intrigue that linked Nadya, Osip, Lyova and Marusya.

This conversation occurred only days before Mandelstam's arrest. Yet our thoughts could not have been further from that almost inescapable event which completely overturned their life.

Chapter 2

After Mandelstam was arrested and we still did not know why, I sometimes reverted, through inertia, to our petty concerns, and so even did Nadya. One moment she was regarding Marusya Petrovykh with an unfriendly eye. The next instant she mentioned, in passing, that Lyova had left someone's book at the Ardovs' on his way back to Leningrad: he refused point-blank to say whose it was. Nina passed it to Nadya. In fact, the copy of Ehrenburg's novel *Moscow Does Not Believe in Tears* belonged to me.

I continued to work at the Central Committee of the Educational Workers Union, occupying the humble post of secretary to the bureau for research staff. In the evenings, I called at Nashchokin Street. Akhmatova stayed there until the Mandelstams left for Cherdyn. After this, I began preparing to go on vacation. The union had given me a paid holiday at Peterhof [a palace outside Leningrad], which I could take up after 30 June.

I went to Leningrad several days before, however, directly after seeing the Mandelstams off to Voronezh. For the first few hours following my arrival, I was in a state of agitation. I urgently wanted to visit Akhmatova and tell her about the Mandelstams, their return to Moscow from Cherdyn and their move to Voronezh. And where was Lyova now? With her? I rang immediately. "Come at once," she replied. But I contrived to lose my way on Nevsky Prospect or, to be more exact, on 25 October Avenue. Somehow I found myself on Staronevsky Street, and it was a while before I realised and turned back. Then I came up the wrong side of Nevsky Prospect and for some reason missed Fontanka. As if mesmerised, I moved down the wide pavement with the stream of pedestrians, the even façades of the buildings drawing me constantly towards the Admiralty spire, glittering in the haze of the hot day. Akhmatova, meanwhile, was expecting me.

Tired and upset, I finally reached Fontanka and house No. 34. There, before the railings of the Sheremetyev Palace, I halted in amazement – for no-one in Moscow had once mentioned this handsome sight. Entering the courtyard, I quickly found the dilapidated right wing, climbed the derelict staircase, and located Apartment 44. I do not remember who let me in. On the coat-stand hung a faded peaked cap and a familiar man's raincoat with a dark line around the collar. I opened the door into a large dining-room with darkened windows. Lyova rushed back and forth, an electric saucepan full of hot water in his hands.

"I knew it was Emma," he babbled. "I knew it . . . as soon as Bobik started barking in the courtyard." In confusion, he wavered about in his worn checked shirt, joy and embarrassment making his features thoroughly childish. From Akhmatova's attentive and perceptive gaze I could tell that happiness was written on my face. "Put the saucepan on the table, Lyova," she said.

Akhmatova and I sat down on a tiny divan in the corner of the room. I told her about Mandelstam, his condition on his return from Cherdyn and how he had left for Voronezh. Lyova listened, sitting a little way off with a textbook in his hands. Within the past month, it turned out, there had been changes in his life, and he now had a chance of going to university, an opportunity firmly denied him until then. A shift in politics meant that Russian history was again in demand: the subject had been replaced since 1917 by the history of world grain prices, but the class instinct of the proletariat was now being supplemented by a still more powerful impulse: patriotic feeling. Addressing some congress, the Party boss in Leningrad, Sergei Kirov, spoke of the disgraceful state of history-teaching in schools. Lyova's application was accepted, it seems, as part of this change in attitude: now they would allow him to take the entry examinations for the history faculty. I said goodbye to Akhmatova, and, without a word, Lyova stood up to accompany me. Akhmatova also said nothing.

I was staying on Vasilyevsky Island at the apartment of Mandelstam's brother Yevgeny. His family were at the dacha, and that evening he joined them, leaving only an elderly maid at home. Dropping by the next morning on his way to work, Yevgeny heard me calling Fontanka. "You were talking to Akhmatova's son, weren't you?" he remarked. "Keep clear of him, he may have some bad acquaintances . . . To be honest . . . from my apartment . . . I'd prefer it if . . ." I went to stay with my childhood friends who were themselves then living on Fontanka, next to the Anichkov Palace. As soon as the head of the family learned that I had been to see Akhmatova, he responded with a then-current journalistic phrase: "Oh, that old witch who has learned nothing and forgotten nothing?" (Incidentally, on my next visit to Leningrad, which was not until 1937, I recall the very same conversation: "You pay visits to the Sheremetyev Palace?" asked the medical relations with whom I was then staying. "They're all reactionaries.[13] We know, we've some acquaintances there. Whom do you go to see? Akhmatova? Keep well away from her son . . .")

At that time, it was the universally shared opinion that Leningrad workers differed from the proletariat of other Russian towns. It was the custom to note their politeness and their habit of wearing suits, white collars and even hats; in a word, they were a European working class and Leningrad was Russia's most European city. On my first visit in 1927, I was astonished by the city's grandeur, its palaces and monuments, and even by the view of the enormous factory in the Okhta district, which someone pointed out to me from the bridge. Everything prompted me to reflect how extraordinarily powerful the October Revolution must have been to overthrow such a stronghold of Tsarism. By now I was accustomed to the palaces but saw the city's inhabitants as creatures out of Dostoyevsky. The skinny men with clay-coloured faces and sharp eyes rushing down the steps into the bar all struck me as either student revolutionaries or Raskolnikovs. And they were indeed quite different from the Muscovites. In the centre of town, though, on Fontanka and the Nevsky Prospect, I no longer felt this so clearly. At Peterhof, meanwhile, I encountered yet another aspect of life in Leningrad.

The schoolteachers' rest home was located in the English Palace. This was an ordinary residential building with high ceilings and spacious rooms. Mine was for four people. Two of the cots were occupied by friends who had little to do with education. One was about 30 and liked to repeat: "I'm no beauty, am I? And yet men love me, I can't think why." The other was younger and would listen to her friend attentively, learning how best to organise her life. They would talk about trysts in the Tauride Gardens, pleasure trips to the Islands and to Strelka. They were accompanied by shop directors or factory managers. The friends discussed which of these admirers were the more generous and boasted of the presents they received.

The third person in our room was an older schoolteacher. When our jolly neighbours were out, she talked politics. She was especially disappointed that we were handing over the Chinese Far Eastern Railroad to the Manchurians. "And Russian Ivan takes the rap for everything," she would announce. We were sitting on the terrace in wickerwork chairs

---

[13] Literally, "members of the Black Hundreds", i.e. supporters of a shadowy pre-Revolutionary nationalistic and anti-Semitic organisation.

when a column of Young Pioneers passed along the walk. "How pale and thin they are," commented my acquaintance. "If only you knew how often they fall ill, the poor children . . ."

At that moment I was reading the newspaper. Sensational news: Hitler had murdered Roehm. The Fascists were seizing power in Germany. Meanwhile, the teacher was telling me about a professor she knew. He was arrested and, during his interrogation, the NKVD [GPU] "made him stand in the corner, with his face to the wall, like a naughty schoolboy."

She described amateur performances at the Scholars' Club in Leningrad and took a gossip's interest in identifying a professor's wife or a certain Academician's son among the actors. This made an impression on her, but I grew bored. It brought to mind amateur theatricals in the provinces before the Revolution: I had heard quite enough about the passions and intrigues they provoked from my older sisters. And how could anyone forget the Chekhov stories which so often wove the description of similar events into the plot and the psychological portraits of the main characters? Did such petty-minded provincialism still exist? It was not continuing, it was only just beginning. As I recalled, Mandelstam had spoken very recently (in 1929) of our future: "It will be small-minded provincialism, the like of which the world has not yet seen . . ."

Lyova came to visit me several times at Peterhof. My bold neighbours christened him the "Half-Wit". An unreliable admirer, in their opinion. We strolled about the gardens, and he read me his poems, which were soaked in Akhmatova's characteristic vocabulary, "misfortune" and other words I do not now recall. His voice modulated expressively. We went out for a walk and lay down on the grass next to the fence of the Scholars' Sanatorium, to which we had no access. By chance, Professor Piksanov was staying there. I could not stand the man. As a Moscow University student, I had attended his seminar on Karamzin and still harboured hostile feelings since he had been dismissive of my work. He was a pedant, in my view. Then, perhaps, I was wrong but when he lambasted Bakhtin at the defence of his dissertation about Rabelais, Piksanov's conservatism could no longer be in doubt. That was in 1947, immediately after the Central Committee decree denouncing Zoshchenko and Akhmatova which was to cast a shadow of philistinism over our entire culture for many years. In a written assessment of Bakhtin's work, Tarle said that his book about Rabelais was of universal importance;[14] Djivelegov described Bakhtin's erudition as devastating and unrelenting; and one young postgraduate, nervously wringing his hands, said that Bakhtin's works were

---

[14] Published in 1965 as *Rabelais and His World* (Eng. trans. 1982), by which time Bakhtin was almost 70.

a source of illumination. Yet Piksanov, extensively citing Chernyshevsky, claimed indignantly that Bakhtin was forcing a genius of the Renaissance back into the Middle Ages! The author became so incensed that, supporting himself on his crutches, he made agile leaps on his one and only leg and yelled at his opponents: "You all need replacing!" Djivelegov tried to defuse the atmosphere: "One more dissertation like that", he declared, "and I'll have a stroke." That day in Peterhof it was almost as if I had a premonition of this. Along the garden paths of the Academy of Sciences' sanatorium the puffed-up Piksanov strolled self-importantly, while on the grass behind the fence, placidly warming himself in the sunshine, lay the son of two outstanding Russian poets and future noted scholar Lev Gumilyov. The spectacle said something about that historical moment.

When I returned to the city from Peterhof and went to Fontanka, I found Akhmatova rather unwell. She was lying, worn out, on the divan, and the palms of her hands were damp. For the first time I noticed the elegant lines of her arms, elbows and shoulders. Despite the heat, her whole being seemed to emanate coolness and mystery. To some, this choice of words may appear fanciful, but I can find none more suitable. The feeling was probably intensified by the trees growing outside the windows. The shadows of the branches shifted fantastically across the ceiling and walls, which were hung with drawings by Boris Grigoryev. We moved to the dining-room. "Nikolai Nikolayevich [Punin] has gone to Sochi with Irochka and Anna Yevgenyevna," Akhmatova said. "He left us his ration card, but we don't have any money to use it."

Both she and Lyova were weak with hunger and did not even have enough to pay for cigarettes. Then, evidently, they borrowed a little money from one of their acquaintances. Nevertheless, Lyova gained a low mark in his last exam because he was faint-headed from hunger. It was then that I came up against Akhmatova's strange domestic arrangements. Punin[15] lived with both families. Although he now shared his life with Akhmatova, he did not cease looking after his first wife (Anna Yevgenyevna, née Arens) and their daughter Ira. All lived in the same apartment and ran the household as one.

Before returning to Moscow, I saw Akhmatova and Lyova several more times. Once I was in the chemist's shop on the corner of Nevsky Prospect and Fontanka and looked through the window at the far side of the Prospect. Unexpectedly, I saw a lonely figure amid the two intersecting streams of passers-by. It was Akhmatova. She was walking very calmly to the Public Library, hatless and in a white linen dress with Ukrainian

---

15 The art specialist Nikolai Punin (1888–1953) was Akhmatova's fourth and last husband.

The House on Fontanka

embroidery that Punin had brought her back from Kiev. As she proceeded with her strange, hesitant gait, something seemed to shield her from the hurriedly passing strangers. I felt that I loved her. It is so easy to tell, when you suddenly see someone dear to you in a crowd or on the street. The person seems so defenceless . . . they'll knock her down or run her over . . . Why can't they see that they should treat her with care?

Now that the Mandelstams had left Moscow, my life would change, Akhmatova realised. What did I intend to do now? she asked. Hearing that I very much wanted to take up the history of literature but had not yet chosen a definite subject, she suggested that I begin studying the life and work of Gumilyov. Akhmatova mentioned two surnames I should remember. Luknitsky and Gornung, she said, had long been engaged in such study. (Only half a century later did the results of their labours appear in print.) Akhmatova promised to give me certain bibliographical materials which she and her assistants had put together. Enthused by all I had seen and heard in Leningrad, I returned to Moscow.

I still had a few days' leave. Yevgeny Khazin and I went to the Park of Culture and Recreation (Gorky Park). I wanted to go to the outdoor theatre, but he couldn't afford the tickets. He never had any money. We entered the hall where they played records. It was very crowded. Some were shouting for Caruso recordings, others demanded that they play Chaliapin. Complete strangers argued with one another about the vocal qualities and performances of the two great singers. For the first time, I was looking at fanatical supporters. Of course, there were then also football fans who even in their daily lives were divided between

Spartak and Dynamo supporters. Such passions, however, lay beyond the scope of my observation. Among these amateur singing enthusiasts I recognised a distinctive category of Muscovite. Historians who gave up teaching in schools to be accountants and secretaries; engineers who exchanged irksome public service for a peaceful life as a construction draughtsman – in other words, all who had sought well-paid, clean work free of ideological pressure. They were ardent radio-listeners (it was then still a novelty), and many had acquired gramophones; their wives were wild about the singing of Kozlovsky and Lemeshev.[16] Ten to fifteen years later, something began to tell me they had all been killed, if not during the war then in the prisons and labour camps. That type of Soviet person had disappeared for many years to come.

When we'd heard enough singing, Yevgeny and I went to the dance hall. A working-class lad, short but well proportioned, was dancing the foxtrot in the Russian manner: he moved with such elegance and such a stonily impassive face (then *de rigueur*) that we could not help admiring him. "A prince of the blood," we decided. An uncle who was doctor at the Tula ammunition plant also used to say that one came across individuals of striking pedigree among the young workers there.

Next day I went to the office. They were just waiting to sack me, it seemed. I had to face Litvin-Sedoi himself, who sat on the Central Council's Presidium. I requested two days to tidy up and hand over my files since I was very proud of my card index and folders. "There's no need to hand anything over. You're to leave today," was the reply. He gave no explanation of the reasons for my dismissal.

I asked for a reference. The director of political education, formerly an inspector, might have come from the pages of Sologub's *Petty Demon* [1907]. On a scrap of paper he wrote: A good employee but did not do voluntary work. What was this?! I sat on the "economic commission" of our Union committee. (For the life of me, I cannot now remember what we did there.) I asked for an explanation. "You have a degree, more is expected of you," the director declared. I remembered that the Union's Central Committee had instructed me to visit schoolteachers' apartments just before the New Year and check that they did not contain decorated fir trees.[17] I firmly rejected such an outrageous request. Perhaps that was why they called me a poor volunteer? The reference I was given had a definite concealed political meaning, but of what kind? That I did

---

[16] Contemporary Soviet tenors with a repertoire of folk songs, romances and classical music.

[17] Until the mid-1930s, this pre-Revolutionary custom was prohibited. The Orthodox Christmas fell on 7 January (New Style).

not know. I appealed to my immediate superior. "They always made remarks to me about you," he responded, "but I told them you were a good employee." Only in 1992 did I learn that Mandelstam not only gave my name as one of those who heard his "seditious" poem about Stalin but also my exact place of work: "The research staff bureau at the Central Council of Trade Unions." Little wonder the Council Presidium lost no time in sacking me.

Once again I was unemployed. Officially, I was a dependant of my father. I went to the Lenin Library to read Gumilyov's books. They were handed out only in the restricted-access room, and I enjoyed working there. Between the bookcases I could look through the windows on the ground floor at the old Kamenny Bridge [replaced in 1935], lightly spanning the river and, beyond it, the Poteshny Palace and the tops of the cathedral cupolas in the Kremlin. Then the railings of the garden in front of Pashkov House formed a calm half-circle that reached far across what is now the main road. Snow was falling. This was the real Moscow. I had forgotten about it as I took the No. 19 tram across the Ustinky Bridge every day on my way to the Central Council.

Lyova sent me a letter. He had been accepted by the university and the day before he had already taken part in a student *subbotnik*.[18]

Chapter 3

Papa was a consultant at the Kremlin hospital and among his high-ranking patients was Shvernik, head of the trade unions. That December, Shvernik sent Father an invitation to a gala evening, at the Central Council itself, as I recall. Freshly shaven and wearing a new tie, Father drove to the event with pleasure in a car provided by the Kremlin medical administration. He returned unexpectedly early. Standing, amazed, by the stove in the dining-room he said: "Kirov's been murdered." There had been an announcement that evening by the event's organisers. Papa repeated the details. When he said Kirov had been shot in the back of the head, I could not help blurting out: "They killed him themselves." "Only you could say a thing like that!" shouted my father, outraged, and quickly left the dining-room, slamming the door behind him.[19]

Nadya came up from Voronezh and told of meeting some "returnees" allowed to live no nearer than 101 kilometres from Moscow. They

---

[18] "Voluntary" (unpaid) labour activities.
[19] The death of Sergei Kirov on 1 December 1934 would soon be used by Stalin to justify the Purges and the destruction of all his rivals within the Bolshevik Party.

described how they had learned of Kirov's murder. During the night, all the doors started opening and shutting; people ran from one building to another, and alarmed voices could be heard. The exiles were already experienced people and realised that this calamity would also affect them.

Papa meanwhile recounted what happened during Kirov's funeral. Stalin went to Leningrad and gave the local Party bosses such a bawling-out that the blood froze in their veins. They literally fell dumb and trembled with fear. It was not hard to believe – one need only take note of Molotov's cowed ears in the *Pravda* photograph of the funeral.

On 20 January, the student vacation began. A very despondent Lyova came to Moscow. Not a trace remained of his initial joy at being accepted by the university. I had flu and could not see him for several days. When he visited he said: "I'm leaving." Before going home he had to call on his granny in Bezhetsk who had raised him until his sixteenth birthday. "There's no way round it – family," he concluded. "What have you been doing all week?" I enquired. "Lying on the sofa at the Klychkovs' and smoking."

Both Sergei Klychkov and his wife, Varvara, had taken a liking to Lyova when he was still living with the Mandelstams. During that first year of our acquaintance, Lyova naively confessed to me: "I used to play among the cabbages in Bezhetsk. Now here I am, staying with a famous poet who reads me his verse. I nonchalantly make critical remarks, and he tells me how Gumilyov chided him when he showed *him* his first poems." In turn, Lyova read his verse to Klychkov. Afterwards Klychkov told me: "Lyova won't be a poet, but he will become a professor."

In March 1935 began the mass expulsion of former members of the gentry[20] from Leningrad. Old ladies, quite unadapted to contemporary life, were evicted from their well-settled communal lairs[21] and, within 48 hours, packed off in all directions.

I was still unemployed. My best friend since schooldays, Lena Galperina, who was married to the artist Osmyorkin, helped me find a job. We had studied together at Moscow University, but she had then also been enthusiastically involved in public readings. This branch of theatrical art played

[20] The term "gentry" denotes the pre-Revolutionary *dvoryanstvo*. A status that might be hereditary and landed, it was also attained automatically on reaching a certain rank within the civil and military hierarchies of the Tsarist system. Hence the eviction of the Rudakovs from Leningrad.
[21] See Appendix 1.3, "Living Space", pp. 425–6.

a very important part in the educational programmes of the 1920s. Literary evenings involved everything from solo performances by acclaimed actors and actresses to thematic lectures given by professional performers in workers' clubs.

Lena worked for the lecture bureau of the Moscow City Education department. On her recommendation I was given a job there but in administration: I could hardly read Marxist lectures on literature, could I? They made me assistant to a very energetic and experienced woman who was popular among the actors. Apart from purely cultural "events", the department also had to organise large variety concerts involving actors, dancers and singers. As the new table of ranks took shape, a novel category of performer began to appear: People's Artists and laureates of State prizes. Slavish praise became common and almost obligatory. In private, my boss still permitted herself to laugh at the universal refrain "Only Comrade Stalin . . ." (knows, understands, etc.), but at work such liberties were quite out of the question. Once I poked fun at the reverence with which a department official referred to the Party's Central Committee. With incomprehension he retorted sharply: "We love and respect the Central Committee." During a May Day or Revolution Day demonstration, another of our officials, a terribly well-read man, gave me a detailed and severe account of *Sous les toits de Paris* [1930]. This bourgeois film, which was only just being shown in Soviet cinemas, was bad, empty and devoid of ideals; but as I watched, I liked it so much that my heart melted within me.

Another noticeable change. They had begun to reconstruct the city. Moscow's famous round squares were being transformed into shapeless expanses. The central flowerbeds vanished and so, naturally, did the diagonal asphalt pathways that gave the individual a sense of scale and direction. Flyovers lifted across the city. A building like the former lycée now found itself somewhere down below, beneath the new Krymsky Bridge.

The Party authorities at work did not like me. "I can't understand what our Party people want from Emma," my immediate superior would say to Lena.

Yet I also found some release here in the mass entertainments we organised for public celebrations, excursion trips, rest homes and so on. Among the performers were accordionists, magicians and amateur jugglers. The actors, lecturers and administrators considered these people beneath contempt; they were just in it for the money. But we established a very special working relationship. They began by informing on one another and even denouncing my boss: she took bribes, they claimed, which was an utterly incredible allegation. Over the telephone someone openly defamed one of the best performers: "He's just a money-grabber," I was told. "So are you," I calmly answered. "Stop peddling gossip." Astounded, he shut up.

Little by little, I introduced a quite different tone, and this educational process gave me a great deal of amusement. Take the following episode, for example. "The GPU club have just been to see me," I said and added, without more ado: "they want a whole day's entertainment, somewhere far out of town, and they're not paying much. As you well know, I can't bargain with them or turn them down. Help me out. Cast lots" (I meant the three or four best performers) "and whoever pulls the short straw gets the very next good order we receive. Just treat this event as though it was unpaid." Since I always kept my word (the most important thing in such circles) and everyone had their turn when I allocated the tours, a strict and orderly system came into being. It felt as though I was running a genuine workers' co-operative. This enraged our bosses. "What's going on here?!" they enquired suspiciously, and soon found a plausible reason to sack me. I had not served a full year in the department.

Again I started going to the Lenin Library. On my way there, I once met the biologist Boris Kuzin. It was pleasant to see the close friend who had been the Mandelstams' constant and welcome visitor. Now that they had left, I invited Kuzin, with a special feeling of friendship, to come and see me more often. But somehow, strangely, he turned down my offer and almost ran away from me. With astonishment I looked at his retreating figure and noticed a painful tension in his back and head. That is how he remained fixed in my memory, hurrying beneath the walls of the Manege past the Alexander Gardens. He was being watched, apparently, and he knew it. Soon he was arrested. I never met him again, but we exchanged letters once. That was not until 1973, shortly before his death.

When Kuzin was arrested, Nadya went to see Smirnov, a gifted entomologist who was his close friend and scientific colleague. She was accompanied by Akhmatova, who had come on a visit from Leningrad. Akhmatova had no particular ties with Kuzin: indeed he had much less admiration for her than for Mandelstam, but she went to support Nadya at a difficult moment. Instead of a friendly discussion, Smirnov cried out as soon as he saw them: "It's your fault, you've ruined him!" and slammed the door. (Perhaps it did not happen quite like that. I was not present, but that was the story I heard from Akhmatova and Nadya.) Kuzin was sent to the camps. After two or three years, he was let out and exiled, his sentence reduced because he had overfulfilled his labour norms. Nadya went to visit him in Kazakhstan, where he worked on a State farm, as an agronomist, I believe. She brought back a photo of him wearing a sheepskin coat, his face changed beyond all recognition.

I cannot establish the order of my next few meetings with Lyova. There he was, seated at my bureau, writing a short poem that was too reminiscent of the early Lermontov. All I recall is the concluding phrase: "And nothing can rejoice my soul." On another occasion he wrote out a poem that was very powerful, despite its archaic vocabulary, and presented it to me. He was dedicating it to me, he said. As I remember it goes:

> The earth is poor, but richer then is memory
> That fears neither leagues nor years.
> We vow by ancient names
> And now from our dark shame
> Dare not look our wives in the eye
> But cast a gaze, humiliated and hypocritical,
> To our cups, our drunken cups of wine,
> And in them drown both envy and ignominy.

On another occasion he came back from church, sad and disappointed. He had ordered a requiem mass for his father, but the priest had not agreed to describe Nikolai Gumilyov as "slain".

From time to time, Akhmatova also appeared in Moscow. Once she stayed the night with me, preoccupied by my relations with Lyova. She would speak only of him. Gazing at me, she remarked, "What pale skin you have." Suddenly, for no apparent reason, she could not contain her feelings and exclaimed: "Emma, I want a grandson." She began to tell me how hard it was living with Punin and that Lyova was her only hope. When he finished

Lyova, Anna Akhmatova and Lyova's grandmother Anna Gumilyova, 1927

university they would live together. "But Lyova has a mad, passionate longing . . . " Akhmatova took so long to complete the sentence that I grew pale with anticipation " . . . to go and live in Mongolia."

She was alarming herself unduly. We had made no plans for the near or distant future. In fact, we gave no thought at all to our relations.

Akhmatova often stayed at the Mandelstams' flat in Moscow, where Nadya's mother looked after her. Of course, I would visit Akhmatova then and a couple of times found Pasternak with her. Once he was about to leave. Ending their conversation, he began to talk of his own domestic affairs. His father-in-law had not long died and left him a fur coat. A warm fur coat. "And now I shall go and try it out," was his adroit farewell, as he quickly donned the coat in the hall and went out into the frosty night. It was odd to observe his comfortable worldly manner in that habitation of woe.

Another time, Akhmatova and I were getting ready to leave for the station. She was going back to Leningrad. Unexpectedly, Pasternak dropped by and wanted to see her off. We left together. On the way, Pasternak got off the tram: "I'll catch you up." We exchanged puzzled glances but indeed he found us at the station waiting-room and was holding a bottle of wine (all he could then find in the shops), which he gave to Akhmatova.

There was some time before the train left, and they began talking about Andrei Bely. Both were critical of his late prose and membership of the Anthroposophist Society. When the conversation turned to Kamenev's article, which, so Nadya asserted, had killed the writer, Pasternak immediately said: "He's not one of us, but I shan't let that lot have him." In the preface to Bely's last book, *Between Two Revolutions*, Lev Kamenev had defined all Bely's literary work as a "tragi-farce" acted out "on the sidelines of history".

After a pause, Pasternak broached a sensitive subject. He began urging Akhmatova to join the Writers' Union. She maintained an enigmatic silence. He described how much good she might do by taking part in public life. He had been invited, for instance, to a meeting of the *Izvestiya* editorial board where he sat next to Karl Radek. They listened to what he had to say, and he was able to do something useful. Akhmatova's fingertips drummed on her little suitcase, and, casting the occasional highly expressive and almost demonstrative glance in my direction, she said nothing in reply.

Chapter 4

A morning telephone call. Lyova: "Can I come and see you now?" These sudden appearances and disappearances called to mind the Gorky novel in which one of the brothers, I think he was called Yakov, was wandering about Russia. Occasionally, he came home, announcing his return with a tap at the window. He would eat supper, talk to his family about some important matter and stay the night. Then he left again, and no-one knew how long he'd be gone, or if he would ever return.

Lyova was standing in the corridor wearing an awful jacket and trousers with enormous patches on the knees. He was embarrassed as he greeted me in our still-respectable apartment. He had grown a thin Tartar moustache that drooped round his mouth. On his way through Moscow, with only a day here, he was returning from an expedition somewhere in the Don area.

We decided to go to Kolomenskoye. In those days, it was a long journey, first by tram, then bus and some way further on foot.[22] Lyova still wore the very same greasy-collared raincoat with sleeves too short for his arms. The tram took a long while to come. People stood all around us. From time to time, they looked us up and down.

As we walked, Lyova told me how he had joined the expedition. The university authorities paid the fares of all involved apart from him. He went to the tutors. "What are you getting worked up about, Gumilyov?" "They're making my life impossible, that's why" (tossing a pile of books on to the floor); "they won't let me go on the expedition." In the end he paid his own fares, and once at the dig M.I. Artamonov made him one of his team. Lyova always told a good story. As with Akhmatova, every word counted. It was always an epic narrative, but neither word nor intonation was exaggerated to stress its tragic nature. (Later, he lost this style.)

We looked round the Church of the Ascension and the chancery buildings which, for some reason, were wrongly labelled the palace of Tsar Alexei Mikhailovich. How low the ceilings and doors were! "They were set at human height, but in the eighteenth century they began making them taller." Lyova always had a historical perspective on everything.

On the way, we had seen women workers digging trenches. "What's the point in making women do such heavy work? They won't be able to have children after that."

It was the last sunny day in October 1935. We sat on a bench beneath the elms opposite the Kazan church. Someone walked past, a little way off. "What's the time?" "Five o'clock." Without a word, we both leaped

---

[22] The seventeenth-century tsars built their summer residence, a fantastic, largely wooden complex, at Kolomenskoye in a park on a bluff above the Moskva River. Only the brick-built churches and gateways have survived. According to mistaken legend, Peter the Great was born there, prompting the poet Sumarokov to refer to it as "Russia's Bethlehem".

to our feet. (Although we had not seen each other for several months, we got on very well.) How the time had flown. This very evening, Lyova was going back to Leningrad, and he also wanted to call on the Klychkovs.

In the bus Lyova's behaviour was provocative. He did everything but trip up the workers coming home from some factory or other. In his crumpled peaked cap he looked like a former officer. They hated him but were intimidated by his audacity. Getting into arguments in the tram was a favourite pastime, and he always made sure he had the last word.

Back home we ate. He was a gloomy sight with his Tartar moustache. Falling silent for a while, he then announced: "When I get back to Leningrad they'll arrest me."

"?"

"Oh, we know all right. A friend of ours was interrogated this summer."

She was released but had confirmed everything.

"What did she confirm?"

"She heard conversations when she visited us."

I did not ask what conversations, probably their "Petersburg", "gentry" kind of discussion. I wept.

It was too late to visit the Klychkovs. He did not ring them but went directly to the station. Once more we were saying goodbye in my room, with the same prospect of never seeing each other again. The visit more resembled a farewell blessing than a lovers' rendezvous. Lyova's parting words to me were: "Become Orthodox."

What did I do the next few days? I don't know. There was no news from Leningrad.

I shared my anxiety with Lena. "Yes, the two of you are involved," she graciously conceded, but could not help adding: "I don't like prison affairs, they don't appeal to me." For Akhmatova, on the contrary, they had a definite "appeal". It was not my visit from Lyova that touched her. Probably she knew nothing about it. Twenty years later, though, when famous Italian films began to be shown in the Soviet Union, she insisted that I accompany her to a cinema on the outskirts of town where they had a repeat showing of the *Walls of Malapaga* [1949].[23] Akhmatova had already seen the film, but was ready to watch it again and again. The hero and heroine meet and say farewell before he is arrested. Inescapable punishment awaits him, and his misdeed is no fabrication but a real criminal offence. Nevertheless, Akhmatova said that it was "our" film, it was about us.

---

[23] Titled *Au-delà des grilles* in French. Directed by René Clement, it won awards at Cannes in 1949.

In the mid-1930s, all you could see in our cinemas were Soviet musical films like *The Merry Lads* and *Circus*, which I detested. During these same anxious and uncertain days, someone dragged me to a matinée showing of such a film. I went against my will and returned home in vexation. In the hall I could see Akhmatova sitting on the small corner divan with her ancient little battered suitcase. Radiating tension, she had already been waiting several hours to see me. We went into my room. "They've been arrested." "Who do you mean?" "Nikolasha [Punin] and Lyova."

She stayed the night and slept on my bed. I watched her burdensome sleep, as though she had been crushed under a stone. Her eyes became sunken and triangular recesses appeared around the bridge of her nose. They would never vanish thereafter. She had changed before my eyes.

The next day I took her to Nashchokin Street. As yet she herself didn't know whom to stay with. No-one could say how she might be received. All day I waited for her call. She summoned me only the next morning. Where she spent that night I don't exactly know; with the Bulgakovs apparently. We met by the entrance into the courtyard. She came out in her blue raincoat, long strands of hair tumbling and waving from beneath a felt cloche. She noticed nothing and looked about her with unseeing eyes.

We went to find a taxi. Kropotkin Square and Volkhonka Street had been dug up and closed off in several places: they were building the "Palace of Soviets" metro station where the dynamited Cathedral of Christ the Saviour had stood. Autumn mud. She was afraid to cross the road. A car appeared in the distance: "No, no, not on your life." "The car's still far away, let's go." She stepped out into the road and pulled back. I tugged her. She wavered. The car drew nearer. Next to the driver sat a man in a leather jacket. They noticed us and, it seems, burst out laughing. As they approached, the man in the leather jacket examined the strange figure, reminiscent of a shot bird, and recognised who she was. Recognised her, with pity and horror . . . Was this crazy, wavering beggar woman the famous Akhmatova? The entire play of emotions on his face flashed before my eyes. Probably he had once been an admirer and had watched her adoringly at poetry evenings. (Now you would hardly recognise yourself, my friend, sitting in a leather jacket next to the chauffeur of your government car.) They drove past.

Somehow we crossed the road and found a taxi. The driver drew out of the taxi rank and asked where we wanted to go. She did not hear. I didn't know where we were going. Twice he repeated the question. She stirred: "To Seifullina,[24] of course." "Where does she live?" I had no idea. Akhmatova muttered something. For the first time in my life, I heard her shout, almost shrieking with anger: "Surely you know where Seifullina lives?!"

Why should I know? Finally, I began guessing: At the Writers' Apartment Block? Akhmatova did not reply. Somehow we got an answer: Yes, in Kamerger Street. Off we went. All the way she cried out: "Kolya . . . Kolya . . . blood." She had lost her mind, I decided; she was raving. I saw her to the doors of the apartment. Seifullina herself let her in, and I left.

Many years later, in calm circumstances, Akhmatova read a lengthy poem to Tolya Naiman and myself. It struck me as familiar. "I think you read it to me once before, long ago," I said. "I was composing it the day we drove to Seifullina's," replied Akhmatova. I suspect that she herself altered a quatrain from this poem to get it past the censor:

> . . . for the "lily of the valley" May
> in my blood-smeared Moscow
> I'd give up the glory and gleaming
> Of the flocks of stars . . .

For "blood-smeared", the printed version reads "hundred-domed", but in her manuscript a blank space was left for the epithet.

We must return to the 1930s and those tense days.

I did not notice how much time had passed. Two days? Four? At last, the phone rang. Again only one phrase: "Emma, he's home!" Horrified I asked: "Who do you mean, he?" "Nikolasha, of course." Timidly: "And Lyova?" "Lyova as well."

She was ringing from Pilnyak's apartment. I went to see her there, at Pravda Street. A celebration was under way. The two of us sat in the bedroom while music could be heard from the neighbouring room. Guests had arrived. An important Party figure from the regional committee, and someone else: "He has three pips," she whispered to me.[25] Everyone wanted to see Akhmatova and to congratulate her . . . on this "royal pardon". But she had a great deal to tell me. Pilnyak came in and impatiently invited her to join them next door. "Boris Andreyevich," she said, "this is Emma!" But he was not interested; he wanted to mark the

---

[24] The writer and playwright Lydia Seifullina (1889–1954); her novelist husband, Valerian Pravdukhin (1892–1939), perished during the Purges.
[25] Literally "lozenges". Until shoulder boards and stripes were restored in the armed forces and security-service rank was indicated on uniform shirts and jackets by small, coloured lapel or collar buttons, varying in shape and number.

event with his guests in the
dining-room. Unwillingly, he
left us.[26]

What did Akhmatova have
to tell me?

It had all taken very little
time. Evidently, Seifullina had
connections in the Party's
Central Committee. Akhmatova
wrote a very brief letter to Stalin.
She gave her word of honour
that her husband and son were
not conspirators, nor had they
committed any crimes against
the State. The letter ended with
the phrase: "Iosif Vissarionovich,
please help!" Pasternak had also
written to Stalin. He had long
known Akhmatova, he wrote,
and observed her thoroughly

Emma Gerstein, 1937

admirable attitude to life. She lived modestly, never complained and never
asked anything for herself. "She is in a dreadful state," his letter concluded.
Pilnyak drove Akhmatova to the Kremlin commandant's office in his own
car; it had already been agreed who would receive the letter and hand it
personally to Stalin.

I noted for myself a difference in the way writers regarded Mandelstam
and Akhmatova. They felt a duty towards the former as a wonderful
poet, but in Akhmatova's case this was enhanced by genuine affection.

Her account was interrupted by Pilnyak. He insisted and she went
into the next room to meet the guests. There was a musical flourish as
Pilnyak put on a new record and grandly announced: "Anna Akhmatova!"

As I waited for her in the bedroom, I wrote a short note to Lyova.

Akhmatova returned from the dining-room for a moment to say goodbye. I asked her to take my letter. "Really! It's no time for letters! I
shan't take a thing." She was fearful of letters, a search in the train,
anything . . . and quite rightly too. Who knows what I might have written about Stalin in that note? "Well, in that case," I asked, "tell Lyova
what I was going to write: he must make use of these exceptional circumstances and seek permission to take his degree as an external student.

---

[26] The writer Boris Pilnyak (1894–1938) was arrested late in 1937 and shot in
April the following year.

He will not cope otherwise. The students won't let him alone, and sooner or later he'll say the wrong thing: 'Stalin himself released me' . . . It's dangerous. They'll accuse him of being boastful and taking the 'godhead's' name in vain."

I was about to go home. Akhmatova followed me out into the hall. I opened the door. Suddenly, the tall, lithe figure bent down and she gave me a rapid and tender kiss.

Some time after, Nadya arrived from Voronezh. Of course, I went to Nashchokin Street, and there I found Mandelstam's Leningrad brother, Yevgeny, and Khardjiev. They continued a conversation begun earlier. Yevgeny finished describing his visits to Akhmatova: it seems they concerned joint efforts on Mandelstam's behalf. Then he began saying how hard her life was and, ending his account, remarked in passing: ". . . And that business with her son . . ." "Nothing helped?" asked a concerned Khardjiev. Startled, I demanded: "What's happened?" "Oh, they've excluded him from university! Some silly student affair." I leaped up and began walking about the room in agitation. Just as I'd feared! Nadya came up to me and asked softly, in amazement, "You love him?"

Soon Alexander Osmyorkin went to Leningrad. (He was in charge of a studio there at the Academy of Arts, and another in Moscow at the Surikov Institute.) With him I sent a note to Lyova.

Two weeks later Alexander returned and brought me a reply. It was an historic letter. Lyova described in detail all the harassment he had endured at the university. Two years later, regrettably, Akhmatova herself threw this letter into the stove in my room. The circumstances, Lyova's arrest in 1938, were indeed exceptional.

I recall only two of the episodes Lyova described, and one in no more than the most general outline. It concerned Peter the Great. Lyova had given a different assessment of the Russian Emperor from that urged on the students during their lectures, and they complained that he considered them idiots. The stupidity and meanness of the other episode remains etched in my memory. "I have no sense of rhythm," wrote Lyova. When they did army drill, he said, he was always out of step. The instructor declared that he was sabotaging the exercise and deliberately discrediting the Red Army. Lyova ended the letter: "The only solution is to move to Moscow. Only with your support can I lead a normal life and at least do a little work."

At the very end of January 1936, Akhmatova came to Moscow – to do what she could for Lyova, of course, and also perhaps for Mandelstam, whom she was about to visit in Voronezh. Yevgeny Khazin and I saw her off at the station. Before she left I showed her Lyova's letter. When she had read to the end, she announced in a voice of iron: "Lyova can only live with me." Thereafter Akhmatova would not let him visit Moscow. I did not know how he spent that winter. I do vaguely recollect yet one more episode.

Probably spring was already on the way. I received a letter from Lyova with a request. In order to join an archaeological expedition, it appeared, he had to complete at least one brief course, say, in agronomy, since he had been expelled from the university. They would not register him even for that, however. I don't remember whether he asked me to intercede with Pasternak or if I thought of it myself. At any rate, I borrowed my cousin's knitted cardigan and went to see Pasternak at home; he then lived on Volkhonka. I liked the room, which was cool and empty. Pasternak was friendly and sympathetic to my request but nothing came of it. I don't remember why.

That summer, Akhmatova again came to Moscow. I told her of my appeal to Pasternak. She commented mildly: "That's not the cleverest thing you've done in your life."

Then she went to stay at Starki, Vasily Shervinsky's estate near Kolomna. The Soviet regime had left him this property in recognition of his outstanding contributions to medicine. The renowned consultant was widely known outside Russia and in our circle was famed for having treated Turgenev. Akhmatova was friendly with Shervinsky's son Sergei. As for me, I went with our family, for the first time in many years, to our dacha in the village of Cherepkovo, not far from Moscow. Yevgeny Khazin often came to visit me there.

In July, Akhmatova returned from Starki and met me as a woman meets a vanquished rival. "Lyova was so keen to see me that he came to Starki from Moscow on his way to join the expedition," she declared. I had no idea that Lyova had been in Moscow and managed to get on the expedition after all. I was disconcerted and quite hurt. But I had not left him my address at the dacha, had I? Somehow that simple idea had not entered my head. Still, on his return from the expedition that autumn he came to me and spoke of his extreme depression at that time.

Meanwhile, much in my life and interests had changed.

Chapter 5

Various episodes from that time fuse in my memory to form a single period, the mid-1930s. Yet other sources help determine, to the day, the date on which certain things happened. I did not remember, for instance, exactly when the events I have just described took place: my trip to

Kolomenskoye with Lyova, Akhmatova's long wait in our hall, our ride to Seifullina's apartment, and the celebration at Pilnyak's. Half a century later, indirect documentary evidence has appeared. From an entry in Yelena Bulgakova's diary we learn that Akhmatova came to her on 30 October 1935 and, with the help of Mikhail Bulgakov, drew up her letter to Stalin. Other publications give 3 November 1935 as the date on which Punin and Lyova were released. Sergei Rudakov's letters establish that Akhmatova visited Voronezh from 5 to 11 February 1936. Therefore, Yevgeny Khazin and I had accompanied her to the station on the 4th (or perhaps 3rd) of that month. In the days that followed I would be distressed and dejected by the misfortune that had struck our family or, to be more precise, by the unbearable grief that had overwhelmed my father.

Alexandra Kanel, my father's friend and dearest companion since the Revolution, died on 8 February 1936. Her death occurred in strange circumstances and was almost instantaneous. There were hard frosts and blizzards that year, typical February weather for Moscow. Alexandra Kanel caught cold, but it was no more than the usual sneezes and running nose. This unexpectedly became acute meningitis and within two to three days she was gone.

My father had lost his closest friend and the beloved woman who was the radiant figure in his life. Shortly before, he was himself seriously ill. I was visiting him at the Kremlin hospital when Kanel came into his room: he gazed at her with devoted eyes, full of love and hope. During the civil funeral, he pointed towards the open coffin and said to me, with inexpressible tenderness: "Just look, how beautiful she is!"

I was totally absorbed with anxiety and compassion for him in his grief. Yet I regarded all else that went on around me with calm eyes. Of course, I was sorry for Kanel's daughters Dina and Lyalya, whom I had known since they were children. I was well aware how passionately they loved their mother, but as adults we had been so distant that I did not know them any more. Coldly, I noted that Dr Levin quoted Nadson[27] in his tribute before the coffin and that among the numerous wreaths was one sent personally by Molotov. Then it was impossible to foresee what a calamity for her daughters Dr Kanel's friendly ties with the families of Molotov, Kamenev and Kalinin would prove to be.[28] She was their personal physician and, of course, knew many Kremlin secrets. Our family was so far removed from this side of Papa's life, however, that we felt for his grief

---

[27] Popular poet of the 1880s, see "Near the Poet", p. 51.
[28] Lev Kamenev was executed, with Zinoviev, in August 1936. Kalinin and Molotov remained prominent government colleagues of Stalin, but their wives were later despatched to the camps.

but did not speculate about the strange course of Alexandra Kanel's illness. At the time, we did not ask ourselves about events and incidents that seared my father's soul with alarm. These have since become better known.

In his memoir about the 1938 "doctors' plot", published in 1988 (*Druzhba narodov*, April), Professor Rapoport made reference to the death of Alexandra Kanel:

> I suspect that the real reason for the conviction of Dmitry Pletnyov and Lev Levin was not their phoney participation in the "murder" of Gorky but a quite genuine event in 1932 – the suicide of Stalin's wife Nadezhda Alliluyeva, who shot herself through the temple.[29] Those who knew the real cause of death were the chief consultant of the Kremlin hospital, Alexandra Kanel, her deputy Lev Levin and Professor Pletnyov. All three were invited to sign a certificate giving the cause of death as appendicitis. All three refused. The certificate was signed by other doctors and the insubordinate medics met a tragic fate (Alexandra Kanel, it is true, "managed" to die in 1936).

Still more definite is the tale of Kanel's elder daughter Dina. She was also recounting her own tragedy, however: arrest in 1939, Beria's involvement in her case, the beatings and torture of her interrogation and what happened to her thereafter. She was finally rehabilitated only after Stalin's death. The fate of Kanel's younger daughter, Lyalya, was even more frightful. She was not released and evidently was shot in 1940. Dina's laconic account has been published in *Till My Tale Is Told*:[30]

> I suppose it was preordained as far back as 1932. In that year my mother as chief consultant at the Kremlin hospital, together with Doctor Levin and Professor Pletnyov, refused to sign the falsified death certificate of Stalin's wife: it stated that Nadezhda Alliluyeva had died of acute appendicitis. Stalin never forgave any of them for this. The fate of Levin and Pletnyov is well known: they were later accused of having murdered Maxim Gorky. My mother was dismissed from her post in 1935 and she died the next year.

---

[29] And see Appendix 1.2, "Alliluyeva's Suicide", p. 424.
[30] Simeon Vilensky, ed., *Till My Tale Is Told: Women's Memoirs of the Gulag*, Russian edn 1989; English edn 1999 (London and Bloomington). One of the 16 authors is Yagoda's niece Vera Znamenskaya.

Dina Kanel's memoir "Meeting at the Lubyanka" tells how she met Tsvetayeva's daughter Ariadne Efron in prison. More detail can be found in *Entwined Fortunes* [1988], a book by Maria Belkina about the life and death of Marina Tsvetayeva and of her children Ariadne and Georgy. These were the details that so disturbed and depressed my father, but I had no inkling of them at the time.

Alexandra Kanel was sick with a mild influenza, Dina told Belkina, when Lev Kamenev's 12-year-old son Yura came unexpectedly to see her, sent by his mother Olga [née Bronstein, sister of Lev Trotsky], from the city of Gorky. (They had been banished there after Olga's first arrest.) Kamenev was already in prison. The show trials had begun. "Yura only spent a short while in Kanel's room because he was in a hurry to catch the train back," writes Belkina. "Alexandra Kanel came to dinner upset, with red blotches on her face. She was distracted, nervy, and after sitting for a short while with the family, went back to her room, saying she felt unwell. Dina pressed her to say what had happened. What did Yura tell her? Kanel insisted he had just called to pass on his mother's greetings." It was after this visit that the cold became meningitis, and within four days Kanel was dead.

Only in 1941 when Dina was in Oryol prison did she learn of the fateful role Yura's appearance played in Kanel's life. Dina found herself in the same cell as Olga Kameneva. Lev Kamenev and their elder son, Alexander, an airplane pilot, had already been shot, and after many enquiries she learned that Yura had died, supposedly of typhus. At that moment, the invading Germans approached Oryol. The Soviet prison authorities shot Olga Kameneva and the other political prisoners: she was led out of the cell to her death when Dina was still there. Shortly before her execution, however, she told Dina exactly what Yura said to her mother.

Olga instructed him to warn Kanel that "they" had asked many questions about her. In particular, they wanted to know who told Olga Kameneva that Alliluyeva had committed suicide. Her daughter-in-law, Alexander Kamenev's wife, said they had heard the news from Alexandra Kanel: she had visited them at home on the day after Alliluyeva died. Kanel had already learned of the event from Molotov's wife, Polina Zhemchuzhina, who had no idea that the news would become a State secret.

Kanel's fear and alarm on receiving such information is quite understandable. Afterwards Dina would be thankful her mother died in her own bed and did not go through the horrors of the subsequent interrogations and executions. When Dina and Lyalya were arrested in 1939, their interrogators tried to make them confess that their mother had spied for three foreign states, since, as a consultant at the Kremlin hospital, she accompanied the wives of Kamenev, Kalinin and Molotov when they went abroad for treatment at various health resorts.

My sister and I tried to ease my father's grief, but did not realise the full extent of his concern. Many in circles with which we had no dealings, however, felt a genuine compassion for a man who appeared to have aged ten years overnight. Among them was Vladimir Bonch-Bruyevich.[31] Wanting to show his respect for my father he gave me a job at the Literary Museum, an institution he had organised not long before. Until then, such work had been beyond my reach. On leaving university, I had not settled into any career, and ten years later this already seemed a hopeless task. Now this great shock disrupted the standard procedures. My father's misfortune brought me work, which led to a great change to my life.

Chapter 6

The job was at the manuscript-acquisitions department. Sums had been specially allocated for contract work to compile inventories and to systematise and annotate archival documents in museums and public libraries. As the need arose to sort the accumulated papers, a large group from the old intelligentsia moved from one museum to another and remained thus engaged until the very outbreak of war. Elderly ladies who knew foreign languages were particularly encouraged to take up this work since the correspondence and memoirs in gentry archives were almost always in French, less often in English or German. My knowledge of languages was poor, but I joined this group and from 1936 to 1940 sorted through the manuscript holdings of the Literary Museum, the Historical Museum, the Lenin Library and then, in 1946, the State Archive for Literature and Art.

I found a distinctive atmosphere at the Literary Museum, an institution that had grown and expanded through the enthusiasm of its director, Bonch-Bruyevich, and his assistant Klavdia Surikova. The staff regarded it as a home from home. Many were related to pre-Revolutionary professors and authors or were the assistants and family members of those now writing. Famous surnames – Turgenev, Bakunin and Davydov – were frequently to be met in the payroll lists and in our

---

[31] An Old Bolshevik and companion of Lenin, Bruyevich commanded the guard at the Constituent Assembly in January 1918. Retired from active politics, he set up the Literary Museum in 1933.

daily conversations. The elderly Davydov[32] sang gypsy romances to his
own guitar accompaniment and personified the culture of the country
estate. Tyutchev's great-nephew K. Pigarev often put in an appearance.
He was working at the Muranovo estate, where he served as the curator and researcher of the Tyutchev and Baratynsky Memorial Museum.
S. I. Sinebryukhov and the renowned N.P. Chulkov rivalled one another
in their exhaustive knowledge of gentry genealogies. Then there was the
daughter of the poet Fofanov. A somewhat odd woman with enormous
dreamy eyes, she would recount her bloodthirsty, criminal nightmares
to us by the fireside during our lunch break. (This ritual element in our
daily labours was elegantly organised, with a specially laid table, exploiting all the comforts of an old-fashioned town house.) One of the most
respected members of our team was Nikolai Antsiferov. Always kindly,
interested in everything and enjoying the work of popularisation, he was
an inspired scholar of the urban milieu, as his famous book *The Soul of
Petersburg* testifies. He also had a most romantic devotion to Herzen's
wife Natalya and was a passionate defender of Herzen's love for her.
When he gave lectures on Lermontov's "Demon", his advocacy of love
as a distinct spiritual condition stirred elevated feelings in his female audience. (When Natalya Herzen's love letters to Herwegh were discovered,
Antsiferov was deeply shocked. The unkind comment was that her infi-
delity killed him; he indeed died soon after the publication of this sensational discovery.)

In conversation Antsiferov would sometimes recall Solovki,[33] where
he was imprisoned for several years. Once there was discussion of the
unusual moral code among criminals. This too had now gone, continued Antsiferov, and they were abandoning their observance of the ludicrous, ugly but rigidly enforced laws of their caste. On another occasion,
the role of religion in supporting a resilience of spirit was mentioned,
and he quoted an example from his own experience as a prisoner.
Somehow he had aroused the particular displeasure of his immediate
boss and was sent to clean the latrines. Antsiferov bore this ordeal with
dignity, aided by a special inward state of mind. In our conversation he
described it as religious, but I do not remember the details.

The kind and very active daughter of Professor U. was tenderly devoted
to her brother and paralysed father. She always spent part of her modest
wages buying her father sweets in our canteen as a treat. We knew how

---

[32] Descendant of Denis Davydov (1784–1839), poet and celebrated leader of a
guerrilla detachment in 1812.
[33] The first permanent prison camp of the Bolshevik regime, set up for their
political opponents in 1923 on islands in the White Sea.

they lived. The professorial apartment had, of course, been taken over, but they still retained the middle room and used it for their meals. As soon as the family sat down to breakfast, the neighbours walked through, carrying their chamber-pots. Such behaviour, to which we were all subjected in one degree or another, must have been a form of self-assertion for those who, 20 years earlier, would not have dared enter the master's living quarters without invitation or sit down in the presence of their "well-born" betters.

U. was going to do some work in Leningrad, and I asked her to give a letter to Akhmatova. She took it but the next day handed it back: "I can't do it. You understand, her son is Gumilyov!" Boris Sadovskoi had exactly the same reaction to Lyova. Antsiferov often visited his apartment at the Novodevichy Convent, and when Lyova's name came up in conversation Sadovskoi exclaimed: "He's unyielding!" Oh, those gentry types! They were themselves particularly scared and always cautious. But why then did they artificially foment such an atmosphere of political unreliability around the name of Gumilyov's unfortunate son? (I am not at all sure, moreover, that Lyova ever visited Sadovskoi.)

The staff of the Literary Museum (and the same was true for other museums, incidentally) were all engaged in research or pretended to be so involved, in order to improve their formal status and earn better salaries. Some chose a subject and toiled away at it year after year, although they were incapable of independent scholarly activity. Others regarded their museum posts as no more than necessary havens and spent the rest of their time wholeheartedly engaged in their favourite areas of study. Apart from Antsiferov, the outstanding figure here was Olga Sheremeteva. Modest, poor and educated, with a profound, glowing gaze and abundant grey hair, she was a true pioneer. With Dmitry Shakhovskoi she was studying Chaadayev's legacy.[34] It was she who sorted the books that had belonged to the Russian thinker into a separate depository at the Lenin library. Chaadayev made numerous comments in the margins of these volumes; Sheremeteva reassembled his personal library. After the war, unfortunately, the books were returned to their old locations (all had remained catalogued under the author's surname), and now it is unlikely that there is anyone capable of tracking them down again.

Olga Sheremeteva was keen to help me in my work. She translated the French letters I needed from the archives and would bring me excerpts that related to my research. The subject was the biography of Lermontov.

---

[34] Pyotr Chaadayev (1794–1856), philosopher, declared officially insane by Tsar Nicholas I for the first of his *Lettres philosophiques* (the rest were published only in 1913). Admired by Pushkin and the subject of an essay by Mandelstam.

This all began as follows.

Boris Eichenbaum was staying at the Mandelstams' apartment in Nashchokin Street. He and his wife had come on a visit to Moscow from Leningrad with Alexander Morgulis (the hero of Mandelstam's "morgulets" and constant companion of the household). Ever since reading Eichenbaum's "Major Issues in the Study of Lermontov" I had dreamed of talking to him. His 1935 article was entertainingly written and not a conventional study in the history of literature but irradiated throughout by an exciting and innovative approach. Eichenbaum identified the gaps in Lermontov's mysterious biography and, by an elegant and unexpected regrouping of the known facts, indicated new avenues of investigation. One problem was the identity of the woman to whom the poet had devoted an early lyrical cycle. As Eichenbaum noted, Irakly Andronikov had taken up this theme energetically. Three years later, Andronikov's research acquired the form of a famous tale, "The Mystery of N.F.I." I had already heard a great deal from those who visited Leningrad about this young man, who was then 26 or 28. He had an extraordinary gift of mimicry, they told me, possessed perfect pitch, and had an irrepressible theatrical temperament that found expression in the improvised performances he gave before small private audiences.

Some sixth sense told me I would find myself here. Very quickly, I had reached a limit in my studies of Gumilyov: the books and magazines were all read, but it was impossible to look at the manuscript materials about Gumilyov in the archives.

I knew Morgulis well and asked him to introduce me to Eichenbaum.[35] As always, Morgulis chattered good-humouredly about everything: how Nadezhda's mother, Vera Yakovlevna, was looking after them, the importance of the sketches by Prince Gagarin that Eichenbaum had used in his work on Lermontov, and the visits Andronikov had paid to the descendants of the now identified Natalya Fyodorovna Ivanova.

Eichenbaum's response when we met made me think later of the Decembrist Batenkov and the comparison he drew between two of Alexander I's ministers. The imperial favourite and tyrant Arakcheyev attributed great importance to all he did and let it be understood that it was well beyond the capacity of a mere mortal's comprehension. In all the reformer Speransky did, he gave the impression that anyone might compile a new legal code, if he so wished, reform the educational system or preside over the State Council . . .

---

[35] Boris Eichenbaum (1886–1959), literary specialist of the Formal school; associated in 1920s with LEF; devoted a lifetime of study to Lev Tolstoy.

Eichenbaum resembled Speransky. He was not taken aback by my lack of research experience, nor did my ignorance of the techniques of bibliographical work deter him. He immediately suggested that I begin tracking down materials about the "Circle of Sixteen". Lermontov had belonged to this group, and nothing apart from that fact was known about the "Sixteen". "But how does one begin?" I asked him doubtfully. "Very simple. First you must work through the name indexes of *Russian Bygones*, *Russian Archive*, the *Historical Herald* and other such publications. Then you will make selections from the *Biographical Dictionary*, and after that you'll be well under way," kindly explained Boris Eichenbaum.

One thing certainly did lead to another, but each step forward at the Lenin Library proved an obstacle course. It became easier when I was given a ticket allowing me to use the "special" reading room. This was located in the gallery of the elegant main hall. The Lenin (formerly Rumyantsev) Library, it should be remembered, was accommodated in the famous Pashkov House. From the gallery one could gaze around at the long black tables between the snow-white columns, the gleaming crystal chandeliers, and the faultless moulding on the ceiling. It was Irakly Andronikov who helped me get a pass to the reading room. He had just moved from Leningrad to Moscow, and we had become friends.

All of this created the feeling that something new had entered my life. I'm convinced that, beyond the immediate content of the work, a love for your subject also includes a passion for the accessories that accompany that activity. They combine to create the sense of vocation, of having found one's path in life.

Identifying the "Sixteen" proved exceptionally difficult. Only ten members of the circle were named in the literature and they were referred to, moreover, without titles or initials, by no more than their surnames. Even such connoisseurs of noble lineage as Chulkov and Sinebryukhov, the experts of the Literary Museum, declared that it was quite impossible to establish their identities. Still, after consulting Irakly, I decided to examine the *Imperial Rescripts*, since a generalised portrait of Lermontov's comrades indicated that many would already have fought in the Caucasus. A new obstacle. The bound volume of the *Imperial Rescripts* was not available to readers at the Lenin Library. The Historical Museum came to my aid. They advised me that these edicts and announcements were also published in the military newspaper *Russian Invalid*. The Historical Museum had issues for every year. A lucky discovery followed. At the end of each issue, lists were published, in the tiniest typeface, of all who had left Petersburg or arrived there. When the names of Lermontov, his friend and relation Mongo Stolypin or

Prince Alexander Dolgoruky began to surface in these tedious columns, it is hard to convey the excitement I felt. It was as though I was breathing the rarefied air of success. Had contemporaries ever imagined that these official reports would be of interest to anyone apart from retired military officers? The poet Ivan Dmitriyev, for instance, composed an ironic epitaph on the theme, published in the early nineteenth century:

> Here lies a brigadier, who died advanced in years.
> This is the lot Fate throws us!
> You live your life and die, and all that remains
> Is a line in the papers: Has departed for Rostov.

For me, however, those ten days spent from morning till night on the fifth floor of the Historical Museum on Red Square opened the way to new discoveries. Thus began the decades of my work in the archives, which expanded from year to year. I was allowed formal access to State archives thanks to the kind support of Bonch-Bruyevich. My life was now divided between the Literary Museum, the manuscript division of the Lenin Library, and the Military-Historical Archive.

Neither Nadya nor her brother Yevgeny could understand this side of my work. The study of literary history, to their way of thinking, either meant the enunciation of critical and, at times, extravagant judgements or the writing of memoirs. As soon as I started to study Lermontov, Nadya began to fear that I would write memoirs about the Mandelstams. I knew too much, she believed. These anxieties surfaced most strongly in Voronezh, where Mandelstam (provoked by Nadya, of course) reproached me with the intention of writing memoirs about him after he died. Such suspicions struck me as laughable; my studies were far removed from the recording of reminiscences, and my attitude to Mandelstam and Akhmatova was purely private and personal, unconnected to a curiosity about famous people.

Chapter 7

On her return from the Shervinsky estate in Kolomna, Akhmatova spent about a fortnight in Moscow. She stayed with me; all my family were either at the dacha or on holiday and I was between jobs. She had sunbathed and recovered at Starki, where she swam in the Moskva River and felt well, surrounded by those who loved her. But in the city, she once again suffered a variety of ailments. We spent much time at home.

Akhmatova's appearance is captured in the wonderfully expressive and truthful photograph that Gornung took at Starki. In this famous portrait, Akhmatova is sitting with her feet on a divan covered in striped ticking. Her figure, arms, neck, fringe and face have all been caught with extraordinary precision. In another small amateur snap, Akhmatova sits, her head wrapped in a kerchief, on a bench opposite the Marinkina Tower. She gave me both photographs, inscribing one "Dear Emma, from Akhmatova in memory of my Moscow days in 1936. 26 July" and, on the same date, dedicating the other "To Emma, as a token of my tenderest feelings, Anna. Me in Kolomna."

As soon as she returned to Moscow, Akhmatova began to ring various influential people on Lyova's behalf. There was an additional telephone in my father's empty study and she called from there. She sat tensely erect on the flat-seated, carpet-covered armchair and held the receiver to her ear. She dialled a Kremlin number and waited for Osinsky to come to the telephone. The humiliation provoked a noticeable tremor and she began to shake from head to foot. I gazed at her with an aching heart. What a noble, pliant and nervous creature, I thought.

When we were relaxing, we talked a great deal and Akhmatova recalled the 1910s with enthusiasm. She told me about her romances and showed me various photos, hinting which poems were dedicated to whom in *Rosary* and *White Flock*. I immediately forgot most of this because I appreciated neither the male type of beauty nor the nature of love affairs during that period. For me the 1910s were "more remote than Pushkin". One of her stories, however, remains engraved in my memory.

She was returning to Tsarskoye Selo with Gumilyov. At the station in Petersburg a "certain someone" (Akhmatova always spoke mysteriously) met them and began a conversation with Kolya, while she "shivered like a thoroughbred Arab pony". I know, I thought tenderly to myself, I've seen what a hot-blooded, proud person you are.

Akhmatova at Starki, 1936

This twofold impression has for ever etched the scene at the station in my recollections, as though I had been there myself. Thirty years later I learned that the "someone" had been Alexander Blok. He noted in his "Diary" on 5 August 1914 that he had met Akhmatova and Gumilyov at the station. And in her memoirs she also named Blok, describing the three poets' luncheon, there at the station, during the first days of the war.

I don't remember if Osinsky or someone else gave Akhmatova their support, but she was referred to the Higher Education Committee. There she saw an official who asked her to ring back in five days' time, then in another three days, thereby putting off any decision. Meanwhile Akhmatova had clearly fallen ill and would soon have to return home. She left for Leningrad and asked me to call the Committee once again. It was the same story: Ring back in five days, in three days, in a week's time and so on. Naturally, I could not abandon this task, and for an entire month my life revolved around those telephone calls to the Higher Education Committee.

In September 1936, Lyova unexpectedly came to see me at the Literary Museum. He had returned from his archaeological expedition. We went for a walk and I told him how things were going with the Committee. When we parted, he clasped my hand so firmly and gazed so gratefully into my eyes that it was as if I had risked my life for his sake. I was surprised he attached such importance to behaviour which was considered quite natural in my circle. Could he really imagine someone giving up halfway after accepting such a request from family friends?! That evening at our apartment he said that the only emotion he could still feel was gratitude; all other feelings had atrophied.

It was the first time we had met since his arrest and release the previous autumn. Now he told me some of the details. The investigation had been conducted as though he and Punin faced severe punishment; perhaps they would even be shot. The interrogators were particularly interested that Lyova had run into the kitchen, during the fateful conversation, to get a knife to cut the bread. The informer had offered this information to "the relevant authorities" as a symbolic gesture that hinted at the terrorist attack they were preparing against Stalin. Lyova therefore felt grateful to Stalin for releasing him. Whereupon he informed me: "Bear it in mind that when they asked whom I used to visit in Moscow, I named the Ardovs – they know that anyway – and you. There was no-one else I could name."

Now here Lyova sat, on the window-sill in my room, pardoned by Stalin but again cast adrift. "Do you know the difference between Jews and Russians?" he mused. "Jews classify everyone as either family or outsiders. They'll savage an outsider but do anything for their own. You, for instance, consider me family. The Russians also divide people into family and outsiders. They'll also savage any outsiders, but if a Russian's in trouble, they think: 'He's our brother, of course, but we still don't give a damn!'" Lyova regarded Jews with "the curiosity of a foreigner".

Incidentally, encountering such difficulties in his attempts to get higher education, he often repeated (according to Akhmatova), "Now I understand the Jews," meaning the *numerus clausus* imposed in Tsarist Russia to restrict the number of Jews entering university.

The Committee had still not reached a decision. Ardov became involved. He exploited the accusations recently brought against Zinoviev[36] to offer the Committee's officials the common account of the death sentence passed on the poet Gumilyov: Lenin supposedly pardoned him, but Zinoviev took the decision into his own hands and ordered Gumilyov's execution. Ardov's assured and relaxed manner always made an impression in high officials' offices.

Ardov lived well at the time. He would take Lyova to the Metropole Hotel, drive him around in taxis and accompany him to the Committee. Lyova confessed to me: "I've come to Moscow to see you, but I can't resist good living."

Lyova was impressed by what he saw as the artistic worldliness of the Ardov home. All of the female visitors were dazzling: Veronica Polonskaya, the prosecutor-general's daughter, the wife of Ilf . . . Above Nina Ardova's divan hung portraits of the famous poets, such as Mikhail Svetlov, who were in love with her, and now, at her feet, sat Gumilyov. My description of that household is probably a distorted reflection but that is what I heard from Lyova and Nadya (Akhmatova spoke differently of the Ardovs but also with an unsettled partiality). Nina flirted with Lyova, and he frankly admitted: "I cannot remain indifferent when she lies with her bosom half uncovered and gazes at me with her brilliant black eyes."

One evening he dashed from Ordynka to see me, quite beside himself. The Committee had finally decided not to reinstate him at Leningrad University since the administration there was resolutely opposed to it. An offer was made, however, that he enter Moscow University as a first-year geography student. Apparently, Ardov had secured this concession. Lyova was mortally offended. He felt himself to be a born historian and had no desire to be treated as a student ready to take up any subject. And to start over again at the age of 24! Nina Ardova, however, took a practical view. Matters of vocation meant little to her, and she had no

---

[36] The show trial of the "Zinovievite-Trotskyist bloc" was held in August 1936.

notion where Lyova's gifts lay. She urged him to accept the situation:
since the offer held out the prospect of relative well-being, he should
do as suggested. In her efforts to persuade him, Nina adopted a moral-
ising tone, and Lyova, in extreme irritation, fled across the landing to
the Klychkovs' apartment. They were very fond of him, and on this visit
to Moscow he was staying with them.

In fact, Lyova gave many funny accounts of that household. An actor
known to the Klychkovs dropped by. Hearing Lyova's surname, he was
so scared that he made as if to leave immediately. Klychkov lost his
temper and, stamping his feet, yelled at the man: "Well, you're a priest!
A priest!" The actor's father was apparently an Orthodox priest. (Varvara
Klychkova gives exactly the same account in her memoirs but says that
the actor's father was not a priest.)

On this occasion, however, neither the Ardovs' practical benevolence
nor the passionate and friendly support of the Klychkovs could still
Lyova's anxiety. He considered his failure nothing short of catastrophe.
Since I believed that he had a vocation, I suffered with him, but still
felt that the tension must now be defused. "Forget them, Lyova," I told
him. "It's not necessary to go to university to study. If it's proving so
difficult, then drop it. You'll be a historian whatever happens."

It was exactly the right thing to say at that moment. With a sense of
enormous relief, Lyova exclaimed: "Emmochka, you are the only woman
I truly love!" But the next morning, resigned and subdued, he wept: "I
feel sorry for Mama."

Appeals to the Committee continued for another two to three weeks.
Lyova began to reconcile himself to the possibility of studying in
Moscow, even as a first-year geography student. But where was he to
live? In a student dormitory? We all realised that was impossible in his
case. The Ardovs found him a room or bed somewhere, although I did
not think that their acquaintances would be suitable neighbours for
Lyova. In the end, all was settled. Lyova left for Leningrad to pick up
his things and then return to Moscow and move into the room the
Ardovs were offering.

November passed, then December, and there was no news of Lyova.
At first, I was simply alarmed for his safety. But Akhmatova sent no news
of a calamity. I had to accept a sad truth; Lyova had deserted me. I
recalled Genevieve, Zola's laundress, whose lover left her, walking off
down the familiar Paris street never to return.

Only much later, and by accident, did I learn that Lyova treated
Klychkov in exactly the same way. (He felt embarrassed to ask anyone
where Lyova had gone.) I now learned that Lyova was living very
comfortably in Leningrad. It was my Lena, having gone there to cele-

brate the New Year, who told me. With her I sent a letter to Akhmatova containing bibliographical references and notes about Gumilyov. Lena brought me a reply in which the Gumilyov materials were surreptitiously referred to as Lermontov's:

<u>31 December 1936</u>

Dearest Emma,

I still have not thanked you for your hospitality this autumn and for the care you showed me. Forgive me. I have been ill for four months, and my heart condition hampers work and life.

Someone is shortly going to bring me your article about Lermontov and I shall read it this New Year's Eve.

They have taken away my pension. You can imagine how that complicates my existence. I should come to Moscow, but have not the strength.

Most affectionately yours,

Anna

Akhmatova's letters require close reading. Written in pencil, this note transmitted in concealed form certain important events in her life. Her heart condition was, naturally, exacerbated by emotional distress, the nature of which I had to guess. I understood not that she would read my notes about Gumilyov on New Year's Eve but that she would be on her own that night. Life with the Punins was becoming unbearable now that Akhmatova had lost an allowance which, however small, was indubitably her own (she had been given an individual pension "for her services to Russian literature"). Not a word about Lyova.

Chapter 8

Meanwhile, life continued. I met many new people and remained on good terms with my friends and acquaintances. We laughed a great deal. Lena was an excellent raconteuse, and I had a sense of humour as well, though she said it was more like that of Shchedrin.[37] When we went out for a smoke at the museum, the staff would exchange critical remarks.

---

[37] A classic satirist of the later nineteenth century, Shchedrin (1826–1889) took a gloomy view of Russia: "… a place of chaotic social conditions, vicious power struggles, demented and unrealisable projects, and senseless cruelty" (Terras).

In the afternoons, we left for the manuscript department of the Lenin Library, on the other side of Mokhovaya Street, and there the scratching of our pens was frequently interrupted by some merry comment.

Many of the permanent and contract staff at the Library's manuscript department also bore the names of famous nineteenth-century artists and philosophers. Sisters-in-law, great nieces, third cousins – these female relatives of departed celebrities were fantastically poor and, as a consequence, all a little mad: they were either hysterically gay or possessed by stormy love affairs which began and unfolded right there in the Library. One of the few male members of staff, or even a reader, might sometimes see me home, and this gave cause for gossip although I never became seriously attached.

The department's daily administration was in the hands of a most severe and punctilious woman, evidently a Communist, with mousy, smoothly combed hair pulled back in a bun. Many years later, I was told that she had been Gershenzon's[38] private secretary when still a girl. She said I was a good worker "but very capricious". "Capricious" was a mild comment. "A difficult person" was the description in all references from places where I worked. Very late I realised that this was a standard euphemism in personnel departments. During my life, I have heard the most varied criticisms from those around me, but the term "difficult person" never appeared again once I stopped going out to work.

Several episodes from that period come fleetingly to mind, but I cannot place them in any chronological order. One impression, of only passing significance, can be dated with comparative precision, since it is linked to a specific political event. At a general meeting of department staff, we were told that we must listen to the text of the new Soviet Constitution.[39] Who would read it aloud? A woman with a small pencil in her hand pointed elegantly at me. This was flattering because she was a decent person, taciturn and slight, who kept her distance from the others. She had nothing to chat to them about: she did not recall literary evenings at the Polytechnical Museum where the unforgettable Igor Severyanin was once crowned "king of the poets"; she did not reminisce about Sologub's "Ghostly Charms"; she did not recount amusing finds in the correspondence of long-departed gentry families. She had to deal with quite different material. In another building, she toiled away on a unique collection of ancient Hebrew manuscripts. From Voevodin, one of the department's administrators, I learned that the Library held invaluable

---

[38] Literary historian Lev Gershenzon (1869–1925) initiated the 1909 collection of essays *Landmarks*, calling on the Russian intelligentsia to abandon its radicalism.
[39] Discussed throughout the year and adopted on 5 December 1936.

documents dating back almost to the Old Testament prophets. They could not make an inventory of these relics, he said, since no-one knew the ancient dead language. Now I saw before me someone who possessed that rare and demanding skill. Her surname was Shapiro.

Then the war came, and the treasures of the Lenin Library were evacuated far to the east. After the war, when they returned to their rightful place, the disastrous period of State anti-Semitism began. Probably no-one then gave a thought to the Library's invaluable collection of ancient Hebrew documents.

Another episode linked to my spell at the manuscript department can be dated with some precision. It concerned the famous cardiologist Dmitry Pletnyov. Even before the terrible trial in 1938, when he was accused and convicted of murdering Gorky, a disgraceful campaign was waged in the press against the respected physician.[40] Under the pseudonym "Citizeness P." (a most suitable letter!), a woman wrote to *Pravda* that when she consulted the professor about a heart complaint he bit her breast, and, as a result, she had suffered chronic mastitis. There followed a full discussion in the newspaper. In particular, Pletnyov was criticised for complaining to the police and asking their protection from this crazy woman who kept pestering him. For her part, she followed the classic pattern: she phoned him, wrote threatening letters, lay in wait on the street, and came to his clinic and caused an uproar. Finally, articles appeared in the main national newspapers which brought this harassment to a deadly conclusion. I remember Akhmatova, who had a very good knowledge and understanding of what was going on around her, remarking that *Pravda* was read aloud in schools during the political-education lesson. What would teenagers, still almost children, make of the filthy details that filled these articles? Our ladies, however, who knew French, English and German, were wholly on the side of "Citizeness P." They were outraged by the old man's perverted sexual appetites and discussed the fantastic story, quoting individual passages. By then, I could stand it no longer and blurted out: "Lies!" There were instant and angry rejoinders: "But it was printed in *Pravda*! We are accustomed to believe what we read in *Pravda*." At that very moment from behind the bookshelves emerged a man with inexpressive, harsh features (one of the "grey ones", as Yevgeny Khazin called them). He looked at us all attentively and, without uttering so much as a word, vanished again among the bookcases. It was the director of the Gorky archive, which had only just been organised, and he was selecting material for it at the Lenin Library.

---

[40] Gorky died in June 1936; see Vitaly Shentalinsky, "Stormy Petrel", in *The KGB's Literary Archives* (London, 1995).

A year later, our educated ladies greeted the announcement that Yagoda had "betrayed the Motherland" with just the same naivety. "What did he lack? He already had everything," they said in amazement, for the first time feeling their moral superiority to this awful figure. A far more direct reaction to Yagoda's 1938 trial came from the policeman who guarded the entrance to the department. At that time, the rules were observed unswervingly. The policeman on duty checked passes but did not exchange a single word with the readers passing rapidly through the hallway. On this occasion, however, he could not help himself: "Just imagine, Yagoda himself! We were scared even to say the word *Lubyanka* and now look what he's turned out to be. A Fascist. And the way he lived . . . I was on duty at his dacha: the ponds there, the fish they raised, every kind of carp . . ." At the Literary Museum, there was an elderly woman, a Bolshevik since before the Revolution, who had been taken on by Bonch-Bruyevich and was trying to compile a card index of literary manuscripts. She repeatedly collapsed with heart trouble, crying, "Yagódka, Yagódka! Of all people . . ."[41]

The Literary Museum was already ceasing to be a comfortable "nest of gentryfolk". One of the researchers told me with bitter regret that they could no longer gather socially since it aroused suspicion. Poor U. now not only bought sweets for her sick father at the canteen but also food for prison parcels. Her beloved brother had been arrested. Soon she began visiting him at the city's Matrosskaya Tishina prison and even twice fell under a tram during these crazy trips. Luckily, she escaped without injury both times. Once she told me, bravely and grief-stricken: "My life is ended," so intensely did she love her brother. Then she moved to another museum and worked there for many years, a well-liked and appreciated employee. What became of her brother I do not know.

Another member of staff at the museum, who bore the name of a great Russian writer and was related to one of the brilliant "Silver Age" authors, submitted a complaint to the special section. She reported that an issue of the émigré newspaper *Poslednyie Novosti* containing a reprinted private letter of Bukharin's, of political significance, was in the holdings of the Literary Museum.[42] Not long before she had astonished me with a remark that came oddly from the lips of the old Moscow intelligentsia. We were smoking in the corridor and saying how ugly the new building of the Lenin Library was. Without thinking, I commented: "Even

---

[41] A common and affectionate diminutive (literally "little berry") that recalls the NKVD (GPU) boss's surname Yagóda but is usually pronounced "yágodka".

[42] The leading Bolshevik Nikolai Bukharin, at one time Mandelstam's patron, was arrested in February 1937. Brought to trial in March 1938, he was then executed as an "Enemy of the People".

Stalin said . . ." and cited the critical words attributed to him about this new structure. "Why 'even'?" she corrected me, with an ambiguous smile.

A young female staff member at the Library, one of the "communoids" (i.e. a non-Party Communist), referred with revulsion to Bukharin's last testament: "What a poser."

Chapter 9

Each person thought he alone was afraid. But everyone was scared. People tried to convince themselves that their arrested comrade, relation or acquaintance was indeed a very bad person: they had always been aware of it, actually. This defensive reaction explains the voluntary spreading of malicious rumours about the latest victim. I remember how those in theatrical circles clung to one explanation for Meyerhold's arrest.[43] Supposedly, he had been caught at the aerodrome, about to board a plane flying to a foreign country. "I believe it," women (for the most part) added with conviction, failing to see an absurdity that Akhmatova pointed out to me immediately: "Do they really think he was about to flee the Soviet Union without Raikh?" Everyone knew how passionately Meyerhold was attached to his wife, the actress Zinaida Raikh. Only he was arrested, moreover, and until the fateful day when she was murdered in her own apartment, Raikh remained untouched. Some consoled themselves with the idea that the arrests were part of a logical and carefully conceived process. "Why worry? What could happen to you? You've stolen nothing and didn't belong to any of the opposition factions. Your son is a manual worker, he's found a job at a good factory, and he's in the Komsomol. What could happen to him? Calm down." Unable to restrain her anxiety, the other would admit: In his application, my son concealed that his father was a priest. There then followed new torments. Why had she let that out and spoken of something that should not be mentioned?

I began to be afraid even before 1937. Fear would come without warning. During one such fit, I poured my heart out to Lena. She reassured me. I returned home very late. As always, even more than usual this time, I was nervous moving through Moscow. The city seemed militarised. One after another, creating an unbelievable racket, motorcycles raced through the city centre. I shied away from them as I crossed the vast, shapeless squares. My sister's words came to mind. She had been walking past the

---

[43] Arrested in May 1939, Vsevolod Meyerhold was shot in February 1940.

House of Unions[44] during some congress (or was it one of the trials?): "Crawling with agents," she said when she got home. Her language was uninhibited because she remembered the Butyrki prison. In the early 1920s, our family had gone there to visit a relation convicted during the trial of the Socialist Revolutionaries.

When the tram reached Shchipok Street, I calmed down a little. I still faced a walk, however, across the enormous, dark and empty

Moscow in the mid-1930s: the House of Unions

hospital gardens. From far off, I could see, with relief, that the light was burning in the administrative wing. I reached it at exactly the same moment as two men ran down from the adjoining veranda. I turned right towards our house. Two people were standing on the porch. One of them was the hospital manager, a very polite Pole, while the other . . . But why mention the other when the figure of a sentry with a rifle at the ready, a hard mouth and a peaked cap pulled down over his eyes emerged from the dark corner of the building. "They've come to see you," the manager warned me cautiously.

"To see me?" There, you see, Lena? I thought to myself, with a kind of pleasure even.

But the manager was already asking nervously: "Why don't they open up?" "They're probably asleep," I answered, shrugging my shoulders; I was trying very hard to maintain my composure. It felt as though I had reached my warm bed after a hard day's work and was snuggling down only to encounter a sharp knife stabbing up at me from beneath the blanket.

I turned the key in the lock, but the door was on the chain. Our neighbours up to their usual tricks. That'll teach you to be out till all hours. When

---

44 The former city Assembly Rooms, now used for public trials, grand meetings and concerts, and the lying-in-state of deceased Soviet leaders.

they finally responded to the bell and banging on the door, I went along the corridor to my room, preserving what dignity I could. With astonishment I discovered that no-one was following me. "They" had remained in the hallway and – so that was it! – began to knock at Father's door. It was then that I grew scared. "Warn him!" I appealed to the manager. Everyone gave me a derisive and gloomy look. When "they" entered his room, a sentry (probably not the one from round the corner) remained sitting on the wooden divan in the hallway. He was a quite ordinary lad. But when I asked him for a light, he first held out a box of matches and then whipped back his arm as though he had touched a toad: "Against the rules." I woke our family. But "they" had a warrant only for Papa, it seems, and – thanks to the tiresome squabbles between the hospital staff and the apartment's other inhabitants – each of us had recently been given individual leases for our accommodation. This was most convenient for us and not at all helpful to the hospital administration. In this particular instance, it saved me from a search. Meanwhile, they continued to search my father's room.

Alarmed and tense, we ran from one room to another. Suddenly, Mother asked in her tender, musical voice: "Emmochka, what do you think? Could this harm us?" and pointed to several copies of Trotsky's *Lessons of October* in her chest of drawers. When her grown children had thrown away these books, like sensible Soviet citizens, Mother had carefully picked them up again. Shocking! You can't destroy books! What were we to do? She must have an entire stock of prohibited literature. Any minute now, I thought, "they" would come into Mother's room since she was not registered separately: both rooms were listed as Father's. I tore thick wads of paper from the books, crumpled them up and, now and again, walked steadily out to the toilet and flushed them away. The sentry paid no attention to me.

It was already light, and "they" were still there. Sitting in my room, I heard with horror how Papa's door opened, someone ran out of the house, and a car drew up. Were they now taking him away? I ran to his door. "They" had disappeared, and Papa came out to us with a deep sigh of relief, holding his hand to the left side of his chest. Evidently, they had been looking for one specific document and, not having found it, had gone.

What were they after? Papa would say nothing to us, and our suppositions revolved around the Kremlin hospital. But there was one other circumstance. I have mentioned our relative who was an SR (Socialist Revolutionary). Lev Gerstein had already served a ten-year prison sentence and was living in exile in Siberia.[45] From time to time, his wife

---

[45] From June to August 1922, the first Soviet show trial was held in Moscow. The accused were leaders of the Socialist Revolutionary party, the Bolsheviks' chief rival for popular support.

appeared in Moscow and often stayed with us. Whenever she came to visit, she always took every precaution. "I don't think anyone's tailed me here," she would say with preoccupied concern, and there were certain signs which assured her that she was right about this. All important addresses and telephone numbers she learned by heart. She did not keep a diary of any kind. Once at home, however, she was very free with her opinions.

In 1936, she lived with us for quite a time. She brought sad news: Lev Gerstein was dead. Naively she hoped that Papa could help get an obituary published in *Izvestiya*, to announce the death of this former member of the SR Central Committee.

Margarita Gerstein was Latvian and had joined the SRs at an early age. She spread revolutionary propaganda among manual workers in Riga and met Lev through the party. Even in 1936 she remained the living embodiment of an SR woman (in 1937 she vanished, and we could learn nothing of her fate; I don't know if Papa tried to find anything out). Her choice of words and her appearance, the calm way she spoke of the sufferings she had endured, and her capacity to enter into the simple daily interests of those around her all helped to make her a woman of exemplary upbringing and tact. With her prominent light blue eyes (she probably suffered from an overactive thyroid gland), smooth, colourless hair, false teeth and limp, she made one think of a schoolmistress. A good schoolmistress since her smile lit up her entire face. The terminology she used had not changed since before the Revolution. She would say "the public", for instance, when the contemporary Soviet word was "masses". With good-tempered humour she recalled various episodes from her life in the underground and in exile: a funny story about the English in Vladivostok or an account of the touchingly primitive life of the Siberian peasants among whom she served a term of exile in Tsarist times.

Much more frightening were her tales of Soviet prisons in the early 1920s, when her kidneys were permanently damaged by the beatings and all her teeth knocked out (hence the false teeth). She gave an epic description of the woman who led her interrogation. Calling the soldiers in to beat the detainees in front of her, this woman would watch "and became unimaginably beautiful". "She was a sadist and was soon relieved of this work," added Margarita placidly. When Lev was in prison, it was the duty guard who tormented him. Twisting the switch in the corridor, he constantly turned the electric light in the cell on and off. The continual flashing of the light drove the prisoners to distraction. Margarita thought the guard was doing this out of boredom, but one might suppose it was a deliberate tactic. She said so little about the sufferings she had endured that it was only from one of her casual remarks that I learned she had also served time in a camp. When that was, I never managed to find out. In any case, by 1922, when the SRs were put on trial, she was no longer in Moscow. Now in the 1930s Margarita often told us how the convicted SRs were living. They were held two to a cell in prison, where they so got on each other's nerves that they applied for transfers to solitary confinement.

She described the conditions under which the SRs lived in Siberian exile after their release from prison – i.e. in the early 1930s. They fell ill and petitioned to be moved somewhere with a better climate, but nothing was done. Lev Gerstein also appealed, but he was likewise refused the right to a transfer. In exile he was given a very important post, but the ceaseless vigilance of his surveillance wore him down. Once he was so infuriated that when he saw a police informer walking towards him, he stuck out his tongue at the man. On the other hand, Margarita assured us that her husband had been feared by all the local thieves and bribe-takers: he was in charge of the State gold reserves (those held in the Orenburg bank, it seems) and was famed for his incorruptible, even rigid honesty. I could believe this since I still remembered old family stories of his character. As a youth, when he was living at home in the Ukraine in some small Jewish settlement, he was once sitting by the window and reading. A house on the other side of the street caught fire. The blaze was extinguished. The young man did not hear a thing. Only when he finished his book did he look up and see that a burned-out ruin had replaced the familiar building opposite. That was the legend about Lev in our family.

Emma at 16

Being banished to a restricted place of residence after he was released from prison, Lev first lived with his wife in some village. Margarita said that young peasants would come through the snow on sledges to see them from 60 or 70 kilometres away. They came to ask what they should do. They were ready for "political struggle". The SRs dissuaded them from taking action, however, assuring them that resistance was useless and would only lead to new bloodshed and pointless sacrifices. Distressed, Margarita added that the younger generation in the villages had taken heavily to drink.

Perhaps I am not recording these tales in strict chronological sequence. But I took little interest in the political activities of the SRs. I had viewed them with indifference ever since Lev Gerstein, seeing me at 16 with a copy of *Thus Spake Zarathustra*, commented immediately: "Have you got to the part where Nietzsche says, 'When you visit a woman take a whip with you'? How do you like that then?" It struck me as an old-fashioned and narrow-minded approach. As far as I could then see, Lev Gerstein did not accept anything apart from Pyotr Lavrov's *Historical Letters* [1870], which he much admired.[46]

Once a widow, Margarita lived with us for quite some time. Probably there were things she had to attend to in Moscow after her husband's death. We had no idea whom she was seeing. But at home she would readily discuss political subjects. It was from her that I first heard how Stalin cleared his way to the top, steadily replacing all the local Party officials with his own people. A striking example was the Urals. Trotsky considered the area his stronghold, but when he came to speak there he could not find any of the region's former Party officials. Quite different delegates now came to congresses in Moscow, and voting in favour of the "general line" was already a foregone conclusion. That was roughly what she told me.

Sitting beside me on the divan one day, she was arguing that political struggle at the present moment was pointless. "Of course, we could rub out Stalin, but . . ." At that moment the door opened and into the dining-room came Polya, our housemaid. I shuddered and was terrified, but Margarita, without altering her lazy pose, rounded off the phrase in exactly the same intonation, with the same clear voice: ". . . so, Emmochka, go ahead and buy the silk, don't hesitate. You deserve a new dress after all you've done!" When Polya had left, Margarita added further instructions to this practical lesson: "Never give the impression that you've been caught unawares. And don't creep about furtively or look uneasily around you."

---

[46] Lavrov was a prominent émigré opponent of Tsarism with an uncompromisingly utilitarian view of art.

Meanwhile, Yevgeny Khazin and I, wary of the neighbours and considering ourselves vulnerable because of the Mandelstam affair, used to speak in hushed voices. Yet disaster passed us by and struck those around us; we could not understand why. My older brother's wife, Nadya, had a ready explanation for all such cases. How, for instance, had a girl from an honest working-class family ended up in the camps? The answer was simple: because of her inappropriate familiarity with foreigners. Nadya worked as a district doctor in the local polyclinic and was interested only in what happened at work each day: what "Grishka", the clinic director, or "Raika", a fellow doctor, had said. This was the main theme in all her accounts of what she did. She tried to draw her husband into this philistine quagmire, but he cared for nothing but his work. He was devoting the enthusiasm of a highly qualified specialist and inventor to the electrical engineering of the new Moscow metro.

My younger brother was in his final, or last but one, year at the Bauman technical institute. At that time, engineers were being trained under a rush programme since the country was industrialising and there was a shortage of specialists. It was in my brother's nature, however, to make the most thorough study of any subject. He would not hand in his coursework until he had prepared fully. This led to persecution by the other students. At the insistence of the Komsomol and the student self-management committee, he was excluded from the institute for "sabotaging the reform of higher education". As a result, he worked as an engineer without a diploma for 15 years until, at the age of 40, he went back to college and completed the course, starting again from the beginning. The entire experience made him very vulnerable emotionally. Our sister-in-law Nadya extended her sway over him.

During these years, she became a full-blooded Stalinist. The social base of Stalin's regime and its main psychological support were the urban white-collar workers of the Soviet bureaucracy. As I then already understood, their place in the social structure of that time was analogous to that of the petty bourgeoisie which, according to Marxist political analysis, supported the Fascist regimes in Italy and Germany.

I have not forgotten scenes from a film documentary of the May Day parade when an air squadron appeared in the sky and together with the ground forces created an impressive spectacle of Soviet armed might. A high-ranking Japanese military commander attending the parade was unable to conceal his shock and envious rapture while Voroshilov, approaching the guest for a parting handshake, could not hide a triumphant smile. Our Nadya overflowed with pride at such scenes. She was especially impressed when Anthony Eden came to Moscow for talks with Stalin. "They can't ignore us," she would repeat. If the British Prime Minister had visited here first, that meant, in her eyes, that he acknowledged Soviet superiority.[47] "They're Europeans, practical people, that's all," commented Khardjiev.

Another relation, Ida, came from an uneducated section of society. Her father had owned a watchmaker's shop, and they lived behind the premises. She longed to escape. After finishing the *gymnasium*, she could not join the Women's Higher Courses[48] and instead, as was the practice, became a pharmacist. Only after the Revolution could she graduate from the medical institute and qualify as a doctor. Her gratified pride knew no bounds. She rightly considered that she had become "someone" thanks to the Soviet regime. Yet in 1936, she was the first of our circle to encounter arrests, trials and prison.

Ida had no apartment. She lived in former servants' quarters – in other words, a small wooden house without any conveniences, not even basic plumbing. This forced her to enter into a fictitious marriage with an engineer from Vilno in Poland; he was helping to build a new apartment block and as one of the builders received a basement flat there. Unfortunately, he was not a discreet fellow. Once at work he exclaimed in exasperation, "Ach, you can't do a thing with the Russian proletariat!" He was immediately denounced, and our relative received a ghastly initiation, taking parcels to the prison and visiting her fictitious husband there. She also attended the court hearing. No, this was not yet the time of the extra-judicial Special Board and troika or of beatings and torture behind bars. The engineer came before the most ordinary people's court, but this did not spare him 20 years in the camps and internal exile. At these open hearings, Ida saw and heard her fill of the life of ordinary Muscovites. A jealous wife reported her husband for smiling, supposedly, when he read *Pravda*. Neighbours in a flat worked together amicably to wreck a new woman-lodger's life. She read only the classics, they had noticed, and disdained Soviet literature. Now she was being sentenced for anti-Soviet attitudes. And how strange it was: our cousin Ida, who owed her higher education to the Soviet regime, spotted its dangerous tendencies, while my sister-in-law Nadya, who came from a highly educated family, in the space of a few years managed to lose all the moral principles of her upbringing. She turned into a typical urban philistine and Stalinist.

---

[47] Eden visited Moscow in the 1930s but as Foreign Secretary.
[48] Before the Revolution women could attend only the Higher Courses, not university.

Chapter 10

Each January, at the beginning of the new financial year, there was a break in contract work. With a letter of support from the Literary Museum, kindly provided by Bonch-Bruyevich, I went in January 1937 to investigate the archives in Leningrad, at Pushkin House, the Public Library and those depositories that came under the central archive administration. The visit promised to be interesting. I had somewhere to stay, since I'd remembered our relatives in Leningrad. I would call on Eichenbaum and boast of my finds in the Military-Historical Archive in Moscow. I knew I would meet Rudakov, who had already returned from exile in Voronezh. At last I would see Akhmatova and thereby quench my need for such human contact. But how would I greet Lyova? I hoped he'd have the sense not to be at home when I went to visit his mother.

At the agreed time, I knocked at the Punin apartment. It was Lyova who opened the door. He flew out and, giving me no chance to shed my fur coat, covered my face, shoulders and legs with kisses: "How glad I am! What a joy!"

He was in his third year at Leningrad University. How he had been re-admitted I do not know. Subsequently, I was told that this was thanks to the efforts of Nikolai Punin. Lyova was no longer living at Fontanka but staying with a friend called Axel, of whom I had never heard. Until Lyova's arrest in March 1938 they would live together. Who was this Axel? I tried to ask. "Someone's got to be dissipated," Lyova replied, "so he's dissipated." Until things had been sorted out, Lyova had been deeply depressed and gone away to some village or little town where he stayed . . . with his brother. The latter's existence had been unknown to both Lyova and Akhmatova until a short while before. The story went as follows. A middle-aged woman had called unexpectedly on Akhmatova. Olga Vysotskaya had formerly been an actress at the Meyerhold Theatre. She had had an affair with Gumilyov, she announced, and in 1913 had borne him a son. And here he was. She called in the young man: "Orest!"

Akhmatova immediately acknowledged him as Gumilyov's son. "He has Kolya's hands," she confirmed. Lyova was rapturous. Orik shared his room that night, and on waking the next morning Lyova murmured (in English): "Brother." How do I know such details? I have not the slightest idea. Probably Akhmatova told me.

Lyova would come to Fontanka to eat.

"Mama, it's time for me to take nourishment . . ."

"Don't close your eyes when you're eating, Lyova . . ."

"But it helps me . . ."

These mealtimes were called "feeding the animals".

The very first day, I was invited to eat with the family. At the table sat Punin, his wife Anna Yevgenyevna, their daughter Ira, Akhmatova and Lyova. On entering the apartment, I had immediately noticed an illiterate note on the door: "Bel not wurking". "Did you write that?" I had jokingly asked Ira, with the lightly patronising tone people usually adopt when talking to teenagers. This girl, however, was not at all like ordinary children. She had given me an unfriendly and mocking look and made no reply. Now Ira cast an expert eye over the meat and gravy that the maid brought in. The two women were friendly, and Ira was always sitting on the table in the kitchen, swinging her legs and chewing sunflower seeds.

Anna Yevgenyevna was 45, with coarse features and smoothly combed hair, tightly drawn at the temples but falling in locks on her neck. She had her own "companion" who was a doctor with the emergency services. Never once did I see him join their common meals.

Ira and her mother sat at one end of the very long table with Lyova and Akhmatova at the other. In silence, Anna Yevgenyevna would periodically down a small glass of vodka and only rarely, like a knife thrust, utter some remark in her low smoker's voice.

One evening over tea, Akhmatova was describing Lyova's conversation with a prostitute on the boulevard. "He didn't hire her," she added in an unnatural voice. Lyova expanded her account, repeating word for word a striking phrase the prostitute had used. "You could get ten years for such words," rang Anna Yevgenyevna's gloomy voice from the other end of the table.

On another occasion, there was talk of idlers. Anna Yevgenyevna suddenly announced: "Who the hangers-on are here, I don't know." Lyova and Akhmatova stiffened at once. For several minutes, I could see nothing but those two proud and offended profiles, seemingly linked by an invisible thread.

Once Punin had made my acquaintance, he expressed his astonishment: "I thought you were a Mme Récamier, but you're quiet." Then he proposed "a toast to Emma's quietness".

During one of my visits, a very animated Luknitsky dashed in. Everyone was in a state of excitement because enormous articles, filled with accusations against the Party opposition, had already appeared in the newspapers. People read and discussed them and kept up the pretence that there was nothing to worry about: "It doesn't concern us. With luck it'll all blow over." Perhaps the show trials had already begun, I do not exactly remember. It was January–February of 1937.[49] Pavel

---

[49] Throughout 1937 numerous people would be arrested, but only some were brought to public trial.

Luknitsky jested that he was above suspicion and totally orthodox. Playfully, Punin denied this. "I'll prove it to you this instant!" cried Luknitsky and rushed out into the hall. From his briefcase he pulled a volume of Lenin's works and triumphantly bore it into the dining-room. He had subscribed to the edition and just been given the latest issue.

Supper was not ready, and people sat around, Akhmatova on the little divan in the corner. "I've written a novel that no-one will ever read," said Luknitsky. Not to be outdone, Lyova declared that he had written a short story no-one would ever read. Even Punin joined in this ludicrous competition and, pointing to one of his articles, said that no-one would ever read it either. At that moment, Akhmatova's sonorous and musical voice came from the corner of the room: "But they'll read me."

A dish of carved slices of meat was brought in. All were to serve themselves. "Pavlik! Lyova!" Punin cried. He was not urging them to take what they wanted, but was "apprehensive" that they would forget themselves and put too much on their plates. Punin had a large family to support!

I managed immediately to adopt the right tone with him. Aware that he was unbelievably stingy, I realised that I had to shock him somehow, and so when he invited me to dinner and asked what I would like to eat I ordered dishes that were an extravagance at the time (among them pork cutlets). He was ecstatic. When this meal in my honour took place, however, his first remark was: "But Lyova's gone off to Tsarskoye Selo." Well, in that case we would eat without him. The sweet was a *compote*, but Ira was running behind and did not serve it on time. We drank it after the meal had ended, having sat down again to table. "Ira, Ira!" Punin exclaimed threateningly, from time to time. The girl said nothing, her lips stubbornly sealed. There must have been a row before the meal. Was that why Lyova had left for Tsarskoye Selo?

With his tic and his domestic dramas, the effusive Nikolai Punin was like no-one else I knew. Often he sat at the table for hours in a red dressing gown, playing patience. At other times, he shut himself up in his study, coming out to gulp down a cup of tea and comment under his breath: "How well the work's going, I've already turned out a whole 25 pages!"

Akhmatova translated excerpts for him from French and English books about art. She herself read them with great interest. She was very fond of the neighbour's boy, Valya,[50] son of the woman caretaker, and once she showed me how they recited Pushkin's "Golden Cockerel" together.

---

[50] Valentin (Valya) Smirnov is thought to have been among the half million inhabitants of Leningrad who died of starvation and disease during the blockade.

Just as three years before, reading Dante with Mandelstam, she restrained her rapture, abashed by her enthusiasm for the poetry. I was very touched by the sight of a bashful Akhmatova.

She eagerly translated French extracts from the archives for me.

If I found Lyova at Fontanka, he always left with me. He was in an uncontrollable state. After a few drinks, he would declaim Mandelstam's poems at table: "In Petersburg we shall meet again / . . . In the velvet black of a January night. / In the velvet of the cosmic void." Akhmatova sent him to take 50 roubles (a loan, of course) from Lydia Ginzburg. We walked out the back way on to Liteiny Avenue. Poetry, nerves and vodka had reduced him almost to tears. The atmosphere was gloomy. Yet in Moscow, Lena had told me what an enjoyable New Year's party they had just been to in Leningrad, and about the pubs on Vasilyevsky Island which she and a crowd of artists had visited. It had all been effortless, dazzling and witty. Could there really be normal life in Leningrad? For me, the entire city was overshadowed by the "House on Fontanka". (At that time, incidentally, no-one, not even Akhmatova, referred to the former Sheremetyev Palace by that name.)

I was staying with my cousin, the SR Lev Gerstein's sister, who was 25 years my senior. She lived with her husband and two student daughters in a cold, spacious Petersburg apartment in a large pre-Revolutionary block built as rented accommodation on Greek Avenue. (During the war, it was wiped off the face of the earth.) The husband resembled a typical Russian academic and, at the same time, a selfless doctor from the provinces. Like everyone in Leningrad, their apartment was superbly furnished with objects from the city's palaces, bought for a song in second-hand shops. In the bookshelves stood sets of *Sovremennik* and *Otechestevennye zapiski* magazines, a tradition of pre-Revolutionary student circles in Petersburg. My cousin who was a doctor, a general practitioner, warned me against Lyova's reactionary "Black Hundred" views. Lyova noticed none of this when he came to see me several times in the cold, clean flat of those high-minded intellectuals.[51]

For a short while, Akhmatova was admitted to the Obukhov Hospital for tests on her thyroid. Once I went to visit her with Lyova. I waited my turn to pass beyond the barrier through which visitors were received and saw how tenderly Lyova clung to his mother and how he pitied the sight of her in the yellowish-brown hospital gown. The wife of the literary critic and philosopher Engelhardt had also come to visit her. I saw

---

[51] The Russian word is *raznochinets*, a classless or "upstart" intellectual. In the *Noise of Time* Mandelstam comments: "A *raznochinets* needs no memory, it is enough for him to tell of all the books he has read, and his biography is done."

her only that one time and admired her elegant figure and her clear gaze and features. Lyova called the Engelhardts "the finest people in Russia". Both would die in the Leningrad Blockade. Somehow they were related to the pathologist Vladimir Garshin, who had long admired Akhmatova's poetry. Unless I'm mistaken, it was then that he first got to know Akhmatova, visiting her on the pretext of organising an examination by the famous endocrinologist Baranov. Perhaps it was not quite like that, but there was some link between her time in hospital and her first meetings with Garshin.

I took Lyova to see the Rudakovs, my Voronezh acquaintances and friends of Mandelstam. Rudakov was again living with his wife in a small student room in a communal apartment on Kolokolnaya Street. Sergei and Lyova read poems the entire evening, showing off their knowledge of Sumarokov,[52] reciting his verse from memory and discussing the eighteenth century in Russia. We stayed very late. When we left, Lyova thanked me for introducing him to Sergei. "That was a tonic; I was getting so depressed without poetry at the university," he said.

After walking only a short distance, Lyova announced: "You just go across the Chernyshov Bridge and you'll come out on Fontanka." (I had moved back to my friends living near the Anichkov Palace on Fontanka since my relations had not registered me and were very afraid to put me up.) It was already after 1 a.m. I had a poor sense of direction at the best of times and was far more nervous at night, especially in a strange city. I was enraged. Having told Lyova what I thought of him, I set off in the direction he indicated, privately feeling most timid. He began to run after me, loudly calling my name. A passing drunk told me approvingly: "You show him, you show him." But after a look at the running Lyova's beardless face, his fur hat like a bonnet and the ridiculous short coat flapping about his knees, the man exclaimed: "It's not a man at all, but some woman!" Lyova retorted: "And you're a flunky!" The man immediately fell silent, totally deflated. I memorised this, storing it away for future use and, after the war, tried it out myself. When a drunken caretaker threatened to kill me, I responded exactly as Lyova had done. It worked beautifully.

Forgetting the tram, on which he had been hoping to reach the Kolomna district, Lyova saw me home. The gates were closed, and there was no way of reaching our stairway entrance. The caretaker in a sheepskin coat examined us suspiciously and demanded to know where I was

---

[52] Alexander Sumarokov wrote the first Russian classicist tragedy for the stage in 1747. With imperial encouragement, he went on to write a further ten tragedies and twelve comedies.

going (after all, I had not been registered there). Finally, he allowed me in. Lyova left, but it was a long time before anyone responded to the doorbell. When the neighbours let me into the apartment, I quickly slipped into the room where I was staying and lay down on the divan, drawing the curtain behind me. "And I thought it was that damned Yagódka," I heard my hostess quip to her husband.

The husband, my childhood companion, was then frequently in demand to address musical evenings dedicated to Pushkin. He was most eloquent, had a photographic memory, and tossed off names and quotations with ease; he always knew exactly what to say on each occasion. He adored music and knew it very well.

The charm of an evidently cultured and well-read man and his knowledge of languages meant that he often received foreign performers touring the country. Describing a conversation in the dressing-room with a famous French conductor, he recalled the following brief scene. One of the Philharmonia administrators came up to him. As soon as the man had left, the conductor gave my friend a knowing look and asked: "*C'est un agent de police?*" Similar digressions from the usual confident and mannered speech of a Soviet public lecturer were pronounced in a quiet voice as though he had shaken off a spell.

My highly successful friend told of a "shock-worker", a Stakhanovite,[53] who was sent abroad with a delegation. Astonished by the material well-being of workers in capitalist countries, he took to the bottle on his return and cried, shedding drunken tears: "They tricked us, they tricked us!" When my friend touched on the conditions in which we were now working he spoke very quietly indeed: "During our lectures we always describe how Pushkin's imperial censor hindered his writing. What they are doing today to our writers – is it not just the same?" Such thoughts, however, would surface only to vanish again; or, to be more exact, people actively suppressed them.

Though my mother was totally incapable of dealing with the rudeness and cruelty of Soviet life, she would nevertheless bless it for the absence of anti-Semitism. She had never forgotten the insult she suffered on graduating from the *gymnasium* in the 1890s: because she was Jewish she had received a silver, not a gold, medal. Proud of her Soviet citizenship, she did not notice the absurdities of our existence. Adult children crowded their parents' apartment and tried to live their own lives, each in their separate corner. With her usual expression, Mama observed how my elder brother, a 35-year-old engineer, received an honoured

---

[53] Manual workers who, like the legendary miner Stakhanov, heroically over-fulfilled their plan targets.

guest in his one and only room. The child sleeping there began to cry, and his mother tried without success to calm him while my brother ran out with the kettle to the communal kitchen: he returned to his guest, trying to keep a smile on his face after hearing a sarcastic remark from the neighbour and feeling unfriendly eyes on his back. As she watched this tense and pathetic procedure, Mama suddenly, and to her own surprise, woke up. "In the old days, Borya would have travelled abroad several times," she sighed. "By now he'd have been a master of his profession and, as befits the respected head of a family, living in his own apartment." And she voiced her feelings with the greatest humility after what was, for our times, an outstanding musical event. Political considerations of some kind justified two performances at the Conservatory of the prohibited "Bells" by Rakhmaninov and Bach's *St Matthew Passion*.[54] We went to hear the Passion. When we got home, Mama said, with a certain timidity: "How do the words go? 'And brother shall deliver up brother to death, and the father his son; and children shall rise up against their parents and cause them to be put to death.'" The scene of Peter's treachery when, realising what he had done, he "went out, and wept bitterly" made a special impression on her.

For his part, my father behaved as if he were a member of the Central Committee. He never permitted himself to criticise the Soviet regime, even at home, or to discuss the members of government whom he treated as a doctor. He merely pitied them, noting how isolated they were and fearful of each other. Papa approved of the reconstruction of Moscow and was joyful that the roads were being widened – he, after all, moved around by car. The shapelessness of the new squares exasperated me. Alexander Osmyorkin shrugged his shoulders and said, derisively: "Kharkov."[55] Lyova did not compare the former appearance of both cities but commented: "It's not the only wild, open space in Russia." When dining at our apartment, I warned him, he should not say such things. Over a cup of tea, Papa asked him how he liked the new Moscow. As I had trained him, Lyova gave a neutral answer: "Spacious."

This was very wrong of me because I permitted Lyova to regard my family with a disrespectful condescension. He even commented that "one feels a certain emptiness" in our home. "At least we are afflicted with a few demons," he said, comparing Shchipok with Fontanka. This was unjust and most unobservant. Our family had quite enough of its own

---

[54] Performances of religious music were rare; the first work was Rakhmaninov's 1913 setting of Poe's "The Bells".
[55] Capital of the Soviet Ukraine until 1934. The city centre retains various Constructivist monuments built around a paved area larger than Red Square in Moscow.

demons and guardian angels, grudges and tears of repentance, fierce quarrels and touching reconciliations.

Papa was told that one of the thoughtful young Jewish men he had known back in Dvinsk[56] (where I was born) now lived in Moscow. He was doing well, but had become addicted to wine and would not stop drinking. Unexpectedly, Papa said, in that same quiet voice: "It speaks well of him. He's not fulfilled, it means."

My elder brother was finally allotted two rooms in an apartment shared by other employees of the metro-construction company. His wife, Nadya, told us how well they got on with their new neighbours, who praised eight-year-old Seryozha for carrying out the rubbish bin and always turning off the light in the toilet. "Frightful," sighed Papa. "They're such philistines."

Ten years later, during the so-called struggle with cosmopolitanism, my sister-in-law Nadya would be shattered by an outburst of anti-Semitism in the same apartment. The year 1937 struck a cruel blow against Jewish members of the Party, but throughout the 1930s anti-Semitism remained formally unacceptable at the domestic level. One incident led me to reflect on the whole situation.

Calling on Lena, I found the poet Vanya Pribludny,[57] recently returned from banishment to Astrakhan. He was accompanied by a friend, the son of the well-known economist Tugan-Baranovsky, who was living in bourgeois Latvia. Why he was now in the Soviet Union I do not know. Jokingly I asked him: "Are you fleeing persecution?" Both denied this and even took offence. Baranovsky talked about his life in Riga. He had a Jewish wife. Along the coast, there were different beaches for Jews and Christians, and he shocked his wife's relations by visiting the Jewish beach while she appeared totally out of place on the beach reserved for Christians. As he talked, he laughed, but I felt that I was hearing tales of prehistoric times. Had I only thought, I need not have been surprised. When we had stayed on the Latvian coast at Dubbeln during the summer of 1914 the owner of the neighbouring beach at Majorenhof had prohibited Jews from lodging there. Once the First World War began, however, the Pale of Settlement within the Russian Empire was abolished.

But let us return to Leningrad in February 1937. I had gone to visit Lyova and admire his bachelor quarters. On the wall was a portrait of Nikolai Gumilyov belonging to Axel. There stood his filthy and repellent

---

[56] Today Daugavpils (Latvia); pre-1914, Dinaburg, a town in the empire's Vitebsk province.
[57] Vanya (or Dmitry) "the Stray", literary pseudonym of the poet Yakov Ovcharenko (b. 1905). A Red Army volunteer during the Civil War, he was shot in 1937.

bed. Lyova slept on the floor on a bearskin and assured me that he took it into the courtyard each day and shook it out. That seemed doubtful. In the chest of drawers lay two rusted forks and an equally rusty knife. Axel was out, and I was already leaving when I bumped into him in the corridor. I never heard anything more about him. Incidentally, two years later when I was sorting through someone's archive I came across a pre-Revolutionary postcard from Klyuev. The poet indicated his return address in Petersburg, and it was the same apartment on Sadovaya Street.

My visit to Lyova coincided with the centenary of Pushkin's death. Only in Moscow did I learn that Akhmatova had spent the day entirely on her own. V.N. Anikiev called at Fontanka that evening and found her alone and very sad. She had not even received an invitation to the memorial gathering on 10 February. I learned this from the Osmyorkins and bitterly regretted that I had not visited her that evening instead of spending the time with Lyova in that repulsive room.

The trip to Leningrad has left confused but very rich memories. Everything differed from Moscow, starting with the low steps of the tram carriages and the even lines of the rails on the flat roadway, which seemed to have been stamped into the earth. Tall, broad windows with regular cross bars. The large, cold apartments of the Leningraders, with rooms subdivided by plywood and cloth partitions. Stone floors and Dutch stoves at the archive, which was located in the former Senate building. Draughts inside and out on the city squares. Struggling through the Leningrad wind and snowstorms on St Isaac's Square. On Nevsky Avenue squeezing into a tram, which grew empty the nearer it drew to the Maltsev Market. A feeling of ferocious hunger because there were no canteens in the city. A sense of dejection at Fontanka. My dissatisfaction with Lyova. While still in Leningrad, I wrote to Lena: "I enjoy your company more than anyone else's. Lyova leads a very dull life here. With Akhmatova I sometimes don't know what to talk about." And, at the same time, a constant feeling that work was going well at the archives: on the low ground floor of the Public Library where the aged curator, the legendary I.A. Bychkov, was still in charge and referred to me as "Mme Gerstein" (this when "there are no masters now!"); at Pushkin House, where Modzalevsky's card index alone provided a store of invaluable information about the personalities of Pushkin's and Lermontov's time; and, finally, in the thick folders of Prince Gagarin's drawings at the Russian Museum. Each foray into this material gave a sense of progress, since it had never been examined for this purpose before. And what a joy it was to visit Eichenbaum and be greeted by his lively interest and encouragement.

Chapter 11

On my return to Moscow, I resumed the way of life I had found so absorbing. The archives, the manuscript section at the Lenin Library, the Literary Museum . . . Soon, however, I fell out of favour with Bonch-Bruyevich. I then worked, as I have said, for the acquisitions department, and material offered to the museum passed through our hands. It so happened that I began to deal with the manuscripts of Sergei Klychkov. They arrived in batches. Certain letters written to him by famous individuals, in particular Voroshilov, were also sold to us. Yet all these items were brought not by Klychkov himself but by the poet Pimen Karpov.

Well disposed towards Klychkov, I went to ask him if he had engaged Karpov to sell his manuscripts. My news created a shattering impression. The impoverished and homeless Karpov, it turned out, often stayed the night with the Klychkovs, who made up a bed for him on the trunk where the manuscripts were stored. He was secretly pulling out Klychkov's papers and selling them, bit by bit, to the museum. "I was just about to go to *Krasnaya nov* [monthly] and speak there about the friendship and trust that is essential between us as writers!" Klychkov exclaimed. "Well, I shan't be going now!"

It then became apparent that the Klychkovs were mildly hurt by Lyova's disappearance. Somewhat diffidently, Klychkov asked me: Was it true that Lyova Gumilyov was in Moscow? Karpov claimed to have seen him in the reading-room at the Lenin Library. On learning that this was a misunderstanding, Klychkov gave a sigh of relief. As we know, Lyova did not then come on visits from Leningrad. Neither did he take the trouble to let me or the Klychkovs know that he had been re-admitted to Leningrad University. Klychkov, however, also proved himself a fine fellow. He went to the Literary Museum and kicked up a fantastic row. He did this without consulting me and must have revealed the source of his information.[58] Bonch-Bruyevich and the secretaries he'd trained for this work realised that in me they had acquired a colleague who could not observe departmental confidentiality or, if you will, protect the firm's commercial secrets. Though perhaps Bonch-Bruyevich had by now also learned of my involvement in the Mandelstam affair?

When they told me that the museum no longer had the funds to renew my contract for the next quarter, I first insisted on seeing the director. But for a month all they would say was, "The director is busy," or, worse, "Wait," and then (after three hours of waiting), "Vladimir Dmitrievich is just leaving." I realised that my career there was over.

---

[58] Sergei Klychkov (1889–1937) was soon arrested and shot.

At the Lenin Library, on the other hand, things were still going well. And my work there was more interesting. For almost a year, I was busy classifying and describing the enormous depository of the Yelagin family. Avdotya Yelagina, who hosted a renowned literary and political salon in Moscow, had a large family. Her elder sons by her first marriage were Ivan and Pyotr Kireyevsky, the leaders of the Slavophils,[59] and they and her remaining children from her second marriage (the student brothers Yelagin and their young sister Lilya) constantly corresponded with one another. The younger children wrote most often to their father in the country, giving a detailed account of those who attended the regular "Sunday" salons, of how people spoke, and of who said what and the subject of their debates. I thus became absorbed in Moscow's cultural life of the 1840s, and these gatherings came alive in my imagination. But before becoming immersed in the atmosphere of those intellectual debates, I was given other smaller depositories to process. Among them was a box that, perhaps, had become separated from the enormous archive of the historian S.M. Solovyov. It contained his unfinished manuscripts and some of his correspondence. Probably no-one before me had opened this box, since I discovered two valuable unpublished letters there. One was from Nekrasov, the other from Lev Tolstoy.

It had become the custom at the Lenin Library to give the right of first publication to the person who discovered an unpublished document. This is not a wise rule. Without the slightest preparatory work, I was lucky to have plucked these valuable letters from the box before anyone else, but there was no merit in that. To provide a commentary for Nekrasov's letter about an article by Solovyov for his magazine *Sovremennik*,[60] or to annotate Tolstoy's request for certain details about the reign of Peter the Great, one had to know the subject thoroughly. Was it worth engrossing oneself in specialist literature for the sake of one incidental publication? Usually, the non-specialist gets away with a few general remarks culled from already published works. The prospect did not entice me, and to the astonishment of my colleagues and acquaintances I declined to publish Tolstoy's letter. I took on the Nekrasov letter, however. Here also, as it turned out, I could not cope without expert aid. I asked Yevgeny Khazin at least to provide my commentary with the obligatory Marxist terminology, but

---

[59] The Slavophile current arose in mid-nineteenth-century Russian culture and thought in opposition to the unthinking and wholesale adoption of Western liberal ideas, especially when imposed on society by the State.
[60] Nekrasov's short letter (20 December 1850) begins: "Dear Sergei Mikhailovich, Your last article about the Interregnum [early seventeenth-century Time of Troubles] was halted by the censor . . ."

he was not strong in that genre either. He dictated certain general phrases to me, but they were so superficial and did so little to uncover the true significance of the document that, in despair, I arranged to see Nikolai Khardjiev. I had long wanted to talk to him, and not just when we met through Nadezhda Mandelstam, when he always greeted me in very friendly fashion. Once I even asked Lyova to bring him to visit me. It was already the late autumn of 1936, and both men arrived in cloth summer shoes for lack of any other. They were very cheerful, nevertheless. Now, six months later, I went to visit Khardjiev in Maria's Grove and show him the plan of my commentary or introductory article to this unknown letter from Nekrasov. He looked through it and began asking questions. How were historical articles selected for *Sovremennik*? Did the magazine often publish such material? What was the subject of the Solovyov article discussed in the letter? Had it been published and, if so, when? I could barely answer a single one of his queries. "Clear this nonsense from my desk," said Khardjiev by way of conclusion. He now outlined the work necessary for preparing the publication.

I began my research in the reading-room of the Lenin Library. As the necessary facts accumulated, I would go to Khardjiev and seek his guidance. (On one such visit, I met the Mandelstams as they fled from those shadowing them.) Discussions of Russian history, it turned out, had so far received very little attention in specialist works devoted to Nekrasov's magazine. At long last, my article on "Russian History in Nekrasov's *Sovremmenik*", which concluded with the newly discovered letter, was ready. When it was published, Yevgeny Khazin's reaction was sceptical: the letter had been pushed to the end of the article. Indeed, it had not been given a journalistic treatment, but, as a result, this new material had been set in its proper context.

Khardjiev became indispensable. I endured his whims and caprices – I knew how to cope with them – and the reward was the company of a highly educated man with a most original mind. He had already done a great deal for literature and was passionate about his work. He was then preparing his collection of Khlebnikov's unpublished writings and the task demanded extraordinary gifts: subtle textual analysis, intuition, a fanatical capacity for work and an inspired determination.

The sixtieth anniversary of Nekrasov's death was approaching. Khardjiev advised me to take my article to *30 Days* magazine. "They're certain to print it," he declared. As indeed they did. The article was published in the first issue of 1938. Without waiting for it to appear, I went to Leningrad immediately after the New Year to work in the archives.

Chapter 12

On my very first day in Leningrad, I went to see Akhmatova. Of course, Lyova was there, waiting for me, and of course, he walked me home ("How happy I am, how I've missed you – I was already thinking of going to Moscow"). We crossed over to Vasilievsky Island. Osmyorkin had given me the key to his studio at the Academy of Arts and stayed on in Moscow. I enjoyed living there, and there was no-one to disturb us. Lyova had grown up a little and become wiser, he was already 25. It was more interesting talking to him. "I've discovered an entire nation east of Lake Baikal," he announced joyfully. Meanwhile I was anxiously awaiting my first publication: perhaps I'd missed something in the proofs?

Things were going well for Lyova at the university. The elected senior of his year came up to him, looked at him ("with her black eyes, she's Jewish") and offered to print an article in their magazine. He readily agreed. We talked about the Mandelstams. For it was only a short while since Mandelstam had come to Leningrad to "raise funds". Lyova was not wholly approving: "He's clutching at life too eagerly." We did not fully realise that Mandelstam's last few months as a free man were his death throes. Some superior intuition told the poet that he was doomed, though he did not want to admit it. All of his actions that year were not deeds so much as a convulsion.

The conversation turned to the religious perception of death. Mandelstam's outlook was monistic, Lyova said, while Christians were dualists: the spirit was one thing, the body another. Only with that under-standing could the doctrine of the immortal soul have developed.

Apart from visiting the archive, I went each day to see Eichenbaum, Rudakov or Akhmatova at Fontanka. At the end of the week, I had a completely free evening. I rang up Lyova and said he could come earlier, only to hear a reply that astounded me: "I can't, I've been invited out." "What do you mean, who's invited you?" I was beside myself with indignation and hurt. The more I said, the worse it became. What pleasure was there to be stranded in a strange city, sitting in an empty studio, all by myself? I was furious. Finally, he was forced to admit: "Well, I'm not visiting anyone, I'm going to church." It was 6 January, Christmas Eve in other words. I knew quite well what the date meant but in Leningrad had lost count of the days. When we had made things up, he reproached me tenderly: "Tut tut, making me talk about church on the phone like that."

Indeed, danger lay in wait for him on all sides. He read me poems he had composed for some long narrative work or even a historical tragedy. "Our arms are strong . . ." and so on: I do not remember the words, but it was the monologue of a captive warrior. "The lads clench their fists when I read them that," he told me. There: so he was reading such poems to the other students. A shiver ran down my spine. This was more serious than the pranks he had told me about in Moscow. The students chanted his verses about the officer in charge of military instruction and training at the university. In those years, someone of such rank in the Red Army should have been addressed, if I remember rightly, as "Comrade Commander". Lyova's composition went: "Colonel Mey, sir, / pour yourself some vodka, / . . . and don't be stingy with the herring, sir!" Or there were humorous verses with the refrain, "We must have orgies". He mentioned a specialist in Oriental studies. She was teaching him Japanese, and, in return, he would recite the poems of Annensky, Gumilyov and Akhmatova to her. I didn't like the sound of that. I never actually enquired about his life there. During the first years of our acquaintance, it's true, I once asked him in Moscow whom he saw in Leningrad. He named a children's writer. "A good writer?" "No, bad." He also visited an artist. "A good artist?" "No, bad." And he was seeing some woman. "Is she interesting?" "No, not very." "Lyovushka, but why such dull companions?" "They're all the good Lord sent me."

Though I do dimly remember that Lyova was seeing Yevgeny Ivanov, Alexander Blok's friend. If so, then probably the 60-year-old was linked to the youthful Gumilyov by their common interest in religion or, to be more accurate, Orthodox Christianity. Perhaps they were parishioners of the same church and met there.

Now in the studio on Vasilievsky Island, Lyova asked yet again about my life in Moscow. But his enquiry was a jealous one, and I refused to answer such primitive questions. Often he would reflect: "What a long and successful affair ours is, four whole years already." "It's not an affair," I objected. "We rarely see one another," I explained, "and so nothing irritating and everyday comes between us. If we lived in the same city, everything would be different." As if he did not hear, caught up in his own thoughts, Lyova commented: "How stupid people are to have children in mixed marriages. When Russia is Fascist in about eight years' time children with a Jewish parent will not be allowed to do anything, and, like mulattos and half-castes, they won't be accepted by society."

On another occasion, lying on Osmyorkin's bed in the far corner of the studio, he was silent for a long while and then murmured: "I keep wondering what I'll say to the interrogator." As always, I asked no questions.

Three weeks passed. I began preparing to return home. Lyova asked me to stay longer. "I can't," I replied. "I've done all I can in the Leningrad archives." In fact, I had run out of money. But I could not say so to Lyova – he and Axel had one shirt between them.

At this point, Osmyorkin came back. "You can live as my guest," he invited. Of course, I agreed. The rostrum split the large studio into two halves. Osmyorkin fed me, and we lived quite happily together. He was a noisy, open and companionable person, and in the evenings he invited people round. Lyova visited me during the day when Osmyorkin was at the Academy.

Osmyorkin and I invited Akhmatova together with Punin. I went to fetch her. Punin was to come directly from the Academy. Akhmatova and I walked for a long while through one of the city's large gardens and then along Nevsky Avenue. Once again, I had an acute sense of the city. The even road surfaces, mild winter, grey sky, damp wind and exceptionally gloomy, preoccupied, even worn-out faces of the passers-by. Akhmatova noticed no-one. She was wrapped up in her own thoughts; to be more precise, she was continuing some conversation with herself. We were walking along the boulevards of the Great Line, and she talked of Blok and my favourite among his poems, "With my bitter tears . . ." Angrily and wittily, Akhmatova attacked it. "What an objectionable piece of verse," she said. "She is crying and begging, if you please, but as for him 'my face was scorched by the tempestuous head wind'." With inimitable humour, sarcasm even, Akhmatova quoted the closing verse and commented: "What male self-satisfaction, 'I do not know, I forgot you.'" Akhmatova was probably thinking of Punin at this time: by the autumn they would part for ever. Talking about him at length in Moscow a short while before she had lightly remarked: ". . . fed up to here with me" and drawn her hand across her throat.

Khardjiev told me how Punin had read his new short story about love during that same January 1938 in Leningrad. "You think that's about me?" Akhmatova calmly addressed Khardjiev. "It concerns a quite different woman." But when we dined together at Osmyorkin's studio there were no detectably prickly moments between Punin and Akhmatova.

Opposite the studio was a market, I think the Andreyevsky market. I bought some food there and prepared snacks to go with the vodka. I was not very good at it, but they all treated me with consideration. Lyova came up in conversation, and they talked of him as if he were a little boy. I meanly supported this attitude. When they were leaving, I quipped: "Alexander, you see the guests out while I tidy up our little nest." Tidying that little nest was impossible. Firewood lay stacked on the floor in the corner by the stove. The cups and plates did not match and were kept in a simple wooden cupboard painted black. An enormous cupid dangled over the head of the iron cot, with gilt shining through a layer of dust. And so on. It was a rash joke. I had forgotten the poisonous mists that drenched the atmosphere about Akhmatova just as they had earlier enveloped the Mandelstams at Nashchokin Street. Not a word slipped their attention, and, when needed, it would be brought up in some new context. I should add that this never went beyond our immediate circle.

The next evening, Lyova came to see us. He was accompanied by his contemporary and friend Vova Petrov (later a famous art specialist). Vova was a rosy-cheeked boy wearing a handsome coat with an expensive fur collar. The more he drank, the paler he grew. Finally, he was white as a sheet. When they left, we laughed and imagined what Vova looked like in various other situations. "He just got paler and paler . . ." Osmyorkin kept repeating. We were seized by a helpless fit of laughter. But the young fellow probably should not have been drinking at all. "What an earthy colour Lyova's face is compared to Vova," I said, "a real drinker's face." "What do you expect? He's been through fire and water." Then we did not know that this was merely the beginning of Lyova's ordeals: the most terrible was still to come. "And what was that shred hanging from his jacket?" "It's a very old jacket of his, and the padding is coming out." "And no-one sews it up?" Osmyorkin continually returned to Lyova's appearance, examining him with an artist's eye: "There is a capricious line to his mouth, like Akhmatova's."

For no reason, Osmyorkin decided to make a pass at me and was very persistent. Lena and I never countenanced anything of the kind: to me, her husband was like a brother or another relation. But he had some scores to settle with her at the time: "And it'll make things more interesting with Lena," he assured me. (Perhaps he would have found it more interesting. The prospect was of no conceivable interest to me.) He took offence at my indifferent rebuff and thereafter, alas, became an enemy – which would have unpleasant consequences for me.

It was time for him to return to Moscow, and, naturally, we were leaving on the same train. The morning of our departure, I arranged with Lyova that he would come round between 10 and 11. He was late, and with an inexplicable sense of relief I decided to go out. First I rang Khardjiev, who was staying with some acquaintances. I wanted to see him, but he became affected and difficult: "Why did you wake me up?" I lost patience and went to the Hermitage. I was leaving that day and had not even managed to visit the museums, if only to look at the Rembrandts. I left the studio.

After the evening meal, a most tedious artist visited Osmyorkin. Lyova arrived to see us off. I withdrew with him beyond the rostrum to talk privately before we parted. He was in a bad mood: "I rushed and hurried, went without breakfast only to find the door locked in my face." He was pale and bitter, and Osmyorkin cast us spiteful glances.

We went to the station. Lyova was clutching a black tin tray decorated with bright flowers that Osmyorkin had spotted and bought at the market. We found our places in the carriage while Lyova stood beneath the window on the platform. I went to the door, wanting to say goodbye to him. Osmyorkin followed. Lyova flung his arms round Osmyorkin's neck with exaggerated affection. I had to say my farewells to Lyova in Osmyorkin's presence. I remember Lyova's broad, white face, crooked hypocritical smile and ridiculous jacket.

In our compartment, Osmyorkin teased me, pretending to be sympathetic: "You're sad. You regret leaving Lyova behind, don't you?" In Moscow, he told Lena: "Emma's so in love with Lyova! But he parted more tenderly from even me than from Emma."

Still, I was content with my last visit to Lyova, despite our unsuccessful farewell. Prickly moments were unavoidable given his character, not to mention my own, but they could not obscure the deep affection that bound us. As a young girl, I used to dream of meeting a man who would be a pillar of strength, a spiritual guide, a friend and a defender. That dream was long forgotten. There were no men around me who lived a serious and steady existence of artistic creativity. All those with whom I could talk were neurotic, tired and dissatisfied, or else they had become rigid, substituting automatic reflexes for the more natural responses of a living spirit. Above all else, they were preoccupied with themselves. Lyova, with his impulsive deeds and tactless behaviour, even though he laid no claims to my innermost thoughts and emotions, was much more acceptable to me than these other strange creatures. I valued him as a friend whom I loved and saw rarely. I loved the ideas that he always expressed with an elegant and original laconicism, inherited from his mother; I loved the heroic and poetic agitation that resembled his father; I admired the nobility with which he bore his terrible burden, comparable to the historical destiny of persecuted under-age heirs to the throne. I pitied him and for some reason privately referred to him in French as "*victime*". Yet this time, I felt encouraged to believe that both his life and mine could change for the better. What a strange, frivolous attitude! Afterwards I would often observe something of the kind. Before catastrophe struck, I would be gripped, for some reason, by a feeling of happiness. For instance, during the night of 21–2 June 1941, as the Germans prepared to invade the Soviet Union, I had an especially blissful dream.

Osmyorkin went to Leningrad again. I came to spend the night with Lena. Several acquaintances had called to see her, and we shared a meal, laughing and enjoying ourselves. This mood buoyed us up even after Osmyorkin returned to Moscow. In early March, Lena again saw him off to Leningrad. Only two or three days had passed when she rang me up and said: "Shura [Osmyorkin] has just called from Leningrad and told me to let you know that Lyova has gone away." There was no need to ask where: this meant he'd been arrested.

That evening, I raced over to see Khardjiev. I found him on his own in the kitchen of the small empty apartment. He was frying himself some potatoes. He sat me down on a clean stool, listened to my news and let out a cry. But then he said: "You know, I must have something to eat – I haven't had a bite all day."

For a short while, he ate. Then he turned to me: "His fiancée's to blame. You do know, don't you, that Lyova had a fiancée?" We moved to his room. Khardjiev was silent; he thought and he gazed at me with his burning eyes. "He's done for." I gathered all the strength I could muster: "And what was this fiancée of Lyova's like?" "Well, now: he summoned Anna Andreyevna [Akhmatova] and myself and he also invited the woman. As though we were looking over a prospective bride." (Khardjiev had returned from Leningrad some ten days after me.) "She wore glasses and was quite pretty. We didn't like her at all. We told him so, and he was somehow very quick to share our opinion. He was court-ing her but didn't appear to be that deeply in love. She's a Mongolian princess, though. From Mongolia, but a princess none the less."

Nikolai Khardjiev, 1940s

Long after, Khardjiev reminded me of a phrase I could not help utter-ing that evening: "You don't know how very dear Lyova is to me." I never reminded him of his words at the time: "Emma, you will never see him again." This was said most severely.

He was wrong. For many years, we would continue to see someone who bore the name of Lev Nikolayevich Gumilyov. But though we still called him Lyova, it was not the Lyova we had known before his arrest in 1938. How Akhmatova suffered from this fateful change in his personality! Not long before her death, at any rate during the last part of her life, she once fell into deep thought, re-examining every stage in her son's life from the day he was born. At last she firmly declared: "No! He wasn't always like that. They made my boy like that."

Khardjiev lived in Maria's Grove. The long tram journey home across the entire city lasted almost an hour. I could not stop thinking or regain my senses. Pity, anger at the GPU, but, all the same, that fiancée . . . In my heart of hearts I suspected that the entire performance with his prospective bride had deliberately been staged to pay me back for missing my last tryst with Lyova before leaving Leningrad. I felt sure that was why he had invited Khardjiev, who would tell me about it immediately on his return to Moscow. The thought did not cross Khardjiev's mind. Our conversations were about quite different matters.

When I got home I lay my head on the arm of the chair and wept openly and bitterly as I had not wept since childhood.

Soon Osmyorkin returned to Moscow. According to Lena, he said: "Akhmatova and Anna Yevgenyevna were so distressed that they kept urging me to let Emma know straightaway. But how could Emma help them?" He did not leave them for two days. Akhmatova was quite delirious. She kept crying some woman's name: "Zina, was it? Zina?" Lena resolutely refused me any sympathy. "None of it has anything to do with you. Neither that fiancée nor some Zina woman. What has your casual affair with him got to do with it? Forget all about it."

It was sometime after 20 March. I wanted to know what was happening in Leningrad so badly that I was going crazy. Meanwhile, I was invited to address the Lermontov commission. Khardjiev helped me prepare. The session was to be held on 9 April. Shortly before, I met Irakly Andronikov on the street; he had just come back from Leningrad. I was still wearing my winter coat, and there was an unexpected springlike warmth in the air. Walking beside Irakly, I barely let him finish his stories about Pushkin House before asking abruptly: "You don't know what they're saying there about Akhmatova's son?" He looked at me in amazement. He knew nothing, and we resumed our cheerful conversation. I felt worn out with the heat and anxiety.

It was then that the Mandelstams left for the sanatorium in Samatikha, still hopeful that things would somehow work out.[61] Nadya's older sister Anya, meanwhile, was seriously ill in Leningrad, where she lived in a Khazin relative's apartment in a dark back room. She had cancer.

---

[61] Mandelstam was arrested there on 3 May.

In June their brother Yevgeny went to be with her. Soon Anya died. After burying his sister, Yevgeny returned to Moscow. The very same day he rang me. As always: "We'll meet in the next few days, I'll come round early one evening." I could not wait. I began to insist, it must be today, now! "We'll meet outside and go for a walk together." He could only agree.

That summer, all the benches had been removed from the Boulevard Ring. Perhaps they were being repaired. Perhaps they had been removed to punish the Muscovites who were in mourning for the boulevards: Stalin had the idea of removing them as part of the plan to reconstruct the city. People whispered that he feared barricades.[62] An old man sat on the boulevard, complaining over and over again. Were they really going to take away the benches? He was arrested.

Yevgeny and I met on Bolshaya Dmitrovka Street and went for a walk along the Boulevard Ring. Naturally, he was stunned by his loss. He could not stop describing Anya's suffering, how Akhmatova nursed her, how the dying Anya gave Akhmatova her bead necklace and how they buried her: "Only the three of us were there: Nadya, myself and Akhmatova. That uncle was also present but he doesn't count." And as he talked of Akhmatova, Yevgeny let fall a few words: "And since Lyova's case has been passed to the Military Tribunal . . ."[63] I reeled with the shock. I began asking him to tell me more, but he stubbornly continued talking about his own concerns and did not want to add another word about Lyova. He talked and talked about Anya, whom I had known and loved, but I could not think of her now. My legs were giving way beneath me and I thought I would collapse. But on we went, walking along the boulevard without a bench in sight.

The whole summer was like that. In my imagination I conjured up the physical tortures and moral torments Lyova was enduring. Then suddenly, I would feel a sense of release, and it seemed at that moment as if he was feeling better and something had happened. Every woman knows the insanity of helplessness when someone near and dear has been imprisoned. Only no-one felt sympathy for me.

On 1 October 1938, a great misfortune struck Lena's family. Her 25-year-old sister suddenly died. After the funeral we all sat in Osmyorkin's large studio. There was no funeral wake: Jews do not have them and that was awful. The parents sat with gloomy, lifeless faces; from time to

---

[62] Two concentric rings of boulevards surrounded the heart of Moscow throughout the nineteenth century. The Garden Ring became an eight-lane ring road; the inner Boulevard Ring has survived.

[63] The Supreme Court's Military Tribunal dealt with the most serious "counter-revolutionary" and "political" offences and handed down death sentences.

time, Lena burst into loud wails of grief and Shura comforted her. Then suddenly, when she was sitting in one corner of that large room and I was in the other on the rostrum, Lena loudly and clearly announced to me: "Emma! I forgot to tell you: Lyova was given ten years, but the Moscow prosecutor objected to the sentence. It was too soft in his view, so they'll probably shoot him."

My head was spinning, and I went into the next room. Some time later, Lena joined me. "Lenochka –" but she replied harshly and loudly: "I don't want to talk about it now. Anyway, what's it to you? It's not your grief."

Apparently, people also had different rights when it came to feeling grief.

Soon Akhmatova came to Moscow to petition for her son.

Of course, I had seen her several times in Moscow before I heard of the prosecutor's objections. She came to visit me, and, at her request, we together burned Lyova's letters and poems in my small tiled stove. Akhmatova was concerned that my room would be searched: "they" should not get their hands on a single unnecessary word, no matter how innocent the subject. Many naive people were caught out in this way. "I have nothing to hide: I say, write and do nothing of that kind," honest Soviet people would tell themselves. As it happened, the "organs" did not need anything "of that kind". All they required was something they could latch on to and then use to astonish their detainee by naming some distant acquaintance or mentioning a petty incident from his every-day existence. "They know everything about us!" thought the detainee after such cross-questioning. In response, experienced people developed their own principle of self-defence: "They should know nothing what-ever about us."

Akhmatova herself threw Lyova's letters to me into the stove. There were not that many. Into the stove flew what I have called his "historic" letter, describing the way he was hounded at the university. And his first letter, which I remembered for the phrase "the weather's bad and I'm out of sorts". And the letter Lena remembered because Lyova, with understanding and approval, had described the Pushkin production staged by actor-manager A. Dikoi with sets designed by Osmyorkin. With difficulty we also managed to burn the thick leaves of a drawing album in which Kuzin had written out Nikolai Gumilyov's "Poisoned Tunic" in full.[64] At some point Kuzin had lent me the album but was soon

---

[64] Verse tragedy on a theme from Byzantine history. Gumilyov composed it in Paris and London before his return to Petersburg via Murmansk in April 1918.

arrested and so the manuscript remained with me. Now it also went up in flames. When this auto-da-fé took place I do not exactly remember. Probably it was after I astonished Andronikov by referring to the arrest of Akhmatova's son but before Akhmatova, Yevgeny Khazin and Nadya, who had made the trip to Leningrad, walked behind Anya's coffin. Osip Mandelstam could not be at the funeral; he was already under arrest and in Butyrki prison.

The terrible year of 1938 seemed much longer in my recollection than it was in reality. Only by consulting certain of my own papers can I establish how compressed time was for me then.

On 9 April, I spoke before the Lermontov commission at the Institute of World Literature. I gave a report on the new documents I had found. Lermontov's friend Prince Sergei Trubetskoi was, it seemed, not at all the high-society fop portrayed in P.E. Shchegolev's brilliant but inaccurate essay "Love in the Ravelin".

They declared me "a poet of the archives", and I requested a research trip to Alupka, Vorontsov's palace on the Black Sea. At the end of his short life, Trubetskoi became related by marriage to Count Vorontsov, the son of Pushkin's "half-lord, half-scoundrel". The institute would cover my expenses but only in late autumn, not until November, so there would be no risk of my enjoying a summer or early autumn holiday at the expense of the State.

At the beginning of October, however, I had heard of the prosecutor's official objection to Lyova's ten-year sentence. Prior to that appeal Akhmatova had been to see Lyova in prison. She told me about it. Lyova said: "I've been given the same as Radek, ten years." And: "Mama, I spoke like Dimitrov, but no-one was listening."[65] He did not want his appearance to distress his mother, so he wore someone else's scarf around his neck, "to look more attractive" as he put it. When they parted, he quoted Blok:

> Not the first warrior am I, nor the last,
> My homeland long shall ail . . .

During this account, Akhmatova casually remarked: "Lyova sent you his greetings." Ladies adopt such an artificial and throwaway tone during a brief social call. It was hard to understand the intention behind this phrase: was she being condescending towards me, or was she concerned

---

[65] Karl Radek, a repentant supporter of Trotsky, was publicly tried and sentenced in 1937 (he died in prison two years later). Georgy Dimitrov, the Bulgarian Communist, defied Göring from the dock at the Reichstag Fire trial in 1934.

to preserve the dignity of her dispirited son? When the time came for Lyova to be convoyed to the camps Akhmatova gave me the address of the transit prison with the words "Now you can write to him". I sat for a long while, a blank sheet of paper in front of me, and could not find the words I needed. My love had been defiled. And I did not write to him then.

I found words of comfort much later, in 1940, and I sent them to Lyova in Norilsk. By then, however, much water had flowed beneath the bridge.

It was still tormenting Nadya not to know (O accursed 1938!) why Mandelstam had been arrested. She stayed the night with me and could not stop asking herself why they had not detained her when they came for Osya. During their last days at Samatikha, she confessed, there was an incident involving another guest who had come to their room. The woman was secretary of a district Party committee, no less. If her complaint was the cause of Mandelstam's arrest, they would also have taken Nadya . . . She was miserable and anguished.

Meanwhile I was leaving for the Crimea. The train journey to Sebastopol took a whole day and night, if not two nights. Every seat, of course, was taken. The men kept visiting the restaurant car and coming back drunk. They got on familiar terms with the female passengers but, for some reason, quickly fell out with them. What quarrelsome people! I paid no attention and lay on the lower bunk, reading a book. The man opposite gave me a disapproving and suspicious look. Finally, he declared indignantly: "Who reads such a book lying down? You should study it and take notes. It's such a profound work." I had decided to pass these two wasted days and nights reading compulsory literature and took with me the just-published *History of the All-Union Communist Party (Bolshevik)*.[66]

It was night when we arrived in Sebastopol. The station buffet was brightly lit, and there were quite a few people round the tables, but not that many. There was a strange agitation in the room, however. The waiter was clearly overexcited and exchanged banter with the passing customers, but his attention was fixed on the kitchen, to which he ran to collect the dishes. Losing any vestige of self-control, he yelled vehemently several times at the woman behind the counter: "Just don't sign anything! Don't sign anything, that's the most important!"

Among the passengers round the tables were many soldiers and officers. This was Sebastopol, after all. Surrounded by the noise and fuss of

---

[66] Stalin's notorious rewriting of the Party's history, subtitled "A Short Course".

the rail station were two modestly dressed girls, mere teenagers in fact, calmly drinking tea at their empty table and eating nothing. They were obviously local and had come to pursue their usual nocturnal profession. O misery!

We went on to Alupka on a bus that was also crowded with soldiers. The only civilians were myself and a woman with a teenage daughter. The men flirted with the girl.

We drove past the famous "Baidar Gates". The name stirred sour recollections. In the 1920s during NEP, Soviet officials flocked to the Crimea and the Caucasus for their vacations. I remember countless proud and self-assured secretaries who holidayed on the Black Sea with their male "acquaintances". My elder brother took his wife there, after they economised on tram journeys for a whole year (the price of a tram ticket then depended on the distance travelled). Back in Moscow they gave a rapturous description of the Baidar Gates and the amazing view of the coast and sea that opened below them. Father sent my sister to the government rest home in Yalta, and she also talked of this view. So did Papa when he returned from the south, bringing back wonderful grapes, pears, apricots and melons. I never went on vacation since I was always unemployed.

Driving into Alupka, we could already hear a noise, some way off. Choral singing and laments . . . In a nearby rest home, a group of vacationers was leaving. Those remaining behind saw them off in accordance with established ritual: they pretended to wipe away tears and would not permit the car to leave. It was all a performance. Other guests did not join in the send-off but strolled not far away, singing their favourite Soviet songs. Alas! It was a rest home for the GPU.

The clientele, however, was evidently already third class. Soon it would be winter, and the women strolled along the deserted beach in felt bootees and winter coats. Solitary male figures in military greatcoats would occasionally appear on the freezing paths. Dark, high waves beat relentlessly against the cliffs. A north-east wind was blowing. I gazed at this threatening sight and thought of all wayfarers and "those in peril on the sea".

At the museum I sat in a large, cold room filled with tall, glass-fronted, locked bookcases. On the table lay volumes I had already examined from the Vorontsov library's rich collection of foreign books about Tsarist Russia. I was copying out a letter of Trubetskoi that would not be published for another 50 years.

Unexpectedly, a loud voice was heard outside the door. A short, stout man and his wife came rapidly into the library. The museum assistant took a volume from a bookcase, very politely handed it to the new arrival and then retreated to the neighbouring room. Without removing his overcoat and or taking a seat, the new reader began to look through the book and, showing certain pages to his wife, expressed his noisy pleasure. Then he turned to me, a complete stranger, and enthusiastically explained the interest and importance of this rare volume. An intense inner energy and kindly disposition could be read in his eyes. After a minute I realised that I was talking to Samuil Marshak. But he was already briskly departing, with his wife behind him. Their car was waiting downstairs. It seems that they were passing through Alupka on their way back to Moscow from the Crimea.

I was given the Empress Alexandra Fyodorovna's letters to Trubetskoi's sister, who became the Countess Vorontsova in 1851, but I could not decipher them unaided. The handwriting was tiny; the text was in French and employed various abbreviations. I did not know the language well enough. "Are there any other materials?" "Yes, but they're kept in the tower. And who's going to climb up there in such a north-easterly gale?" My visit to Alupka so late in the year was a very limited success.

Chapter 13

Documents in my possession illustrate the background against which such important events, both personal and public, took place and provide a number of firm dates.

1. On the copy I made of the letter from Trubetskoi in Alupka is the stamp of the Vorontsov museum with the date 17 November 1938.

2. On 20 November of that same year, I was in the district people's court, successfully defeating a civil action brought against our family by the All-Union Institute for Experimental Medicine.[67] The institute wanted to take away two of our rooms, but at the hearing it was made clear that we did not constitute a single household: each of us was independent, and we all held our own individual entitlement to our rooms. The court rejected the institute's plea.

---

[67] "There was something of the later charlatan Lysenko about the institute and its founders," remembers Lev Razgon ("Ivan Moskvin", *True Stories* [London, 1998]). While those who had organised it "were not frauds ... their scientific ideas were so in tune with those of the bosses that they were swept impetuously upward by a powerful force. Their theories enraptured first Gorky and then Stalin."

3. However, the institute appealed and on 30 December 1938 I answered a summons to appear before the Moskvoreche district prosecutor. This turned out to be a bad-tempered, rude and vicious female. She declared that I should be evicted from the apartment, without bothering the courts, since I had nothing to do with the institute.

4. We all began copying out a declaration that my father had transferred a five-roomed apartment on Malaya Dmitrovka (today, Chekhov) Street to the building's self-administration committee in 1920. Father then went round the present inhabitants of the building, who agreed to witness and confirm such a statement.

5. At that very moment I received notification of a meeting at Pushkin House[68] on 20 January 1939. There, for the first time, I was to deliver a substantial report about Lermontov's "Circle of Sixteen". Consequently, I would go to Leningrad and, naturally, visit Akhmatova. I went there again in November that year. But before then, I had seen Akhmatova many times in Moscow: she made regular trips to appeal on Lyova's behalf. Meanwhile, the attempt to confiscate our rooms would continue for another two years, ending in 1940, when we surrendered one of them.

Father and I suffered most. In his case, the reasons were psychological. I was kept in a state of tension by the constant harassment and the prospect of moving into the same room as my mother. Although my sister was also dragged into court and to the prosecutor's office, she was, for all intents and purposes, invulnerable and went on living in a single room with her husband and little son. My younger brother was no longer with us since he had moved with our older brother into the latter's new two-room accommodation. He had become very attached to that family, and the room at Shchipok Street remained his only in a formal sense.

They all had regular jobs and possessed the relevant documents. I was quite unprotected, not possessing any union membership cards or the like that would have given me at least some rights. I was considered not to be employed. On 10 December 1938, the head of the manuscript section at the Lenin Library handed me a document "for presentation to the Moskvoreche district prosecutor" stating that I was employed at the library "on contract", processing manuscripts and performing independent

---

[68] Pushkin House (founded 1905) was merged with the Academy of Sciences' Institute of Russian Literature in 1931.

research. This letter had no legal validity. But it was all I had! A whole year later I received a memorandum for submission to the district housing section of the Moskvoreche district, requesting that I be placed on the urgent waiting list and provided with accommodation in 1940. It was written by the Regional Bureau of the Section of Research Staff, to which, evidently, I had been admitted in early 1939. But membership of the section had practical value only for those who were established and permanent employees at some research organisation.

Appreciating my lack of rights, the institute lawyer had stressed my unmarried status in his speech before the court. Emphatic in his respect for my sister, the legal wife of a successful husband and the mother of their child, he considered me a second-class being. He did not restrain his irony and felt sure that the judges would share his views. It was as though he was pretending to know nothing of the women's committees and other evidence of the equality of women in our socialist society. My remarks to the court were based on such facts, and I firmly reminded those present that the days of old maids and girls without dowries had passed: I was an independent person who had a profession to follow and was therefore entitled to a separate room. A female lay assessor on the panel of judges threw me a glance filled with respect and even gratitude; I have never forgotten it.

The professional standards of the lawyers were very low. At one moment during this two-year odyssey, we addressed a petition to the Central Committee of the Party. I was the author. Before submitting it, we decided to consult a lawyer who specialised in housing matters. As he read our declaration he expressed amazement: "Who wrote this? How correct and logical it all is." In fact, it was simply a clear and coherent presentation of our case.

I remember going to see some important official in the prosecutor's office; it was by then 1940. The atmosphere there was quite lax and already carried a hint of anti-Semitism. Mocking my father for his parental fondness in settling all of his children in the hospital apartment (where else was he supposed to house them?), the prosecutor made irritable reference to the patriarchs of the Bible.

Father remained a leading consultant at the Kremlin hospital. He was not removed following Alexandra Kanel's dismissal in 1935 nor after her death. They invited him less and less frequently, however, to participate in consultations. Now Papa often did not use an official car but travelled by metro or trolley-bus, taking his oldest grandson Seryozha to the Novodevichy Cemetery or going by himself to see the Kanels at Mamonovsky Street. He remained very attached to Alexandra's daughters Dina and Lyalya and even to her grandson Yura (Lyalya's eldest boy). Everything in that household, of course, was steadily falling apart; it ended with the catastrophic arrest of the two daughters in the summer of 1939.[69] Another incident in our own family had already showed Father the way things were going.

My brother's Stalinist wife Nadya was an incorrigible democrat. She treated their nanny, the stupid and hideously ugly Arisha, as if she was a close relative. You would not believe how Nadya cosseted the nanny. Arisha began an affair with the caretaker's young son. Nadya would leave the apartment so that they could be alone together. Retribution was not long in coming. One day, Arisha came to her mistress in tears and told her she was pregnant. However, the boy had been conscripted into the army. Full of compassion for this lonely woman, Nadya gave her money for an abortion.[70] Arisha took some holiday leave and went away.

Unexpectedly, the phone rang: a trunk call from another town.

Someone wanted to speak to my brother. I watched him talking, an expression of total incomprehension on his face. It was Arisha. She shouted at him and used the familiar "thou". Soon there followed a stream of semi-literate letters, written for her according to the well-established model of experienced blackmailers. To add conviction, the precise date was indicated on which the imaginary event had occurred. My brother treated the whole business very calmly. Receiving a summons to appear at the people's court, he went to see the judge before the hearing and established his alibi, as I remember, by showing him a certified statement that he had been absent from Moscow on the day in question. But the woman defending Arisha was not dismayed: "This poor illiterate woman – can she be expected to remember the exact day and date after what she's been through?" and she deleted the date from Citizen Grachova's plea. The court, of course, decreed that my brother should pay maintenance until the newborn child was 18 years old. A lengthy and wearing case ensued. Arisha found a new, educated lawyer. He even read Dostoyevsky and brushed aside Citizen Grachova's unattractive appearance with a reference to Fyodor Karamazov, who made advances to Yelisaveta Smerdyashchaya. Thus a matter that we had at first regarded as a joke ended with the deduction, for years afterwards, of a third or a quarter of my brother's salary in order to support Arisha's little girl – whom the mother, in honour of her former mistress, named Nadya.

---

[69] See *Till My Tale Is Told* (note 30), chap. 15, "A Meeting at the Lubyanka".
[70] Legally prohibited in 1936, abortion was a criminal offence for all involved.

This story had the most disheartening effect on my parents. Willingly or not, they had to abandon their last illusions about our radiant new existence.

In these changed circumstances, Papa began to commit one mistake after another. He remained on good terms with Yekaterina Kalinina until she herself was arrested.[71] Following the death of Alexandra Kanel, Papa was again admitted to the Kremlin hospital with double pneumonia. I visited him and once, when I was there, so did Kalinin's wife. I could see how highly she regarded him, and as she left she kissed him. When she had gone, however, Papa told me that he had been tactless and asked where her husband was at that moment. It was not done to enquire about the movements of such an important figure of State as Mikhail Kalinin.

Several years in a row Papa spent his summer vacation at Kalinin's dacha (or estate?) in Meshcherinovo. As a doctor, he was there to keep an eye on the health of Kalinin's elderly mother. Once Papa told me of his unfortunate speech on Kalinin's birthday or some other anniversary. Probably this was not an official occasion but a domestic celebration. He made a toast that those present could not understand and found rather convoluted.

On another occasion, wanting to allude to his now advancing years, Papa began his speech with the words: "As the most senior among those gathered here . . ." Poskryobyshev did not like that.[72] Which was rather alarming, for who did not know that Poskryobyshev was close to Stalin and carried out his secret instructions? But nothing came of it.

Another unfortunate public pronouncement, and this time Father was made a pensioner before he was 70. A man of energetic temperament and, moreover, still oppressed by grief, he found it impossible to do nothing. It was my faithful friend Lena Osmyorkina who proposed a solution.

I should add that she was unusually vociferous in private. She could deliver a tirade about the insecurity of the elderly in the Soviet Union. She noted that there was "not one achievement that could not be reversed" in our society. Scornfully she would deride the food on offer in the shops and was especially incensed by the bulls' testicles now being sold at meat counters.

Her maid often intruded into our conversations: "Yelena Konstantinovna, who among us isn't dissatisfied? You're dissatisfied" (meaning

---

[71] An Estonian revolutionary, her arrest in late 1937 and imprisonment in the Gulag until 1945 were used to put pressure on the nominal head of state Mikhail Kalinin.

[72] The feared and detested A.N. Poskryobyshev was Stalin's private secretary.

the intelligentsia), "the peasants are dissatisfied, factory workers are dissatisfied, office workers are dissatisfied . . . So who's satisfied? Party members?" She was a simple-hearted woman who had come into the city from the surrounding Moscow Region. Lena's mother, Nadezhda Isaakovna, was, to be frank, no less simple-hearted, but in her case it took the opposite form. Like many Soviet people she tried not to believe the horrors taking place all around her . . . This became clear when Lena was telling us about a letter she had received from one of her friends in the camps. The unfortunate actress wrote that a smile would never again cross her face. Nadezhda Isaakovna exploded: "That's just a pretty phrase!" A noisy argument developed between mother and daughter, and, as always, it was loud but not hostile. They shouted at one another, and Lena made use of her wonderful trained voice.

My father tried not to grasp what lay behind these events – the complete degeneration of the system he had knowingly and idealistically served since 1918 though not himself a member of the Party. I remember his shock at my comment on the speech Stalin made to the Eighteenth Party Congress [in March 1939]. Detecting a new intonation in the secretary-general's reference to the Germans, I said: "You see, we're going to form an alliance with Germany." Papa was amazed. Worse still, he felt insulted. Still, his reaction was not as sharp as five years earlier when I had said that Kirov had been killed by his own people. Now Papa no longer had the strength to resist my heresies. Until Dina and Lyalya Kanel were arrested, however, he considered that the accusations against "Enemies of the People" might be true.

All this was at a time when, in Khardjiev's words, "the crack of skulls being crushed could be felt in the air" and "people began resembling maggots in a glass jar". Punin then urged his friends not to become apathetic: "Do not lose despair!"

Lena saw a newsreel film taken during one of the famous and bloodthirsty trials of Trotskyists at the House of Unions. Among those shown was Krestinsky, who retracted his testimony in court. At the next hearing, for some reason, he had become rather deaf. Clearly, they had subjected him to vigorous physical persuasion in the meantime. Lena was particularly astounded by the guards who surrounded the condemned men. There was nothing human about them, she said. Irina Shchegoleva, who was appealing for less harsh measures against her sister Musya Malakhovskaya, banished from Leningrad as the wife of "an Enemy of the People", said exactly the same to Lena. "Nothing has any effect on these people," she commented, meaning those who sentenced her brother-in-law to "ten years' imprisonment without the right to correspondence" – i.e. to execution – "not youth, beauty or intelligence, neither human feeling nor talent". A highly gifted cartoonist, Boris Malakhovsky was charming, artistic and extremely witty, and Osmyorkin had doted on him.

Lena and I privately called Stalin the Antichrist. She thought his blood-thirsty nature and cruelty were most important, but for me his defining trait was his corrupting influence. Of course, his bloodlust was no less than the Führer's, but if the ideal for Hitler was a blond sadist, Stalin strove to make scoundrels of us all. History has seen many tyrants and wicked men, but not all of them wanted to corrupt and degrade. Stalin ensured the moral destruction not only of those innocent people whom he allowed to survive but also of those serving in the secret police. Of course, people with sadistic tendencies were attracted to the work, but others had been driven to bestial cruelty by the entire system and the complicity of all their associates. In my view, they were also victims of Stalin.

That was how we talked at home. There were many such homes. People restricted their circle of acquaintances and did not admit outsiders. "*Sans secsautes,*" the late Malakhovsky liked to pun *à la française.*[73]

The post of director fell vacant at the Commissariat of Education's polyclinic where Lena's father worked: he was a general practitioner, a wonderful diagnostician and, incidentally, much loved by his patients. Lena's mother also worked for the dentist at the polyclinic. It was on their initiative that Father was offered the job, and he kept it until his death in 1943.

The work, however, had no links with the Institute for Experimental Medicine, where he had formerly been employed, and this laid him open to a new danger. They began threatening to evict him from our apart-ment. A new neuropathologist appeared at the institute who had, it seemed, come from Kharkov and was desperately in need of lodgings in Moscow. They dug up an edict or decree from the 1920s that had hardly ever been invoked. Medical institutions then were given the right to evict persons who had nothing to do with their organisation, without provid-ing alternative accommodation. Naturally, it had been impossible to implement such an edict in the 1930s when every nook and cranny was filled to overflowing by those fleeing the new collective farms.

But the newly appointed head of the neuropathology department had brought in a new hospital manager, and they decided to defeat Father by wearing him down. The neuropathologist spread slanderous rumours about my father's past while his assistant negotiated with Papa,

---

[73] "Without informers": *seksot* is a Soviet abbreviation for "undercover employee" or "associate".

hinting that one had to forgive the man considerably: if Papa only knew what nerve-wracking work he had formerly performed! We had already realised, some time before, that the neuropathologist had served in the secret police. When he finally settled in our apartment, he not only failed to conceal the fact but, on the contrary, made it public knowledge.

For the time being, however, the new manager was urging Papa in a sympathetic voice to give up his study: "You should not work any more." When Papa returned home, tired after a full working day and his travels on the tram, the hospital manager would meet him at the gates and accompany him as far as our veranda. As they walked, he would mutter all kinds of things, trying out still other arguments.

Papa did not give in. So then they dreamed up the following trick. Father received an official paper demanding that he pay off the debts accumulated on the flat, which he had used free of charge for 15 years. The total arrears proved an astronomical sum. They knew perfectly well that the apartment had been legally occupied as rent-free accommodation but realised that such a demand would greatly upset Papa. It was summer, and the days were very hot. Father with his weak heart dragged himself from one office or archive to another in order to document the former arrangements. They had calculated correctly. Papa told us: "I can't face any more of this" and gave in. His study was handed over to the institute and they erected partitions there, thus creating an apartment for the neuropathologist, his wife and their little daughter. They proved to have a great many relations in Moscow, and all of them, apparently, worked for the NKVD. Even the neuropathologist's father-in-law worked in the book-binding department of that organisation. He moved in with his daughter while other relatives would ring them up during the night, and, when I commented that it was rather late, they insolently replied: "We're ringing from the NKVD."

Somehow we all squeezed in together. I remained in my room, but they did not leave me in peace. They wanted that as well. My one hope lay with the coming Lermontov celebrations in October 1939 to mark 125 years since his birth. The special jubilee collection would be published by then, I supposed, containing my major contribution, which was (as Professor Nikolai Brodsky liked to say) "crammed with new ideas". They would then make me a member of the Writers' Union, I naively imagined, and I would no longer be as defenceless and lacking in almost all rights. But it was decided to postpone publication until 1941, the centenary of Lermontov's death. I would have to wait another two years . . .

Chapter 14

The threat of Lyova's execution receded. Obviously, the prosecutor had to withdraw his harsh demands. All that year there was talk of bringing the "students' case" to court. Lyova was among the accused. Akhmatova therefore met several times with the parents and relatives of those charged with him – the celebrated neuropathologist and Academician S.N. Davidenkov and his wife, and other unfortunate, less famous individuals.

If I remember rightly, Lyova's stepbrother Orest Vysotsky, then a student at the Forestry Institute, was also one of them. Incidentally, on 10 March 1938, when Lyova was arrested, Vysotsky was staying the night with him at Sadovaya Street. The next morning, it was he who came to Akhmatova and told her what had happened. I think he was also charged with involvement in these student cases, but he was either acquitted or released and not brought to trial. I have little information on the subject.

Apart from the gifted Kolya Davidenkov, among the accused there was also a graduate student of Academician I. Yu. Krachkovsky, the country's leading Arabic scholar. His surname was Shumovsky (or Shamovsky). Frequently and sorrowfully, Akhmatova commented that they had taken away the brightest of the younger generation, the future stars of Russian scholarship.

I remember how we searched Moscow for Shumovsky's cousin, who was working at the maternity home on Molchanovka Street (it was destroyed by bombing during the war). Through the Moscow City information service I tracked down her home address, and Akhmatova and I went to see her in Dorogomilovo. We didn't find her at home, but for a long while I kept this note of her address as a reminder of those insane years. When Lyova finally returned, he listened to my tale of our quest with such a warped and scornful smile that I ceased to preserve that pitiful relic.

I took no part in Akhmatova's energetic petitioning at that time. She appealed instead to influential acquaintances and was frequently aided by Victor Ardov. Someone introduced her to the noted lawyer Kommodov, evidently a specialist in political cases, but he refused to take up Lyova's defence. This was a blow for Akhmatova. On her next visit to Moscow, she told me that Kommodov wanted a large fee for taking the case. Yet what fees could one expect from the impoverished Akhmatova?

Sometimes it struck me that her activities on Lyova's behalf were insufficiently energetic. I suggested that she pluck up the courage to take some extreme measure, such as a bold and forthright appeal to the authorities. "But then they'll arrest me immediately," Akhmatova objected. "So they'll arrest you," I bravely proclaimed. "But even Christ in Gethsemane prayed, 'Let this cup pass from me,'" Akhmatova replied severely. I felt ashamed.

That January (1939) in Leningrad I was busy with my Lermontov activities and achievements. Anything that concerned my visits to Akhmatova seemed to me an entirely separate matter. It was strange to call her on Fontanka from the public telephone . . . in the district's Party committee building. A musical and literary evening devoted to the *Lay of Igor's Host*[74] had been held there in the conference hall. The introductory lecture was an enraptured performance by Sergei Rudakov. Then the professional reader Grigory Artobolevsky gave a grave and inspired recital of the great work itself. His wife, Anna Artobolevskaya, a close friend of Lina Rudakova, played the piano. Both their husbands had only a short while to live. Artobolevsky died at the Battle of Kursk in 1943 after going there to perform for the frontline soldiers; Rudakov was killed in a battle near Mogilyov in January 1944.

Ten to fifteen minutes after my call, I was already in Akhmatova's room, since the district Party committee was located on the opposite corner of Fontanka and Nevsky Avenue.

I entered a different world.

Akhmatova's new accommodation[75] was kept on a "wartime" or, to be more exact, "prison" footing. The bottom drawer of one cupboard was crammed with rusks and could never be closed, while Akhmatova was a lonely figure, looked after by Tanya, the caretaker.[76] Tanya would take her to the public baths, pulling her by the hand as they crossed to the other side of the road and urging her: "Come on, walk! Oh, do walk!" Akhmatova was about to deliver a food parcel to the prison. I went to buy tins of condensed milk and other items and also gave her 200 roubles to hand on to Lyova. But he was not there; for some reason they had sent him to the White Sea Canal before passing sentence. We could not understand it at all. You could request them to return the money, I told her, since Lyova had not received it. "What kind of *requests* can you make there?!" a horrified Akhmatova replied. I regretted the money, which I had saved with such difficulty. But I felt ashamed and instantly fell silent.

---

[74] The most famous work of medieval Russian literature, the twelfth-century *Lay* tells of Prince Igor's ill-fated attack on the Polovetsians.
[75] When she separated from Punin, Akhmatova moved into a different room in the same apartment.
[76] The mother of Valentin (Valya) Smirnov, see note 50, p. 219.

Akhmatova lay down almost all the time, and, without even raising her head from the pillow, barely mumbling, she recited her new poem to me:

> Quietly flows the quiet Don
> Yellow moon slips into the house.
> He slips in with fur hat askew,
> He sees a shadow, the yellow moon.
> This woman is ill,
> This woman is alone,
> Husband in the grave, son in prison,
> Say a prayer for me.

It did not occur to me that this was the future *Requiem*. And she herself was not yet contemplating such a work. I did not then wonder why the River Don should find an echo in a Leningrad poem. Only much later in Moscow did I ask Akhmatova about this. Her answer was evasive: "I don't know, perhaps because Lyova went on an expedition to the Don?" She also said that Sholokhov's *Quiet Flows the Don* was Lyova's favourite work. "You didn't know that?" she asked with surprise. Indeed I did not.

Again I stayed at Osmyorkin's studio; he had given me the key. How mournful to be there this time, however! It felt as if I was in a burned-out ruin. One of Osmyorkin's students looked in and for some reason told me how they enjoyed themselves there when the master was away.

The Rudakovs visited me. Sergei enviously went into raptures over Akhmatova's line, "He enters, his fur hat askew". He had heard "Quietly flows the quiet Don . . ." from Akhmatova herself even before I arrived. But he did not know Mandelstam's poem about Stalin by heart. He learned it now from me. I did not say the words twice, fearing the neighbours, but gesticulated to indicate "fat fingers oily as maggots, / Words sure as forty-pound weights", and we slapped our calves with especial pleasure so that Rudakov would not forget "his leather-clad gleaming calves".

Then I fell ill, and Osmyorkin's neighbour, a woman I did not know at all, brought me hot tea or soup. Still sick, I returned to Moscow by train. There, as I have already recounted, I was met by the shattering news of Mandelstam's death. In a letter sent through the post to Akhmatova, I wrote that my friend Nadya was now a widow.

Chapter 15

When I next arrived in Leningrad in November 1939, I was well received at Pushkin House, and the famous Lermontov scholar V.A. Manuilov

came to see me at the Scholars' Club on Khalturin Street, where I was
staying. We discussed our work, and again I went to Fontanka as if entering a different country.

By now Lyova had been sent to the camps. His five-year sentence
was considered very mild and, so people said, was due to the dismissal
of Police Chief Yezhov and his replacement by the "kindly, just" Beria.

Still lying down, Akhmatova read me poems that would become part
of the *Requiem*.[77] Thereafter I always remembered the "blind red wall",
"the house manager pale with fear" and "Crucifixion", a poem that,
after Lyova returned, Akhmatova said I should not have read to him.

In 1939, I saw Vladimir Garshin for the first time, visiting Akhmatova.
He called in the evening, at 7, bringing a packet of tea and some food.
Akhmatova sat with her feet up in a deep armchair, rather huddled, while
Garshin enquired with concern about her health. There was a comfort-
able atmosphere of the kind you meet in adversity when human warmth
and kindness somewhat ease another's profound dejection.

When he had left, Akhmatova said his visits were always like that. He
called on his way home from work and was living on Rubinstein Street.
Recently, I checked this. Garshin indeed lived on Rubinstein (formerly
Troitskaya) Street, in an apartment building that stands on the corner
of Fontanka, while the hospital where he worked was across the river,
on the Petrograd side. Probably he got off the tram on Nevsky Avenue
and after crossing the Anichkov Bridge he had only to turn right in order
to reach his apartment. But he would turn to the left, cross the road
and walk on to the Sheremetyev Palace where Akhmatova lived in the
courtyard, at the rear of the building.

This route became a ritual and is reflected in Akhmatova's *Poem without a Hero*:

> Guest from the future!
> Will he really come to me
> Turning left off the bridge?

A quite different person is meant, people will say, by the image of the
"guest from the future". His name is well known and is mentioned in
commentaries, memoirs and scholarly studies. But the one does not
exclude the other. The *Poem* is neither a documentary record nor the

---

[77] A sequence of poems composed between 1935 and 1940, the *Requiem* was
memorised by Akhmatova and selected friends and not entrusted to a permanent typed version. First published in the USSR in 1987. See "Eight Poems
by Anna Akhmatova", pp. 320–22.

report of some flat-footed agent, observing all those who visited Akhmatova.[78] In works of imagination, we are accustomed to the synthesis of images, using features drawn from a variety of prototypes. Akhmatova herself pointed to one such "borrowing" from her own childhood memories when we talked about the *Poem* in the 1940s. She was referring to the suicide of the infatuated cornet Vsevolod Knyazev and the line, "Now perfume lingers on the staircase". At Shukhardina's apartment building in Tsarskoye Selo, a certain fashionable and modish lady lived on the same staircase as the Gorenko family. Whenever she went out, the scent of her perfume would long remain on the stairs. Akhmatova also mentioned such a scent in a polemical comment written in the 1960s: "In not one residential building in Petersburg could you then smell anything on the staircase other than the scent of the passing ladies and the cigars of the passing gentlemen." These tokens became rooted in the teenage girl's imagination as a symbol of the enticing adult world with its shifting tides of joy and sorrow and, therefore, of her own future life. The second of these tokens also appears in the verse of which I have just quoted the three concluding lines. They are preceded by:

> The sound of steps that are not there
> Crossing the shining parquet,
> The blue haze of a cigar
> And in all the mirrors was reflected
> The man who had not come
> And never could come here.

The "blue haze of a cigar", I suspect, is linked to the image of Boris Anrep,[79] the hero of Akhmatova's lyric verse in 1916. In reality he came to Petersburg only at the end of 1914 and for "The Year 1913" (as the first part of the *Poem without a Hero* is called); he also is "a guest from the future" in that "Petersburg Tale".

The second prototype of the "guest" I consider to be Vladimir Garshin.[80] The lines just quoted did not appear, I should add, until the 1945–6 variant of the typescript copies of the *Poem* with which we are

---

[78] Akhmatova completed a first version of the *Poem without a Hero* in the early 1940s. In its final form it is dated 1940–62 and carries three successive dedicatory prefaces. First published as a whole in New York in 1960, Soviet publication did not follow until the mid-1970s.

[79] Anrep emigrated to England in 1916. For his 1952 mosaic portrait of Compassion in the entrance to the National Gallery in London, he chose to depict Anna Akhmatova.

[80] Vladimir Garshin (1887–1956) remained in Leningrad throughout the blockade, carrying on his work as a doctor.

familiar. After she broke off relations with Garshin in the summer of
1944, Akhmatova systematically expelled all direct dedications to him
from the *Poem*, even where he was not mentioned by name. I have in
mind the "Epilogue", the third part of the triptych. In the 1942 Tashkent
recension, the section was dedicated "To City and Friend" but in the
later versions only "To the City". Garshin did not disappear from this
section, however, but remains in a different capacity. A passage that originally began:

> You are my terrible, my final
> Radiant listener to dark ravings . . .

and continued:

> reliance, forgiveness, honour,
> you burn before me like a flame
> you stand above me, as a banner
> and you kiss me, like flattery.
> Place your hand on my head
> Let time now stop
> On the watch you gave me

became:

> You are not the first or the last
> Dark listener to luminous ravings

and continues:

> What revenge are you planning for me?
> You are not drinking, only sipping
> This grief from the very depths –
> The news of our parting.
> Don't place your hand on my head –
> Let time stop for ever
> On the watch you gave me

The latter version remained unaltered when Akhmatova finally
completed work on the *Poem*, and it depicts the essence of her relations with Garshin.

The third prototype for the image of the "guest" is Sir Isaiah Berlin.
The story of his acquaintance with Akhmatova is well known from

memoirs by contemporaries and the hero's own reminiscences. The circumstances of their first meeting, I may say, were best described in Akhmatova's own poetry. Not in the *Poem without a Hero*, however, but in verse from the "Sweetbrier" cycle: "You invented me. There is no such woman on earth . . ." This was dedicated directly to Berlin though, naturally, did not mention him by name (bearing the date and place, 18 August 1956, Starki). There we read:

> We met in an extraordinary year
> When the powers of the earth were already exhausted
> Everything was in mourning, everything bowed down
>   by misfortunes
> And only the graves were fresh.
> Without lamps the Neva's waves were black as tar
> Dark night stood like a wall
> And that was when my voice called to you!
> What I was doing I did not yet know.
> You came to me, as though star-led
> Walking through the tragic autumn
> To that ever-empty house
> From which a flock of burnt verse fled.

Berlin's memoirs tell us exactly when this was, late November 1945. Immediately after the end of the war, in other words. Long settled in England, the author now saw the city from which his parents had taken him as a teenager. When he arrived in the morning he still did not know whether the author of *Rosary*, the *White Flock*, *Plantain* and *Anno Domini* was alive. At 3 that afternoon he had already been brought to see her on Fontanka. What possible significance could there be, for this tense encounter, whether he turned left or right off the Anichkov Bridge? None whatsoever. If in his essay Berlin gives a very precise description of his route, this was probably under the influence of Akhmatova's lines. When she substantially revised the *Poem* in 1954 she made him hero of the verse, "The sound of steps that are not there", and added a number of verses that identified him.

As concerns Garshin, the emotional impression I received when we met in 1939 of the dramatic path his footsteps repeatedly traced, "turning left off the bridge", to Akhmatova's house remains undimmed.

But let us return to the events of that year as they influenced my life. Nineteen thirty-nine was not yet over.

Chapter 16

The day of my departure from Leningrad I lunched at the Scholars' Club. As agitated as his colleague in Sebastopol the year before, the waiter kept approaching his customers and they would exchange nervous comments . . . I sat at a table by myself and could not understand what was going on. Only when I left the building and saw pale stern people, standing in groups and listening in silence to the voices from the radio loudspeakers, did I find out: the war against Finland had begun.

That evening I walked to the Moskovsky Station with the Rudakovs from Kolokolnaya Street where they lived. We kept to the middle of the road. It was pitch black and even the windows of shops and apartments shed not a glimmer of light. The first night of the blackout.

Then in January and February 1940, as we know, there were exceptionally severe frosts, 40 degrees below zero. Our Red Army soldiers, lacking the right uniforms and equipment, froze to death on the frontline and bore the full force of the hatred with which the Finnish snipers regarded us.

Sergei Rudakov wrote one of his best poems about this campaign. I heard it only later when, seriously wounded near Leningrad, Rudakov was transferred to work in Moscow in 1942. I think the poem is not recorded anywhere. This is how I remember it:

> January in the year 1940
> Whom shall we greet with hospitality?
> A heretical winter holds sway
> And lips are sealed with wax.
> God-brother to the Finnish winter,
> Named gossip of Onega snowdrifts,
> Whom will you now thrice denounce
> With your unprintable words, Avvakum?
> The moon ignores the penalty
> And chills the city with an Arctic silver
> And a young tank-driver lies,
> With a knife in his ribs
> But he died from the cold.

After Finland had been defeated, I happened to call on Lena's mother, Nadezhda Isaakovna. A plumber from the housing association was doing some work for her. He was very upset: "Of course, when such a monster pounced on a little country, of course we crushed it," he said indignantly, "– and how many of our own people we slaughtered." We knew, moreover, that Vyborg was taken on the very day (12 March 1940) that an armistice had already been concluded with the Finns. That assault also cost us many lives.

One of our neuropathologist's relatives returned from the fighting. When he appeared at the apartment, all the neighbours crowded round, expecting stories about the war. He was absolutely furious and suddenly fell to to his knees, roaring: "Stalin's no leader! Mannerheim,[81] now that's a leader!" Before I knew what was happening, the corridor was quite empty and ominously silent. How had they got back to their rooms and hidden away so quickly? This daring outburst was not just a consequence of the Finnish war but also prompted by Beria's replacement of Yezhov, which was a risky operation for the NKVD. The few prisoners who were then released told their families and friends tales of torture and forced labour. Patching things up with our maid Polya after some squabble I remember telling her of Lyova's imprisonment. "Oh, you'll never see him again!" she exclaimed. A man she knew had returned from the camps and said to her: "There's more corpses there than you've hairs on your head." Polya had a full head of curls.

Among those who came back was a friend of my sister and her artist-husband. His story is not only another testimony to the brutalities of the jailers; it also provides a glimpse of the psychological depths plumbed by victim and tormentor.

A Cynic's Tale

We shall call him Georgy. When they were both young, he was friendly with my elder sister. He married her girlfriend, and they both studied at the Conservatory in Professor Goldenweiser's piano class. After graduation he taught in music schools. As I remember, he held two diplomas, one technical and the other in the arts, from different institutions. But he could not settle on any one profession, though he had the most varied interests. Indeed, he was a man of exceptional talents. For his own amusement, he learned to read Sanskrit and after the war worked at the Academy of Sciences' Institute of Oriental Studies. Not yet knowing English, he agreed to give a schoolboy private lessons. Preparing from a teach-your-self textbook, he gradually mastered the language and after a while could read a great deal in English. For a time, he worked as the night editor for *Krestyanskaya gazeta*, a major newspaper (and publishing house of

---

[81] Trained in the Imperial Russian army, the elderly General Mannerheim organised and led the Finnish resistance to the invading Soviet forces.

the same name) where sloppy work would not be tolerated. He coped well with the job. He was friendly with the artists at the publisher and introduced one of them to my sister. They married, and my sister's one-time friend would call to see them. We were not friendly, or, to be more accurate, I took no great interest in the man. But once in a while he would come to my room for a chat.

He lived with his wife and son in her parents' apartment; formerly, they had owned a famous ready-made clothes shop on Kuznetsky Most. The flat was also in the very centre of Moscow, in a brick-built apartment building with high ceilings and solid walls. In the 1920s and 1930s, however, it was already a communal flat, and they were left with one big room not far from the kitchen. As they cooked on their paraffin stoves, the other women would yell and shout, making it hard for him to concentrate. He went off to the Lenin Library. He had no access to the special reading-rooms and had to sit with everyone else in the hall. At the time, no more than a Moscow domicile registration and passport were needed in order to make use of that famous public library. Georgy was quite content with this situation. He had long lost interest in his wife, did not love his son and was an egotist as a matter of principle.

In 1935 or 1936, he left for Kolyma,[82] where salaries were much higher. In 1937, he was arrested there. The charge was the intention to betray the USSR to Japan for money. When Yezhov was shot in 1938 and replaced by Beria,[83] Georgy found himself among those released, apparently because he had signed nothing. He returned to Moscow. My sister and her husband said Georgy's experiences had changed him greatly. I did not see him. But once, quite by chance, I overheard him in conversation with my brother-in-law. They were drinking and speaking quite frankly. The artist showed Georgy his work. I heard his friend's voice: "You're drawing Stalin?!" The composition, produced to order, was very effective: "Stalin Leads the Workers in Their Study Group". My brother-in-law confessed in impossibly sincere tones: "You know, I must go on believing. If I didn't believe, I couldn't get up in the morning." "Don't believe, you son of a bitch, just get yourself out of bed," the experienced *zek* responded.

Once Georgy tapped at my door. The first thing I noticed was that he had no front teeth. "Did they knock out your teeth there?" I asked. His whole body seemed to slacken before me. At first he parried uncer-

---

[82] The most remote, inhospitable part of the Soviet Union, by the late 1930s deportation to this north-eastern tip of Eurasia had killed thousands of prisoners. See Appendix 1.5, "The Soviet Ordeal", p. 428.
[83] Though demoted, Nikolai Yezhov remained at liberty, in fact, until April 1939. He was shot in February 1940.

tainly, "Cracked pots last the longest." But then he began to talk. As a rule, he preferred not to describe what had happened to him, but on this occasion he said a great deal. They kept him standing until the lymph trickled from his legs, and they starved him. He was a large, tall man. Yet still he would not sign a thing. Once the interrogator mocked his ferocious hunger by placing a bowl of *shchi* on the floor in front of him. But that was not enough, it seemed; the interrogator loudly cleared his throat and spat a large glob of phlegm into the soup. "And what do you think?" continued Georgy. "Dignity? Pride? I cautiously pushed the phlegm to one side with the spoon and began to eat." (On all fours, evidently? Mandelstam had foreseen it: "If they dared keep me like a beast / they'd toss my food on the floor". When I talked with Georgy I did not know this poem.[84])

He was lowered into a cellar – in a region of permafrost! – and there stood a safe for storing gold. They made him strip to his underwear, shut him in the safe and kept him there for 36 hours. When they took him out, he was almost unconscious and remembered only that he cried: "Golgotha! Golgotha!" He was taken to the interrogators with their white collars and dazzling uniforms, and they covered their noses: he was smeared with his own faeces.

Another time, he was called out for interrogation and already so weak that he could not walk. He crawled along the mucus- and blood-stained floor of the corridor. A woman who had collapsed there with a uterine haemorrhage after being forced to remain standing upright threw him a glance full of compassion. "Do you know, she was like a sister to me!" cried Georgy. "And the sentry, seeing me crawl, could not stand it and muttered through his teeth: 'Those bastards, those animals.' I burst into tears."

Now he was back in Moscow. Again he started going to the Lenin Library. In 1940 he once burst in on me – "I can't stand it. I must tell someone." This was his tale:

> I'm walking along Gorky Street when I hear someone urgently calling me by my name and patronymic. He's chasing behind me and begging me to stop.
>
> I look, it's my interrogator from Kolyma. If you can believe this, we go into Filippov's café and sit down at a table together. I don't know what to think, is this going to be a conversation with Dostoyevsky's Porfiry Petrovich? He says he could not forget me. There's this man, he says, swaying on his swollen feet with the fluid trickling out of them, and all he can say is:

---

[84] "If Our Enemies Were to Capture Me . . .", written in Voronezh in early 1937.

"I'm just a statistic." We sat there for a long while, and he kept blaming all their evil deeds on orders from above. So I ask him: "And the phlegm in the soup, was that also an order from above?" "Well, you know, you get worked up . . ."

During the war, Georgy came to see us in Moscow. He was on his way to the front. "I'm transporting meat," he said. Several times he repeated the phrase, and I couldn't understand what kind of meat he meant. It turned out he meant cannon fodder. He was escorting reinforcements to various regiments or units.

For a long while we had no news of him. There was a war on; perhaps he'd been killed. Then we found out. At some railway station, his pistol was stolen, he was tried and convicted, and sent to a punitive battalion. But he survived even that. He didn't want to spend a single day in Moscow: "I can't wait, I must go and tell Sonya everything that's happened to me." Sonya, the wife he supposedly did not love, had been evacuated somewhere far away. Now he couldn't wait to see her, as though she were his dearest friend.

After the war, as I already said, he had connections with the Institute of Oriental Studies and either worked on Indian themes or translated from Sanskrit, I don't remember exactly. When the struggle against cosmopolitanism began, or, to put it more simply, there was a virulent outbreak of anti-Semitism, he could no longer work for the Academy of Sciences, being a Jew, and instead went to build the hydroelectric station at Kuybyshev on the Volga. There he worked as an engineer. He would come up to Moscow and calmly describe all kinds of horrors – no, his description was not calm, it had the chilling tone of someone who regards life with pitiless eyes. There were *zeks* working on the project. Once they played football or something of the kind. "I took a look," he said. "They had a funny kind of ball. When they tossed it nearer to me, I saw it was a human head. They were kicking it about with their feet." He claimed that many human bodies had been cemented into the building blocks of the new bridge across the Volga. Horror exuded from his dispassionate words. I love the Volga, but ever after I could never contemplate taking another cruise down that great river.

In the 1950s and '60s, Georgy separated from his wife, who had once more become an unloved stranger. They split their room in two. He dined in restaurants, and he ate lavishly and well, having a particular liking for roast goose. In the evenings he listened to the radio in his now reduced room. Perhaps he loved good music? Not at all. He had a passion for the clichéd songs and romances that Vinogradov and Nechayev sang with such feeling.

Once as he was listening yet again to a sentimental romance he abruptly
died. My sister told us how he lay, very red-faced, on the table while
his former wife and son spent the whole night dismantling the partition
with the help of trusted acquaintances. Some outsider might otherwise
have been installed in the newly available room.

The son was most perplexed. His mother sent him to the undertakers'
office and told him to be at the cemetery the next day. But he had to
go to work. What was he to do? It did not enter his head that his employers would give him time off to attend his father's funeral.

During the last years of his life, the deceased gave the impression,
said my sister, of a totally empty man, while his son was the epitome of
a mechanical, repressed individual. Which is worse? I do not know.

After the announcement of the Nazi–Soviet pact, the monolithic ideological unity of Soviet society was slightly shaken. For year after year we
had lived under the threat of attack by the German Fascists. I cannot
forget one open meeting for all the employees of the Lenin Library, held
in the garden opposite the entrance to the old building. It probably took
place shortly after the 1938 Munich agreement. Most of the speakers
were women, and they worked up a tremendous atmosphere, almost
becoming hysterical when they referred to Hitler's *Mein Kampf.* Suddenly
in August 1939 there was a drastic, abrupt change, and Nazi Germany
became our ally. From that day on, incidentally, up until 22 June 1941,
we somehow managed without any slogans. No longer did we hear
appeals or threats, the authorities did not scare or incite us and nothing especially heroic was demanded of us. It was if that had all died
away. The only fanfares were raised to greet the annexation to the USSR
of the Baltic States, Bessarabia and the Western Ukraine.

I was in Vereya on 1 September 1939, the day the Second World War
began. The local inhabitants were extremely alarmed since they believed
that a major war had begun for us as well. "They're requisitioning the
horses," they said. But the only thing that was happening then was the
partition of Poland.

I was so upset that one of the Vereya women asked me: "Who's going
off to fight, your brother or your husband?" A man sat in the corner of
a neighbour's room, pale green with fright. We knew the woman; her
boyfriend was regarded as suspect by the authorities.

Those still capable of thinking for themselves were dismayed.

My father was extremely depressed. If he had not been so tormented
by the fate of his dearest acquaintances, this unbelievable alliance with
Germany would have finished him off completely. When Pletnyov and
Levin were accused a year earlier of "murdering" Gorky, Papa did not

want to admit the monstrosity of the campaign waged against these two well-known doctors. But the appearance of Yagoda at one of the 1938 trials, and his prior admission under interrogation that he had been intimate with Timosha, Gorky's daughter-in-law, astounded my father.

"What a scoundrel!" he could not help exclaiming. After Gorky died in 1936, they began to release details of the role played by his personal secretary and of the writer's dubious entourage. "He began as a nobody and ended as one," Papa remarked. His remaining energies were entirely focused on his grandsons, especially the four-year-old son of my sister, who was his favourite daughter. They all spent that summer in Vereya, and in August I joined them there. An amateur group portrait survives which shows our entire family (apart from my brothers) and my friend Lena Osmyorkina, who for years had passed every summer there. It is clear from the photo how disconsolate and aged my father had become. My sister said that before I arrived, Papa had been summoned for a talk with the investigator in Vereya and had returned home even more depressed.

Some of Lena's acquaintances and fellow-workers were then also staying in Vereya. She often performed with a literary specialist who excelled in the genre of popularisation. Without the slightest hesitation, he

Emma and her family at their dacha, August 1939 (l. to r.): Lena Galperina, Isabella G. (mother), Emma, Vera with her son Alyosha, Grigory G. and Feodosy Bochkov (Vera's husband)

delivered lectures to club audiences on literature from the Marxist point of view and explained socialist realism to his credulous listeners. Now that he was enjoying the freedom of the summer vacation, however, in the company of those he could trust, I was astonished to find that he understood exactly what was going on. With great sarcasm he described meetings at the Writers' Union and confided to us the marvellous discovery he had made, or so he thought: by camouflaging the information with chapter headings from Gogol's *Dead Souls,* he had written to a friend in the provinces about the arrest of their mutual acquaintances. Another friend of the Osmyorkins, a very modest and quiet artist, listened with great sympathy and interest as I recited for him Mandelstam's most seditious composition, "We live, without feeling the country beneath us . . ." Now that the poet was dead and his case familiar within narrow literary circles, and since I had been named by Mandelstam himself during his interrogation, I could calmly introduce a decent person to that phenomenal poem. Nevertheless, we went out into the woods so that I could do so.

In Moscow, where they did not confiscate the horses (at least I heard nothing of the kind), the reaction to the partition of Poland was an explosive urge to go looting. Among those who went was our neighbour, a Communist doctor, who brought many things back for his wife. She showed us some of these gifts in the kitchen. The doctor, however, maintained his ideological consistency and told us how badly the Poles had lived under the bourgeois regime. Apparently, special places were set aside in the university lecture halls for Jewish students, but they on principle would not sit there and stood for the whole of their studies, from the first to the last year. The doctor, who was thoroughly Russian, described this with great admiration for the students – then our Communists resolutely rejected anti-Semitism. I was proud to hear from our neighbour of the restraint and sense of national dignity of my fellow-Jews.

Many offered accounts of the pleasures of visiting Poland, which still retained traces of a bourgeois existence. Alexei Tolstoy supposedly brought himself back a fountain (!) and erected it in his garden; I do not know where, in Moscow perhaps, or in Leningrad, or at his dacha. I have no idea if this was true, but that was the rumour. On the other hand, my girl friend was certainly asked in Poland: "Please explain why there is nothing in the shops since the Russians arrived." I did not hear anything about the Baltic States, no-one was going there yet. But a gifted folklore specialist from the Literary Museum told very interesting stories about the Western Ukraine. She was enchanted by the dignity and politeness of the region's inhabitants, especially in the rural areas. On meeting a visiting stranger, the peasants would all invariably greet the person – including the old women and the especially friendly children. They went to church, observed all the festivals and decorated their homes on these occasions, she said. Everything was respectful and decorous. She was amazed by the difference between them and Soviet peasants. She had been on expeditions to many Soviet republics and autonomous regions and constantly assured me that the local culture was flourishing and that this was thanks to the Soviet regime. I did not argue, since I could judge only by the official weeks of [ethnic] celebration that were lavishly staged in Moscow. Vera Krupyanskaya was very fond of her work. The most kind-hearted woman, she ran and hid herself in the museum cloakroom and wept out loud when she heard that people had begun starving to death during the Leningrad Blockade.

Chapter 17

Nadya could not settle. In Moscow, she avoided staying with her mother at the apartment on Nashchokin Street; she could not stand the neighbours. But I saw her often. As I mentioned, she would stay the night with me. On one occasion, Khardjiev and I sat in Maria's Grove and listened as Nadya told us how she operated a loom at a spinning mill and lived in the little town of Strunino, outside Moscow. A particular episode she described has lodged firmly in my memory. She was using the lift at the factory and there was only one other worker with her. He could not take his eyes off her. "Such a forehead and you're on the factory floor?" he finally said.

I used to visit her mother, of course, after she was left on her own at Nashchokin Street. For some reason, I have no memory of Vera Yakovlevna leaving the apartment and joining Nadya in Kalinin.[85] Yet before that could happen they had officially to exchange the room in Moscow for permanent accommodation in the other town. Following Mandelstam's death, Nadya had obviously decided that Moscow was dangerous for her: she must firmly break her ties with the city and, until her mother died, take her to live in Kalinin. The war upset everybody's plans. Nadya and her mother were evacuated and carried as far away as Kazakhstan. As we know, Akhmatova petitioned successfully for their transfer to Tashkent. It was there that Vera Yakovlevna died in 1943 and Nadya's life began to take a quite new direction.

---

[85] The city of Tver was renamed in honour of Mikhail Kalinin in 1931.

Probably the move from Moscow occurred when I was in Leningrad and that is why I do not remember the details. At the very end of December 1939, Nadya sent me her first letter from Kalinin:

Emmochka!

I'm writing on the off-chance, without precisely remembering your address.

I can't get away [to Moscow] although I'm spending almost all my time at home. Whether I'll go on waiting much longer, I don't know. They might give me a job at any moment.

I know you're incapable of coming here.

That's very hurtful. Take your old buddy and try to come. I would be overjoyed to see you. You're simply not people but pillars of stone, and I hate the lot of you.

Another thing: Zhenya thought it inelegant to take back the paraffin stove from you. Mine has stopped working altogether. As a result we have nothing to make tea on. Please do bring it with you. (There, that's a reason for coming.) Or, join forces with Zhenya and send it to me by post, only wrap it up in paper so that it doesn't get broken.

Write.

Ask N. I. [Khardjiev] what he thinks [about coming].

I wanted to telephone either him or you but then decided that it would annoy you and rejected the idea.

Stir yourself, and come to visit.

Nadya

Zhenya doesn't even write. I've grown accustomed to that, but it worries Mama.

Probably Nadya was waiting for a teaching job.

She had two occupations in Kalinin. She made toys as a member of some craft workshop and taught German at a school. I remember with what enthusiasm she described, on her visit to Moscow, the methods she used. Together she and her pupils read aloud Goethe's "Erl König" (in the original, of course), catching the intonation of classical German. She thus accustomed her young charges to the language and, at the same time, unveiled to them the mysteries of poetry.

As for the paraffin stove, Nadya had two in Moscow and to spare me squabbles in our kitchen had given me the second. There was no question of her buying a new one now. The country was experiencing yet another shortage of all that a normal person could need.

In the end, it was Alexander Mandelstam who took the paraffin stove to Kalinin. In fact, a considerable share of the worries linked to Mandelstam's arrest was borne by his brother. It was Alexander who took parcels to Butyrki prison when Nadya was not in Moscow, and it was he who went to get information at the NKVD department (I don't remember exactly what it was called) on Kuznetsky Most. Mandelstam's last letter, which was addressed directly to his brother "Shurochka", is testimony to these efforts.

My "old buddy" was Nadya's reference to Khardjiev. We had indeed already known each other for five years, had drunk a quantity of dry wine together, and on innumerable occasions dined on cheese, just the two of us or with Nadya. But there was a problem. Khardjiev was suffering from extreme stress. Shortly before Nadya's letter arrived, Khardjiev's friend Tsezar Volpe rang me up after returning to his native Leningrad. I could save our mutual friend, he tried to persuade me, from being taken into hospital (which would have been awful!) if I went to stay with him for a while. It would calm him down. Volpe added diplomatically: "This merely testifies his deep attachment to you." Undoubtedly, these were Khardjiev's own childish ruses: he had been pleading with me unsuccessfully for several days to perform this same feat. However, the assurances of his friend had their effect and I gave in.

On my arrival, I joked that I was changing my behaviour after receiving confirmation of his attachment to me. "Yes, you are performing a noble deed," he replied, adopting the same tone, "but I see you immediately opening your briefcase. Take out the proofs I must read." He was quite right. Then I did not let a single publication go to the printers before Khardjiev had looked it through and gone over the text with his expert hand. That was how I learned to be laconic and to the point in my research articles, something of which I remain proud to this day.

As a memento of that period I have a copy of Khardjiev's *The Janissary*, which had been published in 1934. To begin with, he gave me only Favorsky's superb engraving, which served as a frontispiece to the book. The dedication shows the author's modesty – "Emma, if Favorsky had illustrated the entire book, it would have suffered by comparison. N.K., 25 November 1939" – and in brackets he included a significant postscript: "(on the eve of total madness)". It was December when Khardjiev gave me the entire book, sprinkled with his stylistic alterations. All the while I stayed with him he was engaged in making those corrections. And then he did calm down, as the book's daft inscription confirms:

"For Emma Grigoryevna. May she keep this in a dry place and preserve it for all Eternity. N.K., December 1939".

Why was Khardjiev in such an overexcited or, on the contrary, depressive state? One, we were all half mad then. Everyone knew someone who was in prison – or had just been shot even – and the person's friends and relatives still worried over his fate. Two, I could clearly see that Khardjiev was tormented by some agonising romance. I was not interested to learn who the other person was. In Akhmatova's words, this was the "higher freedom of the spirit, that which we call friendship".

Some 20 years later, Akhmatova would express the same thought aloud: "I wish to know only as much about my friends as they want me to know of them." That was the discretion I had observed instinctively in friendship before I ever got to know Akhmatova.

It's another matter when people themselves describe their lives. Khardjiev was editor of the first two volumes of Mayakovsky's collected works (i.e. the early Mayakovsky, the best of his work, in my view) and still honoured the cult of the Brik household. He considered Osip Brik to be a highly intelligent man, and as for Lily Brik . . .! At this time, Mayakovsky's muse was beyond criticism for Khardjiev. He felt no need to tell me about that side of his existence, and for my part I was not very interested in the Futurists and all emphatically left-wing art. Of course, I knew a good deal of Mayakovsky and Vasily Kamensky[86] by heart; I read Aseyev and had visited the exhibitions and gone to the Meyerhold Theatre. But I simply did not know the other poets and artists of the avant-garde, as it is now called.

Sometimes, however, Khardjiev would complain to me about his friends and colleagues, hurt by another's words or deed. This relieved his irritation and was entirely innocuous. I had never even met most of these people. It is impossible to forget one of his stories about Meyerhold although I do not recall the details. Probably it was after his theatre had been closed and not long before the director's arrest. Several people had gathered at Meyerhold's apartment, among them Khardjiev. The tragic atmosphere became most intense, and Meyerhold wanted to turn the gas on and leave this life.

Khardjiev considered Alexander Vvedensky a great poet and an original personality but not someone he felt close to.[87] All the more unexpected, therefore, was the poet's sudden appearance at Maria's Grove.

---

[86] One of the first Russian Cubo-Futurists, Kamensky (1884–1961) was the author of *Tango with Cows: Concrete Poems*.

[87] Alexander Vvedensky (1904–1941) was a close friend of Daniil Kharms, belonging to several radical Left Art groups and to Oberiu.

He announced that he had written a new poem and wanted to read it aloud. He recited the now familiar "Elegy". After hearing it, Khardjiev said: "I'm proud that I live at the same time as you." Vvedensky sat down at the table, wrote out the text and gave the page to Khardjiev. He told me of this visit soon after, and, without letting the precious autograph out of his hands, Khardjiev read the whole "Elegy" aloud. I was staggered by this pitiless and piercing transformation of our tragic time into words. This unquestionably brilliant poem was to prove prophetic: "With death keep in step, with death: Poet and Poor Horseman". Death did not keep Vvedensky waiting. Arrested in 1941, he was banished from Kharkov during the first week of the war and perished, without reaching Tambov, in unexplained circumstances. Like Pushkin and Khlebnikov, he died several months short of his thirty-seventh birthday.

All that winter, Khardjiev was preparing to submit his textual labours of many years to the publishers. These were the manuscripts he had collected of unknown poems by Khlebnikov.[88] How often, as he stepped rapidly and lightly into the corridor from the kitchen or the bathroom, returning to his own room, did I hear his exultant voice repeating lines of Khlebnikov which he had been the first to read: "In the 93rd foot regiment / I died, as children perish" or "I am a black raven . . ." The poem "Ailing Russia" left a particularly deep impression on me.

There were also more than enough capricious incidents and irritable outbursts during our December idyll. How then could we consider going to Kalinin? However, Nadya sent him a much more eloquent invitation. I quote from the typescript copy Khardjiev gave me in the 1970s:

Dear Nikolai Ivanovich,

In my new life, which is quite unlike anything else, I often remember you and miss you very much. Are we fated to meet? A separation of three hours' distance is a very difficult thing. I'm afraid that neither you nor I shall overcome it. And then there's the train and the railway station, and for me three-hour journeys are unbearable, reminding me of the last three years of my life.

I often imagine what we would do if you came to see me. You could not, of course, visit me at school and see how my 30

---

[88] The prolific Velimir Khlebnikov (1885–1922) wrote poetry "almost incessantly". The volume of his *Unpublished Works*, for which Khardjiev had compiled the poetry section, appeared in Moscow in 1940.

lion cubs (I have 300 in all) sit on their benches while, like a veritable juggler, I conjure with German verbs at the blackboard. You know: you toss and catch, they're all different colours, and so on.

But we would go with you to the market where people buy pork, liver, honey and both dried and frozen apples. We would haggle long, of course, and return home with the honey jar on our palms. On the way, we'd have our photos taken by the fairground photographer, on a wooden horse in our best sailor's costume or on a ship or, most simple of all, in a car driving through the Daryal ravine. Then the Vozrozhdenie workshop where they sell all kinds of things, and home across the Tmakha River to cook and light the stove.

That's how I entertain my guests. And with you I would be particularly hospitable and deferential. I would surrender the best room in my palazzo, with its view over all the barns and sheds in the courtyard.

I am a fairground barker, but I know that my "roll up, roll up!" is doomed to failure. There are no frankfurters here. Though there are doves. They are altogether too handsome. Apart from the doves I have nothing else. But they are not mine. What was he called, the one who drew the doves? The one you showed me? These are his doves.[89]

It was easier for me when I was not working. Now I'm unbearably miserable. In the mornings I can hardly believe that I'll rise and get on with my life and, most important of all, get through the day: that is hardest of all. I've never been this way before. Just like a wild beast. You know, time is not at all a healing matter. On the contrary. To begin with, it's like a dream. Then everything becomes quite real. I think the further I go, the more real it becomes. I do not try to escape from myself. I am only just beginning to understand now. Earlier I had to walk so much that I had something like concussion. Now I don't, and that's worse.

Of my few women friends, only Emma writes occasionally. Sometimes she says she wants to visit me; sometimes she invites me to come and stay. And that's it. She's a slow-moving creature,

---

[89] E.G.: The "frankfurters" and "doves" allude to the first days following Mandelstam's arrest and the time after news came of his death. Nadya spent both occasions at Khardjiev's room: "I lay prostrated with grief; but Khardjiev cooked frankfurters and made me eat ..." (*Hope against Hope* [London, 1999], chap. 75). The artist who painted the doves was Max Ernst, as Khardjiev indicated on my copy of the letter.

why should she go anywhere else. But I would be very glad to
see her. Of Anna A. [Akhmatova] I hear nothing. That's also
certainly [gone] for ever, since I live too far away.

One more thing. Never have I so strongly felt that there are
acquaintances and close friends. I have a great many acquaintances. But I desperately miss close friends, for instance, you. I
cannot precisely define the degree of our affinity. And our mamas
cannot help us, they've forgotten. How could we find out?

Love
Nadya

She did not reproach Khardjiev. Beyond a sincere and overwhelming
grief, Nadya still possessed so much unspent vitality. Creative energy
poured from her like a fountain. Even when she reproached me this was
clothed in an elegant literary form:

Dear Emma Grigoryevna,

I have not received any news from you for a long while. Nothing
at all, in fact, from Moscow, and I'm becoming very concerned.
Could you not send word of yourself and of all my relatives and
former friends? I'd be most obliged. I would be happy if you came
to visit during these holidays. Of course, I shall come to Moscow,
but I fear that by the time I am free to travel, you will already be
in Vereya. And the journey to Vereya is just as insuperable for me
as the trip to Kalinin for any normal Muscovite.

Therefore, Emma Grigoryevna, we can only trust to heaven
where, after death, we shall choose some well-appointed little
cloud for our posthumous aerial voyages.

My love, until we meet,

N.M.

Soon Nadya herself organised a trip to Moscow. Her friendship with
Khardjiev remained quite unclouded.[90] Several times she spent the night
in my room. Often the three of us met. I can still see and hear a variety of scenes when we all gathered at Shchipok Street or in Maria's
Grove. The atmosphere of these gatherings is well reflected in a letter

---

[90] The final rift between E.G. and Nadezhda Mandelstam in 1968 was prompted
by the latter's "slander" against Khardjiev (see Introduction, pp. xxiv–xxvi).

Nadya wrote to me, dated 7 December 1940:

Emmochka,

My head is clearer now. So is yours, I hope.

Please write to me about all your affairs and in particular what came of my latest matchmaking.

I want a copy of the Khlebnikov. I'm determined to have one. It's not true that editors only receive two copies. I'd like to see that contract.

If he is friends with you (i.e. has enticed you back to his couch), grab a Khlebnikov from him. For me, naturally.

Overall, I'm mad at the confusion and muddle. Moscow treated me badly. It was best of all with Zhenya and with you. On the last day, naturally, when you were not howling but seeing me off.

Are you really not coming to visit me here? How I hate you.

Nadya

I invited her to stay and see in the New Year. But the post was working badly then. Nadya's reply is adorned with three postmarks, separated by an interval of eight or nine days: "Kalinin-Regional, 1 January 1941", and both 8 and 9 January, "Moscow".

Nadya wrote:

Emmochka,

Thanks for the invitation.

Unfortunately, it arrived late. In order to fix up a ticket I would have been running around, pleading and fussing, for a whole week.

So it didn't work out.

I'm very tired. Almost sick. I can't wait to see the last of the school.

The neighbours like listening to the radio for days and nights on end. I'm working 24 hours a day. A good thing I didn't give up the toys.

Wonder when I'll see you.

Anyway, perhaps, I'll see you sometime.

Love
Nadya

Poor Nadya. As we can see from her letters, humour and flashes of her characteristic firework display of wit were what kept her going. But pangs of grief must have assailed her when there was a pause and she remembered she was living in a world in which Osya no longer existed. This was never once discussed. It could not yet be mentioned. The time for that had still not come.

The scars left by her experiences appeared at the most unexpected moments. When I was accompanying her to the railway station (as she mentions in her 7 December letter), we were caught up in a raid. They were looking for black marketeers, the so-called bag-merchants, and this time were after only the women involved. At the entrance to the platform, they checked not only tickets but also people's belongings. Nadya was gripped by something like a nervous tic. She began to shake visibly from head to foot, and her teeth started to chatter. It took all my strength of will to calm her down. This involved pretending to be calm and amiable myself. It had the desired effect on those conducting the search, and they didn't even touch our things. In the carriage we found ourselves sitting next to some ordinary lads, and since I kept up this calm friendliness Nadya concluded that somehow I knew these people.

Nadezhda, 1940s

I have no recollections of Nadya visiting Moscow in 1941. As if under a spell, apolitical people had totally forgotten that our country might be drawn into the Second World War. Of course, we followed events in Europe with anxiety and compassion, but it all seemed far away. Our small circle, if we can call it that, was so preoccupied with its own sorrows, passions and concerns that we did not notice or tried pretending not to know that we were standing on the brink of the abyss.

The dispute between our entire family and the Institute for Experimental Medicine meanwhile continued. The institute administration grew more and more brazen. Now those living in other hospital buildings swelled the number of evicted residents. To gather and collate our common complaints, I had to meet people whom I had not known until then. Among them was an engineer who had long ceased to have anything to do with the hospital. Like all not very clever people he cheered himself and us with the conviction that together we could defeat the institute administration. "They face the fate of France!" he would exclaim. I was deeply offended by this servile crowing over the vanquished. When in the first months of the Great Patriotic War our own forces suffered shattering defeat and Moscow was bombed, I felt like saying to him: "And what shall we call our fate?" But that was already impossible. He had been called up into the home guard and died surrounded by German forces. I felt sorry even for that cheerful philistine.

Nadya continued her difficult life in Kalinin until the very outbreak of war. She did have those on whom she could depend, nevertheless. Her mother was with her, and both her brother Yevgeny and Alexander Mandelstam came to visit them. Furthermore, she had made a new friend in Kalinin. The wife of a leading arrested Communist, the woman had been banished from Moscow with her two children and her mother. Before her own catastrophe struck, she belonged to the most privileged circles in Moscow – i.e. to Soviet high society. She had been a hostess at large receptions with foreign guests; she knew other languages, dressed with taste and was very beautiful. Ordinary Soviet women gave her the admiration befitting a "star" when she was driven up to the entrance of her own home in a large black automobile. Her present changed circumstances found her working very hard in Kalinin, but she did not complain or give in. Her "*savoir-vivre*", as it's called, was highly developed – i.e. she had a healthy, practical outlook and a rational benevolence towards others. It is said that she never once quarrelled with anyone in all her life. Such a temperament was a wonderful foil for Nadya's exaltation and prickly character and set an example of restraint and calm, undemonstrative heroism. They remained friends until Nadya's death.

Chapter 18

Akhmatova presented me with the new collection of her poems *From Six Books* with an affectionate inscription dated 8 July 1940. Probably she had inscribed her copies while still in Leningrad: in midsummer I do not remember her being in Moscow. However, I shall never forget her visit in August 1940.

I went to see her straight after some quite painful treatment at the polyclinic. "How do you stand it?" she asked considerately and, as always,

without any introduction read me two more new poems. One was about
the fall of Paris ("When they bury the epochs . . ."), the other about
the bombing of London ("the twenty-fourth drama of Shakespeare").[91]
I was astounded and, lowering my head, hid my face on the table. "Don't
pretend you're crying," she said, using irony to conceal her satisfaction
at the impression she had made. I was not pretending nor was I crying.
It was as though I had choked on a roaring gust of wind that left the
room filled with ozone. The sensation returned often during Akhmatova's
short August visit to Moscow. The first few days passed in uncertain
hope, the last day in despair.

Lyova was writing gloomy letters to Akhmatova. It hurt to hear his
phrase from her lips: "No-one could care less about me." Quite recently,
I had asked Akhmatova whether he remembered me. "Yes, yes, he named
you among those I should contact if he died." To many, however, it
then seemed that he would be pardoned and released. If, after an interval of 17 years, a Soviet publishing house was issuing Akhmatova's new
book, it was commonly thought this sensational news showed that she
was suddenly in favour with Stalin. Evidently, this would affect not just
her poetry, it was assumed, but also her own position. No gifts could
ease Akhmatova's life, however, if her son remained in a labour camp
beyond the Arctic Circle. That was why Pasternak asked Akhmatova on
28 July 1940: "Is Lev already with you?" In that letter he described in
detail his reactions to almost every poem in the new collection and
referred to its appearance as "a great triumph which has been the subject
of discussion for over a month now".

Such talk was not unfounded. Fadeyev, Alexei Tolstoy and Pasternak
intended to nominate Akhmatova's book for the Stalin Prize. It was then,
it seems to me, that Akhmatova wrote her second letter to Stalin. I myself
do not remember the contents, but Lydia Chukovskaya told me the argument she used in her appeal. Her son had been accused of intending to
kill Zhdanov,[92] she wrote, and she had urged him, supposedly, to perform
this terrorist act. Akhmatova requested that this monstrous accusation
against both of them be withdrawn. Later Akhmatova concluded that her
letter had not been passed on and had not reached Stalin.

For the time being, however, that was still unclear. There were already
noticeable fluctuations in Akhmatova's position. These are reflected in
Lydia Chukovskaya's daily diary entries.[93] At first, the Leningrad admini-

---

[91] See "Eight Poems by Anna Akhmatova", pp. 322–3.
[92] Andrei Zhdanov (1896–1948) was behind the 1946 decree, which condemned
works by Akhmatova and Zoshchenko; until the late 1980s, Leningrad University
bore the name of Zhdanov.
[93] See Lydia Chukovskaya, *The Akhmatova Journals: Vol. 1, 1938–41* (London, 1994).

stration was in a state of euphoria that the disgraced poet's name could now be mentioned again. On 5 January 1940, she was accepted, with pomp and ceremony, as a member of the Writers' Union. Two publishing houses immediately began preparing her books for publication. Literary magazines asked for poems to include in their next issue. There was talk of increasing her pension, giving her a flat and so on. Then these raptures began to cool.

In July, a scathing review of *From Six Books* by V. Pertsov was already being published in *Literaturnaya gazeta*. Writers, it is true, saw nothing fateful in this event. In the same letter quoted earlier, Pasternak wrote: "Pertsov's tone outraged us all, but here people think (among them, Tolstoy) that one of the real writers ought to write about you for a magazine, not in a newspaper." Such an article did not appear. Akhmatova was not awarded the Stalin Prize. Her pension was not increased, and she received only an apartment after the war. Nevertheless, Akhmatova went to Moscow to plead on Lyova's behalf. On 31 August 1940 – immediately after Akhmatova had returned to Leningrad, in other words – Lydia Chukovskaya wrote: "She was amazed and, of course, encouraged that Fadeyev had received her most politely and immediately done all that was in his power. (The last few days before her departure she had asserted: 'Fadeyev will not even see me.') She was also amazed that Fadeyev and Pasternak had nominated her book for the Stalin Prize." Even in her precise and detailed records, Lydia Chukovskaya could not openly describe what had happened in Moscow during Akhmatova's last day there. I remember.

After her meeting with Fadeyev, Akhmatova went to the USSR prosecutor-general's office on Pushkin Street. I accompanied her. When she was called in to see the prosecutor, I waited for her in the vestibule. Soon, far too soon, the office door opened and Akhmatova appeared. In the doorway stood a man far shorter than she who looked her up and down and rudely tossed hostile phrases in her face. Akhmatova walked along the corridor, looking around with unseeing eyes and pushing at different doors in search of the way out. I rushed after her. I have no recollection of where I took her and how we got there.

Without delay she went back to Leningrad. I saw her to the station and helped her on to the train. As soon as I reached home, I began writing to Lyova in Norilsk. Until that day I had not written to him in the camps. What made me break my silence?

For some reason, Akhmatova simply had to let Lyova know that the prosecutor had rejected her appeal. She was scared to do so. Lyova had already begun to suspect that his mother was not petitioning for his release, or was doing so incompetently. Even in the Far North there were those who helped fan this spark of suspicion into a great flame. I could see that Akhmatova had not the strength to write and tell him of the collapse of their hopes, yet neither could she lie to him or keep quiet. It was becoming a disastrous situation. At this point, I could stand it no longer and impulsively started writing to Lyova myself.

All night I wrote, pondering each word. Finally, I realised that there was no need for hints and allusions. What secrets could there be in this case? Akhmatova had openly visited the prosecutor's office and our constant observers had seen me with her, of course, on the platform of the Leningrad Station in Moscow. I signed my name in full, gave my postal address on the envelope and began the letter by announcing that I had only just seen Akhmatova off on the train; she had been to the prosecutor-general's office and was now returning to Leningrad.

Next I openly declared the gloomy result of that visit, without giving any distressing details, naturally. Then followed words of comfort and hope. Since I was writing from the heart, I found a way to say what I wanted. Although I am seeing many new people, I wrote, I should never forget him, he was my sorrow. The principle aim of my letter was to ask him not to write angry letters to Akhmatova; "she is doing all she can" – I well remember including that phrase. There was no reply, but my letter had an effect. Akhmatova told me that Lyova had begun to write more gently to her. I considered this a sign that my letter had reached him. Only after the war did I learn from Lyova himself that he replied to me then, but his letter apparently had gone astray. That was a common occurrence at the time. In the 1950s, on the contrary, every letter to and from the camps reached its addressee, even during Stalin's lifetime.

Let us return to 1940.

After making corrections, deletions and additions, I wrote out a clean version of my letter and dropped it in the post-box. Immediately, my head began spinning with fear. How would Akhmatova react? What if she were to blame me for what I'd done? Yet she herself had given me his address in Norilsk. I should have feared something else. Six months earlier I had had to fill out a form containing a question I had never seen or heard of before: "Who among your relatives and *acquaintances* [my emphasis, E.G.] have been convicted and punished?" I entered two dead men, Mandelstam and my SR relative. I wrote nothing about Lyova. If these two documents were compared, the consequences might be unpleasant. Yet I brushed aside this fear, from either frivolous disdain or common sense. These materials passed along different channels, I believed, and there was little chance they would fall into the same hands. I was hardly important enough for them to keep me constantly under surveillance and track down all my documents. The form would surface a year later. But that is a different story.

Chapter 19

The year 1940 began unhappily for me. A sharp discord wrecked the idyll at Maria's Grove. Khardjiev suddenly dashed off to see in the New Year somewhere else, evidently with his fateful beloved who had summoned him unexpectedly. Naturally, he would not tell me the true reason for his behaviour, which made it seem all the more hurtful. I spent New Year's Eve at home, and this put me in an awkward position with my own family. The timing could hardly have been worse, since I was again without a job. I do not remember why, but my contract with the Historical Museum had not been renewed.

My position became increasingly unbearable. Not surprisingly, I clutched at the only opportunity that arose to find a job. This was at an institution that now went under the most ludicrous abbreviation GAFKE[94] (the State Archive of Serfdom and the Feudal Epoch). In reality it was the oldest and richest of our national historical archives. It was located on Pirogov Street and I imagined how the "youthful archivists" of Pushkin's time had worked in the very same building. And it was here that Alexander Turgenev finally ruined his eyesight, already weakened by his tireless quest in all the archives of Europe for documents relating to Russian history.

GAFKE was famed for the ferocious and ignorant woman who was its director, a Communist from the Latvian Rifle Division.[95] The archive itself came under the control of the NKVD. These circumstances made me hesitate. When they announced that they were hiring contract workers at the beginning of the year, I could not bring myself to approach them. But life became so stressful that in March I went to sign up there. I had to see the director several times before we could reach agreement. I filled out a form and on her instructions went to someone else to have the paper signed and stamped.

I found myself in a large office where there were several desks. By the window was a big writing table, and behind it sat the uniformed head of the department. He asked me to wait, and I sat down at an unoccupied small desk, looking absent-mindedly about me. At that moment, a young woman in a uniform jacket strode rapidly into the room and headed straight in my direction. "You were given the wrong form," she said, tossing a different questionnaire on the table, and hurriedly departed. Lazily, I began filling out the form. Gradually, I

---

[94] The association is with the Russian verb *gafkat'*, "to bark".
[95] Military unit that went over to the Bolsheviks during the Revolution, subsequently forming Lenin's personal bodyguard.

noticed that the questions were growing more and more complicated. Here was the one about arrested and exiled acquaintances; but they also asked if any of my relatives had been in those areas held by the Whites during the Civil War; and, finally, did anyone working in the "organs" know me? With pleasure I entered "No" in both instances, but once again the same woman appeared and tossed me yet another printed form. This was the "official secrets" act. I signed. When I worked in the archives as a researcher, I often signed similar declarations. Similar, but not like this one. Because it followed from the text that I was now employed by the secret police, though the question "In what department?" had been left blank. Alarm made me see double, and I do not remember the exact formulations in those ill-starred documents. I assumed that they wanted to ask me to work in some classified depository. Yet what kind of documents was I leaving behind me? Naturally, I could have asked the department head for an explanation but no fewer than six employees, working away at their desks, were stealing glances at me. I did not want to reveal my true attitude to the NKVD in front of such witnesses. That was not all, though. I was also expected to bring in two character references from members of the Communist Party. I decided to meet this requirement so as not to give the impression that I was someone of dubious reputation. Then, I thought, I'll find some excuse to turn down a job at GAFKE.

While I went about obtaining these references, I was in a state of confusion. I went back to my elder brother for advice. He reacted to my story with indifference. As a senior electrical engineer at the metro-construction company, his work was classified and he filled out many such questionnaires. My friend Lena, on the contrary, showered me with reprimands. When I found myself alone in her room, I remember, I sat holding a razor to my wrist and debated whether to slash my veins or go out on to the landing and toss myself from the fourth-floor window of that tall apartment building. I did not do anything of the kind, however.

Eventually, I calmed down. Yet when I brought in the two references and the same head of department joyfully enquired: "And have you left us your phone number?" I realised I had fallen into a trap.

I never showed my face in that office again. Three weeks later, I went to see the obdurate director and told her I had fallen seriously ill and would not be taking the job at GAFKE.

It is hard to convey how infuriated she became. She quoted the example of certain selfless women who worked, hunched up with pain, but would not abandon their posts. This had no effect on me. Then she began to tempt me with materials that they had not shown even to

Tarle.[96] It was enticing, but I did not give in. She continued to press me and only then did I ask her the question I should have posed at the very beginning, there in that large office. "Do all archive employees fill out the same form?" I enquired. "No," she yelled, foaming at the mouth, "not everyone! You must be *admitted* to the System!" At which point our discussion ended. I never again set foot in that accursed GAFKE until all the archives were reorganised. Then, following the war and the Twentieth Party Congress, I often went to work in the archives now held there, under quite normal conditions, at the building to which I had taken such a liking.

I began to forget this repellent escapade as though it had passed without leaving a trace. Meanwhile, intensive preparations were under way in Moscow and Leningrad to commemorate the centenary of Lermontov's death. I published a number of articles about my research, two of them sizeable compositions,[97] in newspapers and journals and received quite a good fee for them. My material position improved slightly. The editorial board of the "Literary Heritage" series invited me to contribute to the two-volume edition of Lermontov that they were preparing.

The work was interesting. There was a friendly and business-like atmosphere at their office, and, at the same time, it was a very jolly place thanks to the temperament and inexhaustible wit of Ilya Zilberstein, the founder of that well-known series.[98] With him worked Sergei Makashin and Ivan Sergievsky. The latter was in charge of the Lermontov publication and very well disposed towards me.

All three had their own close and subtle relations with the archives. Many resourceful discussions, of which I was quite unaware, were held with the Foreign Ministry archive. As a result I was allowed to see unique documents concerning Lermontov's duel with Ernest de Baranthes, the French ambassador's son. I had already published several new documents relating to this duel, some of which were also held in that archive. The most important of these, however, had been carefully concealed from me until a more thorough agreement was reached with the editors. Now I could publish a fuller study in "Literary Heritage". This was to the advantage of the archive, the editors and myself.

When we were working together, Sergievsky once said to me: "I'd like to talk to you, 'man to man'." "Are you being followed?" the

---

[96] Yevgeny Tarle (1875–1955), Russian historian and author of a biography of Napoleon favoured by Stalin.

[97] "Concerning Lermontov's Duel", *Almanac: The 22nd Year* (1939); "Lermontov and the Circle of Sixteen", *Literary Critic* (September–October 1940).

[98] Zilberstein amassed an art collection that formed the nucleus of the new Museum of Private Collections in the late 1980s.

conversation began. "No." The editors were thinking of giving me another study to complete, he said, based on yet more substantial materials. To do that, however, I must be given official access to classified documents. Could I do that? Would I agree? I confessed to Sergievsky the details of the previous year's incident. "We know about that," he said, quite imperturbably. I requested a few days to think it over.

My enthusiasm as a researcher got the better of me. I came to Sergievsky and announced my agreement. If only you could have seen the look he cast my way! It was filled with reproach and disappointment. My heart sank. But it was too late to back down. We discussed the details of the agreement. Taking my leave, I walked heavy-hearted toward the door. But barely had I touched the door handle when Sergievsky called out to me: "Emma Grigoryevna, come back." Sitting in the same place across the table from him, I heard him say: "It's better not to go there." He explained: "It's a fishy business. Today they'll entrust you with the archive, and tomorrow they might give you a different task." A weight was lifted from my shoulders. Nevertheless, still bewildered, I asked: "But what will Lebedev-Polyansky and the rest of the directors say? It's very bad of me, isn't it . . ." "It's bad," Sergievsky did not disagree. But the matter was decided. I was turning down the offer.

I went home extremely happy. Was it simply because I had avoided this pitfall? No, I was also filled with an exultant sense of joy on Sergievsky's behalf. He was a petty and hard-bitten Soviet literary specialist, but he had revealed to me another, genuinely human side to his character.

I could not then foresee that Sergievsky's name would become linked to the persecution of Akhmatova in 1946, after publication of the Central Committee decree about the magazines *Zvezda* and *Leningrad*. That was already a new chapter in post-war history. But I never forgot how Sergievsky had saved me.

Chapter 20

In December 1940, I again began to work for the Literary Museum. I was not now attached to any of its departments, however, but helping prepare the exhibition to mark the centenary of Lermontov's death on 27 July 1841 (15 July, Old Style). This unique exhibition was open for only a day. From 23 July, Moscow was already being bombed. The day after the opening, we began closing down the exhibition and preparing the valuable exhibits, gathered from museums throughout the Soviet Union, for evacuation. We did not even manage to photograph the displays. No catalogue was prepared, and there were no reviews in the press. No-one today remembers this exhibition; it is as if it had never existed. Yet its structure, design and scholarly method all contributed something new. In so far as is possible, given the total absence of documentary evidence, let me set down what I remember.

The Lermontov jubilee committee was a governmental body, but the necessary administration and research was assigned to the Literary Museum. Bonch-Bruyevich was no longer there. As an Old Bolshevik and companion of Lenin, he was harassed and "squeezed out" of the unique sanctuary he had created in the early 1930s for the preservation of manuscripts and illustrative material relating to the history of Russian literature.

He collected and bought archives from still-living writers. They were all in need of money and readily responded to the museum's offers.[99] The go-between who linked the director and the writers was the charming and beautiful Klavdia Surikova, who was devoted to Bonch-Bruyevich. The writers were happy to invite her to their homes and when they came to the museum treated her as the enchanting hostess of that convivial town house. When I first came there in 1936, she was still playing this role. What a change I now observed!

By chance I learned that Surikova could not spend her vacation at a rest home. The salary of the museum secretary was insufficient to cover the costs, and she could no longer count on a subsidy from the trade union. She lived alone with her little daughter. Her public role at the museum, according to her colleagues, was her one remaining comfort. But that too now came to an end.

I witnessed the following episode. Arriving at work Surikova found another's jacket on the back of her chair. At first she paid no attention, but her astonishment grew as no-one came to claim the item. Opening a drawer in her desk, she found someone else's folders. She directed a bemused enquiry at a colleague who happened to be nearby. With concealed malice, the latter advised her to go and look at the notice board. Surikova, it turned out, was no longer the secretary and had been moved to some other department. This was located on the first floor in a room that the writers never visited.

This technique for removing an unsuitable colleague evidently answered our superiors' pronounced passion, it seems, for humiliating

---

[99] E.G.: In an early foreign publication I came across a very naive interpretation of these relations. Writers handed their archives to the museum, supposedly in order to shield them from the all-seeing eyes of the GPU. It was hardly the right place for that.

people. Similar tactics were common in Nazi Germany. At least I remember just such a scene in the post-war German film *We Are the Wunderkinder*. The only difference was that the hero, a former editor at a publishing house, was not moved upstairs but sent down to the basement to shift and pack books.

Most extraordinary of all, the woman who so brazenly took Surikova's place subsequently proved a thoroughly enchanting person who led a difficult, even heroic life. I have in mind Zinaida Ilovayskaya's selfless turns of duty on the museum roof during the war.

Strange to say, while I established warm personal relations with both of these women, I did not find much in common with the research staff. Our main disagreement concerned the organisation of literary exhibitions. They laid stress on written material. Trying to uncover the "ideas" underlying complex works by great writers using this method, however, only resulted in a collage of quotations. The illustrative material, the mind and soul of any exhibition, was thus involuntarily relegated to a subordinate role. Landscapes and portraits, "texts" and small objects were hung not only on the walls but also on the doors, the tiles of the Dutch stove and the side of the cupboard or placed on a ledge in the wall. The only guiding principle was the logic of thematic development. Such artistic blindness was sharply rebuffed by Nikolai Pakhomov, an experienced museum curator and himself a passionate collector. He was an expert on Lermontov's drawings, paintings and autographs. Naturally, someone of his learning found it difficult to accept the dull exhibitions staged at the Literary Museum: in turn he was accused of not appreciating the meaning of Lermontov's works. There was some truth in what the museum staff said. Pakhomov adhered to traditional rules for hanging paintings and drawings and showed no consideration for the contents of the poet's works. When I arrived in 1940, this internecine strife was at its most bitter. Soon, however, the irreconcilable opponents were to be astounded by a quite new approach that burst in on their dated feud.

Two students and followers of Malevich, Nikolai Suetin and Konstantin Rozhdestvensky, were invited to design the Lermontov jubilee exhibition. Not long before, they had won recognition in official circles for their brilliant (as they were described) designs for the Soviet pavilion at the 1937 World Exhibition in Paris. Pakhomov was outraged. Accustomed to the stylised decor of early nineteenth-century town houses in Moscow or country estates, when shown the new artists' proposals he snorted derisively: "Made in the USA"! He conceived a personal hatred for Suetin and Rozhdestvensky, who, he considered, "just made it up as they went along". For their part, the ladies who had worked under Bonch-Bruyevich contemptuously recalled that Suetin had been totally destitute when he came to the museum: "Instead of a hem, his trouser legs ended in a fringe." However, the new designers found that they had the full support of Irakly Andronikov, who was a member of the government's jubilee committee. "If only you knew what it cost me!" he confessed, as if apologising to me for this great advance in his career.

Until then, we were equal members of the Lermontov commission at the Institute of World Literature. We had both begun by working on areas suggested by Boris Eichenbaum, and shared our finds with one another. It was as though we had established a division of labour. His research was among the living descendants of Lermontov's contemporaries; mine required the archive materials that I sought only in State depositories. He had published three articles in journals and newspapers, and so had I. But Irakly was very popular in theatrical and literary circles thanks to his unique gifts as an impersonator, parodist and raconteur. At the time these performances were regarded as amateur activities. He had not yet tried his hand in public at the Leningrad Philharmonic or the Tchaikovsky Hall in Moscow. Still, his entire daily life was a theatrical performance. No matter what the organisation, he would always make for the director's office. Charming all the employees and secretaries on the way with his anecdotes and routines, he would save the full recital for a selected audience in the director's office. Returning to the exhibition from a symposium in Leningrad, he so impersonated the words and gestures of those who had spoken at Pushkin House that the sometimes dull language of literary studies acquired a colourful gleam and began to glow with his delicate humour. Nikolai Antsiferov was very fond of Andronikov's tales not just for his talents as an actor but also for the intelligent and professional summaries they contained. Irakly knew how to provide an excellent synopsis.

Antsiferov did not side with any party at the museum and took a most lively interest in everyone. Sometimes, I gently reproached him, he wasn't a good judge of character. "You're an optimist," I said, but he would deny it with a sad, wise smile: "No, I'm a pessimist." He was considerate to others because too often he had come into contact with moral freaks, for example during his interrogation or the several years of his imprisonment on Solovki.

Our literary specialists at the museum, on the contrary, did not share Antsiferov's tolerance and were convinced that the new designers knew nothing about literature. Could these practical craftsmen, working from American models, appreciate the great ideas of Russian literary genius? They were dubious. As it turned out, the designers grasped the inner meaning of Lermontov's works better than the professional connoisseurs

of literature. I remember how Rozhdestvensky noticed a self-portrait in
the poem "Mongo" that not one of us, until then, had spotted, inserted
in the humorous and frivolous text of this "hussar" poem:

> He weighed his words carefully
> And was rash in his affairs;
> At times sober, he lied without shame
> And at celebrations held his tongue

Suetin examined portraits of the women who inspired Lermontov's
lyric verse and delved into the nature of the poet's relations with his
muses. Imagination had the upper hand in Lermontov's love affairs, he
commented. The designer expressed his thoughts incoherently or, rather,
in compressed form since he was slow-moving and pensive unlike the
agile and sociable Rozhdestvensky. "A bull with a fiddle," I once described
him in conversation with Khardjiev. He laughed out loud and replied
that one of Malevich's paintings was titled *Cow with a Fiddle*.

My discussions were mostly with Boris Ender, the third designer. He
had not worked at the World Exhibition in Paris, neither was he a student
of Malevich: he pursued his own path in painting. At first a pupil of
Matyushin[100] he had then become an abstract artist. Suetin and
Rozhdestvensky invited him, as a friend and kindred spirit, to join in the
work on our exhibition. He would be responsible for designing my room.

This represented Lermontov's major works, *A Hero of Our Time*, *The
Demon*, "Meditation" and "1st January". Striving to achieve a correspondence between the design of the room and the underlying tonality
of Lermontov's works, we frequently chatted about poetry and art. In
passing, Ender told me a great deal about the artist and writer Yelena
Guro,[101] one of the first Cubo-Futurists. He had a quite profound and
special affinity with her. Ender was constantly seeking out expressions
of Lermontov's childlike quality: without it, a poet could not exist, in
his view. As I introduced him to the significance of my discoveries about
Lermontov, I found him more appreciative than our literary specialists,
who are often inclined to be dogmatic in their own field.

Like me, Ender was incapable of talking to his employers. Apparently,
he did not get on with the administration anywhere and had not yet
been able to obtain the fee for his previous contract. So he came to

---

[100] Modernist composer who, with the poet Alexei Kruchonykh, created the
famous 1913 "opera" *Victory over the Sun*. Malevich created the sets, and
Khlebnikov provided a prologue.

[101] Pseudonym of the painter and writer Eleonora von Notenburg (1877–1913),
wife of Matyushin.

work hungry. This he concealed from me, but once when he was with Andronikov he fainted and only then did it become apparent that he was not eating.

Suetin and Rozhdestvensky were careful that Ender did not draw the attention of our employers, fearing that otherwise he would engage them in a principled argument about art. They themselves were adept at dealing with ideological comrades. You should have seen and heard how eloquently Rozhdestvensky, addressing the members of yet another commission, defended the design for his room. "It will be a work of art!" he said inspiringly, and, as if charmed, they softened and believed him. But he was pursuing a quite different artistic effect in his own paintings. He had a studio where he worked from eight in the morning until he left for the exhibition. This would crop up in conversation between the artists, as did reference to the "crazy paintings" he worked on each morning, supposedly in pursuit of "the secret of the disintegration of living substances"(?!).

Just like the famous Pushkin jubilee exhibition in 1937, Lermontov was given display rooms at the Historical Museum. The Pushkin exhibition had been richer, however, in both contents and the wealth of accumulated scholarship. It had occupied the entire first floor, taking visitors on a circular route that led from the main entrance on Red Square to an exit via a staff entrance opposite the Nikolskaya Tower of the Kremlin and the gates into the Alexander Gardens. We had to lay out our exhibition in three (or perhaps four?) rooms on the very last, fourth, floor. The rooms were enormous, the ceilings high and the windows narrow. The lighting, as a consequence, was uneven, and this inhibited a free and intelligent distribution of the exhibits. Our artists resolved the problem by blocking off the windows. The only light would be electric, and extravagant eighteenth-century chandeliers were purchased, incidentally, to provide the overhead lighting. But that was not the most important effect. The very long walls now offered an even expanse interrupted by wooden frames, and the artistic objects of the past century looked well within these geometrical shapes. The problem of combining modern forms and materials with historical objects was the subject of passionate discussion among those working at the Literary Museum. By tradition, they strove for a stylisation or, to be more exact, an imitation of the era of Pushkin and Lermontov in its every expression – interiors, the framing of watercolours and drawings, and so on. Was it really necessary? Freely and imaginatively, Ender chose any form which would enhance the virtues of the exhibit, and he knew how to achieve a harmonious combination between objects of different styles.

Suetin's design had a most distinctive structure. It was the final room of the exhibition where, traditionally, obligatory official themes were presented: the significance of the Russian author for world literature, and the influence of his work on Soviet poets and writers. I could not stand such subjects. Therefore I have a poor memory of the detail of Suetin's innovations and merely recall that he created a brilliant architectural finale. It was truly an apotheosis.

The first two rooms also employed the principle of placing frames against the solid walls, but it was not intrusive. Colour dominated everything.

The first room covered Lermontov's childhood in Tarkhany and Moscow, and his time at the military cadets' college in Petersburg. It was designed by Rozhdestvensky. The room felt as though it was filled with sunshine, and delicate pastel shades succeeded one another on the walls. I'm talking here of the impression, not the actual materials. Among the exhibits, of course, there were not just watercolours but also oil paintings, engravings and pencil sketches. Still, the overall effect was of brightness or, to be exact, of a rainbow in the literal rather than figurative sense.

Rozhdestvensky had a particular affection for daylight, I think. By chance I heard him speaking on the telephone to the woman who was his neighbour at the flat, trying to find out when someone had come to see him. The words "at what time" and "when" were never mentioned: he was interested to know only where the "dear sun" had been at that moment.

Artists think with their eyes. Colour and line speak to them before logical thought. I became convinced of this during the first days of the war when I created a mobile exhibition with Rozhdestvensky about the "Patriotic War of 1812". We drew our illustrative material from the rich selection of woodcuts held at the Literary Museum. I chose a page that depicted Napoleon on the banks of the River Neman – in other words, just before he attacked Russia. "No," Rozhdestvensky objected. "We shall use this picture." The scene was exactly the same, but on the river bank there stood a solitary tree. I had not noticed that detail. All the branches of the tree pointed in Napoleon's direction. "Do you see? The wind's blowing the other way. That says it all . . ." The withdrawal from Moscow, flight from Russia – in a word, failure and defeat.

Ender had his own reading of *A Hero of Our Time*. He decided to adorn our exhibit with an Oriental carpet, but he was not drawing on some banal idea of the way Tsarist officers decorated their rooms in the Caucasus – a Persian carpet hanging over the divan and decorated with pistols, a dagger and other finely chased weapons. He was not reproducing that standard picture but after re-reading the novel was relying on his own fresh impressions. Ender defended his proposal: "Pechorin died in Persia, didn't he? And, if you remember, he bought a Persian carpet at a stall in the Caucasus."

(Of course I remembered!) So two small Persian carpets served as items of decor and not illustrations to the tale of "Duchess Mary". They were hung horizontally and symmetrically above the exhibit, further reinforcing the shape defined by the wooden frame. At the centre was a portrait of Lermontov, surrounded by depictions of those belonging to the "Circle of Sixteen". The portraits were not of high quality, but Ender also found a way round this problem. He carefully selected subtle tones for the card on which the drawings and engravings were mounted. When these were added to the colourful depictions of a masquerade ball at the Winter Palace and to watercolour portraits of "Countess Emilia" [Musina-Pushkina] and S.M. Vielgorskaya which embodied the soft, feminine beauty that Lermontov adored, the entire stand appeared a symphony of colour. Still, the overall effect was of a glimmering, not a dazzling, light, and that corresponded to my perception of Lermontov's extraordinary prose. Neither was of interest to the regular staff of the Literary Museum. One of its most influential ladies commented, pursing her lips: "Too pretty."

If it had been an exhibition about Nekrasov, Tolstoy or Dostoyevsky, such a remark might have been justified. As we know, there was a sharp decline in the aesthetic quality of everyday surroundings in later nineteenth-century Russia. During Lermontov's time, however, not only he but also his closest friends drew well, many were musically gifted, and the poet himself was particularly attentive to architecture and interiors in certain of his works. When we remember this and such magnificent ballads as "Three Palms", "Gifts of the Terek", "The Tryst" and "Quarrel" any accusation of superfluous prettiness is quite out of place. Anyway, the opinion of the museum's permanent staff had no influence on the fate of the jubilee exhibition. Far worse were the visits paid by high-ranking officials when the work was still unfinished. When Fadeyev came, he saw that I had chosen as the principal motif for the *Mtsyri* stand:

> . . . yes! The hand of fate
> Led me by a different path!
> But now I am sure
> That I might be not the least
> Of daring warriors in my forefathers' land

He was indignant. He remembered very well how the hero had strained to quit "airless cells and prayers" for "that wondrous world of alarms and battles". Fadeyev recited the already clichéd and romantic lines: "I knew but one thought / a single fiery passion . . ."

And it was amazing to watch Andronikov, always so explosive and pugnacious, as he listened with the meekness of a schoolboy to the comments of his highest superior, the secretary-general of the Union of Soviet Writers. He did not even attempt to defend my viewpoint, although at that time he was usually vociferous in my praise. The layout of the *Mtsyri* stand did not alter greatly when the epigraph was replaced. However, the stand devoted to *Hero of Our Time* had to be completely changed due to the harsh ideological criticisms of V.Ya. Kirpotin, a leading Marxist critic who headed the Lermontov jubilee commission.[102] He was indignant at the close proximity of *Hero*'s author to the portraits of the Sixteen. "What are these aristocrats doing here? And where's Belinsky? Where's Herzen? Where's *Otechestvennye zapiski?*" he angrily demanded. Of course, they were all there, but not at the centre of the exhibit. We had been thinking along other lines. We were trying to show how the image of Pechorin had come into existence, not its historical and literary significance. As time passed, the understanding of Lermontov's novel had diverged, naturally, from Belinsky's interpretation. Less than 20 years later, critics assigned Pechorin, together with Onegin and Oblomov, to the category of "superfluous men". Then this interpretation gave way to another. Was it necessary to reflect that entire historical process at the exhibition? We had wanted to avoid such officious tedium by trying to give expression to our present understanding of the novel. To be honest, I was not offering *our* present understanding but my own interpretation of *A Hero of Our Time*. It was not till somewhat later, during the war in fact, that I succeeded in grasping the mysteriously shifting subtexts of Lermontov's novel, and it would take another 30 years before I could fully think out and publish my own concept of the work [*Lermontov's A Hero of Our Time*, Moscow, 1976]. But exhibitions are collective, official affairs. There was no chance for me to argue with our superiors. We acquiesced.

With renewed invention, Ender altered our part of the exhibition. The general appearance did not suffer much, but the conception, my conception, disappeared. I was convinced that when Lermontov drew a picture of "our generation" in the poem "Meditation" and when, in his prose, he depicted the type of "contemporary man" whom he "came across too often", Lermontov was taking the Sixteen as his starting point. The fellow members of his circle or club used to meet almost every evening at the very time he was writing "Meditation" and working on his famous novel. Even in the 1970s, I was unable to voice this suggestion and provide conclusive proof. The hypersensitive attitude of Soviet society to the Russian monar-

---

[102] When Socialist Realism was prescribed for members of the new Writers' Union in 1932, the *Izvestiya* editor Ivan Gronsky and Valery Kirpotin (head of the Central Committee's literary division) were appointed as the two principal enforcers of orthodoxy.

chy and its aristocracy was also a hindrance. For most of the Sixteen had been sons of those imperial courtiers who, in Lermontov's own expression, stood in a "greedy crowd" about the throne. To this day (I write in 1992) our society's attitudes to that titled élite are of an incomprehensible intensity. Either it feels hatred, which finds expression in mockery, or else an admiration that spills over into servility. I still hope that I may write about the Sixteen from a new point of view, that of the nineteenth-century "Russian dandy" who appeared after the defeat of the Decembrist uprising (". . . we are rich, barely from our cradles, with the mistakes of our fathers and their belated wisdom"). Lermontov's "dandies" almost all disappeared before they could disclose their gifts: some did not live to see 30, others barely passed the age of 40. Three of them fought beside Lermontov near the River Valerik in Chechnya. Eyewitness accounts suggest they were themselves in search of death (N.A. Gervais, Prince A.N. Dolgoruky, Baron D.P. Fredericks). Certain Russian commentators detect a self-destructive urge in Lermontov's own behaviour during his last duel with Martynov . . .

Let us return to 1941, however. In early June, I saw Akhmatova and Marina Tsvetayeva at Khardjiev's apartment in Maria's Grove. It's a strange thing, but when I later recalled that meeting, I was always sure it took place in 1940, not 1941. Once I asked Khardjiev when it was, and he also confidently said: 1940. What can explain this aberration of memory? For it required special enquiries and the comparing of various pieces of indirect evidence and, finally, publication of Akhmatova's precisely dated note before all doubts could be dispelled. The first and last time the two poets ever met was a fortnight before the beginning of the Great Patriotic War. The explanation of the mistake both Khardjiev and I made is very simple. Before the war we thought differently, and all the events of that time subsequently blended in our minds to form a single epoch.

It was a strange time, immediately before the war. A quiet and expectant political climate had descended on Moscow. We followed what was happening in the European war, of course. It is enough to recall Akhmatova's poems about "vanquished Paris" and "To Londoners", and her reference (in part three of the *Poem without a Hero*) to the siege of Tobruk in Libya[103] to rebut the involuntary accusation that we were then indifferent and short-sighted:

---

[103] It was the siege of Tobruk, from April to December 1941, not the subsequent battles for the port in 1942, that left an impression on the poet: "All that spring and summer, we anxiously opened the newspapers, hoping to learn that Tobruk had been relieved, but the siege continued. Akhmatova had managed to experience the beginning of the Leningrad Blockade. Now these horrors were not 'somewhere there' but 'just around the next corner'" (E.G., "Notes on the *Poem without a Hero*," *Peterburgskii zhurnal*, 1–2 [1993]).

But the earth beneath me hummed
And such a star gazed down
Into my not yet abandoned home
And waited for the signal . . .
Somewhere there, near Tobruk,
Somewhere round the next corner.

Yet instinctively I persuaded myself, and I was not alone in this, that we would not go to war after the Finnish campaign. I remember that Professor Nikolai Brodsky visited our exhibition and wondered, pre-occupied, whether the USSR was not heading for a war with Hitler. To me, his words sounded like a voice from under the ground or some-where far away.

Our preparations for the exhibition were in their final stages. A great many new people began to appear in the display rooms of the Historical Museum. Artists came who were curious about this new work by Suetin and Rozhdestvensky. Of course, Khardjiev looked in often and approv-ingly examined the finds and discoveries of his friends and colleagues. Quite often Yevgeny Khazin came to see me there. It was difficult to catch me at home during those days, and we should remember that he was very much in his element at dress rehearsals and private views.

As we were about to open, the chaotic last-minute preparations were in full swing. Those who produced the texts were hastily changing some-thing in the inscriptions on the exhibits. The carpenters and builders were putting up the frames and shifting the furniture around. There was a smell of paint and glue, hammers banged away, and saws sang – it was as if we were in some large workshop. It was a cheerful atmosphere. Andronikov and Rozhdestvensky decided to alter the configuration of an exhibit that, it had seemed, was quite finished. They dragged the ladder over and, although they were both quite hefty fellows, took it in turns to climb up to the ceiling clutching a hammer, while the other remained below, steadying the ladder and directing the hanging of a large picture. They joked with one another, and Irakly, at the top of the ladder, was by turns actor and director, an enthusiastic exhibition manager and a punctilious and energetic worker.

Irakly copied my neighbours' maid and called me "Yemma". I called him "Andron". We were not only fellow Lermontov specialists here but also comrades-in-arms, battling against our ecstatic museum ladies. Our alliance with the artists made us a party of our own in the museum. There's little point in denying that we overdid the resistance to our "ideological" opponents. We privately mocked them, and that does us little honour.

Once, Andronikov and the artists unintentionally went too far. I even flew at them and almost issued a reprimand. They were so offhand about the need for a joint discussion of one of the themes in the exhibition that they forgot about the research associate from the museum who had devised the exhibits on that stand. She had prepared to defend her conception, not without a certain anxiety, and had laid all her exhibits out on the floor in the proper order. Her opponents, however, were not there. They were not in the museum, as it happened. I couldn't bear to look at the pathetic figure of this woman who was usually so haughty and self-confident. Yet she could not, for one moment, abandon these priceless exhibits, now scattered over the floor. Finally, the three of them returned to the museum, noticeably cheered and invigorated. It seems they had been to a restaurant and dined as true gentlemen should. Andronikov, it must be said, never drank. He did not need to drink, he said, he was already intoxicated with life. While others drank, he would provide a spirited improvisation. And when Andronikov began to act out his tales, his listeners forget about time. Evidently, that was what had happened on this occasion. It was the weak side, incidentally, of his dazzling gift. Sometimes he would let his impersonations go on too long, and that revealed his dilettante attitude. Several times I watched as he could not shake off a personality. He was not in charge of his grotesque characters; they possessed him. At times, it was even rather awful to watch him during one of those "séances". After the war, when he began to perform publicly in large concert halls, he must have acquired a purely professional mastery. The tempo and rhythm of his work were determined by the packed audiences. This was not the same as stirring the entranced gratitude of a small circle of connoisseurs.

And so I lived life to the full during those six months. I even had a dream, unforgettable in mood, which was a "premonition of bliss", in Lermontov's words.

Its contents I do not remember. But it came against an unusual background. Something was happening outside the window. Vehicles were driving past. The silence, which descended for a minute, was broken by a ragged chorus of rough male voices. Then the monotonous rumble of heavy vehicles began again – God knows how they had wandered into our empty side street. The sound woke me and sent me back to sleep. I finally woke when it was quite light. I lay there and didn't get up, for a few minutes longer trying to hold on to the inexplicable feeling of vague joy that had possessed me all night.

Without a knock the door opened. Mama hurried into the room. No "Good morning", only the words: "Germany's attacked!"

Why do we often have happy dreams before misfortune strikes? I don't know.

But Lermontov's lines (from "My Demon") read:

> He'll show an image of perfection
> And suddenly seize it back for ever
> And having giv'n of bliss a premonition
> Will never give me happiness.

All remember what happened to them on 22 June 1941. One man immediately received his papers, went to the military registration office and from that day was no longer in control of himself. Another was not called up but went there anyway or to the local Party committee and demanded, begged and insisted that he be sent to the front. A third was horrified and took fright. And yet another learned that war had started while everyone else was sleeping: he was staying at the dacha and listening to foreign broadcasts on the radio. He took the earliest local train to Moscow and stood first in line outside the Savings Bank. At exactly 8.00 a.m., he managed to withdraw all the money from his account. He had his wits about him. The order to freeze the nation's savings until the end of the war came a little while after.

I have heard all kinds of stories about those first days of the war. Yet one detail has never appeared in private stories, film documentaries or fictional accounts. They talk of the volunteers and of the appearance in the city of anti-aircraft guns and balloons. But nowhere do they say that all the younger generation went out into the street.

During a good summer, Moscow has its own "white nights" at the end of June and in July. Darkness falls for only an hour or so and passes without notice. No-one wants to sleep. The night of 22–3 June, young people understood that the hour had come to prove themselves or die. Agitated, they could not stay at home. They wanted to be together, not with their families.

During the first day, some groups went in an organised fashion to Red Square. Only shortly before, they had been greeted here on graduating from secondary school and celebrated the beginning of a new life. This time, no-one met them. It was not the time or place. The next groups spread out across the city. They were joined by still others. But they did not form up in columns, link arms, sing or carry posters. Steadily, they filled the streets and simply walked, in twos or threes but mostly on their own, silently, only occasionally exchanging a word with those next to them. Pensive and disturbed, they were saying their farewells to Moscow's streets and courtyards and to one another. A generation went to meet its destiny.

On one such day, I left the Historical Museum together with Khardjiev. We were not very talkative.

"A writer died today," Khardjiev interrupted the silence.

"Who was it?"

"Zoshchenko."

"No!?"

"Zoshchenko's characters have died. And another writer has been born again:

> Like thundering hammers
> Or the waters of enraged seas
> The golden heart of Russia
> Beats steadily in my breast.

The lines were from Nikolai Gumilyov's poem "The Attack" (1914).[104]

Chapter 21

The museum researcher so recently snubbed by the exhibition designers had been a ballerina in her youth, it was said. She preserved the "refined" gait and gestures that professional dancers do not display in everyday life. At the museum, she found herself a devoted assistant, a new boy with an effeminate manner. With love and eagerness, he readily performed the tasks he was given by the former ballerina and future Lermontov authority. He himself had no future. On the first day of war he disappeared: had he been called up, summoned elsewhere or sent on some mission? Soon, very soon, we were informed, in somewhat vague terms, that he had already been killed. He appeared briefly and vanished without trace, the lithe boy with the open smile.

No-one else involved in the exhibition had yet been called up. But of course we could not shut ourselves off from events. These steadily became ever more menacing, but we continued to work with such intensity that we even made a joke of it: "We have only two goals, to capture Berlin and open our exhibition." It seemed to us that Berlin would be taken without our help, and very soon at that. The reports from the Sovinformburo had not yet killed this hope. But gradually, we began to hear that our forces were abandoning one town after another. Ender

---

[104] Published in the October 1914 issue of *Apollon*, the poem was also recited by Gumilyov at the Stray Dog Cabaret in December, when he was in Petrograd on three days' leave from the front.

came into the museum with the news that a truck filled with people had only just driven across Red Square to the Zamoskvoreche district. Unbelievable tension was written on their faces. Had they just escaped from a battle? For the time being, we worked only more furiously on hearing such reports. "Are you all made of iron?" the woman attendant supervising our room asked me in amazement. It was unusually hot in Moscow. The windows had already been sealed for the exhibition; now the museum's other rooms were also blacked out. We gasped in the dreadful stuffiness. Our exhibits, meanwhile, were being stored in the basement. Each day we dragged them in heavy cases up to the very top of that enormous building, directly below the burning-hot roof, clambering up and down the staircases (there were no lifts there) and crossing to our side through the connecting rooms on the second floor.

Our woman attendant said she had met an old colleague in the Party. He described the German tanks as an enormous advancing herd of monsters. There was no way of stopping them: "But we can't just lay down and die. We must fight back," he said.

These extraordinary events prompted memories of her youth during the Civil War. She came from Astrakhan Province and their village constantly changed hands. The women hid themselves, but when the Reds began to gain the upper hand they came out of hiding. They ran round the backs of the houses to greet the victors, crying: "But where are our Communists? Where are our Communists?" "We'll find them," came the answer. They tracked down the local peasant men and with threats led them to the bank of the Volga. "Dig them out!" they ordered. "The men turned white as your kerchief," she continued. "There in the pit all our Communists were lying. There was one woman among them. Then in front of us they shot the diggers . . . And such a beautiful bridge across the Volga and how the scent of acacia hung in the air!"

Among the Reds who entered the village was her future husband. With him she travelled the length and breadth of the country because he became a prosecutor and was sent to different districts. Then he began going away on business, taking a woman inspector with him. "I was so grief-stricken I finished up in hospital, and he came to see me. What was there to talk about, though, if that inspector was already in the family way?"

As always, I popped out of the museum during the lunch break and went to a summer café under large umbrellas.

Not far from me, two men were sitting at a table. In a steady voice, without pauses or exclamations, one was telling the other: ". . . our girls smeared their faces with coal and wrapped themselves up in any old rags in order to look like old women. I walked on, and when I reached the edge of the village there 'he' was . . ." The epic tone betrayed his deeply felt alarm. He had managed to get out of a village occupied by the Germans.

. . . I'm coming back from some club where I have lectured to an audience of policemen about the Patriotic War of 1812. With me I carry a mobile display, and it's so heavy that one of the policeman is accompanying me. We wait to cross the road near the Belorussky railway station. Vehicles race down the Leningrad Highway: trucks, cars and motorcycles. My companion points to certain of the motorcycles: "Those are coming back from the front." And those also, I say, but I'm looking at the wrong vehicles. My escort can tell which is which without fail, by the kind of mud on the machines and the faces of the riders. He knows the people scurrying into the metro. Those are the usual passengers but that fellow comes from somewhere else. . . .

The front was near, and aerial bombing became more frequent. It had begun on 23 July. The attacks came day and night. "Aha! Here comes Adolf!" boasted the young anti-aircraft gunner who had been caught out in the street. We hid under a roof covering the open corner of a multistorey block: there was no time to run to the shelter. Klavdia Surikova was still working at the Literary Museum. She left her first-floor room dressed in a sheepskin coat and boots and came over to my desk to say goodbye: she was going out in a truck to dig trenches on the far approaches to Moscow. Silently, she took a sheet of paper lying on the desk, a programme of lectures for those in anti-aircraft defence, and on the back she wrote:

> Where is it, that far-off gilded horizon
> Of the enchanted Hesperides?

> 1/9-41 For Emma

I have never found out where these two lines come from.

Subsequently, she was evacuated with her daughter to Kazakhstan, returned to Moscow and for many years remained Bonch-Bruyevich's private secretary. She brought her daughter up by herself and helped her acquire a good profession as a doctor.

People were waiting for the new "master", as our maid Polya put it. She equated the possible arrival of the Germans in Moscow with her own experiences. When you go to work at a new place, you worry and wonder what the new master will be like. But you take one look, and you see you can get on with these bosses as well. At the beginning of the war, she was mobilised to work on the labour front. She went to dig trenches. Returning for a day, she told us that there were only women working there, while a male supervisor strode about and herded them like cattle. "If someone clever would only come and see what's going on. If only they saw!"[105]

To replace Polya, we had a temporary maid from elsewhere. During air raids, she would take her basket of belongings and sit clutching it in the courtyard, paying no heed to those still in the house. Even such a heartless egotist, however, spoke truly when she commented on the speeches of the leader of Moscow's Communists that poured from the loudspeakers during the intervals between reports from the Sovinformburo, air-raid warnings and all-clear signals. "At such times you should say something special," she commented. "You want to hear something out of the ordinary." Probably she meant something that suited that exceptional moment. So far as patriotic feeling is concerned, Russians do not need such appeals; it's in their blood.

The monotonous radio broadcasts were also interrupted by pseudo-folk music. The rollicking songs to an accordion accompaniment not only shocked me, a "refined intellectual", but also the ordinary people who made up the mixed and rather odd crowd on the streets of Moscow. One man jeered with irony and hatred: "It's a good accordion too!"

I was going out the gates of our hospital garden. "That's it then," the gatekeeper told me. "You lot are in for it now. The Germans are already in Belye Stolby." I imagined the tanks crushing my parents but somehow pulled myself together and thought in amazement: So that's what it feels like. You're going to face some horror, and yet you don't lose your wits. Only from that day onwards did I stop thinking about our labour camps and cease to imagine the torments, misery, hunger and cold that people endured there. As concerns Belye Stolby, the gatekeeper was probably passing on an inaccurate rumour. The Germans had not yet approached Moscow from that direction during this first part of the war.

The Literary Museum was then almost next to the Kremlin (later the building was taken over by the Kalinin Museum). The Nazis' best pilots bombed the area with a special fury. The deep crater that appeared in the centre of Manege Square after one night-time raid was testimony to their efforts. Even more frightening was the collapse of the house directly adjacent to the museum. There, opposite the "Lenin Library" metro station, stood part of a four-storey residential block (later public toilets

---

[105] Three-quarters of a million Muscovites, the great majority of them women, were mobilised to dig defensive trenches in 1941.

and a café occupied the site). It had been torn in two by high explosive in a direct hit. The apartments on the building's next staircase were left without their fourth wall. The empty room on the last floor made a particular impression. From the street you could clearly see the pattern on the wallpaper, the pictures hung so touchingly over the bed and the bed itself. Many of the inhabitants were buried under the rubble, and it took several days to dig them out.

That was the ominous sight which greeted us when we came to work in the morning.

Ilovayskaya, who had behaved so insolently in taking Klavdia Surikova's job, proved a heroic woman. She had just spent a difficult night on the roof as a firewatcher, bravely and fearlessly extinguishing incendiary bombs. Her life was as hard as Surikova's, but she was living with her mother, not a daughter. A few times I visited her small room with its little painted wooden sideboard, decorated with a colourful curtain behind the upper glass panel of its only door. That was where she took the cleanly washed cups when offering me tea: "Let's enjoy what we have". A male friend, who apparently did not have a job and perhaps suffered from a drink problem, would come to see her. This room was his only refuge in Moscow, the one place where he felt secure. Her colleagues at work took a simpler view: they criticised and pitied her and, putting themselves in her place, asserted that they would never allow themselves to be exploited in that way. But you cannot deprive people of the urge for human contact, as necessary for the one who gives as for the one who takes.

Towards the end of the war, or, more probably, after it was over, Ilovayskaya began to suffer from a brain disease that sharpened her senses and perceptions of other people almost to the point of clairvoyance. This lasted for several years. Eventually, she died of this illness. I had not managed to give back the ten roubles I'd borrowed from her. How can someone take money from a seriously ill woman? You can, it seems, when you are catastrophically short of money yourself and it is offered to you in such a comradely fashion. For this was already the period of the "struggle against cosmopolitanism" or, in other words, of unemployment for Jews.

The reports from the Sovinformburo became increasingly alarming. The Fascist forces were racing towards Moscow. Children were already being evacuated. Still based at the Historical Museum, we modestly played our part, but morale in our "unit" also began to decline. One of the designers referred to his "naked nerves". Irakly Andronikov could not get to the front because Fadeyev had instructed him to join the fleet, but not a single boat had yet sunk. In other words, no vacancy had appeared for Irakly. Soon our designers sent their wives to be evacuated, and then Andronikov saw his wife and daughter Manana off to Kazan. I began to get anxious. I vaguely imagined the existence that awaited me: air-raid alarms, total isolation and confinement to the house. Irakly reproached me for flashes of despondency, saying that he did not recognise me. Of course, I was making frequent visits to military hospitals, but it felt as if I spent all four years of the war at the bottom of some crater.

The siege of Leningrad had already begun. The Communist ladies from the Paris Exhibition, invited to the Lermontov jubilee by our designers, no longer concealed their fear.

Finally, Irakly left. He went to Kazan to join his family. We said goodbye. He found it unbearably shameful and turning to face the wall, like a naughty 13-year-old schoolboy, he burst into tears, wiping his nose with both hands. Then, loudly blowing into a large handkerchief, he mumbled, "I can't help it . . . Manana . . ."

Several years later when he had long returned from the war (he ended up working for a newspaper at the front), he dropped the words "I remember", with a special intonation, into a conversation on quite another theme. It was a hint at our dramatic parting. That "I remember" was all I needed to hear.

In every home and in every family, people discussed whether to leave Moscow or stay. Little was yet known about the atrocities of the Fascists.

Lena's family faced a distressing choice: should they all leave together, or only send away Lena with the children, eight-year-old Tanya and two-year-old Lilya? During one of those days, her friends and a neighbour were sitting in her apartment. With them were a young educated Jewish woman and an actress friend. Both discouraged Lena from going away anywhere.

Tongues wagged freely, and the neighbour suggested that after the horrors of 1937 nothing worse could happen. The actress, who performed at the Maly Theatre and came from the Volga area, was a beautiful woman who spoke wonderful Russian; she agreed.

"But how will we bear the humiliation if the Germans take over Moscow?" I asked doubtfully.

"What of it? We'll take our humiliation like the rest of Europe," was the imperturbable response of the woman from the Volga.

Yet another relative of the NKVD neuropathologist appeared at our apartment. He was an older man in a military uniform with a red band around his cap, just returned from the Baltic States. In the corridor he met my father and, staggered by what had happened, gave an account of their retreat from Riga. "They were shooting at us from every window, firing at our backs!" I quickly returned to my room. That evening, our neighbour, the neuropathologist, said we must leave Moscow. He was travelling with his family on a special train. He offered to take Papa and all his family. Apart from me.

Papa refused. I argued with him, saying that he would find work anywhere. But he pointed out that he could no longer operate: his hands shook and his sight was failing (he had cataracts). In our egotistical way, we, his children, had not noticed this.

I could see the German tanks rolling over his body and begged my father to accept. "But they're already near Mozhaisk," I said in a panic. "Well, if they take Moscow then the same will happen in the most remote parts of the Union." Papa resolutely refused to budge. "Everything will collapse and then it won't matter where we are."

Bombing raids were ever more frequent in our Moskvoreche district, and the bombs were falling nearer and nearer. I lay down to sleep in my clothes. If a bomb hit us, I was afraid to be caught in my nightdress. What a ninny, to be concerned with preserving my modesty beneath the rubble!

I know of another similar case. Refugees came to us from Tula. I was supposed to send these elderly acquaintances to their children and grand-children in Saratov. Their Tula apartment had lost its roof, and, for days on end, they had been sitting unwashed, frozen and hungry as the shells dropped all round. Suddenly, the old man turned to his wife: "Franechka, you really should go to the hairdresser's! Have your hair done."

So we stayed. Without time even to say farewell to our parents, both my brothers were sent away to Magnitogorsk on the metro-construction company's train and thence to a factory. They made the whole journey in carriages from the Underground.

It was during these tense days that Akhmatova appeared in Moscow. She was sent, as everyone knows, on an aeroplane from besieged Leningrad. Although Moscow was being bombed, it was not under artillery fire, which Akhmatova simply could not bear. She was in a bad way. She warned that Moscow would experience the same cold and hunger – there would be nothing left, not food, not firewood, not paraffin.

Only later did I learn of the situation in which Akhmatova had found herself in the besieged city from the stories and letters of Zoya Tomashevskaya. Together with Anna Yevgenyevna, their daughter Ira and grandchild Anya, Punin and the entire Academy of Arts were evacuated to Samarkand. Akhmatova remained alone in the empty apartment on Fontanka. The Tomashevskys took her in. But they themselves could not live in their fourth-floor apartment with a broken lift; they were already much weakened by hunger. The caretaker gave them somewhere to stay, perhaps in the basement. That was where the Tomashevskys brought

Akhmatova. She sent the caretaker to buy her some cigarettes.
On the street he was killed
instantly by an artillery shell. It
is hardly surprising, then, that
Akhmatova reached Moscow in
a distressed and depressed state.

A woman escorted Akh-
matova on the plane after her
relative had requested Akhmatova to take her into evacuation. I was surprised that she
was not at all worried about me.
Akhmatova was greeted in
Moscow as the personification
of bravery and resolution. First
she stayed with Marshak and
then with a sister of Olga
Berggolts[106] in Kislovsky Street.
During those days everyone
was wondering how they would
leave the city, where they would
go and who would take them

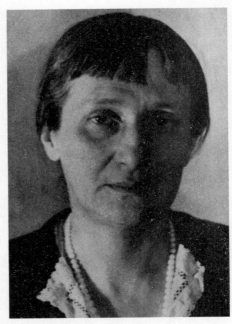

Anna Akhmatova, 1941

there. This anxiety had reached a climax, apparently, by the time I came
to see her. A great many writers had gathered. They talked only about
evacuation. Where would it be best to go? The names of different towns
came up in conversation – Chistopol, Sverdlovsk, Kazan, Kuybyshev,
Tashkent, Alma-Ata . . .

Pasternak was extremely excitable. He told Akhmatova how he was
training with the home guard and, in an imaginary conversation, jokingly
threatened the chief editor of Iskusstvo publishers: "I can shoot as well,
you know!" Pasternak wanted to sign a contract with them to write a
"new, free" play. But the editor turned him down: "We don't yet know
what kind of dramas you write. If you offer us a translation, I'll be only
too glad."

Akhmatova lay on the divan and addressed him in the words of
Chekhov's character Firs: "They've forgotten about someone." Which
meant: I want to be evacuated together with you, my friends. Somehow

---

[106] The poet Olga Berggolts (1910–1975) remained in Leningrad throughout
the blockade, working for the city's radio station and keeping a daily record of
events in prose and verse.

she had not a thought for me. But after leaving her side Pasternak glanced nervously at me several times. Finally, he came up and asked quietly: "And how will you be leaving?"

That evening, Akhmatova realised that I was not among the country's "living treasures" and that no place had been set aside for me in any of the trains. Whereupon she learned that all she had to do was officially inform Litfond that she needed someone to accompany her and give them my name. She was so convinced it would work that we made firm plans. I was to come to her very early the next morning, bringing only a small bag containing the bare essentials. But this also meant resolving to leave my parents. In those critical days, this proved a harsh ordeal.

They would find it easier if I was not with them, I thought. My parents were being looked after by my sister, her husband and their children. The husband was Russian and came from Vologda. We were still naive enough to suppose that this relationship would help my Jewish family survive under the Nazis. And anyway, would the Germans take Moscow? Papa did not believe in their victory. Naturally, that evening was one of the most difficult of my life. Finally, however, I decided to leave with Akhmatova.

At 8 a.m. I rang the doorbell at the Berggolts' apartment. The sister opened the door and said that Pasternak had rushed in during the night and announced that the carriages were standing ready at the platform: They must take their places without delay. And off they went.

I walked along the street in tears. Round about flew scraps of torn documents and Marxist political brochures, swept along by the wind. At the hairdresser's, there were not enough chairs to serve all their clients and the ladies stood in a queue along the pavement. The Germans were coming, they must get their hair done.

When I got to the museum, the staff were about to go to various military units and read them lectures or serve in the anti-aircraft defences. Having glanced at me, our director, Polina Lvovna, immediately saw that I was in no condition to appear before any audience today. Many had a similar appearance then. It was 16 October 1941. A day of panic, unexpected partings, tragic farewells and, quite simply, flight.

On that day, the entire government left Moscow. Papa said that Stalin had told his colleagues: "Do as you like, but I shall return!"[107]

Suetin probably heard the same story. Turning to Khardjiev, he said: "Surely you can see now, Stalin is a genius." Khardjiev argued with him but in the end agreed: "Yes, he's a genius, but in a negative sense." The artists did not accept Khardjiev's "grumbling", as they thought it, but what he said made sense. He laughed at the camouflage draped over all

---

[107] The Soviet dictator did not leave Moscow during the war.

the tall and politically important buildings. The Germans had long ago acquired the most detailed maps of Moscow, and their expert pilots would use them when attacking the Soviet capital.

In those days of flight, Khardjiev jokingly said to me: "Well, I want to go to Iran. The English are there. Now that's a delectable form of oppression." Nevertheless, in the very first weeks of the war he predicted, for all his scepticism, that the Germans were bound to lose. "The coalition always wins," he said with assurance.

Very soon after, Polina Lvovna gathered together all the museum staff who remained in Moscow. She gave a tragic speech and announced that she was leaving the city on foot. She advised us to follow her example. To those who could not walk or leave their family, she offered a few last words of advice: "Burn your Party and Komsomol membership cards, and do not forget to destroy your trade-union workbooks." That struck me as laughable. Did the Germans really hold such a ridiculous view of Soviet life? Every white-collar worker automatically joined a trade union here. However, in the villages – i.e. the collective farms – there were no office employees, but there were activists, managers, agronomists, veterinarians, accountants and supply workers who were all linked to the district centre. The peasants evidently took pleasure in denouncing them. The first indication of their position, probably, was their trade-union card.

Meanwhile in the museum's personnel department they were hastily burning and tearing up our forms and documents, including our workbooks.

There was no way they could conceal the shattering defeat we were experiencing and that our army was surrounded. All you had to do was open *Pravda* and look at the leading article to understand what was happening on the different fronts. When the newspaper exhorted those fighting to cherish their weapons as the apple of their eye, you already realised that soldiers were fleeing the front. You would wait for a tram or trolley-bus, and as it slowed down to pick you up the entire carriage was humming. But as soon as you climbed aboard, with your educated face, everyone fell silent. From the echoes of the dying argument, you could tell that they were all discussing the same thing: how could a fighter abandon his weapon and leave the front? And there he was, the hero of this debate. He defended himself by attacking the high command – it was quite impossible to fight. In a little while, his agitated audience ceased to be inhibited by your presence. One called him a deserter and traitor to the Motherland, others laid all the blame on the authorities but not, of course, on Stalin. Later I asked soldiers who had escaped encirclement how their officers had behaved. "What officers? Everything was a muddle there, and in each group they all decided together what to do, where they should go and how they'd get there. The one who made the most sense was the one they followed." And how had they gone into battle? What were the war cries they had yelled? "What did we shout? 'For Stalin!' What do you expect?"

All the wings at our hospital were reserved for wounded soldiers. When the air-raid alarms sounded, the walking wounded were transferred to the bomb shelter. Once an officer leaped out of the shelter and, swaying and shaking, almost shouted: "It's a hundred times better at the front. You sit shut up here, you can't see the enemy and wait to see whether he'll finish you off or not. Nothing could be worse." The majority of the wounded refused to go down into the bomb shelter.

We had to close the Lermontov exhibition. The terrible events were taking their toll. I was driven out to the anti-aircraft defence units and to the railway depots – in a word, everywhere that those mobilised were living in barracks. With me I took the mobile exhibition about the war of 1812 and read patriotic lectures, which gave me satisfaction. Things went less well with our large exhibition.

Having closed it down, all that was left was to help pack up the exhibits, return them to the museums in Moscow (if that was possible before their evacuation) and prepare the rest to be sent eastwards. In the now empty rooms, we organised another topical exhibition about the war. Fortunately, this was made up of photographs so we didn't have to close it down even after the bombs started falling on Moscow. Now we did not carry heavy loads up the stairs from the basement, but instead hid there ourselves beneath the massive vaults of that typical 1890s building, a solid construction in the pseudo-Russian style preferred by the merchant class.

A great amount of space at the new exhibition was given over to material about the progressive foreign intelligentsia, whom I could not stand because of their rapturous and cheap pronouncements about the USSR. Romain Rolland, who visited Moscow in 1936, particularly irritated me. *Pravda* published his report about the strict-regime penitentiary for juvenile offenders run by the NKVD. It was the living embodiment of Jean-Jacques Rousseau's deepest longings, he said. After such words I lost interest in the author of the nine-volume *Jean-Christophe* saga (1904–12) and the shorter "Enchanted Soul" books of which I had been so fond as an adolescent. I was very glad when we received orders from above to make fewer references to Rolland since he was living in a country occupied by the Germans and our praise might harm him.

With or without Rolland, the patriotic exhibition we organised was quite a phoney and arbitrary presentation. Here I encountered a phenomenon I would observe throughout the war and even into the post-war years: the weekly documentary stills issued by TASS.[108] Our photographers, who genuinely deserved the tag "heroic", took wonderful pictures on the various fronts of the Great Patriotic War. I could call their work "The Human Face of the Frontline". Not because they prettied up the cruel face of war but because among their photos the portrait features of living people could be found. Certain of the reporters chose their subjects with the attentiveness of true artists. Naturally, this was not during the heat of battle, nor in moments of retreat, defeat and encirclement: at least, we did not come across such ominous photographs in the TASS photo chronicle. But there were many pictures of soldiers when they had a little time to themselves, in the short breathing space between battles or arduous marches. These did not show Moscow actors performing for the soldiers on improvised stages or "spontaneous" dancing but human faces. Yet no matter how often I selected such original portraits, my superiors never approved them for the exhibition. Their conventional and empty gaze came to rest only on photos resembling the pictures they had glimpsed in the newspapers. To this day, we see those same images far too often at the cinema and on television. Wretched figures in clumsy greatcoats, running madly, bring shells for the guns, while all around shooting fills the air, the earth is hurled skyward, and someone drops unconscious while another has been killed.

In later years films appeared which showed real people, not these posed saccharine figures. Chukhrai's *Ballad of a Soldier* [1959] and *Clear Sky* [1961] come to mind; a while after came Vyacheslav Kondratyev's *Sashka* [1977], the writer's screen version of his good novella. But these were works of fiction. The genuine daily photo documentary of the war was not shown at the time. So it did not have an impact or fulfil its purpose. The efforts of those devoted and fearless photographers had been in vain.

Often the air-raid siren caught us out in the street. Then we all ran for the nearest bomb shelter. Once I found myself in the cellar of an unfamiliar building and in total darkness. My immediate neighbour distracted me with his tall tales, though he could not see my face. In our village, he said, one woman died of laughter. How did that happen? Well, she began to laugh and couldn't stop, the devil tickled her to death. Two girls interrupted his story: "Let's go and catch some spies!" one said to the other. Just before our December counter-attack, I hid from the raids in a good shelter beneath a tall, brick-built apartment block. There a *chuika* was holding forth. (In the nineteenth century a long coat of that name became the distinguishing garb of, and even title

---

[108] Telegraph Agency of the Soviet Union, the main official news outlet.

applied to, urban petty bourgeois.) The German would come by sea, the *chuika* assured us, but Fritz had no ports he could use, and nowhere to land. That's why he was trying to reach Odessa and other Black Sea ports. The German ate nothing but swedes and was a formidable enemy. This discourse was interrupted by a sensible woman who had a clear goal in mind. Deftly she turned the conversation to Rokossovsky (the December assault was just about to begin).[109] She drew the usual fairy-tale portrait: first he checked the soldiers' food and their boots, only then he turned to military questions. The *chuika* could not help blurting out: "You've fallen for him, have you?" "Women don't love such men," she replied. "They go for the sensitive, tender ones."

She was very well turned out. The plait on her head was neatly tied, her mouth was lightly lipsticked, and all her clothes were pressed and tidy. You came across such types ever more frequently on the streets. The official morale-boosters. It was their job. Once I was walking across Kamenny Bridge and there were almost no pedestrians. A woman walked towards me. As we drew level, she said quietly as she passed: "Our lads have taken Porokhov." Or she named some other town or village, which no less than three days earlier the Sovinformburo had announced that we had abandoned. Only they are deceived, however, who wish to be deceived.

Those who returned briefly on leave from the front displayed a striking-ly business-like attitude. They never indulged in "fisherman's tales" about their military exploits and gave the same answer to all questions: "We're doing our job." Over the phone, fellow-soldiers would part with the phrase, "Stay alive."

By midsummer 1942, we were reassured to find that vegetables were nevertheless growing in the Moscow Region and even in the city itself. Hunger diminished.

Once I glanced out of the window and saw someone in military uniform walking along the path through the hospital grounds towards our house. He limped and was using a stick. I did not immediately recognise Sergei Rudakov. The last time we had seen each other was when the blackout was first put up in Leningrad, on 1 December 1939. Today his eyes were radiant. There was nothing surprising about that. At the field hospital they had believed him to be mortally wounded, and he was also suffering from shellshock. This affected his speech, and

---

[109] Arrested in 1937, Rokossovsky survived the Purges of the Red Army. Made major-general in June 1940, he commanded one of the armies defending Moscow in late 1941.

he muddled up the syllables in words. The tale of his miraculous escape
was recorded in a discursive tract he composed, describing his progress
from the battles at Malaya Dubrovka to the rear in Moscow. (It has been
published in the yearly almanac of the manuscript section at Pushkin
House, and so I give no details here.)

In Moscow began the happiest period of his life, though regrettably
it was soon brought to an end. I witnessed the joy with which Boris
Tomashevsky enveloped Rudakov in a wide embrace, never expecting
to see him alive again. Indeed he asked him: "You've come back from
the other world, have you?" That was in the garden in front of the
Institute of World Literature, where elderly scholars and Tomashevsky,
now evacuated from Leningrad, had gathered for a session of the
Pushkin commission. This was not Rudakov's first appearance in literary circles under the new guise of a valiant warrior who had been
wounded but who retained the dazzling military bearing of his fore-
bears. All the time until August 1943 he soared as if on wings in frontline Moscow. To begin with, he simply had not dared to hope that he
could achieve so much nor that his activities would enjoy such undisputed success. This is evident in his first letters to his wife from Moscow.
Here he was, overjoyed by such an insignificant event, in my view, as
a visit to the Writers' Union: "Today attended the closing session of
the literary criticism symposium at the Writers' Union," he told Lina.
"I got in, thanks to Seifullina (?!). It happened like this: I know her
niece from *Zvezda*, and she proposed that through her aunt (in fact,
with her aunt) we go and listen to the discussion about my profession
as a publisher's reader."

It heartened him to mix with famous writers:

> For the first time, I saw and in part heard Fadeyev, Seifullina
> herself, Sobolev, Shchipachov, Kozhevnikov . . . and again
> Utkin, who has lost his fingers and is now monumentally fat,
> Lebedev-Kumach, Ehrenburg once again, and for the first
> time, Efros, Nusinov and Kirsanov, plump and in a white
> soldier's shirt, as you would like me to appear.
>
> During the interval a very kindly Ivan Rozanov.
>
> And you remember the herald in "Prince Kurbsky":
> suddenly the herald rides in "parting the crowd, a letter tucked
> beneath his hat". Like that, "parting the crowd", Shklovsky
> rushed over to me, thundering: "S.B., I have written a theo-
> retical work that will not be published until we have read it
> together and discussed it . . . And what about your sequel
> to the *Bronze Horseman*?"

In a word, he knows how to advertise himself (in this case, verbally). The crowd turned to look . . . I felt wonderful. The silence is broken. I can talk and I can think, for I cannot think in silence.

After such a start, he delivered a whole series of triumphal addresses at scholarly gatherings in some museum or library where elderly and half-starved professors had gathered. They felt awkward not to be fighting and therefore listened to the oratorical passion of the young scholar with a special paternal affection. The more pleasure he took in his success and recognition, unfortunately, the less satisfied he felt with his position in society. In his letters to his wife, he constantly returned to these themes. I did not know of these hidden disappointments and only saw him as kindly and filled with inspiration. It was not until the 1980s when I gained access to all his letters to Lina that I learned of this worm gnawing away inside him.

Acquaintance with Marina Tsvetayeva's manuscripts and photographs was a breathtaking experience for Rudakov, and he gave a most subtle characterisation of her work and photographic portraits. Yet the experience prompted a return to his constant sense of grievance: "This viewing had a devastating effect on my nervous system. What do I want? With whom should I be among the human mass? Where are my rights?" And he continued once again to develop his *idée fixe*:

> I have the feeling that if somewhere I was recognised for myself, and not just as an educator, teacher, student or draughtsman, then I would feel more at peace. The thing is that I don't like having to work [for money], but I'm ready to edit any blasted devils if only they'd recognise me and not think of me as some government clerk.

Being in roughly the same situation myself, I had no idea how desperately it tormented him. I readily shared with him a feeling of joy that he had survived and also myself did not lose hope of a better future. From other letters to Lina (during her lifetime she read me only excerpts), you may read how we spent our time in frontline Moscow. More than once he recalled the delicious piece of goose I had prepared for him (it came on my ration coupons), and how we either went to the market to sell the vodka he was issued at the military registration office or drank it ourselves. These "pleasures" were a little hampered by the disapproving looks of my sister. It was a pity, she thought, I was feeding the goose to him; she had given me some bread only on the strict understanding

that I would return it by mealtime (she ran a separate household within
the apartment and managed to keep her two children fed with difficulty). This episode is reflected in the merry record I made, witnessed
by Sergei's signature, after we had been drinking vodka together.

Two Quarters

4 February 1943

Here begins the diary I was too lazy to keep in 1942.
However, I shall retrospectively add all the entries for 1942.
That's for later.

With Sergei Borisovich, who truly is the namesake of my
favourite rosy-cheeked 14½-year-old nephew, we today drank
a half-litre of vodka together. But S[ergei] B[orisovich]
corrected me: "Not half a litre but two quarters." And there
is a difference. For two quarters are grander to the tune of
7½ roubles.

For the first time, Sergei visited me wearing his shoulder
boards. He is that same ensign. I have always loved ensigns
and since my Lermontov period have felt closely linked with
them. Poor Irakly (with his wife Viviana Robinson and daughter Manana Vivianovna) imagined, in the simplicity of his
barefaced soul, that all senior lieutenants are the heroes of
our time. How primitive! No, I correct myself, how unimagina-
tive. That's the Moskva Hotel[110] for you.

And so 1 February (or 01.02 as the military say) the caretaker asked S.B. for a half-litre, now he has his shoulder boards,
and some dame, a typical middle-aged lady, said that just such
ensigns had courted her when she was younger and more
beautiful (cf. "Yevgeny Onegin"), since Khardjiev declares that
literature stands between the world and S.B. And S.B. declares
that nothing, alas, stands between Khardjiev and the world.
This polemic arose because I have been a gossip since birth,
and Maria's Grove is the habitation, by turns, of Khardjiev,
Tsvetayeva and Rudakov. I must correct that, Tsvetayeva was
there as a visitor. While S.B. adds, in the words of Davydov,
"I was on the Linde, but only passing through."

---

[110] Symbol in the early 1930s of the reconstructed Soviet capital, the imposing
Moskva Hotel was erected next to the Kremlin.

To which I should add that crazy Mikhail Matveyevich, a noble correspondent, muddled up everything and mistook an angel who appeared at the front for Lyova Gumilyov. S.B. insists I write down that Marina [Tsvetayeva] mentioned this: "There are those with enormous wings and there are those without wings." Though as it turns out, Lyova has long ceased to be an angel, which Mikhail Matveyevich forgot, and is at the museum not as an exhibit but as a research associate. God send him success and a tolerable character.

Yet the most important thing is that Sergei Borisovich turned out to be an angel, unrecognised by anyone, and brought us potatoes, and a great many of them.

The bread would be desirable by mealtime (this was added by S.B. Rudakov).

That was how we amused ourselves or distracted one another from all the mishaps of war. Moreover, Sergei had not yet lost the joyful excitement stirred by his ever-growing success. It should be admitted that he enjoyed not only success in literary and scholarly circles, which was quite proper for his work, but also the purely decorative moments of his essentially innocent activities in the Moscow adult education programme. On the night of 30 April and 1 May, he was already describing in his latest letter to Lina the ceremonial gathering on the eve of May Day: "And there they grandly presented me with a certificate," he rejoiced. "I could not have expected such delicacy from the military commander – to organise and devise these certificates, print them and have me issue them to everyone else and then by special order award one to me and even ring up the department head to bring it round unexpectedly."

I recall this most characteristic detail so as to explain why he was no longer satisfied with my company. By that time I was in a very difficult position. Rudakov made egotistical reference to this: he needed a woman he could talk to, who would serve as a captive audience. This is what he wrote of me in June 1943:

Things are going very badly for her. They not only did not admit her to the [Writers'] Union but also removed her entitlement to some of the residual, intermediary links of the semi-academic [food] supply [system]. She was earning money by giving blood. That also came to an end, for some reason. She's in a state of wild melancholy and real despair. Which is all quite extraordinary since she has dazzling recommendations from the same Tsyavlovsky, Eichenbaum, Brodsky,

Manuilov etc. And she's doing serious work. Her "duels" and "circle of 16"[111] are linked to her name and mentioned in any feeble article and in the volumes of "Literary Heritage" and so on.

"But it is all in vain," Rudakov naively concluded. "She has had more than ten articles published now. There is nevertheless some kind of idiot within her, an incapacity and hostility towards people, a disdain of the Mandelstam kind, which evidently spoils everything else."

This explanation is so primitive that I have no desire to replace it with the true – that is to say, political – reason for such ostracism. Still, from these letters it is clear that husband and wife had already evolved a negative attitude to my publications: "You write about Emma, that things are as they should be. It's not quite like that," wrote Rudakov. "Her works on Lermontov are better than we thought." Essentially, he was a kind and noble man, and it seems that he felt uneasy running me down at the same time as we had spent the difficult wartime days together in such a friendly fashion. Yet his accustomed egotism nevertheless also came into play here: "I no longer have the sense of any competition. All the same, for me these Unions are not enough. They do not define me."

This clannish scepticism towards all who did not belong to the Leningrad school – i.e. who were not working within the narrow bounds of the Formal method – was typical of those who came immediately after the "advance party" but not for its founders. Shklovsky said the recommendations I received were "poems in the form of prose" and himself gave me such a dazzling reference that I remain proud of it to this day. It did not do me the slightest good and I do not know where the original is now, but I have preserved an officially notarised copy:

To the administration of the Writers' Union
Comrade Gerstein is producing a new view of Lermontov.
She is not writing more books about books but is finding a new approach, and already we cannot work without her.
That is what it means to be a writer – that's to say, a primary source and not an editor.

V. Shklovsky
14 May 1943

---

[111] Gerstein's substantial 1940 studies of Lermontov were preceded by her more popular accounts of both subjects in the weekly press.

It was a "positive factor", he told me, that in the aforementioned references nowhere was it said that "you are industrious".

Of course, such recognition gave me a feeling of joy and reassurance.
Such an authority as the sharp and merciless Victor Shklovsky could be
trusted.

But no practical benefit came of his testimonial.

Slowly, I sank into the pit of my desperate situation.

Nikolai Antsiferov tried to help me, strenuously putting me forward
as an author for the Sovinformburo, the most rigidly official of all organs.

I was not able to write a single line for them except for those occasions
when the required note was intended for the All-Union Society for Cultural
Relations.[112] Then they printed two or three of my sketches. That was why
I rejoiced when the first parts of Zoshchenko's new novel *Before Sunrise*
appeared in two issues of *Krasnaya nov*. This stirred in me an appetite that
I had thought quite extinct for understanding literature as a whole. I jotted
down what were, perhaps, unorganised thoughts about the state of contemporary Soviet fiction. Impatiently, I awaited the third part of the novel so
as to analyse this new and topical work. What followed silenced me for a
long while: Zoshchenko's novel was banned and the next instalment did
not appear.[113] I cherish the following perhaps disorganised introduction as
a token of that brief state of heightened awareness:

27 October 1943

Like all contemporary writers, he is interested in psychology.

The great writers of the last century paved the way. But
they worked on different material. Extraordinary and
admirable people who were several decades ahead of their
contemporaries described ordinary, conventional people.
The life of the latter was stable. It had form. At the same
time, this steady form made events possible. Unexpected
events uncovered the unusual qualities of people. The ordinary, average human being had a character and a biography. The writer gazed into the depths of his soul and
uncovered extraordinary inner richness in the unexcep-
tional story of a life. The reader recognised himself and

---

[112] A branch of the Soviet propaganda effort, aimed principally at foreign sympathisers.
[113] Stopped by the authorities as "a piece of outrageous 'subjectivism' and
'psychologism'", the final instalment was published in the USSR only in 1972.

was grateful to the writer. He did not notice that the writer
had passed him through the filter of refined and delicate
art, and was making him a present of himself. There was
hardly any discussion of the methods of this art. The writer
was solitary. The critics barely rose to an understanding of
his mastery. The private life and existence of the writer
differed sharply from that of the average man. That was
in the order of things. But he was writing about what he
had gleaned among strangers. There was something that
made these strangers his fellow-men – and that was their
shared Fatherland, Russia. They wrote about it.

Now everything is different. Character is missing altogether. There are reflexes that are shaped by the pressure of
a multi-ton mechanised force. When the rhythm of that enormous machine is blocked by something, then feelings, tastes,
hopes and passions, sometimes timidly and sometimes with
unusual force, burst out into the open. And, O horrors! It
turns out that they are the same as they were fifty years ago.
Nothing has changed. There has been no enrichment.
Contemporary taste, style and the new personality do not
exist. The new form exists only in rhythm. In art, the contemporary style must be a rapid external tempo and a quite
immobile inner condition. But passions and the sense of
personality . . . without warning they illuminate that already
alien life, which does not belong to itself, and then disappear under the pressure of the insuperable. But who knows?
These flashes of summer lightning are perhaps the promise
of the future. "They shall some day wake in a distant sea
like a wave."

The contemporary writer cannot produce a biography or
novel without artificial and unnatural effort, neither can he
describe a life in which events aid the harmonious development of the personality.

We lack even the most basic qualities. There is no age.
Children, adolescents, adults and old people live one and the
same life. The drastic, astonishing changes that have been our
fate never entered man's dreams in the past century. Yet how
full and long his life was; he went through several meta-
morphoses, each time taking new form. While we remain the
same through all these upheavals. Therefore, a description of
the contemporary individual requires us to rip separate
episodes out of context, not to link them in an extended

narrative. Lev Tolstoy did just the same. His *Childhood, Youth*
. . . These are separate frames, isolated in his memory of
himself. Yet this produces the illusion of a continuous narrative. The air between the chapters aids this. Contemporary
scenes burst into an airless space.

The author does not claim to have created a novel allowing us to follow the life of his hero. He lays his cards on the
table and speaks only of separate incidents. They are different and varied. They do not seem to make us understand the
life of society and of the epoch. And how could we understand? What do we see now?

Zoshchenko does not deliberate or theorise. He has written a book about traumas.

The most astonishing thing is that this note was written on 27 October
and on 14 November 1943 Father died.

The end might have been expected any day. And indeed on 11 November
he suffered a brain haemorrhage, dying three days later in hospital.

He had his contradictions. I have a document in which, during the
First World War, the Red Cross thanks him for treating the wounded
like a true Christian. Papa, in fact, was very irritable, sharp and not above
administering a slap or two.

I constantly recall how my father lay dying before my eyes. There
was a war on, and all his dear ones, his entire "second family", so to
speak (there were already children and grandchildren there), had been
arrested. But we did not go into evacuation – Papa did not want to
leave. We lived as badly as everyone in Moscow. During the first
months of the war, moreover, when the Germans were advancing on
the city, it was almost like Leningrad. The one exception was bread,
which was in uninterrupted supply throughout the war, very good
bread. Manual workers daily received 800g, office workers 600g and
each of their dependants 400g, every day. I do not remember any
disruption of the supplies. But there was nothing else. There was no
heating, it was cold, and the bombing raids had begun. Could it get
any worse?

None of my friends had stayed behind and it was tense at home and
within the family. There was no sense of comfort. Meanwhile, Papa
would lie there and repeat: "Neither house nor home, no friends. And
where would I run to if I left?" He was suffering from sclerosis but
still served as the polyclinic director. He didn't see patients and could
not find the way home. Several times he got lost in Moscow. I went

to fetch him and meet him. Finally, he became worse; it was bitterly cold in the apartment and they admitted him to the hospital. Once when I was there he suffered another brain haemorrhage. And he looked at the corner of the room and saw death; it was incontrovertible. And his eyes read: "Into Thy hands I commit my life", that kind of expression. Resignation is not the word. Then he grew very unwell, and the doctors started doing something with oxygen and I could not go to him: I had the feeling that I would stop him from dying, and that he had already gone.

Later the nurse told me that when he was in great pain, he groaned: "O my poor little children, my poor little ones . . ." imagining all that awaited us.

When he died, all those who knew him said: "He was a great man"; "A great man has died." This, of course, led to a total change in our life as a family.

Everything was changing.

The wounded and those demobilised as invalids began to return from the front.

They told us little about life during the war but were settling mysterious scores among themselves of which I had no conception. Finding themselves at a Moscow market, those who'd been at the front exclaimed: "When are we going to crush you lot!"

Walking along the "Chistye prudy" Boulevard at twilight, I noticed two tank-drivers slashing at one another, silently, not uttering a sound, with short knives. It was some bestial duel. The rare pedestrians shrank away from them, and so did I.

In broad daylight, in peaceful conditions, a taciturn sailor stood at the head of the queue into the beer hall. At the other end was a jolly lad who kept larking around. It took the sailor only one moment to leave his place, approach the lad just as silently and give him a resounding clump on the back of the head. The other merely cried out: "What was that for?"

I noticed the cowed eyes of the inhibited soldiers, filled with shame as they met their beloved women. Their wives and girlfriends were overjoyed that they had survived, but the men were thinking: What kind of husbands and lovers are we going to be? – and were ashamed of their disabilities. Meanwhile, the first defenders of Moscow in 1941 were dying slowly in military hospitals outside the city, having never set eyes on the Soviet capital.

But on the tram I also observed two young soldiers released from hospital who were gazing at streets and houses of which they'd never

seen the like. They were in such euphoria that they peppered their exclamations with ecstatic obscenities. On the front seat of the carriage sat a
member of the Komsomol with a book in her hands. She reproached
the noisy youths, but they wouldn't shut up, and finally she burst out
in an indignant reprimand: "You should behave decently in public." One
of the exultant soldiers replied furiously: "Decently? This young man
only has one arm: tell me, is that decent?!" Only then did I notice that
his sleeve was empty from the shoulder down. And at that moment, he
seemed to wake up and realise that his future was spoiled for ever.

At the bread shop, a man with no legs was behaving hysterically, with
a lost despair, and those around regarded him with compassion. Then I
noted a lean man attentively examining the face of that cripple. Having
recognised him, he came up, bent down and quietly told him something. The unfortunate fellow's hair stood on end.

They took down the blackout, and the Sovinformburo issued triumphant
communiqués. We watched the Yalta and Teheran conferences on the
newsreels at the cinema. The second front was open. In the air you could
sense that the war was coming to an end. It was a time to mourn the
slain and anticipate imminent reunion with those who had survived and
been invalided out of the army. Many had been sent back from the front.
The streets of Moscow became lively, and sometimes you could spot a
pair of lovers, who had halted among the crowds. Happiness was written on their features, though ever more frequently I also saw that hang-
dog expression on the men's faces. It expressed disquiet for the future.
Too soon we found out that the ending of the war had not brought us
happiness either. I shall not describe the succession of staggering events
that ensued. All I can say is that for me a period began of decades "as
empty as a cannibal's yawn", to use Pasternak's phrase about the Thirty
Years' War.

In January 1944, soon after Father's death, came the news that Rudakov,
under arrest since the previous August, had been killed at the front. But
Akhmatova's arrival in Moscow from Tashkent in May as always brought
a fresh current into my existence, and in this case there were two pieces
of news of direct importance to me. Lyova had completed his term of
imprisonment in the camps, and, more important, Akhmatova handed
some of Mandelstam's manuscripts to me on behalf of Nadya for safekeeping.

Lyova's voluntary departure for the front and the resumption of our
correspondence during the war have already been described. Here is his
last, most substantial letter from occupied Germany:

Berlin, 14 September [1945]

My dear, my very dear Emmochka,

I received your angry letter and refrained from replying (for which I'm very pleased). Now I have received a cheerful note and am responding without delay, even point by point.

a) I have determined that no-one treats me better than you. God knows, why ever do you love me? I'm bad, evil-tempered and old and have a difficult character.

b) If all my "fiancées" were brought together in one place, it would make quite a good slave market, less than Stamboul but rivalling those in Trabizond or Jaffa. I never remember them, but I write to you. "Do you feel the difference?"

c) The inspection of the future bride certainly did take place, but it did not at all have the goals you suppose. The error arose, as I now understand, as a consequence of Khardjiev's sexual inadequacy. But I shall give you the details when we meet. Then you'll understand that you are wrong about everything when you took offence at me, although I realise that it was bitter and hurtful for you then.

d) You cannot make poetry out of full-blooded expressions alone for they – those expressions, that is – remain in the background and lose out in the compositional sense, turning into couplets more suited for the Grand Guignol or the Old Curiosity Shop. An example are the failures of Osip Emilievich [Mandelstam].

I have repeatedly had to search for banalities and clichés for the background, and that, at times, is more difficult than striking an extravagant pose. Certainly, the "rabble of dead worlds" is an unusual and local phenomenon, which arises in the midst of the familiar, accustomed sky, which does not attract notice. That was the intention, and that was the result. A success, in other words. But I consider this poem weak and hope in future to show you something more interesting.

e) The idea of the multiple themes in A Hero of Our Time is novel, but in order to accept it I must become acquainted with all your arguments. It is too bold and new a thought.

f) What are these ideas that have got into your head about my supposedly comparing women with female elephants and so on? Naturally, animals have sex and gender, but that's the end of it. One must not object to literary approaches, far less take offence at them. Never do that again.

g) You wouldn't find anything jolly about my life. Three hours a week, I instruct curious officers about history and literature; the rest of the time they instruct me and with an equal lack of success, it seems. I'm totally fed up with Europe. There's nothing to read, and nothing to talk about. Write more often.

h) I am no longer angry with Mama and shall not try your patience.

Love and kisses

Leon

The day after this letter arrived, the long-awaited edict announcing demobilisation was published. Some of the most exciting days had come. Naturally, I began to await Lyova's promised arrival. Time passed, he did not appear, and there was no news from him whatsoever. Tales did the rounds of various catastrophic accidents linked to demobilisation. Gradually, I became infected with anxiety. Finally, I had to settle for the idea that something had happened to him. Peacetime existence, meanwhile, was beginning to assert its rights. Osmyorkin had already received his first pass to travel up to post-blockade Leningrad. This was late in the autumn, and he spent no less than a month there at the Academy of Arts. It was another month before he returned to Moscow. I was visiting Lena at that moment, and he gave a long and excited account of his impressions.

"Well, and how is Akhmatova now?" I asked him. "How is she coping with her solitude?"

"What solitude? Lyova's living with her. He's already working at the Institute of Oriental Studies, after passing his university graduation exams."

I was dumbfounded. I had been sure that I would never see him or write to him again. But just as unexpected as his disappearance was the sudden arrival of a postcard. He told me how many exams he had managed to pass during that time: he had finished university and, to Akhmatova's delight, had secured the necessary marks to attain his master's degree.

"Mama is amazed," he wrote, "and calls me an octopus."

Written late 1980s–early 1990s. First incomplete publication in *Novy mir* (November–December, 1993).

EIGHT POEMS BY ANNA AKHMATOVA

Akhmatova, courtyard at Fontanka (photo N. Punin)

Under her dark veil she wrung her hands . . .
"Why are you so pale today?"
"Because I made him drink of stinging grief
Until he got drunk on it.

How can I forget he staggered out,
His mouth twisted in agony . . .
I ran down not touching the banister
And caught up with him at the gate.

    Panting, I cried: A joke!
    That's all it was. If you leave, I'll die.
    He smiled calmly and grimly
    And told me: 'Don't stand here in the wind.'"

Kiev, 8 January 1911

Published in Evening *(1912), Akhmatova's first collection of verse, which bears the epigraph* "La fleur des vignes pousse, et j'ai vingt ans ce soir" *(André Theuriet). [tr.]*

MCMXXI

    Everything has been plundered, betrayed, sold out
    The wing of black death has flashed,
    Everything has been devoured by starving anguish
    Why then is it so bright?

    The fantastic woods near the town
    Wafts the scent of cherry blossom by day,
    At night new constellations shine
    In the transparent depths of the skies of July –

    And how near the miraculous draws
    To the dirty, tumbledown huts . . .
    No one, no one knows what it is,
    But for centuries we have longed for it.

June 1921

From Anno Domini MCMXXI *(1922), Akhmatova's fifth collection and the last she could publish until 1940. Dedicated to Natalya Rykova (1897–1928), wife of Professor G.A. Gukovsky. In 1919–20, when two-thirds of the population of Petrograd had fled from cold and hunger, Akhmatova visited the Rykov family several times at the experimental farm in Tsarskoye Selo where Rykov senior was an agronomist. [tr.]*

Three excerpts from *Requiem*

They led you away at dawn
I followed you like a mourner,
In the dark front room the children were crying,
By the icon shelf the candle was dying.
On your lips was the icon's chill.
The deathly sweat on your brow . . . Unforgettable! –
I will be like the wives of the Streltsy,
Howling under the Kremlin towers.

1935

For seventeen months I've been crying out,
Calling you home.
I flung myself at the hangman's feet,
You are my son and my horror.
Everything is confused for ever,
And it's not clear to me
Who is a beast now, who is a man,
And how long before the execution.
And there are only dusty flowers,
And the chinking of the censer, and tracks
From somewhere to nowhere.
And staring me straight in the eyes,
And threatening impending death,
Is an enormous star.

1939

Epilogue

Once more the day of remembrance draws near.
I see, I hear, I feel you:

The one they almost had to drag at the end,
And the one who tramps her native land no more,

And the one who, tossing her beautiful head,
Said, "Coming here's like coming home."

I'd like to name them all by name,
But the list has been confiscated and is nowhere to be found.

I have woven a wide mantle for them
From their meagre, overheard words.

I will remember them always and everywhere,
I will never forget them no matter what comes.

And if they gag my exhausted mouth
Through which a hundred million scream,

Then may the people remember me
On the eve of my remembrance day.

And if ever in this country
They decide to erect a monument to me,

I consent to that honour
Under these conditions – that it stand

Neither by the sea, where I was born:
My last tie with the sea is broken,

Nor in the tsar's garden near the cherished pine stump,
Where an inconsolable shade looks for me,

But here where I stood for three hundred hours,
And where they never unbolted the doors for me.

This, lest in blissful death
I forget the rumbling of the Black Marias,

Forget how that detested door slammed shut
And an old woman howled like a wounded animal.

And may the melting snow stream like tears
From my motionless lids of bronze,

And a prison dove coos in the distance,
And the ships of the Neva sail calmly on.

March 1940

In the Fortieth Year

When they come to bury the epoch,
Not with psalms will they mourn it,
But with nettles, with thistles,
They will have to adorn it.
And only the gravediggers jauntily
Work. Business won't wait!
And so quietly, oh God, so quietly
That it is audible, is how time passes.
And afterwards it floats away
Like a corpse on a thawing river –
But the son won't recognise his mother,
And the grandson will turn away in anguish.
And the heads will bow even lower
And the moon move like a pendulum.

And so it is – over ruined Paris
There is now such a silence.

5 August 1940

To the Londoners

Time, with an impassive hand, is writing
The Twenty-fourth drama of Shakespeare.
We, the celebrants at this terrible feast,
Would rather read Hamlet, Caesar or Lear
There by the leaden river;
We would rather, today, with torches and singing,
Be bearing the dove Juliet to her grave,
Would rather peer in at Macbeth's windows,
Trembling with the hired assassin –
Only not this, not this, not this,
This we don't have the strength to read!

1940

The first of these two poems was published, with disastrous consequences, in issue 1–2 of Leningrad *magazine in 1946. "To the Londoners" did not appear in print in the Soviet Union until the mid-1970s. [tr.]*

Gold rusts and steel decays,
Marble crumbles away. Everything is on the verge of death.
The most reliable thing on earth – sorrow,
And the most enduring – the almighty word.

1945

Part of a longer work which Akhmatova read to various friends but which then was lost. Years later, someone mentioned that an academic still recalled parts of the poem. Akhmatova would not rest until her informant took her to see him. With his aid, she restored eleven lines which preceded this solitary quatrain. [tr.]

ANNA AKHMATOVA AND LEV GUMILYOV
[1995]

Wounded Souls

In 1994, fragments of correspondence between Akhmatova and her son, the historian Lev Gumilyov, were published for the first time. The texts in the April issue of *Zvezda* were selected and edited by Gumilyov's widow Natalya and the literary specialist Alexander Panchenko. Though of a different generation, the latter had in recent years become a friend of Gumilyov, as can be seen from their joint publications and his thoughtful obituary of Gumilyov in *Izvestiya* (19 June 1992): "He was a true free thinker."

Unfortunately, in the commentary and introductory article to the correspondence, Panchenko permitted his warm personal feelings to override the demands of scholarship. Making no attempt to analyse this account of Akhmatova's life and work, he gave full credence to the stories Gumilyov told about his mother. Indeed, Panchenko openly admitted as much when explaining the source of the commentary to individual letters: the remarks were based on his "conversations with Lev Nikolayevich". What a pity this declaration was not included in the title! It would have denoted the true subject of the publication immediately and offered invaluable insights into the psychology of Lev Gumilyov, a gifted individual with an extraordinary biography.

The memoir element was also very important in Panchenko's introduction, and again the source was the same. Yet a one-sided description of such a major figure in Russian poetry as Anna Akhmatova could not help but distort our understanding of her and lead to outright errors.

For the two editors were not in possession of all the relevant materials. They themselves noted references in the letters to previous postcards Akhmatova had sent to her son. These were not to be found, Gumilyov's widow commented, either in Akhmatova's archives (now preserved at the National Library in St Petersburg) or in the "private papers of L.N. Gumilyov". Nor could they have been found, since Lev Gumilyov burned most of the letters his mother had sent him. In 1956, he informed an astounded Akhmatova of this during the first days of his return from the Gulag. "You can't keep anything in the camps. Sometimes they move you to another place, and then they search you . . ." he explained. And when I brought up the subject, he replied with noble indignation: "What! Was I supposed to bargain for Mama's letters?!" Nevertheless, as we can see, he did preserve some of them. Soon after his release, we learned of this in the course of a friendly conversation. Nadezhda Mandelstam, myself and another former *zek* were present. Lyova pulled "Mama's letters" out of his pocket to show us how obstinately she had declined to answer his direct questions. He waved about the very letter (19 November 1954) now published in *Zvezda*.[1]

His demand to know about the beloved woman from whom arrest had parted him five years earlier was met by Anna Akhmatova's veiled response, using the coded language he knew so well: "Do write a polite letter to Nat[alya] Vas[ilievna] if you get her note. I must insist that you do so. She has changed little, and is still that same maiden-rose; her marriage has proved unsuccessful and she speaks no more of it. She brings me books and repairs my dressing gown, which is coming apart at the seams." She referred to the lady as Pushkin's "maiden-rose" whose breath might be thoroughly contaminated with the "plague". Contemporary readers need not be told, I hope, that "plague" here did not mean anything like syphilis or AIDS but alluded to the subject of one of Akhmatova's poems: "They bound me within an unseen stockade / With their smooth surveillance." This was an affliction that pursued Akhmatova and Lev Gumilyov all their lives, especially in 1946.

For them, the year began in Leningrad in a boisterous and cheerful mood, but after the unprecedented Central Committee decree concerning Akhmatova and Zoshchenko in August, each visitor to Fontanka was naturally regarded with suspicion. I would hesitate to affirm that this was an accurate estimation of Lyova's girlfriend; Akhmatova herself was convinced and put forward many persuasive arguments in support of her view.[2] Disoriented by long years of isolation, Lyova no longer wanted to understand the meaning of her words. We shall encounter such stubborn incomprehension more than once.

---

[1] See Appendix 3, "Gumilyov, Akhmatova, Gerstein: Letters 1954–7", pp. 448–70.
[2] Oleg Kalugin, "The KGB Files on Anna Akhmatova," in *State Security and Literature in USSR and GDR* (Moscow, 1994).

The ten letters from Akhmatova preserved by Gumilyov became a selective compilation intended to immortalise the image of a bad mother, which Lyova created and cherished in his tormented soul. It is hardly feasible to draw a psychological portrait of Akhmatova from such meagre and tendentious material. Yet that was precisely what Panchenko attempted to do.

Unlike her son, Akhmatova lovingly preserved all his letters. Regrettably, of that numerous collection today held at the National Library only five of the most bitter and unjust letters that Lyova sent his mother were selected by Panchenko for publication in *Zvezda*. Lyova's side of the published correspondence begins with the letter of 5 September 1954, in which he instructs Akhmatova how she should petition for his release:

> The only way you can help me is not to write appeals for a pardon – those will automatically be passed to the prosecutor's office and be just as automatically rejected – but manage to see Voroshilov or Khrushchev in person and explain things to them: that I'm a capable Orientalist, with knowledge and abilities far exceeding the average, and that it would make much better sense to employ me as a scholar than some vegetable-patch scarecrow.

It is almost impossible to correspond through letters that are subject to censorship! How trusting, then, certain readers are when they rely on the tormented Gumilyov's doctored version of the causes of his misfortune. Akhmatova could not explain to him the circumstances under which her appeal had been rejected two months before by the USSR prosecutor-general's office. It was no reply to a "formal" plea or request from Citizen Akhmatova, A.A. but a response to a personal appeal she had made to Voroshilov in early February 1954. The letter was handed directly to its addressee by his adjutant. The architect and painter L.V. Rudnev, then just completing construction of the new Moscow University building[3] on the Lenin Hills, was the go-between: it was known that Voroshilov respected his views. But despite receiving two letters, one from Akhmatova about Lev Gumilyov and the other from Rudnev about Akhmatova, there was no reply, either from Voroshilov himself or from the USSR Supreme Soviet of which he was then chairman. After an exhausting wait of almost half a year, Akhmatova received a note from the USSR prosecutor-general's

---

[3] Tallest of the seven massive "Stalin" skyscrapers built in Moscow after the war. Long-term Gulag inmate Varlam Shalamov referred to them as "watchtowers".

office. There were *no* grounds, it stated, for reconsidering the case against L.N. Gumilyov (see Postscript to this part).

It was a shattering blow. However, Akhmatova was not just "the poet of divine compassion", as Panchenko named her, but also a highly intelligent woman. She immediately realised that as long as the Central Committee's decree about Akhmatova and Zoshchenko remained in force, Voroshilov would not take the responsibility for deciding the fate of her son – especially when Lyova bore the name of his father, Nikolai Gumilyov, who had been shot by the Cheka in 1921. Voroshilov must have consulted the Party presidium or Khrushchev himself, and the new government had decided to offer Akhmatova no favours. Any appeal in her name, therefore, would not only be useless to Lyova but fatally damaging. A way round the situation must be found. This was the only proper approach, but Panchenko interpreted it as the major trait of Akhmatova's character: "She did not protest, she suffered." Two earlier testimonies have been published about this important episode, however, describing the progress of Akhmatova's appeal to Voroshilov.

In the second volume of her memoirs of Akhmatova, Lydia Chukovskaya notes how they compiled the letter to Voroshilov together (12 January 1954). On 5 February, they read Rudnev's letter. I brought them the text, though Chukovskaya was unaware of that. She also did not know that the two texts were handed to Voroshilov's adjutant through someone he had designated, serving in the commandant's office at the Troitskie Gates of the Kremlin. On 12 February, Chukovskaya noted briefly: "She has already sent the letter to Voroshilov." I gave a more detailed account in "Memoirs and Facts: The Release of Lev Gumilyov", an article published in the US in the 1970s and more recently in Moscow.[4] Before going into print, I sent the article to Lyova in 1973. He raised no objections to its publication but made no comment. It is harder to understand why Panchenko ignored these texts.

The interpretation of an anecdote told by Lyova – "a conversation of no little importance for Russian culture", in Panchenko's view – must rank as another such careless oversight. This lively but totally improbable account describes how, after the war, Gumilyov suggested to his mother the image of the "silver age" in the famous lines from *Poem without a Hero*:

> The Galernaya arch grew dark,
> In the Summer Garden the weathervane wailed,
> And frozen over the Silver Age
> Hung the silver moon.

---

[4] *Gorizont*, 6 (1989).

In fact, these lines already existed in the first Tashkent version of the poem, as may easily be confirmed by glancing at the 1976 "Poets' Library" edition of Akhmatova's verse. That variant, including the strophe in question, is there dated 1943. Lyova was then still serving his sentence in Norilsk and could not have known of Akhmatova's new composition. The term "silver age", meanwhile, arose in the 1930s among the first wave of Russian émigrés.[5]

Probably a trick of memory led Lev Gumilyov to claim authorship of this widely known definition. Reunited with his mother in Leningrad after seven years of separation – prison, the camps, the front, victory and Berlin – he listened avidly to Akhmatova's new poems. This gave her joy. She was particularly proud when he approved of *Poem without a Hero*. After a brief period of living together (later, with bitter irony, Akhmatova would call those four years the "Entr'acte"), there followed another seven years of separation. Again prison, this time Lefortovo in Moscow. Thence to a camp near Karaganda in Kazakhstan, another in the Kemerovo Region of Siberia and, finally, four long years in a camp outside Omsk. Try as he might, Lyova could not get back, although many prisoners, among them his own friends, were freed one after the other following the death of Stalin in March 1953. His last year in the camps was too much for him. "The hold-up did not so much embitter him (he was a kindly person) as hurt him," asserts Panchenko, quoting Lyova's words: "I was so deeply hurt I developed an ulcer." Whom did he feel hurt by? The military prosecutor's office? The KGB? Or perhaps the Central Committee of the Communist Party? No, he blamed his mother for everything.

"I'd rather fate be foul and Mama good than the other way round," Lyova wrote to me in one of his numerous letters from the camp near Omsk.[6] Prophetic words! That phrase in itself is sufficient for the reader to sense the psychological background to the conversations between Gumilyov and Panchenko. In the first post-war decade, the latter was too young to appreciate how unique and ambiguous Akhmatova's position was. Her position, I repeat, not her behaviour. Victor Ardov's apt

---

[5] E.G.: So far as I know, it was suggested in 1933 by Nikolai Otsup, repeated in 1935 by Weidlé and then given a fuller interpretation by Berdyaev. Finally, it formed the basis of Makovsky's autobiographical work, *On the Parnassus of the Silver Age* (1962).

[6] "My regular correspondence with Lev Gumilyov resumed in autumn 1954," notes E.G. "After the war ended we met rarely, and, following his arrest in 1949, I restricted myself to helping Anna Andreyevna by assembling the parcels for her son in the camps and taking them to out-of-town post offices" (those in Moscow and Leningrad would not then accept packets for such destinations).

aphorism is applicable to this and to all Soviet history: "You can't board this train on the move."

Everything Panchenko wrote about Akhmatova was a reflection of Lyova's words. For some reason, Lyova needed to portray himself (at 35!) as a devil-may-care reveller. Hence his story of how Olga Berggolts would appear with money and food at the disgraced apartment on Fontanka, and her ribald comments. Hence the disdainful tale of how he cheekily inveigled three roubles from his mother: "There were just the two of us and I was desperate for a drink. But I didn't have a kopeck. So I had to talk to Mama about poetry." As if he had not known all the poems of Akhmatova and Gumilyov by heart since adolescence! It was during this knockabout exchange that Lyova allegedly passed on to Akhmatova his belated ideas about the "gold" and "silver" ages of Russian literature.[7]

Such garish touches are in sharp disagreement with Lyova's tone in Moscow when describing daily life at Fontanka with Anna Akhmatova. He was visiting me in 1948 – i.e. soon after the events described:

> We had finished drinking tea. The skin of a salami lay on the table with a small piece of fat attached to it. Mama threw it to the cat. "Why did you do that? I wanted to eat it," I exclaimed. Mama was terribly annoyed. She began to yell at me, and went on shouting for a long while. I sat there opposite her, not saying a word and thinking: "Shout away, it means you're still alive." Everyone needs to shout their head off once in a while.

How very unlike the Gumilyov who, 40 years on, told his tall stories to Academician Panchenko.

Before the professor's uncomprehending eyes, Lyova acted out the piteous renunciation of his own biography, and Panchenko joined in that stylised game. Akhmatova writes (17 September 1954), through all the impediments of censorship, to the dearest person she knows: "I'm feeling very downhearted. And most ill at ease. At least you should pity me . . ." The commentator intervenes, and his didactic observations echo the irritated tone of Lev Gumilyov towards the end of his life: "A son longs for freedom and, at the least, to learn what's going on outside. His poetess-mother writes about her 'moods', hence his hurt reproaches . . . Just as the well-fed cannot understand the hungry, so the free and the captive." On the contrary, I would say, the prisoner did not understand his free

---

[7] "O Lyova, that's interesting. Sell me that idea," Akhmatova supposedly commented (*Zvezda*, p. 174).

mother. He could not imagine how things had changed – the city, its streets, the room and people that he had left behind seven, ten or even seventeen years earlier. Life, no matter what form it took, went on outside while the prisoner had no more than daydreams, longings and (inevitable in his situation) an irresistible yearning for a past that no longer existed and would never return.

If ordinary correspondents write from a desire to exchange news, correspondence with a prisoner has exactly the opposite aim: the main task is to conceal everything. From his free correspondents the captive hides his most important experience, the daily humiliations and constant danger he faces. From outside it is impossible to write to him about his case (i.e. his chances of being released) or to burden him with additional worries by describing your own difficulties, illnesses or misfortunes. Therefore Akhmatova's letters, and those of Lyova himself, are sometimes abstract and a little dull. Especially when they write about literature and Oriental

Lev Gumilyov, 1953

heroes. For this was camouflage. They wrote of such things so as not to keep silent or deprive their dearest of letters and the chance to see a beloved handwriting. Lyova wrote to me on 12 June 1955: "In my previous letter I inserted quite a brusque letter to Mama. Perhaps you did not pass it on, because of its tone, naturally. Therefore I am repeating the part about Taoism and translations, and so on." These long letters about professional matters were a shield against outbursts of emotion which were painful and almost unbearable.

Panchenko writes about this interest in the East as a "family pastime". Yet for Akhmatova it was no hobby but a genuine urge.[8] One only has to recall her Tashkent poems, "I have not been here for 700 years" and

---

[8] Anna Gorenko's literary pseudonym Akhmatova was derived from the family legend of descent from Akhmat, the last khan of the Crimean Tatars.

especially the poem about the "lynx eyes" of Asia [1945] that had "seen through" and "teased away" something within her:

> As though all my ancestral memory
> Flowed into my mind like red-hot lava,
> As though I'd drunk my own wailing
> From another's palms.

I'm dubious of Panchenko's suggestion that Lev Gumilyov's Eurasian views came to him in the camps. I think it was earlier that Lyova became acquainted with the works of those who founded this theory. Punin was outstandingly well educated and had a fine library at home and of course Lyova read his books. In any case, I remember him mentioning Prince N.S. Trubetskoi, who was living in Prague. (As a young man, incidentally, Lyova had a strikingly Oriental appearance; he was "every inch the Asiatic", one might say.)

In the camps, he learned how to extract the necessary information from works of popular scholarship. Several excerpts from his letters to me in 1956 demonstrate the quiet progress of his work:

10 January: "Please send me more books since I have almost used up these ones."

22 February: "Thank you again for the book. I read it with pleasure, for although it has no inspired moments it has no weak points either. It maintains a level of academic mediocrity and therefore is an adequate aid, thus far, for my subject."

11 March: "So far I have only read one story from your book [The Chinese *Tang novellae*? E.G.] and immediately made a valuable note for my 'History'."

14 March: "The books give me great pleasure no matter what my own fate. If only it were possible to lay hands on two old books: Father Jacinthus, *A History of Tibet and Khukhunor* [1833] and Vasily Grigoryev's *Eastern Turkestan* [1869, tr. from German] . . . Those are the only major works I now lack."

29 March: " . . . For the time being, I accept the condolences of those around me and am studying Si-ma Qian [Chinese historian, first century BC]."

5 April: "I already have all the basic factual material about Central Asia. There's very little of it (on the matter that interests me). Moreover, I am now totally engrossed in Si-ma Qian and will be for a long while yet. It's a very wise book, and one that must not be read quickly."

After his release in May 1956 and when he was already settled back in Leningrad, Lyova wrote to me (7 January 1957): ". . . You cannot begin to imagine how my gratitude to you has grown during the last period. And the reason: books. For if you had not been sending them to me, I would have had to get hold of them and read them now – and when do I have the time?!"

In the camps, as we can see, Lev made effective use of the literature he received and worked enthusiastically, with a clear aim in mind. By the time of his arrest in 1949, he was already sufficiently prepared (having, in particular, defended his master's thesis) not to drown in the superfluous ideas that frequently occur to gifted people when they endure prolonged solitude.

His personal and family relations were another matter. "I do not know whether you are rich or poor," he enquired of Akhmatova on 21 April 1956, "of how many rooms – one or two? – you are the fortunate possessor; or who is caring for you . . ." Improbable rumours reached him about Akhmatova's life. Had a room been kept for him, he wanted to know, at the apartment on Red Cavalry Street? He was well aware that Akhmatova had two homes, one with her Moscow "daughter" Nina Olshevskaya-Ardova and the other with her Leningrad "daughter" Irina Punina. How much bile and malice there is in the expression "fortunate possessor"! This was entirely the influence of Lev's friends in the camps. They had been repeatedly alarmed and upset by rumours and events since the spring of 1953. Stalin's death, the subsequent amnesty (not extended to them) and the general trend towards a reopening of cases had all generated detailed prescriptions for speeding up their release. Time and again Lyova would return to their apparently dependable programme of action. Neither he nor his friends could grasp that the position of certain people was out of the ordinary.

The head of enquiries at the military prosecutor's office handed me a general statement of Lyova's case with an outward show of politeness. He refused to accept Akhmatova's private note, however, and returned it to me. Why? Because Akhmatova was someone with restricted rights. In the 1950s, the Central Committee decree remained in force,[9] and

---

[9] And would not be rescinded, formally, for more than 20 years after Akhmatova's death.

officials were especially fearful of contact with her. They remembered not only the 1946 decree but also what happened before the war when Akhmatova's collection *From Six Books* was published.

The most prominent writers, even the leading functionaries of the Writers' Union, had no idea of the storm that awaited them for publishing Akhmatova's "mystic and religious" book. In September 1940, while Alexei Tolstoy was nominating her for the Stalin Prize with the full knowledge and support of Fadeyev and other members of the awards commission, D.V. Krupin, the chief administrator of the Party's Central Committee, sent an indignant note to Zhdanov. Then one of the Central Committee secretaries, Zhdanov became a specialist on Akhmatova's work. On 29 October 1940, he signed a decree of the Committee's secretariat withdrawing the book from circulation and severely punishing those guilty of issuing "this so-called anthology" in praise of "fornication and adoration of the deity". Akhmatova's book had sold out instantly on its appearance in May 1940, so the print-run could not be recalled. However, the director of the "Sovietsky pisatel" publishing house and of its Leningrad branch, together with the censor, received severe reprimands from their Party superiors. Only recently have these details become known.[10] At the prosecutor-general's office, of course, they had been aware of the fury of the highest authorities even before Krupin's official note was delivered and reinforced by a decree of the Central Committee secretariat. The scene I witnessed in August 1940 when Akhmatova was almost physically bustled out of the prosecutor's office now made full sense to me. I was to meet the same response in 1955 at the military prosecutor's office.

Panchenko and Lev Gumilyov spoke of the prisoner's thirst "to learn what's going on outside". Yet what could Akhmatova write to the camps about her life? That she fainted after she had blessed Lyova and they had parted? That she came round when the secret police told her: "Now you must get up, we're going to search your apartment"? That she did not know how many days and nights she lay there in the cold room? (And when, during one of those days, she asked ten-year-old Anya Kaminskaya: "Why didn't you call me to the phone yesterday?" she heard the reply: "But, *Akuma*, I thought you were unconscious . . .") That enveloped in a fog of grief she burned an enormous part of her own literary archive, which lay in disorder around her? And they were not archival documents but the living manuscripts of her unpublished

---

[10] E.G.: See *The Literary Front: A History of Political Censorship, 1932–46* (Moscow, 1994), and compare A.S. Kryukov, "The Destruction of Anna Akhmatova's Books", in *Philological Notes* (Voronezh), no. 3 (1994).

poems! This act of destruction, she felt, put an end to the underlying purpose of her entire life. That was not all, however. She crowned this impulsive act with a suicidal deed: she now wrote the verse of a loyal subject, even exalting Stalin on his 70th birthday (21 December 1949). Throughout the following year the *Ogonyok* weekly published a cycle of poems, "In Praise of Peace", under her name that would torment Akhmatova as an unhealed wound for the rest of her days. After this public declaration there was always a false intonation whenever she conversed in company.

"I sacrificed name and reputation for him!" she once cried aloud in a paroxysm of despair and distress, reacting to the endless reproaches of her son, back after seven long years. She was haunted by the forced deception of her unknown readers, who had always understood her verse. In 1922 she rightfully declared: "I am your voice, the heat of your breath, / I am the reflection of your face . . ."

And she had been faithful to that union. Until disaster cut her down, she hoped that "on that other shore" where the "heavenly expanse grows dark" she would "not be deafened" by "resounding curses". But this "blessed somewhere" had also deceived her. When the Iron Curtain parted slightly the whisper of philistine gossip could be heard, and, worse still, the "foreigners" all talked of the fading of her talent:

> And they wrote in their worthy newspapers
> That my incomparable gift had died,
> That I was a poet among poets
> But my thirteenth hour had now come.

She abandoned the moral purity of her poetry to save her son and in return received insults from all sides and from her own child. When, indignantly, he yet again quoted the example of other mothers, she was unable to bear it: "Not one mother has done for her son what I did!" The response was a rolling on the floor, screams and camp obscenities. I was there.

Akhmatova's sacrifice was in vain. No-one, so far as I know, had requested this "original sin" or promised her anything in return. She remembered, however, being reproached for her silence following the 1946 decree about the monthlies *Zvezda* and *Leningrad* and her subsequent exclusion from the Writers' Union. Lyova was not released, and a broken Akhmatova was given the right to address the public in a lifeless tone and to translate into Russian the verse of her foreign imitators. Anyone who imagines that this is not torture knows nothing of the joys and sufferings of the artist.

During 1950, Akhmatova went to Moscow once a month to hand over the permitted sum at Lefortovo prison and, in return, receive the prisoner's signed receipt – i.e. proof that he was alive and still there. After the first letter from the transit prison, she received only laconic notes similar to one still in my possession:

Dear Mama

Confirming receipt of packet #277 with my thanks. But from now on send more fats and tobacco instead of biscuits: cheaper and better.

My love.

Dated 19 July 1951, it was sent from the Churbai–Nurinskoe postal district in Karabas (Karaganda Region) and reached the Ardovs' address in Moscow that August. I had sent the packet on Akhmatova's behalf and would send many more. That is why she gave me the postcard. In such a correspondence, what information could you send someone in the camps? She could hardly let him know that the Arctic Institute had begun to squeeze Akhmatova and Ira Punina's family out of the House on Fontanka.

The institute had tolerated their "residence" in its officially owned property until the arrest of Punin in August 1949 and that of Lyova in November. Now that the two women were so vulnerable and defence-less they were literally persecuted. They clung together. Finally in early 1952, Irina rang up Akhmatova who was then in Moscow: "Do as you please, I can't stand any more. I'm taking an apartment on Red Cavalry Street." Akhmatova was presented with a *fait accompli*. She did not wish to part with Ira and Anya, but there was no room for Lyova in the new apartment. At Fontanka after the war, Akhmatova had two rooms; Lyova lived in one of them. Her heart sank when she thought of where he would settle on his return – and she had not lost hope although he had been sentenced to ten years' imprisonment. After suffering a severe heart attack, could she stay on alone to be harassed by the institute's offensive administrators? It was a hopeless struggle and she agreed to the move.[11]

When permission was given to write longer and more frequent letters, she ceased to inform Lyova of the harsh details of her own existence. Whatever she might write, incidentally, he replied with grudges and

---

[11] She would live at the Red Cavalry Street apartment until 1961.

grumbling. These helped to drown out the horror he felt at the unequal blows fate had dealt him.

News that Akhmatova had been elected a delegate to the Second All-Union Congress of Writers in 1954 came as a shock to every educated person in the camp. Lyova's friends were particularly excited. Learning from the papers that the congress would end with a government reception, they imagined that this offered the only convenient chance for Akhmatova to "exploit her position". She could make a loud and demonstrative protest, they thought, against the imprisonment of her unjustly convicted son. It did not say in the papers that members of the government sat behind a table on the stage and were cordoned off from the audience. There sat the writers, dining at small tables, among them Akhmatova with a polite smile frozen on her face. "Mask, I know thee," remarked the actress Rina Zelyonaya as she passed by (they were acquainted through the Ardovs).

At the congress, which was held in late December, Akhmatova did begin cautiously to petition on behalf of Lyova. She raised the subject with Ehrenburg. He undertook to write directly to Khrushchev, adding to his letter as a deputy [of the Supreme Soviet] an appeal from Academician Struve. But Lyova could never rid himself of the false conviction that his mother had missed her only chance of pleading for her son at the congress.

This is no bald assertion on my part. It is based on what Lev wrote to me from the camp, my meetings with his friends who returned earlier, and a remarkable letter from one of them who had been specifically sent to see me by Lyova. They included versifiers, artists and academics but, unfortunately, had little experience of politics and diplomacy. Akhmatova was now very well placed, they thought, and no longer in disgrace. She enjoyed such a high position, in their understanding, that they were amazed that she did not lift a finger to push for the release of her innocent son. This was all an illusion, and it prompted in Lyova the development of his less attractive features: envy, a tendency to nurse grudges and, alas, ingratitude.

This conception of Akhmatova gave rise to much gossip. I suspect that the KGB[12] also lent a hand. It never occurred to Lyova that his solitary mother, who had lived for years with other families, could not eat, drink, fall sick or receive friends and people she needed to see without paying her share of her hospitable hosts' expenses. One episode has been blown out of all proportion and continues to cast a quite unjustified shadow on Akhmatova's reputation: her gift of a Moskvich automobile to Alyosha Batalov, Nina Olshevskaya's oldest son, who was then not a famous film actor but a modest soldier, serving his two years'

---

[12] The Committee for State Security, name of the secret police from 1954 to 1991.

conscription in the army in Moscow. With his young wife, he occupied a room of 7 square metres at the apartment on Ordynka, but whenever Akhmatova came to Moscow they gave it up for her. She would live in the room for at least four months in the year and, when she fell sick, for even longer. In 1953, she earned a great deal of money for translating Victor Hugo's play *Marion Delorme*, which was included in the 15-volume jubilee edition and paid at the highest rates. Naturally, having become so wealthy, in our terms, she gave the friends around her the best gifts she could afford. For Batalov she picked something special, and he deserved it. The little Moskvich then cost 9,000 roubles. It gave Alexei a great deal of pleasure and provided Akhmatova with a sense of moral satisfaction.

Rumours and stories now spread across Russia about Akhmatova (she imperceptibly became "Anna Andreyevna" to friends and strangers alike, rather than the more deferential Anna Akhmatova), but still no books of her verse were published, and she continued to write new poems in secret. At the same time, she began cautiously to collect letters appealing for Lev's case to be reopened from the most outstanding scholars: Academician Struve, Corresponding Member Konrad and the director of Hermitage Museum, Artamonov.[13] Among writers, such leading figures as Sholokhov, Ehrenburg and the secretaries of the Writers' Union, Fadeyev and Surkov, joined in the petitioning on his behalf.

I say she acted "cautiously" because only recently, during Stalin's last years, one could create considerable difficulties for others simply by mentioning the surname Gumilyov or drawing sympathetic attention to what she herself called her "ambiguous fame". How certain could Akhmatova be that these academics would respond to her request if both Struve and Artamonov had been sure Lyova was dead? If not Akhmatova, they could have asked others about him – but they feared to involve anyone else. That was why people at the Hermitage claimed that Lyova was not writing to his mother. Today's readers, it would seem, cannot imagine the malevolent atmosphere in which those years were shrouded. And if that is the case, what right do they have to condemn Akhmatova?

The Torment of Anticipation

The eminent Orientalists and historians who had already joined in the battle to free Gumilyov were, it should be said, enthusiastic and acted with determination and intelligence. Struve wrote twice on his behalf.

---

[13] Mikhail I. Artamonov (1898–1972) had known Lyova since the 1930s.

As Akhmatova's trusted representative, Konrad told me that he himself had failed completely. Yet later he added that we could not imagine the further lengths to which he had gone, though quite without success.

I wanted to send Lyova copies of these scholars' brilliant recommendations but Akhmatova feared this might provoke a nervous breakdown, given his captive and humiliating position. She also suspected that these reports might harm Lyova in the eyes of the camp administration. That proved to be the case. "He must have done something wrong if he's still being kept here," they conjectured and, to be on the safe side, subjected Lyova to stricter conditions. His position was by now very much out of the ordinary. On 22 February 1956 he wrote to me: "It's a pity there's still no reply. This is not only getting on my nerves but affects the camp bosses as well: they simply cannot make out whether I'm bad or good. Therefore, my condition lacks any stability, and that creates no end of difficulties for me." On receiving this, I resolved, despite Akhmatova's forebodings, to send him copies of the letters I had handed to the military prosecutor's office. He replied on 11 March: "It's very good that you've sent me those reports. It's no great misfortune that they were delayed on the way." But things were worse than he admitted. In April, Lyova requested one of his now released friends, a Uniate priest from the Western Ukraine, to come and give me a detailed account of his situation. The friend was unable to stop on his way through Moscow but wrote me a letter. I should treat it, he said, as a "brief and sincere confession" by Lyova, and asked me "so far as you are able, to help ease his difficult position"[14]: "Lev Nikolayevich has come under strain recently. For several months he was left in peace but the latest reports did not please our bosses and they decided to pressure him. It's clear they want to destroy his faith in his own abilities and powers, and perhaps there are other reasons of which you are aware." Lyova's tense situation was reaching crisis point: ". . . without letters I feel as if I've been skewered, smeared with turpentine and dusted with red pepper," he wrote on 29 March 1956, though I had written to tell him that evidently his case would be finally dealt with that month.

It is not at all surprising that the words of these prominent scholars made the local authorities think twice. "In my view, the removal of Gumilyov from the ranks of Soviet historians is a major loss for our discipline," wrote Academician Struve. No-one apart from Gumilyov could take the place of the recently deceased Professor Yakubovsky, he wrote, and boldly referred to Lyova's "profound learning and maturity of

---

[14] E.G.: The letter, dated 26 March 1956, left Ternopol Region in mid-April, but it was not until 24 April 1958 that it reached Moscow.

thought". Professor Artamonov spoke of Gumilyov's "exceptional gifts" and his "dazzling knowledge in his chosen field". Incidentally, Artamonov bore witness that Lyova's "interest in the history of the nomadic Turkic peoples" had been formed when he was still a student.

Both scholars had been his supervisors, to one extent or another, on archaeological expeditions or at the Institute of Oriental Studies. The historian Okladnikov, a holder of the Stalin Prize, did not know how Gumilyov had begun as a scholar, but his brief and forceful letter demands our special attention.

He had come into contact with Gumilyov only, he emphasised, in the course of his own research work. He most emphatically declared that he was not alone in considering Gumilyov a "major, I would even say, outstanding researcher into the past history of the nations of Central Asia", and that many scholars who had carefully read his works shared Okladnikov's opinion as to "the freshness of thought and genuine historical perspective of his views". "Many other specialists would share my joy at Gumilyov's return to his scholarly work," said Okladnikov, covering his own back somewhat. In conclusion, he requested that Gumilyov's case be reopened as quickly as possible "in the hopes [of discovering] that in Beria's time, infringements of Soviet legality might have been committed". There was, it seemed, no more to say. Unexpectedly, Okladnikov adds a phrase that strikes a very different note from all the above-quoted statements: "In any case, if he was guilty in some respect, it was to a far lesser extent than all he has by now endured in captivity."

Apparently, Okladnikov knew something about Gumilyov's guilt which entitled him to compare the degree of punishment with the scale of Lyova's misdeeds. Was the professor perhaps being indiscreet? Or had someone else, unintentionally, been too frank? Of course, the latter was the case . . .

Okladnikov entrusted his document to a reliable intermediary, Nadezhda Mandelstam. When she brought the letter from Leningrad to Moscow, she commented that Okladnikov would not risk a political assessment of Gumilyov or call him unjustly convicted. "Struve is 80 and a member of the Academy. He can take risks, I can't . . ." was how Nadezhda passed on his thoughts. But she could always get round anyone; her powers of persuasion were her chief talent. This was the predominant trait of her character and derived from the combination of a highly temperamental nature, an excitability bordering on hysteria, irresistible will-power and, strange as it may seem, an insouciant frivolity.

Naturally, it was Nadezhda, not Okladnikov, who knew something more about Lyova's case. It was strange that I was not aware of this, since I had been so intently engaged in Lyova's affairs at the time. Two weeks had not passed, however, before I was given an exhaustive account by Akhmatova. She described details I had never imagined about Lyova and Punin's arrest in 1935, an event that left a deep impression on me. A letter I received from Lyova was the spur for Akhmatova's frank admissions.

I had asked him under which article of the Criminal Code he had been convicted and what the charges against him were. At the military prosecutor's office, they had adamantly refused to tell me: "Ask him yourself," was their cynical retort. As I have already noted, they would barely let Akhmatova see such officials and did not want to talk to her. That was why I was keen to go to Omsk, get permission to see Lyova and, at long last, talk to him in person. But this proved impossible. My question about his conviction reduced Lyova to a state of shock. He regarded it as a further sign of his mother's indifference. However, he did reply (19 December 1955):

> Here it is: 17-58:8&10.[15] Substance of the case: twice arrested, in 1935 for conversations at home, and in 1938 "without committing an offence but, being convicted, considered his arrest to be a quite unjustified act of cruelty"; I thought so, but said nothing. Convicted in 1950 as a "repeater" – i.e. someone whose punishment they decided to resume without any pretext on his part (i.e. on my part).

As concerns the last conviction, I may remind readers that Akhmatova, having earned a personal interview with the deputy prosecutor-general, asked whether someone could be punished twice for the same offence. The answer was laconic: "They can."

After receiving Lyova's letter, I said to Akhmatova that she could now go to the prosecutor's office with a more definite complaint. Her reaction was unexpected: "The 1935 case is quoted? Then I can't go there." Why?

In his letter, Lyova acknowledged that in 1935 an offence really had been committed: "conversations at home". If that were so, Akhmatova

---

[15] Article 58 of the Criminal Code concerned "Counter-revolutionary" offences, and Sections 8 and 10 respectively covered terrorist acts, and agitating for the overthrow of the Soviet regime. Here these are linked to the doctrine of complicity embodied in Paragraph 17 of the Criminal Code. "The product of Andrei Vyshinsky's legal genius", this doctrine stated that "each member of a criminal group (and membership in that group was expressed by knowledge of its existence and failure to report it) was responsible not only for his own individual criminal deeds but also for the deeds of the criminal group as a whole ..." (Lev Razgon, "Kostya Shulga", *True Stories* [Ann Arbor, 1997]).

would be forced to admit her own part in this "crime" although at the time she had written a letter of appeal to Stalin, guaranteeing the behaviour of her son and of her husband (also arrested for the same conversations). After publishing her famous post-war cycle "In Praise of Peace" in *Ogonyok*, it was out of the question to remind new judges of the past. As if that were not enough, the cycle contained "21 December 1949", her poem in celebration of Stalin's 70th birthday. I have mentioned the burdensome role of this publication in her life and work. But that was still not all.

In 1935, I learned for the first time, Lyova had read aloud Mandelstam's political satire about Stalin: "We live without feeling the country beneath us". He hid this from me, although I was in some respect also involved in his arrest and in the case against Mandelstam.

There was yet more. A not entirely familiar guest in that house, a student invited by Lyova, was at the dinner table. Staggered by what he heard, the young man immediately informed the "organs". Stalin displayed an unheard-of leniency, and both those arrested were quickly released. Nevertheless, this "case" was again among the formal charges when Lyova was sentenced to ten years' imprisonment in 1950.

One last blow. Until the pardon was issued, the conduct of the investigation in 1935 was very fierce. In the file there remained a copy of Mandelstam's poem written out in Lyova's hand.

But in each letter he continued to complain: "How much time can they spend reviewing an empty charge?" Clearly, he wanted to forget that he had written out Mandelstam's poem, and finally he did so. This was reflected in a primitive yet noble letter from one of his camp companions. On 9 September 1955, the Orientalist Mikhail Khvan appealed to Struve for a rapid intervention not on his own behalf but to save Gumilyov: "All his misfortunes come from being the son of two ill-fated poets, and usually he is remembered in connection with their names.[16] Yet he is a scholar and his brilliant gifts need no reference to the famous for him to be recognised."

"You see, Lyova is already disowning us," said Akhmatova sadly as she passed me the letters received from Struve. Of course, Khvan was repeating what Lyova said. That was clear. While all the petitioners became convinced that some obstruction was holding up his case, Gumilyov only once acknowledged this, in a moment of sober reflection. "There is some jinx here," he wrote to me on 3 February 1956. "The delay is unnecessary, the result of someone's ill will."

---

[16] "I was imprisoned twice," Gumilyov would later repeat, "once for Papa and once for Mama."

If one ignores the two "ill-fated poets", student informers and rival professors, that "ill will" can be located. We must to return to the fateful day in 1934 when Osip Mandelstam gave Akhmatova and Lev Gumilyov an inspired recital of his epigram, a poem of which few were as yet aware.

". . . Lyova especially should not know about it" I remember Nadya's tense voice when she came to see me with that warning. But the poet could not restrain himself within the limits of common sense and entrusted his seditious verse to the "for ever" disgraced Akhmatova and an unformed young man. During his interrogation, Mandelstam decided to be completely honest and made the following comment on Lyova's reaction to the reading: "Lev Gumilyov approved of the work with some vague and emotional expression such as 'wonderful', but his view blended with that of his mother, Anna Akhmatova, in whose presence the work was read aloud to him." Of course, we must not forget that Mandelstam's words are preserved in the version of his interrogator. However, that laid the basis for the case against Lyova. In the documents confirming Lev Gumilyov's final rehabilitation, we can see that the file on him was opened in 1934. It would cast a shadow over him for the next twenty-two years.

That is why, a little earlier, I referred to Nadezhda Mandelstam's "insouciant frivolity": she described all those who heard the satire about Stalin, and were named by Mandelstam, as having "got off with no more than a mild fright". She also brushed aside Fadeyev's direct indication that one of the secretaries of the Central Committee was actively hostile to Mandelstam. In this instance, however, we must turn to her own memoirs.

In 1938, when Mandelstam was leading an unsettled existence in Moscow and Leningrad, trying to legalise his position after exile in Voronezh, Fadeyev "volunteered to sound out higher authority" and "find out what they were thinking". So Nadezhda tells us. The results were very discouraging: "He told us that he had talked to Andreyev but could get nowhere. The latter firmly declared there could be no question of any work for Mandelstam. As Fadeyev put it, 'Outright refusal.'"

Fadeyev referred to the same highly placed official a second time when he and Nadezhda met by chance some years later. Efforts to get Mandelstam's poems published had by then already begun. Nadezhda writes that this was "shortly before the war ended", but she is mistaken: she came back to Moscow from Tashkent for the first time in summer 1946, and it was even later when she stayed with the Shklovskys. In the lift at the writers' apartment building in Lavrushinsky Street, she once again saw Fadeyev:

The lift had hardly begun to move before Fadeyev bent down and whispered that Mandelstam's sentence had been signed by Andreyev. Or rather that's what I understood him to mean. The phrase sounded approximately like this: "They entrusted Andreyev [to deal] with Mandelstam." The lift stopped and Fadeyev got out.

Nadezhda, in her words, "was bewildered. What did Andreyev have to do with it? Moreover, I noted that Fadeyev was a little drunk." Finally, she disregarded this information and exclaimed: "What difference can it make, who signed the sentence?"

However, we cannot ignore these details if we want to find out why Lev Gumilyov's rehabilitation was delayed and whether Akhmatova was to blame. This demands re-examination of many already familiar accounts. By leaving this accumulated material unsifted, we shall remain with an outdated view of Akhmatova.

Suppose that among the sources of the case against Lev Gumilyov, a major role was played by Mandelstam's anti-Stalin poem. We must then look more closely at the history of the poem's dissemination, the fate of its author and that of other individuals involved in the affair. Not many direct testimonies concerning the matter have survived. There are the two incomplete publications of Mandelstam's interrogation; Nadezhda's memoirs and Akhmatova's *Leaves from a Diary*; and testimony as to the part played by Pasternak in easing the lot of Mandelstam, Akhmatova and Lyova. There are also my own memoirs – but people do not like to consult them since they never quite follow the established path. New publications such as Luknitsky's notes we shall leave to one side: this is a major primary source, but it refers to an earlier period of Akhmatova's biography. Unknown materials concerning relations between Stalin and Pasternak, published only very recently in the 1990s, offer a tangible advance in our interpretation of this issue.

My Hypotheses

Neither Mandelstam nor his wife had any doubts that if the poem was discovered, its author would be shot. Hence the arrogant and doomed tone in which Mandelstam read me his satire about Stalin, adding, "If he finds out, I'll be shot."

Mandelstam's pardon struck everyone as a quite exceptional event. I say "pardon" because banishment for three years to a university town in central Russia was a penalty very far from the expected execution. The very manner in which this lenient response was announced, moreover, a telephone conversation between Stalin and Pasternak, was mystifying. The call has led to many different interpretations in the specialist literature. Before turning to them, however, we must recall the text of the conversation as recorded by Nadezhda from the words of Boris Pasternak:

> Stalin told Pasternak that Mandelstam's case was being reconsidered and that everything would turn out fine for him. There then followed an unexpected reproach: why had Pasternak not gone to the writers' organisations or "to me" and petitioned on behalf of Mandelstam? "If I was a poet and a friend who was a poet had run into difficulties, I would do all in my power to help him . . ."
>
> Pasternak replied: "Writers' organisations have not got bothered with such cases since 1927 and if I had not raised his case you would probably have heard nothing." Then Pasternak added something about the word *friend*, wanting to define more clearly the character of his relations with Mandelstam, which naturally did not fall under the term *friendship*. This comment was very much in Pasternak's style and had no bearing on the matter in hand. Stalin interrupted with a question: "But he is a master, isn't he, a master?" Pasternak replied: "That's not the point here . . ." "What is then?" demanded Stalin. Pasternak said that he wanted to meet him and have a talk. "About what?" "About life and death," answered Pasternak. Stalin put down the phone. Pasternak tried to ring him back but he only reached his secretary. Stalin did not pick up the receiver again . . .

Some suppose that Stalin had not read Mandelstam's satire. No-one, it is said, would have dared show it to him. I think this is hardly convincing. Anyone afraid of retribution for knowing the text would be even more fearful of denunciation for concealing it from Stalin, who himself issued the command to "isolate but preserve" the poet. The original text of this resolution with his signature has yet to be found. Who but Stalin, however, could take responsibility for such a decision? A second interpretation, most clearly expressed in the 1989 *Materials for a Biography* of Pasternak, suggests that the phone call was motivated by Stalin's desire to find out whether Pasternak himself knew the poem, and thereby determine how widely it had circulated. Tasks of this kind were entrusted to GPU investigators; there was no need for the Leader himself to make such enquiries. Others suggest that Stalin was hoping that Mandelstam would be his future apologist (we may recall the poet's later "Ode" to the Soviet leader). A fourth interpretation links Stalin's dramatic call with the intensive preparations, then under way, for the first Congress of Writers. This view is strengthened by the permission Pasternak received to conceal neither the contents of the conversation nor the fact that it had taken place. Quite naturally, tactical considerations played a part in any deed of a wily politician like Stalin. Was this sufficient incentive, however, to account for the edgy and strange conversation that has since become famous?

Pasternak repeated the conversation to several writers, mentioning the same details. Nadezhda reproduced it, so she says, "as accurately as if dictated". I fear that Pasternak was not as accurate as that. The thought occurs that his was an edited version, intended for transmission to the public. It diverges in certain respects from the course of events as we now know them. One is Pasternak's successful intervention in support of Lev Gumilyov and Nikolai Punin's release in 1935: yet he considered that the way the 1934 telephone conversation ended was a great failure on his part. Before examining the important episode when Pasternak defended Akhmatova, we may suggest that the motivation behind Stalin's call to Pasternak is wrongly given. Nadezhda quotes Bukharin's message by way of explanation: "In his letter to Stalin, Bukharin added a postscript that Pasternak had come to see him and was alarmed by Mandelstam's arrest . . ." However, there might be other reasons for Stalin's call. For this was not the first time the two had been in personal contact. That was in 1932, and it had taken an unusual form. It was then that Pasternak's fascination with Stalin began, and this story indubitably had an effect on the fortunes of Akhmatova and her son.

The poet's first note to the Leader was reported in a Soviet newspaper but none of us, including Nadezhda, remembered it. This episode has not received attention in Russian publications. It was allotted no place in the *Materials for a Biography*, in the numerous editions of Pasternak's correspondence, or in collections of reminiscences about him. It created more of a stir in émigré literature and Slavic studies in the West. The first response was Mikhail Koryakov's 1958 article "Russia's Thermometer" in *Novy Zhurnal* [New York]. This quotes press reactions to the sudden death of Stalin's wife, Nadezhda Alliluyeva, on 9 November 1932.[17] The newspapers were then full of the condolences

---

[17] See Appendix 1.2, "Alliluyeva's Suicide", pp. 424–5.

of various organisations and members of the Central Committee, and of
the deceased's relatives and fellow employees. A notable place was occupied by the letter that appeared in the 17 November issue of
Literaturnaya gazeta. This message of sympathy was signed by 33 writers, but Pasternak was not among them. He attached a separate note,
and it was published there and then: "Share the sentiment of my
comrades. The day before, for the first time, was thinking hard and
deeply as an artist about Stalin. Next morning read the news. Astounded
as if there, saw and lived it myself."

On 18 November a letter from Stalin to the editors of *Pravda*
appeared, expressing his thanks to all who had sympathised with his grief.
Stalin's reaction to Pasternak's extraordinary words remained unknown.
But when he rang Pasternak about Mandelstam 18 months later, he
could not have forgotten, of course, about the poet's strange and significant addendum. Neither had Pasternak; he never subsequently reminded
anyone of its existence though it had been published. It will not appear
too fanciful, I hope, to see Stalin's telephone call as his reply to Pasternak's
postscript.

A major study of the poet, *Pasternak in the 1930s* [Jerusalem, 1984],
devotes an entire chapter to Mandelstam's first arrest and the famous
telephone call. Its author, Lazar Fleishman, could not reach a definite
conclusion nor did any of the other interpretations that he cites. The
task is impossible, moreover, if each episode is treated in isolation: they
were part of a process that lasted three years. This came to a close in
1936, when two poems by Pasternak dedicated to Stalin were published
on 1 January in *Izvestiya*. The poet would later characterise this cycle[18]
as "a sincere attempt, one of my greatest attempts (and the last in that
period) to live through the thoughts of the time and in harmony with
it". He made no secret that "Bukharin wanted something of this kind
to be written, and the poem was a joy for him."

Everything suggests that Bukharin needed the first poem in the cycle
("I understood: all is alive . . .") with its banal and essentially mediocre
exaltation of the Leader, of leaders even (". . . And Lenin and Stalin /
And these verses now . . ."). This much-desired composition was clearly
quite as "foreign" to the poet as certain lines in another extraordinary
letter he had sent Stalin not long before. The second poem of the new
cycle ("The temper obstinate appeals") was organically entwined with

---

[18] The two compositions later opened a cycle of seven poems entitled "The
Artist" (*Znamya* [April 1936]). Pasternak never republished the first poem, and
the second only appeared thereafter (in his 1943 and subsequent collections)
without the stanzas about the "Kremlin recluse". See Christopher Barnes, *A
Literary Biography of Pasternak*, Vol. 2: *1928–60* (Cambridge, 1998).

his note shortly after Alliluyeva's death in 1932. The first contains clear echoes of one theme in this new letter:

> To begin with, I wrote to you in my own style, wordy and with digressions, submitting to that mysterious something which, beyond all that people understand and share, draws me to you. But I was advised to abridge and simplify the letter, and I am left with the terrible feeling that I have sent you something foreign that is not mine.

Undoubtedly, the poet's adviser in this case was Bukharin. They were already linked by their previous effort to save Mandelstam.

In the interval, there had been another letter, when Pasternak had written supporting Akhmatova's appeal to Stalin in late October 1935. Surprisingly, it was Pasternak, not Akhmatova, who thanked Stalin for the release of Gumilyov and Punin. That says a great deal. It points to the unspoken dialogue that linked Stalin and the poet throughout these three years. Pasternak himself says as much. The new letter (which probably preceded the *Izvestiya* publication)[19] opens:

> Dear Iosif Vissarionovich,
>
> It vexes me that I did not then follow my first wish and thank you for the miraculous and instantaneous release of Akhmatova's family. But I felt ashamed to disturb you a second time and decided to keep to myself a feeling of warm gratitude to you, being assured that it would, in any case and by *means unknown*, in some way reach you. (Emphasis added, E.G.)

There was also a topical theme in the letter. In his later autobiographical essay "People and Situations" (1956), Pasternak described how Stalin's famous comment about Mayakovsky in December 1935 freed him from a life in public view as the country's first poet, a role certain literary critics wanted to thrust upon him. However, he did not cite the letter itself in his essay. Now it has been published we may quote the closing words, which speak of the inner tie between these two striking personalities:

> In conclusion, let me thank you warmly for your recent words about Mayakovsky . . . Now . . . with a light heart I can live and

---

[19] First published in September 1990. For the complete text, see Appendix 1.4, pp. 426–8

work as before, in a modest silence, with the unexpected and mysterious occurrences without which I would not love life.

In the name of that mystery,

I remain your warmly affectionate and devoted,

B. Pasternak

Unfortunately, commentators and various specialists have tried to reduce the authenticity of this attachment to the petty details of contemporary political and literary life.

The urge to provide a rational explanation for the irrational has always struck me as a futile occupation: it is just as unhelpful as asserting a mystery when it is clearly a matter of simple ignorance. Surely Stalin's deed in calling Pasternak is sufficient in itself. Does this not show that the Leader had placed his confidence in the poet? Koryakov used words such as *soothsayer, visionary, diabolism* and *mystical horror* in connection with Pasternak's first note to Stalin. It would be more accurate to pursue a different line of thought, expressed by the same Koryakov: "From that moment onwards, 17 November 1932, it seems to me, Pasternak, without realising it, entered the personal life of Stalin and became some part of his inner world."

But why "without realising it"? Pasternak in fact had recognised this in a rejected strophe from the well-known poem published in *Izvestiya*, "The temper obstinate appeals":

> As in a two-part fugue
> He is not infinitely small,
> He trusts in the mutual understanding
> Of the two most widely separate principles.

This poem was prefigured in November 1932 when "as an artist" he thought about Stalin "for the first time". The word *artist* embraces more than "soothsayer" and the like. A creative mind is greater than that of one who is endowed with special powers of perception but whose vision is without love. Rembrandt could not have painted his portraits had he not combined his creative energy with a feminine sensitivity that does not weigh virtues and vices but grasps the individual as a whole. In this letter, Pasternak confesses to what is, virtually, a feminine love for Stalin. This frees him from possible accusations of servility, literary politicking or diplomacy. For as long as the artist is engaged in the creative battle to master material that resists him, he is above categories of good and evil (which different judges may assess in a variety of ways).

In the *Izvestiya* poems, Pasternak called Stalin an "actor at the height of his powers", a "genius of the deed". This echoes a widespread opinion of the 1920s that, alongside the post-war neurasthenics who as elsewhere had been unbalanced by unprecedented events, a new breed had appeared in the young Soviet society. There was talk of individuals who could change the course of major and minor events by their actions. The meditative and reflective observed these confident newcomers with a greedy curiosity: cheerful atheists, they would stop at nothing, even voluntary service in the Cheka. In such an atmosphere the term *deed* had a grave and meaningful ring.

In Pasternak's poems, the deed of Stalin can be understood to mean his twice-exercised pardon, first of Mandelstam, then of Akhmatova. In this sense, the word leads us back to Pasternak's first note to Stalin. Boris Paramonov offers the following interpretation of this episode in his "Pasternak versus Romanticism":[20]

> Pasternak identified the revolution with woman but gave it an ambivalent interpretation as both the revolt against violence and violence itself. He saw Stalin, the "murderer of the revolution", as quite simply the murderer of his own wife. "Saw", of course, is not the right word. In his own mysterious inner being, he bore such images and unconsciously surmised that this was the case, while Stalin, as unconsciously, guessed what Pasternak had seen. In this Kremlin drama, Pasternak sat in a corner as judge and as witness.

If we extend this "unconscious" contact to these three encounters, the telephone conversation and the two letters, we shall need neither to pose nor answer the question, as Mikhail Koryakov and, later, Boris Paramonov did.

In that first encounter, they saw "the reason why Pasternak survived: he gave Stalin a mystic fright". But perhaps both authors have been in too much of a hurry to deny Stalin's human side. Could Stalin be called the "murderer of the revolution" before Kirov was killed and the subsequent appalling fabricated show trials? This generalisation ignores the formation of character and, in the present case, the gradual transformation of a human being into a bloodthirsty monster. For the time being, Stalin was engaged in a cruel and deceitful struggle only with those of his political rivals (Trotsky, Kirov) who might displace him. This was not the same as murdering, in a fit of rage or perhaps jealousy, his wife and the mother of his two children. Someone had to pity if not

---

[20] *Norwich Symposia on Russian Literature* (Northfield, Vt, 1991), vol. 1, pp. 11–25.

forgive the murderer. Chance helped him learn of the poet's sincere compassion. Furthermore, this was not just one more expression of condolence: here was the potential author of his exaltation in verse. The poems, as we know, came later. After they had appeared, there would be yet another fit of submission to the enchantment of power. Kornei Chukovsky records the following in his diary:[21]

22 April 1936

Yesterday at the congress of the Komsomol, I was sitting in the sixth or seventh row. I looked around and there was Boris Pasternak. I went up to him and took him to the front rows (there was a free place next to me). Suddenly, Kaganovich, Voroshilov, Andreyev, Zhdanov and Stalin appeared. The excitement in the hall! And HE stood, a little weary, pensive and majestic. One had a sense of power, an enormous assurance of authority and, at the same time, something feminine and soft. I looked about me. Everyone had enamoured, tender, inspired and laughing eyes. To see him – simply to see him – was a joy for all of us. Demchenko [a Komsomol leader] kept turning to him with some comment or other. We were all jealous and envious – how lucky she was! Each of his gestures was received with reverence. I would never have believed myself capable of such feelings. When he was applauded, he took out his (silver) pocket watch and showed it to the audience with a delightful smile. We all whispered one to another, "His watch, his watch, he's pointing to his watch," and when we were leaving we again recalled that watch as we collected our coats and hats.

Pasternak whispered words of adulation all the time, I did the same, and with one voice we said: "Tsk, that Demchenko is now blocking our view of him (for a minute)."

Pasternak and I walked home together and were both elated with joy.

This was probably the last twinge of Pasternak's psychological infection by Stalin's forceful personality. The reversal began in June 1937, when he refused to sign the writers' collective demand for Marshal Tukhachevsky's execution. Sharing the general sense of horror at the depredations of the terror, he was then personally shaken by the death

---

[21] Kornei Chukovsky, *Diaries, 1930–69* (Moscow, 1994).

Akhmatova and Boris Pasternak, 1946

of his friends the Georgian poets Titian Tabidze and Paolo Yashvili. In the familiar pages of *Izvestiya*, he read the words of a deflated and crushed Bukharin before his death. Pasternak now rejected the terrible figure of Stalin.[22]

Mandelstam's path led him in the opposite direction. Beginning with the sharp political satire in 1933, it ended with the contrived "Ode to Stalin" of early 1937. The latter was something written for the moment and not worth the attention of the researcher. But in a poem from January 1937, Mandelstam succumbed, as Pasternak had done, to the attraction of a great historical figure:

> Mid the noise and bustle of the people
> At the rail stations and on the wharves
> Gazes the epoch's mighty landmark,
> And his eyebrows start soaring in flight.

Astounded by Stalin's pardon, Mandelstam talked of him emotionally and thankfully: "And with the caress of a gentle reproach, / his eyes on the wall drilled through me." The poem's closing quatrain is repentant:

---

[22] On 21 August 1936, a collective letter demanding the death penalty for Zinoviev and Kamenev carried Pasternak's signature, though he had given neither assent nor permission. He refused twice to sign a similar demand in June 1937 for the execution of the leading Red Army officers (despite his objections, the name Pasternak was nevertheless published in two such lists). See Barnes (note 18).

And without a pass I entered the Kremlin,
To his heart of hearts I went,
Ripping through the canvas of distance,
Weighed down by my penitent head . . .

At this point the unforeseen occurred. Alongside these poems of recon-
ciliation, when Mandelstam was no longer thinking of Stalin but of the
looming "wholesale deaths" of the twentieth century, something
surfaced. Evidently it was from the poet's subconscious, where he
"dawdled and glowered", that there arose almost beside Pasternak's
"genius of the deed", "the overcast, pockmarked and disparaged genius
of the plundered graves" (*Verses on the Unknown Soldier*, 1937). What
is this, if not a portrait of Stalin?

It is interesting to compare all of these poems with Mandelstam's first
response to Nadezhda's account of her conversation with Pasternak.
Unfortunately, from her hurried version we can pick up only incomplete
and not always intelligible phrases from her private conversations with
her husband:

> . . . He was most content with Pasternak, particularly his
> remark about writers' organisations which "since 1927 had
> not got involved in individual cases".
>
> "That was an accurate statement," he laughed. But he was
> dissatisfied that the conversation had taken place at all. "Why
> was Pasternak brought into this? I should sort it out myself,
> it's nothing to do with him." Later: "He's quite right that
> the main thing is not about mastery . . . Why is Stalin so
> afraid of 'mastery'? It's a kind of superstition on his part. He
> thinks that we can cast a spell on him . . ." Finally: "But
> those verses must have made an impression if he kicked up
> such a row about re-examining the case."

The poet proved right. In his conversations with Rudakov in Voronezh,
Mandelstam would return several times to his thoughts about the power
that was locked up in poetry.

If we are to trust the accuracy of Nadezhda's record, it was in this
sense, perhaps, that Mandelstam understood Stalin's question about his
mastery. However, in Nadezhda's first verbal account of Pasternak's tale,
I did not detect such a nuance. For it was not a matter of the sense of
her words so much as one of intonation and gesture. They indicate that
the replies of Stalin, who twice lost his self-control, should be thus interpreted. He probably broke off the conversation abruptly, not because

he felt angry but because he was suddenly disconcerted: Pasternak's request to meet and discuss "life and death" directly recalled Alliluyeva's tragic end. The nervous repetition, "But he is a master, isn't he? Isn't he?" indicates Stalin's wish to hear confirmation from his qualified interlocutor that Mandelstam was right. My interpretation finds support in a phrase from Nadezhda's appeal to Beria, which she made after Mandelstam's death (though she did not then know that he had died). Among her reproaches was a reference to his mastery, which should be a positive factor for the authorities: ". . . And also to clarify what is rather a moral than a judicial issue: Did the NKVD have sufficient grounds for destroying a poet and *master* during a period of his active and loyal poetical activity?" (Emphasis added, E.G.)

When Mandelstam was still living in Voronezh it was as if he had guessed that the "verses" had made an impression on Stalin. How had he "cast a spell" on him? Above all, by the very image of the ruler who as the supreme authority administered punishment and pardon. In his depiction of this great figure, such details as "oily fingers" and "cockroach eyes" fade into the background. Even "executions" did not embarrass the leader: Lenin had also demanded that people be shot, since the Revolution must defend itself. The heart of the matter lay elsewhere.

Again, let us look around us, at the context. The phone call to the communal apartment where Pasternak then lived was made on 11 June 1934. On 28 January of the same year, the Seventeenth Congress of the Communist Party had begun its proceedings. It ended on 10 February with elections to the Central Committee. Historians tell us that Stalin did not receive the largest number of votes; Kirov was more popular.[23] All that year, which ended with Kirov's murder, Stalin was preoccupied with strengthening his personal authority and taking revenge on his enemies among the Party's highest bodies. In this context, one strophe from Mandelstam's seditious poem must have been balm to the ears of the secretly plotting Stalin:

> Around him a rabble of chicken-necked leaders
> He toys with the service of such semi-humans.
> They whistle, they meow, and they whine:
> He alone merely jabs with his finger and barks . . .

---

[23] In the newspaper reports, Stalin's name headed the list of the new Central Committee. At the Congress, the names were announced in order of the number of votes cast, and there some eight or nine names preceded that of the General Secretary (see Razgon [note 15], "Ivan Moskvin").

It was as if the poet had granted him an indulgence for the crimes that the tyrant had not yet consciously decided to commit!

Such words might be muttered in the hidden corners of the Kremlin palaces as, one by one, Stalin selected from the "rabble" a "chicken-necked leader" and set him against another. *It seems that this Mandelstam is a great master. I must find out more about him* . . . I shall refrain from looking any deeper into the soul and plots of this malefactor. The events of 1937–9 are known to all and speak for themselves.

There are no traces in the circumstances of Mandelstam's last arrest to indicate that Stalin had again cast a baleful glance in his direction. After such a bloodletting, the show trials and the mass executions, imprisonment and banishment of innocent people, he evidently no longer had time to take any interest in the poet. The authorities would have forgotten all about him if he had not set about attracting the attention of his "brother writers" in Moscow and Leningrad. They feared him. At any moment, they might be accused of knowing about that awful anti-Soviet poem, yet its author, for some reason, was a free man. Stalin himself had once treated him with mercy. But what now? It would be best to keep clear of him and quietly send him as far away from Moscow as possible.

The presently accepted account of his second arrest in May 1938 is laughable. By then, people who had just undergone operations were being dragged from their hospital beds and carted off to the Lubyanka. Who would go to the trouble of hiding Mandelstam away in the Samatikha sanatorium, in order to create less of a fuss when arresting him? What nonsense. Why, in those circumstances, should the Writers' Union have magnanimously provided Mandelstam and his wife with two months' free vacation at a rest home not far from the capital? While they were there, several calls enquiring about Mandelstam's health came from the Writers' Union. It is clear that some plot to remove Mandelstam and his wife from Moscow, where their position was not clear, had been thought up. This was all fairly described in Pavlenko's letter to the secretary of the Writers' Union in which he wanted to make a "filial or fraternal" complaint about the disquiet that the fussy poet was causing. We cannot tell from the published documents who decided the fate of Mandelstam the second time; we only know who carried out the orders.

Nadezhda was haunted by the suspicion that a private incident involving a woman in the Communist Party had played its part. In her complaint to Beria, she requested him "to check if someone's personal interest had not been involved in this banishment". She was also uneasy that Mandelstam was singled out. She herself remained at liberty though both had been involved in the incident. So long as we do not possess all the necessary documents, we shall not be able to disentangle this knot.

It is much clearer why Lev Gumilyov was kept imprisoned until 1956. He could be released only after the Twentieth Party Congress had issued its decree, condemning the Cult of Personality and its harmful consequences. Only then was there a decline in the power of Andreyev, who had been dealing with Akhmatova since 1940. Her collection *From Six Books* was then vetoed by three Central Committee secretaries, Zhdanov, Malenkov and Andreyev.

Zhdanov had shown himself to be an incomparable obscurant in 1946, but he died in 1948. Following Stalin's death, Malenkov was very soon removed from power. Only Andreyev remained as a member of the USSR Supreme Soviet's presidium though not of the Politburo. There is no doubt that the ban on any re-examination of Lev Gumilyov's case originated with Andreyev. (Perhaps he had never forgotten or forgiven the above-quoted insulting verse from Mandelstam's poem?) The confirmation of this theory is that Lev Gumilyov was rehabilitated immediately after the Twentieth Party Congress. That did not cure his obsessive and unfounded grudge against his mother, however.

"Good luck was not enough; bad luck must lend a hand," Russians say. As far as Gumilyov's release is concerned, the reverse is true. The good fortune was that one of the "Mikoyan" commissions, established to speed up the re-examination of the cases against those wrongly convicted, was based in Omsk. It freed Lyova. He returned to Moscow, where his file now lay on Prosecutor-General Rudenko's desk: once the latter had returned from Baku, he would formally object to the original decision. That it would require an official objection from the prosecutor-general himself to free Lyova, incidentally, is just one more indication of the complexity surrounding Akhmatova's political position, the fate of Nikolai Gumilyov and the situation of their son, Lev. The two stages whereby he was rehabilitated for ever reinforced his false conviction that he had secured his own release. I remember his unexpected reaction when I remarked: "Lyova, it was the Twentieth Party Congress that released you." "There!" he cried, somehow amazed by my words. "So! That means Mama did not make any pleas at all for me!" The outburst that followed was so passionate that I could clearly see it was impossible to change his mind.

Only occasionally did Lyova shake off this obsessive idea and talk normally of his mother with the tenderness and concern he had often shown towards her in his youth. Saddest of all, however, is that this legend of the bad mother became fixed in the imagination of those who moved in semi-literary circles (and even among those with purely literary interests). This satisfies the insuperable passion for melodrama that, strange as it may seem, has taken root in Russian society as we contemplate the great tragedies of the twentieth century, which we have endured and suffered up to the present time. Let us free one of Russia's best poets from the grips of this saccharine genre and restore to Akhmatova that which is hers by right, her tragic biography and the voice of Tragedy that was her muse. For his part, Lev Gumilyov survived his mother by a quarter century, living in peace and freedom with his devoted wife, Natalya. He went on to write several major works about the history of Russia and Central Asia, and we should approach them as scholarship demands, without rapture, tearfulness or derision.

The Roots of Tragedy

Among Anna Akhmatova's manuscripts at the National Library in St Petersburg two poetic fragments long lay concealed, jotted on the draft of an article about Pushkin. They are not linked thematically to Akhmatova's studies of the poet but belong to the category of "vagrant" lines (this definition often occurs in Akhmatova's correspondence and in Nikolai Gumilyov's "Letters about Russian Poetry"). With no recipient or evident purpose, they are essentially notes from a diary: the presence of rhyme and the lack of a date do not nullify such an interpretation. From the draft text of the Pushkin article it is easy to establish that they were written in 1958–9. Rhyme came easily to Akhmatova, who had been writing poetry since she was eleven. Verse more precisely expressed her innermost thoughts than prose – she herself often said as much, both in conversation and in what she wrote.

Neither fragment, one a couplet, the other six lines long, has hitherto been published as written. Editors were probably deterred by the naked revelation of the first and the mysterious obscurity of the second. Unable to trace a continuous thought in the latter, those who first examined Akhmatova's poetic legacy divided the six lines into two poems. Following the earliest editors the first four lines were accordingly included in one volume and the remainder in another. Ten years, moreover, separated the two publications [*Neva* monthly, June 1979, and *Collected Works in Two Volumes*, 1990]. Clearly, these fragments need to be reinterpreted and provided with a proper commentary.

"The ring of coins". That was how Akhmatova began, but the line ends there and became a title for the first fragment, the following two-line poem:[24]

> No thoughts, no roof
> Nor even a hearth.

The verse grew from a rhyme [in Russian] with the title phrase but acquired a meaning that left such a formal connection behind. An extreme expression of inner devastation is linked to an acknowledgement of how unsettled Akhmatova's domestic circumstances then were. Strange as it may seem, her comfortless life was due to a relative well-being in material terms, an unfamiliar state for her. This introduced a new element in relations with friends and those she lived with.

The "ring of coins" was to be heard after Akhmatova began translating verse, an activity that was fatal to the poet's creative energy. She discussed this with Lydia Chukovskaya more than once. Asked whether she was writing new poems, Akhmatova once replied: "Of course not. The translations do not permit it. You lie there, trying out different variants. What poems could you expect?!" That was in 1952. When Akhmatova began to translate yet more systematically and professionally, she again complained to Chukovskaya: "I feel as if I'm doing hard labour. Today I picked up my article about Pushkin, the 'Duel', for twenty minutes and put it down almost immediately. Not allowed. That's playing truant." These words were spoken in 1958, and Chukovskaya's diary entry is dated 19 December. The fragments under discussion, I would say, date roughly from that same time.

How did Akhmatova live then? Anyone who saw her regularly during the last ten years of her life remembers that she was living between two cities and, naturally, two apartments. Age and sickness no longer permitted her to live alone. She could not stay longer than four months at a time in Moscow because of the extremely strict registration rules. If someone officially occupying a room or an apartment was absent for longer, the police had the right to cancel his or her domicile registration – i.e. prevent the person living in their native town. It's easy to imagine how Akhmatova feared that. Frequently urged to exchange her Leningrad room for another in Moscow, she would give the melancholy reply: "But where then will you bury me?" She feared exclusion from Petersburg not only during her lifetime but also after her death. In her beloved city she lived with her stepdaughter, Irina Punina, and the latter's daughter Anya (Anna

---

[24] *Zvon monyet: "I dumy nyet, i doma nyet, / I dazhe dyma nyet."*

Kaminskaya). She had watched both grow up, and the atmosphere of that household was different from that of the Ardovs at Ordynka: it was more familiar and, at times, altogether too casual. But for Akhmatova this had its charm: "Ira is the only person – apart from Lyova, of course – who addresses me as thou," she frequently remarked. As for Lyova, he was still in the camps and sending his mother what I can only describe as "difficult" letters. When he returned in 1956, he was so antagonistic towards her that it was impossible to imagine them living together. Both were sick and in need of treatment, and Lyova was impatient to create a new, free life for himself. In the end, he set up on his own. His visits added a further tension to that strange "family". Unfortunately, those around Akhmatova made little effort to ease the situation and, on the contrary, only hastened the coming total estrangement.

The son's long-awaited return had proved a wretched event, and this is part of the sorrowful self-revelation, "I have no thoughts." Clearly, Akhmatova was referring not to mental sloth but to something akin to Job's lament (17:11): "My days are past, my purposes are broken off, even the thoughts of my heart."

As to the third phrase, "nor even a hearth", she lacked not just a roof but even a home of her own. The old meaning of the word she uses [lit. "smoke" in Russian] was long preserved in the Russian countryside and denoted the household and all that was in it. This line says, in other words, "I have no family" and adds a further tinge of mournful deser-tion to the fragment.

Akhmatova did not make her "vagrant" lines public. But what we hear in the couplet curled up in the margin of this manuscript found its way into a finished poem she wrote at the same time. During the author's lifetime, it was not published due to the constraints of censorship. However, Akhmatova gladly read it to her friends. I even remember how acute my response was to one line, "Can you thus dispel the hurt?" (probably because of its harmonious interplay of vowels and consonants):

> In vain you cast at my feet
> Grandeur and glory and power.
> For well you know, this is no cure
> For the radiant passion of song.
> Can you thus dispel the hurt?
> Do they heal longing with gold?
> Perhaps I shall mimic surrender
> And not put the gun to my head.
> Yet Death still waits at the door:

Drive her off or call her in,
But behind her darkens the road
Down which I crawled in blood.

Behind her lie the decades
Of tedium, of fear and that void
Of which I'd sing many a song
Did I not fear you'd break into tears.
Farewell then, I live not in a wasteland,
Eternal Russia and Night are with me.
If you'll only save me from pride
The rest I shall manage myself.

9 April 1958

There are many allusions in this poem. "Imagination casts before him its motley hand of cards," it says in the eighth chapter of *Yevgeny Onegin*.[25] And there is another source in the first strophe or, to be more exact, an instance of self-repetition that ultimately derives from the 15-year-old Lermontov's "Prayer" ("From the terrible thirst for song / Let me, Creator, free myself"). In Akhmatova's poem of 1913, we read: "I prayed again, slake the mute thirst for poetry!" In "The Suicide" [1920], notes Kralin, the Acmeist poet Narbut writes:[26] "And you . . ., Imagine I'd put the gun to my temple? Me?!" "Night is with me" refers back to "Oceano Nox" (night rises from the sea), a chapter title in Herzen's *Past and Thoughts*. From Akhmatova alone in this completed poem we find "Eternal Russia" as the bulwark, and "pride" as the unvanquished sin.

Elucidating these allusions also helps us to unravel the puzzle posed by the second draft, the six lines scribbled on the back of that same page from Akhmatova's manuscript article about Pushkin:

Not with you shall I eat the repast
Not of you I shall ask forgiveness
Nor fall at your feet
Nor fear you at night . . .
The bells tolled early in Uglich
The Tsarevich lay wounded to the heart.

---

[25] E.G.: When Akhmatova was reflecting on this chapter, she tried to remember where else Pushkin had used the image. On 5 November 1830, writing about current political events to Vyazemsky, she discovered the poet had complained: "They deal us the purest nonsense and still we keep on punting."

[26] E.G.: See Kralin (ed.), *Akhmatova: Works in Two Volumes* (Petersburg, 1990).

What subterranean currents had brought these lines to the surface I guessed immediately. But suspicions alone would convince no-one, and I said nothing. Not long ago, however, my private interpretation received unexpected support. Many more unpublished drafts of Akhmatova had been preserved in M.S. Lesman's collection, and these were now analysed in Roman Timenchik's article "Pages from Akhmatova's Drafts".[27]

Although the scattered pages were gathered together by pure accident, Timenchik could discern the characteristic themes of Akhmatova's last creative period in these wandering lines. As he rightly observed, these drafts centre on two lyrical cycles, "Cinque" and "Sweetbrier in Blossom". Both are dedicated to one and the same person and linked by a particular subject: Akhmatova's 1945 meeting with Isaiah Berlin, who had come from England to Leningrad, and her refusal to see him in 1956 when he visited the Soviet Union again. Evidently, our second fragment also relates to the same subject and is linked by a variety of echoes to the fragments in the Lesman collection.

The theme of "his" guilt adorns the eleventh poem in "Sweetbrier ": "You do not know for what you were forgiven." Guilt remains the subject in a later verse but now falls on a new character, on "her": "Whether she expected to hear forgiveness, / Whether she foresaw farewell . . ." But no, "she" is not guilty before him. "It wasn't you I once destroyed". An inner dialogue can be heard in the six-line poem. The heroine feels guilt but not before Berlin. So for whom does she experience such a terrible guilt? "The Tsarevich . . . wounded to the heart."

The Tsarevich Dmitry Ivanovich, slain in Uglich according to legend, was guilty only of having been born. Ivan the Terrible's grandson should not have existed and was a hindrance to other pretenders to the Russian throne. At the same age, the nine-year-old son of Akhmatova and the executed poet Gumilyov became just such an innocent martyr. The very fact of his birth condemned him to misfortune,[28] and he became the central figure in the tragic denouement of a highly dramatic conflict.

All these fragments, whether in "Cinque" or "Sweetbrier", refer to encounters with a guest from abroad that left a powerful trace in Akhmatova's poetic consciousness. Why does this third figure force his way into the "old argument of two"? He is there "in the twilight of

---

[27] E.G.: In *Books and Manuscripts from the Collection of M.S. Lesman* (Moscow, 1989).
[28] E.G.: Strange as it seems, no-one better expressed his catastrophic fate than Marina Tsvetayeva in exalted lines from her "Poems for Akhmatova" cycle. "The child's name is Lev" was written in 1916, some while before Nikolai Gumilyov's execution. But how often poets are proved correct in their insights!

rotten plank beds", and in the distant echo "of long-perished bell-towers"; or descending "once more the flagged steps, / Ancient as the Battle of the Don". In the Lesman collection, yet another "constant feature" makes itself felt and is addressed one way or another to the "stranger from Europe": the motifs of "Everlasting Russia". This observation by Timenchik ties in with the appearance of the Tsarevich Dmitry, one of the meekest heroes in Russian history.

It is time for us to descend from the region of poetic visions to the "swarms of lowly truths". In Sir Isaiah Berlin's memoirs, there is a chapter recounting his Leningrad meetings with Akhmatova and their failure to meet in Moscow. He describes events in sober, humdrum tones.[29]

> I did not see her on my next visit to the Soviet Union in 1956. Pasternak told me that though Anna Andreyevna wanted to see me, her son, who had been rearrested some time after I had met him, had been released from his prison camp only a short while before and therefore she felt nervous of seeing foreigners at the present time, particularly as she attributed the furious onslaught upon her by the Party at least in part to my visit in 1945. Pasternak said that he doubted whether my visit had done her any harm but since she evidently believed that it had, and had been advised to avoid compromising associations, she could not see me.

This seems a conversation not between a Poet and a Philosopher, as we are accustomed to think of them, but between two upright gentlemen. Boris Pasternak's friendly aid to Akhmatova indeed put him in an awkward position. The gentleman who was declined the opportunity to meet her must have felt no less awkward. Especially since a policy was involved that must have struck the citizen of one of Europe's most law-abiding states as quite fantastic. In their conversation, both forget their own observations of Soviet life in which the irrational could so distinctly be conjectured. But their true sense of History betrayed them here, and they sought for common sense where it had never existed and, by definition, could not be present.

Lyova was very harshly interrogated about the visit the foreign diplomat made to his mother. In the first days after his return from the camps, when his mind could not cope with everything, Lyova was unable to provide a continuous account of all he had endured during the past

---

[29] Isaiah Berlin, "Meetings with Russian Writers in 1945 and 1956", in *Personal Impressions* (London, 1980).

Nikolai Gumilyov, Anna Akhmatova and their son, Lev, 1916

years. This made the words that burst from him involuntarily all the
more convincing. For instance, he was disturbed that he had referred
disdainfully to Akhmatova ("Mama fell victim to her own vanity,") in
all that concerned that fateful visit. A minute later and he was passionately recalling that he was supposed to take care of the burned papers
lying in the ashtrays. "What was she burning?" they had asked him.
These were the famous burned scraps of paper on which Akhmatova
jotted down any sinister news: justifiably she feared that all her words
were being recorded but did not observe how these burned papers gave
her away. For they would be found after a close friend had left her by
one of the usual informers. Once Lev could not help recalling how his
interrogator seized him by the hair and beat his head against the strong
walls of Lefortovo prison, demanding that he admit that Akhmatova
had spied for England.[30] He did not pass on the interrogator's words
to me precisely, but just the other day (February 1995) I read Oleg
Kalugin's seminar comments in which he spoke plainly of this claim by
the KGB.

Gradually, Lyova forgot the political aspect of his fate and reduced
relations with his mother to a domestic, psychological level that was,
moreover, very trite. I remember how tears came to Akhmatova's eyes
– and she rarely cried – when cruelly hurt by my incautious tale. This
concerned Lyova's determined courting of one of Akhmatova's friends.

---

[30] In 1950 Abakumov, then head of the MGB, would demand that Akhmatova
also be arrested. See Introduction, p. xix.

"Mama did not love Papa, and her loveless attitude was transferred to me," he complained to this woman. Amazed, Akhmatova exclaimed in tears: "He's using us!" Of course, it was terribly interesting to learn from an "authentic source" about the relations between the two famous poets, and this boosted their beloved son's chances of attracting the lady's attention. For that reason, she would then tell me about these conversations.

Akhmatova was dispirited by this conscious trivialising of the tragic fate that bound them together. She was astonished by the extreme egocentricity he now displayed. "He's collapsed into himself," she noted many times, or, "There is nothing left now, nothing but gossip and informers." With assurance she would declare, "He was never that way; they gave him back to me like that!" Where then does that strong note of guilt come from: "Nor fall at your feet / Nor fear you at night . . ."?

Listening more than once to Akhmatova's heavy-hearted reflections about Lyova, I did not appreciate (perhaps I simply did not know) that she had a real chance to leave Russia soon after Gumilyov's execution. "What would have happened, if he'd been brought up abroad?" she often asked herself. "He would have known several languages, gone on archaeological expeditions with Rostovtseff, and the way would have been open for him to become an academic, for which he was destined."

Her intention to emigrate is directly mentioned in two documents. Vladimir Weidlé tells of seeing Akhmatova before he quit Russia for ever: "Akhmatova asked me to find out the terms on which her son would be accepted by the Russian *gymnasium* in Paris, if she decided to send him there . . . She herself was not planning to go anywhere . . ." Weidlé recalled this conversation when Akhmatova was already dead, and her negative attitude to emigration was widely known from her poems and behaviour (*Anna Akhmatova: After All*, Moscow: MPI, 1989).

But Akhmatova's clear intention to leave Russia is reflected in another document. On 26 November 1926, Tsvetayeva wrote from Bellevue:

I'm writing in response to the joyous prospect of your arrival . . . I want to know whether you will be alone or with family (mother and son). Whatever the case, don't hesitate, come . . . Conquer your "agraphia" . . . and write back to me this minute: the dates, alone or with family, a decision or a daydream. Be assured that I will meet you at the rail station . . .

[*Unpublished Letters*, Paris: YMCA Press, 1972]

That was the only chance of saving Lyova. Many mothers leave their own countries in order to save their children from harassment and persecution. Akhmatova could not deny her vocation. Duty as a mother conflicted with her duty as a poet. There lay the roots of a tragedy that was genuine and not imagined. It was this that predetermined Lev Gumilyov's harsh fate.

Written 1994–5. First published as "Akhmatova and Lev Gumilyov: Reflections of an Eyewitness", in *Znamya* (September 1995).

Postscript: The Decisive Letter [1996]

In articles published abroad in the 1970s,[31] I mentioned the presumed reason for the delay in reopening Lyova's case. They had dropped such hints at the military prosecutor's office when I went there on Akhmatova's behalf. From early 1955, a letter from Ilya Ehrenburg to Khrushchev on the same subject was receiving special attention there. A year earlier, however, Akhmatova had received a refusal from the USSR prosecutor-general's office in reply to her letter to Voroshilov. That document was now preventing the military prosecutor's office from investigating the case against Lev Gumilyov.

Today we can finally read the text of Akhmatova's letter and the lengthy and detailed refusal of Prosecutor-General Rudenko. (My thanks to Vitaly Shentalinsky for providing me with photocopies of these historic documents from the State Archive of the Russian Federation.)

1 Architect Rudnev to Voroshilov, date stamped 10 February

5 February 1954

Highly esteemed Klement Yefremovich
    The poet Anna Akhmatova is profoundly disturbed by her separation from her only son, a historian, who has now spent five years in the camps. And this is having a bad effect on her creative work.

---

[31] "Memoirs and Facts: The Release of Lev Gumilyov", *Russian Literature Tri-Quarterly* (Ann Arbor), 13 (1977); "Memoirs and Facts: The Release of Lev Gumilyov", in E. Proffer (ed.), *Anna Akhmatova* (Ann Arbor, 1977).

I beseech you, Klement Yefremovich, to aid the poet Akhmatova in her anguish.

Respectfully yours
Architect L. Rudnev

2 Akhmatova to Voroshilov, date stamped 10 February

Leningrad, 4 Krasnaya Konnitsa St, apt 3
Moscow, 17 Bolshaya Ordynka, apt 13 (c/o the writer Victor Ardov)
<u>8 February 1954</u>

Highly esteemed Kliment Yefremovich

I implore you to save my only son, who is in a corrective labour camp (Omsk, PO box 125) and has there become disabled.

Lev Nikolayevich (b. 1912) was arrested in Leningrad on 6 November 1949 by the MGB and sentenced by the Special Session to ten years' imprisonment in a corrective labour camp.

Not one of the charges brought against him during the investigation was confirmed, he wrote to tell me that. The Special Session nevertheless convicted him.

My son is serving his second sentence. In March 1938, when he was in his fourth year at the history faculty of Leningrad University, he was arrested by the MVD and sentenced by the Special Session to five years. He served this sentence in Norilsk. On completing his term of imprisonment, he worked as a free employee in Turukhansk. In 1944, after his insistent demands, he was allowed to go to the front as a volunteer. He served as a private in the ranks of the Soviet Army and took part in the storming of Berlin (he has a medal "For the Capture of Berlin").

After the war was won, he returned to Leningrad, where, in a brief space of time, he graduated from the university and defended his master's degree. From 1949, he was senior research associate of the Ethnographic Museum in Leningrad.

His teachers, M.I. Artamonov, director of the Hermitage Museum, and Professor N.V. Kuner, could provide information about the value of his scholarly activities for the discipline of Soviet historical studies.

My son is now 41, and he could still work for the good of his country, pursuing his beloved subject.

Dear Kliment Yefremovich, help us! Until very recently, I was still able to work, despite this grief, and translated the play Marion Delorme for the jubilee edition of Victor Hugo's works and two epic poems by the great Chinese poet Ch'u Yuan. But now I feel that my strength is fading: I am over 60, I have suffered a serious heart attack, and despair is destroying me. The only thing that might preserve my powers is the return of my son, who is suffering, of this I'm sure, for no crime.

Anna Akhmatova

To this letter were added the following comments, both dated 12 February 1954:

(i) To Rudenko, R.A.
Please examine and assist,
K. Voroshilov

(ii) A copy bearing Comrade Voroshilov's resolution has been sent to Comrade Rudenko, [signature]

3 Rudenko to Voroshilov

Confidential
Prosecutor General of USSR
15a Pushkin Street, Moscow
6 July 1954

To: Chairman of Presidium
USSR Supreme Soviet
Comrade K.E. VOROSHILOV

An examination of the charge against GUMILYOV Lev Nikolayevich has established that he was sentenced on 13 September 1950 by the [now] disbanded Special Session attached to the USSR MGB to ten years in corrective labour camps for belonging to an anti-Soviet group, having terrorist intentions and conducting anti-Soviet agitation.

Earlier, on 26 July 1939, he was sentenced by the Special Session attached to the USSR NKVD for his participation in 1937 in an anti-Soviet group to five years in corrective labour camps.

During the 1949–50 investigation, GUMILYOV testified that his anti-Soviet views came into being as early as 1933 under the influence of the anti-Soviet attitudes of the poet MANDELSTAM and of GUMILYOV's stepfather PUNIN. He and PUNIN gathered around themselves like-minded sympathisers in the person of students BORIN, POLYAKOV and MAKHAYEV, and by 1934 they had formed an anti-Soviet group. It was effectively at GUMILYOV's apartment that they repeatedly voiced various slanderous fabrications concerning the leaders of the Party and the Government, derided living conditions in the Soviet Union, discussed methods of struggle against the Soviet regime and whether terror could be applied in the struggle against the Soviet government, and read verse of a counter-revolutionary content. GUMILYOV recited a lampoon of similar character, "Ekabatava", in response to the murder of S.M. Kirov, in which he vilely slandered I.V. Stalin and S.M. Kirov. He also spoke of the necessity of establishing a monarchist system in the USSR.

Concerning anti-Soviet activities in the period 1945–8, GUMILYOV deposed that after being released from a place of confinement in 1944, his views remained hostile to the Soviet regime; he slandered the penitentiary policies of the Soviet regime and made remarks in an anti-Soviet spirit about certain individual measures of the Communist Party and the Soviet government.

Thus after the publication of the Central Committee decree concerning the magazines Zvezda and Leningrad, he several times condemned the decree and declared that there was no freedom of the press in the Soviet Union, and that a real writer could do nothing for he had to write as instructed, to a set model.

The instances of GUMILYOV's anti-Soviet activities laid out in his depositions were confirmed by the depositions of PUNIN, BORIN, POLYAKOV, MAKHAYEV, MANDELSTAM and SHUMOVSKY.

In 1951, GUMILYOV appealed for his case to be reopened, indicating that his conviction was the result of a negative attitude to his mother, the poetess AKHMATOVA, and also the negative attitude to himself as a young Orientalist scholar.

GUMILYOV was refused a re-examination of the Special Session's decision by the main military prosecutor's office.

AKHMATOVA in a complaint addressed to yourself wrote that the charges brought against GUMILYOV during his investigation were not confirmed; however her assertion does not correspond to reality.

On the basis that GUMILYOV, L.N. was correctly convicted, the Central Commission for the re-examination of criminal cases adopted the decision on 14 June 1954 to refuse AKHMATOVA in her petition for the decision of the Special Session attached to the MGB USSR on 13 September 1950 concerning her son GUMI-LYOV, Lev Nikolayevich, to be re-examined.

State Judicial Councillor
[signature]
R. Rudenko

We may add to these unique documents the last official paper in the case file. This graphically illustrates how the same Prosecutor-General Rudenko then recognised that there had been no case against L. Gumilyov. It required Khrushchev's astounding speech to the Twentieth Party Congress in February 1956 to achieve such a dramatic reversal.

4 Military prosecutor to Emma Gerstein

USSR Prosecutor-General's Office
Chief military prosecutor's office
To: Citizen Emma Gerstein
27, Greater Serpukhovsky St, apt 67
Moscow
(for Citizen Akhmatova, A.A.)
<u>30 July 1956</u>

I am informing you that the case under which GUMILYOV, Lev Nikolayevich, was convicted in 1950 has been examined.

It is established that there were no grounds for Gumilyov L.N.'s conviction.

By official protest of the USSR Prosecutor-General, dated 2 June 1956, the decree of the Special Session attached to the MGB USSR on 13 September 1950 with regard to GUMILYOV Lev Nikolayevich is annulled, and the investigation has been closed for lack of a corpus delicti.

Military Prosecutor,
Lieutenant-Colonel Karaskua

Apart from the actual contents of the carelessly compiled list of accusations signed by Rudenko, attention is drawn to the dates at which the above correspondence passed through official channels. Rudnev's cover note (5 February) and Akhmatova's letter (8 February) were registered by the chancery of the Presidium on 10 February, but Voroshilov's resolution, added to the letter's top left corner, is dated 12 February. Perhaps he used this two-day interval to get instructions from Khrushchev on how to deal with Akhmatova, whose name continued to be abhorrent.

She herself, incidentally, guessed at such a delay and soon had the chance to confirm that her hypothesis was correct. In May 1954, she participated, with Zoshchenko, in a meeting in Leningrad with students from Oxford. Sitting next to her was the Party's literary critic A.L. Dymshits, and he managed to whisper to her that the 1946 decree had not lost any of its political force. I remember how distraught Akhmatova was that she could not warn Zoshchenko: seated between them were high-ranking official writers, and there was no way that she could approach him in full view of the public.

The date on Rudenko's letter testifies to the minimal influence Voroshilov then exercised in the new administration. Despite the peremptory tone of the Supreme Soviet's chairman he received a reply only on 6 July – i.e. five months later. The extensive text of the USSR prosecutor-general's decision has its interest as an example of the way in which such documents were compiled. Following Gumilyov's return from his first imprisonment in the camps, it says, he retained hostile attitudes to the Soviet regime: the document confuses the date of his release (he left the Norilsk camps in 1943, not 1944) and, most important of all, remains silent about his voluntary participation in the Great Patriotic War in 1944–5. He made counter-revolutionary statements, it is asserted, to students in his apartment. However, Lyova did not have his own flat. He lived with his mother at the Punin apartment, and only from 1936 did he spend the nights at his friend Axel's room (I do not know the latter's surname). In other words, he left the Punin apartment after his first arrest in 1935, when Punin was also arrested. They were both then released by Stalin, but of this most important episode not a word is said in the prosecutor-general's rejection of the plea.

However, there is mention here of Punin's depositions against Lev Gumilyov. Their paths would again cross in prison only in 1949 after Gumilyov's third arrest. Punin had been arrested for a second time, two months earlier. He was then an aged and half-blind man. That August, the rest of the Punin family were not in Leningrad, and Akhmatova and Nikolai Punin were left almost alone in the apartment. Punin had a foreboding or was expecting to be arrested. He constantly told Akhmatova:

"*They*'re hiding behind the trees." As he was descending the stairs, under escort, he mournfully uttered, "Akuma, Akuma . . ." That is what Akhmatova told me. She was deeply upset by Punin's arrest and pitied him.[32] The evident strain in relations between her son and Punin had arisen after their very first arrest, and this caused her additional pain. Evidently, there were some grounds for this tension, if the prosecutor-general's decision darkly mentions Punin's depositions against Lyova.

Reference to Mandelstam having testified against Lyova creates a still more distressing impression. Evidently, this concerns Mandelstam's depositions during his first arrest for the political satire on Stalin. Mandelstam had mentioned Lyova among the approving audience of that poem.

Among the crimes Lyova is listed as having committed, I think the mention of his conversations about freedom of the press, the position of writers and, especially, the 1946 decree is a complete fabrication. Lyova swore to me that he had never said a word to anyone about the ill-fated decree and was very proud of himself for not doing so. And he paid little heed to literature then; all his thoughts were for his research.

Still the documents published here are of prime importance. Apart from their undoubted historical interest, they clear up one of the central problems in Akhmatova's biography. The accusations that she did little to help Lyova during her son's imprisonment are without foundation. It was beyond her capacity to save him. She began to press for his release in exactly the manner Lyova had indicated, though her son little suspected or, to be more exact, had deliberately forgotten how shaky her position was. Henceforth, I hope, this question will no longer be raised in biographical literature about Akhmatova.

The appearance of such conclusive evidence in response to my publication gave me enormous satisfaction as a researcher. Among the reactions to that study [*Znamya*, September 1995] was a fragment of memoir, concerning the complex and at times puzzling relations between Stalin and Boris Pasternak.

By linking certain known but scattered facts, I threw new light on their telephone conversation concerning Mandelstam's arrest. I began with the suicide (or murder) of Stalin's wife, Nadezhda Alliluyeva, in 1932. There are several interpretations of the brief message of condolence Pasternak then sent, but I had not come across any acknowledgement of the possible influence this note had had on Pasternak's later contacts with Stalin. Now, however, I received encouraging support in a letter from my friend Tatyana Litvinova, daughter of the former Soviet

---

[32] Punin died in the Vorkuta camps on 12 August 1953.

Foreign Minister Maxim Litvinov. She was well acquainted with Ilya Ehrenburg and would visit him at home.

Their conversation about the indirect contacts between Stalin and Pasternak occurred when the latter was being harassed over his novel *Doctor Zhivago*. Litvinova writes (29 December 1995):

> Once we were discussing why Pasternak was never arrested. Ehrenburg told me that Boris Leonidovich [Pasternak] himself had a theory that the Chekists could not believe he was still at liberty, and that the Pasternak living in Peredelkino was not the same Pasternak they had locked away long before. "In actual fact," said Ehrenburg, "the following might be the case."
>
> And he told me about the "Alliluyeva letter" (hallelujah!) but I got the impression from his tale that this was not a postscript but a long, "rambling" (pre-Bukharin?) letter in Pasternak's usual style[33] and that the main thought running through his descriptions of his sleepless reflections was: How should one respond to the personal tragedy of the super-personal Man-Leader? The most important of E.'s assertions was that the letter supposedly lay under the glass covering Stalin's desk in his study. This supposedly was sufficient to deter the "chicken-necked" from touching Pasternak. Whether that was really the case, I don't know . . .[34]

Whether Pasternak's letter lay on Stalin's table or not, it is important that such a supposition existed in circles close to the highest authorities. This episode probably has no historical significance, but it is most important in psychological terms.

Written 1996. First published 1998.

---

[33] "Much later Pasternak reported that he refused to sign the collective message [in November 1932] and 'wrote Stalin a long letter on the occasion of Alliluyeva's death'" (Barnes [note 18], p. 75).

[34] E.G.: Litvinova continues: "That the psychology of lackeys is of this kind, however, I can testify. When Papa was excluded from the Central Committee in 1942 on certain nonsensical accusations, he was sitting in the auditorium while the entire suite headed by Stalin presided on the stage. Papa leapt up and shouted: 'So you consider me an Enemy of the People, do you?' Stalin had already got up, and the entire train was about to follow him into the wings. He half-turned, his pipe in his hand, and answered (slowly and meditatively, I think, from Papa's account): 'We don't consider you an Enemy of People.'"

III

NADEZHDA
[1998]

When Khardjiev lived by himself on Kropotkin Street I would often go to see him. Once during our conversations he recalled a curious comment Akhmatova had made about Mandelstam's poetry: " . . . do you know, . . . it is neither the early . . . nor the late poems I love best . . . but those somewhere in between . . ." Khardjiev could then still remember even her pose and tone: "She was lying on the sofa, her head turned towards me and, for some reason, she pronounced each and every word slowly." I was familiar with Akhmatova's unhurried diction, pausing as she spoke. This happened when she was putting a new thought into words.

By "in between" she evidently meant Mandelstam's Moscow poems of the 1930s. Later she would mournfully repeat: "I'm a tramcar cherry in a terrible age / and I don't know why I'm alive . . ." (lines from his 1931 poem: "No, I can't hide from the Great Shambles"). Then she also liked to quote a stanza from the 1935 poem in memory of Olga Vaksel: "And the firm swallows of rounded brows/ Flew to me from the coffin/ To say that they'd been resting/ in their cold Stockholm bed."

There's no question that Mandelstam's "Moscow verse" appears poorer than the philosophical poems in *Stone*, which are suffused with the poet's astonished awareness of Creation, of surrounding nature and of himself. They pale beside the solemn poetry of the early 1920s in its tense assimilation of the historic significance of that sick era. The Moscow verse can appear simple-minded when set beside the polychromatic and ornamental design, woven from hidden associations and reminiscences, of the full-throated Voronezh poems – those same poems of which Kornei Chukovsky, contradicting me one time in Peredelkino, said, "Not weird, wonderful."

For Akhmatova it was most important to hear a living human voice in the verse of a great poet and the individual intonation she referred to as a new harmony. In Mandelstam's work of the 1930s a direct auto-biographical element makes itself distinctly felt. This was a demonstrative confirmation of his words that poems are written under the influence of unexpected and deep experiences, whether of joy or sorrow. There is a note to this effect in Akhmatova's episodic reminiscences of Mandelstam.

Of his late poems Akhmatova singled out only one: "You have not yet died, you are not yet alone". In her characteristic way, she would often chant the two lines she particularly liked: "And poor is he, who himself half-dead/ begs alms of a shadow". In the personal not philosophical sense, however, the theme of life and death was no less resonant in other Mandelstam poems, "those somewhere in between". It is these that I want to discuss. I am trying to get closer not to the principles of his poetic style, nor to the pattern of his thought (contemporary philolo-gists have already said much of value on those subjects), but to those things that tormented and wearied him at the time. To enter this preserve I must surmount considerable obstacles: the influence of Anna Akhmatova's *Leaves from a Diary* and of Nadezhda Mandelstam's *Hope against Hope* and *Hope Abandoned* (as well as the *Third Book* of her writ-ings compiled by Nikita Struve).[1] My own observations will aid me, for it was during those years, from 1928 to 1937, that I was close to the Mandelstams.

Leaves from a Diary

After Mandelstam's posthumous rehabilitation in 1956, Akhmatova wrote the poem "I bow before them, as over a chalice". The immedi-ate pretext was an examination of Mandelstam's manuscripts, which Nadya had finally retrieved from various hiding places. Yet for many years to come this poem, the best among her best, could not be published in full. Even in the authoritative Poet's Library edition of her work in 1976 only stanzas three and four were offered as the basic text: we find the

---

[1] Until the late 1980s, these works could only circulate illegally in Russia. When Nadezhda Mandelstam's books were published abroad in English translation, she suggested the titles, a word-play on her name, which translates literally as "Hope". The *Third Book* (Paris, 1987) appeared posthumously.

others in the section of variants and listed as "other versions".[2] Now, in the 1990s, when the poem is published in full, I shall recall the text in its only complete version:

For Osip Mandelstam

I bow before them, as over a chalice,
The secret notes too great to count
In these dark, these tender tidings
Of our blood-spattered youth.

The same air, as above an abyss,
I once breathed in the night,
In that empty, iron night
Where you call and shout in vain.

O how heady the breath of carnation
That I once dreamed of there,
These are the swirling Eurydices
The bull bears Europa cross the waves.

These are our shades as they fly
above the Nevà, the Nevà;
This the Nevà as it laps the step,
This your pass to eternal life.

These the keys to an apartment
Of which we cannot now speak,
The voice of the mysterious lyre
As it sings in the fields beyond death.

1957

Akhmatova opened the original version of her *Leaves from a Diary*, which she conceived as a prose study of Mandelstam, with the two "legitimate" verses. However, it did not form a coherent whole. Her understanding of the destiny of the poet, of her brother-in-arms and friend, only found expression in the poem dedicated to his memory.

---

[2] The complete text finally appeared in the long-delayed volume of Akhmatova's selected prose and verse published in Leningrad in 1976 (see Introduction, p. xxv).

At the beginning of the *Leaves*, Akhmatova sketched an image of the poet, with characteristic laconicism, selecting a few individual traits. Her views on the nature of Mandelstam's memory, for instance, are very important: "He was incapable of recollection or, to be more precise, it was for him a different type of process. For the moment I cannot give it a name but it was undoubtedly close to creation." We learn that he was "a brilliant conversationalist – considerate, inventive and wide-ranging". His discussion of verse was "dazzling but partisan, and sometimes he was monstrously unfair, for example, to Blok". At the same time "he knew and well remembered the verse of others, and often fell in love with particular lines". Only in Akhmatova's account could we hear Mandelstam's admission that "he had thought so long about Pasternak that he had even grown tired" or his categorical "I am an anti-Tsevetayevite". It was Akhmatova who stated, with authority, what an "enormous event" the revolution was for Mandelstam, who was then "a fully-formed and already acknowledged poet, if only in narrow circles".

Unfortunately, these first drafts were set aside when Akhmatova, unexpectedly, began to concern herself with issues affecting Mandelstam's "personal life". Perhaps this digression occurred because a special, and in part polemical, purpose lay behind the *Leaves from a Diary* . . . I should describe this in more detail, though, since I witnessed and even collaborated in the early stages of that process.

Following Mandelstam's partial rehabilitation,[3] Akhmatova said to me: "Now we must all record our memories of him. Otherwise you know what tales will be told: 'the tuft of hair . . . below average height . . . fussy . . . always causing rows'." She had in mind the stories about Mandelstam that had long circulated in the literary world.

Nadezhda also thought it important to stem the flow of gossip with live descriptions by people who had loved Mandelstam and known him well. With reason she placed me in their number. Her second book, *Hope Abandoned*, denied me that role and assigned me another. That was after 1968, however, when I broke off all relations because of her slanders against Khardjiev. For the time being, we are still in 1957.

Nadya had not yet considered writing her own memoirs. She had other worries: pushing through an edition of Mandelstam's works, agreeing the membership of the commission on his literary heritage with the Writers' Union, gathering together the poet's manuscripts,

---

[3] E.G.: Mandelstam was then rehabilitated only in relation to the second 1938 arrest. The 1934 charges concerning the Stalin satire were not re-examined until 28 October 1987, i.e. after the death of Nadezhda.

and working with Khardjiev who, on her recommendation, had already signed a contract with the Poet's Library series. Moreover, she was not yet living in Moscow. Teaching at colleges in Tashkent, Ulyanovsk, Cheboksary, Pskov and even Chita [in eastern Siberia], she came to Moscow only out of term-time. On these visits she often met with dissidents, particularly those who had been in the camps, and naturally was swept up by the political atmosphere of the "Thaw". She confessed to me that she still could not decide whether to send a forthright letter to Khrushchev or begin writing her memoirs. The choice was made some time later.

When she began to write her first book, Nadya found herself in something like a state of shock. She became immersed in her past life with Mandelstam, gradually reliving, step by step, all its twists and turns. It was a merciless rehabituation to that apparently forgotten life which, in reality, had only been pushed temporarily into the background. An understanding of the essence of their life together did not return immediately. "I was his friend, not just his wife," she said to me with some astonishment, as she once more thought over the meaning of her union with Mandelstam.

Those days when Nadya and I would meet at the Shklovskys' flat in Lavrushinsky Street were touching and affecting. Soon, however, she began using old material to mould an image of herself that clearly damaged the depiction of Mandelstam. We shall return to this phenomenon.

Nadezhda's first book of memoirs began to circulate in samizdat in the early 1960s. Akhmatova heard of this from her adoptive granddaughter. "*Akuma*,[4] there's a lot about you there," Anya naively told her, after reading the prohibited volume. "You'd think Nadya would have shown me this before distributing her book," remarked the bewildered Akhmatova. She herself had been more attentive to the poet's widow, the wife of her friend. Not one word in the *Leaves* diverged from the accounts given by Nadya. From the outset, moreover, they were conceived as a tendentious composition. My own experience convinced me of this.

Following Akhmatova's wishes, I began to put my scattered notes about the Mandelstams in some order. I showed her the very first drafts of a continuous text. Without reading to the end of the second page Akhmatova cried out: "No, no! You can't write about that!" This prohibition referred to passing mention of the squabble between Mandelstam

---

[4] Affectionate family name first given to Akhmatova by her second husband, the Assyriologist Shileiko, and subsequently adopted by the Punins.

and Gornfeld. I was astonished. That literary row was widely known, it had been discussed repeatedly in the press, and a great many documents relating to the affair had survived – Mandelstam's entire *Fourth Prose*, after all, had arisen from the conflict. "Why can't we at least mention it?" "Because, because" (she was incoherent with agitation), "because Osip was in the wrong!"

This was a guiding principle. There was prior agreement that the literary portrait of Osip Mandelstam should ignore entire layers of his tangled and stormy life. I could not accept this set of rigidly enforced omissions. Moreover, the one-sided description of Mandelstam's personality led to a series of distortions. In *Leaves from a Diary* one encounters episodes where this supposedly *ennobling deception*[5] becomes translated into the crudest untruths. The time has come when all these obscure moments can and must be illuminated.

Some Direct Errors

"During his interrogation, says my son, they read him what Osip Emilievich had said about Lev and myself. His depositions were irreproachable," wrote Akhmatova. "Could many of our contemporaries say as much of themselves?"

These words stir nothing but bewilderment. Could she have forgotten that when Nadya came back from seeing Osip at the Lubyanka she turned to me, and announced in despair: "Emma, Osya named you . . ."? As we immediately discovered, Mandelstam had named the other 9 or 11 people to whom he had read the poem that was the reason for his arrest (the Stalin satire). Among them were Akhmatova and her son Lev Gumilyov. Today we have documentary confirmation of this event. Some of the legal records have been published [*Ogonyok* 1/1991, and *Izvestiya* nos. 121–5, 1992] and though these provide only excerpts from the investigation file, whatever materials are added in a full and exhaustive publication no-one can now describe Mandelstam's depositions about Akhmatova and Lev Gumilyov as "irreproachable". He described Lyova's reaction to the poem he had just heard: "Lev Gumilyov approved the piece with an indefinite emotional expression like 'great' but his opinion agreed with that of his mother Anna Akhmatova, in whose presence he heard the poem read."[6] And how did Akhmatova react? According to the Lubyanka deposition she pointed out "the monumental, rough-hewn, penny-ballad character

---

[5] Which is too often preferred to the "swarms of lowly truths" (Pushkin).
[6] See Vitaly Shentalinsky, "Mandelstam Street", in *The KGB's Literary Archive* (London, 1995).

Akhmatova, Nadezhda and Emma Gerstein, 23 June 1965

of the piece". It is hard to understand what noble testimony by the poet the interrogators could show Lyova in 1949–50. It was interpreted quite unequivocally by the Special Session[7] and the USSR Prosecutor General: "The instances of Gumilyov's anti-Soviet activity laid down in his depositions are confirmed by the testimony of Punin, Borin, Makhayev, Mandelstam and Shumovsky."[8] Clearly Lyova could not call Mandelstam's behaviour at the Lubyanka "irreproachable". Only by going against her conscience could Akhmatova so elevate Mandelstam's image as a prisoner under interrogation. Perhaps these were all "white lies" to save the honour of a great poet. Yet having once strayed, it was already hard for her to return to the straight and narrow.

The effects can be felt in the uncertainty with which Akhmatova, whose prose was usually so precise, narrated important events in Mandelstam's life as a poet. It is perplexing, for instance, to read the following passage from the *Leaves*: "Concerning the poem where he praised Stalin, 'I feel like saying not Stalin but Djugashvili' (1935?), Mandelstam told me: 'I now understand it was a kind of sickness.'" Anyone who knows when Akhmatova and Mandelstam met during those years cannot fathom what that "now" refers to. The date entered by

---

[7] Extra-judicial body that rubber-stamped prior decisions, convicting dozens (if not hundreds) at each sitting.
[8] Lev Gumilyov was arrested a second time in 1949, as was Nikolai Punin, and both were sent to the camps.

Akhmatova, with understandable hesitation (1935?), is of no help. As
she remembered all too well, it was in February 1936 that she visited
Mandelstam in Voronezh. Then the "Ode to Stalin" simply did not exist.
This we know from Rudakov's letters to his wife, which describe the
entire course of Mandelstam's work on his poems from April 1935 to
June 1936. The next time Akhmatova and Mandelstam saw one another
was in Moscow, in May–June 1937. They met almost every day until he
was deported from the city. This was a totally unexpected blow for him
since his attitude to the authorities was very loyal at that time. Their last
meeting was in Leningrad in autumn 1937. Describing in retrospect how
the Mandelstams spent that year, Akhmatova writes: ". . . it became
impossible for them even to visit the Moscow apartment . . . They would
come up from Kalinin and sit out on the boulevard. In Leningrad Osip
read me all his new poems but did not allow anyone to write them down
. . . He was by then seriously ill but with an inexplicable obstinacy
demanded that the Union organise an evening recital of his poetry."
Much that Akhmatova did not yet know lies concealed behind the phrase
"inexplicable obstinacy". She did not know of the love poem Mandelstam
had dedicated to the "Stalinist" Lilya Popova (which concludes "Prepared
to live or to die, / In a pledge of tender affection, / She utters with
fondness/ The thunderous name of Stalin.") A series of letters from
Mandelstam to other writers and to the Writers' Union remained unpublished at that time: he then requested and demanded that they hear and
discuss his account of the work he had done in his three years of exile.
Nor did Akhmatova know that when he was illegally staying in Moscow
with the Osmyorkins in 1937–8 Mandelstam gave impassioned readings
of the self-same "Ode" to their acquaintances who dropped by. In my
view it was undoubtedly a kind of sickness. Yet Mandelstam could not
have admitted as much, he did not have time to.

A remark about Mandelstam as a friend radiates the same anachronism. "The last time I saw Mandelstam was autumn 1937," we read in
the *Leaves*. "He and Nadya had come to Leningrad for a couple of days.
It was an apocalyptic moment. Each one of us was closely pursued by
misfortune. They had nowhere at all to live. Osip breathed with difficulty, catching the air with his lips." Nevertheless, Akhmatova continues: "For me he was not just a great poet. When he learned (probably
from Nadya) how difficult I was finding things at the House on Fontanka
he said, as they left Leningrad from the Moskovsky railway station:
'Annushka' (he had never called me that in his life), 'always remember
that my home is your home.' This could only have been just before the
end." What home could Mandelstam then offer Akhmatova? The entire
poignancy of his existence as a free man before his last arrest lay in his

homeless condition. This parting at the station, however, perfectly fits 1933 when, for the first time, the Mandelstams had been allotted an apartment of their own, on Nashchokin Street in Moscow. As we know, Akhmatova then accepted Mandelstam's invitation and came to stay in February 1934; and as many do not know, she complained a great deal to Nadya about her now burdensome life with Punin, sharing the same apartment with his first wife and daughter. Nadya enjoyed telling the curious about the elegant "swan's neck", the "regal gait" and Akhmatova's other striking poses and, on the sly, she mocked her domestic clashes with Punin's wife. "She's getting on . . ." Nadya remarked condescendingly (Akhmatova was then 44).

In 1957 Akhmatova, with her precise associative memory, became thoroughly confused by the constant, self-imposed obligation to give an idealised portrait of Mandelstam. This was despite her own maxims (in the *Poem without a Hero*) that ". . . poets are above sin": "in no way is he guilty". There the sinner was being offered absolution; in her *Leaves from a Diary* the very fact of sin is denied. Indubitably Akhmatova, being under the strong influence of Nadezhda's guiding hand, did not write freely.

Marusya

The influence of Mandelstam's widow can be quite distinctly felt when Akhmatova refers to Maria Petrovykh (1908–1979). Enumerating for some reason Mandelstam's romantic involvements since 1914, Akhmatova continues:

> In 1933–4 Osip Emilievich felt a stormy, brief and unrequited love for Maria Petrovykh. The "Turkish Woman" (my title) was dedicated or, to be more exact, addressed to her and is, in my view, the best love poem of the 20th century ("Mistress of Shamefaced Glances"). Maria says there was another quite bewitching poem about the colour white. Evidently the manuscript has been lost. Maria remembers certain lines by heart.
>
> There is no need, I hope, to repeat that this "Don Juan" list does not record the women with whom Mandelstam was on intimate terms.

The account is full of hints and veiled suggestions. The impression remains that the author was not trying to convey something important so much as leave the most significant unsaid. The thoughtful reader cannot help posing a succession of perplexed questions.

For example, the lines from Mandelstam's "bewitching" poem are not cited. Yet Maria Petrovykh knew them by heart when Akhmatova was writing the *Leaves* and they often then met on friendly terms. Why the omission?

If a brief romantic attachment influences a poet to write "the best love poem of the 20th century" then he must be an "impressionist" poet, inspired by a momentary mood or a "chance infatuation", as Nadezhda wrote of her husband's involvement. But Mandelstam was not a Balmont or an Igor Severyanin. He was a poet of a deeper formation.

Nadezhda is particularly insistent that Mandelstam's attachment to Maria Petrovykh was brief. This is incorrect. The Mandelstams and Marusya saw one another throughout the 1933–4 season. Let us go back to the day I met her at their apartment, as they listened affectionately to her chatter or, shall we say, charming babble. That was in October or November 1933. Later, on 13 January 1934, Lyova, then staying with the Mandelstams, saw in the Old New Year[9] at Maria Petrovykh's apartment.

When Nadezhda went into hospital for some tests, Mandelstam and Lyova, who were both in love with Marusya, urged and implored her to come and live with them: how would they survive without a woman to run the home? This role did not attract her but she gladly went to visit them at Nashchokin Street; evidently she found it interesting. Everything points to an established acquaintance.

Therefore, Nadezhda's last account of this affair (in *Hope Abandoned*) strikes a sharply dissonant note. In her version Maria Petrovykh

> for a moment wormed her way into our life, thanks to Akhmatova (Mandelstam even asked me not to quarrel over this with Akhmatova, which I had no intention of doing). For two or three weeks, losing his head completely, he kept telling Akhmatova that if he weren't married to Nadenka, he would go away and live only for his new love . . . After Akhmatova had left, Maria Petrovykh kept visiting us and he would spend the evening with her in his room, saying that they were holding "literary conversations".[10]

But they did not only meet at Nashchokin Street. Osip visited Marusya somewhere near Polyanka Street, where her family (mother, sister or

---

[9] Until January 1918, Russia preserved the Julian calendar. The Old New Year continued to be celebrated (as it is now).

[10] The English translation of *Hope Abandoned* (London, 1999), chap. 23, erroneously suggests that there was only one such evening of literary discussion in Mandelstam's room.

brother?) lived, and at Granatny Street where she lived with her husband. The affair lasted longer than 3–4 weeks, was a deeper involvement than that depicted by Nadezhda and, as will become apparent, ended most dramatically.

The version Akhmatova offered in *Leaves from a Diary* differs in no way from what Nadya says – if one disregards the highly vulgar expressions employed by the author of *Hope Abandoned*. Such clichés, "chance infatuation", "losing his head", jar on the ear when applied to a poet who always found other words to denote his feelings: "For a wild, a strange blood/ Mine was changed" in the 1920 love poem addressed to Olga Arbenina, not to mention the "Mistress of Shamefaced Glances".

Nadya's interpretation is undeniably correct when she says that Akhmatova introduced Maria to the Mandelstams. That was back in the autumn, when Akhmatova briefly visited Moscow. On her longer visit in February 1934 she introduced Maria to her own select Moscow literary circle. The Mandelstams' flat became unrecognisable. Zenkevich and Narbut, old friends from the Poets' Guild, came to see Akhmatova and for some reason Pasternak's first wife, Yevgenia, visited her on her arrival and when she departed. The well-known Pushkin specialist Bondi also came and Akhmatova took Marusya to see other Pushkin scholars. I remember Akhmatova saying what a strong impression Maria made on Grigory Vinokur when she read him her own verse.

In Maria Petrovykh's later notes, published after her death [*Selected Works*, Moscow 1991], there is an interesting story about this period in Moscow and her first acquaintance with Akhmatova (in Leningrad) and with Mandelstam.

"I first saw Akhmatova and made her acquaintance on 3 September 1933. I went of my own accord to visit her at the House on Fontanka. Why did I go? I had a vague knowledge of her poems. I had never felt an urge to associate with the famous. Somehow I just went – call it destiny, an inexplicable attraction. I did not simply 'go', I had to go. 'The led woman', Nikolai Punin wrote, referring to me. It's true. I came like a junior to her elder."

The following entry is of direct relevance: "In 1934, together with Akhmatova and Mandelstam I was invited to visit Yevgenia, Pasternak's first wife (at 25 Tver Boulevard). There I read my own poems and heard invaluable comment from Boris Pasternak – approval and appeals for a greater boldness. Then I saw him at his own room (on Volkhonka St.) and the more I knew him, the more I liked him. He was a man of passionate emotions and brilliant intelligence. A kind, extremely responsive person for whom another's woe immediately became his own."

In a further entry she speaks of her attitudes to the three named poets: "My feelings for both of them [Pasternak and Akhmatova, E.G.], and my relations with each, were quite different but both poets have remained with me always." She goes on: "I am astonished and entranced by Mandelstam's poetry but for some reason it was not instinctively mine."

Akhmatova introduced Marusya to Georgy and Nadezhda Chulkov, old and close friends of hers. Akhmatova's young acquaintance also enjoyed success and recognition with them. A memento of this introduction is the well-known photograph taken at Nashchokin Street. It strongly conveys the character of the Mandelstams' apartment. The wall is white and bare, and the hanging weight of the kitchen clock (not in the picture) can be faintly seen. Four writers stand against this background (from left to right): Chulkov, Petrovykh, Akhmatova and Mandelstam. Marusya, small and delicate, is clearly abashed at finding herself among renowned and leading figures from an already past but acclaimed epoch in Russian culture. The photograph is symbolic of her induction to the order of *true* poets. Nadezhda emphasises this in *Hope Abandoned*. "There is a photograph showing Mandelstam, Akhmatova, Chulkov and Petrovykh. It was taken in our apartment at Furmanov Street [name for Nashchokin Street after 1934]. Akhmatova wanted the first picture to be literary and the second, of the family. I am there, and so are grandpa and Alexander." Maria Petrovykh, however, was included in both photographs. In the second she sits next to Nadezhda. To the right are the distinguished poets; to the left of Mandelstam are his wife, Marusya, his father and brother, all in free and relaxed poses.

I cannot help seeing this photograph as a veiled reference to the arrangement of family life proclaimed by the Mandelstams. The *ménage à trois* was widely practised in the '20s. Its roots went back to the 1890s and though it had almost disappeared in the '30s, it remained the ideal for the Mandelstams, particularly for Nadezhda. She would praise such a way of life and repeat her husband's own views: a three-way marriage, he said, was a fortress no enemies – i.e. outsiders – could take. I did not hear him say such things but that was hardly necessary. We all recalled the example of Merezhkovsky, Zinaida Gippius and Filosofov; that of Osip and Lily Brik plus Mayakovsky was before our eyes. In our conversations, it is true, Mandelstam made fleeting allusions to some other variations on the same subject. But for a long while these would remain not entirely clear to me.

As for Marusya she merely expressed extreme astonishment at Nadezhda's second book, *Hope Abandoned*. There it was said that she "wormed her way" into their home. Staggered, the now 60-year-old

Maria told common friends of Akhmatova that it was Nadezhda who so insistently invited her not just to come more often but also to spend the night there, offering some trunk for her to sleep on. Though not grasping their intentions, Maria did not forget the emphatic interest of the Mandelstams. This is clear from an entry in her diary that, as she herself indicates, was made before the appearance of *Hope Abandoned* – i.e. before Nadya's unexpectedly rude comments about her:[11]

> I often felt sorry for Nadezhda during those long years when things were hard for her. I am glad that now (so late!) her life is going well, at least in the practical sense. She has a place to live, money to live on, and she can survive. I appreciate how much she has suffered; I do not understand her super-human malice.
>
> I find this animosity unpleasant. It is a demeaning not an uplifting response. Moreover, she is malevolent by nature, and was like that before those terrible ordeals, even when she seemed to feel kindly towards me.

Let us remain for a while in this eventful period.

On a small stage within a very compressed span of time the drama of Osip Mandelstam's last weeks as a free man was acted out. Several poorly dressed individuals, of varying ability, played their part. Each contributed a portion of heightened passion to the performance, thereby creating an atmosphere of high tension. A hidden source of additional illumination cast an ineradicable hue over the entire scene. As if by agreement, all pretended to ignore it. Yet they knew that the "shining calves" and swingeing decrees of the "Kremlin crag-dweller" had been denounced in their hero's "penny-ballad" poem. Only the elderly Emil Mandelstam was unaware of his son's perilous verse. The other participants had heard the poet himself recite it, each convinced, however, that he (or she) alone was initiated into the secret.

In *Leaves from a Diary* Akhmatova said that whenever she now passed the turning from Kropotkin Street on to Gogol Boulevard she recalled Mandelstam that winter, telling her, "Poetry today must have a civic conscience." And a second phrase: "I am prepared to die." When the two went on their walks, we also know, Mandelstam would confess to Akhmatova that he had fallen in love. I think he also mentioned the story, which she knew, of his passion for Arbenina and rivalry with Gumilyov.

---

[11] ". . . M.P. was the sort who chased men . . .", ". . . just a silly girl trying out her powers on another woman's husband" (*Hope Abandoned*, chapter 23).

After all, he exclaimed in my presence (when Nadya was absent): "How interesting! I had just the same experience with Kolya . . ."

Akhmatova did not appreciate the linking of that love story, 15 years earlier, with the present affair. Either she was jealous of Lyova (some mothers are like that) or feared his lack of political restraint. She took an extravagant step. He had not yet begun to see Marusya regularly in Moscow but to forestall anything of the kind Akhmatova unexpectedly appeared at Marusya's apartment and urged her to stop flirting with Lyova. "What use is this boy to you?" she said offhandedly, recalling an intonation once so magnificently perfected as the "Cleopatra of the Neva".[12] The era of Columbine, Salome and Pallada[13] was past, however. Marusya had a great many unresolved problems of her own. She began to confide in Akhmatova.

Maria intended to divorce her husband. This would not be easy since he was deeply devoted to her. His adoration even led him to write down her words (our common acquaintances told me this, not Marusya herself). He was older than she and, most importantly, a graduate of the Timiryazev Agricultural Academy who had no connections with art or poetry. At that very moment the close friend of Marusya's youth, a former student, returned from internal exile. She faced a difficult decision. And now there were not two but three rivals circling about her "with noiseless gulping mouths".[14]

Lyova's hatred was directed towards the younger rival whom he contemptuously dismissed as an "intellectual in a pince-nez". Marusya, meanwhile, confessed her deepest secret to Akhmatova: she loved an actor who performed on the second stage of the Arts Theatre. Her long poem, *The Bronze Spectator*, was dedicated to him and published only after her death. The obvious analogy with *The Bronze Horseman* is explained by Vladimir Gotovtsev's most famous role. In Alexei Tolstoy's play of that name he acted Peter the Great. He was then almost 50 but that did not prevent Marusya loving him, while explaining her complete indifference to Mandelstam because he was an old man. Even as a poet, she said, he was alien to her. I do not fully believe this. Sitting in the next room, I myself heard Mandelstam, his voice wound to the highest pitch, as he declaimed his inspired orations; I myself saw Marusya, with

---

[12] "I only heard of this episode from Arina Golovachova, Maria Petrovykh's daughter, in 1997," notes E.G. Maria then shared a room in a communal apartment on Granatny Street with her husband and sister.

[13] Celebrated pre-1924 contemporaries and friends of Akhmatova: Salome Andronikova (Halpern), Pallada Gross and Columbine (Olga Sudeikina).

[14] The goldfish image comes from "Mistress of Shamefaced Glances", p. 396.

an ecstatic gaze and burning cheeks, as she left his room and tossed a careless "goodbye" to Nadya, myself and a third person who was dining with us.

I do not know whether Akhmatova spent a whole month in Moscow on her February visit. She was in Leningrad by the beginning of March, of that I'm sure. I remember and shall never forget what a sigh of relief Mandelstam had drawn at her departure: "Nadenka, how good that she's gone! That was too much electricity for one home."

They were now hopelessly caught between revelations and things never said.

The High Tide of Revelations

At that time Akhmatova had no close woman friend and felt the need of someone to whom she could speak frankly. During a friendly and sometimes frivolous conversation with Nadya she once in passing referred to "my mother-in-law" and mentioned a Jewish first name and patronymic. "You're joking?" I asked in amazement. "Not at all," was Akhmatova's reply.

Later I learned that the composer Artur Lurye had been her third husband; Punin was her fourth. Whereupon Lyova with a certain bravado and evident exaggeration said that Mama had had four official husbands. We now all know, thanks to the *Poem without a Hero*, that after divorcing Shileiko Akhmatova lived with Olga Sudeikina and they were then joined in the same apartment by Artur Lurye (their life together is described most vividly in Yury Annenkov's reminiscences). From much later conversations with Nina Olshevskaya I learned that Akhmatova told her in confidence: "We could never decide which of us he was in love with." At the beginning of the 1920s Lurye emigrated to the West, and Sudeikina followed some time after. Akhmatova remained in Russia. These facts are widely known.

The nature of the relations between all three is well described in Lydia Ginzburg's diaries, published only in the 1980s. Her informant was Grigory Gukovsky: his first wife, Natalya Rykova, who died early, had been a close friend of Akhmatova. "Gukovsky once said that in biographical terms her poem about Jacob and Rachel[15] was an extremely emotional composition for Akhmatova," writes Lydia Ginzburg. "In his view this narrative Biblical poem was a far more personal work than the 'Grey-

---

[15] E.G.: The reference is to the first printed version of the poem "Rachel" in the third *Archer* anthology (St Petersburg, 1922).

Eyed King' and others. It refers to Artur Lurye." Thus we learned that
the two women were linked by friendship and rivalry.

But Nadya wanted to believe there had been a closer bond in their
friendship. Then knowing nothing of that *ménage à trois*, I was astounded
by a phrase that escaped her lips when we were talking about Akhmatova:
"What a stupid woman! She doesn't know how to live as a threesome."

She burned with an insurmountable need to be more specific on the
subject. Nadya began to expound a rigid arrangement that, in her view,
was compulsory in such a situation. Shunning euphemisms and "mysti-
cism", she imbued her uninhibited talk with something additionally
unpleasant. It is hard to convey the secret of this overprecise language
(perhaps it lay in the timbre of her voice?) but beside it any obscenity
sounded as pure as spring-water. Her system consisted of a strictly calculated sequence of exhibitionism and voyeurism.

Nadya was bisexual. These tastes had formed very early, when she was
fifteen or sixteen. That was just before the Revolution, during the First
World War – i.e. a time when things had been turned upside down
anyway. The youngest in the family, Nadya had access to a Bohemian
life through her older brothers and sister. Well-read, she flaunted with
especial delight Zinovyeva-Annibal's *Thirty-Three Monstrosities*[16] and
Théophile Gautier's novel *Mademoiselle de Maupin* (then not yet translated into Russian). Certain sources listed these works as pornographic.
Nadya herself could invent stories that were more suggestive than daring,
and built up a repertoire of anecdotal episodes from the lives of her still-
living contemporaries. During this last year, however, such amusements
were displaced by excursions into political subjects that she drew from
world history and our Soviet existence. Her range of interests was wide
but frequently the ideas were not her own. They were picked up elsewhere and then raised to fever pitch by her fierce temperament and
unbridled imagination.

When I first got to know her Nadya retained many of the ways of
her youth. She was capable of eccentric escapades. Suddenly she might
bunny hop the length of the staid sanatorium corridor or, alternatively,
settle comfortably somewhere in an armchair and, with a bashful smile,
quietly fashion indecent figures out of Plasticine. In their room at Uzkoye
she would leap up and down on the armchairs like a shameless monkey.
Both the Mandelstams loved to romp about in my presence.

Stubbornly I did not grasp what they wanted from me. It should have
become clear during my walks in the park with Mandelstam. In my earlier

---

[16] This 1907 novel by the wife of Vyacheslav Ivanov was the first in Russian
literature to describe lesbian affections openly.

memoirs these have already been described in outline. Too preoccupied
with my own feelings and impressions, however, I did not try to decipher many of his hints. Neither did I then attach the necessary significance to Nadya's behaviour, when she subjected me to a full-scale
interrogation: What exactly were you two talking about? She listened to
my answers most intently. With a rather dim-witted honesty I did not
so much relate what Mandelstam said as enumerate certain of his themes
or phrases. Among these was passing reference to an affair he'd enjoyed
with two sisters who both acted in films. Nadya exploded. "He's lying
his head off," she yelled in agitation. "Before we met he knew nothing.
It was I who taught him that kind of thing."

Nadya called her union with Mandelstam "a physiological success".
At that time all her pranks and pronouncements were permeated with
erotic themes. How did I react? The moral and aesthetic aspect of such
matters did not in the least perturb me. We were living in an era of
sexual revolution, we were free thinkers and we were young: in other
words, we had a natural and healthy sensuality but adopted the manner
of true snobs who are not surprised by anything. The sole criterion of
behaviour in our sexual relations was personal taste, who liked what.

I now understand that my head was filled with an absurd mishmash
of artificial theory that did not at all suit my own way of behaving.
Mandelstam realised this. "Where do you get this mixture of chastity
and shamelessness?" he once asked me.

The complete lack of sexual inhibition, Nadya asserted, combined
with the unparalleled novelty of the days in which we lived, and the
danger hovering in the atmosphere, had created a favourable soil in which
a great love might flourish. Often she talked of her wish to write a book
about love and contemporary (read, Soviet) man. Even without these
lofty words I had a living example of such love before my eyes: Osip
and Nadya Mandelstam.

Gradually, much was revealed to me about their relations. Once I
missed the last tram and stayed the night. This was in the same apartment on Brest Street where they led such a gloomy existence. It was
there that Mandelstam wrote "Midnight in Moscow". That evening he
was unexpectedly aggressive and began making open passes at me, while
Nadya guffawed and leaped about us, her clothes and hair in disarray,
but not forgetting to follow, with a sharp-sighted and expectant gaze,
what would happen next. But nothing ensued. My indifferent rejection
of this contact and my total unwillingness to join in the game simply
enraged Mandelstam. He reproached me, using all the cheap phrases
then in fashion, "for night-time you are behaving indecently" and so
on. But this struck him as insufficient and he tauntingly compared me

to Yevgeny Khazin's wife: "Lena would certainly have behaved differently." Nadya cautiously remained silent. It was she who had brought her brother Zhenya and myself together. She was good at that. Indeed she continued to amuse herself in this way with various people to the last days of her life.

An affair with a married man is a banal predicament, with its constant shift between resentment and exultation and the daily possibility of unexpected insult. Zhenya's unplanned-for seaside vacation with his wife was just such a blow. It would last exactly three weeks and no more, he assured me, since they hadn't any money. Three weeks passed, and then another three, but they did not return. At this moment Nadya was admitted to hospital for yet another round of tests. I went to see Mandelstam on Pokrovka Street and found him with Yakhontov. They were discussing aspects of a work the actor had himself written for his "One-Man Theatre". Suddenly Mandelstam started fussing about "Zhenya and Lena" who had got lost somewhere in the Caucasus. There were anxious telephone conversations with his mother-in-law. He began dashing out to the phone in the corridor and then confiding who said what to Yakhontov. Now it was Lena's father ringing up: he'd found the date of their last letter from Kislovodsk. Very far, incidentally, from the therapeutic sea. Mandelstam began discussing with Yakhontov the route the travellers might possibly take on their return journey. He spoke with his usual nervous eloquence but I suspected rather than saw the hidden smile that flitted across his face: he was finding it entertaining to sneak glances at me. Yakhontov, I think, knew what was going on. The show was for my benefit, after all, to observe my reactions to each of these wounding remarks. I said nothing. And that maddened Mandelstam who was incapable of ever remaining indifferent.

Similar "gibes" were repeated more than once the following year when the Mandelstams moved to Herzen House (25 Tver Boulevard). I continued to visit them as often as before. Our conversations covered every conceivable subject. As always, entire days might be devoted to Mandelstam's latest fit of letter-writing, eloquent complaints in which all his skills were deployed to transform petty episodes into vast events, bathing them in streams of sarcastic invective, demands and lofty expressions. How skilfully he, indeed both the Mandelstams, involved vast numbers of people in promoting their interests! It was impossible not to be swept up by this crazy commotion and, like one hypnotised, join in the latest feud. These bursts of noisy activity were succeeded by periods of quiet (the writing of verse). In other words, the days were so hectic I quite forgot about their earlier erotic advances. But once I stayed late, again missing the tram, and spent the night there. Mandelstam seemed to remember the previous scenes and almost repeated one of them, but this time with an emphatic appeal that Nadya take part. Given our close and friendly ties, it could all have been treated as horseplay had I not recalled the earlier episode in their old room – and had Nadya not enjoyed reproving me with tales of a new female acquaintance who "knew how to behave decently at night-time". The conclusion of this last onslaught at Tver Boulevard was exactly the same as that previous most explicit instance: I rejected their advances with indifference.

This forced Mandelstam to return occasionally to his old grudges, exaggerating and inflating the drama of my relations with Nadya's brother. In one of our private conversations Mandelstam assured me that the affair was a sickness as far I was concerned. He claimed he could cure me. "Really? And how exactly?" Quite cold-bloodedly he replied: "Take off your clothes, and I shall whip you."

Thereafter I could no longer regard him in the same way, as an older friend to whom I was bound by our candid relations. None of the previous events had stirred feelings of distaste or alienation because they had an aura of distinctive levity that emanated from Nadya. But the thought of sadism never entered my head until then. Nadya, it is true, had hinted at this side of his behaviour towards her. But they were very faint hints. Mandelstam could not write down his poems, she said, but dictated the texts to her. We know this from the manuscripts we now possess, written in her hand. But she also described, not without pleasure, how as he dictated he cursed and even hated her – and that this stimulated his creativity.[17] I was prepared to believe this, but who then had he bullied when writing *Stone* or "The Horse", the brilliant poem he dedicated to Olga Arbenina? Nadya was not yet beside him. However, for me the most uncertain sensation is prompted by Mandelstam's letters to his wife. Akhmatova wrote, in *Leaves from a Diary*, that he had an "incredible, unbelievable" love for Nadya and she cited his letters as evidence. Certainly they are an astonishing expression of the strength of his tenderness, concern and longing for his wife. But I cannot pretend they do not leave me with the unpleasant impression of an excessively cloying kind.

A letter Nadya wrote to him from Koktebel in early October 1926 uncovers a concealed meaning behind these endearments: "I'm going around here with an enchanting young thing called Anya. She is from Peter[sburg], 26 years old, and very attractive. She has just dropped by and is giggling. Dear Nanny, I shall send her to you with some grapes

---

[17] Cf. Rudakov's similar reports, "Working on Poems", in Appendix 2, "Mandelstam and Rudakov", pp. 437–43.

and pebbles. Well, Kitten dearest, goodbye . . ." The parting postscript reads: "Osik, don't go looking at pretty little things without me!" In that same letter she mentions Olga Vaksel with whom Mandelstam had by then broken off relations. Vaksel was now being filmed in crowd scenes for the "Factory of the Eccentric Actor".[18] Nadya writes: "If you watch the Factory, please close your eyes."

In her diary Olga Vaksel also wrote that Nadezhda was bisexual and she describes scenes that equal and even exceed those recounted here. In later life Nadya firmly disavowed this, referring in *Hope Abandoned* to Vaksel's "preposterous erotic memoirs". Olga wrote of Nadya: ". . . she called him Mormon and was very approving of his fantastical plans for the three of us to go to Paris together."

In all her passions Nadya always kept half an eye on ideology. She admitted to creating about her an atmosphere neither of love nor friendship but of a sect with its own rites and distinctive ethics. The cult of deformity played a major role in their household. This elaborate system for playing up their physical shortcomings gave rise to a special freedom of speech and behaviour among all who visited them.

Yet why was Nadya's urge to combine a solitary exclusivity with an openness that exceeded all bounds reborn now? Why in 1934, when the attitudes of the Mandelstams and all around them were changing so dramatically, under the impact of the ominous "Great Breakthrough"?[19] The heightened interest in "sexual issues", as they were then called, was, it seemed to me, partially excluded by Nadya's delirious obsession with politics. Our domestic Soviet politics, naturally, not international affairs. It is enough to recall the responses in Mandelstam's poetry to the horrors of collectivisation, which they saw for themselves during summer 1933 in the Crimea. And could I possibly forget Nadya's feverish state when she rushed into my room with news of the "subversive" poem "We live without sensing the country beneath us . . ."?

Not the least influence on both the Mandelstams' political mood was their friendship with Boris Kuzin. From the first time they met him in Armenia in 1930 he was accepted as a member of the family or, to be more precise, of a severely restricted circle. As a scientist Kuzin rejected Marxism, as a man of common sense he saw the economic absurdity of our "socialist" regime and as a patriot he detested the whole situation.

---

[18] Avant-garde theatre group founded in Leningrad by Kozinstev and Trauberg in 1921.
[19] Term in official propaganda for the vast forces of change set in motion by the First Five-Year Plan (1928–32), notably collectivisation of agriculture and forced industrialisation – with the consequent famine and rapid extension of labour camps.

Kuzin was one of the first to introduce the GPU as a real theme in the Mandelstams' life. He was pestered by a certain "comrade" who was recruiting informers. His firmness and outright refusal to co-operate made an indelible impression on Nadya. One episode in particular remained engraved in her memory. A GPU plainclothes "investigator", who was attempting to cajole Kuzin and simultaneously threaten him with arrest, tried to exploit his exceptionally strong attachment to his mother. "Just think: what will happen to her if you're arrested?" Kuzin responded in a single courageous phrase: "Mama will die." The investigator reproached him: "What a cruel man you are." As she learned directly from Kuzin of these discussions, Nadya developed for herself the ideal of the Roman wife who is prepared to defy death with her husband. But for the time being she was still caught between amorous and civic exaltation. Kuzin introduced not merely a political but also an emotional theme. The Mandelstams had just returned from the Crimea, and had taken Kuzin with them: he had been briefly imprisoned and was in need of psychological repose. However, Boris unexpectedly became Nadya's defender from the egotism of Mandelstam. Could I forget the ringing, deep-chested baritone of the infuriated Kuzin – "What? Is she just a typewriter for producing his verse?" – in response to my words of restraint, that it was our duty to forgive the poet a great deal. In Stary Krym relations formed that fed a new current of tension into the atmosphere of those days.

Incidentally, I have forgotten yet one more powerful current flowing into that small fourth-floor apartment: the appearances of the beautiful Arts Theatre actress Nina Ardova-Olshevskaya. She first visited the Mandelstams to see Akhmatova, long the object of her adoration. She was delirious at the chance of meeting her in person. Lyova was invited to visit the Ardovs as well, as an intermediary and bearer of the renowned surname Gumilyov. There Nina's friends would gather, among them Nora (Veronica) Polonskaya who was then still married to Mikhail Yanshin, an actor at the Arts Theatre. (She had already been named, however, as a member of Mayakovsky's family in the poet's last letter [1930]: "Comrade government: My family is Lily Brik, my mother and sisters, and Veronica Polonskaya.") Contacts between the experienced Nadya and Nina gave peculiar expression to a particular aesthetic. A member of a sect professing the cult of deformity displayed a bogus affability towards a woman from an alien profession, who as an actress had learned from Stanislavsky himself how to carry her youth and beauty with freedom and simplicity. They understood each other perfectly. Adopting the special dialect of sophisticated ladies, they traded trivial remarks in which the voices, respectively, of the convoluted

Mandelstam and the bawdy humorist and raconteur Ardov could be heard as distant echoes.

Perhaps these are sufficient ingredients? No, that is still not everything.

The Dénouement Approaches

On the street Nadya met a young translator who recited from memory a poem Mandelstam had dedicated to Marusya. Apparently, it was already being passed around.

> Mistress versed in shamefaced glances,
> Suzerain of little shoulders!
> Pacified the dangerous headstrong male;
> The drowned words sound no more.
>
> Fish pass, fins redden,
> gills pulsating: Here, catch me!
> Feed their noiseless gulping mouths
> With a half-repast of flesh.
>
> We are no handsome golden fish,
> Our sisterly custom is such:
> In a warm body, thin slender ribs,
> While pupils damply shine in vain.
>
> Poppy-seed brow marks a perilous path.
> Why, like a Janissary, do I prize
> That swiftly reddening, tiny, piteous
> Crescent of your lips?
>
> Don't be cross, my Turkish love,
> I'll be sewn up with you in a sack,
> Swallowing your dark words,
> Drink deep for you of evil waters.
>
> You, Maria, sustain the failing,
> We must forestall death, fall asleep.
> I stand at a hard threshold.
> Go. Go, I say! – Yet, stay a while.

Nadezhda knew nothing about it. Staggered, hurt and at a loss, Nadya was in a state of shock and for once her reaction was normal, without affectation. "Just think," she complained to me, "I could already be the mother of a 17-year-old son." She recalled how she became a woman very young and her affair in Kiev during the stormy Civil War period when the city passed constantly from one side to another.

Later Nadya would demand that the final poem to be printed in the "Voronezh Notebooks" should be "As along the streets of monstrous Kiev". I am

Maria Petrovykh, early 1930s

convinced this was for the lines "She was seeking her husband, I do not know whose wife. And not one tear slid down her waxen cheeks." Nadya considered this her portrait at the moment in May 1919 when her principal lover, a former member of the Rada [the independent Ukraine's Parliament], was forced to flee as the Reds entered Kiev. Mandelstam, her new hero, had already left the city. They were reunited, as we can see from their letters, only in 1921. Therefore she recognised herself as "I do not know whose wife", tearless and courageous in misfortune.

Soon she pulled herself together, and took charge of the "Mistress" poem. She provided an interpretation and herself read it aloud, particularly insisting that the line "You, Maria, sustain the failing" actually read differently and that she should not be named there. Then the justification was that "Maria" would be identified in literary circles as a married woman known to many, as Maria Petrovykh: she should not be compromised in this way. It was only much later, when Nadezhda and Maria had both died, that a handwritten original of the poem was found in the Petrovykhs' family archive. There in Mandelstam's own handwriting the line read: "Our tenderness sustains the failing." This line has been interpreted in various ways. I shall refrain from comment.

Nadya began to regard Marusya with concealed hostility. She even started to harbour a suspicion: Perhaps Petrovykh was linked to the secret police? It was still a most naive period. Neither Lilya Popova, nor Kuzin nor Marusya herself concealed that they had been called in for a talk

with plainclothes "investigators" who pressed them to become informers, now threatening arrest, now offering various enticements.

Lilya Popova had by then married a second time, to a composer and
one of the founders and performers of the "One-Man Theatre".
Yakhontov and Lilya never ceased to work together but at that moment
she was concerned for the fate of her husband. As was the custom, the
investigator who had talked to him made him sign a document, she told
us, agreeing that he would never tell a soul about their meetings.
Naturally, no normal person could keep such a secret, and so her husband
blurted it out hysterically not only in conversation with her but also with
friends and even over the telephone. One such conversation was interrupted by the self-same investigator: "So that's how you keep your word?"
his voice sounded in the receiver. Following which the unhappy man
was arrested and sent to the camps where Lilya visited him. And then
– if you can believe it – she became enchanted by the camp's commandant and thought him a wise, humane person who was helping to
"reform" the neurotic musician.

Certain of Marusya's acts and gestures set Nadya on her guard. Nadya
had begun to speak frankly about the possibility of Mandelstam's imminent death and put together a collection of all his poems on cigarette
papers, including the unpublished Moscow verse. She was astonished to
note that Marusya had not taken the copy given to her as a present but
left it lying on the window-sill at Nashchokin Street.

Later, when Osip was under arrest and until Nadya was summoned
to the Lubyanka, we sat waiting for several days to learn his fate, she
would grow irritable and say of Marusya: "And why does she come
round here, ringing her hands?"

But most important of all (and it was very typical of the time), Marusya
frankly admitted that she sometimes felt like Raskolnikov who could
barely resist throwing himself on the mercy of Porfiry Petrovich, and
admitting his crime to the investigator. From time to time she experienced similar impulses. She told Nadya this and, probably, Mandelstam
as well. Of course, Nadya passed it on to me. At the beginning of the
war I heard the very same tale from Yelizaveta Efron, who knew Marusya
well from vacations in Koktebel.

Hitherto we have talked about Maria Petrovykh's behaviour at the
Mandelstams' apartment in Nashchokin Street. But what happened when
they met elsewhere and Mandelstam, as we have noted, faced the rivalry
of her two young admirers, Lyova and Vitaly Golovachov?

First, we must examine a sonnet by Mandelstam, "I recalled an ancient
legend". Published very late, posthumously of course, it probably found
its way to the editors thanks to Lyova. In my view, its content is rather

unpleasant and as verse it is almost weak. It expressed the one definite idea that the patriarch Joseph "after eccentric behaviour" is ceding his place to a young "lion cub" [in Russian *Lev* means *lion*, tr.]. As was his custom, Mandelstam turned real incidents from his life upside down and twisted them into a new subject that was entirely the author's.

Lyova immodestly complained, "I would leave her covered in scratches" (meaning that she remained unapproachable). Mandelstam, on the contrary, depicted her in this poem as the victim of the lion that had triumphed in their tussle. This is very characteristic of the man and his poetic approach and even affects this primitive subject. In reality, both Lyova and Mandelstam had already ceased to solicit Marusya's love. It was I who "distracted" Lyova: he left Maria after writing an epigram in which he called her Manon Lescaut. From then on, it seems, he never gave her another thought. Mandelstam parted from her in a quite different fashion.

Having ceased to pursue her, he acted as though he were her friend and I am sure he was being sincere. He approached me with a request: I was to persuade Father to petition for a Moscow residence permit for the disgraced Vitaly Golovachov. I refused to get involved in the affairs of someone I did not know at all, especially since my father lacked the authority to intercede for anyone arrested or exiled, in this case a student.

To anticipate, I may add that Marusya finally married Vitaly and bore him a daughter. Unhappily, in 1937 he was again arrested, apparently sent to the camps, perhaps to Kolyma, and there died of hunger in 1942.

The Mandelstams greeted Lyova's return to Moscow in April 1934 with great dissatisfaction. He had withdrawn from the amorous rivalry for Marusya's affections and this did not suit Nadya. I think it was she who sent Lyova downstairs to stay with the Ardovs where Nina was very flirtatious with him.

That did not stop Mandelstam seeing Lyova. He ran up from the ground floor to their apartment and they would go out somewhere together. Mandelstam greeted him with mischievous proposals, "Let's do something naughty!" and they began to telephone Akhmatova in Leningrad. Mandelstam had completely forgotten how dissatisfied he was during her visit in February. Insistently he demanded she return to Moscow.

After a phone conversation with Akhmatova, in which he had repeatedly said goodbye, he declared in a flash of temper, in my presence (no-one else was there), and before replacing the receiver: "We're members of the same party. Her party comrade's in trouble. She's obliged to come."

And indeed Akhmatova packed her things. Three days later, on 13 May, she arrived and that night when everyone in the apartment was getting ready for bed, the GPU men appeared with a warrant for the arrest of Mandelstam. I cannot shake off the feeling that he himself had hastened his downfall.

The night of that search when Mandelstam was taken off to the Lubyanka has been described in detail by Nadezhda in *Hope against Hope* and by Akhmatova in *Leaves from a Diary*.

I turned up at Nashchokin Street the following morning, probably after a call from Nadya, and was too late to see Mandelstam. Later, I may add, when the Mandelstams were moved from Cherdyn to Voronezh, a telephone bill arrived at Nashchokin Street that was so enormous it took Zhenya many months to pay off. It was Vera Yakovlevna, Nadya's and Zhenya's mother, who took on responsibility for this debt since she stayed behind and lived in the apartment.

It seemed that all the tempestuous events of Mandelstam's arrest and exile had completely brushed aside any memory of Maria Petrovykh. And this was not appearance but reality. Akhmatova writes, and I remember it well, that after his arrest she next saw Mandelstam only in February 1936 when she went to Voronezh. There, she says, he told her all the details of his interrogation and the charges against him: Akhmatova never passed them on to anyone else, however, nor did she reveal them in her *Leaves from a Diary*.

Throughout the pre-war years, as far as I could observe, Akhmatova and Maria Petrovykh hardly saw each other. In any case, Akhmatova only reported other people's remarks about her. For instance, Marusya had proved a passionate and pedantic mother, especially when she was feeding her little daughter. She and Akhmatova were evacuated to different cities: Akhmatova went to Tashkent and Maria to Chistopol. After the war, however, their friendship resumed or, perhaps, only became close for the first time.

Marusya regarded her with an unchanging and devoted love and became one of Akhmatova's dearest friends. I judge not solely from my own impressions over many years but also Akhmatova's rare dedication to "the radiant guest of my life", dated 9 May 1959, in the 1958 volume of her poems that she gave to Maria.

Naturally the question of how Marusya had behaved during the year that preceded Mandelstam's arrest in 1934 was dropped. Unexpectedly, it surfaced again in the 1950s, in quite new circumstances and in a new form. This concerns a poem by Mandelstam that became known only at that time.

The Black Candle

The strange image of the black candle occurs in "Your slender shoulders shall redden with the lash". A special history is attached to these lines. Apparently, Mandelstam was in Voronezh when he wrote the poem, almost a year after his transfer from Cherdyn. By that time, April 1935, Sergei Rudakov, the young literary specialist banished from Leningrad, had appeared. Leaving him to keep an eye on Mandelstam, Nadya went up to Moscow on business. Finding himself alone and, moreover, with a new acquaintance who stimulated him to write and discuss poetry, Mandelstam wrote works dedicated to two different women. Their fate had shaken him deeply.

Olga Vaksel, as we know, played a major role in the Leningrad life of Nadezhda and Osip Mandelstam during the '20s. In 1935 they received belated news of her death. Three years earlier she committed suicide in the foreign city to which, upon marrying a Norwegian, she had moved. Tidings of her tragic end shook both the Mandelstams. Nadya learned of this in Moscow. She grieved and sighed, but her recollections of Olga were erotic: "Lyutik, Lyutik!" she kept repeating, "she could never refuse anyone." Mandelstam's poem to Vaksel ("Can one praise a dead woman?") is suffused with deep feeling: "I treasure your painful memory".

At exactly the same time Rudakov copied down a poem dedicated to another woman and sent it to Leningrad, enclosed in a letter to his wife. It became known again only in the 1950s when, gathering material for the first posthumous edition of Mandelstam's poems, Khardjiev visited Rudakov's widow.

It was hard to grasp to whom the poem was dedicated.

> Your slender shoulders shall redden with the lash,
> Redden with the lash and burn in the frost.
>
> Your child's hands shall labour with flat-irons,
> Labour with flat-irons and tie up sacks.
>
> Your tender feet shall walk barefoot across glass,
> Barefoot across glass, and the bloody sand.
>
> While I must burn as a black candle for you,
> Burn as a black candle and not dare to pray.

Nadezhda talked and wrote about it. She put forward reasonable arguments in favour of her own candidacy but could not dismiss no less convincing indications that there was another woman for whom the poet was fearful. And not just fearful. He was to blame, he felt, for her possible ruin: it was unambiguously stated in the closing couplet of this baffling work. "I do not know what to think of this poem," Nadezhda writes at the end of her commentary: "and that distresses me." After her death, however, and that of Maria Petrovykh, documents were published that threw light on its origins.

They are the depositions of Mandelstam's interrogation in 1934. When Nadya returned from the Lubyanka she gave us the following information. During his cross-examination Mandelstam had seen his satirical poem about Stalin written out in someone else's hand. The handwriting, it seemed to him, was that of Maria Petrovykh. Yet he did not name her among those who had heard the poem. Naturally, after his first encounter with the investigator he returned to the cell in a highly excitable and, at the same time, depressed state. I cannot believe that doubts did not begin tormenting him. If "they" already had a copy of the poem in Maria's handwriting then why did he not name her as one who had heard it?! For he was staking everything on being entirely frank with his inquisitors.

At the following cross-examination he resolved to correct his mistake. Without waiting to be asked, he hurriedly told the investigator that there was another woman, Maria Petrovykh. In Nadya's first accounts the investigator grinned on hearing this name: "Ah! The theatre-lover." Apparently Mandelstam did not then have a chance to tell Nadya any more.

In fact, he not only mentioned the name Petrovykh. He admitted that she had written down the text of the anti-Stalin poem. "To be truthful," he added, "she did promise to burn that copy immediately." With admissions such as these did Mandelstam appear before his investigator – a naive and crafty, noble and perfidious figure.

He himself realised how little this resembled the behaviour of a stalwart and spirited oppositionist. Some verse that Rudakov copied in Voronezh suggests that Mandelstam assessed his conduct in a fable composed on the way to Cherdyn – i.e. five days after his release from the Lubyanka:

> A quick-witted tailor, sentenced to hang,
> deftly eased that stiff collar and lives to this day.

But Mandelstam's main hope of acquittal or an easing of his lot was that no-one had written down the "seditious" verse. Naming the sole person who had copied it out meant exposing her to a more serious charge:

"the distribution of counter-revolutionary material". It was this, probably, that tormented Mandelstam's conscience. The poem about the "black candle" is either self-justification or repentance. It lacks any erotic motif and is addressed to a woman he loved. We find such a direct statement once and once only in Mandelstam's lyric verse.

I am not sure that Nadya knew of the additional evidence Mandelstam had provided against Marusya.

Having forgotten or never known these circumstances, Nadya was in a state of feverish anxiety for another reason four years later. She was disturbed that only Mandelstam had been arrested at Samatikha. Why had they not picked her up as well? She thought she knew and, indeed, she repeatedly told me. Or, to be precise, she could not remain silent about the tormenting uncertainty as to why Mandelstam was unexpectedly arrested on 3 May 1938.

Nadya spoke plainly. At the Samatikha rest home they had drawn another guest into their erotic games. She turned out to be a member of the Party's district committee. In *Hope Abandoned* the account of this incident is so opaque that the main reason for Nadezhda's fears is not apparent: perhaps this episode had directly provided a pretext for denouncing Mandelstam to the authorities?

This anxiety was reflected in her letter to the new head of the NKVD, Lavrenty Beria, written on 19 January 1939.[20] Mandelstam was no longer alive but Nadya was not yet aware of that. The desperate appeal wavers between a heroic if belated desire to follow Mandelstam to his death and a fear of falling into the grips of the NKVD. It is a paltry and unseemly text when set beside Nadezhda's subsequent life as an ardent anti-Soviet.

Moscow
19 January 1939

Dear Comrade Beria,

In May 1938 the poet O.E. Mandelstam was arrested. From his letter I know that he was sentenced for Counter-Revolutionary Activities by the Special Session to five years in the North-East Corrective-Labour Camps. In the past Mandelstam was convicted under Article 58 (for counter-revolutionary poems).

The repeat arrest in 1938 was totally unexpected. Mandelstam had just finished a book of poetry, and the question of publishing

---

[20] And see Shentalinsky (note 6).

it had been constantly raised by the Union of Soviet Writers. We could more likely have expected complete reinstatement [of his rights] and a return to open literary activity than his arrest.

I do not understand how the investigation concerning counter-revolutionary activities by Mandelstam was conducted. As a consequence of his illness over a number of years I did not leave his side for one moment and yet I was not brought into the investigation either as an accomplice or at least as a witness.

Let me add that during his first arrest in 1934 Mandelstam suffered a severe psychosis and the investigation and exile, moreover, took place when he was already ill. At the time of his second arrest Mandelstam was physically in a seriously ill condition and in an unstable mental state.

I request that you:

1. Assist in having Mandelstam's case reviewed and clarify whether there were sufficient grounds for his arrest and deportation.

2. Verify the mental health of O.E. Mandelstam and clarify whether deportation was appropriate in this respect.

3. Finally, check whether someone did not have a personal interest in his deportation.

And one more thing: to clarify the moral rather than the legal side of this matter – did the NKVD have sufficient grounds for destroying a poet, a master [of his craft], when he was actively and loyally writing poetry.

Nadezhda Mandelstam
Furmanov Street, 3/5, apt. 26
tel. G 64667

The entire tone of this note does not just indicate Nadezhda's extreme desperation. She had also quite lost her bearings in the new situation since 1937. The peremptory style of her appeal could no longer exert the same effect on the authorities. In 1934, on the eve of the First Congress of Writers, it had been possible to influence the position not just of Bukharin but of Stalin as well.

The letter is governed throughout by her striving to share the fate of her husband and to emphasise her solidarity with the new trend in Mandelstam's poetic work, which showed him to be a loyal and law-abiding citizen. Her role in 1937 in aiding and shaping his new attitude is the more striking when we recall how, two years earlier, she resisted what Mandelstam had written about *Chapayev*, after seeing the Vasilyev brothers' film of that name.[21]

Then, she tore up the drafts of two poems ("The day was five-headed" and "From the damp talking sheet") that voiced his enthusiasm as an artist when he saw talking films as if for the first time and, after escaping from prison, absorbed the sights and scents of the northern Russia landscape. Yet most important were his inner conflict and doubts and the wounded awareness that he had opposed the enormous swell of enthusiasm that the directors of *Chapayev* now managed to instil in the poet.

Nadya was well aware of the "Ode to Stalin" and the thoroughly "loyalist" poem Mandelstam addressed in his last year to Lilya Popova. She knew of all Mandelstam's reversions to a legal existence and activities or, more precisely, his desire to start living and acting legally. Perhaps in 1937 they were even inspired by Nadya herself. Another sign of her disorientation at that moment was her crazy demand that Osip fake a heart attack in order to avoid expulsion from Moscow. Under her guidance, I was supposed to play an active part in this production (I refused). Narbut, Klychkov, Ben Livshits and Klyuev had been arrested. Yet Nadya continued to hope that my loud and deliberate cries in the street would inhibit the GPU men . . .

In this entire sequence of events, which followed a clear logic of their own, one circumstance still demands explanation. How did the Mandelstams, released from their three-year exile in Voronezh in May 1937, return to Moscow unaware that the poet was banned from the two capitals and, it seems, the next twelve largest cities in the Soviet Union as well? Their actions and demands strengthen the conviction that they did not receive such an instruction on leaving Voronezh. How could that happen? The thought occurs that Mandelstam was not subject to the law whereby those convicted in a certain category were deprived of the right to settle and live in the mentioned towns. Only after he and Nadezhda, misreading the new situation of the Great Terror, had appealed insistently to official literary organisations did they begin to alarm their "fellow" writers.

It is most unlikely that any of these writers knew the poem "We live without sensing the country beneath us . . ." They could not help being

---

[21] Immensely popular 1934 film about the legendary Civil War hero Vasily Chapayev, based on the 1923 novel by Dmitry Furmanov. (In the mid-1930s, Nashchokin Street was renamed in honour of Furmanov.)

aware, however, that it was an outspoken and anti-Stalinist work. That rumour had reached them. In the bloody turmoil of 1937 they became flustered. How should they deal with the author of such a work? He had been pardoned in 1934 but perhaps he was already doomed by 1937?

Now we know that these anxieties found expression in Pavlenko's self-assured letter to Stavsky, the general secretary of the Writers' Union; he in turn made cautious approaches (letter of 16 March 1938) to the then secret-police chief Yezhov. Who gave the final signal for Mandelstam's arrest remains unknown. Yet we cannot regard the entire last year of his life, when he was still a free man, as anything other than protracted death throes.

Playing at Death

The documents from Mandelstam's investigation file throw light not only on the poem about the black candle but also on "Mistress of Shamefaced Glances", the major work he dedicated to Maria Petrovykh. It was written not after his 1934 arrest and exile, as in the former case, but before those events.

That crucial turning point in Mandelstam's life nevertheless casts its shadow over the poem's last stanza:

> You, Maria, sustain the failing,
> We must forestall death, fall asleep.
> I stand at a hard threshold.
> . . .

A primitive interpretation suggests itself. If the author was seeking protection from unavoidable downfall then this must refer to the imminent execution he had foreseen. When he wrote the anti-Stalin poem he was ready to be shot: as the first to hear it, I remember his proud words to that effect. Now he was seeking refuge in a woman's love.

But from the investigation file we know that Maria Petrovykh was quite the wrong person to defend the poet from political retribution. Mandelstam had entrusted her with the text of this dangerous poem. If she wrote it down and they had even agreed that she would destroy the text then, according to GPU logic, they had acted as conspirators.

In that case from what or from whom was he fleeing? The answer can be sensed in the preceding stanza. It has, in my view, been correctly interpreted by the classical philologist Sophia Polyakova. The "closed sack", according to legend, was the punishment for unfaithful wives in Turkey. Moreover, not only the adulterous woman was sewn into the sack and cast in the sea but also her seducer. Polyakova quotes a most relevant verse from Nikolai Gumilyov's poem, "Constantinople": "How many, many other lovers/ Lie in remote inlets/ Entangled, drowsy and taciturn". The image of "evil [lit. crooked] waters" clearly suggests deception and unfaithfulness to his wife.

Why did Mandelstam seek refuge from death not with his devoted wife but with another woman? At first sight, it seems obvious. He turns away from his wife because he has fallen in love with another. But the new woman he desired does not feel kindness, special sympathy or devotion towards the hero of the poem.

Mandelstam paints her portrait in negative features. There is a "futile, moist gleam in her pupils". Perhaps she's a hysteric? (Akhmatova expressed herself more delicately when she anxiously enquired of me: "So, is she some kind of siren?") She lowers her eyes, expertly "versed in shamefaced glances". A coquette? The "piteous crescent" of her lips suggests a woman of the harem who incites crude male desire. The Janissary is a rapist, a foot-soldier in the Ottoman infantry which was made up of renegade Russians and other captives.

If we recall the portraits of the women with whom Mandelstam was in love they are very precise and always perceptive. He knew how to sketch the inner and outward likeness of a woman and did so as an artist, not at all as a lover who had "lost his head completely".

In late 1920 he devoted an entire cycle of most important and profound poems to Olga Arbenina, and in one of these ("I am sorry that winter is here") he paints her informal portrait. Before the reader stands a frivolous young actress who "talks of everything without a thought", "seems made for comedy squabbles", while "all about her teases and sings, like an Italian roulade". His other love, Olga Vaksel, "spoke on impulse, for no reason, out of turn", her unexpected smile revealing a "clumsy beauty" (1924): she was a "wild timid creature", a "little bear cub" (1935).

Finally there are the four undisputed portraits of Nadezhda. One is late, "Your pupil in its heavenly rind", 2 January 1937; another though late refers to the past, "As along the streets of monstrous Kiev", April 1937; and there are two early poems that belong, roughly speaking, to the honeymoon of their relations, "On the stone spurs of Pyrrhea" (1919) and "Return to the incestuous bosom" (1920).

In the earliest of these poems Nadezhda is easily recognised in the fifth and sixth lines of the opening stanza:[22] "And a high chill wafted

---

[22] Published in *Tristia* (1922) under the title "Tortoise". The poem "is permeated with motifs from fragments of Sappho, as translated by Vyacheslav Ivanov in 1914".

from the bulging girlish brow". Still more strongly is her appearance related to Ancient Greek poetry in the third stanza where, likening her to a "tortoise-shell lyre", Mandelstam animates her actual physical form. Here the cult of deformity, mentioned earlier, dominates triumphantly: ". . . barely the toeless one crawls by" mimics the gait of the desperately bowlegged Nadya. Her pose exudes the carefree spirit of the Golden Age as she ". . . lies in the sun of Epirus, gently warming her golden belly . . ." The clarity of the artist's vision throughout the third verse is astonishing.

Was there not then something in the poet's relations with his wife that forced him to withdraw within himself and grow estranged from her? Most certainly. Nadezhda herself speaks of this many times in *Hope Abandoned*. But there it is done with a practised hand, which wraps these amazing confessions in rhetoric and a well-judged bitter humour.

While Mandelstam was still alive, Nadya, faithful to her new ideal of the "Roman wife", took as her model one of the heroines in Tacitus. The consul Caecina Paetus had been sentenced to death. His wife Arria appealed to him to commit suicide together and, wishing to boost his spirits, stabbed herself first with the sword. Pulling it from the wound she passed it to her husband with the famous words: "See Paetus, it does not hurt."

Let us gather some of Nadya's summons to joint suicide from *Hope Abandoned*:

> Noting my glassy gaze when he would speak about the future, M. laughed and comforted me: "There's no hurry, what will be shall be. We're still alive, don't give in . . ."

> Frequently, at various unbearable periods of our life, I suggested to M. that we commit suicide together. My words always provoked a sharp rebuff. His main argument was, "How do you know what will happen later . . . Life is a gift which no one would dare to reject."

> Most often he would dismiss it with a joke: "Commit suicide? Impossible! What would Averbakh say? It would be a positive literary fact.

> And on another occasion: "I can't live with a professional suicide."

> On the way to Cherdyn he was afraid of being shot. Upon which I said to him: "Well, it's all to the good if they shoot

[us]: it saves us committing suicide." Already sick and delirious, obsessed by one dominant thought, he suddenly burst
out laughing: "Back to your old theme."

From then on life took such a course that the subject came up
again and again, but M. would say: "Wait . . . Not yet . . .
Let's wait and see . . ."

Thankfully I learned quite quickly of M.'s death and began
to think where I might retreat and take shelter.

It's easier for me to understand the triumph of death, as M.
over the years perceived it, than regard it as a tragedy.

M. was allowed no respite but, on the other hand, he was
saved by death. Such a release by death is truly a hundred
times more uplifting than all we strive towards in life. I await
death like my best friend. I've done everything and am now
ready to die.

As reflected in *Hope Abandoned*, Nadya's attitude to death during the
last years of Mandelstam's impoverished existence has partly been stylised.
In certain letters, though, it comes across in all its harsh nakedness.

I have in mind one noteworthy description by Sergei Rudakov of
Mandelstam's mental state in Voronezh, uncovered by Khardjiev in the
1950s. On 2 August 1935 Mandelstam experienced a fit of despair because
of the rejection of his essay about the State farms. This left the poet feeling he was trapped in a blind alley. Mandelstam's nervous confessional
words were framed, in that text, by Nadezhda's statement: "Osya grasps
at anything to stay alive. I thought the prose would work but he doesn't
know how to conform and please. I am in favour of dying . . ." Such a
direct, crude statement now alarmed Nadya. Anxiously she wrote "Lies!"
on the margins of Khardjiev's copy. All the false accusations rained down
on Rudakov by Nadezhda (and, following her, by Akhmatova) have their
beginning here.

Despairing at the intolerable hardness of their lives, Nadya occasionally allowed a slip of the tongue. In a letter (never sent) to the
Litfond doctors she exclaims hysterically: "Putting Mandelstam in a
psychiatric clinic as opposed to a sanatorium, which he needs, will mean
to kill him. But, evidently, there is no other solution," (Rudakov copy).
In *Hope Abandoned* Nadezhda herself published another letter written
but never sent to Mandelstam in the camps. Though she quotes it

lightly Nadya could not conceal that the idea of his death had become her *idée fixe*.

Thus far we have relied only on Nadezhda's words about Mandelstam. Can we not find an echo of this serious issue in his poetry? For the moment, we shall examine only one poem. "No, I cannot hide from the Great Shambles" was written in 1931, in other words, well before the Stalin satire. Let's read through the entire text:

> No, Moscow, the horse-cabby's back,
> Cannot hide me from the Great Shambles.
> I'm a tramcar-cherry in a terrible age
> And I don't know why I'm alive.
>
> You and I will take 'A' and 'B'
> And see who shall be first to die.
> But the city squeezes small as a sparrow
> Or spreads up and out like a rising pie,
>
> And barely can menace round the corner –
> Do as you like, I shan't risk it!
> Who hasn't enough warmth in their glove
> To ride round that great Tart, Moskva?

Nadezhda has given a published commentary. Their homeless condition once forced them to part. Taking different tram routes, Mandelstam went to spend the night with his brother near Nogin Square while Nadezhda went to Zhenya on Strastnoi Boulevard. The poet offers a historical picture of Moscow at the time, and the bewildered situation of its contemporary visitors and inhabitants. With astonishing mastery Mandelstam combines a general view of Moscow's importance with the visual impression from a particular journey along the city's streets. Here one both feels how the rails lead the carriage into a narrow side street ("small as a sparrow"), how the expanse of a large square opens out ("spreads up and out like a rising pie"), and how Moscow "barely can menace round the corner", as it flashes past the eyes of the passengers.

Specialists have debated what the "tramcar-cherry" means and how it is linked with the "terrible time". It has no meaning other than the sight that greeted every Muscovite each day on the street: a full tram carriage, festooned with people clinging to the handrails and dangling from the steps like bunches of cherries. Cherries are usually picked not one at a time but plucked from the tree, with the stem, in bunches. What Moscow was like in a terrible time the Mandelstams knew all too well; and this is reflected in many of his poems of a period so aptly named "the Great Shambles".

Still, the mainspring of this poem is a sinister private quarrel, quite audible here, that had been going on for a long while between Mandelstam and his wife: "Who shall be first to die?" There is reason to hear Nadezhda's bravado in the draft ("Do as you wish, I'm not afraid") and the life-loving Mandelstam in the final version ("Do as you like, I shan't risk it"). Even in the first years of their life together in Leningrad Nadya admits that her failure as an artist gave her the right to kill herself: "I was sure that I had the right to take leave of life if it did not treat me well. But M. categorically denied this."

The covert revulsion from Nadya over the central question of life and death permeates all Mandelstam's poems of the '30s. A defensive movement fills the poem "Petersburg, I do not yet want to die" [*Literaturnaya gazeta*, 28 November 1932], written in December 1930, and the fragment, then unknown to Nadya, "Help me, Lord, to live this life to the end" [January 1931]. The second line, "I fear for life, for Your servant . . ." in particular echoes his retort in their 1920s quarrel: "Life is a gift, no one would dare to reject it."

The Terrified Eagle

In the series of poems where Nadya's veiled image is present, the work about Lot's incest with his two daughters ("Return to the incestuous bosom" 1920) is particularly complex. In a late commentary Nadezhda recognised herself as one of the two incestuous daughters and called the poem "harsh and strange". One can agree on those two matters but overall her interpretation does not stand up to criticism. She takes the closing lines as her starting point: "No, you will love a Judaean/ you will vanish in him, and God be with you." The argument may be resolved by examining the biographical details of the two Mandelstams.

For Nadya it is most important that she was the only Jewess in Mandelstam's "Don Juan" list of conquests. This made him feel "a sharp sense of his Jewishness", she suggests. On the contrary, by falling in love with Christian women of various nationalities, I would say he could feel himself more intensely a Jew by being a traditional renegade. "He felt Jews to be one family, hence the theme of incest," continues Nadya. Such sophistry leads to absurdity. Jews are well known for being family-centred, so does that mean they have all come from the "incestuous bosom"? Then the problem of the entire nation's degeneration would arise. The legend of Lot, on the contrary, holds the clan in such high respect that it forgives the righteous man's daughters their incest in order to uphold this principle. They are the victims of their elevated duty not oath-breakers.

Nadezhda then rebuked the poet for "mixing up" two Biblical legends when he gave Lot's unnamed daughter the name of Jacob's unloved wife, Leah. I do not agree. Mandelstam had not confused someone with anyone else. Here I rely on his remark about the composition of the *Egyptian Stamp*: "My thoughts leap implicit links". Mandelstam could not stand descriptive poetry. He selected individual traits of the present, those that he had seen and absorbed at that time, and then with the evanescent impulsiveness of brilliant thought transformed them into independent subjects, thereby re-drawing the world.

During the stormy period of the Civil War Mandelstam lived an extremely intense life. He travelled to many towns, was twice arrested by secret police of various political persuasions, and spent the summer of 1919 in Kiev where he met and became intimate with Nadezhda. Nevertheless, that September they parted. He went to the Crimea and only on 5 December 1919 did he again think of her. Then he understood how much he needed Nadya, and felt he was bound to her not just by love but some kind of kinship. Of course, there was an area of his life, his writing, to which she still had no access. He was so expressive, however, that he was in need of a friend and someone he could talk to every minute. In his letter of 5 December he calls her "sister", "daughter", "little one" and "friend"; he asks her forgiveness for something ("pardon me my weakness") and confesses, "I cannot forgive myself that I left without you!"

After such a tender and touching letter, they could have joined forces immediately and remained together for ever. But yet another regime came to power in the Ukraine and there was no way back to Kiev. Mandelstam found himself in Petrograd. There he often gave public recitals and was greeted with recognition and success. In late October 1920 he met Olga Arbenina. They would continue to meet for almost three months.

His passion for Arbenina gave birth to an entire cycle of first-class poems. The poem about Lot and his daughters, written that same year, evidently grew out of reflections on his own private life. He saw Arbenina as the mythical Helen of Troy. Her "seductive image" forms the centre of the brilliant "Horse" in the Arbenina cycle. This passion separated him from Nadya. For good reason when his correspondence with his future wife resumed in 1921 he no longer addressed her as "thou" (*ty*) but formally as "you" (*vy*). In other words, everything had to start again from the beginning.

In her memoirs Arbenina says: "Our friendship with M [andelstam] lasted until January 1921 . . . I then occasionally met M. and his wife when visiting the Livshits'. We would converse with some embarrassment."

Nadezhda, Moscow, 1923

This brief aside shows that the poem about the daughters of Lot had little connection with the Bible but contained an important autobiographical confession. If we remember "As along the streets of monstrous Kiev" where the biographical motif provides the entire structure of the poem, we shall understand a great deal more about Mandelstam's life and death. "I know not whose wife" in the latter poem, we can guess, refers to the old and new loves of this brave woman, wandering about the city. Let us assume her former husband was not a Jew. Then we read:

> Return to the incestuous bosom
> Whence, Leah, you came.
> . . . because you preferred a yellow twilight
> To the sun of Ilion.

Then the "fateful change" in that poem, and love for a Judaean and, most important of all, the declaration "You shall be Leah, not Helen" all represent the true balance of forces within the Mandelstam marriage. They were not united by passion but something else and no less powerful – the feeling of a complete lack of inhibition.

We can observe the same process in the poem "I enter with a smoking splinter". Usually this is interpreted unequivocally and even entitled "Untruth", having been first printed as such in *Mosty*, the undependable Munich almanac. In acting thus, commentators ignore a fundamental quality of Mandelstam's writing and interpret the poem as an allegory – most certainly political and most certainly anti-Stalinist: supposedly ordinary people called Stalin "six-fingered"– i.e. a wizard or the devil (or so Nadezhda claims). But Mandelstam's writing has many layers and offers several meanings. Of these the deepest often remained not entirely clear to the poet himself. This explains how Mandelstam could be "unbelievably" tender and caring (Akhmatova) in his letters to Nadya but mention her with harsh rudeness in his poetry. The hidden meaning of his relations with Nadya is immured in the very foundations of the many-storeyed structure of his writing; it forces its way into the poetry against his will. As far back as 1912, reviewing *Dandelions*, a collection of Ehrenburg's poems, Mandelstam had good reason to declare: "True poetic chastity makes a shamefaced attitude to one's own soul unnecessary."

Nadya's special gift for encouraging confidential frankness in tête-a-tête conversations was recalled by the philologist and writer Eduard Babayev at the end of his life. He spent his youth in Tashkent to which the widowed Nadezhda Mandelstam had moved during the war. Soon he fell beneath her all-consuming influence. The process whereby she possessed the souls of the young he denoted as a "coil" and described its application as follows:

> . . . to begin with she removed one still superficial layer of
> doubts, that were inhibiting the behaviour of the boy.
> Gradually she increased her interest in him and towards the
> end guessed the most painful area of his self-awareness; this
> she lightly removed by a liberating but apparently acciden-
> tal phrase. It was already more than sympathetic under-
> standing, it was a real absolution of sins. That was what
> created an unusual lightness in contacts with her.

The entire second half of Nadezhda's life was spent in such games. It was not that easy, however, when she lived side by side with a great poet. An attentive new reading of the poem "I enter with a smoking splinter" [April 1931] will help us get to grips with that complexity:

> With a smoking splinter[23] I enter
> The cabin of six-fingered untruth.

---

[23] A glowing splinter, often birch and up to a foot in length, was used as a fixed and portable light in peasant homes.

> Just let me have a look at you
> For I must lie in a coffin of pine.

This poem belongs to the "Wolf" cycle of 1930–2. Yet although the metaphor "six-fingered untruth" makes a momentary appearance in drafts of "For the resounding valour . . ."[24] the poem itself brings a quite uncharacteristic motif of repentance and guilt to the cycle. What was he guilty of? Whom had he betrayed? Where does that final awful admission come from:

> – never mind, you're all right,
> for, my gossip, I'm just the same.

"I'm just the same"? Who is this favourite girlfriend whom he calls "gossip"?

Left to her own devices after Mandelstam's death, Nadezhda began to make demands on everyone and battled over the slightest trifle. She was hurt that Akhmatova did not put the date of Mandelstam's death in her *Poem without a Hero* but, instead, talked about the suicide of a certain Knyazev.[25] She began to quarrel with Khardjiev because, as an experienced and perceptive textologist, he corrected three mistakes in her copies of the poems. And she insisted that Mandelstam's erotic life had depended entirely on her. If we judge the poet by his widow's books, instead of gauging his life from what he wrote and said, we shall never reach the truth.

During the first years of their union Mandelstam devoted himself, with Nadya's technical assistance, to inspired work on lyrical prose. In 1924–5 they both became involved in the most banal adulterous relationships. She intended to leave Mandelstam for the artist T. He turned to the greedy accumulation of money from literary hack-work and with these funds he repaid certain moral debts to Nadya; but, most important, the money also paid for the hotel room where he would meet Olga Vaksel (Lyutik). The affair became intense. So intense that Lyutik's mother felt the right to demand of Mandelstam that he take her daughter somewhere to a sanatorium in the south. When Nadezhda, with her bisexuality, intervened in this relationship, his wife was transformed from a "daughter" and "sweetheart" into "my gossip". As I remarked, the poet himself could not sometimes identify the origin of particular images in his poems.

---

[24] The first variant of the last stanza reads: "Lead me off in the night where the Yenisei flows / to the cabin of six-fingered untruth / because it's not wolf's blood that flows through my veins / and I must lie in a coffin of pine."

[25] The first dedicatee of the "Poem" was Cornet Knyazev, who killed himself on 27 December 1913 for love of Olga Sudeikina (to whom, on her death in 1945, the work's second dedication was addressed).

The capacity to see far into the future or, in other words, the sooth-saying power of genius, came to Mandelstam in his early youth. He was 20 when he fully understood his fate. I have in mind the poem about the terrified eagle, the best of three works (see "The Seashell", 1911, and "Self-portrait", 1914) that develop a common theme, the dramatic duality of frail flesh and an elevated almost cosmic spirit:

> Within my being like a snake I melt
> About myself I twine like ivy
> I ascend above the Self.
>
> I long to return, fly back to myself,
> fluttering dark wings
> widespread over water . . .
>
> And, like a terrified eagle
> Returning, no longer found
> the nest, tumbled in the abyss.
>
> I shall wash in the lightning fire
> And, cursing the laden thunder,
> Within a cold cloud I'll disappear!
>
> 1911

Perhaps Mandelstam was afraid to expose his own weakness, or he did not appreciate the magnitude of this poem.[26] For whatever reason, he did not include it in his first collection, *Stone*.

Written 1990s. Published in *Znamya* (February 1998).

Epilogue

Readers and specialists today seem to relish the theme of premeditated suicide, elevating it to a matter of melodramatic interest. In fact, Mandelstam arrived at such a thought only when he realised that he was doomed. Few suspect that the private argument over suicide between

---

[26] E.G.: Two images from classic Russian verse are concealed in this poem. One is the "frightened eaglet" of Pushkin's "Prophet". The other is Tyutchev's "stone", which was hurled from the mountain heights into the valley by some mysterious hand, remaining there as a bulwark.

husband and wife, which they also each confronted within themselves, was the constantly present theme of their last years together. As we can judge from *Hope Abandoned*, it would pursue Nadezhda to her death. The nervous agitation with which she there surrounded the portraits of those whom she knew is striking. She wrote of three suicides[27] with such powerful hatred and disparagement that it becomes quite indecent. Nadezhda did not spare her palette when proving the insignificance and weakness of the "feeble" Mayakovsky and the "cowardly" Dligach, or in deriding the Tashkent NKVD man with whom she had been on close terms.

We can now offer an answer to Akhmatova's strange dependence on Nadya. I have spoken of the powers of persuasion with which Nadezhda was endowed. Akhmatova was not a weak person, and did not easily succumb to the influence of others. What was it that forced her in *Leaves from a Diary* to repeat, in essence, the portrait of Mandelstam already outlined by Nadezhda?

Mandelstam brought misfortune on himself by his open and staggeringly credulous trust in official literature during that terrible time. This thought could comfort many, but not Pasternak and Akhmatova. While dousing themselves in a cold shower of determined rationality, they could not escape an unconscious feeling of guilt for his downfall.

Successful or not, brilliant or in places lame, Mandelstam's satire

Mandelstam, prison photo, May 1938

---

[27] See also her remark about Yakhontov, who jumped out of a window and killed himself "in a fit of panic that he was about to be arrested" (chap. 14).

nevertheless expressed feelings and judgements about the personality of Stalin that were shared by Akhmatova. As concerns Pasternak's reaction to the epigram we cannot overlook the testimony of a contemporary: "This is suicide," she remembers him saying, "and I do not want to be any part of it." As is well known, in 1932 he wrote a personal letter of sympathy to Stalin, on the death of the latter's wife Nadezhda Alliluyeva. But when the political trials of the Leader's former comrades-in-arms began, Pasternak came to his senses. Still, he could not help feeling that his human, all-too-human behaviour had saved him from the fate of Mandelstam. And no matter how brave Akhmatova's repentant verse in *Requiem*, that work remained hidden from inquisitive eyes until it ceased to be dangerous. Faced by the real death of a poet, Pasternak could only regard his own expression of the poet's vocation, "utter ruin and downfall", as an actor's rehearsal compared to what actually happened to Mandelstam.

Like all great poets they were demanding of themselves and could not mute the absurd (in rational terms) feeling of guilt for Mandelstam's tragic end. Nadezhda suspected the existence of this secret feeling and this encouraged her to write letters from Voronezh in which she made unprecedented demands on both Pasternak and Akhmatova. Later she could not forgive either for having survived. The other insistent note in Nadezhda's books is self-justification for her own survival. Compensation for her ambiguous position was now found in the idea of her mission. Having continually urged Mandelstam towards joint suicide, Nadezhda used her singular obligation to preserve and publish his manuscripts to justify her long life without him.

A poet is cast in the same mould as a prophet. As far back as the early 1930s Mandelstam had already foreseen the bloody lawlessness of Stalin's purges and executions. Yet when the events actually unfolded before his eyes it was as if he did not see that terrible reality. Creatively he was then engrossed in a vision of the future world war. In the *Verses on the Unknown Soldier* we encounter "kidnapped cities", "the humble spirit of bursting tombs", the union of "human and cripple", "millions of dead, slaughtered wholesale" and the cosmic theme.

"And a brood of wooden crutches stumps round the century's furthest fringes": that was what then filled Mandelstam's inner ear. There is no sense in making of him a consistent champion of the rights of the individual and freedom of thought. His nervous constitution was not created for systematic political struggle. Yet Mandelstam fulfilled his duty as a poet in that unprecedented epoch and died, sharing the fate of millions of his fellow-citizens.

From "The Fraternity of Poets", *Znamya* (October 1999).

OF MEMOIRS AND
MORE BESIDES
[1999]

I began thinking about memoirs when still a child. Ours was a large and
complicated family, and I was convinced that on becoming an adult I would
write a "novel" about us all – I did not then know the word *memoirs*.
Fortunately, my intention to write something resembling *La Famille
Thibault* was not realised, and I did not expose each of my relations to the
general gaze. Then I began writing letters. Adults praised them, but my
older female cousins would tell me: "Literature is not just writing letters.
Don't get the idea you'll ever be a writer." There was one uncle, however,
to whom I also sent my letters. I was older by then and wrote about
Weltschmerz. "You'll be a writer," he said and gave me a beautiful little pen
with a fine No. 86 nib: subsequently, in my frivolous fashion, I lost it.

My sister and cousins, however, would recognise only "finished"
expressions – i.e. existing models – and assured me that literature was
not composed in the extraordinary language I used. Now I was in the
older classes at our Moscow *gymnasium,* and the woman who taught us
Russian literature was a pupil of the philosopher Lev Lopatin.[1] "Free"
barely describes the composition topics she would hand out. "Sodom or
Madonna?!" The words she exclaimed rang in the air. Such subjects I
found simply wearisome. They did not attract me then.

I also kept a diary. But my patience was limited, and so scraps of paper
with my scribblings could be found, scattered in every corner of the apartment – for which my brothers and sister would shame me in concert.

---

[1]Psychologist and philosopher (1855–1920) who was friendly with Vladimir
Solovyov.

Today memoirs have become
very popular. They were popular in the 1920s as well. It was
Kornei Chukovsky who began
it all. With relish he republished
the reminiscences of Avdotya
Panayeva in a single volume[2]
in 1926. There followed several similar publications. The
select nineteenth-century salons
aroused particular interest. This
was stimulated by Aronson and
Reiser's *Literary Clubs and
Salons* (1929), where we learned of the Karamzin establishment that so impressed us all.
That household was part of our
literary memory until the
1950s and '60s when sensational new material appeared
about the unique salon organised, after the historian Karam-

Emma, aged 7

zin's death, by the numerous members of his family.

In the late 1920s every young lady longed to host a literary salon
that would be regularly attended by at least one renowned film director or writer. In my mind, that fashion is associated with the vogue
for "free expression and movement" as taught by the barefoot Isadora
Duncan. Young ladies with little suitcases, hurrying to their dance
classes, were an inescapable feature of the Moscow streets in those
years.

I would prefer, though, to speak not of the popularity of memoirs in
Russia, but of how we should read and make use of them. In the 1920s,
the study of sources was taught at philological faculties. Each student
knew that he or she should be able to indicate the source of the text
being cited – i.e. was obliged to know the literature on a subject. Today
this is a forgotten skill. How often in memoirs and articles we encounter
the phrase "I have read somewhere . . ." followed by the author's own
conjectures which are actually without any foundation.

A few examples.

---

[2] Avdotya Panayeva-Golovachova (1820–1893) wrote many novels about women
in contemporary Russian society.

An author most experienced in his field of the arts has recently issued an appeal. The most important thing, he says, is to make notes about everyone and everything: write, write, write. Yet one has to know how to write. Any police informer can write – or, on the contrary, is incapable of writing, but has to do so by virtue of his occupation. Literary texts, however, always depend on selection. Too often nowadays people write down the first thing that occurs to them, and the trusting consumer of such memoirs then irresponsibly repeats those statements that happen to stay in his mind.

A striking example is the incident involving Mandelstam and Alexei Tolstoy. Why did the poet slap this famous writer's face? To my astonishment, I have now several times read extraordinary fantasies about this literary row. The event took place in Leningrad, we are told, at the editorial offices of the monthly *Zvezda*. Among the writers present was Mandelstam. Also in the room was the poetess Sofia Parnok. At that moment with a demonstrative din Alexei Tolstoy entered the office. All the seats were occupied. Someone suggested that Parnok give him her chair, and it was then, supposedly, that the indignant Mandelstam slapped Tolstoy's face.

The only truth in this account is that Mandelstam slapped Alexei Tolstoy across the face in the presence of many other writers at the *Zvezda* offices in Leningrad. Anyone who has read Mandelstam knows that the incident was linked to the comrades' court, chaired by Tolstoy, which investigated the poet's dispute with the writer Sargidjan (Borodin). There are at least three detailed accounts of this dispute. Two belong to individuals who attended the hearing: F.F. Volkenstein (Krandievsky), Tolstoy's stepson, and the famous poet, translator and memoirist Simeon Lipkin. A third account ["Near the Poet"] may be read in my *New Look at Mandelstam* (Paris 1986), where the beginning of that furious quarrel and the subsequent scrap are described.[3] There I also give the story told by Mandelstam's brother-in-law Yevgeny Khazin, who came to see me immediately after the hearing and provided a detailed account of all that took place there. And still the legend about Alexei Tolstoy remains alive to this day. In the commentary to Akhmatova's *Leaves from a Diary*, republished in 1996 in a collection of her prose and poetry, we read: "The all-powerful Alexei Tolstoy insulted Nadezhda Mandelstam and the poet interceded for her and gave him a slap across the face." Here we have an arbitrary assessment of the behaviour of the two protagonists and a total ignorance of the subject under discussion.

The Russian mass media, meanwhile, continue to repeat the passionate versions retailed in Nadezhda Mandelstam's three books of memoirs.

---

[3] In this volume see "Near the Poet", pp. 43–4, 58, 64.

These also refer to the offence given to the poet's wife by Tolstoy. According to my information, the affront lay in the following. After the scrap described earlier Nadezhda was left with a black eye. In effect, Tolstoy's decision stated that "both sides should be ashamed of themselves", but did not even mention the injury Nadezhda had sustained.

Another example. Recently there were celebrations to mark Andrei Voznesensky's 65th birthday.[4] One journalist could think of nothing better by way of congratulation than to cite Mandelstam's moving letter to Tynyanov of 21 January 1937. This was sent four months before the poet was released from exile in Voronezh. He was then experiencing a surge of creative energy, but there was no-one for him to talk to, who could appreciate as fully the explosive culture of that moment. "Please do not consider me a shadow," Mandelstam writes. "I myself can still cast a shadow. But recently, I have become intelligible to virtually everyone. That's ominous. For a quarter of a century now, blending the important with the frivolous, I have advanced towards Russian poetry. Soon, however, my poems will flow into Russian poetry and merge with it, thereby altering something of its structure and composition." The correspondent applies this unique letter to the imagined position of Voznesensky, someone who has always contrived to remain in the public eye.

And that is not the chance ineptitude of a hasty journalist; it is a general phenomenon. Mandelstam's verse has been plundered for quotations that sound apposite only in rare cases: more often, his words are cited on any pretext or, most frequently of all, without a hint of relevance. Probably the universal application of Mandelstam's lines is linked to the appearance of the most complete volume of his work in the New Poets' Library series (St Petersburg, 1995). Undoubtedly liberation from the insistent chaperoning of his widow, who died almost twenty years ago, has also played its part. For her apologists, though, she remains a more authoritative interpreter of Mandelstam's work and life than the poet himself.

Not everyone, I repeat, can write memoirs. In his time, Pushkin urged his contemporaries not to be lazy about writing things down, but straightaway taught them how to do it. It was essential to indicate "I heard this from so and so . . ." Then such a note became a document. Its reader might check the accuracy of the information received and could gather material about the person who had served as the source for Pushkin's diary entries.

---

[4] A popular poet since the late 1950s when, with Yevtushenko and others, he declaimed his verse before audiences packed into football stadiums.

Alexander Pushkin also cultivated the genre of "table talk", but never presented these anecdotes about famous people as established fact. On the contrary, when speaking of an unjustly fought duel in the eighteenth century, he concluded: "Rumour laid the blame on Potyomkin." Thus rumour became, in his hands, a genuine historical fact.

The memoirist has a special type of recall. Somewhere in the recesses of consciousness, the true author of reminiscences can preserve a particular character's intonation or gesture for decades and thereby resurrect certain important episodes in the life of an individual or of society as a whole.

I think an exception to this rule, however, must be made for the writings of those who were once arrested and by chance escaped death in the Gulag. They cannot help but tell what happened to them. It is a need as compelling as that which led early men to draw on cave walls. For whom, for what reason, did they do it? They could not do otherwise. The writings of former camp inmates simply must be published. Once in Russia there were the almanacs of "Former Political Prisoners" and regular issues of *Hard Labour and Banishment*.[5] In a similar publication these memoirs will not be overshadowed by other reminiscences and will stir their intended readers to the depths of their being. Such authors need not know how to write: each word is a heart-rending cry.

First published in *Voprosy literatury*, no. 1 (1999).

---

[5] Periodical, published 1921–35, by the Society of Former Political Prisoners, an organisation of those who had been imprisoned as opponents of the Tsarist regime.

APPENDICES

I. Five Notes

1.1 The Gornfeld Affair [tr.]

In 1928 Mandelstam revised the Russian version of the *Legende de Uylenspiegel*. When it was published in September, the title page erroneously credited him as translator. Arkady Gornfeld (1867–1941) was understandably indignant. Despite a formal apology from the publisher, the original translator began a series of heated exchanges with Mandelstam in the press: "If as I walk through a flea market I recognise, even in its altered state, the coat that yesterday hung in my hall, I have the right to say: Look here, this is a stolen coat." The dispute rumbled on for a year and prompted Mandelstam to write his *Fourth Prose*.

Early in 1929, Narbut's replacement as director of the "Land and Factory" publishers tore up all contracts with the poet. Mandelstam broadened his attacks to include the entire translation "industry" and provoked both denunciation and support. Among fifteen prominent signatories to a public letter defending him in *Literaturnaya gazeta* (13 May) were Pasternak, Pilnyak, Fadeyev, Zelinsky and Averbakh. Not until December 1929 did a writers' commission issue an ambivalent judgement reproving both Mandelstam and those who had accused him of plagiarism.

1.2 Alliluyeva's Suicide [tr.]

On the night of 8–9 November 1932, shortly after the fifteenth anniversary of the October Revolution, Nadezhda Alliluyeva shot herself. The death of Stalin's wife was briefly announced in *Pravda* on 10 November, but no explanations followed. The strange pause continued for almost a week until collective letters of condolence from writers, the Central Committee and other organisations began to appear. Attempts were meanwhile being made to hush up the event and present it to the world as the result of a tragic and unexpected illness (appendicitis, perhaps).

Some thought Alliluyeva's desperate act had political motivations – she came from a family of old Revolutionaries. Others suggested purely private reasons: "That poor woman!" exclaimed an acquaintance not long before, referring to her difficult family life. A perhaps understandable suspicion that Stalin himself might have killed the mother of his two children was mistaken. The cult of Stalin had begun to take shape in December 1929, on his 50th birthday. As the entire economy was being wrenched into a different gear (famine was only months away), the suicide came as a dramatic reminder of the Leader's vulnerability.

1.3 Living Space [tr.]

Following Russian usage, the living accommodation described here has been referred to as an "apartment" or flat. Those in Moscow and Leningrad whose lives form the subject of this book were better off than the thousands of families then living in barracks. But not by much.

The accompanying ground plan (adapted from L.M. Vidgof, *Mandelstam's Moscow* [Moscow, 1999]) was drawn from memory by Mandelstam's nephew and shows a classic communal flat of the Soviet period. The various tenants (individuals, couples, entire families) had one room each and shared the rest – the large kitchen where "sixteen primus stoves sang," the bathroom and toilet, and the wide corridor where neighbours smoked, children played, and the phone was always ringing. Some flats had fewer tenants; some had more. This plan depicts Apartment 3 at 10 Starosadsky Street in Moscow, where Alexander Mandelstam lived and, on occasion, Osip and Nadezhda as well. The poet made an evocative poem of these conditions when he immortalised as Alexander Herzevich (or Scherzevich) the musical Bekkerman brothers in the neighbouring room, who "from morn to night" polished their Schubert, till it shone "like a real cut gem".

As the years passed, such flats grew increasingly crowded. Service apartments allocated in the early 1920s to the chief physician Gerstein in Moscow or the art historian Punin in Leningrad gradually acquired more and more inhabitants, each with a claim to living space. The intrusive and claustrophobic side to life in a *kommunalka* was recalled by one

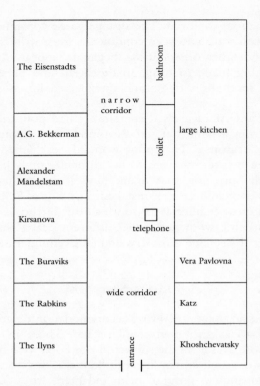

Communal apartment 3, 10 Starosadsky Street, Moscow

raised in such an apartment: ". . . as you enter . . . you hear the flutter of slippers and the squeaking of floors, and you notice many pairs of eyes scrutinizing you through half-opened doors" (Svetlana Boym, *Common Places* [New York, 1994]). The telephone, where one existed, was also shared property. The strange story of Stalin's telephone conversation with Pasternak on 11 June 1934 loses much of its pathos if the sequence of events is not visualised in such a setting: the communal apartment on Volkhonka; the neighbour knocking to say that someone was ringing Pasternak, supposedly from the Kremlin; the poet cautiously noting down the number dictated by Stalin's secretary Poskryobyshev, on which he was then to call back and speak to the Leader himself.

1.4 A Letter to Stalin [tr.]

At the First Congress of Soviet Writers in August 1934, the Party spokesman Nikolai Bukharin declared Mayakovsky and Demyan Bedny to be anachronistic phenomena. It was the poetry of Pasternak, he said, which expressed the aesthetic demands of the epoch. The "intimate" and "incomprehensible" poet's new pre-eminence would remain officially unchallenged for a year and a half. Then, in a *Pravda* article of 5 December 1935, Stalin intervened. The dead Mayakovsky, he pronounced, was "the best and most talented poet of the Soviet epoch".

Boris Pasternak to Stalin, late December 1935[1]

Dear Iosif Vissarionovich,

It vexes me that I did not then follow my first wish and thank you for the miraculous and instantaneous release of Akhmatova's family. But I felt ashamed to disturb you a second time and decided to keep to myself a warm feeling of gratitude to you, being assured that it would, in any case, and by means unknown, in some way reach you.

Yet another uncomfortable feeling. To begin with, I wrote to you in my own style, wordy and with digressions, submitting to that mysterious something that, beyond what all people understand and share, draws me to you. But I was advised to abridge and simplify the letter, and I am left with the terrible feeling that I have sent you something foreign that is not mine.

I have long dreamed of offering you some modest fruit of my labours, but it is all so talentless that the dream, evidently, shall never come true. Or perhaps I should be bolder and without further ado follow my first impulse?

"Georgian Lyric Poetry" is a weak and derivative work, the honour and glory of which belongs wholly to the authors themselves, for the most part wonderful poets. In rendering Vazha Pshavela [1861–1915], I deliberately avoided a faithful reproduction of the form of the original for reasons that I shall not weary you with, in order to convey more freely the spirit of the original, immeasurable and thunderous in its beauty and conception.

In conclusion, let me thank you warmly for your recent words about Mayakovsky. They correspond to my own feelings; I love him and have written an entire book about that. However, your lines about him have also indirectly had a saving effect on myself. Recently, under the influence

---

[1] First published in *Glasnost: CPSU Central Committee Weekly* ("From Stalin's Personal Archive"), 16 September 1990. E.G. comments: "There it was given a date of March 1936, but when Lazar Fleishman published it (see "Pasternak's Letter to Stalin," in Literary Supplement 12, *Russkaya mysl*, 28 June 1991), he dated it more convincingly as having been written immediately before the *Izvestiya* cycle in January."

of the West, I have been terribly over-praised, and an exaggerated importance has been attributed to me (it even made me ill): they began to
suspect a major artistic force in me. Now that you have put Mayakovsky
in first place, I have been freed of this suspicion, and with a light heart I
can live and work as before, in modest silence, with the unexpected and
mysterious occurrences without which I would not love life.

In the name of that mystery,

I remain, your warmly affectionate and devoted

B. Pasternak

By the end of 1935, notes Lazar Fleishman, works praising the Leader
had been widely promoted in the Soviet press. Fleishman also comments
that the collection *Georgian Lyric Poetry* (Moscow, 1935), which Pasternak
enclosed with this letter, "reprinted his own recent translations of odes
to Stalin by the Georgian poets Yashvili and Mitsishvili. The gift served
as an inventive message that the poet was not ready to compete with his
Georgian friends in a genre then still new for Russian literature."

1.5 The Soviet Ordeal [tr.]

Among countless others despatched to the Gulag, Mandelstam never
reached his destination. On the longest and most murderous "Middle
Passage" of the Soviet camp system, he died in Vladivostok, having arrived
too late in the year and too sick, after months in prison and the slow,
cramped train journey eastwards, to make the further sea voyage to Kolyma.

By 1953, the year of Stalin's death, some 18 million had been sent
to the camps. There are no such statistics in these memoirs, but for
decades the life the author describes was attended by the constant menace
and growing depredations of internal repression and punctuated by
repeated upheavals on an unprecedented scale (revolution, war, famine,
mass arrests and deportations). Gerstein ceased to wonder each day what
was going on in the camps, she remarks, only when war began in 1941.
Any attempt to describe that history without assessing the long-term
effects of such trauma on the rest of society is clearly inadequate.

The entire population was trapped in the various circles or zones
of the system created by Stalin (and Lenin). At its heart lay a casual
and arbitrary brutality, most clearly expressed by the seizure and execution of hostages. An effective form of terror from the Civil War, the
practice would evolve and acquire a veneer of legality, but the principle remained the same. Eight hundred were rounded up in 1921,
suspected of participation in the Tagantsev "conspiracy". There had

been seditious conversations but there was no such counter-revolutionary plot. More than a hundred, including Nikolai Gumilyov, were shot. The unpredictable threat in the 1930s, and thereafter, of summary execution, banishment or hard labour in the Gulag (on criminal charges often as flimsy as the imaginary political offences) served to extend and systematise a proven method for keeping society under control.

This was both a shared and a highly divisive experience. In a characteristic oration that exemplifies the pressures and suspicions of their existence, Nadezhda Mandelstam once denounced the quest for high-ranking scapegoats: they would have achieved far less, she suggested, without the "agents, informers, petitioners, delegations and advisers" who actively aided and supported them. Gerstein's closing note "On Memoirs" mentions the agent's reports and the written denunciations, recalling two of the most widespread "literary" genres of the Soviet era. Mandelstam's first 1934 imprisonment offers a glimpse of the deeper degradation imposed by the system, of informing against oneself and others in the ever more fantastic confessions extracted during interrogation. In 1938 the poet was held for four months, then convicted of "counter-revolutionary" activities and sent to the Gulag to serve a five-year sentence. In the indictment he was described as being of the merchant class and "a Socialist Revolutionary".

None came through these ordeals unscathed. The incomplete statistics for the numbers shot and imprisoned are at last available; they begin to acquire meaning, however, only when attached to individual biographies. Furthermore, the effects lasted more than one lifetime. The intimidation and lesson of conformity was absorbed by subsequent generations who lived, as a consequence, in a more "vegetarian" era. Critical of the many garrulous and tendentious voices of the *glasnost* era, in 1989 Emma Gerstein sought out the obscure compiler of a volume of Gulag memoirs to commend him and his authors for having preserved a record not just of horrors but of the qualities of compassion and dignity that had helped them survive.

2 Mandelstam and Rudakov [E.G.]

The Missing Key

Mandelstam's collaboration with Rudakov had its high and low points. The poet was incapable of systematic work. After the tumultuous first two months of their acquaintance and the writing of new poems, the

creative and poetic energy began to ebb. Mandelstam turned to paid
literary work with Nadezhda: reviews, their radio drama *Goethe's Youth*
and other commissions for the radio and, finally, work in the theatre.

However, he could not exist outside his poetry. Together with
Rudakov, Mandelstam began to reassess all his poetic work, from 1907
until the most recent Voronezh poems. On first acquaintance Rudakov
struck Mandelstam as a bold, cocksure fellow, who had dreamed up an
enormous book on the theory and history of Russian poetry. Now his
tasks narrowed. They decided to prepare a collection of Mandelstam's
verse with a full commentary and there was even suggestion that
Rudakov would write a monograph about Mandelstam. Always prone
to extravagant enthusiasms, the poet accompanied the enterprise with
approving exclamations. As we read his comments we should not forget
that we are learning of them from Rudakov. Still, the latter was sufficiently objective and, most important, possessed a sensitivity to word
and intonation.

They began to implement their plan on 23 May 1935. That day
Rudakov noted:

> I am writing in pencil because I am living at the Mandelstams'.
> Today we have been taking *dictation* (already about 300
> poems!), can you imagine, Lina? In this way I *artificially*
> halted and neutralised the destruction of new poems. He is
> absorbed by his recollections. Lina, it's a miracle we met.
> Now he insists every day: work, write – and I shall write new
> things, and the work about him will be amazing.

"Now he may be leaving here earlier than me," writes Rudakov, on 26
May:

> It's not certain. Nadya has still not returned and that's one
> of the reasons. That we were together for these months is an
> astonishing and historic event. He has bequeathed all the
> poems to me after his death, in his own words: "You will be
> the sole heir and publisher of Mandelstam." Now Nadya
> perhaps will bring the old things from home. If Leningrad
> [takes us back] there are hopes of a new evening recital, with
> me.

The work continued intensively. When Mandelstam was dictating the
1930–33 poems that Rudakov did not know (a total of 406 lines) they
also started to discuss his poetry.

29 June: I've only just returned from M. Tired as if I'd been working for 100 hours. I copied more than 150 lines under dictation into your white notebook and, most important of all, discovered major works that he had completely forgotten. At times they're first-class pieces. A handful of the Koktebel poems are irretrievable but these parrots are more upset about the loss of some pebbles they gathered there. N.'s lack of trust in me (or to be more exact, unwillingness to give me access to Oska's legacy) is gradually melting away . . . She promised to write down, on the quiet, the things that O. himself did not give me.

Dictation of the new unpublished poems continued until 30 June. By then Rudakov had accumulated up to 1,000 lines of poetry (including the verse published in literary journals), for the period 1930 to 1934. "Your little white notebook is completely full," he reported to his wife. (Where is that little notebook? Neither it nor any others were subsequently found in Lina Rudakova's archive.) A letter of 1 July indicates a slump in their work: "He's very difficult and at times I feel it's not worth it. But perhaps only he knows how to write poems today."

At one moment the recollection of Mandelstam's early poems led, in Rudakov's words, to a tragic love story: "Mandelstam and Nadezhda went out and 'chatted, walking up and down' and each confided past sins to me, talking one about the other." On 2 July he continued:

Today there's a suppressed drama between them. And I'm to blame. O. has some women's pieces that are not dedicated to her, written at times when she was not thinking about him (she doesn't mention them aloud, and does not like them) . . . It seems that a row will break out at any moment but the poems, it must be said, become the clearer and more powerful for that.

This recollection was to prove fruitful for future readers. Unknown to Nadya, Mandelstam dictated two poems to Rudakov: "Your slender shoulders", dedicated to Marusya Petrovykh[2] and "Volga, dash your steep slopes", dedicated to Lilya Popova.

The Mandelstams spent all July preparing radio broadcasts and making trips to collective farms in order to write an article (unpublished) for the newspaper. Regular work with Rudakov was interrupted. Only on 5 August did Rudakov write:

---

[2] See "Nadezhda": "The Black Candle", pp. 401–3.

From the post office I shall go to M. Yesterday they finished
writing the article and perhaps things will quieten down, then
I shall start to milk Oska historically. To be prepared I am
taking with me paper and the elaborate little programme I
drew up yesterday. He's an impulsive character and it's important to involve him and give him a push in the right direction: then he gets going himself. If only I can bring it off!

It was as though Mandelstam had again cooled to those "recollections".
However, his wife was showing an indubitable interest in the work. On
6 August Rudakov wrote:

Nadezhda helps a little but very sincerely. But I'm worried
. . . The Voronezh [material] is very rich but the plan should
not remain an illusion, it's very necessary. I'm having all
kinds of literary conversations with Nadezhda, and they have
led to the idea that they'll push to get me access, through
Akhmatova, to the Gumilyov materials. God, if I could only
live and work! Yesterday, to recover from the [newspaper]
article he read Dante aloud . . .

10 August: My work on M. proceeds in two directions.
Retrospective biographical notes and plans and thoughts
about the analysis of a particular poem. The first are written
down, for the most part, the second largely remain in my
head.

18 August: By the time you arrive there will be an entire
exercise book about Osya. When I look at what I've done it
seems it's needed in its own right and as a future incentive
for theoretical work.

Rudakov gained Nadezhda's full confidence.

21 August: I cunningly let her know about my programme
for O. She promised: 1) to give his humorous verse, 2) to
bring all the drafts and her own diaries about him from
Moscow, 3) everything in verse she can remember, 4) to write
out his life history by dates.

But if Nadezhda recognised Rudakov's work, his wife, on the contrary,
was becoming concerned. Mandelstam was taking up too much of her

husband's time, Lina feared, and this prevented him from writing his own verse. Their shared household also had its negative side, she believed. She considered that the Mandelstams were exploiting him. In his letters Rudakov had to defend them and justify his own behaviour to Lina. In September, when she spent her vacation in Voronezh, this led to a general discussion with her participation. Of course, Rudakov did not write to her that month but references and allusions to those September conversations occur repeatedly in later letters. Her visits did not help establish peaceful relations. It was after her first trip to Voronezh that the tone of Rudakov's reports about the Mandelstams changed markedly: the overfamiliar names that so grate on the ear (Nadka, Oska or even "the madman") then began to appear.

The work and real contact resumed at the end of October. Until then Rudakov was making notes of a biographical character only from Nadezhda's words. Finally on 22 October we read: "It hasn't happened for a long time but today I came home late from O. Unexpectedly there were again literary conversations and reminiscences."

October

25: Now I'm doing a lot of work on O. I pinched a copy of the personnel form he filled [for the theatre]. He was born on 3 January 1891 and gives an interesting statement of his social origins. A curious document! N. is trying to cajole me by dictating his biography. That's a help but she includes complaints in her account of events, which is disrespectful and cheap in tone, not the way O. speaks.

26: N. is systematically dictating his (and her own) biography to me. We've done 1919, 1920, 1921 and early 1922.

27: O. is going crazy about his position. I'm gathering notes about this.

November

2: You write that I don't want to tell you about my own literary life (and that of O.). It's just that those conversations were a separate tiny part and, two, what it's now been possible to extract are pure commentaries and they immediately found their place in the notebook and naturally were not repeated in letters . . . The theatre, sickness etc. should

form part of the commentaries in the Second Book. That's
how I see them.

4: Today was a turning point for me. The beginning of literary work. We worked for almost an hour on *Tristia* and
furthermore I got a lot of relevant stuff from him. Through
cunning conversations . . . I lead Oska to reflect on general
issues. The method is as follows. I talk of my own viewpoint
(or of someone else's) and he objects and then takes off in
the given direction, revealing himself.

5: We've been working a lot and well and shall finish the
1928 collection in another 3–4 sessions. A mass of invaluable
[information] is being entered in a notebook with annota-
tions. Once again a dead end: I realised that I am extracting
these comments myself – i.e. from O., and testing out a great
number of my own thoughts, which with his permission I
note down. I shall always be able to separate the two, but it
makes no sense to write two sets of comments now. There's
a gamble here: if it's M. then all will believe him but if it's
me, there are doubts. But if I passed it all off as M. then I
would be "effacing" myself. Under normal circumstances it
all ought to be sorted out and described somewhere in supple-
mentary and introductory words. Isn't that right? Meanwhile
my technique is growing. As soon as he gives less detail I
toss in some provocative question: he livens up, and off we
go again.
     I beat Nadya at chess all the time now and we chew
sunflower seeds. A brazen liberty: O. likes neither.

From 25 November 1935 until 11 January 1936 Rudakov was in the
Plekhanov Hospital in Voronezh.
     On 5 January Mandelstam returned early from the Tambov sana-
torium and immediately rang the hospital to find out when Rudakov
would be released. The poet was on his own, Nadezhda was in Moscow.
Mandelstam told Rudakov over the phone that his poems had been
accepted by the *Krasnaya nov* monthly in Moscow. On 11 January
Rudakov was allowed home and on 15 January they were expecting
Nadezhda to return, "With the papers!" added Rudakov. "O. said
three times that we are going to work." That same day he reports her
arrival:

January

15: All the Moscow news is deadly discouraging. *Krasnaya nov* was a comforting myth. O's nerves are very bad and he does not know everything about Moscow.

NY has brought me so much that I felt triumphant and terrified at once. I'll tell you more later. It's a priceless treasure. Then she began quietly to tell me of Moscow pleasures but I was egotistically joyful at what she'd brought. She has a saying: 'I want to preserve what already exists' – i.e. what's been written, without worrying whether he will still be able to write. There's an element of rhetoric but she's sincere and it seems that everything will really pass on to me.

16: Today I got home early, at 7 p.m., and shall work the whole evening, reading "Conversation about Dante" and other bits and pieces. With my fondness for the landscape of written texts Nadine gave me a wild delight, Oska's manuscripts. There are forests, parks, meadows and even waterless deserts. Up to 300 pages, from smudged drafts to neat final copies, which are strikingly laid out (very simply, of course). The range of poems from the 1907–20 period is unbelievably extended. You simply can't imagine. Then the variants! If only I can complete what has been proposed.

23: I woke up very late. On the sideboard was a card from Moscow . . . the USSR prosecutor-general's office, 19 January 1936: "No action is to be taken in response to your appeal for a re-examination of your case."

All efforts proved useless, our hopes have collapsed.

I continue to work on the manuscripts. They're very interesting. But it's hard to live without a future. We'll hope for the best but at the same time we must ask ourselves, perhaps nothing will ever change?

(Lina Rudakova continued to appeal but success would come only in July.)

31 January: Today with OE we examined [works] from 1907 to 1912. We checked in detail where and when pieces were written. We also wrote down certain comments. Then together we read in Italian the eleventh canto of Dante's *Purgatory* . . .

February

3: It's a miracle that something has started to work with O. and we have filled 15 notebooks of textual criticism . . . Day (and evening, of course) with M.: work, Dante, everything mixed up together . . .

6: I looked through some portions of my textual criticism with Akhmatova . . . She did not expect to find what she saw there, it seems.

7: Pushkin House wants to buy O.'s archive. He will not give it. He's keeping it for me to work on but retains his rights of ownership.

19: It's now 9 p.m. I'm alone in my room. There's a pile of notebooks in front of me. I'm going to work and you'll be pleased with this work: it's now progressed to fundamental issues, since the textual criticism is already approaching the end.

20: The worse things get, the more natural and good N. becomes. With her the biographical outline has now been brought up to 1930 (from 1919) – i.e. to the new period of poetry.

23: I am finishing 1932 for O. 1933 and 1934 are very insignificant in size.

29: O. was infinitely frustrating today and the textual criticism gave me no rest. By evening I was so tired that I couldn't stay any longer.

The refusal of the procurator to re-examine Rudakov's case, Mandelstam's overexcited and pessimistic condition, and Lina's long and jealous silence all contributed to a break in the work. Rudakov referred less often to their work together and his last letters concern his expected return to Leningrad.

2 March: I've been working a lot. I'm sending one page with the "Wolf", it's the only thing I've filched. Hide it. The variant of the last line is interesting.[3]

---

[3] See "Near the Poet": "Return to Poetry", pp. 22–3.

On 10 June before Mandelstam left for the dacha in Zadonsk and Rudakov returned to Leningrad, he wrote to Lina:

> About the manuscripts we've decided that I'll hand over the finished portion and leave the rest in Moscow when I pass through. I've given back 1908 to 1924. My departure has been postponed.
>
> 20 June: Yesterday, by tradition I spent the whole day with them: this involved sending their belongings by train, my selection of some other papers, and his remarks and captions for certain materials (in particular *Stone*, 1913). In the notes I received from them there were certain of Nadka's references to me (concerning our polemic with O. in September 1935). Everything had been done to leave no documentary proof of my role.

In *Hope against Hope* Nadezhda describes the help they received in Moscow from Rudakov in 1937. According to Khardjiev, Mandelstam then introduced him to Rudakov, glowing with paternal tenderness. "I have dictated to him the 'key' to all my poems," announced Mandelstam and nodded with satisfaction when Khardjiev recalled Derzhavin, the poet's only predecessor in this genre. "Both of them looked as if they were united by some joyful mystery," added Khardjiev, in his account of the meeting.

Alas, this "key" which had cost so much labour, exaltation and quarrels, was lost. The biographical outline, compiled by Nadezhda, and her notes also disappeared.[4]

Working on Poems

Rudakov's time in Voronezh ended happily. For the Mandelstams, on the contrary, now began the most difficult part of their stay in that city. Difficult but wonderful since it was marked by an unprecedented flowering of Mandelstam's creative energies and was crowned by his "Unknown Soldier", a poem that defined the epoch.

Mandelstam could not stand solitude. In Voronezh, temporarily parted

---

[4] E.G.: In Mandelstam's copy of the 1928 *Poetry*, on the other hand, there remain corrections made as a result of the re-examination undertaken with Rudakov. Mandelstam wrote in Indian ink undoubtedly taken from Rudakov, who preferred it for writing.

from Nadya, he latched on to Rudakov. By the fourth day of their acquaintance, when Rudakov described to his wife a visit to some well-established inhabitants of the city, he added: "Meanwhile M. is moping in the café, waiting for me." Mandelstam adored disputes and drew inspiration from verbal and intellectual contests (with other men). He complained, as we recall, that the contemporary vocabulary was much thinner and people's intellect had become impoverished: he accused Rudakov of weakening as an opponent. Most extraordinary of all, this was how he composed poems.

After marrying, Mandelstam dictated his poems to Nadya. This was not dictation of a ready text. He tested each word, and made her read back to him what she had written, and demanded her opinion – only to reject it with indignation. In the process, Nadya admitted to me, he abused her with every conceivable insult. Nevertheless, it was essential for him to work in this way and Nadya talked about it with tenderness. That is why, as if admiring this habit of Mandelstam's, she said to Rudakov: "All night Oska cursed you with the most vivid phrases and did not let me sleep. As a result the poem is finished. You're a magnificent fellow. Without you he would not have completed the verse." The following typical dialogue illustrates the unchanging creative habits of Mandelstam. The conversation arose when they were all three working together for the radio. On 10 October 1935 Rudakov wrote:

I got so annoyed that I said it was impossible to work with him.

He: Am I really so petty that I would deliberately push myself forward in other work because you led me when we were working on the poems?! I'm the most open to advice.

She: Yes, but only in poetry. For the rest you're sure you do everything better than anyone else.

This is not just Nadezhda's witticism or Rudakov's self-satisfied exaggeration ("you led me"). Mandelstam's need for someone to talk to when he was writing finds expression even in the late Voronezh poems ("Reader, adviser, physician:/ A word on the thorny staircase!") However, he did not need advice in order to be guided blindly: on the contrary, he lacked "thorny" – i.e. antagonistic – discourse. That was what stirred in him a flow of creative energy. This is very accurately defined by Rudakov in his further account of their famous commission from the radio:

Concerning poems we (that is, I) argued endlessly: there was
an absolute responsibility, I insisted, for the verse of perhaps
the best poet in the world. And I would argue to the bitter
end but in this hack-work it was simply impolite since the
output would be low quality. Moreover, his insults did not
undermine me as concerns poetry (*and for him insult was the
background for creativity*) [my emphasis, E.G.]. He would
curse a line with every expression imaginable and, it seemed,
had totally discarded it but it would nevertheless remain; in
Italian translations, on the other hand, and even on the radio
this motley genius was incomprehensibly dictatorial.

When they worked together on literary adaptations Rudakov was a quite
unacceptable collaborator for Mandelstam. His pedantry, rationalism and
inclination towards strict logic paralysed Mandelstam. Rudakov describes
the process:

When I showed him the list of selected quotations Osya was
complimentary but in a lukewarm way. When we began working together, he rejected my pieces and the linking texts. . .
I didn't calm down, as before, but yelled back at him, as over
the poems and methodically insisted on my concept . . . he
threw himself down on the bed with a groan, he was tired
and didn't understand a thing, Nadine was uneasy but I kept
pushing.
    . . . We went from one dead end to another and then
things got going. We are now at work. The pressure gauge
shows that we're almost ready for verse . . .

During this period of close association with Mandelstam, Rudakov developed and grew. When they first met he regarded Mandelstam as an
Acmeist, the author of *Stone*, *Tristia* and *Second Book*. For he did not
know the majority of Mandelstam's new Moscow poems, less than half
of which had been published. The transition to a new style, Mandelstam's
advance beyond Acmeism, thus was unexpected for Rudakov. With theories he had built up from the works of Tynyanov and Eichenbaum, and
soaked in Gumilyov's theoretical constructs about verse, Rudakov was a
suitable sparring partner. In his first letters Rudakov repeatedly illustrated
how Mandelstam had "reneged" on Acmeism. On 12 May 1935 he
wrote:

> . . . we were reading Vaginov. He grew bad-tempered and
> said that this was the elevation of sound [they were discussing
> Vaginov's handwritten collection, the *Semblance of Sound*,
> E.G.] but is enchanted by certain pieces . . . It is precisely
> when he sees things that are close to his own work, the epoch
> of 1908–25, that he becomes infuriated . . .

Perhaps Rudakov's persistent return to conversations about Acmeism and
his own idol Gumilyov provoked Mandelstam's resistance and a number
of his negative pronouncements on the poetry of the Acmeist leader. At
the same time these discussions aided Mandelstam in his work on fundamentally new poems. Rudakov attacked the mature poet with criticism
of his new poetic lines and that was just what Mandelstam needed. "He
reads me every line," wrote Rudakov on 26 April 1935, "and I have a
pile of objections (see my letter to Grigory Leokumovich) that are based
on my experience as a poet, which is somewhat objectified. Again there's
an argument (his wife is afraid)."

Arrogantly he traced the influence of his conversations in Mandelstam's
very first Voronezh poem, which was prompted by Galina Barinova's
violin concert. Yet Rudakov's "corrections" show that he had not yet
grasped Mandelstam's poetic system and the latter disregarded his
suggested change. Returning to this poem two and a half months later,
however, Mandelstam sat Rudakov next to him. "Today 'Barinova' (23
lines) is finished," wrote Rudakov on 18 June. "During the work Nadine
intervened, pushing me aside and muddling my conversation. He:
Nadyusha, we need to be alone, only Sergei Borisovich can help with
this. She acquiesced and was in her own way contented."

I think we can believe such assertions. During that period, we must
remember, Mandelstam was working intensively on his "Bolshevik" poem
cycles. Rudakov emphasised the stormy character of this process, which
coincided with the move to a new apartment and quarrels with the land-
lord. That was the chaos from which grew poems that, to Mandelstam's
great anger, many listeners called filigree work. This period of storm and
stress continued in Lina's presence. She came to Voronezh during the
May 1935 holidays and on 10 May Rudakov was already writing to her
in Leningrad. Here we learn of the doubts and hesitations that the first
Voronezh cycle caused Mandelstam (the emphasis is mine):

> You were there when he threw out the "Stanzas". Then he
> (with Nadine) destroyed all the drafts of the Stanzas and
> Chapayev, which he had begun. He said they were gibberish
> and wanted to destroy the drafts that I had (not guessing

that they had been copied?). Nadka called him "my Gogol" (in the sense of destroyed "discreditable" manuscripts) and rejoiced. I did not manage to memorise the Stanzas. Now, cautiously – a line at a time – I draw them out of him with indirect questions. I memorise them and write them down at home (I already have 32 of 46 lines). There are 9 lines of Chapayev. And when I get a grasp on the text I see it's not so bad but requires correcting so as to *remove sloppy parts*. As I dictate them back to him, he returns to the pieces and *finishes* them while I preserve the "accursed" first variant, which is essential in its naked form for my work. I'm writing of things you did not see since there was a period when his nerves were feeble (the apartment, the Koktebel pebbles, his raving wife).

The words I have emphasised vividly demonstrate the nature of Rudakov's "help". He restored poems that Mandelstam had abandoned and the poet completed them after listening to Rudakov's advice. He did not follow his recommendations. This form of co-operation can be clearly traced in subsequent letters, especially from the phrases I have emphasised.

18 May . . . vast amount of work with M. . . . from the snippets and drafts that were added to "Black Earth" and "Kama"; we (first I and then he) made a little over a hundred alterations to the poems of the "Bolshevik" cycle. Here I reworked Stanzas (the initial text *"was saved and rejected"*).

This seems quite straightforward, the usual work an editor performs with an author. Strange that such a master and mature poet as Mandelstam should need editing. But these were poems with a special intention. They may take confessional form, but they are openly political verse. They had to reach and be understood by their audience. So Mandelstam wavered, testing out on Rudakov whether the new poems fitted that purpose. Rudakov asserted:

The frightening thing is that this is no longer "advice" but truly my work (mine) . . . *Based on his material* I make corrections that cannot be rejected, I make insertions and replacements (lines, half-lines) before the existence of which the material was dead. Before all else *I put the entire jumble in an order that provides logically the only complete form*. I have all the drafts, and when you see [them] you'll understand

what was involved. I even have a horrible feeling: they'll read
the brilliant M. but without me, I swear, there would only
be "Kama", "Black Earth" (which I finished off, moreover)[5]
and a handful of lifeless and scruffy trifles.

Mandelstam had exactly the same opinion of his cycle, it seems, despite
Rudakov's "help". On Sunday 24 May Rudakov went to visit relatives
at Sosnovka and did not get to Mandelstam until 10 p.m. He wrote:

> Depression. He lies there and moans that he's only written
> Kama and Black Earth and the rest is rubbish. The cycle is
> getting him down and he's weaker . . . I take up the sheets
> of paper, read them all through (as an educational process),
> and after each piece: "You see, it's good not rubbish, this is
> good about it and that is good." He says nothing but has
> some semi-variants that are interesting but don't fit (the
> cycle). Overall he's uncertain. He says I read wonderfully
> (that's better than a diploma). I'm so happy when people
> appreciate my reading, most of all, perhaps, because I'm not
> always sure of myself. The most important is only just begin-
> ning. As I go off to make a phone call, I say to him: "Listen,
> the period of 'I think we (i.e. I) OUGHT to speak' has come
> to an end, since the cycle of openly political poems is complete.
> Now you're a free man and at liberty, not under obligation.
> These last works have a life of their own, and that's the most
> important thing now." He was happy when he understood
> that. These half-variants will be a new piece, about children,
> that's all. OK? Good night. . . . This letter has expressed
> everything very fully.

Evidently this referred to a new poem by Mandelstam that in some hand-
written versions Nadezhda called "Haircuts for the Children". Alas, it
would upset Rudakov but we cannot sympathise. Perhaps the internal
rhyme and rhythm of that poem was influenced by a previous work of
his own that he had read to Mandelstam (26 May: "Lina, what can I
do!?! I can't go and stand on Nevsky Prospect and tell everyone. He
knows my poem by heart"). Yet that does not detract in any way from
Mandelstam's achievement, which for Rudakov was unattainable.

---

[5] Dedicated to Rudakov. In the "Tashkent manuscript" of Mandelstam's poems
compiled in 1943–4 by Nadezhda Mandelstam (with the assistance of Yevgeny
Babayev), it bears the note "For Sergei" in her hand.

As a student of the formalists he could not get away from the conviction that art was the sum of the techniques employed. Therefore, ignoring the literary work as a whole he naively sought competitors and jealously defended his prior claims, comparing the poems of outstanding contemporaries with his own efforts. At his first contact with Mandelstam's new work he exclaimed: "And here there's something inexplicable and inordinate but not indisputable. Lina, he's doing what I began to do a year and a half ago." He lamented that Pasternak had "beaten him to it". If Rudakov had developed normally, in other words, if he had been published and read his poems to those who were professional judges, he would soon himself have realised that it was not a matter of inventing "approaches" and that he was not a poet: his calling was the history of literature, verse theory and textual analysis.

The necessity of discussing Rudakov's poems was, of course, burdensome for Mandelstam. I think he pitied Rudakov, realising that his urge to write poetry was insuperable and not far from a manic obsession. Sometimes Mandelstam would let something slip, however, whether by accident or intention. On 6 August 1935 Rudakov complained to his wife: "I don't have the inclination to argue about poetry and do not show my verse to O. He's convinced that I don't know how to write. Evidently, it's more peaceful that way. He announced: 'There are four writers in Russia: myself, Pasternak, Akhmatova and P. Vasilyev.' I suppose the cats got me." Mandelstam's own attitude to Rudakov's poetry was expressed in a brief epigram (recalled by Natalya Shtempel) that he wrote after Rudakov had left Voronezh: "Tears froze, and forty-pound chains of ballast/ weighed Sergei Rudakov's studious ballads."

Mandelstam remained indifferent to this concealed feud and respected Rudakov as his future biographer and editor. Lina maintained the secret as part of their private married correspondence: throughout my subsequent years of friendship with the Rudakovs, I never heard from them of Sergei's mania in this respect. We should not be reading his letters, in fact, had not all the other important materials concerning their literary relations been destroyed.

Rudakov in Moscow

Much is already known about the tragic life and death of Mandelstam. In the introduction to *Mandelstam in Voronezh* the fate of Rudakov was sketched in general terms. Since his Voronezh chronicle has been used

to write a chapter in the biography of Osip Mandelstam it is fitting to
talk once more of the chronicler himself. What follows comes from
wartime correspondence, which is always of interest not just for its heroic
aspects but also for the private, domestic details. On 25 February 1945
Lina wrote from Leningrad to Rudakov's first wife, her former friend,
informing her that he had been killed:

> Everything radiant, joyful and creative in life is over for me.
> Life itself has ended, indeed, since daily concerns and the very
> fact of existence do not in themselves constitute life.
>
> Seryozha was wounded as early as November 1941, gravely
> wounded near Leningrad. By some miracle he survived.
> Throughout the terrible winter of the blockade he lay in a
> military hospital. At that very moment his sisters were dying.
> Irina and Alyosha [Vaginov] died, and then Lyudmila. Only
> Alla survived because she was later evacuated to the Molotov
> Region. By that time I was in the Urals; Seryozha had sent
> me there at the very outbreak of the war.
>
> In spring 1942 Seryozha was sent to a reserve regiment
> in Ladoga. From there he transferred, as a disabled officer,
> to Moscow where he worked for the military commandant's
> office. It was in Moscow that he finally found his feet. He
> was about to defend his dissertation when he was again sent
> to the front and killed during the first battle.
>
> I'm afraid that even you did not know how gifted he was,
> and what an unlimited reserve he possessed of creative energy.
> And for a whole series of circumstances not one of his works
> was ever published. Only now are they going to print his
> Katenin work in the "Pushkin Annals". And he will never
> know that now.
>
> So I still have one cause in life, to see all Seryozha's works
> in print . . .
>
> I came back to Leningrad in the autumn of 1944. Only
> Seryozha's books and manuscripts have escaped destruction
> here. Papa died during the Finnish war. Mama is now with
> me. There is nothing left in Kiev . . .

Here is the documentary confirmation of when Lina returned to Leningrad.
The manuscripts were safe. She could have given the news to Akhmatova
only at a chance meeting: for more than six months after Akhmatova
returned from Tashkent in May 1944 she lived not at the House on
Fontanka but with L. Rybakova. Lina could not have known that.

Whatever the circumstances of his military service Sergei was always concerned about the manuscripts. He arrived in Moscow on 23 June 1942 and on 11 July, his name day, he wrote to his wife:

> Today I gave myself books as a present, in your name, if you like: the seventh volume of Kheraskov's *Works*[6] and Osip Emilievich's 1928 collection! I was missing it but, of course, it is inseparable from the manuscript version that in size exceeded this volume. It's a very hard feeling – a natural physical delight and a heartache that it might all be lost.

6 August 1942:

> My stay in Moscow is one success after another. If we were not parted, and if I was not terrified for the books and manuscripts, I would feel satisfied with my present situation.

In December Rudakov had an amusing encounter at the commandant's office; he was billeted in Maria's Grove. Not surprisingly, Rudakov had fleeting memories of Mandelstam and Akhmatova there. These are reflected in his letter of 13 December 1942:

> I went to fetch a form from next door at the commandant's office. There were people waiting at the counter and one was holding the book *To Mayakovsky*. My sociability and lack of literary conversation over a long period prompted me to ask to look at the book. The man was a bit like Shcherbina, stocky, brown and yellow, with large eyes but perhaps a little ragged, neglected and perhaps thin. Just the type who takes refuge from misfortune in a book. "I know you, what's your surname?" "Khardjiev." "Don't you recognise me?" and so on. He grasped my hand in both his ("What a pleasure"). He came to visit me: Annushka, Nadya, Oska . . . His collection of books has survived. The manuscripts have been evacuated. He is not living at home (not in Maria's Grove where Tsvetayeva visited him) since it's cold there. We exchanged telephone numbers. We agreed to meet. He has only just returned from Alma-Ata. His place is cold, so's mine, and we agreed to meet at Emma's . . . On his own initiative he rapidly

---

[6] Mikhail Kheraskov (1733–1807), leading poet of the Sumarokov school.

decided to give me the Mandelstam manuscripts in his possession (a couple of small pages).

Khardjiev's intention accorded with his conception of Rudakov as the
future editor of Mandelstam's poems. Like everyone else Khardjiev
remained unmoved by Rudakov's own poetic compositions. On 28
January 1943 Rudakov wrote: "A moderate entertainment, the evening
at Emma's with Khardjiev. I read him my poem about Marina, the
Leningrad verse and about the expanse of Ladoga. He says that he liked
them but, as was said in *Woe from Wit*, 'Who thus shows their joy?'"

Ignorance of the fate of the Mandelstam and Gumilyov manuscripts
continued to torment Rudakov. On 1 June 1943 he again tells Lina:
"Khardjiev telephoned. He's received a letter from Nadka, enquiring
about me. She asks me to write. But what can I say? It's a torment."

But soon arrived the letter from the house manager in Leningrad stating that the books and manuscripts were safe. The reaction to this news
was exceptionally strong. 2 July 1943:

> Once more about the things. It can't be right that they were
> "all" sold off? But one must not even try to explain without
> experiencing the conditions of that winter. Uncle Sasha, for
> instance, said something to the effect that he couldn't under-
> stand how people could burn chairs and so on to heat the
> rooms. But what would he have said in Alla's place, when
> the glass in the windows (barely covered by plywood) was
> smashed and first Irina and then Lyudmila lay dead next to
> her in the bitter cold and darkness. It is only the fetishising
> of my collection and the old-fashioned idea that my litera-
> ture was all that remained of our family, which explains why
> the books were not burned.

Lina was jealous of all Sergei's acquaintances. This explains the light self-
justification and, at times, mocking tone of his letters when he refers to
me and Tsvetayeva's sister-in-law Yelizaveta Efron. 17 July 1942: "Emma
today took me to see the sister of Marina's husband. The latter is a middle-
aged (old) tall, grey-haired lady who organises public readings . . . I
immediately disarmed her and won her favour by reading three pieces
about Misha." He was referring to Misha Remezov whom he saw die of
hunger in blockaded Leningrad.

In another letter (6 February 1943) he describes conditions in
Moscow: "similar to last February [in Leningrad, E.G.]. In my company
Emma tries to take an interest in literature. The same with Efron.

Touching and for me infinitely pleasant that when I am there [the war] if not forgotten is not mentioned or recedes into the background." Here Rudakov, as was characteristic of the man, exaggerated his own role. Yelizaveta Efron never stopped working and devoted much attention to children who, for a variety of reasons, had not been evacuated from Moscow. She taught them and organised amateur theatrical productions to entertain them. Meanwhile I continued to research the biography of Lermontov and seminars were held both at the Literary Institute and the All-Union Theatrical Society.

After hearing of Rudakov's contributions during discussions of the Society's Pushkin group, and learning of his dissertation on the "Rhythm and style of the *Bronze Horseman*", Shklovsky invited him to come and discuss his new theoretical article. 4 July 1943:

> Lina, I'm writing at night, so it's really 5 July, about 2 a.m. . . .
>
> For some reason it's a white night. I'm exalted and disappointed. Don't laugh, that's not a contradiction. I've just come back from Shklovsky. He's 50. Extraordinarily handsome. Not in the sense that his portrait would look good in the hairdresser's window but with the intelligent good looks of a thinking man . . .
>
> Shklovsky says that crickets like listening to people read. So I shall do such work as makes the cricket in the corner squeal with delight.

Unlucky Rudakov's farewell letter to me was written on 2 December 1943:

> Dear Emma Grigoryevna,
>
> How good that you have heard at least part of the poems. When you write you always imagine your audience – i.e. your closest collaborator . . .
>
> How sad that you have moved to a new room, I so loved yours. I'm talking nonsense and your father's death lies behind it. I greatly appreciated that he, it seems, was very well disposed towards me. It seems that not only you but the house favoured me.
>
> Thank you for your certainty that all will end well. But (to share a secret) I myself feel dreadful physically. And no less than Lermontov, I think, on his last journey through Moscow do I feel I shall not return from the frontline.

Lina has copied down almost all the poems. What a joy her arrival is. You must understand that with particular intensity, against the background of all our telephone conversations.

Greetings to your mother and the Merzlyakov residents.[7]

Military post box 44698-A

Yours Rudakov

Greetings to Nadya and Annushka.

The letter arrived on 5 January 1944, ten days before Rudakov was killed.

3 Gumilyov, Akhmatova, Gerstein: Letters, 1954–7

From autumn 1954 Emma Gerstein was in regular correspondence with Lev Gumilyov. Between March 1955 and April 1956, as he waited impatiently to be released from the camps, he wrote to her at least three times a month. A selection of his letters to Emma Gerstein is included here, as are certain key letters exchanged by Lev Gumilyov and Akhmatova in the same period. As noted earlier, many intervening postcards and letters sent by mother to son have not survived.[8]

A few months after Stalin's death on 5 March 1953, many prisoners were released in an amnesty from the Gulag. They were among those sentenced for criminal offences, however, and their sudden appearance in society helped create a crime wave outside the camps. In 1954 commissions began re-examining the cases of those sentenced for "counter-revolutionary" offences, the "political" prisoners who then formed a quarter of the 2-million-strong prison-camp population. Some of Lev Gumilyov's companions in this category were freed. Gumilyov continued to wait and hope. Evidently he also reminded himself, from time to time, that unless something happened, his sentence would end only in 1960. [tr.]

---

[7] Tsevtayeva's sister-in-law Yelizaveta Efron and her friend Zinaida Shirkevich.
[8] Many of the letters are abridged here.

Lev Gumilyov to Akhmatova, 5 September 1954

Dear, kind mother,

I have received your postcard in which you say you are going to Golitsyno for a vacation and the packet with the jam, honey and enchanting tea caddy . . . It's understandable why your efforts were unsuccessful: you took the wrong approach. There's no point in proving my innocence, it's already quite clear to any informed person. Remember that my disgrace began back in 1946, that's the root of the problem . . .

. . . The only way you can help me is not to write appeals for a pardon – those will automatically be passed to the prosecutor's office and be just as automatically rejected – but manage to see Voroshilov or Khrushchev in person and explain things to them: that I'm a capable Orientalist, with knowledge and abilities far exceeding the average, and that it would make much better sense to employ me as a scholar than some vegetable-patch scarecrow . . .

I've nothing to say about myself, my life is totally uneventful. I did expect, though, that the second volume of the Three Kingdoms[9] would surface from below the slab of lard . . .

Love
Leon

Lev Gumilyov to Emma Gerstein, 14 September 1954

Thank you, Dear Emma, for the letter.

It was a pleasant surprise. The food in the packages was charming and reached me without problem. I drink my tea out of the tin cans as if they were glasses.

Thank you for your kind concern for me though I'm surprised that you and Mama have not become fed up with my constant misfortunes. I'm so very fed up with it all that I've even ceased to be upset, let alone worry about myself. I live one day at a time, like a moth, and try to draw pleasant impressions from a life of contemplation. I've fallen for the works of the Soviet writer

---

[9] Historical novel of the fourteenth-century Chinese writer Lo Guan-chun.

Prishvin,[10] which were sent to our library here. It's extraordinary how he heals the soul. I've become quite old and grey-bearded and soon the stuffing will start leaking out of me at the seams. But in return I've grown wise and calm as a little bronze statue. That will strike you as laughable: you're accustomed to my extravagant moods.

Once again my thanks for your letter and your efforts on my behalf. I kiss your little hands

Leon

Akhmatova to Lev Gumilyov, 17 September 1954

My dear son Lyovushka,

I've now received your 5 Sept. letter and hasten to reply: the second volume of the *Three Kingdoms* has not yet been published. Much in your letter seemed unclear to me – probably there was correspondence that went astray in 1950 . . . It's autumn in Leningrad but there are still intervals of good weather. I read in an anthology: "Altyn was a Tatar who served the Chinese in order to train their soldiers 'after the manner of the Huns'" . . . But enough of Chinese affairs. I'm feeling very downhearted. And most ill at ease. At least you should pity me.

Love
Mama

My cold has made me quite deaf and I live in total silence.

Lev Gumilyov to Akhmatova, 9 November 1954

My dear Mama,

I've received your postcard and the 100 roubles . . .
They showed the Indian film *The Tramp* here [1951, director

---

[10] Mikhail Prishvin wrote popular works of nature study, offering one of the few then officially licensed literary means of escape from heroic narratives of industrial and agricultural progress.

Raj Kapur]. Everyone was enraptured, and so was I . . . And how feeble the English film *Thief of Baghdad* [1940] seemed to me. Asia and Europe are indeed changing places and I become ever more certain that Europe will soon turn into the provincial region it was in the sixth century [AD].

My health has improved and I left the hospital a stronger man but have again been classified as an invalid. The attempt to turn me into a navvy has so far only led to me being confined to bed for half the time . . .

It strikes me as naivety to make plans and think of the future. Everyone around me receives heartening letters and to begin with they were pleased but now they ignore them since nothing good has come of it. It's good that you don't write senseless words of encouragement but if you do undertake something practical you must let me know, so that it doesn't turn out like last year . . .

I have no idea how you live now: what rooms you have, whether they're warm and comfortable. But somehow I think you are bored . . . I am studying history with determination every free minute . . .

My love, dear Mama

Thank you that you do not forget your son
Leon

Akhmatova to Lev Gumilyov, 19 November 1954

Dear Lyovushka,

I have again kept to my bed for the whole week but for some reason I feel that I'm over that sickness completely. There was no need to ask anyone about An Lu-shan (eighth century AD), I myself came across him in Fitzgerald's book [C. Fitzgerald, *China: A Short Cultural History*, (London: 1935)]. What made you think he was a Hun? My author says he was a "Turk of the Kitan tribe", of very lowly origins and born beyond the Great Wall in the land of Liao Tung (southern Manchuria) . . . He was distinguished by his cunning and amused the emperor with his rough humour and lack of etiquette. An Lu-shan became the favourite of the beauty Yang Kuei-fei, the mistress of the emperor (Ming-Huang), and had a brilliant career . . .

Rebellion flared in the army of the emperor and the soldiers demanded the head of Yang Kuei-fei, An Lu-shan's protectress. She was suffocated. Po Chu-i [Chinese poet, AD 772–846] wrote a didactic poem on the subject: "Everlasting Wrong". (See Eidlin's preface to Po Chu-i [*Lyrics*, 1935] concerning An Lu-shan).

After capturing Ch'ang An, An Lu-shan enjoyed no further success. The new emperor Su Tsung sent the population of the north-east against him and received considerable help from nations friendly to China: the Central Asians, Turks and even the Arabs, who were sent by the Caliph. An Lu-shan and his son were killed and replaced by other pretenders. The war went on for another ten years and ended in 766.

That's everything I can tell you about An Lu-shan and you yourself are aware that all this took place during the golden age of Chinese poetry.

It's winter here now, but I have still not gone out since my illness.

All my love. Don't get depressed.

Mama

P.S. Also look in Po Chu-i's book on p. 222 for a mention of An Lu-shan and p. 223 for an amusing episode with a swan and a letter from the *History of the Han Dynasty* [written by Ban Hu, AD 32–92] . . .

They wouldn't accept my parcel for you at Pavlovsk and Aristide [Dovatur, philologist] was kind enough to send it from Luga on 16 November. Yesterday I heard on the radio that it was –22 degrees centigrade in Omsk. Poor Lyovka! Yakov Markovich [Borovsky, philologist] came to see me yesterday and read me his translations – it was he who organised the despatch of the parcel and asked to send you his greetings. I changed my mind about sending the postcards, they're out of date now. How did you like volume II of the *Three Kingdoms*? . . .

Do write a polite letter to Nat[alya] Vas[ilievna][11] if you get her note. I must insist that you do so. She has changed little, and is still that same maiden-rose; her marriage has proved unsuccessful and she speaks no more of it. She brings me books and repairs my

---

[11] N.V. Varbanets (1916–1987) was a philologist who worked from 1938 until 1982 in the rare-books department of the Public Library in Leningrad.

dressing gown, which is coming apart at the seams because it's made of brocade. Well, you don't understand such things. This letter has also been lying about a few days; today it's already the 24th.

Once again, my love. I'm waiting for your news.

Mama

Lev Gumilyov to Emma Gerstein, 7 December 1954

Dear Emma,

Forgive me that I did not immediately answer your kind, friendly letter. I was very touched by your desire to come and see me here but, unfortunately, that is impossible. Only parents, children and registered wives have the right to a visit so only Mama can come to see me. But to get Mama to travel that distance, without a night in Omsk, for the sake of a 2-hour [meeting] is impossible. Apart from which my appearance will only distress her. Therefore I have decided not to disturb her unnecessarily. I'm most grateful to you for your attention and kind feelings towards me. Your feelings and letter are all the more valuable since, in all likelihood, we shall not meet again. My health is steadily deteriorating and I shan't hold out to the end [of my sentence, tr.] no matter what medicine they give me. Yes and it's about time too, that's enough suffering, I'm fed up with it all.

I kiss your dear hands

Sincerely and tenderly
Leon

Lev Gumilyov to Emma Gerstein, Telegram: 22 December 1954

REMIND MAMA TO MAKE EFFORTS
ON MY BEHALF. LYOVA

Emma Gerstein to Lev Gumilyov, Telegram: 23 December 1954

WE REMEMBER. TRY TO KEEP CALM.
THAT'S THE MOST IMPORTANT. EMMA

The Second All-Union Congress of Writers (the first was in 1934) was held in Moscow in late December. [tr.]

Lev Gumilyov to Emma Gerstein, 15 January 1955

Dear Emma,

I received your kind letter and telegram and this evening the parcel you packed for me arrived. My dear Emma, your attention and thoughtfulness toward me exceed all possible joys. It makes it that much easier for me to breathe. I also received Mama's post-card, which made me very happy. Not that I had begun making plans for my life [in future], I've had quite enough disappoint-ment already, but the recognition of my scholarly achievements and potential was pleasing. As concerns the rest I live as before but respond to any pleasant occurrence with joy. My health is improving. The operation was successful since our surgeon is a master [of his craft]. If I am not again inundated with physical tasks beyond my capacity I hope that my bodily condition will stabilise.

How is Mama getting on? I wrote her an enormous letter but perhaps she will not soon return home [to Leningrad] and so will not soon receive it. Kiss her for me and order her to write me a postcard. I have developed an appetite for letter-writing.

It seems as though it's become easier and merrier to live[12] during the last year. Many of my acquaintances have written to me. Emma, my dear, write to me sometimes, it gives me great joy. My associ-ations with you are exclusively pleasant. Now I'm grey and wear a beard; the others call me "Dad" but the soul cannot develop here and mine is still the same age as it was five years ago.

---

[12] Allusion to Stalin's 1934 declaration: "Life has become easier, comrades, life has become more joyous."

Lev Gumilyov to Emma Gerstein, 8 March 1955

Dear Emma,

O, how angry I am with you. Why ever did you mention my illnesses to Mama? I almost did not write to you [about them] but then realised you were one of the few of my acquaintances who had never done me a bad turn. Now that life is nearing its end I try to remember all the good things and then inevitably I remember you.

Forgive my shaky handwriting. I had a relapse yesterday lifting something heavy and am now again in the hospital and my movements have acquired the distinctive grace that is reflected in my writing. You didn't say anything about Mama in your letter to me, how she is, her appearance, etc. Mama's style of letter-writing rather resembles teasing but I know that it's not deliberate or, to be more precise, comes of a simple lack of attention to me. You are a sensitive, observant and level-headed person and I would be most grateful if you could offer me some advice about Mama. That she loves me I know, but such a variety of content is lodged in the concept "love" that it is too little to say "she loves you". She keeps me so much in the dark about her own daily existence, situation, and her activities and amusements etc. that I began simply to lose heart. I consider that one parcel a month does not fulfil all a mother's duty to her perishing son and that does not mean that I want two parcels. . . . The lamentations about the state of my health simply infuriate me. It's time she understood that I'm not in some sanatorium although conditions now have improved greatly but my depressed state of mind remains as before and my organism's lack of immunity is the result. One cannot live without joy, it functions as a vitamin. At times I begin to suspect that Mama loves me by inertia and that (as a woman) she is no longer accustomed to me, since everyday concerns dominate her. I cannot forget how difficult it was to find the right tone in which to approach her in 1945 [after returning from the front, tr.]. Nor can I forget my incredulity then. And now, recently, I sense some kind of emptiness, a profound loneliness. Well, I think you've understood me and I hope will reply and I'm depending on you not to deliberately mislead me . . .

They've come to collect our letters. I must stop if this letter is to catch the post. I kiss your little hands, my dear; I'm no longer angry with you and await your reply,

L.

A poet from Omsk [Sergei Zalygin] came here and gave a report about the [Second] Congress [of Writers]. I stood up and asked a question about Mama. He said she was "in a creative mood" and that English students had come to visit her and ask about her health. All I know about her is that she likes seventeenth-century Korean verse and that she "went to pay the telephone bill". I know nothing even about her material situation. You must agree that this is a little cruel and my life is not very cheerful as it is.

Waiting for your answer

L.

Lev Gumilyov to Emma Gerstein, 25 March 1955

Emma, my dear, forgive me that I was a little angry with you. I was quite in the wrong and you did the right thing. She'll shed a tear or two there, but it means nothing to her [closing couplet of Lermontov's "Testament" (1840), E.G.].

Yes, you're right that Mama now suffers from senile dementia and a disintegration of her personality;[13] but for me that makes things much worse, not easier. I'll begin at the end. You write that Mama is not the culprit of my fate. Who else then? Were I not her son but the son of some ordinary woman I would be, whatever else might happen, a flourishing Soviet professor, a non-Party specialist as many have become. Mama herself knows everything about my life and that the sole reason for my difficulties was my kinship with her. I understand that she was afraid to draw breath in the first few months but now it is her duty to save me and prove my innocence; neglect of this duty is a crime. You write that she is powerless. I don't believe that. As a delegate to the Congress she could approach a member of the Central Committee and explain that her son was unjustly convicted . . .

I wrote to Mama about this in the autumn. She seemed to understand but it's hopeless.

There is only one way to save me: make a member of the government or the Central Committee look into my case and re-examine it without preconceived ideas. I can't do anything to achieve

---

[13] E.G.: Of course, I had not written in such terms but mentioned certain age-related changes in Akhmatova's psychology.

that from here; there's nothing I can do, in fact, but she not only can but also should have done something. She managed to save her husband in 1935, didn't she?

I know what the problem is. Her poetic nature makes her frightfully lazy and egotistic, in spite of her extravagance. She can't be bothered to think about unpleasant things and that she must make some effort. She is very sparing of herself and does not want to be upset. Therefore she is so inert in all that concerns me. That is fatal, however, since not a single normal person can believe that a mother couldn't care less about her son's death. For her, however, my death will be a pretext for a graveside poem: How poor she is, she has lost her son. Nothing more. She wants to calm her conscience, though, hence the parcels like scraps from the table for a favourite pet and those empty letters, with no answers to the questions I pose. Why does she mislead herself and others? I perfectly understand that the parcels are bought with her earnings or, to be more exact, from money given to her by the government. There's no need to be naive: her needs have been considered and I am included in the calculation. Therefore if we're talking of justice she should send me half of her earnings. But now I really do not wish to feed on scraps from the master's table. It's her duty to me and our Country not to feed me but gain my rehabilitation, otherwise she's fostering "wrecking attitudes" of which I have fallen a victim.

Does she really not understand that?! Strange.

During a difficult period [1946–9, E.G.] when we both went hungry I nursed her through six illnesses. I knew no rest and denied myself everything. And, at the same time, I tried to get her re-established and urged her not to give way to grief but work for Soviet Literature as I myself have worked all my life for Soviet Oriental Studies. I did so tactfully, avoiding her sore spots. But now, when she is well provided for, with benefits that I by right should share, if she does not understand her duty then what should be my attitude to this?

Her behaviour might be justified only if I was myself the cause of my misfortune. But that was not so. I must admit I did in part suppose that she could be frivolous, for I know her character. But she has truly exceeded my expectations and forebodings. Yes, her dream was prophetic [I had described Akhmatova's jealous dream about Tatyana Kryukova, E.G.]. Tatyana Alexandrovna is an old lady who fell in love with me and, evidently, without thought of gain. We did not become intimate and for my part there was no more than a friendly disposition. But she wrote warm words to me and sent me parcels, as you do. Emma, dear sweet Emma, how I want to kiss your hands and you but that is hardly likely to happen. I write about my health without concealment. My nervous system seems irreversibly damaged by this heightened tension. At times my heart gives way and I black out, without any cause apparently. My stomach functions so badly that I now have a duodenal ulcer. They refused to operate and treated me with compresses, palliatives. I collapsed when lifting something that was not so heavy, which means my muscular system is giving up. Taken together this means that I shall no longer be able to work in six months' time and things will be even worse for me then; I shan't be able to study history which is the only thing that now keeps me going. Then I won't have any need to return.

One more thing. Mama's visit and just a little affectionate warmth, of course, would support me and give me an incentive to live. But I thought, she is short of money, as before, and sacrificed myself. The train journey to Omsk is no more arduous than that to Leningrad [from Moscow] and, with money, one could also fly. But now that's beyond repair, may her conscience be her judge.

What does the future hold? Evidently I shall gently relapse into disability and death, which does not frighten me. It's just sad that my scholarly gifts are now developed and I could provide our research science with that which it now has most need of – a general approach to Oriental Studies, introduction to the discipline, without which any work is incomplete. Just as the translations of the incomparable Ch'u Yuan are inadequate. To understand him the translator must know the history of China and not just the language; the historical gift is as rare as the gift of poetry. To this letter I attach a note that, once you have read it, you are to pass on, please, either delivering it yourself or sending it by the local city post.[14]

Emma, dear, sweet Emma, thank you. During these 5 years the ignorance, silence, and empty letters were harder to bear than everything else. Now I feel more at ease.

---

[14] E.G.: Lyova sent a naive and offensive note to Victor Ardov that opened with the ludicrous and foolish phrase: "What harm did I ever do to you?" I used the right entrusted to me and destroyed the note.

Please, there's no sense in dragging out my death throes with more parcels.

Once again I embrace you, my dear

L.

Akhmatova to Lev Gumilyov, 27 March 1955

Dear Lyovushka,

On 19 March I received your letter, which contained a heap of grudges against me. Ever since I have been writing you my reply. Let my try to clarify everything in full and coherent detail: for a long while I did not give your address to Nat. Vas. [Varbanets] although she was very insistent in demanding it and I asked you, in a postcard, whether I should let her have it. You did nothing to forbid me doing so. She did not once talk about you to me and does not do so now. Even now she conceals from me that she had sent the letter that upset you . . . How and why was I supposed to think that she loved you?!

I asked you to answer her because one must always be considerate, especially with Maiden-Roses. I was sure you would find a tone that fitted the moment . . . What Nik[olai] Al[exandrovich] and Vasya[15] wrote to you about her, I do not know. Probably they just wanted to cheer you up.

As concerns Tatyana Alexandrovna [Kryukova]. She came to me yesterday and is going to Kostroma and will send you the April packet from there. She is in good health, lively and, as always, engrossed in her work at the Museum. I am also very grateful to her for her kind attitude to you but she doesn't like me very much or, to be more precise, does not like it when I go to see her in order to hand over the money I'm allowed to send you . . .

An "inaccuracy has crept" into the answer the Omsk writer gave in response to your question about me. No students came to visit me or enquire about my health. A year ago, indeed, some Fascistic football-playing young people from England [students from Oxford, tr.] asked me a rather tactless question at a meeting of

---

[15] N.A. Kozyrev and V.N. Abrosov, astronomer and ichthyologist respectively, had been with Lev Gumilyov in the camps.

the Writers' Union. But my categorical reply prevented further discussion.[16] I did not address the Congress of Writers; my name was mentioned there once by Pavel Antokolsky in his speech, in connection with the Rainis and Salomen Neris [collections of] translations. That was reported in the newspapers.

A short while back (the 15th I believe) I sent you a very long and detailed letter containing the historical reference you wanted (90 BC) with a superficial description of my existence. But the letters "UKh" were not included in the address since that was the address in your previous letter. It would be a great shame if the letter were mislaid.

On the 24th the editor returned my manuscript of the Korean Anthology [published in 1956] with his commentary. On Tuesday I shall take the text to Moscow where I must deliver the work as quickly as possible. Academician Struve told me that, in his opinion, you could give very helpful advice on my Asian translations . . .

In all this history with the Bird[17] I am most of all enchanted by the unceasing concern of Fate, which, evidently, considers that I have still not received my "full due". I can say of myself, "Thus smiles the pale-faced gambler, able no more to count the blows of fate" [Innokenty Annensky, "August"].

If you want, I shall give an even more extended presentation of my thoughts on this subject. However, I am rewriting this letter for the seventh time (since 20 March) and no longer understand what's of interest and what is not.

I'm very hurt and very upset that you could write me such a letter. I could not believe my eyes. What Nik. Al. and Vasya wrote to you about the Bird I do not know . . . You've chosen a fine person to ask! . . . Have you really forgotten how she openly enchanted Nik. Al. in our presence and we couldn't stop laughing at it.

It's very good that you're engaged in Oriental Studies, particularly the Huns, but you should not forget classical Russian poetry, especially Pushkin. Re-read the *Little Tragedies* of 1830. How profound and percipient! Recently I read somewhere that both the songs in the "Feast . . ." (Mary's and that of the Chairman)[18] are not translations but composed by Alexander Sergeyevich [Pushkin] himself.

Re-read my letters and see for yourself that I least of all wanted to assure you that Nat. Vas. had some special attitude to you. How

---

[16] They asked whether or not Akhmatova considered the 1946 decree to be just.
[17] Natalya Vasilievna Varbanets (see note 11, p. 452).
[18] One of the *Little Tragedies*, Pushkin's "Feast during the Plague" is loosely based on a Scottish original. Commentators have long noted that Pushkin himself composed these two songs.

could I suppose that after her five-year silence, marriage and so on, you would attribute some significance to her epistolary efforts? When you suggested in a letter that I treat her as a daughter-in-law I was most surprised.

There, Lyova, this is the longest letter I have written in my long life. That life is already coming to an end, and that's to the good.

Love
Mama

I have a heavy cold. I'm sniffling and have a headache but I've already bought my ticket. Misfortune.

Good night!

Did you receive the postcard where, quoting V.V. Struve, I told you that since the death of Academician Yakubovsky only L.N. Gumilyov could conduct a scholarly polemic with bourgeois specialists concerning the Turks? How's that!

Lev Gumilyov to Akhmatova, 14 April 1955

Dear Mama,

My greetings for the coming festival [Easter] and wishes that you finally cease to be ill. I assumed you were in Moscow and sent a letter for you there, and now I'm writing to the City but perhaps you by this time will already be in the editor's office surrendering the Koreans. I shall hope that the letter will catch up with you.

Your reply was very disappointing for me . . . All I would like from you is a little attention, e.g. that you would answer at least those questions that I have asked you concerning my personal affairs. But it seems that is also an unfulfillable wish. You wrote just the same kind of letters to me when I was at the front and I was just as disappointed and upset. Well, enough of that.

I've long thought how I could help you in your Oriental activities. Were I at home I would simply explain certain features of Eastern psychology, history and culture, but no-one apart from me, perhaps, could do that . . . There's no point in your studying the history and ethnography of the East, and it would be impossible moreover, but here is a way in which one could establish for oneself a true if approximate impression of Ancient China and

Korea: look at their pictures. There are a great many excellent publications there, *Ars Asiatica* [Paris], *Ars Sinica, Sizin* . . . and so on.

But don't just look at the pretty pictures, note the epochs and when you sense the consistency with which the style evolves you will capture the feeling you have been looking for and then the Chinese and the Koreans will be satisfied with your translations. . .

Compare the epochs and you'll sense the way the East thinks. With your intuitive ability you will quickly master this method. It doesn't matter that you cannot express the difference between one epoch and another in words – you will see and feel it and then you'll master the rhythm of history. It's an imperfect method but better than the kind of advice Orientalists like — offer . . . Such people have only two qualities: aplomb and ignorance . . .

I received the packet and 100 roubles. Thank you.

Love
L.

Akhmatova to Lev Gumilyov, 29 April 1955

Lev,

I have only just received your letter of 14 April. Of course, I shall carry out to the letter your instruction concerning Natalya Vasilievna,[19] all the more so, since it is entirely reasonable . . . Your un-Confucian letters (excluding the last of them) have very much distressed me. Please believe that I am writing absolutely everything about myself, my domestic arrangements and my life to you. You forget that I am 66, that I am afflicted by three serious illnesses, and that all my friends and contemporaries are dead. My life is gloomy and lonely, and none of that aids a flowering of epistolary style.

My dear boy, I have to upset you deeply: your teacher Nikolai Vasilievich Kuner has passed away. He was so fond of you that he wept when he learned what had happened to you. I have set aside the news of his death, published in *Leningradskaya pravda* [daily newspaper], in memory of that radiant individual.

Iskusstvo publishers are issuing all Shakespeare's works in old

---

[19] Excised from Gumilyov's letter in the *Zvezda* publication.

and, in some cases, new translations. They asked if I would do *Timon of Athens*. Do you remember it? There's no contract yet and I doubt if I'll have the strength for such a big job.

At last it's spring here. Today I'm invited to visit someone and will wear a new summer coat. This will be my first outing.

Much love
Mama

Moscow is beautiful and radiant. The festival approaches and all is somehow fresh and clean.

[E.G.: In April I informed Lyova that I had been to the chief military prosecutor's office. There they told me the number of his case, which had reached them on 19 April, and suggested I return in exactly a month's time.]

Lev Gumilyov to Emma Gerstein, 2 May 1955

. . . Your practical letter was a great joy for me, perhaps the first this year. I do not count on a rapid result. Staff at the prosecutor's office are in no hurry and it will be good if there's an answer not in two months but by the end of the year . . . About visiting . . . A visit would be very desirable because of Mama's epistolary style. . . . You could come with her and, I hope, everything would go well and be pleasant. Additional materials on my case are to be found in the *Great Soviet Encyclopaedia*: biographical excerpts were appended as part of the case against me.

Just write to me from time to time . . . For the meanwhile I don't need books. After my illness I read with difficulty and only light literature. This was the most serious illness in my life. But now I'm considered on the road to recovery, working a little and watching films, which are now often shown here.

Lev Gumilyov to Emma Gerstein, 10 May 1955

I've been waiting for your letter for a long time and it still hasn't come. I very much want to know whether Mama has decided to come and see me or is still wavering, Stanley spent less time preparing to search for Livingstone than Mama to visit me. And this is the most suitable time of year, weather-wise, but I don't know whether she has money for the trip. I am waiting patiently for a response to Struve's "complaint" but I am not as well as during the winter . . .

[E.G.: As she prepared in May 1955 to travel to Omsk and see her son (at her request I was to accompany her), Akhmatova encountered such forceful opposition to the trip that she was completely abashed. One of the main arguments employed by the Punins and the Ardovs, and those around them, was the citing of imagined cases when prisoners had suddenly died due to the emotional stress of such meetings.

Disturbed by Lyova's long silence, I sent him a telegram before the last two letters had reached me. His telegraphed reply (13 May 1955) read:

YESTERDAY SENT SECOND LETTER. NEED YOUR HELP. AWAIT NEWS OF MEETING. LOVE KISSES LYOVA]

Lev Gumilyov to Emma Gerstein, 26 May 1955

Dear kind Emma,

Let me inform you that I am again in hospital . . . The weather here is magnificent, a sweltering fine summer but the mood is sad, for we victims of Beria and Abakumov are being forced to wait too long for the slightest attention . . . Most likely I'll be rehabilitated posthumously. You ask my opinion of Ira [Punina]. Nina [Ardova] is better, more sincere. Irka is a leech who will cling to Mama for as long as there's something to suck. That's the base Punin nature for you . . . I was especially amazed by the message that the visit was off: Mama could have let me know herself . . .

There's just one thing I can't understand: does she really suppose that family feeling – i.e. on my side – can remain after all her attitude and behaviour towards me, as revealed in the last period? Do kind friends so lick her arse that she considers herself absolutely infallible? In her letter of 17 May she writes that she finds it "dull" without my letters – but I don't write to amuse her, that's what the cinema is for . . .

I authorise you to tell her everything that you consider necessary. I'm not writing to her any more for even when I explained why I was dissatisfied she either did not understand or pretended that she had not understood.

I was very disappointed by your reference to the "annulment" of sentences. That is applicable only to those who were sentenced in court. What about us poor sinners, for whom there were no materials, depositions or even charges?! . . .

Lev Gumilyov to Emma Gerstein, 9 June 1955

I have been waiting long for your letter and now it's come . . .

I got three postcards from Mama, which I could not bring myself to answer for a long while, they so upset me. People write such things when they're holidaying on the southern shores of the Crimea. What is she thinking of? . . . I enclose a letter to Mama in this envelope. Please pass it on to her . . .

Lev Gumilyov to Emma Gerstein, 12 June 1955

Dearest Emma,

After receiving your two letters I was even more upset. Of course, I shall write immediately to Mama [I had told Lyova of Akhmatova's very serious illness, E.G.] . . .

Lev Gumilyov to Emma Gerstein, 15 September 1955

On 12th of this month the prosecutor summoned me for a cross-examination and it continued from 10 a.m. until 6 p.m. (with a break for lunch). In one day we covered what took them 10 months before. He wrote everything down properly but did not raise hopes about a rapid decision. If there is a just, legally proper re-examination of the kind Rudenko is saying he wants in the newspapers then there can only be a positive outcome. But how long it's dragging on!

And I don't know if my health will hold out since I've been put back on to physical work. That was a result of Mama's appeal: an official enquiry about my health came from Moscow and since I have been getting better over the one and a half months, the commission decided I could go back to work . . .

I don't understand why people show incompetent initiative in matters of which they don't have the faintest understanding. Let Mama do what I request or not, but not dream up anything by herself.

Lev Gumilyov to Emma Gerstein, 27 September 1955

Dear, kind Emma,

Both your letters arrived at the same time . . . Your perspicacity is beyond praise: our censor has indeed been unwell but we all so wished for his recovery that, thankfully, he is now better and order is restored . . .

Lev Gumilyov to Emma Gerstein, 19 December 1955

That the prosecutors are all tired of your face is nothing compared to my opinion of them. Officially my appeal has now been with them 20 months. It's four months since my cross-examination even, whereas the law says the investigation should be completed within two months . . . I find it even more amazing that you still do not know what the charges against me were. 17–58: 8&10 . . . There's nothing to make clear here and so if there's no progress that means that it's held up waiting for some important decision-maker. Evidently they are discussing not the crime but my person. How I wish they were less interested in me! Then there would have been a result six months ago . . .

Lev Gumilyov to Akhmatova, Saturday 24 December 1955

Dear kind Mama,

A happy new year. I wish you the very best, viz. to translate Chinese lyrics with the advice of a competent Orientalist, e.g. myself.

There are severe frosts now, today –42 degrees. The workers did not go out to work and are relaxing. The wind cuts your face and the snow rings beneath the feet and is very firm. The climate, it must be said, is abominable. It was much better in the Kemerovo Region.

There are no notable events or changes in my existence . . . for the time being all is comparatively satisfactory if one does not consider my state of mind, but it's not the custom to pay it any attention. It's become lonely and empty around: many of my acquaintances have left and many are sitting on their suitcases and nervously waiting to go. Although I'm sitting on a stool I can't help be infected by the general nervous atmosphere and so it's become harder to ponder about the Huns, Uighurs and An Lushan. I have not received an answer from you to my last three letters but I'm not worried . . .

The frost is holding and I keep stoking the stove and, for the meanwhile, sit next to it without my jacket, which is something. Now I'm sending this letter to Moscow since I think you're there.

My love, dear Mama
L.

Lev Gumilyov to Emma Gerstein, 1 March 1956

Dear Emma,

I've received everything! . . .

My love and thanks for your a) concern, b) attention, c) rebukes, for they are deserved, d) books, e) reviews, f) forgiveness of Serunchik [camp friend released early], g) efforts on my behalf and h) loyalty in misfortune – that's the most important of all.

[E.G.: On 25 February 1956 the 20th Congress of the Communist Party came to a close. Several days later I went to the chief military prosecutor's office to collect yet another document and received the long-awaited news: the USSR prosecutor-general, Rudenko himself, would uphold the protest against Lyova's conviction. I wrote to tell him on 1 March.]

Lev Gumilyov to Emma Gerstein, 10 March 1956

Yesterday I sent you and Mama a letter and today your postcard of 1 March arrived. I am overwhelmed with joy . . . A friend said to me: "You have a future but you don't have a present." That's partly true but my thoughts and knowledge are growing, thanks to the books I've been sent, and that's already something . . .

Please embrace Mama and reassure her, cheer her up as much as you can.

Lev Gumilyov to Emma Gerstein, [3 April 1956]

All personal relations that I had with others have been severed by the scythe of Chronos . . . So I simply do not know what to wish for . . .

If you send a telegram on Wednesday it'll reach me on Friday. Not only I am waiting – the entire post-office staff are interested. Meanwhile I accept the condolences of those around me and study Si-ma Qian.

Akhmatova to Lev Gumilyov, 6 April 1956

Hello, Lyovushka,

I've only just finished (5 p.m.) a translation of Chao Chian's "Funeral of Flowers" [eighteenth-century Chinese writer]. There is a kind of dreamy excellence in this poem, which is very difficult to translate.

Vasily Vasilievich [Struve] had pneumonia and heart complications but, apparently, everything has passed satisfactorily. I shall not go to the dacha[20] today in order to work: I have little strength and a vast amount of work has built up . . .

There is a large exhibition of French paintings in the Hermitage. Were it not for the staircase I would go.

Don't fall sick, my dear son, write to me. It is my only joy.

Love
Mama

Lev Gumilyov to Akhmatova, 13 April 1956

This is for Mama.

Thank you, dear Mama, for the delicious food you sent. It is already spring with us, and a large pile of optimistic rumours, or *parasha*[21] as they're called, have melted away. I was expecting a

---

[20] In 1955 the Leningrad branch of the Writers' Union allocated Akhmatova a small summer house (she called it the "Booth") in Komarovo.
[21] Literally "night bucket". In the Gulag and the Soviet prison system, those who carried the night buckets (*parasha*) out of cells and barracks comprised the unofficial news network (cf. scuttlebutt).

copy of your Koreans[22] but take comfort in my disappointment in Si-ma Qian. What a shrewd man! But the incomplete nature of the translation spoils everything. It is far too free a treatment of the works of a genius. I understand why you're not writing now. You find it a burden when the fate of your son is about to be resolved, but all thanks to Emma [Gerstein], she keeps writing and I am not wrong to be concerned. The days pass quickly. In the daytime I work, in the evenings after drinking tea I read about ancient China. My creative urge has dwindled; evidently I've grown old.

My love, dear Mama, and thanks once again for your concern about me. But how long this tiresome process is proving!

Leon

Akhmatova to Lev Gumilyov, 26 April 1956

Dear cub,

I'm still home [in Leningrad]. I came for a week but fell ill, suffered a serious heart attack, and now cannot travel. Meanwhile spring and the white nights have arrived. Your postcards are waiting for me in Moscow. Thank you for them . . .

A photographer from TASS came and took thirty snaps, trying to catch some likeness. But you know that I'm not at all photogenic. He said it was for publication abroad so they needed a recent photo. Forgive me that I write to you about such trifles . . . but I have so few new impressions because of my sickness and the last few days I have not even been able to read.

Vladimir Georgievich Garshin has died.

Love
Mama

Lev Gumilyov was released in May 1956 and that month returned to Leningrad, where he rented a room in flat 218 at 195 Mosvoksky Avenue. He was now 44; his mother was almost 67. [tr.]

---

[22] *Korean Classic Poetry* (1956), a collection including translations by Akhmatova.

Akhmatova to Lev Gumilyov, 13 February ?1957

My dearest son Lyovushka,

I'm writing to you to say, once again, what joy your phone calls bring me. They are the only thing that keeps me going these last few days. It was so tormenting in Moscow when I could not speak to you. I'm home all the time, please ring. I was recalling our life, quite a majestic spectacle.

Please believe that I least of all want to do things my own way and shall wait quite patiently until you come and explain everything to me yourself.

Very much love
Your aged Mama

BIOGRAPHICAL NOTES

Akhmatova (pseud. of Gorenko), Anna Andreyevna (1889–1966), poet. Born in the south; family, then comprising four children, moved to Tsarskoye Selo. Father a retired naval engineer; mother, in her radical youth, a member of People's Will: parents separated in 1905. Educated at *gymnasium* in Tsarskoye, then in Kiev 1906–7. In 1910 married Nikolai Gumilyov. Only child, Lyova, born in 1912, when her first collection of poems, *Evening*, appeared. From 1925 to 1940, works were banned. The 1946 denunciation "half nun, half whore" was a caricatured rephrasing of remarks made in a 1923 lecture by Eichenbaum concerning erotic and religious motifs in her work. Died at Domodedovo outside Moscow; buried at Komarovo.

Gumilyov, Lev (Lyova) Nikolayevich (1912–1992), historian and Orientalist. Faced numerous obstacles and dangers as son of executed father and disgraced mother. Arrested and imprisoned in 1938 and again in 1949, pursued his studies with determination and lived to write many works on the history and culture of Asia. In 1961 broke off almost all relations with his mother.

Gumilyov, Nikolai (Kolya) Stepanovich (1886–1921), poet, leading Acmeist. Akhmatova's first husband, they separated during the First World War. Co-founder of the literary and art magazine *Apollon*; in 1912–13 was leading figure in new Acmeist movement (with Akmatova and Mandelstam), opposing a Pushkinian clarity, precision and restraint to the Symbolism then current in Russian poetry. Two lengthy African journeys preceded wartime enlistment in the Russian army. From 1905 produced seven collections of poems and two short prose works. In February 1921 was popular choice as head of Petrograd branch of Union of Poets; shot in August of that year (see Appendix 1.5). Not published in the USSR, and his name barely mentioned, between 1923 and 1988.

Khardjiev, Nikolai Ivanovich (1902–1996), art and literary specialist of mixed Armenian and Greek origin. After studying law at the university in Odessa, moved to Moscow in 1928. Expert on Futurism and co-editor of the collected works of Mayakovsky (1935) and unpublished poems of Khlebnikov (1940). Chosen by Nadezhda Mandelstam to be editor of the posthumous Soviet edition of her husband's collected poems. Emigrated in old age to the Netherlands with a rare collection of art (including works by Malevich).

Khazin, Yevgeny (Zhenya) Yakovlevich (1893–1974), *literatteur.* Nadezhda Mandelstam's older brother. Married, in succession, to Soviet designers Sophia Vishnevetskaya and Yelena Fradkina. Member of 1957 commission appointed by Writers' Union to preserve and publish his brother-in-law's works.

Mandelstam, Alexander (Shura) Emilievich (1893–1942), Mandelstam's middle brother. Died in evacuation during the war.

Mandelstam (née Khazina), Nadezhda (Nadya) Yakovlevna (1899–1980), wife of Mandelstam. Born in Saratov, youngest child of a well-read lawyer. Grew up and educated in Kiev; taken on trips to Europe; graduated in 1917. Studied under artists Exter and Murashko. First met Mandelstam in 1919. Tubercular condition caused concern in 1920s. Following Mandelstam's death, taught Western languages to schoolchildren in a variety of provincial Soviet cities, during and after the Second World War.

Mandelstam, Osip Emilievich (1891–1938), poet. Born in Warsaw, eldest of leather merchant Emil (Chatskel) Mandelstam's three sons. Family moved to Pavlovsk, then St Petersburg. Educated 1900–7 at Tenishev college in Petersburg. Travelled to Paris and Germany. In 1911–17 registered at Petersburg University. First poems published in *Apollon* in 1910. From 1928 until 1973 no collected edition of his poems appeared in the USSR; first publication of *Conversation about Dante* (1967) marked culmination of his first return as a writer. An uncensored two-volume edition of his works (Averintsev, Nerler and Mikhailov, eds) was published in Russia only in 1990.

Pasternak, Boris Leonidovich (1890–1960), poet and translator. Born in Moscow, son of an artist; first intended to be a musician. A 1914 verse collection was followed in 1922 by acclaimed poetry collection *My Sister Life*, epic poem *Lieutenant Schmidt* (1927) about 1905 revolution, and autobiographical prose *Safe Conduct* (1931). In later 1930s he retreated to the greater safety of translation. After the war began work in secret on what would become the novel *Doctor Zhivago* (Emma Gerstein was invited to hear the author read early versions of the text). Under particular pressure after Olga Ivinskaya, a romantic inspiration for his heroine Lara, was sent to the Gulag from 1949 to 1954.

Petrovykh, Maria Sergeyevna (1908–1979), poet and translator from Armenian and other languages of the Soviet Union. Her husband, Vitaly, was arrested and died in the camps. In early 1960s Solzhenitsyn's first meeting with Akhmatova took place at Petrovykh's flat.

Punin, Nikolai Nikolayevich (1888–1953), art historian and critic; Akhmatova's last husband. In 1922 challenged Trotsky's definition of Akhmatova in *Pravda* as an "internal émigrée". Passionate supporter of the avant-garde in art (wrote book about Tatlin), Punin worked in Russian Museum from 1913 and was among founders of the icon collection there (publishing *Andrei Rublyov* in 1916). Akhmatova lived at his apartment on Fontanka from 1926 (with his first wife, Anna Arens, and daughter Irina), staying on after she and Punin separated in 1938. Forced to leave the Academy of Arts and dismissed by the university, Punin was imprisoned in 1949. Determined to outlive Stalin, died at Abez in Vorkutlag in August 1953.

Rudakov, Sergei Borisovich (1909–1944), literary specialist. Banished to Voronezh, where he became acquainted with Mandelstam and gathered materials about his life, Rudakov died at the front in January 1944 after a six-month imprisonment.

Stalin (pseud. of Djugashvili), Josif Vissarionovich (1879–1953), Soviet leader 1924–53. Bolshevik revolutionary, repeatedly banished to remote areas by Tsarist goverment after 1903; in 1913 exiled to Turukhansk. By mid-1930s established personal dictatorship and associated cult.

INDEX

This index includes the names of people, places, institutions, historical events and literary works. Pages with illustrations are indicated in italics. Actual surnames follow pseudonyms in brackets, as do married (or maiden) names; diminutive and familiar forms of first names are likewise indicated.